IMPORTANT:

HERE IS YOUR REGISTRATION CODE TO ACCESS

YOUR PREMiUM McGRAW-HILL ONLINE RESOURCES.

Registering for McGraw-Hill Online Resources

To gain access to your McGraw-Hill web resources simply follow the steps below:

1. USE YOUR WEB BROWSER TO GO TO: **www.mhhe.com/siedentop5e**

2. CLICK ON **FIRST TIME USER**.

3. ENTER THE REGISTRATION CODE* PRINTED ON THE TEAR-OFF BOOKMARK ON THE RIGHT.

4. AFTER YOU HAVE ENTERED YOUR REGISTRATION CODE, CLICK **REGISTER**.

5. FOLLOW THE INSTRUCTIONS TO SET-UP YOUR PERSONAL UserID AND PASSWORD.

6. WRITE YOUR UserID AND PASSWORD DOWN FOR FUTURE REFERENCE.
   KEEP IT IN A SAFE PLACE.

Thank you, and welcome to your McGraw-Hill online Resources!

REGISTRATION CODE

NA8L-MK3L-G7N6-HNIS-FOYV

Introduction to Physical Education, Fitness, and Sport

FIFTH EDITION

Daryl Siedentop

The Ohio State University

Boston   Burr Ridge, IL   Dubuque, IA   Madison, WI   New York
San Francisco   St. Louis   Bangkok   Bogotá   Caracas   Kuala Lumpur
Lisbon   London   Madrid   Mexico City   Milan   Montreal   New Delhi
Santiago   Seoul   Singapore   Sydney   Taipei   Toronto

Again, for B. J.

Higher Education

INTRODUCTION TO PHYSICAL EDUCATION, FITNESS, AND SPORT,
FIFTH EDITION
Published by McGraw-Hill, a business unit of The McGraw-Hill Companies, Inc., 1221 Avenue
of the Americas, New York, NY, 10020. Copyright © 2004 by The McGraw-Hill Companies,
Inc. All rights reserved. Previous editions © by Mayfield Publishing Company. No part of this
publication may be reproduced or distributed in any form or by any means, or stored in a database or retrieval system, without the prior written consent of The McGraw-Hill Companies,
Inc., including, but not limited to, any network or other electronic storage or transmission,
or broadcast for distance learning.

Some ancillaries, including electronic and print components, may not be available to customers outside the United States.

2 3 4 5 6 7 8 9 0 FGR/FGR 0 9 8 7 6 5 4

Vice president and editor-in-chief: *Thalia Dorwick*
Publisher: *Jane Karpacz*
Sponsoring editor: *Vicki Malinee*
Development editor: *Gary O'Brien*
Marketing manager: *Pamela Cooper*
Production services manager: *Jennifer Mills*
Production service: *Matrix Productions, Inc.*
Manuscript editor: *Carole Crouse*
Art director: *Jeanne M. Schreiber*
Design manager: *Violeta Diaz*
Cover designer: *Brad Greene*
Interior designer: *Richard Kharibian*
Art manager: *Robin Mouat*
Photo research coordinator: *Alexandra Ambrose*
Production supervisor: *Tandra Jorgensen*

The text was set in 10/12 New Caledonia by G&S Typesetters, Inc. and printed on acid-free,
45# New Era Matte by Quebecor World, Fairfield.

Cover images: golfer: © PhotoDisc/Getty Images; biker: ©Stockbyte; basketball: © Rick
Gomez/Corbis

The credits for this book begin on page C-1, a continuation of the copyright page.

Library of Congress Cataloging-in-Publication Data

Siedentop, Daryl.
    Introduction to physical education, fitness, and sport/Daryl Siedentop.—5th ed.
        p. cm.
    Includes bibliographical references (p.) and index.
        ISBN 0-07-255739-7
    1. Physical education and training.   2. Physical fitness.   3. Sports.   4. Sports
sciences.
I. Title.

GV341.S479 2001
613.7′1—dc21

2003048789

www.mhhe.com

Contents

Preface   xv

PART ONE   Understanding the Context of Lifespan Sport,
Fitness, and Physical Education   1

CHAPTER 1   Lifespan Sport, Fitness, and Physical Education   3

Lifespan Physical Activity—A Revolution Not Limited
by Age or Gender   5

The Early Years   5
Preschool Physical-Activity Programs   6
Children's Sport   6
Elementary Physical Education   7

Youth—The Transition Years   8
The High School Interschool Sport Program   8
Out-of-School Sport   9

Young Adulthood   10
University Recreation Program   10
Community Recreation   11
Fitness Involvement   12
Informal Participation   13

The Older Adult   13
The Masters Athlete   13
Physical Activity Forever   14

The New Settings for Sport, Fitness, and Physical Education   14
Multipurpose Athletic Clubs   14
Sport Clubs   15
Specialized Sport/Fitness Centers   15
Sport-Medicine Centers   16
Home Gymnasiums   16
Worksite Programs   16
Sport/Games Festivals   17

The Emerging Characteristics of Lifespan Physical Activity   17

Limitations   19

A Framework for Understanding the Possibilities
for Professional Service   20

Summary   20

Discussion Questions   21

CHAPTER 2   The Emergence of a Profession: 1885–1930   22

The Heritage of Physical Education, Sport, and Fitness in the United States   23
The Birth of a Profession   23

The Scene before 1885   24

The Context for the Emergence of the Profession   26

The Battle of the Systems   29
The German System   30
The Swedish System   30
The Beecher System   31
The Dio Lewis System   32
The Hitchcock System   32
The Sargent System   33
The Boston Conference in 1889   33

The Emergence of Organized Sport   34
Sport on the College Campus   35
Faculty Control and the Beginning of a National Intercollegiate System   36

The New Physical Education   37

The Spreading of the Physical-Education Umbrella   39

The Golden Age: Post–World War I   40
Education through the Physical   41
The Beginnings of a Science of Physical Education   42
Access and Equity   43

Summary   44

Discussion Questions   45

CHAPTER 3   Consolidation and Specialization: 1930–Present   46

The Cultural Context: 1930–1940   47

Sport, Fitness, and Physical Education: 1930–1940   48
A Shift to Participation   48
Federal and Private-Sector Intervention   49
Organizational Consolidation and Standardization   49

Sport, Fitness, and Physical Education during the War Years   50

Expansion and Growth during the Postwar Years   52
The Expansion of Sport   53
The Postwar Years in Physical Education   54
The Fitness Crisis   55

The Mid-1950s and On: Forces That Shaped Our Current Culture   56
Sport in the Post-1950 Era   57

The Fitness Renaissance and the Aerobics Era   58
School Physical Education since the 1950s   59

The Academic-Discipline Movement   60

Summary   64

Discussion Questions   65

CHAPTER 4   Changing Philosophies for Sport, Fitness, and Physical Education   66

Philosophical Influences in Early American Sport, Fitness, and Physical Education   67
The Gymnastic Philosophies   68
Muscular Christianity   68
Masculinity–Femininity Ideals   70
Amateurism, Fair Play, and the British Ideals   71
Character Education through Physical Challenge   72

School Sport and the New Physical Education   73
The European Antecedents   74
The Reemergence of Play as a Philosophical Concept   75
The Early Twentieth Century: Philosophies Come Together   76

Philosophical Forces in Sport, Fitness, and Physical Education since 1950   77
Human Movement   77
Humanistic Sport and Physical Education   79
Play Education and Sport Education   80
Experiential and Adventure Education   81
The Fitness Renaissance and the Wellness Movement   82

Summary   84

Discussion Questions   85

PART TWO   Sport   87

CHAPTER 5   Basic Concepts of Sport   89

Sport—The Natural Religion   91

Leisure, Play, Games, and Sport   92
Leisure   92
Play   93
Games   95
Competition in Sport and Games   97

The Institutionalization of Sport   98
The Codification of Rules   99
The Role of the Referee   99
The Genesis of Sport Organizations   99
The Importance of Records   100
The Public Nature of Institutionalized Sport   101

Sport Spectating   102

Sport Aesthetics   103
Aesthetics of Form Sports   104
Aesthetic Quality of Other Sports   104

Sport Ethics   106
Fair Play and the British Tradition   106
Rules and the Nature of Games   107

Summary   108

Discussion Questions   109

CHAPTER 6   Sport Programs and Professions   110

The Leisure Myth   111

Child and Youth Sport   112
Organization of Child and Youth Sport   114
Coaching for Child and Youth Sport   115

Interscholastic Sport   116
Organization of Interschool Sport   117
School Coaches   120

Collegiate Sport Programs   121
Intercollegiate Sport   121
College Recreational Intramural Programs   123

Professional Sport   124

Organized Recreational Sport   125
Sport for People with Disabilities   126
Masters or Veterans Sport   128

Nonparticipant Sport Involvement   129
Sport Management and Administration   130
Athletic Training   131
Nonparticipant Sport Vocations: By Whom?   131
Sport and Technology   132

Summary   133

Discussion Questions   134

CHAPTER 7   Problems and Issues in Sport   135

Sport Problems or General Social Problems?   136

Cooperation and Competition   137

Child and Youth Sport   138
Premature Entry into Organized Sport   139
Overuse Injuries   139
Developmentally Inappropriate Sport   140
Specialization   141
Lack of Adequate Training of Coaches   141
Outside Pressure to Win   142

Impact of Sport on Family Life   143
Dropping Out by Children and Youths   143
Unequal Access Based on Socioeconomic Status   143
Aussie Sports: An Example of a National Program   143

School Sport   144
Exclusion and the Varsity Model   145
School Sport Injuries   146
Eligibility and Pass-to-Play Rules   147
Specialization   148
Performance-Enhancing Supplements   148
The School Coach as Teacher–Coach   149
Parental Pressures and Booster Clubs   149
Pay-to-Play Plans   150

Intercollegiate Sport   151
Recruiting Violations and Pressures   151
Drugs That Enhance Performance   152
Economic Disparities among Top Powers   152
Economic Pressure to Win   152
Treatment of the Student–Athlete   153

Equity Issues in Sport   154
Women's Issues   154
Minority Issues   157

Sport Systems   158
Alternative Goals for Sport Systems   158
Sport for All   159
Sport in Perspective   160

Summary   161

Discussion Questions   163

PART THREE   Fitness   165

CHAPTER 8   Basic Concepts of Fitness   167

A Contemporary Understanding of Fitness   168
Health Fitness   170
Motor-Performance Fitness   172

Cosmetic Fitness   172

The Dose–Response Debate   173

The Social Gradient in Health and Fitness   176

Fitness-Training Concepts and Principles   178
General Training Principles   179
Health-Fitness Training   180
Continuous and Interval Training   181
Anaerobic Training   181
Strength Training   181
Flexibility   184

The Measurement of Fitness   184
   Measuring MVPA   187
   Informal Measurement of Fitness   188
Summary   190
Discussion Questions   191

CHAPTER 9   Fitness Programs and Professions   192

Fitness Levels among Children and Youths   193
Activity Patterns among Children and Youths   196
Fitness Levels among Adults   198
Fitness and Activity Patterns among Older Adults   200
Fitness and PA Programs for Children and Youths   201
   Comprehensive Schoolwide and Community-Linked Programs   205
   AAHPERD Efforts to Promote Physical Activity and Fitness   206
Worksite Fitness and Wellness Programs   208
   Informal Home-Based Fitness Activities   209
   Federal Efforts to Promote Fitness and Physical Activity   210
Physical-Fitness Instruction: By Whom?   212
Sport Medicine and the Rehabilitative Sciences   213
   Athletic Training   213
ACSM Fitness-Instruction Certification   215
   Strength and Conditioning Specialist Certification   215
   YMCA Fitness Instructor Certification   217
   Physical Therapy   217
   Bachelor's Degree in Adult Fitness   218
   Master's Degree in Fitness   218
Summary   219
Discussion Questions   220

CHAPTER 10   Problems and Issues in Fitness   221

The Costs of Inadequate Health Fitness   222
Fitness Behavior: Short and Long Term   224
Developing a Fitness-Educated Public   225
Equity Issues in Fitness and Activity   227
Certification of Fitness Leaders   229
Fitness Tests or Activity Estimates?   229
Fitness and Aging: Changing Views and Expectations   230
Fitness Issues in Physical Education   231
Research Issues in Fitness and Physical Activity   234
Toward a Physical-Activity Infrastructure for the United States   235

Summary   237
Discussion Questions   237

PART FOUR   Physical Education   239

CHAPTER 11   Basic Concepts of Physical Education   241
Education through the Physical   242
NASPE's Move toward National Goals and Standards   245
Other Important Curriculum Influences   246
Movement Education   246
Health-Related Physical Education   248
The Academic-Integration Model   248
The Social-Development Model   249
The Sport-Education Model   251
The Adventure-Education Approach   253
The Eclectic Curriculum   255
What Is the Subject Matter of Physical Education?   255
Physical Education for Students with Disabilities   256
State Requirements for Physical Education   257
Liability   259
Title IX   259
Does Physical Education Have a Central Meaning?   260
Summary   261
Discussion Questions   262

CHAPTER 12   Physical-Education Programs and Professions   263
Exemplary Physical-Education Programs   265
A Comprehensive Health-Related Elementary-School Model   265
Preschool Programs   266
A High School Lifetime Physical-Activity Program   267
An Upper-Elementary Sport-Education Program   267
A High School Personal-Growth Curriculum   268
An Elementary Adventure Program   269
A High School Fitness Emphasis   270
A Research-Based National Elementary Program   270
An Early-Elementary Movement Program   271
A Comprehensive High School Program   272
The "New PE" at Middle School   272
A High School Program Emphasizing Community Linkages   272
A Districtwide Wellness Initiative   273
A State Wellness Curriculum for High Schools   273
What Makes These Programs Work?   274

Technology in Physical Education 274

The Physical-Education Teacher 278
What Do Physical-Education Teachers Do? 278
A Day in the Life of Two Teachers 278

Preparing to Become a Physical-Education Teacher 279
Differences among States 279
National Standards for Beginning Physical-Education Teachers 280
Certification for Teaching Adapted Physical Education 282

Summary 282

Discussion Questions 283

CHAPTER 13 Problems and Issues in Physical Education 284

Issues in Elementary-School Physical Education 285
Time 285
Elementary Specialist Teachers 286
Facilities 287
Developmentally Appropriate Practices 287
Curricula 288

Issues in Secondary School Physical Education 288
Busy, Happy, and Good 288
Multiactivity Curriculum 289
Difficult Teaching Situations 289
Coed Participation 290
Rethinking Secondary Physical Education 292
Physical Education in Urban High Schools 292
The Intramural Program 293

General Problems in Physical Education 293
Can Physical Education be a "Basic" Subject? 294
Assessment 294
Outcomes and Credibility with the Public 295
Should School Physical Education Have a National Curriculum? 295
Liability 296
Gender Equity 296
Skill Equity 297
Good and Bad Competition 298

Physical Education in the Sport / Fitness Culture 299

Summary 300

Discussion Questions 301

PART FIVE   The Scholarly Study of Sport, Fitness,
and Physical Education   303

CHAPTER 14   Exercise Physiology   305

Definition of Exercise Physiology as a Field of Study   307

Development of Exercise Physiology   308

Current Status of Exercise Physiology   309
What Do Exercise Physiologists Do?   310
How Does a Person Prepare to Be an Exercise Physiologist
or a Fitness Specialist?   312

Current Issues and Problems in Exercise Physiology   313

Summary   314

Discussion Questions   314

CHAPTER 15   Kinesiology and Biomechanics   315

Definition of Kinesiology and Biomechanics as Fields of Study   317

Development of Kinesiology and Biomechanics   319

Current Scope of Kinesiology and Biomechanics   320
What Do Kinesiologists and Biomechanists Do?   322
How Does a Person Prepare to Be a Kinesiologist or a Biomechanist?   323

Current Issues in Kinesiology and Biomechanics   323

Summary   323

Discussion Questions   324

CHAPTER 16   Motor Behavior   325

Definition of Motor Behavior as a Field of Study   328

Development of Motor Behavior   329

Current Status of Motor Behavior   330
What Do Specialists in Motor Behavior Do?   332
How Does a Person Prepare to Be a Specialist in Motor Behavior?   332

Current Issues and Problems in Motor Behavior   332

Summary   334

Discussion Questions   334

CHAPTER 17   Sport Sociology   335

Definition of Sport Sociology as a Field of Study   336

Development of Sport Sociology   338

Current Status of Sport Sociology   339
   What Do Sport Sociologists Do?   341
   How Does a Person Prepare to Be a Sport Sociologist?   341
Current Issues and Problems in Sport Sociology   341
Summary   343
Discussion Questions   343

CHAPTER 18   Sport and Exercise Psychology   344

Definition of Sport and Exercise Psychology as a Field of Study   345
Development of Sport Psychology   347
Current Status of Sport and Exercise Psychology   348
   Academic Sport Psychology   348
   What Do Sport and Exercise Psychologists Do?   349
   How Does a Person Prepare to Be a Sport and Exercise Psychologist?   351
Current Issues and Problems in Sport and Exercise Psychology   353
Summary   354
Discussion Questions   355

CHAPTER 19   Sport Pedagogy   356

Definition of Sport Pedagogy as a Field of Study   357
Development of Sport Pedagogy   359
Current Status of Sport Pedagogy   360
   What Do Sport Pedagogists Do?   362
   How Does a Person Prepare to Be a Sport Pedagogist?   363
Current Issues and Problems in Sport Pedagogy   363
Summary   364
Discussion Questions   365

CHAPTER 20   The Sport Humanities   366

Definition of the Sport Humanities as Fields of Study   368
Development of the Sport Humanities   370
Current Status of the Sport Humanities   371
   What Do Sport-Humanities Specialists Do?   374
   How Does a Person Prepare to Be a Sport-Humanities Specialist?   374
Current Issues and Problems in the Sport Humanities   375
Summary   377
Discussion Questions   378

PART SIX   Future Problems and Prospects   379

CHAPTER 21   Relationships to Allied Fields   381

    Recreation   382
    Health   387
    Dance   391
    Allied or Integrated?   393
    Summary   394
    Discussion Questions   395

CHAPTER 22   Sport, Fitness, and Physical Education in the Twenty-First Century:
Themes Defining Our Present and Future   396

    Theme 1: Meeting the Public Health Challenge   397
    Theme 2: Distributing Opportunity More Equitably   398
    Theme 3: Focusing on New Populations   400
    Theme 4: Gender Equity in Sport, Fitness, and Physical Education   401
    Theme 5: Child and Youth Development: The After-School Hours   401
    Theme 6: Collaboration between Disciplines and Professions   402
    Theme 7: The Activity and Leisure Industries   403
    Theme 8: Toward an Expanded Physical Education   404
    Theme 9: Toward an Inclusive Rather than Exclusionary Culture   405
    Theme 10: Wellness as the Center of Lifestyle Education   406
    Summary   407
    Discussion Questions   407

Glossary   G-1

Bibliography   B-1

Credits   C-1

Index   I-1

Preface

Most of the readers of this text already share an important kind of knowledge about sport, fitness, and physical education—they have experienced them. Although those experiences are different, they provide the starting point from which the material and issues in this text are addressed. On the basis of these experiences, readers will bring a point of view to the issues raised in the text.

Introduction to Physical Education, Fitness, and Sport will help students to acquire new perspectives and to test the points of view they bring to the subject matter. The text covers the history, ideas, events, people, and programs that have led to the current status of these fields. The best of current knowledge and programs is presented, as well as the issues and problems that confront the fields today and perhaps into the future. Readers are introduced to career possibilities and are given information about preparing for professional service in all areas of sport, physical education, fitness, and kinesiology—in careers as diverse as athletic trainer, fitness leader, sport manager, physical education teacher, biomechanist, and sport psychologist.

Throughout, this text emphasizes activism and professionalism. Both the ability to think critically about sport, fitness, and physical education and the will to act decisively are hallmarks of competent professional practice. Every effort has been made to encourage readers to reflect critically on important issues, to recognize and confront the problems that exist in the various fields, to understand the facts related to those problems and to seek further information to shed light on possible solutions, to weigh the merits of alternative solutions, and to respect divergent points of view. No single answer to any issue is presented as the only answer. On the contrary, because there are likely to be multiple solutions to problems, the discussion questions at the end of each chapter were chosen specifically to spark debate.

Sport, fitness, and physical education have the potential not only to touch the lives of individuals but also to positively affect the nature of our common cultural life. Cultures evolve, but they do not necessarily always "progress." If sport, fitness, and physical education are to become inclusive, positive forces in the twenty-first century, professionals will have to learn about and provide solutions to the many problems that exist in the various fields. Problem solving and leadership require knowledge, skill, and perseverance. This text can help you acquire the knowledge and the skill and will make it clear to you that perseverance is necessary for success.

ORGANIZATION OF THE TEXT

The fifth edition of *Introduction to Physical Education, Fitness, and Sport* is divided into six parts. Part 1 provides the foundation for understanding the current status of the various fields and the important issues within each of them. The emphasis in this part, and throughout the text, is on the desirability and possibility of ensuring a physically active lifestyle for all people. Part 1 examines the extraordinary time we live in related to those fields, examines the important influences that have led to this historic period of our professions, and presents the philosophical positions that have supported the past and current development of the professions.

Parts 2, 3, and 4 present detailed information about the fields of sport, fitness, and physical education, respectively. Each part begins with a chapter that examines the basic concepts of one of these fields and its current stage of development. That chapter is followed by a chapter describing current programming efforts within the field and the qualifications for professionals who work within the field. Each part concludes with a provocative look at the major issues and problems that confront the field.

Part 5 focuses on the scientific and scholarly disciplines that support the sport, fitness, and physical-education professions. These chapters describe the development of the disciplinary fields and the new knowledge the fields have developed. Each of the seven chapters describes the research and scholarship carried out in a particular discipline and the qualifications for entry into that discipline, as well as the current issues being discussed within the discipline.

Part 6 includes two chapters, one of which examines the allied fields of health, recreation, and dance. The final chapter identifies and discusses themes that are crucial to influencing the future of sport, fitness, and physical education as we move into the twenty-first century.

FEATURES OF THE FIFTH EDITION

The fifth edition continues to update information about and expand coverage of the major developments in sport, fitness, and physical education. Special new emphasis is given to issues and problems that seem to be of major importance for the near future, the following of which are exemplary:

- Physical activity in relationship to epidemics of obesity and diabetes
- Problems associated with adult violence in youth sport
- Changes in physical-education programs to meet public health goals
- Advances in professional certification in athletic training and other fitness-related professions
- New approaches to school physical education that emphasize lifetime physical activity

- Implications of *Healthy People 2010* goals and progress made in reaching *Healthy People 2000* goals
- Federal, state, and local efforts to develop infrastructures to support physical activity
- Continuing problems in interscholastic and collegiate sport
- Recent developments in the kinesiological disciplines that support sport, fitness, and physical-education professionals

As fields progress, the problems in those fields change, sometimes subtly and sometimes quite drastically. Each section of the text deals with problems in ways that attempt to reflect the latest information from the various fields. As has been the custom in previous editions, I will often state my view, but not to the exclusion of other views and always in a way that encourages young professionals to develop their own views based on sound evidence and information.

Finally, the *Introduction to Physical Education, Fitness, and Sport* Online Learning Center (www.mhhe.com/siedentop5e) includes a variety of tools for both instructors and students. Password-protected instructor's resources include downloadable PowerPoint slides and Instructor's Manual. Student resources include a wide variety of elements keyed to each chapter in the text: chapter outlines and learning objectives, interactive study questions, and more.

ACKNOWLEDGMENTS

My professional life and work have been influenced by a number of bright and caring people who took the time to share with me their own insights and experiences, and who cared enough about me to offer me their honest and sincere criticisms. My brother, Larry, a Fellow of Keble College, Oxford University, is a world-class scholar in political history and theory. He has always been an inspiration to me. Ken Weller was my first mentor. Russ DeVette and Gord Brewer helped me to understand and care about sport. Larry Locke, Charles Mand, Don Hellison, and George Graham have been close professional colleagues, providing me with honest criticism of my work. The many years I worked on a day-to-day basis in physical-education teacher education with Mary O'Sullivan, Deborah Tannehill, and Sandy Stroot were the best of my professional life.

I wish to thank the following individuals for their helpful reviews of the fifth edition:

Robert H. Cummings,
Christopher Newport University

Jennifer J. Gorecki,
Illinois State University

B. Sue Graves,
Florida Atlantic University

Nancy Halliday,
Hofstra University

Daniel B. Hollander,
Southeastern Louisiana University

Mel L. Horton,
Winthrop University

Kathy LaMaster,
San Diego State University

Gerald E. Landwer,
University of Nevada, Las Vegas

The doctoral students with whom I have worked have been a constant source of pride and inspiration. That many of them have gone on to important professional careers of their own is the greatest source of pride in my professional career. My collaborative work with teachers in central Ohio has always been a continuing source of information and inspiration—and a constant reality check for me. My thanks particularly to Chris, Gary, Bobbie, Molly, Jane, Bob, and Carol.

I would like to thank all the folks at McGraw-Hill who have helped to make the transition of this text to the McGraw-Hill list after the Mayfield Publishing acquisition. My special thanks go to Gary O'Brien, who is quite simply the best editor I have ever worked with. Gary was tremendously helpful and competent in navigating this edition through the revision process.

PART ONE

Understanding the Context of Lifespan Sport, Fitness, and Physical Education

Chapter 1   Lifespan Sport, Fitness, and Physical Education

Chapter 2   The Emergence of a Profession: 1885–1930

Chapter 3   Consolidation and Specialization: 1930–Present

Chapter 4   Changing Philosophies for Sport, Fitness, and Physical Education

When you become a professional in any area related to sport, fitness, or physical education, you must think critically about the issues related to your professional endeavors. Other people will expect you to have the knowledge and the ability to analyze issues differently from the way laypeople do. Put simply, you will be expected to know and to do things that nonprofessionals do not know and cannot do. To fulfill the expectations people have for you as a professional, you must know something of both the history of events and the philosophical positions that have characterized your profession. You will, of course, develop your own philosophy, but you should develop it critically, with respect for competing points of view. Your professional philosophy is not just your opinion; it is a coherent way of looking at your professional world, informed by an understanding of the events that have led to the current state of affairs.

The four chapters in Part 1 provide an overview of the current context for **lifespan involvement** in physical activity through sport, fitness, and physical education; of the history of these fields; and of the evolution of diverse philosophical perspectives in these fields.

1

PART ONE

Understanding the Concept of Lifespan, Sport, Fitness, and Physical Education

Lifespan Sport, Fitness, and Physical Education

Eventually, what we now call physical education, reformed and refurbished, may well stand—as it did in ancient times— at the center of the academy, providing the strong foundation from which all education can rise. Education in the formal sense, however, is only part of the story. For the body opens us to larger realms. And every game we play, whether old or new, invites us to consider the larger game, our life itself.

George Leonard, 1974

LEARNING OBJECTIVES

- To explain and justify lifespan involvement as an important new possibility

- To describe the possibilities for involvement at various developmental stages

- To describe the new settings for sport, fitness, and physical education

- To discuss and analyze the emerging characteristics of lifespan involvement

- To discuss both the possibilities and the problems of the current sport and fitness booms

We are living in an era during which people in the developed world have changed fundamentally their perception of human life and of how it can be lived. It is now clear that lifespan involvement in sport, fitness, and physical education is *possible* and *desirable*. People can become involved in purposeful physical activity very early in life and can continue to pursue those interests throughout their lives. Unfortunately, that possibility has not yet been realized for many people. Increasing the likelihood of lifelong involvement is what this book is about.

This is an extraordinary era for people interested in sport, fitness, and physical education! There certainly has been no period in the history of the United States to match it. Sport is central to much of our cultural life. The neighborhood turns out to watch a youth soccer game. The community is brought together as it follows the fortunes or misfortunes of the high school basketball team. Students, alumni, and fans rally around sports teams from universities. Professional teams draw more spectators than ever and, in a good season, capture the imagination of entire regions. Watching events such as the World Series, the Super Bowl, or the National College Athletic Association (NCAA) basketball finals has become a national ritual of immense proportion.

Do not get the idea that we are simply a nation of spectators, however! As spectating has increased (both attendance at games and television viewing), so too has participation. More adults than ever before are participating in sports such as softball, golf, volleyball, running, cycling, and swimming.

If you enjoy physical activity, you are already well aware of trends that range from serious fitness work through regular, moderate physical activity to brief strolls in a park. Fitness centers and sport clubs with fitness facilities have sprung up everywhere, and the "athletic look" has replaced the "slim look" in fashion magazines. Activity clothing and athletic shoes have become standard dress, not only for physical activity, but also for dining, going to movies, and casual outings.

In addition to influencing fashion, the activity movement is part of a larger health movement that influences diet, exercise, and other habits of lifestyle. The emphasis on looking healthier and actually being healthier are often referred to as *lifestyle management* and are part of the *wellness movement,* which promotes a lifestyle focused on feeling and staying well through the prevention rather than the remediation of illness.

The focus on wellness through lifestyle management is good for the nation as well as for individuals. The promotion of a physically active lifestyle is a major public health issue because of the increasing costs associated with health care and insurance, especially for an aging population. In 1991, in its landmark publication *Healthy People 2000,* the United States Public Health Service created a new strategy to deal with the broad issues related to public health. A series of goals were established and regular progress reports are made. In 2000, *Healthy People 2010* was published. The report noted the progress made on goals in the initial 10 years and established revised goals for the next decade. (See Chapter 9 for details.) Physical activity and fitness is focus area 22 in HP 2010, and the stated goal is to "improve health, fitness, and quality of life through daily physical activity" (Spain & Franks, 2001). Within this focus area, there are fifteen specific objectives for which progress reports will be forthcoming during the decade.

Physical education in schools is obviously one important setting for achieving the goals of a physically active and healthy lifestyle. Recognizing that, the U.S. Congress passed House Concurrent Resolution 97 in 1987, calling for high-quality, daily physical education. The fact is, however, that few students participate in daily physical education and that in many places at various grade levels there is no quality physical education. (See Chapter 11 for details of state requirements for PE.) It is clear that physical education is undergoing serious examination and that stronger programs need to be developed to both meet the challenges related to the public health issues and gain the confidence of the public.

LIFESPAN PHYSICAL ACTIVITY— A REVOLUTION NOT LIMITED BY AGE OR GENDER

Someday, historians will describe the current era as a watershed period characterized by the emergence of the possibility for lifespan physical activity—in sport, fitness, and physical education. We have not yet achieved lifespan physical activity, but we now know that it is both possible and desirable. What we have to do now is to create the opportunity to achieve it.

When we consider the topics of sport, fitness, and physical education, what age and gender groups come to mind? If we observe our cultural traditions, our thoughts may turn to children at play, youths involved in sport, and young adults perhaps continuing for a time in recreational sports, with involvement slowly diminishing as people grow older. Very young children are not typically included in such a scenario. We also may be less likely to imagine the involvement of girls than that of boys. In addition, although we may think of men as continuing some moderately active recreation as they age, we may not think of them as engaged in strenuous activity, and we will be less likely to think of older women as participating in even moderate physical activity. The traditional stereotype is that older people are largely inactive, except perhaps for a quiet walk in the afternoon.

Thus, historically, sport, fitness, and physical education have been limited primarily to older children, youths, and young adults. Most people have believed that adults become much less active as they age. Furthermore, many people have viewed appropriate participation for girls and women as being less rigorous than male participation, and some have considered female participation to be out of bounds altogether. Leaders, who typically have been men, have been especially susceptible to those historically stereotypical views.

Many of us who have entered this current of dramatic change continue to think in terms of such stereotypes, but they are now being dismantled. We are replacing our old ideas with a vision of lifespan involvement in sport, fitness, and physical education—not only for adolescents and young adults, but also for very young children and for older people (at almost any level of intensity); not only for boys and men, but also for girls and women (with equally intense activities). These changes in perception, and the changes in opportunity that accompany them, lie at the heart of the revolution we are now experiencing—and these changes make this era unlike any before it. The possibility of lifespan involvement potentially touches every person. This revolution is not limited by age or gender.

Does this vision of lifespan involvement mean that every person must be a committed athlete from childhood through old age? Clearly not! Indeed, from a public health perspective, regular, moderate physical activity appears to be more important than vigorous, athletic activity (Morrow & Gill, 1995). What the new vision does mean, however, is that people who want to be physically active, at any level of intensity, can now be so. It also means that people are increasingly likely to view involvement in some regular physical activity—sport, dance, fitness, or walking—as fundamental to living well, regardless of their age or gender.

The purpose of this chapter is to provide glimpses of the kinds of opportunities available in sport, fitness, and physical education, which together constitute the possibility of lifespan involvement. Each vignette presents a snapshot of involvement for particular people at particular points and places in their lives. None of the scenarios has been contrived. Each is based on *real* programs or people. Together, they paint a picture of lifespan involvement in sport, fitness, and physical education.

THE EARLY YEARS

Physical movement is the basic language of the early-childhood years, from birth to age 6 or 7 years (Boucher, 1988). Young children learn about their world chiefly by moving about and physically exploring their immediate surroundings. In seeking to foster children's physical, social, and mental development, child-development experts have long recognized the fundamental importance of providing opportunities for physical movement and, later, for motor play. Traditionally, the movement experiences of young children have been only informally arranged and monitored, often with no specific purpose other than to keep children involved in some activity. Furthermore, those early movement experiences have been almost exclusively the responsibility of parents, most of whom have little or no knowledge of or training in motor development or early-childhood physical education.

Preschool Physical-Activity Programs

An organized early start to physical activity is more available now than ever before. Typically, these opportunities are in the private sector, with franchised preschool programs for children ages 2–8 years. One is called "Little Gym." Another is called "Fit by Five." Such programs often emphasize activities that foster skill in bodily control and in eye–hand, eye–foot coordination, typically through fun, noncompetitive activities. A preschool movement curriculum for children of all abilities, called "Smart Start" (Wessell & Zittel, 1995), has been developed by physical-education professionals, for use by parents, preschool teachers, Head Start, and private programs.

Sport opportunities are now being made available to children at an earlier age than in the past. It is no longer unusual to see 5-year-olds enrolled in a children's soccer or gymnastics program. Many infant swimming programs are available. Children's playgrounds are increasingly being designed with apparatus to accommodate activities that are developmentally appropriate for young children and that encourage children to explore and to use their entire movement repertoire.

Most evidence (Gober & Franks, 1988) indicates that children who have enriched motor experiences as infants tend to be more fit and more likely to participate in sport throughout their lives. Sport psychologists even speculate that the drive to excel

in sport may originate in infancy, when parents or child-care workers recognize and respond lovingly to infants' early motor efforts. There seems little doubt now that fitness habits originate in childhood and that the longer a child's bad habits are allowed to persist, the more difficult they are to change.

There is much debate about the *nature* of early-childhood motor-activity programs. Should they be mostly exploratory, with adults providing only encouragement, support, and reinforcement? Instead, should they aim to develop specific skills? At the moment, there is not enough evidence to decide the issue. Experts all agree, however, about the importance of providing rich, stimulating motor experiences for very young children:

> Enhancing and expanding the movement vocabulary of a young child is just as important as improving word and reading vocabularies. Since movement is the child's *first* language, a variety of experiences will help make that language as precise and expressive as possible. (Boucher, 1988, p. 42; emphasis in original)

Children's Sport

Sport opportunities for children have grown enormously in the recent past. (See Chapter 6 for details.) Both the number of children participating and the kinds of early sport opportunities available to these children have increased. Some sports, such as swimming and gymnastics, have age-group programs that are highly specialized, with children sometimes beginning to train year-round in their early elementary-school years.

Typical of this boom in children's sport are the many children's soccer programs that have sprung up across the land. The quality and appropriateness of these programs differ dramatically from place to place. Typical of the better programs is one in a midsized metropolitan area, in which 2,000 boys and girls learn and compete. This soccer association was started by parents and is maintained by them. Together, they purchased a 76-acre tract of land on which they gradually have built a huge soccer complex to accommodate their age-group program.

Young children are capable of extraordinary skill development.

The program begins as an instruction-only program for 5-year-old boys and girls. From ages 6 to 12 years, the children are given continued instruction and are involved in intramural competition. Teams are separated by age and sex when enough children are available, and children from the same neighborhood typically are grouped together to make the transportation easier for their parents. A 10-week season costs $50 for the first child, $40 for the second, and $20 for the third.

All children are guaranteed a chance to play at least one half of each game, and teams are kept fairly small, so that most children get a great deal of playing time. The demand for participation is so strong that leagues are typically formed by age and sex; for example, there is a league for 10-year-old boys and a league for 7-year-old girls.

This soccer program is an all-volunteer association. Parents, of course, provide the bulk of the volunteers, serving as referees and coaches. Individuals or businesses can sponsor teams for $85; all players wear shirts that bear the team name.

As Chapter 10 shows, there are many issues and problems in children's sport. I believe that well-designed, careful programs can provide a positive developmental experience.

Elementary Physical Education

Not all elementary-school children attend physical-education programs, and nearly half of those who do are taught by their classroom teacher rather than by a physical-education specialist. In many schools, elementary physical education is hardly more than a recess recreation period; in some schools, recess actually is counted as physical education.

There are, nonetheless, extraordinary school physical-education programs. In one school of 670

Developing skill through exploration has become a favored method for elementary physical education.

children in the South, there are two teachers who are physical-education specialists, as well as one physical-education teacher's aide. Each child, from kindergarten through sixth grade, attends physical-education classes daily. Part of the program is fitness oriented. Teachers have adopted the FITNESSGRAM® to communicate regular fitness-test results to parents on a regular basis. In addition, anyone who walks down the school's halls will see posters listing children's names and adjacent different-colored stars. Closer inspection reveals that each poster shows the level of performance each child has attained in a specific fitness activity.

Children also learn what are most often called "adventure skills." In the gymnasium, there is a climbing wall, which is brightly colored to represent a mountain scene. At the top of the climbing course, there is a place for each child who makes it to write

his or her name. Children also participate in cooperative games and group initiatives, learning the value of working together and depending on one another to reach specific goals.

Sport is part of the curriculum, too. On one side of the gym is a volleyball schedule for the fourth-through sixth-grade intramural program, which takes place during the recess after lunch. Next to it is the schedule of games for the floor-hockey unit in which the fifth- and sixth-graders currently play.

A visitor to a first-grade class finds the children playing in a unit in which they explore different ways to strike objects. They strike balloons, yarn balls, very soft rubber balls, and balls that bounce more like tennis balls. They strike with different kinds of implements, some of which look like stubby tennis rackets, others like paddles. As the teacher directs their exploration, the visitor can begin to see that the children will eventually explore forehand stroking, backhand stroking, overhead stroking, and even something that begins to approach a tennis serve. The children are all active, and they all seem to enjoy what they are doing—for its own sake, not as an activity they eventually will utilize in sport. Observers can see this additional benefit, however.

YOUTH—THE TRANSITION YEARS

It is not difficult to think of many ways in which adolescent boys and girls are involved in sport, fitness, and physical education. Many of us find that our memories of our own youth are dominated by those kinds of experiences. In fact, those experiences may have been so influential that we decided to explore a professional career in these fields.

The High School Interschool Sport Program

Virtually every high school in the nation has some kind of sport program for its students. The programs differ according to the financial resources of the school district, the size of the school, and the state regulations under which the school operates. The programs are, however, more similar than dif-

Softball is a popular sport for girls in high school and college and the most popular sport for women and men in recreation programs.

ferent. The program described here is from a ninth-through twelfth-grade suburban high school with an enrollment of 1,650 students. The school competes in twelve varsity sports for girls and boys. Football, boys' basketball, girls' basketball, and girls' volleyball have ninth-grade, reserve, and varsity teams. The others have reserve and varsity teams. Eight hundred fifty of the students in the school compete at one time or another on one or more of these teams.

The school has a year-round weight-training facility and a full-time athletic trainer. Nearly every sport has a parents' or a booster club, which supplies extra funds for the program and acts as a communication link between coaches and parents. The school district cannot find enough qualified people to act as coaches from the ranks of certified teachers in the district, so they take advantage of a state regulation that allows them to hire noncertified people to coach if they cannot fill vacancies within the district.

Out-of-School Sport

Not all high school students participate in the inter-school sport program, and some of those who do not participate have an active sport involvement outside the school. Two examples are Andrea and William. Andrea owns her own horse and has trained and competed for years in equestrian sports. She boards her horse at a nearby stable and goes there nearly every day after school to train and care for her horse. She hopes someday to compete in equestrian three-day-event competitions. Thus, she trains both in *dressage* (precise replicating of figures and moves) and in jumping. Last summer and autumn, she competed in fifteen events, most of them

Some kinds of elite sports develop completely outside school programs.

against boys and girls her own age, but sometimes in more open competition against adults. Although her sport involvement is quite expensive, her training and competition are every bit as intense as those for less expensive sports, such as basketball or volleyball. Nonetheless, many of her classmates do not know that she is such an accomplished athlete.

William has taken karate lessons for 6 years. He has slowly advanced in local karate competitions and is beginning to make a name for himself. He trains at a small karate studio that occupies a storefront in one of the area shopping malls. He has grown very strong and can make very quick movements. His room at home is filled with trophies he has won in local competitions. Like Andrea's athletic accomplishments, however, his are not known by many of his classmates. He, too, has never played on a school team.

YOUNG ADULTHOOD

Young adults are women and men who have finished high school and have gone on to further education or have entered the workforce. They are in a time of separation from youth and of establishment of patterns of work and play that will last a lifetime. Young adults participate in sport, fitness, and physical education in so many ways that these ways can only be sampled here.

University Recreation Program

For the 50,000 undergraduate and graduate students at Ohio State University, an important part of campus life is the intramural and recreation program. More than 100 activities are offered each year in a variety of indoor and outdoor facilities, from weight lifting to team sports to fitness activities. Special events are frequent. A H-O-R-S-E tournament (a basketball-shooting game wherein the lead competitor chooses a shot and the other competitor has to replicate it) attracts more than 400 competitors during winter quarter. Billiards, bowling, rowing, and 16 martial-arts programs allow students to

Coed competition is popular among young adults.

learn and compete in activities not often available in high schools. The three indoor swimming pools seem to be busy every hour they are available. During a typical quarter, nearly 500 fitness classes are offered, and more than 13,000 students participate.

The Recreation and Intramural Sports Department also sponsors 56 sport clubs throughout the school year. Some clubs, such as the equestrian, women's rugby, and water-ski teams, participate in regional and national competitions. Some, such as the alpine ski club, take trips during break periods. Each club has a faculty advisor.

A large number of sport competitions are offered each quarter. The department trains student officials and managers for these competitions. During winter quarter, 386 basketball teams compete in nearly 900 games in men's, women's, and co-rec leagues. During the same quarter, competitions are also offered in ice hockey, inner-tube water polo, wallyball, wrestling, badminton, racquetball, squash, and table tennis. Sports change with the seasons, but participation remains high, especially in spring quarter when outdoor facilities can also be used.

Facilities are open and available for drop-in recreation and fitness on a first come, first served basis.

University Recreation Program Fitness Classes

Making fitness fun and attractive to the diverse interests of university students.

- Step kickboxing—Step aerobics combined with kickboxing
- Aero Step—Step combinations combined with hi-lo impact aerobics
- Super Step—Step combinations with power movements for a hi-cardio workout
- W.E.T.—Water exercise training using buoyancy belts and resistance equipment
- H_2O Boxing—W.E.T. classes that incorporate martial arts movements
- Yoga—Exercise and stress relief
- Power Yoga—Functional strength training combined with yoga
- Kickboxing—Athletic and kickboxing movements for a total body hi-cardio workout

- Step and Sculpt—30 minutes of strength training and 30 minutes of step aerobics
- Butts and Guts—Lower-body toning with focus on lower back and abdominal stabilizer muscles in addition to glutes
- Body Sculpting—Resistance tubing, fitballs, medicine balls, and hand weights for shape and strengthening all muscle groups
- Cardio Funk—Combined dance and workout session
- Latin Rhythms—Fun-filled, hi-cardio workout to Latin music
- Cardio Sculpt—Hi-lo aerobics combined with strength training
- High/Low—Alternating high- and low-impact aerobics

SOURCE: Ohio State University, Department of Recreational Sports, Handbook 2001–2002

Students work out in the weight rooms, play tennis on the seventy tennis courts, swim laps, or play pickup basketball. During the 2001–2 academic year, in both indoor and outdoor facilities, more than 1.5 million participants were counted.

The staff comprises 14 full-time professionals and more than 400 student assistants, many of whom are interns from various academic programs in recreation and sport management. More than 200 sport officials are trained each year.

Miami (Ohio) University has also recently built a major student fitness and recreation center. One of the advantages of having a large, new facility is that it can accommodate new and exciting programs. At Miami University, more than 6,650 students compete on 475 teams in intramural "broomball," an indoor hockey-type game played with a small rubber ball and an aluminum stick with a rubber head. In the most recent season, all the slots for the three winter-season broomball competitions were filled

in under 30 minutes after registration began, and 30 teams had to be turned away (Conklin, 1999). What this shows is that fun competitions in good facilities can attract the enthusiasm and loyalty of young adults.

Community Recreation

Most towns and cities have recreation departments that organize learning and participation opportunities for citizens within their geographic boundaries. Although children and older adults often take part in these programs, young adults are the main consumers of community recreation services. Recreation opportunities include classes organized for people to learn new skills, drop-in recreation for a variety of sport activities, and various organized sport teams and sport events.

Community recreation departments try to provide a wide variety of activities, in much the same

Aerobic exercise sessions can take on the look of a festival.

way a university program does. Rather than describe the scope of such a program, as was done for the university program, this section describes in more detail the organization for one sport—softball.

Softball is the most popular participation sport in America. In 2001, through the auspices of the Columbus, Ohio, recreation department, 124 softball leagues competed in 126 city-owned softball fields involving 981 local teams in organized league play and nearly 100 tournaments for 4,000 local and regional softball teams. More than 13,000 games were played by some 35,000 players. The center of this activity is Berliner Park, where there are 31 softball diamonds, 2 batting cages, 2 concession stands, and 2 play areas for children on 226 parkland acres.

Competitions are provided for all levels of skill and interest: men's leagues, women's leagues, and coed leagues, as well as slow-pitch and fast-pitch leagues. Some of the leagues are primarily social, with everybody out to have a good time. Others are very intense, with players who are highly skilled and perhaps even playing in up to four leagues each season. The city trains and employs umpires, and city maintenance personnel keep the facilities in

top shape. The city recreation department, which manages the entire operation, consists of trained professionals.

Fitness Involvement

All across the land, **fitness** facilities of various kinds have sprung up in recent years. Some are franchised; they run television advertising campaigns and display familiar logos on their facilities. Others are more local, often occupying storefronts in shopping areas. Some offer a range of fitness activities, often including workouts using the latest in exercise equipment. Others focus more on group activities, such as the many variations of aerobics. Still others focus more on strength development, with weight lifting as the primary activity.

The young adults who constitute the main clientele for these establishments are concerned with how they look and with their levels of fitness. This increased concern with fitness (and particularly with looking fit) is an important phenomenon in current American life (see Chapter 9). The various fitness facilities also allow a range of participation modes and motivations. As is true of sport participation, some people's fitness involvement is as much social as it is physical. Other people, however, undertake serious workouts.

Informal Participation

Although young adults' participation in organized sport and fitness is impressive, it pales compared with their levels of participation in informal activities. Accurate statistics on informal participation are difficult to obtain. The evidence that informal participation levels are high, however, is all around us.

When you travel around your area on any weekend, what do you see? If you have tried to play golf on a local course, you know that you often have to wait to get a tee time. If you live near water, then you probably have seen people sailing, water-skiing, canoeing, and fishing. If you live in a more wintry climate, you have witnessed ice skating, cross-country skiing, snowmobiling, and other winter activities.

In my area, I see people walking the bike–walking paths near the river where I live. On Saturday morning, the main street in my neighborhood is crowded with small groups of cyclists headed out for a trek, all brightly clad in the latest cycling gear. Joggers, of course, are everywhere. When the weather is good, the local tennis courts are filled during most afternoons.

As is apparent, young adults are increasingly incorporating physical activity into their lifestyles. In doing so, many have become lifelong learners who are continuously seeking out opportunities to learn or to improve their skills as they pursue physical education.

THE OLDER ADULT

One of the myths that pervaded physical education and sport as late as the 1940s was that of the "athlete's heart." The myth was that vigorous exercise was inappropriate for young people because of the potential damage to the heart. We now know, of course, that lack of exercise is more likely to be detrimental.

Similar myths kept older adults from participating in many kinds of sport and fitness activities. Traditionally, only nonvigorous sports such as golf or bowling have been considered appropriate for older adults. If older adults cycled or jogged, they tended to do so in a leisurely fashion. Since the 1980s, the prejudices accompanying these traditional myths have been breaking down rapidly.

The Masters Athlete

Master's athletics begins at age 35 or 40 and continues in 5-year age groups up to the 95-year-old division. The first World Masters Games were in Toronto, Canada, in 1985. Eight thousand athletes from sixty-one countries competed in twenty-two sports. The fifth World Masters Games were held in Melbourne, Australia, in 2002. More than 20,000 athletes competed in twenty-nine sports. No monetary prizes are involved and no material riches are to be gained. Nearly all participants pay their own way to compete.

The biennial World Veterans Track and Field Championships also appeals to mature athletes, often attracting more than 5,000 competitors, who have won the right to participate by meeting qualification standards in their local areas. The friendly, yet extremely serious competition motivates athletes in their 50s, 60s, and 70s to train diligently to perform at their top levels. Through the masters sport movement, former Olympians sometimes extend their careers beyond their young adulthood.

The performances of masters athletes are extraordinary. Sprinters in the 60- to 65-year-old group run 100 meters in less than 12.5 seconds. Male long jumpers age 50 to 55 regularly jump farther than 20 feet. Women age 45 to 50 run 200 meters in less than 26.5 seconds. Women age 55 to 60 run 5,000 meters in less than 19 minutes.

The masters track-and-field movement is perhaps the largest of masters-level movements across many different sports. It is no longer uncommon to find vigorous competition among groups of older adults in swimming, volleyball, and basketball. What has changed most dramatically is our conception of what is possible for the older adult. Vigorous training and serious competition are *not* for youths and young adults only!

Physical Activity Forever

People in the developed world now live longer than ever, so the number of elderly people is rising, as is the proportion of older people relative to other age groups. The 65–84 age group will increase to 12 percent of the total population in 2010 and to nearly 17 percent by 2025 (Cordes & Ibrahim, 2003). Estimates suggest that by 2030, more than a half-million Americans will be over the age of 100. It is increasingly clear that regular physical activity is important in helping elderly people maintain the quality and length of their lives. Whereas young people can increase physical function by 10 percent through regular exercise, older people can achieve an increase of 50 percent. A sedentary lifestyle, on the other hand, is estimated to account for 50 percent of the decline in strength, flexibility, and aerobic functioning among older people. The cost to the nation's public health bill for this loss of capacity is staggering.

The men and women who now constitute our "senior" generation grew up in an era that did not promote fitness in the same ways our current era does. Women particularly tended to be socialized away from vigorous activity and were exposed to the prejudice that it was not feminine to exercise or to compete vigorously. Also, the detrimental effect of tobacco smoking and of eating a poor diet were less well known.

Thus, the current senior generation is actually *learning* to be more active. Many contemporary seniors prefer *low-impact activities,* such as walking or water aerobics, which are designed to minimize the stressful impact of exercise on aging joints. Others, however, work out in much the same way that young adults do, using exercise machines or cycling. Many senior-citizen centers now offer fitness facilities to their clients. These fit seniors also provide excellent role models for their younger counterparts. The generations that follow them, who

grew up in the current climate of knowledge about and support for sport and fitness as lifetime endeavors, are likely to alter further our perceptions of what is possible for the senior citizen.

THE NEW SETTINGS FOR SPORT, FITNESS, AND PHYSICAL EDUCATION

Traditionally, sport, fitness, and physical education have been restricted primarily to children, youths, and adults. Facilities, therefore, have most often been those associated with schools, communities, and family-oriented organizations, such as the Young Men's Christian Association (YMCA). These agencies still provide such facilities and are expanding their programs. There is, however, a host of facilities more widely available to more people than ever before. Many of these sport and fitness facilities are in the private sector, with users paying direct fees for the opportunity to use them.

Multipurpose Athletic Clubs

Historically, the term *athletic club* has referred to a social club for wealthy men in a big city, but these facilities have changed. The modern multipurpose athletic club is one of the most important examples of the shift toward lifespan sport, fitness, and physical education. The new athletic club attracts singles, married couples, and families. The facilities typically include indoor and outdoor swimming pools (the latter with large decks for sunbathing), racquetball courts, several exercise rooms, a sportswear shop, a snack bar, and locker rooms that include a steam room, a sauna, and a jacuzzi. At any time during the day, the facilities bustle with activity. At peak hours—from 5:00 to 8:00 in the evening, for example—virtually every piece of equipment and every inch of space is utilized.

Multipurpose athletic clubs provide more than just facilities. Through such clubs, racquetball leagues are formed, aerobics classes are offered several times daily, and swimming and jogging clubs meet regularly. Special competitions are organized, as are classes to help people learn and improve skills. In the exercise areas of such clubs, individuals can track their progress on computer-based records and can receive guidance from a staff member on what exercises to do and how to use the exercise machines appropriately. A supervised nursery cares for young children while mothers and fathers work out. The typical price range for a family membership for 1 year is $400 to $850. Classes and racquetball-court time are charged on a per-use basis.

The private, multipurpose athletic club is a modern version of what for years has been offered in family YMCAs. The YMCA has also updated its operations and now offers a similar range of instructional participatory opportunities.

Sport Clubs

Private-sector sport clubs are now regular features of any metropolitan area. Tennis may account for the largest number, but there are many types of clubs, with foci ranging from skating to trapshooting to racquetball. Typical is the Olympic Tennis Club, where 2,500 tennis players of all ages play each week, primarily outdoors in the summer and indoors in the winter.

Sport clubs offer three primary services: instruction, organized competitions, and social play. At the Olympic Tennis Club, 350 adults take lessons each week. Lessons might range from a 30-minute private lesson for $30 per lesson to a 1½-hour group lesson costing $16 per lesson. Beginner lessons are typically given in groups of six, last for 1 hour, and cost $11 per lesson. Competitors are organized in several ways, but primarily on the basis of skill level—that is, beginners, intermediates, and advanced. Leagues are formed so that players can participate regularly for an extended period of time.

Social play and practice require only that members sign up for court time. The cost of court time depends on the hour of the day and day of the week, with popular times more costly than off-peak times. Many members have regular court-time reservations and often play with the same person each

Exercise facilities are found in many private and public venues.

week, thus emphasizing the social element often associated with adult involvement in sport.

Sport clubs often have attractive lounges, weight-training facilities, and child-care services available, as well as some kind of food service. The facilities are typically bright, clean, and attractive. The service at sport clubs is typically quick, courteous, and friendly. Amenities such as these keep customers returning.

Specialized Sport / Fitness Centers

While multipurpose centers have grown in importance, so too have the specialized sport and fitness centers. These centers are differentiated from the public type of facility, such as a golf course or a bowling alley, where participation is defined mostly by a pay-per-use arrangement. More recently, sport/fitness centers have developed that are defined by a monthly or yearly membership, and participation is restricted to members. Typical of these are swimming clubs, racquetball clubs, indoor tennis clubs, weight-lifting and body-building clubs, aerobics centers, and gymnastics centers.

Activities are often organized by these specialized centers. Lessons and classes are available, as are regular competitions, such as tennis leagues or water-polo tournaments. The membership feature of these centers tends to produce a social network in which friendships develop and are sustained around the common activity interests of the members.

Sport-Medicine Centers

People who participate in sport and fitness activities often need health-care treatment and rehabilitation—sometimes to remediate problems and sometimes to prevent problems from developing. Unheard of 20 years ago, specialized **sport-medicine** facilities and programs are now common in metropolitan areas.

A sport-medicine program serves varied clientele. It might provide care for high school athletic programs, serve adults who have sport-related injuries, implement sport/fitness education programs, or treat children in either remedial or preventive modes. The staff of sport-medicine organizations might include orthopedic surgeons, family-practice physicians, podiatrists, nutritionists, physical therapists, X-ray technicians, athletic trainers, and even sport psychologists.

Initially, sport-medicine programs were attached to hospitals or were operated out of a regular group medical practice as an additional service to clients. As their popularity has grown, however, they have tended to become separate facilities, specialized to serve clients of all ages.

Home Gymnasiums

As sport, fitness, and physical education grow in importance across the lifespan, adults find ways to accommodate these interests within the home or, by extension, in public facilities available within their immediate area. Ellis (1988) has noted that the do-it-yourself approach that has traditionally characterized some leisure activities, such as gardening, is spreading quickly to sport, fitness, and physical education.

Just as people are increasingly using private-sector sport and fitness facilities, people are also developing informal sport and fitness opportunities within their homes and immediate neighborhoods. Many new houses now include small areas for exercise equipment. Many more basements and family rooms have been converted to accommodate exercise bicycles, rowing machines, and weight-lifting setups.

While many people are paying to gain access to sport, fitness, and physical-education opportunities in private facilities, others are developing the capability to produce these opportunities themselves, often at home.

Worksite Programs

Increasingly, employers are converting older facilities into space for recreation and fitness programs. Newly constructed buildings often include specially designed fitness and recreation centers. Corporations have found that a healthy and physically active workforce is a more productive and less expensive workforce. The costs of employee health care can be reduced substantially by an effective fitness program. Employees who have the opportunity to use company fitness and recreation facilities at times convenient to their workday tend to be not only more productive but also more loyal to the company.

Many corporations and organizations make employee wellness a major goal in their business and personnel planning. Tenneco, Inc., one of America's largest corporations, has a 25,000-square-foot wellness facility that houses fitness equipment, racquetball courts, and large spaces for group fitness activities (Baun & Landgreen, 1983). A four-lane walking–jogging track encircles the building. The headquarters of the Adolph Coors Company includes a wellness center that houses a gymnasium, a clinic, and a counseling office. IBM Corporation has a "Plan for Life" wellness program, which includes wellness screening for employees on company time (Goetzel et al., 1994). Other companies support their employees with memberships at local fitness facilities.

Improving employee fitness and health is now a common goal of corporations simply because of the enormous costs incurred by an unhealthy workforce. General Electric Corporation reported that employees participating in a worksite fitness program reduced health-care costs by 38 percent compared with employees not participating, whose health-care costs actually increased during the course of the study (www.fitwellinc.com). The Coors wellness center estimates that the corporation saved $1.4 million in health-care claims from employees over a 6-year period.

Corporations now regularly provide incentives to employees who exercise regularly and do not smoke. Incentives are most frequently reductions in the premiums paid for health insurance, as well as support for and access to worksite fitness programs on company time. Other corporations provide disincentives. Hershey's Food Corporation, for example, charges higher rates for health insurance if employees have high blood pressure, smoke, are overweight, or don't exercise regularly. Worksite fitness is now big business. It opens up a range of new professional opportunities for women and men who aspire to careers in the fitness and wellness professions.

Sport/Games Festivals

A type of sport festival recently added to our cultural landscape illustrates well the theme of lifespan physical activity. All across America, states have developed highly successful summer sport festivals for athletes of all ages. The first such event, New York's Empire State Games, attracted 5,000 participants in 1978 (*Albany Times Union,* 1992), and the idea spread quickly. Sport festivals in more than forty-five states now attract hundreds of thousands of athletes, young and old. In Montana, a state with only 800,000 residents, the Big Sky State Games attract more than 10,000 competitors each year.

In 2001 Kentucky's Bluegrass State Games attracted 17,000 participants, who ranged in age from 2 years to 85 years and competed in forty-two sports. Athletes from 101 Kentucky counties received 3,799 medals (www.bgsg.org). Many sports include categories for people with disabilities. A festival nature pervades the entire event, and people of all ages and skill levels celebrate the joys of amateur sports.

Thirty-seven states now conduct statewide amateur sport festivals known as State Games. Nearly a half-million amateur athletes participate in State Games each year. Most of those states are members of the National Congress of State Games (www.state games.org). Thirteen states now conduct Winter State Games as well as summer games. State Games are open to participants of all ages and abilities.

THE EMERGING CHARACTERISTICS OF LIFESPAN PHYSICAL ACTIVITY

Lifespan physical activity is an emerging phenomenon. Although we cannot now predict how it will continue to develop and mature, we can predict some characteristics of its future development, based on observations of its early stages.

1. *The importance of an early start.* Habits of participation in physical activity clearly begin in childhood. In addition, the skills developed in childhood can be used throughout life, whereas new skills become increasingly difficult to learn as people age. Also, many fitness problems may have a pediatric origin; that is, unfit children tend to become unfit adults. Although some programs aim at producing "superbabies," making exaggerated claims and, perhaps, doing more harm than good, most early programs do not. Given the importance of early-childhood physical education, physical educators must develop appropriate programs that reach all children.

Obesity Trends in the Age of Physical Activity

The explosion of research and information about the health benefits of regular physical activity is changing our culture, but not everyone has yet heard the message or found a way to change his or her lifestyle.

- The incidence of childhood obesity has increased by more than 50 percent in the last decade.
- Nearly 20 percent of the adult population can be classified as obese.
- More than 55 percent of the adult population does not engage in physical activity at all or is not regularly active.

- A marked increase in diabetes is associated with the increased incidence of obesity.
- The incidence of overweight is higher in minority populations and among the poor.

All of this has occurred despite consistent emphasis on regular physical activity and a greater awareness of the importance of a healthy diet.

There is still much work to do!

SOURCES: Mokdad et al. (2001), Strauss & Pollock (2001)

---

2. *Breakdown of gender stereotypes.* We are approaching the time when girls and women will have full opportunities for lifespan physical activity in ways similar to those men now enjoy. Being fit is not gender specific: You do not have to be male to be an athlete. Sport, fitness, and physical education can no longer afford to organize or categorize activities or roles based on gender rather than on skill or interest. An important professional goal is to eliminate gender bias from how children and youths are socialized into physical activity and from what opportunities are available throughout their lifespans.

3. *Breakdown of age stereotypes.* People now live longer than ever before. In the developed world, a large proportion of the population is in the postretirement age group. Health problems related to aging represent a major investment of national resources. Unfortunately, stereotypes have sometimes contributed to behavior that increased the likelihood of health problems. For instance, traditional stereotype dictated that older adults should not engage in vigorous physical activity; based on such a stereotype, an older woman, for example, would be expected to avoid doing weight training. We now know that vigorous physical activity not only enhances older people's quality of life but also reduces their health-care costs—by decreasing the

incidence and the severity of osteoporosis in postmenopausal women, for example. People who are currently in middle age are likely to change this stereotype as they advance to their postretirement years, but until then, we must encourage contemporary older people to be active, providing them with opportunities to do so.

4. *Shift in emphasis from youths to adults.* The median age of our population increases with each passing decade—America is becoming grayer! The median age is now over 30 years, will reach 35 by the year 2010, and will be above 40 by the year 2020. Sport, fitness, and physical education have traditionally been viewed primarily in terms of programs for children and youths. It is quite clear now that these fields are undergoing an important transformation, shifting their focus to primarily serving adults rather than children and youths (Ellis, 1988). This transformation will require new programs, new facilities, a newly trained group of professionals, and an entirely new outlook on program goals and the processes through which those goals can be achieved.

5. *Shift to the private sector.* Historically, opportunities for sport, fitness, and physical education have been most widely available in the public sector: in schools, community recreation, and public facilities such as parks. In the past several decades, we have witnessed the emergence of an enormous private-sector industry dealing with sport opportunities (the tennis club, the gymnastics center), fitness (the weight-training center, the aerobics center), and physical education (the multipurpose athletic club). The emergence of this new industry has brought bright new prospects for participation; it has also revealed certain problems, such as the increasingly strong relationship between wealth and opportunity in sport, fitness, and physical education. There is no doubt, however, that sport, fitness, and physical education now represent major industries in America. Also, like most other industries, these are market oriented, catering to the interests and desires of the consumer and trying to influence those interests and desires through creative advertising.

6. *Increasingly strong scientific base.* Our scientific understanding of sport, fitness, and physical education has increased dramatically since the late 1960s (see Chapters 14–20). This knowledge has become widely available not only to physical-activity scientists and professionals but also to the general public. Many physically active people are highly knowledgeable about their activity, and they increasingly demand that professionals know the best and latest information. In addition, the high cost of medical services and health insurance provides a strong impetus for researchers to continue investigating the preventive benefits of lifespan physical activity.

7. *The new professionals.* Many of the professional roles described in this text have emerged only in this generation—sport management, cardiac rehabilitation, worksite fitness, and early-childhood physical education, to name a few. Each profession requires a somewhat different preparation, and, increasingly, each requires a professional certification or license to practice. The new professions develop organizations and a specialized literature, often spawning an even more specialized role, such as the sport-marketing specialization within sport management.

8. *Greater amounts of more readily available information.* Check the sport and fitness sections of your local bookstore or video store. What will first impress you is the volume of books, magazines, and videos, particularly the how-to books and videos, such as how to stay fit, how to scuba dive, or how to help your child become more skilled in a sport. Cable television now has specialized sport channels—for example, a 24-hour golf channel that offers instruction, as well as events. Not all the information represents the best of what sport and fitness sciences have taught us, but consumers are getting more knowledgeable and selective.

9. *The use of technology.* Technology is transforming our lives in many ways, including both knowledge about sport, fitness, and physical education and how we do sport, fitness, and physical education. The World Wide Web is an extraordinary source of information as the number of Web sites cited in this text will attest. High-tech exercise equipment allows for more specific workouts and more fun too! Nearly every sport has been influenced by technology breakthroughs in equipment—golf clubs, poles for vaulting, and shoes, to name just a few. The professional work of coaches, personal trainers, athletic trainers, sport managers, and physical-education teachers has been changed by information technology. We should expect that this trend toward technology will continue to change how we exercise, how we play, and how we learn.

LIMITATIONS

Although it is desirable for all of us to be physically active throughout our lifespans, we clearly do not now have equal opportunities for doing so. There is no doubt that socioeconomic status and race limit our opportunities in the current sport, fitness, and physical-education worlds (Siedentop, 1996c).

Most of our educational and political efforts to improve physical-activity opportunities for people of all ages have focused primarily on individuals, as a matter of individual responsibility. People who are unfit or inactive are usually considered to have individual problems, and the programs to effect change in fitness target those individuals. While acknowledging the role of individual responsibility, we must also recognize our collective or structural responsibility to make lifespan physical activity more likely and available, regardless of gender, race, or socioeconomic status. We cannot fulfill our collective responsibility simply through advertising campaigns that say "Just do it." We need to make a national commitment to provide education, facilities, and programs that are accessible to and affordable for all citizens.

A FRAMEWORK FOR UNDERSTANDING THE POSSIBILITIES FOR PROFESSIONAL SERVICE

A major purpose of this text is to offer you a framework within which you can understand the prospects, problems, and possibilities for professional service in sport, fitness, and physical education. The choice of a professional role should be informed not only by the immediate framework for that professional role but also by the larger history from which the role has emerged and the alternative possibilities derived from that history.

This textbook treats sport, fitness, and physical education as both discrete areas of interest and an integrated professional field. This presentation reflects the reality of professional life today. Clearly, professionals in sport are concerned with fitness and physical education. Just as clearly, physical educators teach sport and fitness. The separation of these areas is, therefore, somewhat artificial and arbitrary. On the other hand, preparation for these professional roles is typically specialized in today's colleges and universities. If you major in adult fitness, you will receive a curriculum substantially different from that offered to students preparing to become physical-education teachers; the curriculum leading to a degree in sport management is different still.

Thus, the seeming ambiguity that results from treating these areas separately in some instances and together on other occasions simply reflects the ambiguity of professional life in these disciplines today. Part 1 of this text deals with the historical roots of sport, fitness, and physical education. Parts 2, 3, and 4 explore the basic concepts of sport, fitness, and physical education, provide a survey of what is being done by whom within each field, and review the issues and problems within each field. Part 5 explores the scientific disciplines that not only support professional life but also represent career choices themselves—careers of biomechanist, sport psychologist, and exercise physiologist, for example. Finally, Part 6 discusses relationships to allied fields and examines the prospects and problems awaiting us in the future.

The *consumer* of sport, fitness, and physical-education activities will not recognize the differences that form the structure of this text. The woman or man who goes to a local fitness club or recreation center for an aerobics class or a volleyball match typically does not know or care about the distinctions among sport, fitness, and physical education that form the structure of this text. For the average consumer, the fields of health, recreation, sport, fitness, and physical education are all the same. For the people studying these fields, however, it is important to understand the differences that do exist and the history from which these differences have emerged. In the final chapter of this text, these differences are addressed again; a major theme of that chapter is the possibility of some reconvergence of what have now become separate and distinct fields.

SUMMARY

1. Recognition of the possibility and desirability of lifespan involvement in sport, fitness, and physical education represents a fundamental change in our perception of human life.

2. Sport and fitness are in boom eras, whereas school physical education has perplexing problems but bright prospects.

3. The era of lifespan sport, fitness, and physical education represents a watershed period—one not limited by age or gender.

4. Physical activity in the early years represents a new and exciting field for the sport, fitness, and physical-education professions.

5. Sport, fitness, and physical education for children occur in both the public and the private sectors; each has its own problems and prospects.

6. Activity programs for youths are extensive, with opportunities both within and outside schools.

7. Young adults find many outlets for activity in community programs and in the growing private-sector activity and fitness industry.

8. Adults increasingly have activity programs available at their worksite, and the adult fitness and sport industry has become big business. The masters sport movement has shown that older people can stay active as competitive athletes throughout their lives.

9. The new settings for sport, fitness, and physical education include multipurpose athletic clubs, sport clubs, specialized sport/fitness centers, sport-medicine centers, home gymnasiums, worksite programs, and sport/games festivals.

10. The emerging characteristics of lifespan involvement include the recognition of the importance of an early start, the breakdown of gender and age stereotypes, the shift in emphasis from youths to adults, the shift from the public to the private sector, the increasingly strong scientific base, the creation of new professional roles, the increased availability of information, and the use of technology.

11. Although the consumer of sport, fitness, and physical education typically does not recognize the specialized nature of each field, professional specialization is typical of career preparation. The resulting ambiguity forms the framework for this text.

DISCUSSION QUESTIONS

1. What stereotypes do you hold about who should or can participate in activities? How did you acquire them?

2. Describe three new facilities or programs that you have seen firsthand that are typical of the current boom in sport and fitness.

3. Describe five private-sector facilities for sport, fitness, and physical education in your region. What socioeconomic groups use these facilities most?

4. What specific experience have you had, or what specific evidence can you present, that shows that there is gender, race, or age discrimination or stereotyping in sport, fitness, and physical education?

5. What might the possibilities be for lifetime involvement of a boy or a girl born into an upper-middle-class household in America in the year 2000? What might they be for a child born into a household with lower socioeconomic status?

CHAPTER **2**

The Emergence of a Profession: 1885–1930

Physical education must have an aim as broad as education itself and as noble and inspiring as human life. The great thought in physical education is not the education of the physical nature, but the relation of physical training to complete education, and then the effort to make the physical contribute its full share to the life of the individual, in environment, training, and culture.

Dr. Thomas Wood, 1893, speaking to the International
Congress on Education at the Chicago World's Fair

LEARNING OBJECTIVES

- To describe the cultural influences on the emergence of sport and physical education in the middle to late nineteenth century

- To discuss the historical role of formal gymnastic systems

- To describe the emergence of national sports forms

- To discuss the birth of the physical-education profession

- To discuss the institutionalization of sport

- To evaluate the influence of progressive education

- To describe the twentieth-century emergence of the new physical education

- To identify the contributions of important early leaders

- To discuss the emergence of a national sport culture

THE HERITAGE OF PHYSICAL EDUCATION, SPORT, AND FITNESS IN THE UNITED STATES

In Chapters 2, 3, and 4, you will learn a great deal about how physical-education, sport, and fitness professions developed in the United States and about the philosophies that drove that development. Space does not permit a full rendering of the historical influences that shaped these movements in the United States and, indeed, in most of the Western world. Although there is ample evidence of the importance of sport and physical activity in all ancient cultures, the development of these fields in North America was influenced predominantly by the early Greek and Roman cultures in Europe, particularly by the civilization of early Greece. The city-states of ancient Greece contributed a great deal to the government, literature, and arts of all Western cultures. In no area, however, was the contribution more profound than in physical education, sport, and fitness. The *gymnasium* was the center of ancient Greek education and culture. Education was focused as much on physical pursuits as on intellectual pursuits; indeed, for the Greek citizen the two were inseparable. The often-cited aphorism "a sound mind in a sound body" captures part of that heritage, as does the central guiding ethic of early Greek society, *arete,* or a quest for excellence.

Sporting venues and temples were the two main gathering places for Greek citizens. A regular series of sporting events dominated the Greek calendar, the Olympic Games being the most important festival. Greek city-states were often at war with one another and with other nations, but during the Olympic Games a series of truces allowed contestants to cross battle lines to compete in the games.

When the Roman Empire overcame the Greek dominance of the known Western world, sport and games thrived, and as the empire spread, its favored forms of physical activity and games spread with it. Under the Roman emperors, however, the beauty, grace, and educational centrality of physical activity, sport, and games so dominant in early Greece gradually degenerated into professionalism and corruption. The fall of the Roman Empire in A.D. 476 ushered in a period of 1,000 years known as the Dark Ages, in which physical activity, sport, and fitness diminished in importance amid political and economic chaos. Nonetheless, as we consider the development of physical education, sport, and fitness in the United States beginning in the nineteenth century, we should not lose sight of the enduring legacy of early Greece and Rome to the modern world.

The Birth of a Profession

In 1885 William G. Anderson, who was to become the first secretary of what we now know as the American Alliance for Health, Physical Education, Recreation, and Dance (AAHPERD), was deeply concerned about his own lack of training and preparation to be a professional physical educator (Lee & Bennett, 1985a). Anderson, who was then 25 years old, had graduated from medical school and was employed at Adelphi Academy in Brooklyn as an instructor of physical training. His only real experience in his field, however, had been as a young participant at the German *Turnverein* (a social, gymnastics, and sports club) in Quincy, Illinois.

In 1885 there were no institutions that prepared people to be what was then called a "gymnastics teacher." To become an instructor in physical training, apparently, a person needed only some knowledge of medicine and some experience in gymnastics (a kind of gymnastics very different from what we now know as Olympic gymnastics). There were no professional organizations to bring together people who had common interests. There were few texts available to help people acquire understanding of the field. There were no professional journals. In fact, there was no profession.

Anderson, as his life's work makes clear, was a leader. He wanted to create a forum within which people interested in physical training, physical education, and the various gymnastic systems could discuss with, debate with, and learn from one another.

To that end, Anderson invited a group of people interested in the fields to meet at Adelphi Academy on November 27, 1885. Among those attending were local clergy, school principals, members of the news media, college presidents, and, of course, physical-training instructors. Sixty interested people gathered for that historic meeting. Among them were the famous cleric Henry Ward Beecher; the founder of the Women's Christian Temperance Union and well-known advocate of physical education, Dio Lewis; and the author of the then-well-known book *How to Grow Strong and How to Stay So,* William Blakie (Lee & Bennett, 1985a).

On that day, the participants decided to form an organization, the Association for the Advancement of Physical Education. Dr. Edward Hitchcock, who had founded the first college department of physical education at Amherst College 24 years earlier and was still its head, was elected to be the first president. The director of the gymnasium at Harvard College, Dr. Dudley Sargent, was a vice president. The young Dr. Anderson earned the privilege of being the association's first secretary. Forty-nine of the sixty assembled participants took membership in the new organization. The distribution of their interests and affiliations is testimony to the breadth of interest in physical education at that time: Eleven were college teachers, thirteen were academy–seminary teachers (secondary level), three were practicing physicians, six were active in the early YMCA movement, and two were ministers. The remainder represented private gymnastic clubs, other disciplines such as anthropology, and the business world. Nine of the new members were laypeople. Six of the new members were women, all of whom were physical-training instructors.

That meeting marked the birth of a profession.

THE SCENE BEFORE 1885

Although the Adelphi Conference of 1885 was the symbolic beginning of the sport, fitness, and physical-education professions, these disciplines had a prior history rich in ideas, people, and events. Many of those ideas are considered in subsequent chapters.

The second half of the nineteenth century marked the change in the United States from a predominantly rural, colonial, and frontier nation to a more urban and industrialized nation. Sport, fitness, and physical education were certainly not unknown before 1885. In 1791 the first private swimming pool was built in Philadelphia. In 1820 the first college gymnasium was built at Harvard College. The first competitive football game was played in 1827. John Warren, a professor of anatomy and physiology at Harvard, published the first theoretical treatise on physical education in 1831; in the same year, Catherine Beecher, sister of the cleric who attended the Adelphi Conference, published a book titled *A Course in Calisthenics for Young Ladies.*

Although there was virtually no **physical education** in schools before 1885, the idea of free, universal, public education was growing in the United States. In 1839 the first teacher-training school was founded in Lexington, Massachusetts. The idea that physical training (or physical education, as it was soon to be called) was to be a part of the school curriculum also took hold during that period. In 1866 the first state legislation requiring physical education in schools was passed in California.

The American Civil War was largely responsible for many of the subsequent developments, particularly in the field of sport. Many historians refer to that period as the transition time between local games and institutionalized sport (Spears & Swanson, 1978). The post–Civil War era saw an extraordinary development of organized sport. Development during that pre-1885 period was not confined to universities and sport associations. Sport also grew rapidly in the programs of social agencies. Baseball was first played as an intercollegiate game in 1859; the first intercollegiate football game was played a decade later, in 1869. Tennis was introduced into the United States by Mary Outerbridge in 1874. The National Bowling Congress was formed in 1875, and badminton was first played in

An early twentieth-century physical-education class for college men.

the United States in 1878. In 1879 the National Archery Association and the National Association of Amateur Athletics were formed.

Development during that pre-1885 period was not confined to schools and colleges. The YMCA movement had begun in England in 1844 and was devoted to character education and physical activity. In 1851 the first American YMCA was formed in Boston. The YMCA movement was so successful that it created the need in 1883 for the development of the International Training School of the YMCA in Massachusetts, later to become Springfield College. Springfield College has a long and noble history of contributions to the development of sport, fitness, and physical education. In Cincinnati, in 1848, German immigrants formed the first Turnverein, a forerunner of a movement that was to be widespread for the next half-century in cities where there was a significant population of German descent.

Those events portended what, in the first half of the twentieth century, would blossom into the profession of physical education—encompassing during that later period not only sport, fitness, and physical education but also recreation, the playground movement, dance, and outdoor education.

Although there was no such overarching profession in the pre-1885 period, the roots of its eventual development are clear.

In 1825 Charles Beck became the first recognized teacher of physical education in the United States. He developed a program of German gymnastics at the Round Hill School in Northhampton, Massachusetts. Just 1 year later, another advocate of the German system, Charles Follen, started a gymnastics program at Harvard College. In 1837 Catherine Beecher founded the Western Female Institute, where her own Beecher system of calisthenics was an integral part of the curriculum. In the same year, the Mt. Holyoke Female Seminary offered a course in physical education to its students (Leonard & Affleck, 1947).

As Chapter 4 shows, a dominant philosophical movement of the first part of the nineteenth century was *muscular Christianity,* a philosophy that made exercise and fitness (if not yet sport) compatible with the Christian life. It was this philosophical movement that allowed a still-conservative nation to move gradually away from the Puritan prohibitions against play and exercise. This was an important shift in thought because many of the leaders of society in those days were members of the clergy, and education and religion were still intertwined. It is no accident that the history of that period is so marked by references to people with strong religious affiliations and to institutions with religious missions, such as Dio Lewis, Catherine Beecher, and the YMCA (Lee & Bennett, 1985a).

As religious prohibitions began to loosen, the idea that exercise and fitness were educationally important began to become accepted. (In contrast, recognition of the educational value of sport is much more a twentieth-century phenomenon.) That philosophical shift allowed physical education to become part of the school and college curriculum. In 1861 Edward Hitchcock became the director of the department of hygiene and physical culture at Amherst College, marking the first such organizational arrangement in the United States. In 1879 Dudley Sargent was appointed assistant professor of physical training and director of the

Hemenway Gymnasium at Harvard College. Hitchcock and Sargent were among the most important early leaders in physical education, and their emphasis on scientific approaches provided fundamental direction for the emerging field.

The attitudes and institutions developed before 1885 would later allow the full development of sport, fitness, and physical education (Lucas & Smith, 1978). The young nation was still conservative. Work was valued, and there were still many formal and informal prohibitions against play. In schools, programs of manual labor were more common than were those of physical education. Sport was developing, even in colleges, but that was at the demand of students rather than of people in charge of the curriculum. Still, it was clearly in this transition period that the ideas, expectations, and institutions were forming that would allow for the emergence of sport, fitness, and physical education in the twentieth century:

> New England Puritanism—the traditional inhibitor of sport—was in truth one of the powerful American influences that led eventually to the introduction of voluntary school competitive athletics and compulsory physical education. National stability, rising expectations among middle and merchant classes, the beginning of colonial university education, and an atmosphere of intellectualism received its most significant thrust in New England. This Puritanism was not, as we have seen, an immediate catalytic agent for the rise of sport in the American colonies. Rather, it was a substantial portion of the bedrock upon which certain moral traditions, intellectual origins, and capitalistic institutions rested. Only out of these beginnings of the new nation was a pervasive system of sport and physical education slowly to emerge. (Lucas & Smith, 1978, p. 37)

Those ideas, events, and people were, therefore, forerunners of the great expansion of sport, fitness, and physical education. They certainly did not constitute *physical education* in the sense that we now know it. It is difficult to label each of these movements and the ideas that undergirded them; the terms *physical training, physical culture, gymnastics, sports,* and *play* were all used at one time or another. The term *physical education,* however, as an umbrella concept under which all the others might be understood, was not appropriate to those times.

> First, physical education, as we know it, largely had its origin in the United States. Second, although the name "physical education" appears in the literature before 1900, physical education is by and large a twentieth century phenomenon. (Bookwalter & Vander-Zwaag, 1969, p. 44)

Although the pious, hardworking Puritan is a common stereotype of early Americans, by the 1800s Americans certainly had sporting interests. For example, in 1862 (during the Civil War), more than 40,000 spectators watched a baseball game involving a New York regiment. In 1844 more than 35,000 spectators gathered at a racetrack in New York to watch a 10-mile footrace among professional runners. Horse racing, boxing, distance running, and rowing were popular spectator sports in the pre-1885 period (Lucas & Smith, 1978). People also participated in a variety of local sports and games, many of which later became standardized as national sports.

THE CONTEXT FOR THE EMERGENCE OF THE PROFESSION

Our attempt to analyze and understand the emergence of the sport, fitness, and physical-education professions from 1885 into the twentieth century has to be framed in the context of the general culture. We want to know why things happened as they did—and why some directions rather than others were taken. We cannot answer those questions satisfactorily without first painting in the background of the picture of the developing culture within which sport, fitness, and physical education began to emerge toward the end of the nineteenth century and to blossom as the umbrella profession of physical education in the first half of the twentieth century.

CHRONOLOGY AT A GLANCE—The Emergence of a Profession

Western frontier expansion	1825	Charles Beck hired as first teacher of physical education in United States
	1827	First competitive football game played
	1827	First public swimming pool opened, in Boston
	1834	First rules of baseball published
Era of muscular Christianity	1837	Western Female Institute founded by Catherine Beecher
	1848	First Turnverein formed, in Cincinnati
	1851	First YMCA formed, in Boston
	1861	Hitchcock appointed director of hygiene and physical culture at Amherst
American Civil War	1861	Boston Normal Institute for Physical Education founded by Dio Lewis
	1866	First state legislation requiring physical education passed, in California
	1874	Tennis introduced in United States
Expansion of Industrial Revolution	1879	Sargent appointed assistant professor of physical training at Harvard
	1883	YMCA Training School started at Springfield, Massachusetts
	1883	Swedish gymnastics introduced to United States by Nissen
	1885	Adelphi Conference held; Association for Advancement of Physical Education formed
Free, universal education	1885	Professional physical education program at Oberlin started by Delphine Hanna
	1887	Softball invented in Chicago
	1889	Boston Physical Training Conference held
	1890	Hartwell named supervisor of physical education for Boston
Urbanization	1891	Physical education recognized as curricular field by National Education Association
	1893	Department of physical education and hygiene formed in NEA
Substantial immigration	1895	First public golf course built
	1896	Olympic Games revived in Athens, Greece
	1896	Volleyball invented in Holyoke, Massachusetts
	1897	Society of College Gymnasium Directors formed
Expansion of public schooling	1901	First master's-degree program in physical education started at Teachers College
	1903	Gulick appointed director of physical education for New York schools
	1903	Delphine Hanna appointed first female full professor of physical education
	1905	National College Athletic Association formed

(continued)

		CHRONOLOGY AT A GLANCE—The Emergence of a Profession *(continued)*
	1906	Playground Association of America formed
	1908	First high school swimming pool built, in Detroit
	1909	National Association of Physical Education for College Women initiated
	1910	Four objectives of physical education identified by Hetherington
	1911	National Park Service formed
	1913	Intramural programs established by Michigan State and Ohio State
World War I	1916	First state supervisor of physical education named, in New York
Roaring Twenties	1924	Doctoral programs in physical education first offered by Teachers College and New York University
	1926	First dance major formed at University of Wisconsin
	1927	*The New Physical Education* published by Wood and Cassidy
Stock market crash	1930	*Research Quarterly* first published by Education Association
	1930	National Recreation Association formed

Let us consider a few of the more important cultural influences on the emerging sport, fitness, and physical-education professions:

1. *Decline of religious opposition to sport and exercise.* The early development of physical education and leisure pursuits had been seriously hindered by religious sanctions. In the nineteenth century, however, religion and sport reached an accommodation in the philosophy of muscular Christianity, the idea that the body and physical pursuits were not antithetical to a good, Christian life. The YMCA movement, and others like it, served to consolidate that philosophical position, using sport and exercise as activities through which to reach and serve youths.

2. *Immigration.* Between 1820 and 1880, 10 million immigrants came to America. From 1880 to 1890, 9 million more came! Immigrants brought with them new games and new attitudes, greatly enriching the sport and fitness culture of their new country. Sometimes, sport was a mechanism through which they became acculturated as Americans. They settled mainly in cities and, with the rise of professional sport in large cities, found common

loyalties with other immigrant groups and with groups already established in this country.

3. *Industrialization.* The American Civil War greatly intensified the move toward industrialization. Industrialization produced wealth—and some of that wealth helped to develop sport, fitness, and physical education. Industrialization created technologies for the development of facilities and equipment.

4. *Urbanization.* As immigrants poured into the country and industries developed in and around major cities, the population of America inevitably shifted from predominantly rural to predominantly urban. Whereas hunting, fishing, and other outdoor activities might sustain the leisure needs of a rural population, new activities had to be developed to meet the leisure needs of an urban population. Concentrated populations in cities and the wealth produced by industrialization were also necessary for the development of professional sport (Lucas & Smith, 1978).

5. *Transportation and communication.* The developing technologies in transportation and communication were especially important to the development and spread of sport. In 1830 only 23 miles of rail track existed in America; by 1880 there were 90,000 miles of track! The telegraph, invented in the 1840s, allowed instant communication of sport results. City newspapers became sufficiently sophisticated to have separate pages, or even sections, devoted to sport. In the twentieth century, the development of radio and television was to have an even larger influence on sport and fitness.

6. *Education.* So much of the development of sport, fitness, and physical education has occurred in schools that the development and extension of education was a fundamental influence. In 1862 the Morrill Land Grant Act created institutions of higher education, which provided greater access to university education; those same land-grant institutions would become leaders in the development of sport and physical education in the twentieth century. The American ideal of free, universal education began to become a reality in the middle to late nineteenth century. The courts decided that tax dollars could be used to support secondary education and paved the way for the model of the American comprehensive high school. Compulsory-attendance laws and emerging child-labor laws put more children into school and kept them there longer.

7. *Intellectual climate.* The nineteenth century was one of the most active eras in history for the development of *ideas.* That was the century in which Charles Darwin challenged accepted theories about the development of human life, Sigmund Freud challenged prevailing notions about human psychology, Jean-Jacques Rousseau introduced ideas for a new view of the education of children and youth, and Karl Marx wrote *Das Kapital.* Even the beginnings of what we know as modern science were primarily a nineteenth-century phenomenon. All of that intellectual ferment created a climate within which change was possible, institutions might be challenged, and normal operating procedure might be called into question.

Those influences were crucial to the emergence of sport, fitness, and physical education toward the end of the nineteenth century. Together, those early influences created a context for fantastic development in how people played and watched sport, in how they viewed physical activity, and in what sport and fitness programs were available. We now turn to that development.

THE BATTLE OF THE SYSTEMS

The period from 1885 to 1900 was marked by a competition among several approaches to what was then called "gymnastics" (which we now call "physical education"). That competition was for new converts to the systems and for places in school and college curricula. For that reason, at least for physical education, this period is most often referred to as "the battle of the systems" (Weston, 1962).

Almost all the early programs of physical education in America were **gymnastic systems** imported from Europe. Remember, this was a period of immigration—and immigrants brought with them their own approaches and loyalties. Most of these gymnastic systems were described as *formal* approaches to exercise, meaning that the movements were prescribed and were done in unison by a group of students. Our contemporary view of such approaches is often quite critical, but we should remember that to view these developments fairly, we have to view them in context. What is important is not how they appear to us now but how they appeared to people in the days in which they were popular.

To understand the various systems and why they were so popular as forms of early physical education, we must understand two elements of the context within which they were practiced and debated. First, Europe in the nineteenth century was a hotbed of nationalism. Nationalistic fervor was often accompanied by a strong military spirit. Adherents of a "German" system or a "Swedish" system were advocating more than allegiance to a particular kind of gymnastics. Indeed, loyalty to the gymnastic system was partially a manifestation of pride in country.

Second, a dominant psychological theory of those days was *faculty psychology.* This theory held that the mind could be trained by precise, repetitive practice and that orderliness and precision in activity made valuable contributions to mental development. Thus, the gymnastic systems from the physical domain were deemed to have benefits similar to those derived from the conjugation of Latin verbs from the academic domain—each helped to train the mind.

The early European-oriented systems quickly gave rise to a number of American systems; systems then battled for dominance in physical-education programs. A brief overview of each of the most prominent systems follows.

The German System

Perhaps the most widespread system in this period was the German system, developed originally by Friedrich Ludwig Jahn. Jahn's aim was to develop a system that would help to build a strong, united Germany by balancing academic education with physical education. Much of Jahn's system was designed to take advantage of outdoor spaces and was often practiced in an outdoor gymnasium termed a *Turnplatz* (exercising ground). A variety of exercises and skills were practiced using a variety of apparatus. Horizontal bars, balance beams, vertical ropes, ladders, vaulting horses, and parallel bars were all used; activities included jumping, climbing, running, and throwing (Weston, 1962). Games were also included, but these were reasonably simple games designed to create vigorous activity with running and dodging. Running tracks and jumping pits were typical, and what we would describe as competitive track-and-field activities took place.

Gymnastic societies for the practice and further spread of the system developed—the Turnvereins previously mentioned. In 1816 Jahn published what was to become an influential book, *German Gymnastics.*

The German system was brought to America by three of Jahn's students—Charles Beck, Charles

An early twentieth-century rhythmic gymnastics class for college women.

Follen, and Francis Leiber. In 1825 Beck was appointed teacher of physical education at the Round Hill School in Northhampton, Massachusetts, where he promptly installed the German system. At the same time, Follen was hired by Harvard College to set up indoor and outdoor gymnasiums in the German style. Leiber followed Follen at Harvard and also opened the first public swimming pool in America in Boston in 1827.

In 1848 a failed revolution in Germany brought a flood of German immigrants to America; by 1860 there were more than 150 Turnvereins in operation. By 1890 the number had grown to 300, with over 40,000 members; in many midwestern schools, the German system of gymnastics had become the physical-education program.

The Swedish System

The development of a Swedish system of gymnastics also had its origins in an attempt to regain lost national pride. Sweden had suffered badly in the Napoleonic era and had been severely compromised when Russia took over all of Finland in 1808 (Weston, 1962). Per Henrik Ling was a fencing master who had a serious interest in anatomy and physiology. He had traveled extensively in Europe and had been impressed with the work of Jahn in Germany. He was also enthralled by the Norse history of early Sweden and was determined to regain the vigor and spirit associated with Norsemen. From that mix of nationalism, education, and science was born the Swedish system of gymnastics.

What differentiated the Swedish system from the German system was its scientific–therapeutic basis. Ling's interest in the bodily sciences convinced him of both the developmental and the therapeutic value of scientific exercise. In 1814 Ling assumed the position of director of the Royal Central Institute of Gymnastics in Stockholm, and he began to influence the course of school programs.

Ling's gymnastic system was often referred to as *medical gymnastics* because of its developmental–therapeutic emphasis. The system involved a complex series of exercises done primarily with apparatus such as swinging ladders, rings, vaulting bars, and stall bars, and many swinging exercises involving ropes. These were Ling's *active* exercises, which formed the basis for his school and military programs. Ling also developed a series of therapeutic exercises involving both a *passive* role for the patient, where a therapist manipulated the patient's limbs, and a series of *resistance* exercises, where a patient exercised against resistance offered by a therapist (Colfer, Hamilton, Magill, & Hamilton, 1986). Ling's therapeutic system was remarkably similar to those practiced in modern rehabilitative programs.

The Swedish system was introduced in America in 1883 by Hartwig Nissen, a Swedish diplomat. (If you have been around gymnastics equipment, the name *Nissen* will be familiar to you.) A wealthy Bostonian, Mary Hemenway, provided financial support and influence to help spread the system. Hemenway had provided the support for the Hemenway Gymnasium at Harvard College, built in 1885. In 1887 Hemenway invited Baron Nils Posse to provide a workshop on Swedish gymnastics in Boston. Posse was a graduate of Ling's Royal In-

stitute of Gymnastics and became influential in the spread of the Swedish system in America, founding the Posse Normal School of Gymnastics, which provided a 2-year teacher-training program. In 1909 the Boston Normal School became the department of hygiene and physical education at Wellesley College. A close friend of Hemenway's, Amy Morris Homans, was employed as a teacher at the Boston Normal School and later became influential in having the Swedish system integrated into the Boston public-school program. The Swedish system was thus incorporated into the Boston schools in 1890, and Edward Hartwell was appointed the first director of physical training. Homans and Hartwell were prominent figures in the development of American physical education.

The Beecher System

Catherine Beecher (mentioned previously) was director of the Hartford Seminary for Girls and founded the Western Female Institute, where she developed the system of calisthenics and activities that was to bear her name. The motivation for the Beecher system is embedded in the view of women that was prevalent at the time—namely, that the typical gymnastic system for men was too vigorous and required too much strength for women. Remember that the prevailing ethic for women during those days was based on the four so-called womanly virtues: piety, purity, submissiveness, and domesticity (Spears & Swanson, 1978). Given that view, it is remarkable that *any* system of exercise was developed and deemed suitable for girls and women! The Beecher system was built around twenty-six lessons in physiology and two courses in calisthenics, along with appropriate "female" activities, such as archery, swimming, and horseback riding. The calisthenics were accompanied by music and were designed to produce grace of motion, good carriage, and sound health. Light weights were used, and wands were incorporated into the graceful movements. The Beecher system did *not* win widespread acceptance because even its scaled-down activity

Even in competition, activity costumes for women reflected nineteenth-century views of women.

Smith College women's basketball in 1904. Senda Berenson tosses up the ball.

was thought to conflict with the ideas about femininity widely held in those days.

The Dio Lewis System

Dioclesian Lewis was a radical thinker and a dynamic speaker. His wife's battle with tuberculosis gave him the interest in exercise and hygiene that ultimately led to the development of the Lewis system of gymnastics. Lewis was opposed to the vigorous nature of the German system and greatly admired both the grace of the Beecher system and the scientific nature of the Ling system. Thus, his efforts represent one of the first American systems that used elements from more than one of the other systems.

Lewis used musical accompaniment for his exercise routines, which were vigorous enough to increase the heart rate but were not as vigorous as the German approach. Beanbags, wands, dumbbells, clubs, and hand rings were used in exercises that were graceful and flowing. Social games and dance routines were also emphasized within the system.

Progressive schools were quick to accept the lighter approach to gymnastics, and by 1860 there

was sufficient interest in the Lewis system in schools for Lewis to found the Boston Normal Institute for Physical Education, to prepare teachers for teaching light gymnastics. Lewis also published in 1861 the *Gymnastics Monthly and Journal of Physical Culture,* which can be considered the first American physical-education journal (Weston, 1962).

The Hitchcock System

In 1861 Edward Hitchcock was appointed director of hygiene and physical culture at Amherst College, an action taken because the president of the college was concerned about the physical development and health of the students. The influence of the Civil War required that marching and unison calisthenics be part of the program, but the lasting contribution of Hitchcock was a scientific emphasis, based on measurement, in which health and exercise were approached from a developmental basis.

The Hitchcock system involved a battery of tests (Hitchcock became one of the great pioneers in *anthropometrics*—the measurement of bodily development) for the establishment of a baseline from which comparisons could be made over time to establish progress. The program itself used horizontal and rack bars, ladders, weights, rings, Indian clubs (weighted hand clubs shaped like bowling pins), ropes, and vaulting horses, and it included some sports and games, too.

Hitchcock's system of gymnastics was, perhaps, the first truly American program. Its scientific basis and emphasis on measurement provided a model that would later form a distinct thread in American physical education in the twentieth century.

The Sargent System

Dudley A. Sargent was appointed assistant professor of physical training and director of the Hemenway Gymnasium at Harvard University in 1879. With a background in gymnastics, a medical degree, and the support of a prestigious university, Sargent was in a position to develop a comprehensive program of physical education that combined the best of what was known at the time—and that is what he did.

What came to be known as the Sargent system was an amalgamation of most of the systems reviewed in this section, modified and enhanced by Sargent's own training, experience, and ingenuity. Students underwent a comprehensive medical and anthropometric testing program, on which a prescription of exercise was based. One of Sargent's most important contributions was the development of specialized exercise machines through which those prescriptions could be specifically practiced. A gymnasium using the Sargent system was a place of specialized activity. Calisthenics, German- and Swedish-type gymnastic exercises, and specialized machine exercise were all used.

In 1881 Sargent, recognizing the need to prepare teachers for this scientific brand of physical

education, organized the Sanatory Gymnasium in Cambridge. This later became the Sargent School of Physical Education and still exists today as the Sargent College of Boston University. Dudley Sargent was destined to become one of the most influential leaders in the development of American physical education.

The Boston Conference in 1889

In 1889 Mary Hemenway financed a conference to promote Swedish gymnastics. The **Boston conference** was organized by Amy Morris Homans and was presided over by the U.S. commissioner of education, William Harris. The theme of the conference was an evaluation of the various physical exercise programs then in use—thus, giving to the conference and to the era it represented the "battle of the systems" label.

A list of featured speakers at the conference now appears as a who's who of the fledgling profession of physical education: Hitchcock, Sargent, Hartwell, Anderson, and Posse. Also delivering papers at the conference were prominent American figures such as Henrich Metzner of the New York Turnverein, and international figures such as Baron Pierre de Coubertin of France, who was soon to revive the Olympic Games (Lee & Bennett, 1985a).

That conference is considered by most historians to be pivotal in the development of American physical education. It brought together important persons in a context in which each was called to examine and evaluate current activities in physical education. Although each no doubt tried to promote her or his own system, it is also clear that the door had been opened to the larger question: To what purposes should physical education be devoted, and by what means might such purposes be achieved?

The conference also served to add legitimacy to the beginnings of an *American* physical education; it is interesting that it was a European, Baron Nils Posse, who made that abundantly clear:

If the American nation consists chiefly of Germans, by all means teach the German system. If it is made up of Swedes, teach the Swedish, but if the chief bulk is made up of Americans, teach them *gymnastics* based on the laws of the nation; and if you need a prefix to the system, call it "American." (Lee & Bennett, 1985a, p. 22; emphasis in original)

Sport was not a major topic at the conference. Sports and games were not fundamental to any of the systems and, at that time, had no place in physical education. If we look at what was happening with sport in the larger culture during the same period, however, we can easily see that the days during which physical education was defined as gymnastics were numbered.

THE EMERGENCE OF ORGANIZED SPORT

If the late nineteenth century is interesting for its early development of gymnastic-oriented physical-education programs, it is even more remarkable when viewed as a period of development in sport. During the post–Civil War period, sport grew up: It changed from loosely organized games having many local variations to standardized sports with widely recognized rules and national overseeing bodies. The standardization of sport could not have happened, of course, except in an increasingly industrialized, urbanized culture in which increasing wealth, transportation, and communication and an emerging middle class provided the framework for such developments.

When a sport becomes *standardized* (or *institutionalized*), rules governing its conduct become standard, bodies are formed to enforce those rules, standards of competition are set, the sport is promoted for both participants and spectators, championships are formed, records are kept, and traditions and rituals are developed and shared by people who participate and watch. What a remarkable period of history that was for sport! Sports that can be described as having "come of age" during the period were the following (Lucas & Smith, 1978):

archery	pedestrianism
baseball	polo
bicycling	roller skating
billiards	rowing
bowling	rugby
boxing	sailing
canoeing	shooting
cricket	skiing
croquet	soccer
cross-country running	swimming
curling	tennis
fencing	track and field
football	trapshooting
golf	trotting
gymnastics	volleyball
handball	water polo
ice hockey	wrestling
lacrosse	yachting

Baseball was probably our first truly national sport, having been spread widely by soldiers during the Civil War and having achieved professional success with its attendant organizational apparatus. Although many players were paid and teams competed for money in the very early days of baseball, and especially right after the Civil War, it was the Cincinnati Red Stockings of 1868 who provided the model that was to be emulated not only in baseball but in other sports as well. An entrepreneurial lawyer, Aaron Champion, hired an outstanding manager, Harry Wright, who then put together the best and most complete team of professionals he could hire. The team was undefeated for more than 1 year, during which time they played before an estimated 200,000 spectators (Lucas & Smith, 1978).

Many of those developing sports, of course, had their roots in other countries. Some, like golf and tennis, were played in the United States as much as they were played in Europe. Other American sports, such as baseball and football, had origins in European games but had been modified substantially so as to become unique sports rather than variations of sports practiced elsewhere. Still other sports that came a bit later were derivations of American sports that had origins in other countries.

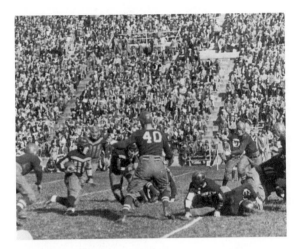

Intercollegiate football was a big spectator sport in the 1920s.

Softball, for example, which was invented in Chicago in 1887, was a variation of baseball, modified for use in smaller places and with less equipment. Basketball, on the other hand, which was invented by James Naismith in the YMCA school at Springfield, Massachusetts, in 1891, was strictly American and was created to meet the need for an indoor sport of skill and activity in the winter months. Likewise, volleyball, which was invented by William Morgan at the YMCA in Holyoke, Massachusetts, in 1896, is a particularly American sport that has since spread throughout the world.

Women were involved in this sport expansion from the beginning. For example, in the same winter that Naismith invented basketball, Senda Berenson adapted the game for her students at Smith College, a nearby institution. By 1899 a committee had formalized a set of women's basketball rules, and the game was being played widely by women (Spears & Swanson, 1978). Volleyball, too, was played by women from the outset.

The revival of the Olympic Games in Athens in 1896 provided a fitting climax to a half-century in which sport had begun to assume the central role it would occupy in the cultures of developed countries for much of the twentieth century. The strongest impetus for reviving the games came from Baron Pierre de Coubertin, who greatly admired the moral and spiritual strength of ancient Greek culture as embodied in the early Olympic Games. Along with the revival of the games as a major sporting event, de Coubertin articulated the philosophy of "olympism," an educational program of peace and cultural understanding that sought to unite the modern world.

Sport on the College Campus

Perhaps the unique feature of the development of sport in America is the phenomenal way in which sport grew on college campuses and came to be an integral part of college and university life. In 1850 there was very little sport participation of any kind on American college campuses, and nowhere did intercollegiate sport exist. Yet, by the turn of the century, sport had assumed a critical social function on most campuses, and intercollegiate competition had begun to move to the central position it was to occupy in the general sporting scene in the twentieth century (Lucas & Smith, 1978).

A brief chronology of growth-period events:

1852   First collegiate competition—a crew race between Yale and Harvard

1859   First intercollegiate baseball game—Amherst versus Williams

1869   First intercollegiate football game—Rutgers versus Princeton

1873   First track-and-field competition, as part of Saratoga regatta

1875   Intercollegiate Association of Amateur Athletes of America formed

1883   Intercollegiate Lawn Tennis Association formed

1890   First intercollegiate cross-country running meet—Cornell versus Penn

        First women's tennis club at University of California

1891   Basketball invented at Springfield College

1892   University of California's women's basketball team formed

1895   First intercollegiate hockey competition at Johns Hopkins

1895   Intercollegiate Conference of Faculty Representatives formed (later became the Big Ten Conference)

1896   First intercollegiate swim meet (Columbia, Penn, Yale)

1900   Oberlin College hosts six-team women's basketball tournament

By the turn of the century, most universities had athletic associations that arranged schedules, purchased supplies, and generally began to offer the array of services now commonly found in athletic departments in universities. What is perhaps most remarkable about all of this rapid development is that it occurred largely through the efforts of students and, at the outset at least, despite the often serious opposition of administration and faculty. Still, as schedules grew more ambitious, travel became more costly, training tables began to become popular, and equipment became more necessary, it was clear that financial support was necessary. Although the student-organized athletic associations could handle those problems at the beginning, the problems soon became sufficiently complex that faculty and administrative intervention not only was necessary but also seemed to be the only way to solidify the venture and ensure its future success.

Thus, while early pioneers in physical education promoted gymnastic systems in school programs and began to develop college departments emphasizing scientific measurement and prescriptive exercise, the students were busy bringing organized sport into the life of the college and university, particularly for male students. The control over schedules and team membership was vested in the team captain, a student whose many roles included those now played by athletic directors and coaches. Little wonder that captains were called "big men on campus" and wielded significant power among the other students.

No doubt there were many college athletic programs in the early days where the captain was a hero worthy of emulation and all the right reasons for playing sport and competing vigorously and fairly were kept in proper perspective. However, there is a tendency to romanticize that period and the student-captain's role. The truth is that the abuses in intercollegiate sport for males toward the end of the nineteenth century were so widespread that only faculty intervention and control could save the system. Intercollegiate sports for women, on the other hand, were controlled by faculty from the outset, accounting perhaps for both slower growth and fewer abuses in women's sports.

Faculty Control and the Beginning of a National Intercollegiate System

As mentioned, sport was not officially welcomed on campus with open arms. Many faculty and administrators were against it, especially in the early days. However, it became so popular among students and so integral to campus life that an accommodation had to be reached. In many cases, **intercollegiate sport** was replete with bad practices and serious abuses—some of which make current abuses look minor in comparison.

Lucas and Smith (1978) attribute the early abuses to two separate threads in the fabric of American society in the nineteenth century: the existence of the Puritan work ethic and the lack of a substantial "gentleman" class. The work ethic was straightforward. If there is a job to do (win the game), then you do everything you can to get the job done. The lack of a gentleman class meant that there were few restraining influences on that work ethic. Rather than "win within the rules," the practice often became "win at all costs." Although sport was well on its way toward standardization, with subsequent enforcement of rules and procedures that would provide a restraining influence, it had not yet matured to the point where the restraining influences provided by sport organizations (conferences, associations, and so on) were effective. In England, from which many of our sport practices derived, the desire to win was restrained by a sense of honor, fair play, and respect for rules that was taught to young British gentlemen in their schools. In England, therefore, the restraining influences were personal as well as institutional. In England also, the work ethic among the sporting classes was entirely different from that in America.

The major abuses had to do with eligibility (there were no rules about it) and with how athletes were treated by their universities.

> One outstanding example was the captain of Yale's football team, James Hogan, who was twenty-seven years old at the turn of the century when he began his intercollegiate career. He occupied a suite of rooms at Yale's most luxurious dormitory and was given his meals at the University Club. His tuition was paid and he was given a $100 a year scholarship. He and two others were additionally given the privilege of selling game programs from which they received the entire profit. Furthermore, Hogan was an appointed agent for the American Tobacco Company and received a commission on every package of cigarettes sold in New Haven. If that wasn't enough for this "amateur" collegian, Hogan was given a ten-day vacation trip to Cuba during the school term after the football season was successfully completed. (Lucas & Smith, 1978, pp. 212–213)

Athletes often competed for different colleges or universities within the same season. Many intercollegiate athletes were paid, and many were for hire, often being enrolled as "special" students for a short time while they competed. Intercollegiate sport became so popular on campus, thus encouraging even greater abuses, that it threatened the real purpose of university education. Yet its very popularity was seductive even to university officials. It was not uncommon for presidents and trustees to try to use the promotional value of sport to build their young universities. That certainly was what the University of Chicago, founded in 1891, did when it hired Amos Alonzo Stagg as its football coach, gave him professional rank—the first such occurrence in America—and set out to dominate intercollegiate football.

The beginning of faculty control was an important step in the continued development of intercollegiate sport. Because it was brought under the normal institutional control of faculty, sport was accepted as an appropriate and useful aspect of university life and as a contributor to the overall goals of a university education. The first faculty athletic committee was formed at Harvard in 1882. By 1888 the composition of this committee had changed to include representatives of alumni and students, and the committee's authority had been extended considerably. This pattern was gradually adopted by most universities.

The next important step in extending faculty control was the formation of associations of universities—what we now know as *athletic conferences*. In 1895 the Intercollegiate Conference of Faculty Representatives was formed, which immediately established eligibility requirements for entering students, for continued participation, and for transfer students. It also placed severe limitations on athletic aid and on how coaches were hired and retained. That conference, later to be known as the Western Conference or Big Ten, became the model through which other institutions, in other parts of the country, joined together to exert institutional control over intercollegiate athletics and, in so doing, ensured a continued role for sport in university life.

Intercollegiate sport for women was always under better control. On many campuses, women's athletic associations were formed; in 1917 Blanche Trilling of the University of Wisconsin organized a meeting from which the Athletic Conference of American College Women was formed (Spears & Swanson, 1978). However, the explosion in collegiate sport for women was to come more than a half-century later, with the advent of Title IX (see Chapters 3 and 6).

THE NEW PHYSICAL EDUCATION

In 1893 an International Congress on Education was held in conjunction with the Chicago World's Fair (Lee & Bennett, 1985a). Because the National

An early twentieth-century gymnastics class at a school for black girls.

Education Association (NEA) had two years earlier recognized physical education as a curricular field, a physical-education section of the congress was organized. That enabled physical educators from Europe and North America to meet for the first time as specialists in a fully recognized school subject. It is also fair to point out that from that time on, the physical-education profession began to view education rather than medicine as its parent field. At that symbolically meaningful conference, a 28-year-old physical educator from Stanford University, Thomas Wood, presented to the audience a view for a *new physical education:*

> Physical education must have an aim as broad as education itself and as noble and inspiring as human life. The great thought in physical education is not the education of the physical nature, but the relation of physical training to complete education, and then the effort to make the physical contribute its full share to the life of the individual, in environment, training, and culture. (Lee & Bennett, 1985a, p. 22)

That conference symbolized the end of the era in which gymnastics dominated the physical-education curriculum, and it marked the beginning of the modern era of physical education. Wood's ideas about a physical education that had broad goals and contributed to a student's complete education were to become the dominant theme in physical education in the twentieth century—and they still dominate today. One of Wood's best students at Stanford was Clark Hetherington, who was to become a major force in the new American physical education, as was Luther Halsey Gulick, then director of the YMCA training school at Springfield. In 1927 Wood and Rosiland Cassidy, another great pioneer, published *The New Physical Education*, a landmark test.

The **new physical education** was to be embraced by many people but was articulated most clearly by four leaders—Wood, Cassidy, Hetherington, and Gulick. Wood went on to head the department of physical education at Teachers College, Columbia University, which became the great early training ground for leadership in physical education, marking the transition from medicine to education for advanced training in the field. Cassidy earned her doctorate at Columbia and became a major leader through her work at the University of California at Los Angeles (UCLA), later becoming a pioneer thinker in the field of human movement. Hetherington had a distinguished career at several major universities, later becoming supervisor for physical education for the State of California. Gulick went from Springfield to become director of physical training for the New York City schools and was a major figure in the development of the playground movement.

The new physical education was consistent with and was greatly influenced by the modern ideas being advanced in psychology and education. In psychology, major figures such as G. Stanley Hall and Edward Thorndike were revolutionizing thinking about childhood, adolescence, and learning. Hall was a frequent speaker at early professional meetings in physical education and showed a great interest in using physical education for educational purposes. His historic book *Adolescence* (published in 1904), which was the first to define that developmental stage and to attach educational importance to it, was then being formulated.

Those ideas were accepted by and further articulated in the educational theories of John Dewey and William Heard Kilpatrick. Formalism was out. Natural play and expression were in. The model of the miniature adult was out. Childhood and adolescence as distinct developmental stages were in. The rigid, highly disciplined, often negative classroom was out. The school as a microcosm of life was in. The school as an enforcer of rigid class structures in society was out. The egalitarian school that would reshape society was in. That was the intellectual climate within which the new physical education emerged and prospered.

The development of the new physical education was not the result of the influence of ideas alone. It is important to remember that the intellectual leaders in psychology, education, and physical education in the early part of the twentieth century were a small group of people who had frequent personal contact with one another. Wood went to Teachers College at Columbia University. The great psychologist Thorndike was also on the faculty there, as was John Dewey, America's greatest philosopher–educator. Hetherington was brought to Teachers College by Wood. Cassidy took her degree there also. Hetherington had studied under Hall, who was a close associate of both Thorndike and Dewey. These people knew one another well and interacted both formally and informally—and it was from this important intellectual circle that the philosophical and programmatic foundation for the future of American physical education was formed in the early years of the twentieth century.

THE SPREADING OF THE PHYSICAL-EDUCATION UMBRELLA

In the years between the turn of the century and World War I, the character of American physical education took shape. An umbrella profession—physical education—was created; it embraced a number of growing movements, including dance, YMCA/YWCA, playgrounds, recreation, outdoor education, sport, fitness, health education, and intramurals. It was during this period, as the umbrella profession formed, that much of the early organizational work in those separate yet related fields took place.

Dance, especially folk dance, became popular in school physical-education programs in the early years of the twentieth century. Together with the growing recognition of sport and games as curricular areas in physical education, dance helped to push gymnastics out of the center of the curriculum. In 1916 the American Folk Dance Society formed.

The playground and camping movements grew out of a genuine social concern with the welfare of children, influenced strongly by the same philosophical and psychological theories that came together in the progressive-education movement. The Playground Association of America was founded in 1906 to guide that movement.

The Industrial Revolution of the nineteenth century had created a national concern about health, especially about the health of children. The emerging school health, health-education, and health-sciences professions were strongly backed by medical societies. In 1903 New Jersey passed legislation making a health examination compulsory for all schoolchildren.

Although this period was characterized primarily by the inclusion of sports and games in the school curriculum and by the development of a national sport culture, fitness was not neglected. In 1902 Dudley Sargent developed his widely used Universal Test for Strength, Speed, and Endurance. In 1910 James McCurdy set up standards for measuring blood pressure and heart rate. In 1915 William Bowen published his influential *Applied Anatomy and Kinesiology*. In 1920 Charles McCloy developed a classification index that was to be influential in later years.

Intramurals became important, particularly as a way of allowing guided sport competition in colleges and universities. In 1913 Michigan State and Ohio State appointed intramural directors, the first such positions recognized. By 1916 a survey indicated that 140 institutions had intramural programs (Weston, 1962). This development at the college level influenced the beginning of intramural programs in high schools a decade later; by 1930 such programs were national in scope.

The recreation movement began to form from a number of sources, including the YMCA/YWCA, the playground movement, camping, and parks. In the days when America was predominantly rural, there was little need for formal recreation organizations. As America became more urban, however, the need for formal recreation grew. The National Park Service was formed in 1911; by 1930 the National Recreation Association had formed from the Playground and Recreation Association.

During this period, America also was building a national sport culture. In 1911, 80,000 spectators watched the first Indianapolis 500 race. A championship boxing match between Jim Jeffries and Jack Johnson was a worldwide spectator event. In 1903 the first World Series was played. In 1905 the National Collegiate Athletic Association was founded. Ty Cobb in baseball and Jim Thorpe in football became national heroes of immense popularity.

In physical education, this period marked the transition from a gymnastics-oriented curriculum to one in which dance and sport began to share more equally. Physical education became associated with education rather than with medicine. Just after 1900, several universities—including Nebraska, Oberlin, California, and Missouri— offered professional preparation courses in physical education, expanding on the pioneer program begun in 1885 by Delphine Hanna at Oberlin College. In 1901 Teachers College offered the first master's degree in physical education. In 1905, at the University of Illinois, the first department of professional preparation in physical education was formed. By 1924 there was sufficient interest and need that both Teachers College and New York University began to offer doctoral programs in physical education.

In 1918 the NEA asked a commission to form national goals for education. The commission produced the now famous Cardinal Principles of Education. Among the seven principles identified as national goals for education were "health" and "worthy use of leisure time." The physical-education professions had been born, had begun to develop their separate and combined organizational structures, and had been recognized officially as important in contributing to national goals for education of all children and youth. The stage had been set for a golden age for physical education and sport.

Another important element in the maturation of the health, physical-education, and recreation professions was the creation of an academy of national leaders. In 1904 Luther Halsey Gulick created the Academy of Physical Education, whose membership was open only to those elected by fellows. That led in 1926 to the formation of the American Academy of Physical Education (AAPE), whose first elected members were Clark Hetherington, R. Tait McKenzie, Thomas Story, William Burdick, and Jay B. Nash. The purpose of AAPE was to create a forum of national leaders who could address major issues in annual meetings. The "Academy," as it came to be known, soon published the proceedings of its annual meetings as *The Academy Papers*.

AAHPERD and AAPE are companion organizations that were formed for different purposes. AAHPERD is a primarily professional organization that seeks to serve its many members with professional services and leadership. AAPE (now AAKPE) has remained an elected group of national and international leaders whose purpose is to assess current issues and chart future directions for the academic and professional represented in its membership.

THE GOLDEN AGE: POST–WORLD WAR I

The era between World War I and the beginning of the Great Depression in the early 1930s was a particularly interesting time in American history; it was

---

Professional Organization Evolution toward AAHPERD

- 1903—Association for the Advancement of Physical Education (AAPE) becomes the American Physical Education Association (APEA).
- 1937—APEA becomes the American Association for Health and Physical Education (AAHPE).
- 1938—The growing field of recreation is added to AAHPE to become AAHPER.
- 1974—The emergence of district associations and the change from older divisions into national asso-

ciations (such as the National Association for Sport and Physical Education—NASPE) causes AAHPER to become an alliance of associations, named the American Alliance for Health, Physical Education, and Recreation

- 1979—The current name is created through the formal addition of dance: AAHPER becomes AAHPERD.

---

an active period for the sport, fitness, and physical-education professions, too. America ended the war as an international power of the first order. The giant American industrial economy had moved into high gear. A middle class was emerging. People had money and wanted diversions. National interest in sports grew at all levels. The radio and the automobile had come within the means of many people—and each was important to the growth of sport, as had been the telegraph and the railroad in the mid–nineteenth century.

This was the era of Bobby Jones in golf, Babe Ruth and Lou Gehrig in baseball, Jack Dempsey in boxing, Man O'War the racehorse, Red Grange in football, Gertrude Ederle and Johnny Weismuller in swimming, Bill Tilden and Helen Wills Moody in tennis, and Charlie Paddock and Mildred "Babe" Didrikson Zaharias in track and field and golf. It was an era of heroes and heroines, of huge crowds (120,000 watched a high school football championship in Chicago), and of previously unparalleled media interest.

Except for media coverage of then hugely popular boxing matches, African American athletes were largely invisible in the majority-controlled media. These athletes were not allowed to participate in most professional and intercollegiate sports, but in sports such as baseball, Negro professional leagues developed and drew many fans, despite media ne-

glect. Institutions of higher education for African American students, particularly in the South, developed intercollegiate sports programs of their own and organized into distinct leagues.

Education through the Physical

In physical education, this era was a time when most states passed laws requiring physical-education instruction in schools. Typically, state directors of physical education were appointed. Teacher education in physical education became available in more colleges and universities. Graduate study in physical education, still dominated at the doctoral level by Teachers College and New York University, began to develop in other parts of the country. The first school of physical education within a university was formed at the University of Oregon. The first dance major was started by Margaret H'Doubler at the University of Wisconsin.

The new physical education, first advocated by Wood and later articulated most clearly by Hetherington, became the dominant theme in American physical education. Those ideas were stated cogently in Hetherington's 1910 paper titled "Fundamental Education."

> This paper aims to describe the function and place of general neuromuscular activities, primarily general play activities, in the educational process. We use the

term *general play* to include play, games, athletics, dancing, the play side of gymnastics, and all play activities in which large muscles are used more or less vigorously. . . . To present the thesis four phases of the educational process will be considered: organic education, psychomotor education, character education, and intellectual education. (p. 630)

Hetherington's four objectives for physical education (organic, psychomotor, character, and intellectual) were to be adopted with only slight variations in language and concept by virtually every important American physical-education spokesperson for 50 years (Siedentop, 1980).

The leadership of the new physical education began to pass in this era from the Wood–Cassidy–Hetherington–Gulick generation to the generation of physical educators trained by those pioneers, most notably to Jesse Fiering Williams and Jay B. Nash. Williams took his M.D. degree at Columbia in 1915 and joined the physical-education faculty at Teachers College in 1919, where he became an articulate and prolific writer. Jay B. Nash took his Ph.D. degree in physical education from New York University in 1929, where he already was a faculty member. Williams became the primary interpreter of Wood, whereas Nash became the main disciple of Hetherington. Both were dynamic and inspiring leaders, and it was through their teaching and writing that the modern curriculum in physical education was developed.

The ensuing battle was a then-contemporary version of the earlier arguments between gymnastics and sports, except now extended into a broader educational context. Williams described beautifully the issues and how they should be decided.

No one can examine earnestly the implications of physical education without facing two questions. These are: Is physical education an education *of* the physical? Is physical education an education *through* the physical? . . . Education of the physical is a familiar view. . . . In effect such a narrow view is a physical culture and has the same validity that all narrow disciplines have had in the world. . . . Modern physical education with its emphasis upon education through the

physical is based upon the biological unity of mind and body. This view sees life as a totality. . . . There is in such a view something of the loftier virtues of courage, endurance, and strength, the natural attributes of play, imagination, joyousness, and pride, and through it all, the spirit of splendid living—honest, worthy, and competent—so much desired by each individual. (Williams, 1930, p. 279)

The notion of **education through the physical** became the modern interpretation of Wood's new physical education. This view placed physical education clearly and securely within the context of general education. It created the vehicle through which sports and games came to dominate the curriculum. It solidified the four objectives of fitness (organic), skill (psychomotor), social development (character), and mental development (intellectual) that still today dominate the rhetoric of physical education.

The Beginnings of a Science of Physical Education

The early contributions of Hitchcock and Sargent had established the American gymnastic systems on a more scientific basis than that of their European counterparts. Emphasis on measurement and prescriptive exercises based on test data were unique features of those systems. Thus, as an American physical-education profession developed in the late nineteenth century, a scientific emphasis was ever present.

As sports, games, and dance began to move gymnastics out of the center of the curriculum, and as the new physical-education philosophy gained strength, the scientific emphasis so notable early in the profession seemed to become less important. In fact, it was simply temporarily overshadowed by the rhetoric and program changes that accompanied the new physical education.

The Sargent tests, McCurdy measurement innovations, and McCloy classification index provided continuing evidence of the scientific direction of the profession, firmly rooted in its medical ancestry.

In 1921 Sargent developed his Sargent Jump Test, which is still widely used. The beginning of doctoral programs in 1924 provided a strong impetus for the research movement within the profession, as doctoral candidates were trained in research methods and began to complete doctoral dissertations. In 1927 the Brace Motor Ability Test was developed, followed 2 years later by the Cozens' Tests for General Athletic Ability. In 1930 the APEA formally recognized this important emphasis within the profession by publishing the *Research Quarterly.*

A major figure in the research movement within the profession was Charles H. McCloy. A graduate of Columbia University with a doctoral degree in biology, McCloy began a career that would include being a university professor, a YMCA director, a YMCA physical-education specialist in China for 13 years, secretary for research in the National Council of the YMCA, and research professor at the University of Iowa, where he provided leadership and influence at a national level (Gerber, 1971). McCloy was the alter ego of Williams and Nash. He tempered each of those leaders' brilliantly written and dynamic pieces advocating education through the physical with sobering thoughts about the fitness level of students in schools, the need to demonstrate important outcomes in skill and fitness, and the need to document those outcomes with scientifically valid data.

This beginning of a research focus within the sport, fitness, and physical-education professions was vital for their increasing acceptance in university programs and as an important educational subject matter. It foreshadowed a period when the physical-education scientific subdisciplines would emerge to stand on their own.

Access and Equity

This era of expansion, in which our professions were born, needs also to be viewed realistically in the context of the inegalitarian nature of the times. Remember, most of the history reviewed in this chapter occurred *before* women were allowed to vote and *well before* blacks were granted their full constitutional rights. Women such as Delphine Hanna, Ethel Perrin, Jessie Bancroft, Amy Morris Homans, Elizabeth Burchenal, and Blanche Trilling were important and courageous pioneers, their advocacy of women in sport, fitness, and physical education made more difficult by the narrow and stereotyped views of femininity in those days. Their names appear less often in this history not because their roles were less important but because the power structures of almost all organizations were dominated by men.

Delphine Hanna, for example, is one of the remarkable figures in the history of American physical education. She graduated from Brockport State Normal School in New York in 1874, earned an M.D. degree at the University of Michigan and then a Bachelor of Arts degree from Cornell University. She taught in public schools, where she became concerned about the health and physical status of children. She completed a course at the Sargent Normal School of Physical Training in 1885 and then took a position at Oberlin College in Ohio, where she developed the nation's first teacher-preparation program in physical education. Among her students at Oberlin were Luther Halsey Gulick, Thomas Wood, and Fred Leonard, all of whom went on to important positions of leadership and influence. In 1903 she became the first woman to be appointed a full professor of physical education.

Nor is there much mention in this history of black people. To be sure, black institutions, such as Hampton Institute and Howard University, pioneered sport and physical education for black students. To their credit, some notable institutions in the history of physical education and sport—such as Oberlin College, Springfield College, and the Sargent School for Women—admitted black students (Zeigler, 1962). In this period of emergence and growth, however, access and *equity* remained restricted to and dominated by white males.

That is where physical education stood as America finished the era of affluence that was known as the Roaring Twenties and plunged into the Great Depression of the 1930s.

SUMMARY

1. The sport, fitness, and physical-education professions were born in the United States at the Adelphi Conference in 1885, at which time forty-nine new members from a wide variety of fields pledged to work toward improvements in the discipline and a more professional standing for it.

2. The pre–Civil War era was a time of transition from local games to institutionalized sport. The war itself helped to spread and standardize many sport forms.

3. Many sports were introduced in America in the period between 1850 and 1900.

4. Several important sports, such as basketball and softball, were invented in America during the same period.

5. The decline of religious opposition to sport, fitness, and physical education, and the philosophy of muscular Christianity, greatly accelerated the growth of those fields.

6. Immigration, industrialization, urbanization, and advances in transportation and communication created the context within which sport and physical education rapidly developed in the late nineteenth century.

7. Formal gymnastic systems developed in Europe were adopted in America and competed with American systems for dominance in school and university programs.

8. The Boston Conference of 1889 debated the various systems. It was most important because it brought together many national leaders and marked the beginning of a distinctively American approach to physical education.

9. By the turn of the century, sport was becoming highly institutionalized at both the professional and the amateur levels through organizations, governing bodies, and sport conferences.

10. Abuses and problems in college and university sport led to the beginnings of faculty control and the formation of sport conferences.

11. The new physical education was heralded by Thomas Wood and marked the transition from a medical approach to an educational approach, ending the domination of physical education by formal gymnastic systems.

12. As a result of this gradual move away from medicine and toward education, physical education was recognized by the NEA as an official curricular field in 1891.

13. Wood, Cassidy, Hetherington, and Gulick became the early leaders of the new physical education, aligning the movement with the emerging progressive education movement and the childhood- and adolescent-psychology movements.

14. From the turn of the century to World War I, an umbrella profession of physical education was created, under which gathered professionals from physical education, health, recreation, dance, playgrounds, camping, and sport.

15. In the early twentieth century, a national sport culture emerged, with widespread participation and spectating and the beginnings of national traditions, as well as sport heroes and heroines.

16. The original physical-education organization (AAAPE) underwent many changes as it evolved into the parent organization we know today (AAHPERD).

17. The era between World War I and the Great Depression was the golden age of sport, fitness, and physical education. Schooling developed nationally, with physical education as an accepted subject; states passed mandatory physical-education laws; teacher education developed fully; graduate study in physical education began; and sport continued its domination of American popular culture.

18. "Education through the physical" became the dominant philosophy for the umbrella profession, as articulated by Hetherington, Williams, and Nash.

19. A science of physical education began to develop, tracing its roots from the work of Hitchcock and Sargent and led in this era by McCloy.

20. Access and equity for women and blacks were not features of this era, even though pioneering work was accomplished by women leaders, and black students had access in some institutions.

DISCUSSION QUESTIONS

1. What do the pictures of the "gymnastics" classes in this chapter tell you about the quality and seriousness of those early models for physical education?

2. Why do you think sport had such a difficult time becoming part of physical education during the "gymnastics era" even though sport was clearly emerging in many forms?

3. How did you react to the stories of early abuses in collegiate sport? Were those abuses worse than abuses today?

4. Does the education-through-the-physical approach sound familiar to you? What type of philosophy would you say supported the physical education you experienced in middle or high school?

5. How did the popular view of fitness change during the time period examined in this chapter?

6. What were the significant events between 1900 and the start of World War I that influenced physical education?

7. How many of the sport heroes and heroines were you familiar with when you first read this chapter? Did it surprise you that in the early part of the twentieth century 120,000 fans witnessed the high school football championship in Chicago?

CHAPTER 3

Consolidation and Specialization: 1930–Present

I suggest that there is an increasing need for the organization and study of the academic discipline herein called physical education.

Dr. Franklin Henry, in a 1964 *JOHPER* article
heralding the beginning of the academic-discipline
movement in physical education

LEARNING OBJECTIVES

- To describe the umbrella profession of physical education

- To analyze the cultural context within which the profession consolidated and specialized between 1930 and 1960

- To analyze the emergence of professional sport

- To describe changes in recreational sport

- To explain the incorporation of lifetime sports into the school curriculum

- To analyze the fitness crisis of the mid-1950s and the fitness renaissance of the '80s and '90s

- To describe the development of research specializations and the academic discipline of physical education

- To analyze the cultural factors affecting sport, fitness, and physical education in the post-1950 years

As we saw in Chapter 2, school physical education in America began as systems of gymnastics and emerged in the twentieth century as a new physical education devoted to the general goals of education. Sport became organized and institutionalized and grew in popularity. Through student interest and leadership, sport found its way onto college campuses; by the turn of the century, it had come under faculty control, beginning its full integration into university life. Professional organizations were formed and grew. A professional literature developed. The post–World War I era—known as the Roaring Twenties—was an economically productive time in which both physical education and sport expanded rapidly. By 1930, at the end of the emergence era, sport, fitness, and physical education had begun to consolidate under the umbrella profession called "physical education."

The signs of approaching maturity for that umbrella profession were everywhere. In 1930 the APEA was on firm footing as *the* organization providing an umbrella under which physical educators, sport administrators, health educators, recreationists, and fitness experts found common ground and support. The APEA had just started two professional journals, the *Research Quarterly* and the *Journal of Health and Physical Education.* The organization also elected its first woman president, Mabel Lee of the University of Nebraska, and presented its first honor awards to thirty-eight men and women who had been instrumental in building the profession (Lee & Bennett, 1985b).

The battle between gymnastic systems and the new physical education had been clearly won by the adherents of "education through the physical," and physical education became firmly established within education rather than within medicine. Many states passed legislation requiring health and physical-education instruction in schools. Research on fitness and performance testing was being established within the profession. Sport was immensely popular within the culture, and there was a general perception that physical education was a vital and necessary aspect of the school curriculum.

By 1930 twenty-eight universities offered graduate study in professional physical education—and many more were offering teacher-preparation programs. In 1931 twenty-eight state associations were affiliated with the APEA, and there were 6,269 members in the parent organization (Lee & Bennett, 1985b). A profession had been born and had matured. Then came the Great Depression.

THE CULTURAL CONTEXT: 1930–1940

The years between 1930 and 1945 marked an important transitional period in American history. The Great Depression following the stock market collapse of 1929 shook the foundations of American society, as well as the assumptions of free enterprise and rugged individualism on which the society had grown and prospered—businesses failed, savings were lost, banks closed, and unemployment rates reached intolerably high levels.

In the face of those economic and social threats, the nation elected Franklin D. Roosevelt as president in 1932 (and again in 1936, 1940, and 1944). President Roosevelt presided over a recovery era in which major changes were made in the social and economic systems within the nation. For example, the Social Security Act of 1935 created a national pension system, as well as unemployment insurance and certain health benefits. The Wagner Act of 1935 encouraged the organization of labor, and unions grew in strength, securing wage and benefit improvements for workers. To pay for all these government programs, legislators developed new tax programs.

The Great Depression produced not only changes in the foundational structures of the government but also programs designed to provide immediate relief from the suffering brought about by the economic collapse. The Civilian Conservation Corps (the CCC), the Works Progress Administration (WPA), and the National Youth Administration (NYA) were three programs, among many, that had a direct effect on the sport, fitness, and physical-education professions.

World War I, the Russian Revolution of 1917, and the Great Depression produced worldwide problems that were to manifest themselves again in international conflict by the middle to late 1930s, as Germany and Italy went to war to expand their territories and influence. By 1940 it was clear that the war would involve more than continental Europe; by 1941, with the declaration of war against Japan by the United States after the Japanese bombing of Pearl Harbor, World War II had begun, and the era of the Great Depression had ended.

Other factors of major importance in understanding the continued evolution of the sport, fitness, and physical-education professions were the development of the automobile as a primary means of transportation, the widespread influence of the radio, and the beginnings of television. It also became clear that the airplane would soon further revolutionize the concept of travel and distance. Urbanization continued, and the emerging middle class grew.

SPORT, FITNESS, AND PHYSICAL EDUCATION: 1930–1940

Sport, fitness, and physical education faced major difficulties during the Great Depression. With unemployment high and families having little money for the necessities, let alone for entertainment, professional sport found it difficult to produce the revenues necessary to continue the expansion of the 1920s. University sport was also very dependent on gate receipts to fund programs, and many programs had to be curtailed. The public's view of college sport had been seriously harmed in 1929 with the publication of the *Carnegie Report*, which had found widespread evidence of abuses, including professionals masquerading as amateurs, eligibility violations, and compromises of academic rules. The report had been widely used to suggest that universities had lost sight of their primary academic missions and needed to cut back their commitments in sport (Spears & Swanson, 1978). The negative publicity from the *Carnegie Report*, combined with the economic collapse at the start of the Great Depression, made it difficult for universities to maintain their athletic programs; many cuts were made.

School physical-education programs also suffered as local communities found it difficult to fund education at pre-Depression levels. Cuts had to be made; and people often argued that physical education was one of the subject areas that could be cut, because it was not a central one—it was considered a frill subject. That attitude surprised the leadership in physical education because the cuts were the first challenge to what had been for most of the twentieth century a well-accepted part of the school curriculum (Freeman, 1982). Interscholastic athletics, which had begun to develop and expand rapidly in the previous era, also experienced serious budget problems, and many programs were curtailed or dropped.

A Shift to Participation

Although spectator sport and school physical education fared poorly during the Depression, the field of recreation prospered. It is true that few people had enough money to attend professional or university events regularly; yet, their interest in sport had not abated. Instead, that interest shifted from spectator forms of sport to participatory forms. Local sport, youth sport, family sport, and other informal kinds of sport participation increased substantially.

The sport through which the shift from spectating to participating can be seen most easily is softball. Invented in Chicago in 1887, softball required less space, less equipment, and less highly developed skills than did baseball. It had spread gradually since its inception, and in the 1930s it became America's most popular recreational sport, a position it still holds today. By 1934 more than 200,000 players were taking part in the game; at the end of the Depression, in 1940, there were more than 300,000 organized clubs, and the Amateur Softball Association had more than 3 million affiliated players (Gerber, 1974), indicating the remarkable growth during the decade of the Depression.

The Depression was a difficult time for America; yet, it was also the period in which sport became democratized, and patterns of participation were established that complemented the already developing patterns of spectating.

> Millions of urban workers—men, women, and children—were finally enjoying the organized sports that had been introduced by the fashionable world half a century and more earlier. Democracy was making good its right to play the games formerly limited to the small class that had the wealth and leisure to escape the city. No exact totals can possibly be given as to the number of active sports participants in comparison with attendance of sports spectacles in the 1930s. . . . There is every reason to believe that in the 1930s the public was spending far more of its leisure . . . on amateur than on professional sports. (Dulles, 1940, p. 349)

That participation pattern, formed initially during the Depression, was to be further developed a decade later, as war veterans returned to normal life after World War II.

Federal and Private-Sector Intervention

The intervention of the federal government in economic and social matters was, of course, the key factor of the Depression era. That was also true for matters of sport, fitness, and physical education. During that period, no fewer than ten federal agencies developed recreation or sport-related programs that were to have a substantial immediate influence as well as long-term effects (Spears & Swanson, 1978). Those agencies included the National Park Service, Forest Service, Tennessee Valley Authority, Public Works Administration, NYA, CCC, and WPA (Spears & Swanson, 1978).

The NYA supplied part-time work for high school students, keeping them out of the labor market and in school. The part-time employment was in the federal government's massive construction projects, many of which were for athletic and recreational facilities.

The CCC opened camps in different parts of the country. Men between the ages of 18 and 25, whose families were on relief, could go to camp for 2 years. At camp, they were provided with housing, food, and minimal pay. Their work was mostly in national and state parks, part of which was directed toward recreational and sport facilities. The CCC men lived in military-style barracks and engaged in well-organized intramural sport programs.

The WPA was responsible for, perhaps, the most visible and lasting influence of federal Depression programs: the building of sport and recreational facilities. The WPA constructed gymnasiums, swimming pools, auditoriums, ski facilities, and stadiums. Many of the facilities where high school and university sport events are still held today were WPA buildings.

The intervention of the federal government was based on clear social needs in society. Those needs did not go unnoticed in the private sector either. Youth agencies in particular expanded their programs and influence during the Depression. The Boy Scouts, Girl Scouts, YMCA/YWCA, and Catholic Youth Organization all developed programs for youths and contributed particularly to sport opportunities for youths. This "youth sport movement," which really began in the Depression, was evident toward the end of the decade when, in 1939, Little League baseball began in Williamsport, Pennsylvania, foreshadowing the enormous growth of youth sport in recent times.

Organizational Consolidation and Standardization

The emergent physical-education profession weathered the Great Depression fairly well. In 1930 the APEA membership was 5,700, but by 1940, when it had become AAHPER, membership had reached 10,000. At the national level, AAHPER began to exert influence to bring about more uniform standards within the profession. Three examples serve to demonstrate the professional gains made during that period (Lee & Bennett, 1985b).

- In 1931 the NEA organized a national committee to evaluate teacher education in physical education. The work of the committee became known as the *National Study of Professional Education in Health and Physical Education.* In 1935 the committee presented a code of standards that was to exert influence over teacher-preparation programming for years to come.

- In 1937 the newly named AAHPE (formerly APEA) became a department of the NEA, forming the organizational structure that would guide the profession for the next thirty years.

- In 1927 the College Physical Education Association created a committee to study the school physical-education curriculum. Chaired by William Ralph La Porte, the committee published its findings in 1938 as *The Physical Education Curriculum.* Over the next thirty years, this monograph would go through seven editions, exerting enormous influence over the structure of the school PE curriculum. The La Porte model advocated a block or unit approach in which activities would last from 3 to 6 weeks, and that quickly became the standard model for organizing the yearly curriculum.

SPORT, FITNESS, AND PHYSICAL EDUCATION DURING THE WAR YEARS

The war in Europe had begun in 1939, spreading over most of Europe by 1940. With the Japanese attack on Pearl Harbor, the United States was drawn into the conflict in 1941. More than 15 million people served in the American armed forces during World War II, including 216,000 women in newly created branches of the Army, Navy, and Coast Guard. The entire economic power of the United States turned toward the war effort and, in so doing, lifted itself out of the Depression.

The events associated with World War II had immediate and far-reaching effects on sport, fitness, and physical education. One of the most important was in the area of fitness, which had been the most important field in physical education during the nineteenth century, only to be gradually moved more to the periphery as the new physical education became popular in the early part of the twentieth century. Professional debates during those days often had to do with physical-fitness outcomes and their relative importance in the goals of physical education. As shown in the writings of C. H. McCloy, the arguments *for* fitness were not necessarily arguments for a return to the gymnastic systems:

> For a profession that has glorified the physical side of man from before 500 B.C. until, shall we say, A.D. 1915, the physical education literature today is strangely silent about the more purely body-building type of objectives. From the time of Homer to shortly after the time of Thorndike, the emphasis will be found to have been on the physical—education *through* the physical surely, but also education *of* the physical, for its own sake as well as in Education's sacred name. Then came the leavening influence of Thorndike's psychology and of Dewey's philosophy, enlarging our concepts of how to educate, and as a profession we made real progress. But this progress was made at the expense of the old model. (McCloy, 1936, p. 5)

Fitness was not a major issue in society during the Depression simply because basic needs such as food, shelter, and employment were dominant concerns. With the beginning of World War II, however, fitness became an issue immediately.

All the many women and men who were inducted into the armed forces underwent physical tests and then basic training. A large number failed the tests, and many had trouble with the physical aspects of basic training. At the War Fitness Conference in 1943, the assertion was made that school physical education had been a complete failure and that the emphasis on sports and games had to be replaced with fitness programs. Although that did not happen completely, it was clear that an emphasis on fitness would reemerge not only in school programs but also in society as a whole. Research on fitness and fitness testing was greatly accelerated, and new fitness programs were put into place (Weston, 1962).

Spectator sport continued in the holding pattern it had entered during the Depression. Many great athletes were in the armed services, travel restrictions were severe, and discretionary leisure money was often diverted to the war effort. Participant sport, on the other hand, continued the growth it had begun during the Depression. The War Department had invested substantial monies in sport equipment and personnel to provide activities for service personnel. Coaches and athletes often found themselves called to duty as trainers, coaches, and sport administrators. War training camps developed large sport facilities and encouraged active participation both among camp personnel and between camps. The so-called recreational sports—such as badminton, archery, shuffleboard, volleyball, and table tennis—were promoted as *rest and recovery* activities for service personnel on leave.

School programs of physical education were forced to emphasize fitness objectives and activities more clearly but also fought to hold on to the more balanced approach that reflected the then-30-year-old development of the new physical education. Regardless of the objectives emphasized, physical education was once again considered to be an important part of the school curriculum; it had outlived the frill problem it had encountered when school budgets had been cut so drastically during the Depression.

CHRONOLOGY AT A GLANCE—Consolidation and Specialization		
	1929	*Carnegie Report* published
	1930	*Journal of Health and Physical Education* first published
Great Depression	1935	NEA national study on teacher education in PE
		College Physical Education Association formed
	1937	AAHPE added as a department of NEA
	1938	La Porte curriculum guide first published
World War II	1943	*The Physical Educator* published
	1948	National conference on professional preparation
G.I. Bill	1950	National Intramural Association formed
	1951	National Athletic Trainers Association formed
Baby boomers	1953	Kraus–Hirschland fitness reports published in *JOHPER*
	1954	American College of Sports Medicine founded
Sputnik	1956	President's Council on Youth Fitness established
	1959	Operation Fitness started by AAHPER
	1960	President Kennedy's "soft American" article published
Civil rights	1961	President's Fitness Council's "blue book" published
	1963	*Quest* published
Environmental movement	1964	Henry's "academic discipline" article published
	1965	Dance added as a division of AAHPER
Women's rights	1972	Title IX passed
		AAHPERD's *Tones of Theory* published
	1975	Public Law 94-142 passed

There is little doubt that a major influence of World War II on sport, fitness, and physical education was the beginning of research specialization—a movement that would explode 20 years later as the physical-education discipline movement. Before World War II, research activity in physical education was limited mostly to physical and motor testing. There were few funds available for research, and most of the work was undertaken by doctoral students completing dissertation requirements.

During World War II, the government funded a great deal of research that was to influence physical education (Weston, 1962). The obvious area was fitness, where more had to be learned, and testing and programming had to be improved. There were, however, other important areas. The beginnings of what we now call motor learning are clearly traceable to the war effort. Airplane gunners and aircraft lookouts needed to be trained. Those kinds of war skills were really motor skills and visual discrimination skills. The psychologists who studied them and produced both the knowledge and the programs for training were the first motor-learning specialists (see Chapter 16).

Adapted physical education also began as a major enterprise in World War II. Although rehabilitation had been a part of the American physical-education scene because of the influence of the Swedish gymnastic systems, the real impetus for the development of this specialization came during World War II, as thousands of wounded soldiers needed both rehabilitation *and* activities in which they could experience satisfaction from leisure participation. Thus, the war years provided great pressure for research in physical education and set the stage for the later period in which the specialized research fields would develop more fully into a discipline.

When the war ended in 1945, the nation settled back from the 15 years of turmoil and dislocation experienced in the Great Depression and the war. Service personnel came home with high hopes, new expectations, and the G.I. Bill, which could finance their college educations. Women, who had contributed significantly to the war effort both abroad and at home, had developed a new sense of what was possible for them and of what roles they could occupy in peacetime. The economy geared up to produce all of those things that had been put aside during the years of struggle. A boom time lay just ahead—and it was to be an important growth period for sport, fitness, and physical education.

EXPANSION AND GROWTH DURING THE POSTWAR YEARS

America survived the war in Europe and Asia as a result of a total effort in both the military and the private sectors. Now, as service personnel returned to private life and families, and industries redirected their efforts to more normal pursuits, that same energy seen in the war years produced a period of growth that was to include sport, fitness, and physical education.

Service personnel came back to jobs, education, and relative prosperity. The nation had postponed its desire for consumer goods for 15 years. The economy boomed. New housing was among the most wanted benefits of prosperity, and housing developments sprang up all over the country, giving rise to a new form of living—the *suburb.*

College and university enrollments soared as former service personnel took advantage of a grateful government's programs, known collectively as the G.I. Bill. Many young couples had postponed marriage and family because of the war. Now, families were started quickly, producing what was perhaps to be the most significant and lasting influence of that era—the *baby boom.*

The number of children born in the postwar era was startling. It represented a major shift in population demographics for America. The *baby boomers,* as they would come to be known, changed the social fabric of American society as they moved through childhood in the 1950s, through adolescence in the 1960s, and into their young adulthood in the 1970s. There were simply a lot of them. That created an economic factor: Money spent on them and by them became a driving force in the economy. Their education, their clothing styles, their musical tastes, their political and social views, and their spending habits dominated both the cultural and the economic life of America for the next 30 years.

The Expansion of Sport

Both professional and intercollegiate sport had limped through the Depression and war years. As explained earlier, however, the nation during the same time had continued to build a solid foundation of participation in sport, and there was no evidence that people's interest in higher levels of competitive sport had diminished. Now, that interest could show itself clearly, as an expanding economy made leisure-time money available to many, rather than to just the wealthy.

To catalog fully the enormous growth of professional and intercollegiate sport during that time, we would have to write a separate book. A few examples here, however, should help us to understand the scope of that expansion. The National Football League (NFL) had ten teams in 1946. By 1977 that number had expanded to twenty-eight. Several leagues had started to compete with the NFL but were eventually absorbed into it. In Major League baseball, there were sixteen teams after the war, expanding to twenty-five teams by 1977. The National Basketball Association (NBA) was just barely starting as a financially shaky organization after the war, but by 1977 it had become a financially sound twenty-two-team organization (Spears & Swanson, 1978).

Nor was the expansion limited to the big three professional sports (football, baseball, and basketball). In fact, it is hard to cite any sport activity that did not expand markedly during the postwar period. Golf changed from a country-club sport of the wealthy to a mass-media, mass-market sport-for-all enterprise. Large numbers of golf courses were constructed, some of the private country-club type, but many others municipal or public fee-for-use courses. The weekend golf game, long a privilege of the wealthy, now became a social ritual for many. More people began to make their living from the sport as it increased in popularity. Ben Hogan, one of the all-time greats, led the list of prizewinners in

1946 with $42,000. In 1975 the figure had increased sevenfold, when Jack Nicklaus led the list with over $300,000 in tour earnings.

The Olympic Games began again in 1948. The modern Olympic movement had begun in the late nineteenth century and had continued to grow gradually in importance, reaching its greatest status with the 1936 games in Berlin (known now as the *Nazi Olympics*). However, war in Europe and Asia had caused cancellation of the next two games. The games resumed in London in 1948. In 1952 Russia entered the games for the first time, and the Olympics became the international festival for major athletic competitions among what were then being called the "Cold War superpowers." Since 1952 the growth of the Olympic movement has been remarkable, with each new host of the Olympic Games trying to outdo the last in pageantry and competitive brilliance.

What happened at the professional and international levels also occurred at both the intercollegiate and the interscholastic levels. Competitive sport captured the nation's interest far more than in the past. Teams began to play regionally and then nationally. Scholarships for athletes at larger universities became commonplace. Interest in local high school teams provided a major social dimension to life in rural and suburban communities. Conference, state, and national championships became contests of widespread interest. More sports were made available, and more people took part in them.

The baby-boom generation was the first to experience a major effort at what we now call "youth sport." Little League baseball had begun in 1939, and other sports for youths followed in the 1940s. It was in the 1950s, however, that youth sport exploded on the scene. Not only baseball but also football, basketball, swimming, and hockey began to be played in age-group competition, typically sponsored at the local level. Later, soccer, gymnastics, tennis, and golf would also develop age-group programs.

Thus, sport at all levels grew substantially during the postwar era. The growth was apparent in many different ways. More money was spent on sport.

Little League baseball became the first highly organized youth sport.

The sport-equipment industries grew. More people attended sport contests as spectators, more people participated in sport, and more people read the sport pages of newspapers. Sport magazines became prominent on the newsstands and in stores. Books on sport for general consumer interest were published. Most notable of all, of course, sport was televised.

There is no doubt that television became *the* major influencing factor on the growth of sport in the 1950s and 1960s. At the outset, many people within the television industry doubted that viewers would watch sport on television. How wrong they were! Television brought sport to every part of the nation and eventually to the world. It made national celebrities of sport heroes and heroines—Willie Mays in baseball, Arnold Palmer in golf, Wilma

Rudolph in track, Billie Jean King in tennis, Willie Shoemaker in horse racing, and Joe Namath in football, just to cite a few.

Major sport events on television became national celebrations: the World Series, the NCAA basketball finals, the Rose Bowl, the Kentucky Derby, and later the Super Bowl and Monday Night Football. Television was both a cause and a manifestation of the growing American sport culture.

There can be no doubt that the postwar era saw the blossoming of a sport culture the likes of which had not been seen before. That expansion, of course, presented both opportunities and problems, many of which are discussed in Part 2 of this text.

The Postwar Years in Physical Education

School programs of physical education, financially troubled during the Great Depression and World War II, participated in the economic well-being of the postwar years, along with most other subject areas. Programs were typically conceptualized in the traditions of the new physical education and were built around the model popularized by the La Porte curriculum group. Although the goals of physical education (fitness, skill, knowledge, character) remained consistent with those of previous eras, and the structure of the program stayed the same (block units in a multiactivity model), the activities selected for inclusion in the program began to change.

During the Depression, the nation had turned from a spectator to a participant approach. During the war, much effort had been made to provide recreational sport for service personnel. The idea of recreational sport took hold during the postwar years while a substantial middle class began to emerge in the economic recovery. The sports pursued most vigorously by that group included golf and bowling—activities that would have been unlikely to be included in school physical-education programs before the war. The rationale for inclusion of those sports in the school curriculum was based on the perception that they could be played for a lifetime—with the implication that team sports, such as football, basketball, and baseball, were to be played only during youth. The lifetime sport movement flourished as physical-education curricula were rebuilt after the war, and it soon became a dominant theme in physical education.

At the organizational level, the postwar years were characterized mostly by efforts to provide services to professionals in an era of rapid expansion. With transportation no longer a major problem, conferences became important to the further development of the professions.

From 1951 through 1960, AAHPER sponsored no fewer than twenty-four professional conferences designed to serve specific professional needs. Specialized conferences focused on leisure, fitness, the mentally retarded, intramurals, secondary-school physical education, elementary-school physical education, sport and fitness equipment, athletic directors, and city physical-education directors. The range of those conferences is one of the best indications of the degree to which physical education was expanding, and of the degree to which it remained an umbrella profession, serving the needs of an increasingly specialized group of professionals.

The Fitness Crisis

The general concern with fitness that had characterized the war years was put aside in the general prosperity and expansion that followed the war. Sport was the major physical-education topic, and in schools, **lifetime sports** (most of which had very low fitness components) became more important. Although fitness remained as a goal of physical education, there was not much done about it in school programs and no apparent concern about it among the public.

That all changed in the mid-1950s. In December 1953, Hans Kraus, a physician, and Ruth Hirschland published an article in the *Journal of Health, Physical Education, and Recreation* (*JOHPER*) titled "Muscular Fitness and Health." The article reported the results of what soon became widely known as the Kraus–Weber tests.

These tests of minimum muscular fitness had been given to a wide sample of European and American children. The results were shocking. Whereas less than 9 percent of European children had failed the test, 60 percent of American children had. It did not matter that the tests were, in fact, not complete fitness tests. (They tended to focus primarily on flexibility.)

The results of the Kraus–Weber tests were brought to the attention of President Dwight Eisenhower by John Kelly, a prominent sports enthusiast from Philadelphia, and by Senator James Duff, who had served as director of the Division of Physical Fitness during the war. President Eisenhower, an avid golfer and former great military figure, was said to be shocked by the reports. National magazines and news sources picked up on the story and quickly turned the entire affair into a national crisis in which American youths were pictured as frail and soft compared with their European counterparts. What followed for the next decade was a national emphasis on fitness that was, in many ways, the forebear of the era of fitness in which we now live (Weston, 1962).

In 1955 President Eisenhower convened a conference of experts to examine fitness problems. Soon after, the president suffered a heart attack, which he survived but which further focused the nation's attention on cardiovascular fitness. In 1956 a national conference on youth fitness was held, which resulted in an executive order to form the President's Council on Youth Fitness. National and state professional organizations were soon holding similar conferences, and in 1958 the nation celebrated its first "Presidential Fitness Week."

In 1960 newly elected President Kennedy published an article in *Sports Illustrated*, titled "The Soft American." He also appointed legendary Oklahoma football coach Bud Wilkinson to head the President's Council on Youth Fitness. In 1961 the council published a widely read and influential document on youth fitness that came to be known as the "blue book."

This extraordinary amount of activity and publicity concerning fitness began to bring to the attention of professionals and the public some of the real facts about physical fitness, particularly its relationship to health and, more specifically, to prevention of cardiovascular disease. Many school programs began to emphasize physical fitness. There was also, however, a strong effort within physical education to resist making entire programs fitness oriented and to continue to focus on a wide range of educational goals. Nonetheless, as the Cold War developed in the 1950s and 1960s, the idea that American youths needed to be more fit stirred a substantial amount of activity at national, state, and local levels.

THE MID-1950S AND ON: FORCES THAT SHAPED OUR CURRENT CULTURE

In the mid-1950s, events began to occur that would shape the social and cultural landscape in America for the remainder of the century. Those changes would be both tremendously exciting and very difficult. During the 1950s and 1960s, the baby boomers went through childhood and adolescence, changing our culture's language, clothing styles, and musical tastes—creating social turmoil between the generations that had not been seen before and has not been seen since.

In 1954 the Supreme Court upheld the decision in *Brown v. Board of Education* (Topeka, Kansas) that eliminated the "separate but equal" ethic that had created segregated schools in America. That landmark decision ushered in the era of what many would refer to as the "civil rights movement." The movement was set off nationally in 1956, when Rosa Parks, a cleaning woman in Montgomery, Alabama, refused to give up her seat at the front of a bus when asked to do so by a white person. (At the time, blacks in the South were allowed to sit only in the back seats of public buses.) Her action led to a boycott of white-owned businesses in Montgomery. The boycott was led by a little-known black minister named Martin Luther King Jr., and attracted

national attention through televised reports of the manner in which the protesters were treated. Eight years later, Congress passed the historic Civil Rights Act.

In 1957 Russia launched the space satellite *Sputnik,* marking the start of what would be called the *Sputnik* era. When Russia essentially beat America into space, it startled both the education and the scientific communities, who had assumed that America was well ahead in such technological breakthroughs. *Sputnik* sparked an era of educational reform and scientific activity designed to regain our competitive advantage. The concern about America's educational system persists to the current day, after a series of national reports and committees have questioned the quality of the school systems. Fifteen years after *Sputnik,* the concern about the quality of education was taken to an even higher level with the publication of *A Nation at Risk,* the report of the U.S. National Commission on Excellence in Education (1973).

In 1962 Rachel Carson wrote a book titled *The Silent Spring,* intended to warn Americans of the environmental dangers of pesticides and chemicals. Little did Carson know that she had identified a major theme for the next 20 years and that environmental issues would occupy an increasingly central role in decision making. Certainly, the growth of wilderness sport and adventure education has direct ties to the environmentalist themes of that era.

In 1965 an unknown named Ralph Nader wrote a book titled *Unsafe at Any Speed.* The book revealed the degree to which the automobile industry neglected safety concerns in the production of cars—and the book launched a consumer movement that is still growing and is beginning seriously to affect sport, fitness, and physical education through issues such as product liability, teacher or coach malpractice, and consumer participation in decisions about sport.

It was during the *Sputnik* era that America also entered into, fought, and eventually withdrew from what was initially called a "police action" in a small country in Southeast Asia. The country, of course, was Vietnam. The conflict cost thousands of American lives, drained American resources, and generated upheavals in the fabric of American society that are not yet fully understood, causing the nation to examine seriously both its national purpose and its role in world affairs.

Above all, that era encompassed major changes in the social ideals of a nation. The civil rights movement is perhaps the clearest example, but the era generally can be characterized as one that dealt seriously with rights of all kinds. In 1972, toward the end of the era, **Title IX** of the Education Amendments was passed by the U.S. Congress, creating the framework within which girls and women might finally have equal accessibility to sport, fitness, and physical-education opportunities. Title IX was one manifestation of what became known as the *women's movement.* In 1975 House Bill S.6 was signed into law and became Public Law 94-142, a far-reaching piece of legislation designed to ensure the rights of disabled Americans, particularly in education.

It was within that tremendously difficult and complex set of social events that sport, fitness, and physical education continued to develop in the contemporary era. Much of what happened in sport, fitness, and physical education in that era forms the basis for the remainder of this text and, therefore, is reviewed only briefly here.

Sport in the Post-1950 Era

The growth in sport in the postwar era was merely a prelude to the even more startling expansion in more recent times. America has become a great sporting nation! During any week of the year, look around you. As I write this, the end of winter approaches. This weekend, there will be fourteen basketball games televised in my viewing area. The high school tournaments are just beginning, for girls and boys. There will also be wrestling, boxing, auto racing, golf, tennis, hockey, and bowling contests on television. Thousands will compete in a local road race. Many will travel to nearby ski resorts to enjoy one of the last weekends for that popular winter sport. All the sport, fitness, and physical-education enterprises described in Chapter 1 will be busy. What is most amazing is that this is a business-as-usual week—nothing special, just a nation at play.

So much has happened within sport in recent years that it is difficult to catalog the main changes. Some trends do seem clear:

- Title IX and the women's movement provided the framework for an explosion in women's sport, from youth sport all the way to the most elite levels of international sport. Not only do more women take part, but also the growth of women's sport has helped us partially to reconceptualize the role of women in society.

- The environmental movement provided the framework for engaging in sport outdoors, especially in wilderness areas. Sports such as cross-country skiing and backpacking have grown enormously.

- The civil rights movement provided the framework for further collapse of racial barriers in sport. University teams were integrated. Black and Hispanic players became great professionals in the newly integrated competitions.

- Road racing has become a national participant sport as well as a spectator sport. Nearly 30,000 people run the 26.2-mile New York City Marathon; millions more watch it on television.

- Youth sport expanded to include many sports other than football, baseball, and basketball; in fact, youth soccer may now be the largest program for boys and girls.

- Sport training started to become more specialized and to begin earlier in children's lives. Not too long ago, most high school athletes competed in a different sport each season, but now they tend to specialize, with year-round training and competition.

- Sport camps have developed for summer participation and have become highly specialized.

The camps are seen by many parents and coaches as necessary adjuncts to year-round participation.

- The money made by elite athletes has increased astronomically. Winner's purses for golf and tennis events are huge. Multimillion-dollar contracts are now commonplace.

- The sport-equipment business has expanded, along with the explosion in participation and spectating. Sport clothes have become fashionable, and athletes have major endorsement contracts with equipment and clothing companies.

- The line separating the amateur from the professional has blurred considerably. Many sports have moved to *open competition,* in which there is no distinction (as in tennis, for example). Many amateurs (in track and field, for example) are able to make a good living while pursuing their sport on a full-time basis.

With the rapid growth and the economic overtones, sport has had more than its share of problems during the post-1950 era. Betting scandals, recruiting violations, point shaving, emotional trauma of young athletes, poor graduation rates for university athletes, and drug involvement have all created national concern. (Those issues and others are addressed in Chapter 7.)

The Fitness Renaissance and the Aerobics Era

Americans have been periodically concerned with physical fitness, set off, for example, by draft rejects in World War I, the polio epidemic of 1916, draft rejects and basic-training problems in World War II, and the Kraus–Weber test reports comparing performance of European children with that of American children. Those concerns have typically been responded to, but for only a brief time. Until recent times, there has been no abiding concern with fitness among the general population; now, however, fitness is very fashionable.

Environmental concerns and aerobic training come together in some outdoor recreational pursuits.

It is probably too early for historians to analyze how the present concern with fitness got started and, more important, how it has managed to be sustained. Clearly, the Kraus–Weber tests and the resulting activity set off by them in the late 1950s and early 1960s laid a foundation for what has happened since then. It also seems likely that we simply know more about fitness and about how important it is to health. (See Chapter 8 for a full explanation.) The most powerful influence, however, is that to be fit became the "in" thing. The athletic appearance—slim, muscular, active—became the model to which many women and men aspired. Sport clothing became popular. No longer were there taboos on going out for a jog or a bike ride. In fact, such activity was strongly supported.

When fitness became fashionable, the private sector became involved—it was clear that there was money to be made from catering to the fitness interests and needs of the society. Whereas several generations ago the thought of going to a gym for a workout was associated with dingy facilities and smelly locker rooms, to go to one of the fashionable spas or fitness centers today is a social event. The facilities are bright, colorful, and clean. The clientele is fashionable. The workout is social, as well as physical.

In 1968 Dr. Kenneth Cooper published a small, paperback book that would wield enormous influence over the fitness movement for a generation and give us a new term that would become commonplace in our language system—the book was simply titled **Aerobics.** By 1973, just five years later, the book had gone through its twentieth printing and the term had come to represent an entirely new approach to cardiovascular fitness. Aerobic exercise became the preferred approach to fitness training. Aerobics classes became popular. Aerobics shoes were marketed. Aerobics videos sold well.

This is not simply a façade of fashion with no substance behind it. On one autumn weekend, within a 400-mile distance in the northeastern United States, there are three major **marathons** (26.2 miles) in which close to 50,000 runners participate. **Triathlons** (swim, bike, and run) have become large participant events also. Local 5-mile and 10-kilometer (10K) races attract a regular stream of new and veteran runners. People who train for and compete in events such as these work very, very hard. So do many of the people who regularly visit exercise centers and work on stationary bicycles or with weights, or go to aerobics classes.

The fitness renaissance and aerobics era has not touched everybody. In the past fifteen years, it has become clear that despite all the efforts to emphasize fitness and wellness, the incidence of obesity among children and adults has increased to the point where it is now officially of epidemic proportions (Mokdad et al., 2001; Strauss & Pol-lock, 2001). It is also clear that people in lower socioeconomic brackets are most seriously affected, and that, of course, also means people of color and ethnic minorities, since race, ethnicity, and socioeconomic status in America are highly correlated. It is also unclear what contributions school physical and health education have made to the fitness/aerobics movements, since too many American children continue to be judged to be unfit (see Chapter 9).

School Physical Education since the 1950s

The curriculum of physical education expanded greatly in the last half of the twentieth century. Lifetime sports (tennis, bowling, golf, etc.) had come into the curriculum after World War II and during the 1950s were fully incorporated into existing philosophies and models. In later decades, the curriculum continued to expand and a new curriculum philosophy challenged the primacy of the education-through-the-physical that had dominated since the early part of the century.

The curricular changes were interesting. They reflected a continuing trend for activities in school programs to be selected on the basis of what was popular in the larger culture. Martial arts and adventure sports began to work their way into school programs. The academic reform movement that followed *Sputnik* in the early 1960s resulted in a countermovement in which competition was downplayed in favor of cooperation. Physical-education programs participated in this general trend by including activities such as new games and cooperative initiatives within its curricula.

The growth of scientific activity in what was coming to be called the "discipline of physical education" created a new emphasis on *knowing,* as well as the more traditional emphasis on *doing.* In school programs, that trend was reflected in *foundations* courses. The courses typically used a lecture–laboratory approach and often focused on fitness and on the scientific aspects of sports, such as sports biomechanics.

Learning to cooperate to complete a task can be fun too.

Adventure education made its way into the curriculum. Not only did physical education go off campus to take part in the natural environment, but also school facilities were modified so that adventure skills such as climbing and rappelling could be learned. After-school, weekend, and vacation trips to adventure sites became common.

The largest conceptual change in the post-1950 era was **movement education,** the first serious philosophical challenge to the new physical education since the latter's inception early in the century. Movement education developed in England in the 1930s and was transported and developed even further as a curricular philosophy and program in America. Important physical educators such as Rosiland Cassidy and Eleanor Metheny helped to articulate the new philosophy of human movement. The goals and values of movement education had great philosophical appeal to many professionals and were widely proclaimed in the 1960s and 1970s. Even AAHPERD began to define its subject matter as "the art and science of human movement." This approach has had a substantial influence on physical-education programs for young children but seems not to have been programmatically influential otherwise.

In the 1990s two new approaches to teaching games and sports gained popularity in the United States, as well as in Britain, Australia, and New Zealand. **Sport education** (Siedentop, 1994) offered a way of organizing students into teams for the length of seasons (rather than units) and created multiple roles for students in a model that was very high on student responsibility and created excitement for students in ways that more traditional approaches to teaching sport in physical education had been unable to do. A related model, Teaching Games for Understanding, developed in Britain. Its approach to teaching started with student understanding of the tactics involved in games and used that as a motivation for students to learn the skills so they could play the game better. Both of these approaches led physical educators to a much stronger focus on *tactical awareness* in their teaching. All of the post-1950s models are described at length in Chapters 11 and 12.

Title IX resulted in coeducational physical education beyond the elementary school, which, in turn, created new problems for both curriculum planners and teachers, as they tried to cope with an entirely new set of demands. The changes were also deeply felt in interscholastic sport programs, where boys' teams and girls' teams now had to share their budgets and facilities more equitably.

THE ACADEMIC-DISCIPLINE MOVEMENT

"I suggest that there is an increasing need for the organization and study of the academic discipline herein called physical education" (Henry, 1964, p. 32). Franklin Henry's now-famous statement appeared in a 1964 *JOHPER* article that was a milestone in the physical-education literature—the birth of the discipline movement. In a scholarly manner, Henry outlined the relevant issues concerning the viability of physical education as an **academic discipline** and defined that discipline's parameters. The article also foreshadowed a major period of reconstruction for the umbrella profession under which the sport, fitness, and physical-education professionals had gathered early in the century and through which they had gained strength and legitimacy in the ensuing years.

Henry's call for an academic discipline of physical education can be seen as a logical outcome of the post-1950 reformist movement in education and the growing scientific activity within physical education that had developed during World War II. As the baby-boom generation began to go through the K–12 school systems of America, more teachers were needed—and they were needed in a hurry. That need was met with greatly expanded teacher-education programs in colleges and universities. The expanded teacher-education programs, in turn, promoted a substantial increase in doctoral-degree programs in physical education. Because the doctoral degree is most often thought of as a research degree, this activity created a context within which research became a major agenda item within sport, fitness, and physical education.

The post-1950 reformist movement in education was aimed at producing more scientists and increasing the rigor of educational programs at all levels. As part of that sociopolitical movement, the state of California in 1961 had passed a bill (called the Fisher Act) requiring that all departments in the state university system have an academic base. Because physical education was, at that time, considered to be an applied, professional field (rather than an academic discipline), passage of the bill caused considerable concern among faculty in physical-education departments in those institutions. It is no coincidence that many of the early leaders in the physical-education discipline movement came from those institutions (R. Cassidy, F. Henry, E. Metheny). These physical educators were forced to begin to redefine their field as an academic discipline rather than as an applied, professional enterprise. It was within that political–intellectual climate that programs for human-movement studies, kinesiological studies, human ergonomics, and exercise science developed.

Many physical educators at the college and university level immediately and enthusiastically welcomed the idea of an academic discipline. As Rarick pointed out, "physical education has within its scope a body of knowledge which is not the concern of any other academic discipline" (1967, p. 51). The formalization of that body of knowledge became the main agenda of the academic-discipline movement.

The most well developed scientific area at the outset of the academic-discipline movement was **exercise physiology.** Research in this field had a long and honorable history within the profession, and productive relationships with other scientific disciplines had been established. In 1954 the American Academy of Sports Medicine (www.acsm.org) was founded by physiologists, physical educators, and physicians. Joseph B. Wolffe, a cardiologist, was elected as ACSM's first president. In 1969 ACSM began to publish *Medicine and Science in Sports,* which quickly came to be one of the most respected research journals in the field. In 1974 ACSM began to certify practitioners, and now there are six certification fields. (See Chapter 9 for full information on certifications.) The fitness renaissance and the phenomenon of aerobics served to greatly increase interest in the exercise sciences, as they would come to be known, bringing in new research funds and also bringing the results of research to the general public.

The early **subdiscipline** areas to develop were **biomechanics, motor learning, sport psychology, sport sociology, sport history,** and **sport philosophy.** The North American Society for the Psychology of Sport and Physical Activity was founded in 1967, to provide a collegial group for the growing number of young professionals who saw themselves as either motor-learning or sport-psychology specialists and also to host the Second International Sport Psychology Congress after the Mexico City Olympics in 1968. Eventually, two journals were started to provide research outlets in those areas: the *Journal of Motor Behavior* (1968) and the *Journal of Sport Psychology* (1978).

The same pattern describes the development of sport history and sport philosophy in the early 1970s. The Philosophic Society for the Study of Sport was founded in 1972 at a regional meeting of the American Philosophical Association. In 1974 the first issue of the *Journal of the Philosophic Society for the Study of Sport* appeared. In 1973 the North American Society for Sport History was formed, an event soon followed by the appearance of the *Journal of Sport History.* Each of those scholarly associations was, from the beginning, of interest to researchers from the older, parent disciplines—in these cases, philosophy and history. One of the characteristics of the emergence of subdisciplines within physical education has been to build bridges between people trained in physical education and people trained in parent disciplines—physiology, psychology, history, philosophy, engineering, and so on.

The national umbrella association, AAHPERD, was quick to recognize the academic-discipline movement and to respond to it. In 1972 AAHPERD published its monograph *Tones of Theory,* in which physical education was defined as the discipline of human movement, and the emerging subdisciplines were accorded equal stature under the new, more academically oriented umbrella. AAHPERD also changed, in 1974, from an association to an alliance, a reorganization that gave greater visibility, self-determination, and autonomy to the seven member associations. The National Association for Sport and Physical Education (NASPE), one of the largest of the associations, formed academies that strongly reflected the academic-discipline movement—for example, the Kinesiology Academy. Much of that organizational restructuring represented an effort to maintain an umbrella and to minimize the splintering that inevitably occurred as the subdisciplines formed their own groups and developed their own loyalties and traditions.

AAHPERD is now composed of seven affiliated associations and six affiliated district organizations. It remains the primary professional and academic organization seeking to hold together and serve a very diverse group of professional and academic interests. The box on page 63 shows the mission, purposes, and organizational structure of the alliance.

The discipline movement had an immediate and strong effect on the physical-education curriculum at the university and college levels. As graduate programs developed in the areas of specialization (sport sociology, biomechanics, and so on), so did new undergraduate courses that reflected the knowledge being developed in the subdisciplines. Because, at the beginning of the academic-discipline movement, most undergraduates were preparing to become teachers, many of the new courses found their way into teacher-education programs. Thus, it became common for teacher-education programs to include courses in motor learning, sport psychology, sport sociology, and other academic-discipline-oriented subjects.

Inevitably, that produced a backlash from the leaders in physical education and teacher education. They argued that studying the discipline of physical education was perhaps important but did not replace the learning of sport skills and the acquisition of teaching skills. As teacher educators in physical education began to publish more research and to join together in their effort to make the teacher-education curriculum relevant to teaching physical education, they emerged as a specialized group themselves (concerned with *sport pedagogy*—see Chapter 19), with a journal of their own, the *Journal of Teaching in Physical Education.*

Since then, separate undergraduate programs have begun to develop in the exercise sciences and sport studies. These programs help students to understand the knowledge developed within the subdisciplines, without any expectation that these students will enter professional service as teachers. Some teacher-education programs, on the other hand, have begun to use the special research knowledge developed within sport pedagogy and the other educational research disciplines.

In the early 1990s, sport-sciences faculty members launched an initiative to change the name of university programs from "physical education" to "kinesiology," thus reflecting the academic,

---

The American Alliance for Health, Physical Education, Recreation, and Dance

Mission

To promote and support creative and healthy lifestyles through high-quality programs in health, physical education, recreation, dance, and sport, and to provide members with professional-development opportunities that increase knowledge, improve skills, and encourage sound professional practices.

Purposes

1. To develop and disseminate professional guidelines, standards, and ethics

2. To enhance professional practice by providing opportunities for professional growth and development

3. To advance the body of knowledge in fields of study and in the professional practice of the fields by initiating, facilitating, and disseminating research

4. To facilitate and nurture communication and activities with other associations and other related professional groups

5. To serve as their own spokespersons

6. To promote public understanding and improve government relations in their fields of study

7. To establish and fulfill other purposes that are consistent with the purposes of the alliance

Alliance Associations

American Association for Active Lifestyles and Fitness (AAALF)

American Association for Leisure and Recreation (AALR)

American Association for Health Education (AAHE)

National Dance Association (NDA)

National Association for Girls and Women in Sport (NAGWS)

National Association for Sport and Physical Education (NASPE)

Research Consortium

Alliance Districts

Central District—Iowa, Minnesota, Colorado, Kansas, Nebraska, North Dakota, South Dakota, Missouri, Wyoming

Eastern District—Connecticut, Delaware, Maine, Maryland, New Hampshire, New Jersey, New York, Pennsylvania, Vermont, Rhode Island, District of Columbia, Puerto Rico, Virgin Islands

Midwest District—Illinois, Michigan, Ohio, West Virginia, Wisconsin, Indiana

Northwest District—Alaska, Idaho, Montana, Oregon, Washington

Southern District—Georgia, Florida, Kentucky, Louisiana, North Carolina, South Carolina, Virginia, Texas, Arkansas, Tennessee, Oklahoma, Alabama, Mississippi

Southwest District—Hawaii, California, New Mexico, Arizona, Nevada, Utah, Guam

---

rather than professional, focus of the programs (Newell, 1990b). The American Academy of Physical Education voted to call the discipline *kinesiology* and became the American Academy of Kinesiology and Physical Education (AAKPE). Many departments in colleges and universities voted to become departments of kinesiology, and others became departments of sport science or exercise science.

An even more recent trend has been an outgrowth of the emergence of health-enhancement and leisure-services industries (Ellis, 1988). Physical activity has become big business! As a result, these service industries need a steady flow of trained professionals whose primary role is to deliver services—from sport management to adult fitness—to increasingly diverse clients. New client populations such as young children and increasingly numerous senior citizens have health and leisure needs that require specialized professional skills, backed by sound academic knowledge. We can hope that in seeking to fulfill the needs of these emerging service industries, the research-oriented academics and the application-oriented professionals will find new common ground for cooperation.

Part 5 of this text examines in detail each of the contemporary scientific and scholarly disciplines in the fields of sport, fitness, and physical education, charts the history of their development, discusses their current status, and addresses career options and relevant issues.

SUMMARY

1. By 1930, at the close of the emergence era, the sport, fitness, and physical-education professions were firmly consolidated under the umbrella of APEA, sport had reached new heights of cultural popularity, and many universities had begun to offer graduate-level programs in physical education.

2. The cultural context of the consolidation and specialization era was dominated by the Great Depression, World War II, the postwar recovery, and the post-1950 social ferment.

3. The Great Depression caused the first serious financial problems for sport, fitness, and physical education since the turn of the century, forcing both government and private sectors to seek new ways to fund programs. Participation rates increased, however.

4. The organizations supporting sport, fitness, and physical education were forced to consolidate further, with the APEA affiliating with NEA and changing its name to AAHPE.

5. Teacher education in physical education began to become standardized through efforts at the national level.

6. World War II showed that fitness levels in the population were low, caused professional and other spectator sport to continue on hold, and further enhanced participation.

7. Research specializations developed, greatly aided by the needs of the war effort, with areas such as motor learning and adapted physical education being created.

8. During the postwar economic recovery, college enrollments soared, and the baby boom led to a major increase in the need for schools and teachers.

9. Professional sport began to develop in the postwar years, becoming popular and taking on its modern forms. Recreational sports, such as golf, tennis, and bowling, also became popular.

10. Youth sport, school sport, and intercollegiate sport also developed rapidly in the postwar years, assuming the central importance they now occupy in American culture.

11. In school physical education, lifetime sports became central to the curriculum. Specialized professional interests began to develop and spawned new national, regional, and state organizations catering to those interests.

12. In the mid-1950s, the nation experienced a fitness crisis when American children were shown to perform less well than did European children on so-called fitness tests. That new awareness led to a series of national programs to promote and improve fitness programs in schools.

13. The cultural context of the post-1950 years was dominated by consumerism, concern for ecology, the civil rights movement, and the Vietnam War, producing major changes in sport, fitness, and physical education, such as wilderness sports, Title IX, Public Law 94-142, and the racial integration of sports.

14. Sport in the post-*Sputnik* era became substantially more specialized and economically important, with the lines separating amateur from professional becoming less clear.

15. A fitness renaissance occurred among middle- and upper-class adults. Women took part fully in the fitness movement for the first time.

16. In school physical education, the post-*Sputnik* years were dominated by curricular innovations such as movement education, adventure education, cooperative games, the discipline movement, and expanded opportunities for girls and for people with disabilities.

17. The academic-discipline movement in colleges and universities changed the nature of academic programs and created a series of subdisciplines focusing on specific academic areas of physical education.

DISCUSSION QUESTIONS

1. How did the Great Depression affect the development of sport and physical education?

2. How did World War II affect our views of fitness, sport, and physical education? What activities grew in importance as a result?

3. What cultural factors allowed sport for children and youths to grow in importance during this era?

4. How do the sport and fitness opportunities today differ from those of your parents' and grandparents' eras?

5. What factors seem to make fitness more or less popular as a general concern among the American public?

6. How has the physical-education curriculum changed in the past 100 years?

7. Why have intercollegiate and professional sport become so popular?

8. Has professional specialization been an asset or a liability to those who implement sport, fitness, and physical-education programs at the grassroots level?

CHAPTER **4**

Changing Philosophies for Sport, Fitness, and Physical Education

Running, then, is my discipline, my speciality, my secret. And these golden days of perfection on the road are the whole-ness that results. . . . In those moments my philosophy be-comes, "I run, therefore I am." And from that point I view all creation.

Dr. George Sheehan, physician, elite age-group runner and foremost philosopher of the running movement
1982

LEARNING OBJECTIVES

- To describe the philosophies underlying gym-nastic systems, muscular Christianity, Arnold-ism, and amateurism, and to assess their impact

- To analyze the influence of nineteenth-century masculine and feminine ideals

- To describe how progressive education influ-enced the development of the new physical education

- To describe the education-through-the-physical approach

- To discuss human movement, humanism, and play education as recent physical-education philosophies

- To analyze the academic philosophy underly-ing the academic-discipline movement

- To describe the current wellness movement

As a professional, you will be expected to examine issues in your field and to make judgments about them. Parents, students, customers, and clients will want to know how your particular professional expertise relates to their lives and goals. Part of what you tell them will derive from the technical expertise you have acquired in your professional preparation. Much of what you relate, however, will rely on the philosophy you have developed about the profession you practice, whether you are a teacher, a coach, a sport manager, a fitness consultant, or an athletic trainer.

The term "philosophy" as used here relates more to professional and daily life than to the formal field of academic study. It refers to the set of values and principles you have adopted that form your views about your professional field, your work, and those with whom you interact in your work. In its most fundamental sense, a professional philosophy is what guides your professional life.

It is important that you form a coherent professional philosophy; that is, the principles that guide your professional work should be applied consistently. You also need to be able to clearly articulate your philosophy to other professionals in your field and to those you serve. Your philosophy will be your own. It will likely be informed by what you know about various philosophical positions in your chosen field, but in the end it will be yours alone. If you are a teacher, you will have philosophy about what goals are most important, the curriculum that is most likely to achieve those goals, the instructional practices that will be effective, and how you should treat your students. If you are a sport manager, you will have views about the value of sport, the right and wrong kinds of sport practices, and a philosophy of management and business. If you are a fitness coordinator, you will have a view about the importance of fitness in overall health and well-being, the relative importance of various kinds of fitness activities, and how you need to engage with clients.

A striking example of the influence of a coherent professional philosophy was that of the late George Sheehan, known internationally as the *runner's philosopher*. Sheehan was a physician and a long-distance runner who interpreted the running movement of the 1970s and 1980s to a generation of men and women who found meaning in training for and competing in road races. His books, which sold widely throughout the world, focused on finding meaning in running and on the role of running in a healthy lifestyle. Although not trained in philosophy, he became one of the most prominent sport–fitness philosophers of recent times.

Your professional philosophy is more than a collection of your opinions. It is more than wisdom gained solely from your own experience. To be effective, your philosophy has to be reasonable and coherent, as well as connected to the evolution of philosophies in your field, whether it be sport, physical education, or fitness. To develop such a philosophy, you must know a great deal about the issues in your field and about various points of view regarding those issues. You must also be able to think critically about these diverse points of view. In developing your own philosophy, you will profit from finding out how philosophies within your field have evolved and how they connect to the past and point toward the future. The remainder of this chapter offers you the opportunity to establish some of those connections.

PHILOSOPHICAL INFLUENCES IN EARLY AMERICAN SPORT, FITNESS, AND PHYSICAL EDUCATION

The nineteenth century was an extraordinary time for the developed world, especially for the United States. (See Chapter 2 for details about sport, fitness, and physical education in the nineteenth century.) Revolutions in France and America had created new forms of government. The Industrial Revolution had been triggered by breakthroughs in science and technology—and, in turn, had unleashed powerful changes in economics, population demographics, and social institutions. It was in the nineteenth century that the sport, fitness, and physical-education professions formed and began to mature.

The nineteenth century was just as important in the realm of ideas as it was in programs and institutions. The range of philosophical beliefs that vied for influence in sport, fitness, and physical education was extraordinary. The emergence in the twentieth century of physical education as a school subject, the acceptance of competitive sport into school programs, the development of intramural sport, the acceptance of fitness as a value in its own right, and the recognition of the role of play in childhood were all results of philosophical debates. Such is the power of philosophy and belief systems. What follow are brief descriptions of the more important philosophical influences on the development of nineteenth-century sport, fitness, and physical education.

The Gymnastic Philosophies

Physical education in America in the latter half of the nineteenth century was dominated by the European and American systems of gymnastics. (See Chapter 2 for descriptions of these various systems.) The German system that was transported to America was influenced primarily by Friedrich Ludwig Jahn. The Swedish system was developed primarily by Per Henrik Ling. These two formal systems of gymnastics were far from identical, but the conditions under which they developed and the philosophies undergirding them had a great deal in common.

The common idea that gave rise to these European systems was *nationalism*. Jahn's entire life was devoted to one purpose: the unity of Germany and the development of German patriotism (Gerber, 1971). He admired the self-reliance and independence that seemed to be a by-product of growing up in a rural area dominated by hardworking peasant farmers, whose life was spent outdoors and for whom physical tasks were a part of daily life. The gymnastic system he developed was designed to produce those qualities. The motto he adopted for

his gymnastic society (the Turners) was *"Frisch, froh, stark und frei, is die Turnerei"*—which means "gymnasts are vigorous, happy, strong, and free" (Gerber, 1971, p. 131).

Ling's great mission was to restore to the Swedish people the spirit and grandeur of the ancient Scandinavian race, particularly the glory that emanated from Norse mythology. Ling was a literary giant in his day and a fencing master. It was during his own training in fencing in Denmark that he became acquainted with gymnastics, which he later took home and developed into the complex and multifaceted program that came to be known as Swedish gymnastics.

Both Germany and Sweden were at low points in their national histories when Jahn and Ling were developing their programs. Each of the gymnastic systems had goals for individual development, yet there was also a distinct group dynamic to the programs—one that lent itself particularly well to military training. Thus, the philosophy of gymnastic training, although clearly to the benefit of the individual participant, was also linked to the health and well-being of the state. A strong and morally upright state could develop only from the firm foundation provided to young men (and, to a lesser extent, to young women) by an education that included a substantial involvement in gymnastics.

The nationalism that undergirded European gymnastics in the nineteenth century could not survive in America. In competition with American gymnastic systems, the proponents of the European systems began to emphasize the physical and health benefits and the individual moral growth that were thought to accompany regular participation in these programs.

Muscular Christianity

Much has been written about the *Puritanism* philosophy that pervaded early American history. It was indeed a stern view of human life, which left little room for physical activity that was unrelated to work and took a harsh view of anything that was

CHRONOLOGY AT A GLANCE—Changing Philosophies	
Pre-1800	Puritanism, democracy, frontier spirit, individualism
1800–1850	European gymnastic philosophies introduced to United States
	Emerson's philosophy of self-reliance
	Muscular Christianity
1850–1900	*Tom Brown's Schooldays*
	British "fair play" ideals
	Arnoldism
	Battle of gymnastic systems and philosophies
	Masculinity–femininity ideals
	Institutionalization of sport
	European antecedents of progressive education
1900–1950	Reemergence of play philosophies
	The new physical education
	Progressive-education theory—John Dewey
	Faculty control of college sport
	Professionalization of sport
1950–1996	Human-movement philosophies
	Academic-discipline movement
	Humanistic education and physical education
	Fitness–wellness movements
	Kinesiology movement

playful. The new world of America was in many respects an inhospitable place, one that could be developed only through a strong work ethic and a climate in which codes of behavior were strict. Thus, Puritanism—a set of beliefs deriving from the stricter forms of religion that grew from the Reformation—served a genuine purpose in the development of America. By the mid–nineteenth century, however, the eastern half of the nation was well developed, the Industrial Revolution was at hand, a middle class was emerging, cities were developing, and the once-strong hand of the Puritan philosophy was gradually losing its grip on the social

life of the young nation. It was within this context that religion and sport reached an understanding through the philosophy that was to be known as *muscular Christianity.*

This philosophy was not necessarily associated with any one person or group or movement, but it was an idea whose time had come for America. One important force for the move away from Puritanism and toward muscular Christianity was the American philosopher Ralph Waldo Emerson. Greatly influenced by what he saw as the best in English education and life, Emerson developed an American philosophy of self-reliance and faith in human perfection. His philosophy contained a central place for sport and fitness:

> Emerson reckoned that moral and physical courage were partly dependent on body fitness. "For performance of great mark," he said, "it (the body) needs extraordinary health." In his *The Conduct of Life*, Emerson noted that "the first wealth is health." He admired the great men of the past and urged young people to read their exploits. Yet sometimes youth does not take readily to books, he noted. "Well, the boy is right; and you are not fit to direct his bringing up, if your theory leaves out gymnastic training, archery, cricket, gun and fishing rod, horse and boat, all are educators, liberalizers." (Lucas & Smith, 1978, p. 88)

The idea that participation in sport had moral benefits was almost directly opposite to the Puritan philosophy—and, gradually, the idea took hold.

Muscular Christianity is the label given to the philosophy that physical fitness and sporting prowess were important avenues through which mental, moral, and religious purposes were developed and sustained. An important source for this philosophy was the educational ideals of aristocratic British education. Charles Kingsley, a prominent American cleric, greatly admired the combination of sport, fitness, and intellectual–moral training that boys received in elite British schools. He borrowed those combinations as he wrote and spoke about the new vision of the religious person in whom moral, intellectual, and physical characteristics were equally important (Lucas & Smith, 1978).

The philosophy of muscular Christianity spread quickly and was made even more popular through the novel *Tom Brown's Schooldays*, a best-seller in the 1850s. The book told the story of life at the Rugby School, an elite British boys' secondary school. The headmaster of the Rugby School was Thomas Arnold, a figure of major proportions in British philosophy and education. Arnold believed in an education that produced manliness, courage, patriotism, moral character, and team spirit, as well as intellectual independence. Sport and fitness were considered to be important activities through which such goals were achieved. In the late nine-teenth century in England, this philosophy was termed **Arnoldism;** it is virtually identical to what is described here as muscular Christianity.

The novel *Tom Brown's Schooldays* was a highly romantic book in which sport and fitness occupied a more important role than they did in the real life of the Rugby School. Nonetheless, this novel was read widely by educators, clergy, and common people, all of whom were influenced by the idea that competitive sport was an attribute of the virtuous, moral life. It was the general acceptance of those notions that allowed sport to develop so quickly in the last part of the nineteenth century in America.

Masculinity–Femininity Ideals

No examination of the philosophies that influenced the development of sport, fitness, and physical education in the nineteenth century would be complete without an examination of the then-prevailing views of masculinity and femininity. If the muscular Christianity movement allowed sport, fitness, and physical education to become more philosophically acceptable, it did so much more for boys and men than for girls and women.

The nineteenth-century views of masculinity and femininity were highly stereotyped. In England in that period, the Victorian era, women occupied narrow and circumscribed roles. The prevailing philosophy in the United States was much the same. Girls were socialized to the "feminine virtues"—piety, purity, submissiveness, and domesticity (Spears & Swanson, 1978). Although mild forms of "proper" exercise were thought to be useful for women, vigorous exercise and competitive sports were generally thought to be inappropriate, both because women were assumed to be genetically unfit for vigorous exercise (such activity would harm them) and because vigorous and competitive activities were presumed to promote behavior that was unladylike.

This narrow view of femininity changed very slowly, partly because of the companion views about masculinity. To be "masculine," one had to be virile; to express virility in one's behavior, one had to avoid behaving in ways that might be perceived as femi-nine. Men were supposed to be tough, physical, and aggressive. There were many Americans in the nineteenth century who believed deeply that American men were becoming too "feminine" and that these men needed to be more "masculine" for America to become a great nation. In one of his popular novels, the famous American writer Henry James had one of his characters express the prevail-ing beliefs—that Americans were suffering from "the most damnable feminism . . . the whole gener-ation is womanized . . . the masculine character is passing out of the world" (Lucas & Smith, 1978, p. 288).

The cultural focus on masculinity and virility was evidenced in the most popular literature of the day—the series of stories and novels known as the *Frank Merriwell sagas.* In serial form in magazines and in popular novels, the character of Frank Mer-riwell became the prototypical American male, the ideal model for the age. Merriwell attended a prep school and then Yale. He was bright, wealthy, fit, skilled, and highly moral. In each new episode or novel, Merriwell would be confronted with some seemingly impossible obstacle to his goal, which he would promptly overcome, most often through an act of physical skillfulness and courage. He typified all the manly virtues, and his high moral stature was intertwined with his virility.

Programs of sport, fitness, and physical educa-tion for girls and women did begin to develop dur-ing the nineteenth century, but they developed much more slowly than and in ways different from the programs for boys and men (Spears & Swanson, 1978). Girls' sport programs were controlled al-most exclusively by physical-education depart-ments. Games were designed to be less strenuous. Spectating was discouraged. Fitness programs were decidedly less vigorous. Sport had to be done "ac-ceptably." Even so, there was much criticism during this time that programs for girls and women were too strenuous and thus were of potential physical harm and promoted unladylike behavior among participants. Such attitudes changed very slowly until more recently, when the feminist movement and the federal law known as *Title IX* began to bring some parity for girls and women in sport, fitness, and physical education.

Thus, even though the nineteenth century was a period of growth and importance for sport, fitness, and physical education, we must recognize that it was so for males more than for females. The pre-vailing philosophies of masculinity and femininity would not allow for full participation for girls and women.

Amateurism, Fair Play, and the British Ideals

The philosophy of muscular Christianity brought religion, sport, and fitness together in a way that bred a new civil religion—one that, according to a British writer in the 1860s, "enjoined its disciples above all to fear God and run a mile in four and a half minutes" (Lucas & Smith, 1978, p. 139). Much of the growing American sense of sport behavior and preparation for sport also was influenced by British ideals. As sport grew in the latter part of the nineteenth century, it grew partially along the lines of amateurism and **fair play** that character-ized much of British sport.

For the most part, amateurism in the late nine-teenth century was the province of the wealthy, and being an amateur in sport typically meant that you were the son of a privileged family. It also meant that you did not train full-time for your competition and that you did not receive any real coaching. Cer-tainly, the notions of fair play and of the well-played game were part of the moral codes of the upper classes in England—and those values were adopted by the wealthy sports enthusiasts of America.

Nowhere can this code and all of its inherent meaning be seen more clearly than in the begin-ning of the modern Olympic Games in 1896. The French Baron Pierre de Coubertin wanted to revive what he saw as the pageantry and almost mystical meaning of the Olympic Games, but he revived the games on the model of amateurism and fair play that represented the nineteenth-century ideals. The now widely proclaimed motto of the Olym-pic Games—"The most important thing in the

The revival of the Olympic Games made sports such as gymnastics popular throughout the world.

Olympic Games is not to win, but to take part"—probably would have been considered silly in ancient Greece, where only the winner of an Olympic contest received any prize.

The ideals of amateurism and fair play were taken seriously by emerging sport groups in America. The Amateur Athletic Union was formed in 1888 and quickly became the most powerful force in amateur sport in America (Spears & Swanson, 1978). Local clubs, such as the New York Athletic Club, were also vanguards of these traditions.

Character Education through Physical Challenge

In 1934 Kurt Hahn, a German Jew who had fled from his homeland to escape Nazi persecution, founded the Gordonstoun School in Scotland.

Hahn's primary educational goal was to train character rather than intellect. He was interested in action rather than reflection. Students (all boys at that time) at Gordonstoun were always active, starting with a 6:30 A.M. wake-up to take a cold shower and go for the morning run. They learned track-and-field, seamanship, and water-rescue skills. They were taught about appropriate character and were assessed on elements of character such as public spirit, sense of justice, persevering in the face of obstacles, and civic courage (Skidelsky, 1969).

Physical fitness was a high priority at Gordonstoun. Classroom activities were interrupted each morning for a 40-minute strenuous workout. Physical challenges were constantly presented to test the fitness of the students, their courage, and their willingness to persevere under difficult conditions.

Character education was generally important in England in the late nineteenth and early twentieth centuries. The philosophy of Arnoldism (see page 70) stressed courage, team spirit, and character. The YMCA movement, which began in England, quickly began to focus on training in discipline, obedience, health, and patriotism. These movements shared the belief that national weaknesses were related to character weaknesses in men. It should be noted that all these initiatives were focused on boys.

The YMCA movement was very successful with young boys but less so with youths. Kurt Hahn believed that youth needed education through adventure; that through expeditions focused on physical adventure, such as treks, mountain climbs, dangerous sailing expeditions, and the like, young men would develop character, experience important achievement, and form significant friendships. Thus was born the Outward Bound movement. Outward Bound courses were organized in several places throughout England and Scotland. Expeditions would typically last four days, present significant tests of courage and skill, and result, it was hoped, in a sense of accomplishment and confidence that would transform young lives. The belief that character could be developed through demanding physical experiences would remain strong in educational philosophy and later in the twentieth century would find a home in experiential and adventure education, described later in this chapter.

This notion has recently been generalized to a current form of education redesign known as Expeditionary Learning Outward Bound (www.elob.org or www.aasa.org/reform/approach/explearn.htm). This is a whole-school reform model for which there is strong research evidence of improved student performance. Students pursue all subjects through a series of expeditions, a series of extended periods of study focused on single themes, which average 10–16 weeks to complete. Schools form into communities of learners in which there is shared decision-making, and learning is assessed through real-world performances related to each theme. Citizenship and character are central to the model.

SCHOOL SPORT AND THE NEW PHYSICAL EDUCATION

When Thomas Wood presented his vision of a new physical education to the International Conference on Education in Chicago in 1893, his talk set the stage for the transition period from a gymnastics curriculum to the education-through-the-physical philosophy that was to dominate twentieth-century physical education. (For a more complete description of the historical development of the new physical education, see Chapter 2.) The philosophical basis for the new physical education was rooted in **progressive-education theory.** Because this philosophical rationale for sport, fitness, and physical education was so completely to dominate the profession in the twentieth century, it is important to trace briefly from where it came and how it came to be adopted.

The main figure in American progressive education was John Dewey, who was not only a premier educational thinker of the nineteenth century but also one of America's foremost philosophers. Dewey was educated at Johns Hopkins University at a time when the major new theoretical issues of the nineteenth century—Darwinism, the philosophy of pragmatism, the scientific theories of em-

The fact that children love to play was central to the development of progressive education.

piricism—created a spirit of inquiry and experimentalism. Dewey took his newly formed ideas about education to the University of Chicago, where he opened a laboratory school, to experiment with and further develop those ideas. In 1897 he published *My Pedagogic Creed,* followed in 1899 by his book *School and Society.*

Dewey's main agenda for education was social reform through a child-centered, natural education. One has to remember that in the 1890s, child labor was still common, sweat shops were everywhere, and common people suffered enormously, especially in cities. It was a time in American history when a collective social conscience began to form.

To look back on the nineties is to sense an awakening of social conscience, a growing belief that this incredible suffering was neither the fault nor the inevitable lot of the sufferers, that it could certainly be alleviated, and that the road to alleviation was neither charity nor revolution, but in the last analysis education. (Cremin, 1961, p. 59)

Dewey believed passionately that the road to peaceful change in a democracy was through education and that education had to be viewed as lived experience in which students were active participants rather than passive recipients. In progressive education, *doing* was every bit as important as *knowing*. He also believed strongly in what he described as the *unity of man*, the notion that mental and physical could not be separated and that all educational activity had intellectual, moral, and physical outcomes. Because of those beliefs, activities such as natural play, sports, and games were valued by Dewey and his followers. Dewey was a firm supporter of physical education, especially when it was directed toward the achievement of social goals.

Dewey was, without question, the most important figure in the history of American education. In 1904 he left Chicago to be professor of philosophy at Columbia University, where he stayed until his retirement. Thomas Wood had been appointed as head of physical education at Teachers College, also at Columbia University, in 1901. He was joined there later by Clark Hetherington, another major interpreter of the education-through-the-physical philosophy. In 1924 Teachers College, in cooperation with New York University, started the first doctoral program in physical education. Thus, many of the early leaders in physical education received their advanced training at the institution that was the main center for progressive education and the education-through-the-physical philosophy.

Dewey's education philosophy had clear antecedents in European educational thought; because that history of thought is so important to sport, fitness, and physical education, we examine it briefly here.

The European Antecedents

The chain of influence that led to the development of both progressive education and the new physical education originated in the mid-eighteenth-century philosophy of *naturalism,* articulated most prominently by the French philosopher Jean-Jacques Rousseau. One of Rousseau's major works was *Emile,* which described his ideal of education for boys and girls. This book was considered to be so radical that it was banned in France, but it was quickly published and eagerly read elsewhere in Europe and later in the United States.

Simply put, Rousseau's argument was that children were born good and then were ruined by their contacts with society. His educational program was *natural,* designed to help children and youths grow up in perfect freedom. He strongly supported sensory experiences of all kinds and was particularly enthusiastic about physical activity, gymnastics, sports, and games. His views of the interrelatedness of mind and body foreshadowed the *holistic* view that became central to Dewey's philosophy.

Rousseau advocated having physical-education facilities in schools and promoted the use of games and sports because he believed that these activities were important in developing two major traits of character: cooperation and competition. Rousseau's philosophy had immediate and long-term influence on education through the work of educators who read and interpreted his philosophy.

- *Johann Bernhard Basedow* founded a school in Germany in 1744 that put the natural philosophy into practice in a real setting. Basedow advocated treating children as children rather than as miniature adults, thereby leading the movement to establish childhood as a distinct developmental stage. Physical activity was central to the curriculum in this school.

- *Johann Heinrich Pestalozzi,* perhaps the most influential of all European educational reformers, believed that all knowledge had a basis in action; thus, he made sensory learning and physical activity central to the school curriculum. The German physical educator Ludwig Jahn taught in a school inspired by Pestalozzi's educational theories.

- *Friedrich Froebel* believed in the unity of life and action, expressed in observing, creating, discovering, and exercising. He created the word "kindergarten" to express his belief in educating the natural talents of young children just as gardeners tend to the natural growth of plants. He, too, believed that sports and games had the power not only to develop the physical talents of students but also to strengthen intelligence and develop character.

Physical education could never have developed as it did as a school subject in America were it not for this chain of influence from Rousseau to Dewey, with the major European naturalist philosophers and educators acting as the links in the chain. Dewey extended this chain through his progressive educational philosophy, and it was within the context of progressive educational theory that Wood argued for a *new* physical education and Hetherington articulated the goals for education-through-the-physical, bringing the philosophical basis for sport, fitness, and physical education clearly within the realm of progressive educational theory.

The Reemergence of Play as a Philosophical Concept

A fundamental concept in the aforementioned philosophical linkages is **play.** Rousseau recognized the value of natural play in the education of children. Basedow and Pestalozzi not only made room for natural play but also made formalized play, through games and gymnastics, a basic part of the school curriculum. It was Froebel, however, who was to make play the cornerstone of children's education. For Froebel, play was the most natural expression of childhood and therefore the most fundamental medium through which children learned about themselves and their world. Dewey made play in childhood a basic tenet of progressive education. Thus, as progressive education influenced more powerfully the course of American education, the notion that play was not only a legitimate but indeed a fundamentally important education focus was widely accepted.

The concept of play, and of its role in education and life, was central to many ancient philosophies. Our knowledge of ancient cultures and customs indicates that playful activities were often central to individual and community life. With the rise and spread of Christianity, however, the concept of play found disfavor with theologians and philosophers. This is not to suggest that people were less playful, because it is now clear that people in all cultures and throughout history have found ways to play. It is only to suggest that as a philosophical and educational concept, play began to be viewed negatively rather than positively. Work was the appropriate form of activity for virtuous women and men. Play was thought to occasion idleness and sinful behavior. This general philosophical trend gained strength in the Christian theologies of the Reformation.

Thus, for several hundred years, religious leaders tended to frown on playful activity. Even children at play were barely tolerated, rather than encouraged. Play in the form of games and sports was often branded as anti-Christian behavior. The renaissance of the concept of play can be traced to important thinkers such as Rousseau, but it was in the nineteenth century that the concept was fully reborn as a positive human attribute. Froebel's work was important in recognizing play as a positive educational process.

Whereas Froebel helped to reestablish play as a legitimate educational concept, it was the German poet-philosopher Friedrich von Schiller who helped to make play a respectable concept in general philosophy and intellectual thought. Schiller did not focus only on child's play, nor was he concerned with leisure-time activity, nor, indeed, can his ideas be viewed simply as a reaction to the pervasive antiplay theology of the Reformation. Schiller argued that play was a basic, integrating mode of human behavior throughout life and across all cultures. He believed strongly that people experienced the wholeness of life most clearly when at play: "For to speak out once for all, man only plays when in the full meaning of the word he is a man, and he is only completely a man when he plays" (Schiller, 1910). Schiller's now-famous statement about play does not sound extreme in today's philosophical climate, but how radical it must have sounded in the early nineteenth century, when people at work and people as pious creatures were the ideal models for human life!

Schiller influenced the work of Froebel in education and of Friedrich Wilhelm Nietzsche in philosophy. By the beginning of the twentieth century, play had returned to respectability both as a central philosophical concept and as an educational theory. The manifestations of this perspective can be seen not only in American progressive education and in the rapid expansion of sport during that time, but also in equally important yet less well known movements such as the expansion of the playground movement in early-twentieth-century America and in the widespread adoption of sport and fitness activities by organizations such as the YMCA and the Catholic Youth Organization (CYO).

The idea of play is clearly evident in the work of Hetherington and of other prominent leaders of the new physical education. Education-through-the-physical utilized the medium of playful activity to accomplish its various goals, especially its social goals. We must understand that the program *utilizing* play could have developed only after the *concept* of play had been accepted in philosophy and education. Again, we see the power of ideas!

The Early Twentieth Century: Philosophies Come Together

The nineteenth century was, as we have shown, an extraordinary period of development in both *ideas* about sport, fitness, and physical education and *participation* in those fields. Muscular Christianity allowed activity and competition to become not only acceptable but also favorable. Moral development began to be tied to sport and fitness. The ideal person was portrayed as fit, skilled, and moral. Education began to change from a narrow, academic view to a more child-centered view in which playful activity was seen to be central to an appropriate education.

As has been shown, each of these philosophical forces developed from a different source, and each had somewhat different initial effects. In the early twentieth century, the forces began to coalesce to form a unified philosophical position that was to undergird sport, fitness, and physical education for the next 50 years. People who were prominent in physical education were also influential in fitness movements, in sport, and in other areas, such as the playground movement and the YMCA movement. Thus, because these people tended to adopt a common philosophy, all those areas were influenced in many of the same ways.

What an exciting and marvelous period that must have been for sport, fitness, and physical-education professionals! Just after the turn of the century, Theodore Roosevelt won the presidency and advocated the "strenuous life" for all Americans. Universal schooling was becoming more of a reality, and physical education was beginning to be seen as a necessary part of basic education. America was quickly becoming a major sport culture—more people were participating and more people were spectating. Graduate study in physical education was now available. The long period of Puritanism was over, and America had begun to embrace fully the value of physical activity.

The major philosophy that undergirded the next 50 years was an amalgamation of many of the ideas described here. It was represented most clearly in the new physical education of Wood and was elaborated most articulately by Hetherington, Cassidy, Williams, and Nash (see Chapter 2). The philosophy, simply stated, asserted that participation in sport, fitness, and physical education was useful because of the contributions it made to intellectual, physical, social, and moral development.

Those contributions were thought to be extremely important in the lives of children and youths; thus, the inclusion of physical education and sport programs in schools was of major importance. Play was accepted as the mode of behavior through which children learned most naturally. Competitive sport, properly organized and administered, was thought to be an important educational experience.

Although activity forms and opportunities for women were still less than equal with those for men, this period also marked a dramatic change in what was considered appropriate for women in sport and physical education. In addition, participation during adulthood was considered to be an important recreational balance to the demands of modern life. It was this unified philosophy that was widely accepted in the first half of the twentieth century, the period during which these professions developed and began to form an identity of their own, leading to the more recent periods of specialization.

PHILOSOPHICAL FORCES IN SPORT, FITNESS, AND PHYSICAL EDUCATION SINCE 1950

The period from 1900 to 1950 was one of unified professional consolidation and growth; the period from 1950 to the present was one of diversity and ferment. The education-through-the-physical philosophy, the dominant underlying belief system for the profession in the early twentieth century, was not seriously challenged until the 1950s. Then a series of societal and professional developments provided the context for a period of diversification, specialization, and accompanying philosophical ferment within sport, fitness, and physical education.

A more complete description of the events underlying this new period of philosophical ferment appears in Chapter 3. In summary, when cul-

tural factors such as the post-1950 reformist movement in education, the civil rights movement, the fitness renaissance, and the era of specialization in universities all came together in a fairly short time span, they produced serious questioning of basic philosophical assumptions of the field. In one sense, much of the remainder of this text involves descriptions of the *effects* of that philosophical ferment. At this point, however, I describe briefly the major philosophical movements since midcentury.

Human Movement

The first serious challenge to a half-century of unified philosophical belief in physical education came during the 1950s, with the development of the *human-movement philosophy.* First developed in England during the late 1930s by the German immigrant Rudolph Laban, and foreshadowed clearly in the work of Rosiland Cassidy, the notion that a philosophy of human movement could underlie physical education took hold in England in the 1940s. After World War II, American physical educators began to learn about this philosophy and saw in it a more satisfying intellectual and emotional approach to their subject matter.

In 1948 Laban published *Modern Educational Dance,* an important and influential book not only for its curricular implications but also for its articulation of the underlying philosophy. In 1952 the British Ministry of Education produced a new curriculum syllabus in physical education for British

Movement education allows children opportunities to explore their movement potential in ways that are fun.

schools titled *Moving and Growing*, which gave an official stamp of approval to the theoretical and curricular innovation called "human movement."

Exactly how and when human movement became an important concept in American physical education is difficult to determine. In the middle to late 1950s, the philosophy and its implications began to appear regularly in the American physical-education literature. Cassidy had identified movement as the "stuff" of physical education as early as 1937 (Caldwell, 1966). In 1954 Eleanor Metheny, one of the early and most important advocates, published an article that provided a basic definition of the human-movement approach, a definition that would still find widespread acceptance today:

> If we may define the *totally educated person* as one who has fully developed his ability to utilize constructively all of his potential capacities as a person in relation to the world in which he lives, then we may define the *physically educated person* as one who has fully developed the ability to utilize constructively all of his potential capacities for movement as a way of expressing, exploring, developing, and interpreting himself and his relationship to the world he lives in. (Metheny, 1954, p. 27; emphasis in original)

In 1958 the physical-education faculty at UCLA began to define and develop an undergraduate curriculum for training professionals in human movement.

During the same period, physical education at the university level was also undergoing a revolution of sorts. Many departments were forced to justify the academic nature of their program—and they found it difficult to do so relying solely on the teacher-education program undergirded by an education-through-the-physical philosophy. Thus began the period of specialization that eventually led to the academic-discipline movement in physical education, which is the focus of Part 5 of this text. Areas such as sport psychology, sport physiology, and sport sociology began to develop. They needed a philosophical framework within which to relate to one another; they found that framework in the human-movement philosophy. In 1966 Warren Fraleigh called for the adoption of human-

movement philosophy as the unifying theme on which the discipline of physical education should be built. In 1967 the influential journal *Quest* devoted an entire issue to this topic; it became clear that most professional leaders saw human movement as the most useful and relevant philosophy on which to develop the young academic specializations.

The philosophy of human movement was sufficiently strong and appealing that it was able to provide the framework for the early development of academic specializations in universities, the reworking of the undergraduate professional curriculum, and the beginning of change in school programs of physical education. At the school level, the philosophy of human movement advocated a more open, exploratory approach to teaching physical education, as compared with previous approaches. Equipped with a new vocabulary and a new curriculum, movement educators began to redirect the nature of physical education in schools, especially for children in elementary schools.

Movement education was the only serious challenger, as a curriculum philosophy, to education-through-the-physical in the twentieth century. In its purest form, it was meant to be an entirely new approach, both to program development and to teaching.

> There is a fundamental distinction that must be made between the organizational structure of contemporary Physical Education and Movement Education. In the former, *the activity itself* (volleyball, track and field or folk dance) provides *the structured basis* for developing a curriculum. Skills within each area are arranged from the simple to the complex and presented to children in accordance with their physical maturity and general readiness.
>
> Within the organizational structure of Movement Education, the concepts and underlying principles of "body awareness," "space," and "qualities" of movement provide a basis for *understanding* all movement. In Movement Education, *all* activities are selected on the basis of how well they can foster and develop the concepts and movement principles described under *body awareness, space,* and *qualities* of movement. These concepts or *elements of movement* thus become the *framework of a Movement Education Curriculum*. (Kirchner, 1970, pp. 16–17; emphasis in original)

The movement curriculum began to be divided into educational gymnastics, educational dance, and educational games. The approach was through exploration and guided discovery. The climate was noncompetitive and success oriented. Most of the elementary texts in physical-education methods used in universities today reflect the rather substantial changes that occurred in physical education during the period from 1955 to 1975, as the human-movement philosophy began to develop adherents.

As the academic specializations of physical education began to develop and mature, they tended to rely less often on the underlying philosophy of human movement to bind them together and, more recently, have utilized the concept of sport as the unifying theme (thus the *sport-sciences* and *sport-studies* programs of recent times). Nonetheless, the philosophy of human movement continues to be a major influence in American physical education, especially in professional teacher education and in school programs.

Humanistic Sport and Physical Education

Philosophies in sport, fitness, and physical education often reflect ideas and ideals that are popular in the intellectual and social climate of the surrounding society. Nowhere is this more clearly seen than in the **humanistic philosophies** in sport and physical education of the 1960s and 1970s. One of the important factors in American culture in this period was *third-force psychology* or *humanistic psychology*. These ideas reached maturity as a popular movement in America during the social turmoil of the 1960s and 1970s. Third-force psychology focuses on the full development of individual potential through personal growth and self-development. (These ideas are often referred to as the "self" psychologies.)

The two major educational movements of the post-1950 era were the renewed emphasis on science and mathematics and the humanistic-education movement. In education, this philosophy —really a set of loosely related philosophies—promoted open education, affective education, values clarification, and less emphasis on competition for grades and academic outcomes. The personal and social development of children was thought to be more important than—or at least as important as—their academic development.

In 1973 Donald Hellison published his influential book *Humanistic Physical Education*, setting forth the conceptual and theoretical basis for the emerging humanistic movement in physical education. This approach to physical education in schools stressed personal development, self-expression, and improved interpersonal relationships as primary goals for physical education.

During the same period, a companion movement developed within the world of intercollegiate and professional sport, fueled by the same societal factors that led to the humanistic physical-education movement. In 1969 Jack Scott published *Athletics for Athletes* and became an early leader in the movement. This text was followed by a series of popular books condemning abuses in sport, criticizing how athletes were treated, and advocating reforms that would allow sport to be more devoted to the personal development of the athletes. Typical of these books were Dave Meggyesy's *Out of Their League*, a strident criticism of Meggyesy's experience in football; Olympic medalist Don Schollander's *Deep Water*; Leonard Shector's *The Jocks*; and Glenn Dickey's *The Jock Empire*.

The proponents of humanistic sport and physical education were critical of then-current practices and were advocates of new forms of participation:

Visualize a nation of sadistic people who get their kicks out of humiliating others or ensuring that others do not get what they want. I am fearful that this is what lies ahead unless we are capable of reversing the present direction of our contemporary games and lives. (Orlick, 1977, p. 33)

In fact, the counterculture ethic reverses every value of the Lombardian ethic. Cooperation replaces competition, an emphasis on process replaces an emphasis on the product, sport as a co-educational activity replaces sport as a stag party, a concern for enjoyment replaces a concern for excellence, and an opportunity for spontaneity and self-expression replaces authoritarianism. (Scott, 1974, p. 159)

The humanistic movement had an enormous influence on many people while it was popular. Although it is no longer described in the terms used during its developmental period, this movement has some clear ties to several current philosophies in physical education. The work started by Donald Hellison has developed into a major curricular and pedagogical force within physical education, known now as "the personal and social responsibility" model (Hellison, 1984, 1995, 1996). Although it has been applied widely, especially in elementary physical education, it has manifested its strong social commitment most clearly in programs for at-risk urban youths. I would also argue that the *critical theory* movement of the 1990s owed some of its popularity to the same concerns that evoked the humanistic movement a generation earlier. Critical theory focuses on structural inequities in society and organizes programs to make people more aware of power relationships that produce inequities and to produce more equality.

Play Education and Sport Education

The traditional philosophy of physical education emphasized *using* activities to reach valuable educational goals—physical, mental, social, and moral goals. In the 1970s, some professionals began to argue that the activities of physical education were valuable *in and of themselves.* Metheny's (1954, 1970) influential work had long promoted this basic idea. A philosophy expressing this point of view was put forth by Siedentop (1972, 1976, 1980) as **play education.** The goal of play education was to help students acquire skills and develop an affection for the activities themselves. Play educators were to be seen as transmitters and transformers of valuable cultural activities:

Play is the proper classification for physical education, both from a logical and psychological perspective. Classifying physical education as a form of play puts it clearly in perspective alongside other primary institutionalized forms of play—art, music, and drama. . . . This classification allows us to recognize that the activities of the weekend golfer or skier, the after-dinner tennis player, and the noon-time handball player are analogous to those of the painter, the member of the community theater, or the musician. Each is at play, at an institutionalized form of play, and it is only the play form that distinguished one from the other. (Siedentop, 1980, p. 247)

From the point of view of play education, physical education did not need to be justified by reference to outcomes beyond involvement in the activities:

We must have the good sense and courage to stand up and defend our field on the basis of the personal and cultural meaning in our subject matter. . . . We do not have to *use* our activities. There is no doubt that they can be used, and often for quite legitimate and noble purposes. But those other purposes are of a different order than play education. In play education we can let our subject matter be just what it is—institutionalized forms of play that are of fundamental importance to the culture in which we live and grow. (Siedentop, 1980, p. 259; emphasis in original)

The philosophy of play education did not directly influence curriculum development in schools. Nonetheless, many physical educators began to argue more boldly that their subject matter (however defined) was valuable in and of itself and did not need to be justified by reference to external objectives or outcomes. Play education never became a reality because it was more a philosophy than a prescription for a program.

In 1986 a similar philosophical point of view was expressed as **sport education** (Siedentop, Mand, & Taggart, 1986). The purpose of sport education was to educate students in the skills, values, and attitudes of good sport so that they might enjoy and participate themselves and also so that they would be active contributors to a healthier sport culture.

The rationale for sport education rests on a few very basic and important assumptions. The first is that sport derives from play; that is, sport represents an institutionalized form of competitive motor play. The second is that sport is an important part of our culture and that sport occupies an important role in deter-

In sport education, students compete in modified games as members of a continuing team.

mining the health and vitality of the entire culture; that is, if more people participate in good sport, then the culture is stronger. The third assumption follows from the first two. If sport is a higher form of play and if good sport is important to the health and vitality of the culture, then sport should be the subject matter of physical education. The development of good sportspersons and the development of a better sports culture should be central to the mission of physical education. (Siedentop, Mand, & Taggart, 1986, pp. 188–189)

If play education lacked a clear program prescription, sport education did not. In sport education (Siedentop, 1994), students become members of teams for the duration of a season (unit), a schedule for competition among teams (or individuals, in the case of an individual sport) is established, a culminating event through which a seasonal champion can be determined is arranged, and records are kept that infuse the competition with greater interest and meaning for students and that begin to develop a sense of tradition in that sport in that school.

This, of course, was all to be done within the structure of the physical-education class. Students would learn skills, and they would still practice skills and strategies, but they would do so as a team. They would compete as a team for the duration of that season (unit). As the season (unit) progressed, less time would be devoted to skill practice and more time would be spent in competition and in preparation for it (strategy).

Experiential and Adventure Education

The emergence of character-education models in England in the 1930s (see pages 72–73) was a prelude to the current focus on experiential and adventure education. Much of what is done in experiential and adventure education grew from the Outward Bound movement. Note that the five core values of Outward Bound are consistent with much of adventure education (www.outwardbound.com):

- Adventure and challenge
- Compassion and service
- Learning through experience
- Personal development
- Social and environmental responsibility

Many school physical-education programs now include adventure activities, and it is not uncommon to see climbing walls and challenge courses on school sites. Adventure-education curricula have also led the way in moving physical education outside the regular class schedule and away from the normal facilities of schools. Day trips and weekend trips are common. Activities such as cycling, climbing, hiking, and canoeing are typical in adventure-education curricula.

The concept of "expedition" has always been central to the educational philosophies attached to these movements. Expeditions have clear goals, a series of challenges, an extended time frame in which to complete goals of the activity, and an authentic form of assessment that is built into completing the challenge.

The Fitness Renaissance and the Wellness Movement

It is impossible to watch television for any length of time or to read a popular magazine without realizing quickly that fitness is "in." Most of the people who appear in advertisements are fit and active—they look strong, they are active, and they let you know in some way (mostly to sell their product) that the active lifestyle is the current definition of the "good life." Fitness is big business in America (see Chapter 9). Not *everybody* is involved in fitness, of course; we know that many children are unfit and that the contemporary fitness renaissance is mostly a phenomenon of the middle and upper classes. Nonetheless, many adults in America have adopted being active and fit as an important part of their lifestyle.

The fitness renaissance is still too recent to analyze *why* it has happened. Obviously, we know more now than in the past about fitness and about how a lack of fitness can contribute to medical problems. All the medical issues put together, however, cannot possibly explain the enormous increase in adult participation in regular fitness activities, such as running, swimming, cycling, aerobics, weight lifting, and triathloning. The contemporary philosophical views that have provided the context for the fitness movement no doubt have much to do with health, but they also have to do with living well—and being active clearly is considered to be part of living well.

The recent popularity of fitness seems to coincide with a number of other movements in society that refocused popular attention on quality-of-life issues. For example, the fitness movement has developed in the same era as have the consumer movement, the ecology movement, the civil rights movement, and the human-rights movement. Each, in its own way, focused attention on what living well meant and on what impediments to living well existed in modern American culture.

If there is a discernible philosophy underlying the fitness movement, it has been most clearly articulated by the health-education and allied medical professions. The relevant philosophical concept is *wellness*. Traditional definitions and views of health all related to *illness*. *Health* was viewed as the *absence* of illness. Ways of measuring health were to assess the "five Ds"—death, disease, discomfort, disability, and dissatisfaction (Edlin & Golanty, 1982). Like a washing machine or a refrigerator, your health was assumed to be good if your body and life were "working." You did not pay much attention to your health until it "broke down."

The concept of wellness took a much broader, more holistic, and more proactive view of health. The factors that define wellness include not only traditional criteria, such as freedom from disease, but also a number of positive criteria, such as adaptability to cope with everyday stresses, feelings of accomplishment and personal growth, ability to express a positive and creative lifestyle, and feelings of contentment and happiness. To be *well* in this more holistic sense, a person must be active, in good spirits, and free from disease and pain, to the extent possible.

A main feature of the wellness philosophy is that to achieve wellness, you must work toward it—it will not "happen" to you. The holistic view suggests that physical, mental, and psychological problems are all related and that to achieve wellness, you must make sure that your work, play, and social lives not only are positive in themselves but also are appropriately balanced.

The fitness and wellness movements have now evolved to incorporate the concept of lifespan physical activity as a main ingredient of a healthful lifestyle, leaving behind an older, more narrow concept of physical fitness. (See Chapter 8 for a discussion of this distinction.) Research has established physical activity as contributing positively to increased longevity, enhanced work capacity, a healthful lifestyle, and general well-being (Karvonen, 1996). Regular involvement in moderate to intense physical activity is seen as a necessary component of achieving and maintaining wellness (Blair & Connelly, 1996). The movement now focuses on *lifestyle* changes that include nutrition, physical activity, useful and satisfying work, and recreation.

Aerobics is a central activity in the fitness movement.

Fitness, wellness, and lifestyle education programs have focused primarily on individuals and have been treated as matters of individual responsibility. More recently, the soaring cost for public health has focused attention on the collective concerns associated with a nation where too many people are inactive and eat unhealthy diets. The publication of *Healthy People 2000* (U.S. Public Health Service, 1991) made it clear that diet and physical activity are *public-policy* concerns. The assessment of the 2000 goals and the setting of new goals in *Healthy People 2010* (U.S. Department of Health and Human Services, 2000) further emphasized that the nation's health was both an individual and a *collective responsibility*. Evidence suggests strongly (Siedentop, 1996c) that people in each socioeconomic group tend to be healthier than

the people in groups below them and to be less healthy than the people in groups above them. In the United States, socioeconomic status also correlates strongly with racial/ethnic status. In nations where socioeconomic differences are less widespread or where they have been reduced over time, the health status of citizens tends to be better. This suggests that improved health and the achievement of physically active lifestyles are socioeconomic and political issues as well as medical and health issues (Siedentop, 1996c; Sparkes, 1991).

Although the fitness–wellness movement, and the philosophy undergirding it, is often identifiable in school physical-education and health programs, this philosophy and the programs developed from it have spread mostly through the private sector in adult society. The wellness movement may develop further by taking into account the lifestyle of children and youths, with school and nonschool programs to promote wellness and to provide activity. If so, then the wellness philosophy and the movement representing it could form the underlying rationale for lifespan involvement in sport, fitness, and physical education. Chapter 1 argued that the opportunity for lifespan involvement is now available. As of yet, however, there is no widespread societal understanding of those opportunities or of why lifespan involvement is beneficial. The philosophy of wellness might provide that understanding.

A number of current developments might affect the further evolution of professional philosophies in sport, fitness, and physical education. For one thing, so-called *risk sports* are gaining in popularity. A whole new "alternative-sport" movement seems to be arising through well-publicized "extreme games," or now "X-games," shown on American television. Another development is the emergence of new sport forms among children and youths, perhaps as a response to the highly structured nature of most youth sport; in these new sport forms, children and youths, rather than adults, have control over the rules, skills, and competitions (Coakley, 1994). In addition, the women's movement continues to coalesce politically and philosophically, and sport has become a major arena for this movement.

Further, the baby boomers—the population group that has so dramatically affected American culture through their teen and early-adult years—are in their midcareer years and looking toward their retirement years. All evidence suggests that they will continue to influence the culture, and it may well be that they become the first generation for whom lifespan physical activity becomes a reality rather than a vision.

SUMMARY

1. Our use of the term *philosophy* refers to the set of values and principles that guide work in a professional field.

2. Professional philosophies should be coherent, reasonable, and connected to the evolution of the professional field.

3. The gymnastic philosophies of Europe promoted nationalism through formal programs of gymnastics aimed at physical, mental, and emotional development of the individual to produce and maintain a strong state.

4. *Muscular Christianity* broke down religious opposition to sport and fitness and endorsed the belief that moral courage was related to physical courage and fitness.

5. *Arnoldism* was a philosophy that promoted an education in which physical activity had a central role in developing manliness, patriotism, moral courage, and intellectual independence.

6. Nineteenth-century philosophies and ideals emphasized masculine–feminine differences and relegated women to a lesser role, in which physical activity was seen as unladylike and potentially harmful.

7. American sport and physical education were strongly influenced by British standards of fair play and amateurism, those ideals being highlighted with the rebirth of the Olympic Games in 1896.

8. The beginnings of an American physical-education philosophy borrowed heavily from progressive-education theory, which was directly traceable to a series of eighteenth- and nineteenth-century European philosophers and educators.

9. Philosophers, psychologists, and educators rediscovered the concept of play near the turn of the twentieth century and began to recognize its importance in the development of children and youths, as well as in adult life.

10. The "new" physical education emphasized education through the physical as the philosophical basis for sport, fitness, and physical education, a philosophy in which activity was believed to contribute to physical, mental, social, and intellectual strength.

11. The education-through-the-physical philosophy dominated American professional thought for the first half of the twentieth century and remains today the most influential philosophy, even though it has more recently been challenged by several competing philosophies.

12. The philosophy of human movement emphasized the ability to move as a means for expressing, exploring, developing, and interpreting one's own self and one's relationship to the world.

13. Humanistic philosophies in the post-1950 era influenced both sport and physical education, focusing attention on abuses and emphasizing self-development, self-growth, and interpersonal relations.

14. Play education developed as a philosophy in which the activities of physical education were seen as culturally important in their own right, not needing justification by reference to educational outcomes. Sport education developed as a companion framework that offered a specific program through which the philosophy could be realized.

15. The philosophy undergirding the development of the sport sciences and sport studies suggested that more academic rigor was needed in college and university physical education and that school programs ought to focus more on

the knowledge base of sport, fitness, and physical education.

16. Experiential and adventure education focus on academic and character education through challenge and responsibility.

17. The fitness and wellness movements were undergirded by a philosophy of holistic health that eschewed the traditional absence-of-illness model and replaced it with a proactive view, in which people actively strove to produce a lifestyle through which positive physical, mental, and emotional health would result.

18. The physical activity needs of the nation cannot be met by focusing solely on individuals but must include public-policy initiatives at local, state, and federal levels.

DISCUSSION QUESTIONS

1. Can you trace the origins of your professional philosophies? How coherently can you articulate these philosophical positions.

2. What current views reflect the influence of muscular Christianity, the gymnastic philosophies, or the British fair-play tradition? In what forms have these notions survived?

3. How have masculine and feminine ideals changed? What vestiges of the former views still linger?

4. What physical-education philosophy best represents your views? How would you describe the philosophy underlying the physical-education program in the high school you attended?

5. To what extent does progressive education still dominate school aims and objectives? Is progressive education compatible with current educational reform?

6. How does the current wellness movement differ from the gymnastic philosophies? Will wellness supplant fitness as a primary concern?

7. Which philosophy seems to dominate professional sport? Which one dominates activity at a local fitness club? Which one dominates youth sport?

PART TWO

Sport

Chapter 5   Basic Concepts of Sport

Chapter 6   Sport Programs and Professions

Chapter 7   Problems and Issues in Sport

Most people who read this text have had a positive experience in sport. For many, like me, sport has been at the center of their lives and has helped to form many of the fundamental experiences of their development as individuals. The sport culture in which we live is a dynamic, evolving enterprise. In many cases, the sport culture does well; in other cases, however, it does poorly. How will it evolve in the future? Who is responsible for helping sport to evolve in ways that serve everyone in the future more fully than it serves us now?

These are important questions that we cannot answer without a thorough understanding of what sport is, how and by whom it is practiced, and the major problems and issues that specialists in this field must face and solve. The three chapters in Part 2 will increase your understanding of and critical thinking about sport.

CHAPTER 5

Basic Concepts of Sport

*The very elaborations of sport—its internal conventions
of all kinds, its ceremonies, its endless meshes entangling
itself—are for the purpose of training and testing and rewarding the rousing motion within us to find a moment
of freedom. Freedom is that state where energy and order
merge and all complexity is purified into a simple coherence,
a fitness of parts and purpose and passions that cannot be
surpassed and whose goal could only be to be itself.*

A. Bartlett Giamatti, former commissioner of baseball
and president of Yale University, 1989

LEARNING OBJECTIVES

- To explain Novak's concept of sport as a natural religion

- To define the concept of play and to explain how it relates to sport

- To define the concept of a game, including the notions of primary and secondary rules

- To explain and provide examples of the game-classification system

- To discuss the several meanings of "competition"

- To analyze how sport becomes institutionalized

- To describe the aesthetic values of sport

- To discuss sport ethics

Sport has been a part of civilized societies throughout history. In some cases, as in Greece in the fifth century B.C., sport was of central importance to the culture. At other times, as during the repressive asceticism of the Middle Ages, sport was officially frowned on but still enjoyed by common people in villages and towns. At the height of the Roman Empire, athletes formed a strong labor union, bargaining for higher appearance fees and prizes and keeping out athletes who would not support the union. Sport even flourished in varied forms in early America, despite the Puritan sanctions against it. Until recently, however, few people tried to examine and analyze sport—to understand what it is, from what human motivations it springs, and what role it occupies in culture.

Sport has been studied and analyzed by scholars in many disciplines since the 1950s—and increasingly since the mid-1970s, when a national and world sport culture developed beyond what anybody could have imagined 100 years ago. The main argument in this chapter is that sport derives from the play impulse in human behavior, as do art, music, and drama. Yet few artistic or dramatic performances draw 80,000 spectators on an autumn afternoon, nor do musical events capture the national interest in the way the National Collegiate Athletic Association's annual basketball championship, known simply as "the Final Four," does. The extraordinary success of recent Olympic Games throughout the world foreshadows the development of a global sport culture that knows no boundaries of race, gender, ethnicity, or age. Understanding sport better, and forming judgments about its role in culture, is what this chapter is about.

Most people who read this text have had significant experiences in the world of sport. Many people who aspire to a career in the sport, fitness, and physical-education professions had childhood and youth experiences in sport that were the primary motivating factors in their choice of career. You probably *know* sport from an experiential point of view, having participated and been a spectator, perhaps having been an official or a coach. The purpose

The intensity of sport involvement is not defined by gender.

of this chapter is to provide a conceptual framework from within which you can understand your own experience of sport, as well as that of the individual and the society.

We should take seriously the topic of *sport*. Some people make fun of those of us who take sport seriously, ridiculing sport as "games kids play" and suggesting that because there are corruptions within sport, all sport is unworthy of serious, adult attention. That is a narrow view, not shared by many serious thinkers—and certainly not shared by any person who has taken the time to study the role that sport plays in people's lives.

By any measure, sport is important. The statistics on the number of people who spectate and who participate are impressive. The amount of money spent on sport is enormous. Sport heroes and heroines are used by corporations to advertise their products. Events such as the World Series and the Super Bowl have become national celebrations, but these kinds of celebrations are also repeated endlessly in cities and towns everywhere during each of the sport seasons that together compose the sport year. For many people, young and old alike, sport has an almost religious significance.

SPORT—THE NATURAL RELIGION

Michael Novak (1976), in *The Joy of Sports,* argues that sport is a natural religion and that we must understand it as such to grasp its fundamental importance. He describes what it is like to be a *believer* among unbelievers.

> Faith in sports, I have discovered, seeks understanding. . . . Other believers know how hard it is to put into words what they so deeply and obscurely know. They have also argued with their wives and friends, and even in their own heads. All around this land there is a faith without an explanation, a love without a rationale. (Novak, 1976, p. xiii)

Novak's argument, like those of many people who for the most part agree with him, is not based on using a simple religious metaphor to explain sport, does not come from a sportswriter talking about "sacrifice" of an athlete, and is not an athlete saying "you gotta believe." His serious argument is based on qualities and characteristics fundamental to the sport experience and to the role that experience plays in individual and social life:

> I am saying that sports flow outward into action from a deeper natural impulse that is radically religious: an impulse of freedom, respect for ritual limits, a zest for symbolic meaning, and a longing for perfection. The athlete may of course be pagan, but sports are, as it were, natural religions. (Novak, 1976, p. 19)

How is sport a religion? Sport is organized and dramatized in a religious way. There are rituals (the coin toss, the opening lineups, etc.). There are costumes (or "vestments," to use the religious phrase). There is a sense of powers that are outside one's control (the ball bounces to the left, the wind blows at an inopportune moment). There are figures who enforce rules and mete out punishments (referees). Sport also can, when done well, teach qualities that are religious in nature, such as perseverance, courage, and sacrifice. In sport, athletes often strive for perfection, just as do many people in religious orders. In sport, as in religion, there are heroes and heroines who provide models of perfection to strive for, who are admired for what they did, and become almost saintlike. Such is the *religious* nature of sport.

Believing in sport does not preclude being Christian, Jewish, or Muslim. However, believing in sport does require that you take sport seriously and, as you will see in the next two chapters, that you be concerned about its health and well-being.

Sport, like religion, can be intensely personal, yet, in its fullest sense, it is *communal.* What we see and experience in sport takes us out of ourselves and lets us glimpse something more perfect than we know ordinary life to be. A. Bartlett Giamatti, former president of Yale University and former commissioner of baseball, argues that sport can do this for both participant and spectator, thus further enhancing its communal nature:

> To take acts of physical toil—lifting, throwing, bending, jumping, pushing, grasping, stretching, running, hoisting, the constantly repeated acts that for millennia have meant work—and to bound them in time or by rules or boundaries in a given enclosure surrounded by an amphitheater or at least a gallery is to replicate the arena of humankind's highest aspiration. That aspiration is to be taken out of the self. (Giamatti, 1989, p. 34)

Believers in sport should neither be ashamed of their beliefs nor be reluctant to defend those beliefs. Being better able to explain and defend your commitment to sport can be a source of personal satisfaction, as well as a powerful professional tool. In addition, you should not have to tolerate having others make fun of sport.

> Sports are not merely fun and games, not merely diversions, not merely entertainment. A ballpark is not a temple, but it isn't a fun house either. A baseball game is not an entertainment, and a ballplayer is considerably more than a paid performer. No one can explain the passion, commitment, discipline, and dedication involved in sports by evasions like these. (Novak, 1976, p. 23)

Thus, as we examine the basic concepts underlying sport, let us do so with the seriousness and respect due a phenomenon of such clear cultural importance. Paul Weiss (1969), Sterling professor of philosophy at Yale University, has written what many people regard as the definitive work on sport philosophy. Weiss argues that sport provides humans with their greatest opportunity to achieve human excellence—and it is that striving for excellence that he sees at the heart of sport.

It is clear that for many people—perhaps for you, too—sport participation provides a source of deep personal meaning. Eleanor Metheny (1970), one of America's leading physical-education scholars of the mid–twentieth century, describes how sport creates conditions within which people test themselves and find out a great deal about who they are in moments of self-revelation during competition.

> Or, as the competitors in the early Olympic contests put it, every man who would submit his own excellence to the test of sport competition must "stand naked before his gods" and reveal himself as he is in the fullness of his own human powers. Stripped of all self-justifying excuses by the rules of sport, he must demonstrate his own ability to perform one human action of his own choosing, and naked of all pretense, he must use himself as he is, in all the wholeness of his being as a man. (Metheny, 1970, p. 66)

Sport has the power to teach. As Wilfred Sheed (1995) points out, sport is not necessarily a force for good, but it is indeed a force. It is such a powerful force that it not only tells you much about yourself as an individual but also reveals a great deal about the society within which sport is pursued. There is good reason, then, for us to consider sport seriously.

LEISURE, PLAY, GAMES, AND SPORT

To understand sport, we have to examine the motivations from which it arises, the forms it takes, and the ways it has developed historically. We also have to understand four related concepts: *leisure, play, games,* and *competition*. We use the terms in our ordinary language when we discuss sport, but we also should understand their specific, technical meanings.

Leisure

Sport developed historically as a leisure-time activity. Leisure can be distinguished from work by examining the attitude of the person, the nature of the activity, and the time dimension of the activity.

1. Leisure can be viewed as an attitude of freedom or release from the demands of ordinary life. This is the subjective component of an understanding of leisure, indicating the great joy and satisfaction derived from leisure activities.

2. The notion of leisure as an activity shifts the focus from the person to the event and those who are responsible for providing the services the event represents—for example, going to a golf course to play a round of golf. Leisure activities are often distinguished from work activities, in that leisure is freely chosen and not obligatory.

3. Viewed as time, leisure has traditionally been the discretionary time left over after work, family, and personal maintenance commitments are handled. The time aspect of leisure shows the leisure–work distinction most readily because the leisure attitude can be found in work and because leisure and work activities are not always easily distinguishable. Some activities are work for some people but leisure for other people.

Leisure attitude, leisure activities, and leisure time are often thought to be related to play—that is, a playful attitude, play activities, and play time. It is in the linkage to the concept of play that we see the fundamental meaning of sport.

Play

Sport as a Form of Play   Most scholars agree that sport is a manifestation of play and that sports are institutionalized forms of play. Play is also thought to be the motivating impulse underlying the development of drama, art, and music. It was the Dutch historian Johan Huizinga who first conceptualized the role of play as a basic motivation in human activity. Huizinga defined play as follows:

> Summing up the formal characteristics of play we might call it a free activity standing quite consciously outside "ordinary" life as being "not serious," but at the same time absorbing the player intensely and utterly. It is an activity connected with no material interest, and no profit can be gained by it. It proceeds within its own proper boundaries of time and space according to fixed rules and in an orderly manner. It promotes the formation of social groupings which tend to surround themselves with secrecy and to stress their differences from the common world by disguise or other means. (Huizinga, 1962, p. 13)

Play, then, is different from ordinary life, different certainly from what we typically refer to as "work." Play does not produce the products that work does, yet it seems to absorb us at least as completely, and often more so. Play, anthropologists tell us, is something that all people everywhere do, in one form or another.

Sociologist Roger Caillois (1961) refined Huizinga's definition. His characteristics of play are now most commonly cited when sport and play are discussed and analyzed. Caillois suggested that play is free, separate, uncertain, unproductive, and governed by rules or by make-believe. It is through an analysis of these characteristics of play that we can see how sport derives from play. Note that each characteristic represents a continuum; at one end is

the most playful situation, and at the other end is the least playful situation.

1. *Free.* Sport is most playful when people enter into it voluntarily. To the degree that sport is required or that the player cannot choose when to participate, sport becomes less playful.

2. *Separate.* Sport is conducted in places where the time and space limits are fixed in advance. It is often conducted in places designed especially for that activity—for example, the stadium, baseball field, golf course, or tennis court. The playful nature of the activity seems to be enhanced when the space for doing it is separate in this sense.

3. *Uncertain.* Sport is most playful when it is uncertain, when the contestants in a competition are evenly matched. Uneven competition is not fun for participants and is boring for spectators. Much effort is made in organized sport to ensure equal competition. Handicaps are provided, as in golf. School competition is often grouped by size of school, wrestling by weight class.

4. *Economically unproductive.* Activity is most playful when it does not result in any new wealth being created (as opposed to work, where creating wealth is the main purpose of the activity). A game itself typically produces no wealth as a *contest*, even though participants may be paid and much money may be made from other sources—television, concessions, parking, and so on. To the extent that new wealth is produced, the playfulness of the activity decreases.

5. *Governed by rules.* Play is almost always regulated. Even young children at play typically begin by creating rules. Sport, of course, is governed by rules that standardize the competition and are agreed to by all participants as necessary for the contest to proceed. Rules are typically established to define the activity, to ensure fairness, and to produce a winner. Further, rules in sport are completely arbitrary, which is one way that play differs from work, where rules tend to make sense. Why three strikes? Why two serves in tennis but not in badminton? Why 10 yards for a first down? The point is that sport is a social agreement to compete within arbitrary rules—which makes it playful—and violating those rules denies the agreement and tends to destroy the playfulness (Giamatti, 1989).

6. *Governed by make-believe.* Play that is not rule governed is dominated by make-believe. Sport typically relies on the rule-governed characteristic of play, whereas drama relies on the make-believe characteristic. Still, we can see in the sport play of young children the union of these two characteristics, since the children often assume the identities of their favorite players as they take part in games.

It is in these ways that we can see sport as a form of play. Clearly, *sport does not have to be playful.* We can imagine forms of sport in which each characteristic is barely present, so much so that the sport activity is totally devoid of the play element. Such sport forms seldom survive long; it appears that for people to want to continue in sport, the play element must be present. How to maintain the play element in sport is a major focus in Chapter 7.

It is in this sense that we need to think when we use *play* as a verb—that is, I *play* basketball, or let us go *play* a game of golf, or did you *play* racquetball last night? The term does not mean merely that you have participated. Instead, it means that you have *played.*

Play is viewed by most scholars as an irreducible form of behavior present in all animal life, finding its fullest expression in human behavior. Play, therefore, represents a fundamental category of behavior that needs no further explanation. People play. Why? Because play not only is fundamental to life but also is the mode of behavior through which some of life's most meaningful moments occur.

> Play is the answer to the puzzle of our existence. The stage for our excesses and our exuberance. Play is where life lives, where the game is the game. Some of the good things that play provides are physical grace, psychological ease and personal integrity. Some of the best are the peak experiences, when you have a sense of oneness with yourself and nature. These are truly times of peace the world cannot give. It may be that the hereafter will have them in constant supply; but in the here and now, play is the place to find them, the

place where we are constantly being and becoming ourselves. (Sheehan, 1982, p. 51)

Play, then, is not a trivial concept. It is a concept rich with psychological, sociological, and historical meaning. It is also a sufficiently strong and rich concept to provide insight into what sport is, what sport means to people who play and watch it, and what role sport occupies in culture.

Child's Play and Adult Play   Children clearly play. Most developmental psychologists believe that play is the most basic form of behavior in young children and that it is through play that children acquire much of their early knowledge about the physical and social world in which they live. Do adults play also? They say "let's play," but do they play as children do? Adults in a racquetball court or on a golf course or in a football game certainly do not look the same as children do when they play. We have to recognize that there are *different ways of playing.*

Caillois (1961) has suggested that ways of playing can be placed on a continuum according to the degree of spontaneity, orderliness, and regulation present in the play form. At one end of the continuum is what we typically see in the play of young children: turbulence, gaiety, spontaneity, diversion. At the other end of the continuum is what we typically see when adults play their sports: calculation, subordination to rules, contrivance, and ritual.

This is not to suggest that one way of playing is necessarily *better* than the other way of playing. Each is appropriate at different times and for different purposes. Typically, as children grow and develop, they change their play activities toward the adult end of the continuum. It is this end of the continuum that is characterized by practice, training, rituals, costumes, skill, and strategy. That way of playing obviously appeals to the more mature person—it simply has more sustaining motivation. The appreciation for practice, strategy, skillfulness, ritual, and tradition is the main characteristic of mature involvement in play.

As play forms mature and as players mature in those forms (sport), it becomes necessary to create

Sport involvement often combines fun and seriousness.

obstacles that must be overcome to achieve the goal of the play. The creation of new obstacles and the overcoming of them to produce a definite result are essential to continued motivation in play. Golfers, for example, as they improve at the sport, continually look for new challenges in the courses they play. A good golf course, in this sense, is one that has obstacles that a player must overcome to shoot a good score. Thus, narrow fairways, sand traps, water hazards, and strategically placed trees all create obstacles that require strategy and skill to overcome. These obstacles make the play of golf more challenging and interesting, and they considerably increase the rewards of shooting a good score.

Sport, then, derives from the play instinct in human behavior and the play element in culture. When sport is most playful, it is most meaningful to the participants. When sport loses its playfulness, the meaning is lessened for the participants (but not necessarily for the spectators).

Games

Although the terms *game* and *sport* are often used interchangeably, there are important distinctions between them. One way to view sport is as a game occurrence—but sport can be viewed in other ways, too. Some games are sport, but some games are not sport. Therefore, the two concepts are related in some ways but not in others.

A **game** is "any form of playful competition whose outcome is determined by physical skill, strategy or chance employed singly or in a combination" (Loy, 1969, p. 56). There are three important parts of this definition. First, games derive from play. Second, games involve competition. Third, the outcome of the game is determined by use of physical skill, strategy, or chance. Not all games are sport, but sport is always a game. This is true, according to the definition, even though we do not typically describe some sport involvement as game involvement; competing in a mile run is not described as "playing a game," but it does fit the definition. Some scholars differentiate games from *contests* and describe activities such as swimming or marathoning as contests rather than as games, but the activities are so similar that each can be referred to as a "game" in the sense defined here.

Competition is a defining characteristic of games and a fundamental quality of sport. I say more about competition in a later section of this chapter; here we note that the term *noncompetitive games*, which appears frequently in the physical-education literature, is a contradiction in terms. Without some element of competition, the activity ceases to be a game.

Sports are games that involve combinations of physical skill and strategy. Games that have outcomes determined primarily by chance—dice, for example—are not sports. Even though there clearly are *chance elements* in sport, such as weather changes or the errant bounce of a ball, these are not the primary determinants of outcomes. Games that involve strong elements of strategy but involve no physical skill are also not sports; bridge, chess, and other board games are examples.

Each sport game is different because each game poses a problem to be solved—what Almond (1986a) termed the game's **primary rules.** The primary rules of a game identify how the game is to be played and how winning can be achieved. The primary rules of a game are what make basketball basketball, and not volleyball.

Games also have many **secondary rules,** which typically define the institutionalized form of the game, or what we might call the *parent* game. Secondary rules can be altered or modified to make the game more developmentally appropriate or different in some other way without changing the essential character of the game, which is defined by the primary rules. The 3-second zone or the 10-second half-court rule in basketball are examples of secondary rules. They can be changed without changing the essential elements that define the game as basketball. The primary rule of volleyball is to strike the ball over a net in a divided court in a way that it either cannot be returned by opponents or hits the floor within their side of the court. Secondary rules include the height of the net, the size of the ball, the size of the court, and the number of hits per side.

Sport games can be categorized in several ways, but for our purposes, it will be most useful to examine a category scheme based on the similarities among the primary rules that define the games (Almond, 1983). This game classification has four categories: (1) territory or invasion games, (2) target games, (3) court games, and (4) field games.

1. *Territory or invasion games* are defined by the problem of needing to invade the space of the opponent to score. Two types of territory-invasion games are those in which goals are used (basketball, ice hockey, soccer, team handball, lacrosse, water polo, etc.) and those in which lines are used (American football, Australian rules football, rugby, speedball, etc.). Territory-invasion games can be further subdivided according to whether the game involves the use of the hand with a ball (basketball), the foot with a ball (soccer), or a stick with a ball (hockey).

2. *Target games* are defined by the primary rules of propelling objects with great accuracy toward targets. Target games can be subdivided according to whether the opponents are directly opposed (croquet, horseshoes, curling, etc.) or indirectly opposed (golf, bowling). In the former, one plays directly against one's opponent, often hitting the other player's ball, for example. In the latter, one plays against the target (the pins, the par on the golf hole), then compares scores with an opponent.

3. *Court games* are those in which an object is strategically propelled in ways that cannot be returned by an opponent. Court games can be subdivided according to whether the court is divided (badminton, tennis, table tennis, etc.) or shared (handball, squash, jai alai, etc.). Court-divided games typically utilize a net. Court-shared games typically rely on rebounds from walls.

4. *Field games* are defined by primary rules that require one opponent to strike an object such as to elude defenders on the field. The shape of the field might differ somewhat (fan shaped or oval shaped), but the basic natures of the games are similar. Cricket, baseball, softball, and rounders are examples.

A knowledge of games—of their meaning and function—is fundamental to the person interested in understanding sport. There are no doubt thousands of games in the world that meet the definitional requirements we have stated but that are not thought of as *sport.* New games develop all the time. Sometimes the new games become sports, sometimes they do not. Frisbee is a good example. On any spring afternoon, you can see students throwing Frisbees in open spaces, but there is seldom a *game* going on, and no one would call it a *sport.* Yet Frisbee has developed into a sport called "ultimate Frisbee"—one for which there are rules and growing traditions. Frisbee as a sport is in the process of becoming *institutionalized;* that is, it is changing from an informal game to an institutionalized sport. To become institutionalized, a sport must be defined with standardized rules to which all players adhere, must have a governing body, and must encompass a growing sense of tradition that bind people to it.

The institutionalization of sport also applies to what one might call *personal performance sports,* such as wrestling, track and field, swimming, and gymnastics. Here too, new activities are constantly being created, particularly by the young people of "generation X"—for example, the very creative and demanding extreme sports that have led to the X Games competitions. The winter skiing sport called moguls, for example, has made it all the way to the Winter Olympic games.

Competition in Sport and Games

Sport and games involve competition. Without competition, there is no game. Yet competition is among the most seriously misunderstood concepts in sport, fitness, and physical education. Almost everybody has strong views about competition. Some people advocate competition at all costs as a positive virtue. Others view competition as inherently bad and want to make sports noncompetitive, as though that were possible. Because competition is a controversial issue, it is necessary for us to examine the concept closely and to understand its different meanings in relation to the concepts of sport and games. Competition is almost always defined first as a rivalry in which opponents strive to gain something at the expense of each other. This kind of definition tends to emphasize the use of the term in economics and business. Far too often, competition in sport is defined exclusively in this economic sense. One form of competition, stemming from the world of economics, is **zero-sum competition.** In a zero-sum competition, whatever is gained by one competitor must necessarily be lost by the other competitor; that is, to the extent that I win, you must lose. One sometimes hears overzealous coaches state that "winning isn't the best thing, it's

the only thing" or "defeat is worse than death." Those kinds of remarks reflect a zero-sum view of competition.

The concept of competition is far richer than that—especially when used in reference to sport. There are three important and related meanings of the concept of competition (Siedentop, 1981). The first meaning is *to come together,* which denotes the festival aspects of competition. When the term is used as a noun (as in "Let's have a competition"), we can sense the notion of a festival. All the world's great sport competitions are clearly festivals—the Olympic Games, the Super Bowl, the World Cup in soccer. We find similar festivals, on a smaller scale, at high school football games, children's soccer games, or an adult equestrian competition. This festival nature of sport is the clearest evidence of its communal importance.

Sport involves rituals and traditions. The *festival* nature of competition is where the rituals and traditions are most easily seen, and the festival nature of sport competition is one of its most appealing attributes.

A second meaning of the concept of competition is to strive to achieve an objective, what I call the *competence* meaning of the term. The words *compete* and *competence* derive from the Latin word *competere.* Competition provides a forum within which people strive to become competent, to become excellent. The institutionalized nature of sport means that rules and conditions are standardized so that performance can be compared fairly. It is within this standardized forum of tradition that sportspersons can learn about their own strengths, limitations, and competence and can strive to improve their performance.

Many scholars believe the pursuit of competence, trying to get better, is a fundamental, sustaining motivation for sport involvement (Alderman & Wood, 1976; Coakley, 1994; Eitzen & Sage, 2003). This belief comes from evidence that shows that young athletes rank wanting to get better as a primary motivation for their continued participation. They also rate being with friends and being part of a team (affiliation) as a strong motivation. It also should be noted that these are ranked higher than the excitement of competition or beating another person or team.

The third meaning of the concept of competition is the one with which we are most familiar—to be in a state of *rivalry*. The opportunities for rivalry within sport are many and varied: team against team, individual against individual, individual against a record, individual now against a previous best performance, individual against a physical barrier. Many of these rivalry motivations coexist in one contest. When 30,000 runners start the New York marathon each year, it is difficult to describe their competitive motivation as a zero-sum rivalry. If that were true, there would be 1 winner and 29,999 losers! The fact is that few athletes view their own competition as a zero-sum phenomenon. Occasionally, a coach does, or a parent, or a sportswriter. Other forms of competition, however, are much more prevalent in sport.

Competition, therefore, involves individuals and groups striving for excellence within the rules and traditions that make up a sport, including all the festival characteristics that give the sport additional flavor and meaning. Within the boundaries of a sport, individuals and groups compete, but seldom, if ever, is that competition a zero-sum arrangement. There are many ways to win and to lose within a competition, and the winning and losing have meaning only within the competition and, even then, only momentarily. If winning or losing has meaning that carries over from the competition to other aspects of life, then it clearly diminishes the play element in the competition.

Sport, therefore, can be understood as a game occurrence in which playful competition is the primary motivational force. The *players* can practice diligently, train seriously, prepare strategically, and compete vigorously, yet still manifest the play element in its fullest. Factors such as unevenly matched opponents, required participation, economic consequences, and pressures for winning that carry over to real life outside the sport event can seriously diminish the play element in sport.

THE INSTITUTIONALIZATION OF SPORT

Somewhere, sometime, someone thought of a new game to play. Rules were suggested, the goal of the game was explained, equipment was probably designed, and special space was acquired. The game was played and enjoyed. Perhaps it was enjoyed sufficiently that others wanted to play it. The rules were then written down, a sketch of the space (field, court, etc.) was made, and the needed equipment was listed. Each time the new game was played, it was, no doubt, changed slightly to meet local needs and interests and to accommodate local problems with equipment and facilities. Eventually, however, some *common form of the game* was needed because many people wanted to try the game. At that point, the game began to become institutionalized.

No doubt, something akin to this process happened for the several games invented in America in the late nineteenth century—basketball, softball, and volleyball. They started as local games for local purposes. Today, they are international games with rules, traditions, rituals, governing bodies, and championships. When volleyball is played in a developing nation, it is essentially the same game as that played here and everywhere else. The game has a common form that is recognized internationally. It has become a fully institutionalized sport.

It is important to understand sport as a social institution. Most people who enter the various professions associated with sport can do so because sport is thoroughly institutionalized in developed societies. Think for a moment of the role that the following professionals occupy relative to sport:

- The orthopedic surgeon who is a sport-medicine specialist
- The sportswriter
- The radio or television sport commentator
- The sport manager
- The referee or umpire
- The sport administrator

- The coach
- The trainer
- The equipment specialist
- The sport promoter
- The sport strength coach

Conspicuously absent from that list is the sport performer! The sport performer is the *only* person necessary for sport to take place at a local level, at a level that is casually organized, flexible, and *not yet institutionalized*. (How many of these other sport types are necessary for a sandlot softball game?) All roles other than participant develop as sport becomes more highly institutionalized to the point where all these sport specialists far outnumber the people who actually play the game.

The Codification of Rules

As a sport becomes institutionalized, it adopts certain characteristics. First, the rules governing the sport are *codified*. The same rules are supposed to govern all contests, and, typically, there is a system through which the codified rules are enforced and, from time to time, changed. How people are to play the game and what is expected of them within the game are defined primarily by the rules and secondarily by the traditions that develop within the sport as it becomes institutionalized. Why does the crowd get so quiet when a golfer putts, whereas in basketball the crowd makes extra noise when an opponent shoots a free throw? The answer cannot be found in the nature of the two skills or in the official rules of the two sports, but only in the traditions of how the two games have developed over time.

The Role of the Referee

The codification of rules for a sport typically produces the need for trained officials and referees. The importance of a referee to a sport is misunderstood by the public and often by sportspersons, too. The nature of sport is to strive for victory within a set of rules and conditions that are similar for all

The referee plays a crucial role in ensuring a fair contest.

contestants; that is, sport is meaningful only when it is a *fair* contest. The main role of the referee is to ensure fairness by seeing that all contestants honor the rules and that no contestants get an advantage that is disallowed by the rules. The more highly institutionalized a sport becomes, the greater the need to train and supervise referees so that the contests are played as much in accordance with the rules as is possible.

The Genesis of Sport Organizations

As sport becomes more institutionalized, it is natural that those associated with the sport want to see whether they, or their teams, are the best for that particular sport season. It seems to be in the nature of sport competition to want to find out who is best at the moment. For people to find out who is best, certain conditions need to be present. First, of course, all participants and teams have to be playing the same game, using the same rules. After the game becomes standardized, there has to be a schedule of playing that allows individuals and teams to compete against others. Also, an agreement has to be reached for a means through which the best can be selected each season. This all requires organization—and these very motivations led to the formation of sport associations and sport conferences.

A group of local teams might form a league to arrange a predictable schedule and to determine a local champion at the end of a sport season. A city or a state might organize a competition that allows a champion to be determined at that level. A national organization such as the Athletic Congress or the NCAA might organize individual and team championships for its members nationwide. An organization has to be created to arrange these competitions, to schedule facilities, and to secure officials. At most local levels, these organizations can be staffed by volunteers. As the sport becomes more institutionalized, however, the organizations become more formal and require full-time workers. This creates the need for trained people to do these specialized jobs and leads to the development of professions such as sport management, sport promotion, and sport administration.

The Importance of Records

As soon as a sport begins to become standardized, records begin to be kept. Records are important to sport in many ways. Many people have argued that the central motivation in sport is striving for excellence. Records are one important way that excellence is defined and preserved. They provide standards against which participants measure their improvement and set their goals. They also provide items of great interest to those who follow the sport but do not necessarily participate in it.

Without standard rules and good officiating, records could not assume the importance that they do

in sport. When we can be reasonably sure that the competition was fair, then the record produced becomes part of the legend of the sport. The records that are of most general interest are those describing the limits beyond which men, women, or teams have yet been unable to go (Weiss, 1969).

Think of the almost magical importance assumed in sport when Michael Johnson obliterated the world record in the 200 meters at the 1996 Olympics. Recall how it was compared to that moment when Bob Beamon not only broke the world record in the long jump at the Mexico City Olympics but also moved completely through the 28-foot barrier and jumped more than 29 feet. These moments—the first 4-minute mile by Roger Bannister, Joe DiMaggio's 56-game hitting streak, Wilt Chamberlin's 100-point National Basketball Association (NBA) game, or Wilma Rudolph's four gold medals at the Rome Olympics—not only set new standards but also provide a glimpse of what is possible in human endeavor.

Records become standards through which young athletes define their improvement. Research has clearly indicated that for many young athletes, the primary motivation for continued participation is increased *competence,* the desire to get better at some event or skill that has value in the sport culture. *Getting better* is most easily judged in reference to standards within the sport, and standards are typically records of past performances by others in similar age groups and settings. For example, most aspiring age-group swimmers know exactly what a new personal best time means for them. They know what the time means not only with respect to their local swim team and local competition but also compared with regional, state, and national norms for the same event and the same age group. Their progress and their potential will be defined and charted by those kinds of comparisons.

In other sports, the comparison of performance and the establishment of competence cannot be accomplished so neatly through records as it can in swimming or track and field. In sports such as basketball or baseball, the records are important— batting average, points per game, rebounds, strike-

---

Sport Institutionalization in Progress

Twenty-five years ago, sports such as snowboarding, BMX, wakeboarding, and freestyle motocross were just being discovered. Now, they are becoming institutionalized with organizations, rules, and regulated competitions.

Vans, a shoe company, sponsors regular North American competitions in snowboarding, supercross, freestyle motocross, surfing, wakeboarding, skateboarding, and BMX.

See www.vans.com for event information.

A similar series of competitions has multiple sponsors and is called Gravity Games (www.gravitygames.com).

Another series is the X Games (www.expn.go.com), which appears regularly on ESPN.

These new sports have much in common. They are typically individual rather than team, involve a fair amount of risk, and are very gymnastic in their performances, whether on wakeboards, snowboards, or skateboards.

---

outs—but they are all established under slightly different conditions against different kinds of opponents. Thus, in sports such as these, it becomes necessary to test oneself directly against the competition to find out one's own limits.

Records, however, are not just benchmarks that provide goals that define excellence. Performing in record fashion or witnessing a record-setting performance is deeply important to the nature of sport, and it is one reason people pursue sport, both as athletes and as spectators.

> When in the midst of that free time activity a person on the field or fairway, rink, floor, or track, performs an act that surpasses—despite his or her evident mortality, his or her humanness—whatever we have seen or heard or could conceive of doing ourselves, then we have witnessed, full-fledged, fulfilled, what we anticipated and what all the repetition in the game strove for, a moment when we are all free of all constraint of all kinds, when pure energy and pure order create an instant of complete coherence. In that instant, pulled to our feet, we are pulled out of ourselves. (Giamatti, 1989, p. 35)

Records play a vital role in sport. They provide much of the tradition of a sport. They define its heroes and heroines. They provide standards for measuring one's improvement. They provide goals for which to strive. For the aficionado who follows the sport, they provide endless hours of pleasure in reading, discussing, even arguing about the relative merits of one performance versus another, one performer versus another, or one team versus another.

The Public Nature of Institutionalized Sport

As sport becomes institutionalized, it assumes a public role. It becomes part of a culture, locally at first, but then perhaps regionally, and for some sports, nationally and even internationally. The general importance of the sport at any of these cultural levels is proportional to the number of people who are interested in following the sport—the more fan interest there is, the more public attention is devoted to the sport.

It is this facet of institutionalized sport that is responsible for sport journalism, sport broadcasting, and sport literature. The first two, at least, are historically recent phenomena, depending as they do on modern technologies. It is no simple coincidence that the late nineteenth century in the United States was not only the period of the emergence of organized sport as a major cultural phenomenon but also the time at which communications technologies began to emerge in their modern forms (see Chapter 2).

The invention of the telegraph in the 1840s made it possible to communicate sport results over long distances. By the 1880s, newspapers had begun to devote separate sections to sport in their daily editions. The emergence of radio allowed for immediate vicarious enjoyment of live sport events across great distances. Television, of course, completely revolutionized sport spectating and is probably mainly responsible for the recent, enormous growth in sport. Now cable and satellite capabilities provide immediate worldwide access to endless numbers of different sporting events.

The public is hungry for sport, both as information and as entertainment. Check the sport section at your local bookstore, or the number and variety of sport magazines at your local drugstore or supermarket. When you next rent a videotape, check the sport section at the video store to see both the instructional and the entertainment videos available. Each article, photograph, and video was produced by someone who pursues a nonparticipant sport vocation.

Sport literature and sport films have come of age. Browse through the sport section of any bookstore and you will see endless "technique" and "how to do" books, many reflecting the views of successful athletes and coaches. There is also now a serious literature with sport as the main theme; books such as David Halberstam's *The Breaks of the Game* (basketball) and *The Amateurs* (rowing), Mark Harris's *Bang the Drum Slowly* (baseball), and W. P. Kinsella's *Shoeless Joe*, from which the film *Field of Dreams* was made. When *Chariots of Fire* won the Academy Award for Best Picture in 1981, it marked the start of an era of sport films that both won critical acclaim and were box-office hits—for example, *Bull Durham, Any Given Sunday, Tin Cup, A League of Their Own*, and *The Legend of Bagger Vance*.

The World Wide Web, of course, has made information about sport available more readily than ever before. A listing of important sport Web sites is provided at the end of Chapter 7. I was born and raised in Chicago and am a die-hard Cubs, Bears, and Bulls fan, so nearly every morning I read the sports page of the *Chicago Tribune* and the *Chicago Sun-Times* on the Internet. Chat rooms, newsgroups, and listservs are available for every imaginable sport.

All of this public attention has made sport a part of our everyday life in America. It has created a number of new sport professions, and it has contributed to the further institutionalization of sport—more rituals, more traditions, more attention to records. It has moved sport from the periphery of American culture, where it was in the 1850s, to the center—all in the relatively short period of one century.

SPORT SPECTATING

Sport spectating is among our most frequently mentioned leisure-time activities. Early in the twentieth century, watching sports was considered to be an inappropriate behavior, especially if done too often. The term used by physical-education professionals was *spectatoritis,* and its medical connotation was purposely chosen. It was thought to be like a disease.

Most of us enjoy watching sports on occasion. Many of us enjoy watching sports often. Are we wasting our time? Should we be using our time in a more productive way? We cannot completely understand sport without including sport spectating in the analysis.

It appears that in most countries, there is a high correlation between sport participation and sport spectating; that is, the more people who participate in sport, the more who watch it (Page, 1969). This does not suggest that one statistic is causally related to the other in any way. It merely means that whatever factors influence the development and popularity of sport in a culture tend to influence participation and spectating in much the same way.

There is more than a bit of snobbishness about sport spectating in certain circles. The idea persists that intelligent, mature people would not get very excited about watching sports. This idea, according to Novak, is a prejudice all believers live under. "To love sports is to love the lowest common denominator, to be lower-class, adolescent, patriotic in some corny way." The *intellectual* thing, the *liberal* thing, the *mature* thing is to set sports aside. This severe prejudice is not usually fatal, not at least to persons of goodwill, but it *is* evidence of insufficiently developed perception. (Novak, 1976, p. xii; emphasis in original)

The sport spectator is not just a fan who responds emotionally but not intellectually to sport. The sport spectator is also often a sophisticated, knowledgeable, and appreciative viewer. Fans watch sport not just to see the contest, not just to see who wins, but also to see athletes perform within a contest in which the standards are clear and rules are enforced so that the playing field is indeed "level." Modern television communications have created new generations of informed spectators. Instant replay, telestrators, slow-motion replay, and technical analysis by commentators have provided viewers with an in-depth education in the skills and tactics of the sport being viewed. The subtle nuances that show the individual excellence of players or the collective excellence of a team offensive or defensive maneuver are revealed immediately after an exciting moment during a contest, so that the viewer not only participates in the excitement of the moment but also gets an immediate education in what produced the excitement.

Often, however, the sport spectator is not just a knowledgeable observer, a detached connoisseur who lacks emotion and passion about sport events. The sport spectator is also often a fan. Some sport events can be watched for the sheer pleasure of seeing grace in action, an excellent contest, or a well-played game, but other sport competitions must be viewed from one side or the other. How often have you sat next to a seemingly calm, mature person who at some point in a game was transformed into a raving lunatic? How often have you experienced the same transformation yourself?

Sport loyalties often run deep. Modern society is extremely mobile. People move often. Sport is one of the few cultural institutions that has provided a sense of enduring meaning and continuity in the midst of mobility and change. A person's allegiance to a local team, to a university team, or to a professional team can form a sense of belonging and permanence. This is one of the important meanings of being a fan. Fans *root* for their team. The choice of terms is important. A *root* is the attached or embedded part of any structure, the part that holds the structure in position, the essential or core part of the structure. To root for a team means to *be rooted* in the fortunes of that team:

> To watch a sports event is not like watching a set of abstract patterns. It is to take a risk, to root and to be rooted. Some people, it is true, remain detached; they seem like mere voyeurs. The mode of observation proper to a sports event is *to participate*—that is, to extend one's own identification to one side, and to absorb with it the blows of fortune, to join that team in testing the favors of the Fates. (Novak, 1976, p. 144; emphasis in original)

The behavior of the sport fan, then, is an important part of the sport; to understand what sport is and how it has become so important to us, we must consider the role of the fan. The term *fan*, short for *fanatic,* is related to the Latin word *fanum,* which translates as "temple" or "feast." The original relationships of these terms take us full circle to the religious nature of sport, where we began this chapter.

SPORT AESTHETICS

Have you ever watched a game or a sport performance and seen something done by an individual or a team that made you say, "That's beautiful"? If so, you have reacted to the aesthetic quality of sport, the beauty that sometimes seems so evident in sport performance.

Sport and athletes have always been subjects for art. In early Greek culture, where sport was so fundamental to social life, artists often used athletes as subjects, creating sculpture and decorating vases with athletes in action. Throughout history, artists have been intrigued by the physical beauty of the athletic body and the visual beauty of athletic performance. The fact that sport and athletes have been the subjects for artists' portrayals, however, does not mean that sport itself has aesthetic value.

To understand the aesthetic value of sport, we must find beauty *in sport* rather than in paintings or sculpture. As sport became the object for intellectual analysis and investigation during the twentieth century, aestheticians, as well as historians, psychologists, and sociologists, began to consider it seriously. Their work has helped us to understand the artistic dimensions and qualities of sport.

If sport *is* art, then it most certainly is a performing art—like music, dance, and drama. The beauty of the art is found in the performance itself, and it is through understanding the source of that beauty in performance that we can begin to appreciate the aesthetic qualities of sport. When considering **sport aesthetics,** we must divide sport into two categories: (1) form sports, and (2) all other sports.

Aesthetics of Form Sports

In some sports, the physical form of the performance is the determining factor in the competition—diving, gymnastics, and figure skating are prime examples. In these sports, the performer consciously works toward achieving a physical form that is aesthetically pleasing, that is beautiful. These kinds of sport performances are typically decided by a judging system, and the judges look for aesthetic qualities in the performance.

The aesthetic qualities evident in **form sports** are harmony, form, dynamics, flow, gracefulness, rhythm, and poise (Lowe, 1977). *Harmony,* for example, refers to the correct relation of parts to a whole, the way in which a sequence of movements brings about a harmonious whole. The instructions in an international gymnastics handbook describe it this way:

> While in all exercises on the apparatus we are always involved with harmony, this concept and evaluation factor will have to be given even greater attention in

the floor exercises, where handsprings, Saltos and kips are combined with pauses and gymnastic elements; where strength and movement have to follow in a harmonious manner, harmony will play an ever greater role. (Lowe, 1977, p. 176)

It is in form sport that the aesthetic qualities of sport are most easily seen and most often commented on. Commentators, spectators, and sportswriters often use descriptive aesthetic language when talking or writing about gymnastics, ice dancing, synchronized swimming, and diving.

What is important to remember about form sports is that they are *sports!* The goal of a sport performance is to achieve victory, to strive to do the best you can to win. In other artistic performances, this competition element is less obvious. In form sport, the athlete wants her or his performance to look beautiful in order to gain a position as high as possible in the competition. Does this mean that in sports other than form sports the aesthetic quality is lost? I do not think so.

Aesthetic Quality of Other Sports

The beauty and artistry in figure skating or diving are easily seen, but what beauty can we find in a rugby match, a marathon run, or an ice-hockey game? Of course, games and contests do not have to be beautiful to be enjoyable, for spectator and competitor alike. It is common, after a hard-won victory, to hear a coach or player say, "It wasn't pretty, but we got the job done." Nonetheless, both competitors and spectators feel enhanced enjoyment of sport when a good competition also has an aesthetic quality.

In what ways do we experience sport as beautiful? Carlisle (1974) has suggested four types of beauty present in sport:

1. *The beauty of a well-developed body in motion.* The high hurdler, the agile football running back, the field-hockey player winding between defenders, and the slalom skier all show efficient, graceful effort applied to solving a particular performance problem.

One kind of aesthetic beauty is seen in form sports such as gymnastics.

2. *The beauty of a brilliant play or a perfectly executed maneuver.* This quality combines the beauty of the physical performance with strong competitive intelligence in which decisions are made quickly and then well executed. This happens especially in team sports where all the players on a team move as if in some intricately choreographed series of maneuvers to achieve a competitive outcome. Bill Bradley described that beauty in this way: "In my Knicks days, there was no feeling comparable to the one I got when the teams came together—those nights when five guys moved as one. The moment was one of beautiful isolation, the result of the correct blending of human forces at the proper time and to the exact degree" (Bradley, 1998, p.21).

3. *The beauty in a dramatic competition.* Sport is most aesthetically appealing when the outcome is uncertain. Competitions that ebb and flow in favor of one team or competitor, then the other, produce a dramatic tension that is among the most attractive of the aesthetic qualities of sport. This quality is experienced more strongly by the spectator who is involved, who roots for one team or the other, than by the more detached observer.

4. *The beauty in the unity of an entire performance.* No doubt, each of us can remember a game or competition that engendered a high level of excellence for all competitors, in which the dramatic tension of competition produced a unified experience that is perhaps the ultimate beauty in sport. In outstanding sport events, such beauty is apparent from the outset through to the dramatic conclusion of the game or event.

Sport in which athletes exhibit some or all of these aesthetic qualities helps to explain why sport is so popular and has achieved such a central role in culture: "If we wish to show that sport has aesthetic values comparable to those of art, then I think the qualities to be stressed, in the context of opposition, are swiftness, grace, fluency, rhythm, and perceived vitality—the qualities which in various combinations constitute beauty" (Elliot, 1974, p. 112). Despite the efforts of Elliot and others, as in many aspects of sport, the experience of beauty in sport is often better than the explanation.

SPORT ETHICS

Ethics is a branch of the subdiscipline of philosophy termed *axiology,* the study of values. Ethics, or *moral philosophy,* is concerned with how people *ought* to behave, particularly in situations in which there is potential for behaving well or poorly. For many reasons, sport has always been considered to be an important place in which to learn about ethical or moral behavior. The general term used to discuss and examine ethical behavior in sport is *sportsmanship,* although a better, gender-neutral term is *fair play.*

Many people believe deeply that participation in sport builds character and that some of the character traits it develops predispose people toward ethical behavior. Coaches often ascribe this power to sport when they talk at banquets about the developmental experiences that youths get through sport. On the other hand, we do not need to have had much experience in sport, as either a participant or a spectator, to know that players sometimes cheat, that coaches bend rules, that fights occur, and that it is possible for youths to learn unethical behavior through sport experience. How, then, does sport relate to ethics, and how does ethics relate to sport?

Fair Play and the British Tradition

The concept of **fair play** encompasses how a sportsperson behaves, not only during a contest, but before and after it as well. The notion of fair play means that one plays by the rules, does not take unfair advantage of an opponent even when the op-

Competitors are often bonded together in their quest for excellence.

portunity arises, treats the opponent with respect, and shows modesty and composure in both victory and defeat. Although elements of fair play can be seen historically in many sport cultures, it was the aristocratic British sport of the nineteenth century that elevated fair play to a way of life, as well as a way of competing in sport.

As I mentioned in Chapter 4, the philosophy of fair play in nineteenth-century England was termed *Arnoldism,* after the popular headmaster of the Rugby School, an elite secondary school. Thomas Arnold believed that sport should be played fairly and vigorously, with opponents always honoring one another, showing both moral character and team spirit. This *fair-play philosophy* was popularized in literature through the novel *Tom Brown's Schooldays* and through a series of books in which the main character, Frank Merriwell, exemplified the qualities of honesty, courage, and humility (Lucas & Smith, 1978).

Because American sport was strongly influenced by British sport, it is not surprising that the philosophy of fair play still permeates sport today, especially sport in schools. This philosophy not only prescribes how one ought to behave within sport but also uses sport as a metaphor for how life should be lived. It is the antithesis of a "win-at-all-costs" approach to sport competition. Within the tradition of fair play, the primary goal of sport is victory within the letter and spirit of the rules, but not victory at any cost.

> Honorable victory is the goal of the athlete, and, as a result, the code of the athlete demands that nothing be done before, during, or after the contest to cheapen or otherwise detract from such a victory. (Keating, 1973, p. 170)

Rules and the Nature of Games

Those who study the ethical nature of sport often focus on rules and on how rules relate to the purposes of games. The argument made is that the game is changed when the rules are bent, broken, or misused and, therefore, that it is not possible *really* to win unless the rules are kept:

> The end in poker is not to gain money, nor in golf to simply get a ball into a hole, but to do these things in prescribed (or, perhaps more accurately, not to do them in prescribed) ways: that is, to do them only in accordance with rules. Rules in games thus seem to be in some sense inseparable from ends. . . . If the rules are broken, the original end becomes impossible of attainment, since one cannot (really) win the game unless he plays it, and one cannot (really) play the game unless he obeys the rules of the game. (Suits, 1976, pp. 149–150)

The rule violations referred to in such an analysis are, of course, those done intentionally. Rules are often broken in games, and referees are there to notice the infractions and to apply the appropriate penalty so that the game may continue. The purpose of the penalty is typically to restore evenness to the contest, to provide for the offended player or team some measure that makes up for what was lost—a free throw in basketball, a loss of yardage in football, or time off the ice in hockey.

When considering rule violations, the intentional foul, the strategic foul, and the purposeful cheating to gain advantage are of greatest concern to sport ethicists. The question is this: What have you won if you do these things? Not the game, because without rules, it is not the game. What have you lost? Perhaps the respect of fellow sportspersons and ultimately your own self-respect. It is clear that outside pressure to win or to gain from winning are likely culprits in serious violations of sport ethics. A competition should be viewed as a test among opponents in which all have agreed what the test will be, as defined by the rules. When players or teams purposely cheat, they change the test, thereby reducing or even eliminating the meaning of victory (Fraleigh, 1985).

Does sport build character, as so many sport enthusiasts and educators have argued for centuries? Or does sport corrupt character, teaching children and youths how to cheat cleverly and take advantage of rules and opponents? The answer is, Sport teaches! It has the capacity to teach positive lessons, and it has the capacity to teach negative lessons. Sport, when done well and properly, can raise the individual and the group, transcend the ordinary and mundane in life, and teach valuable lessons of perseverance, teamwork, and loyalty. Sport also can be corrupted. It can corrupt those who compete. Whether any sport experience is more likely to build character than to corrupt it is up to those in control of that experience and what they do with it.

Sport cannot ultimately survive, however, if participants regularly abuse the rules and conventions that define the sport. If winning at all costs means breaking rules, either in preparation for the contest or during the contest itself, the game will deteriorate and eventually lose its capacity to attract players and spectators. Sport is, in essence, a playful competition in a rule-governed atmosphere that is meant to make the competition as even and fair as possible. When that context is jeopardized, the contest loses its essential meaning. It may survive for a while, but eventually it will deteriorate and disappear.

SUMMARY

1. Sport has been a part of every civilized culture but has been taken seriously by scholars only in recent times—a fact that is surprising given the amount of money and attention devoted to sport by people of all ages.

2. *Sport* has rituals, costumes, symbolic meaning, a striving for perfection, a system of rules, and a means for enforcing the rules—all the elements of a natural religion. These elements underscore the seriousness with which we should view sport.

3. Sport derives from play—activity that is free, separate, uncertain, economically unproductive, and governed by rules or make-believe. Although sport does not have to be playful, participants enjoy it most when it is.

4. *Play* is an irreducible form of human behavior that provides meaning in life and is thought to be a creative element in culture.

5. Child's play is characterized by spontaneity, exuberance, and gaiety; adult play is typically characterized by practice, training, ritual, skill, and strategy.

6. A *game* is a playful competition where outcomes are determined by combinations of physical skill, strategy, and chance. Games derive from play, and sports can be thought of as games or contests in which skill and strategy predominate.

7. Games are, by definition, competitive; a "noncompetitive game" would be a contradiction in terms.

8. Sport games have *primary rules*, which define the problem to be solved, and *secondary rules*, which give form to the game but can be altered without changing the essence of the game.

9. Sport games can be categorized as invasion games, target games, court games, and field games.

10. *Competition* has three related meanings. First, it is a festival that provides a forum for contests and carries with it traditions and rituals. Second, it is a striving for competence within the rules of the forum. Third, it is a rivalry for victory.

11. Competition in sport is seldom a zero-sum arrangement, in which losers must lose to the extent that winners win.

12. As sport becomes more institutionalized, an increasing number of professional roles develop. The process of institutionalization ranges from local to international.

13. Sport becomes more institutionalized as rules are codified, referees are specially trained, organizations form to manage and administer activities, records are kept formally, and public communication develops through radio, television, newspapers, magazines, books, and videocassettes.

14. Spectating is an important part of institutionalized sport. Sport spectators are among the

most knowledgeable and sophisticated spectators for any cultural pastime.

15. Spectators are also often fans who have deep
loyalties to teams and who contribute to the total meaning of the sport experience.

16. Sport has aesthetic value and can be viewed as
an art form. Form sports, in particular, have
high aesthetic value, in that performances are
judged by the degree to which they achieve
beautiful physical form and motion.

17. There are four types of aesthetic value in sport:
the beauty of trained bodies in motion, the
beauty of a brilliant play or performance, the
dramatic tension produced by competition
that is uncertain, and the unity of a well-played
game or match.

18. *Sport ethics* is the study of values in sport. It focuses primarily on sportsmanship.

19. The fair-play tradition of British sport involves
both how to compete and how to behave before, during, and after the competition.

20. Most of sport ethics focuses on rules and their
violation because rules give the sport its form,
and violations of them break the contract between opponents to compete fairly.

DISCUSSION QUESTIONS

1. How do important local sport events, such as a
high school football game, show the characteristics of sport as a natural religion?

2. Can scholarship and professional athletes still be
engaged in play when they are playing their
sport? Explain your answer.

3. To what extent does the game-classification system depend on similarities and differences in
primary rules?

4. How do views of competition among the general public differ from views among athletes
themselves?

5. What kinds of rules and practices should be
adopted to ensure that competition is as good as
it can be?

6. What might happen to a sport such as "ultimate
Frisbee" if it becomes completely institutionalized, as basketball has become?

7. What kinds of sport events or performances have
you found to be aesthetically pleasing? What
about them has caused you to react this way?

8. What personal experiences have you had that
highlight controversial issues in sport ethics?
How did you and other people involved react?

9. Are "extreme sports" a passing fancy, or are they
here to stay?

CHAPTER **6**

Sport Programs
and Professions

Sports are the highest products of civilization and the most accessible, lived, experiential sources of the civilizing spirit.

Michael Novak 1976

LEARNING OBJECTIVES

- To describe the dimensions of the sport culture

- To discuss issues related to leisure time

- To define and provide examples of the different kinds of sport participation

- To analyze youth sport, interscholastic sport, and collegiate sport

- To discuss issues related to coaching in youth, interscholastic, and intercollegiate sport

- To analyze the various ways in which sport is organized and implemented, from youth sport to professional sport

- To describe recent movements that have extended sport participation

- To describe nonparticipant sport vocations

Will historians and anthropologists of the future refer to our times as the "era of sport"? When you look at all the data about sport—data on participation, spending, and so on—you may get that impression. If you look through a listing of television shows for any weekend, you may get that impression. If you go out for a leisurely drive in many areas, seeing the various indoor and outdoor sport spaces and facilities, you may get that impression.

There was a time, not too long ago, when sport was primarily for youths and young adults. Children played, but they did not *do* sport. Older adults watched, but they did not *do* sport. Children now often begin sport participation by the age of 5 or 6. Young swimmers and gymnasts may undergo several years of intense training and competition before they reach puberty. In addition, many sports offer a large and growing number of masters-level or veterans competitions for people over age 40— competition graded in 5-year blocks all the way to age 70 and beyond. Most states now hold summer sport festivals that include competitors from young children to seniors.

How big is sport in our society? Very big! Are we the biggest sport culture in the world? We might be the largest in absolute size, but in relative importance of sport in a culture, you would get a real argument from an Australian, a Brazilian, or a German. Suffice it to say, in America and in many developed countries, sport has, in the second half of the twentieth century and the early part of the twenty-first, assumed an unprecedented role of economic and cultural importance. The evidence for the centrality of the sport culture is impressive (Becker, 1996; Gorman & Calhoun, 1994; Houlihan & DeBrock, 1991; Quain, 1990; *Sports Illustrated,* 1986).

- Ninety-eight percent of all Americans participate in sport, read about sport, or watch sport on television at least once per week.
- Seventy percent of adults say they are sport fans.
- More than 80 percent say they watch sport on television each week.

- Thirty percent of adults bet on sport each year, with the average amount bet nearly $100 per year.
- The gross national sport product (GNSP) was well over $60 billion in the early 1990s, making it one of America's largest industries.
- The largest component of the sport industry (over 30 percent of the GNSP) is leisure and participant sport.
- Participation in youth and school sport has increased steadily since the late 1970s.
- Participation in adult, recreational sport has increased steadily.
- Spectator attendance is at an all-time high.
- Sport apparel has become the "in" fashion, even when no sport participation is involved.
- The athletic-looking body has become the model look for which many people strive.
- High-profile athletes now command multi-million-dollar contracts.
- Many advertisements for products now feature high-profile athletes.
- Women's sport is becoming highly visible and economically strong.
- In some sports, successful senior competitions attract wide audiences.

All these data support the claim that we live in a culture where sport has become centrally important. The purpose of this chapter is to describe what kinds of sport are done, who does them, what specialized roles have developed to support the sport culture, and what qualifications are necessary to work in those roles. First, however, we examine the assumption that a growing sport culture must be built on increased leisure time for participating and spectating.

THE LEISURE MYTH

The conventional assumption about the relationship between leisure and sport is that in cultures where people have more leisure time, there is more sport involvement. So, do Americans now have more leisure time than they used to have? No! What is most surprising about the current era of sport development is that it is not based on any widespread increase in leisure.

The fact is that except for a relatively brief period during the industrialization of developed countries in the late nineteenth and early twentieth centuries, people in most cultures throughout history have had substantially more leisure time than modern Americans do now (De Grazia, 1962). The ancient Greeks and Romans, in particular, had as many festival days (what we would now call vacation) as they did workdays. Although the workweek is shorter today than it was during the early twentieth century, it is probably longer than in most times during recorded history.

Most workers now report that they are working longer hours than they did five years ago (Cordes & Ibrahim, 2003). The number of paid vacation days for U.S. workers is slightly less than it was fifteen years ago. Though this leaves less time for leisure and recreational pursuits, it is clear that we are spending more on leisure than we ever have before. When people have less leisure time, they must make choices. It seems clear that people are increasingly choosing to spend time and money on sport-related pursuits, which is strong evidence of the tremendous power and attraction of sport in our culture.

CHILD AND YOUTH SPORT

Child and youth sport includes all organized sport activities that take place outside the school, under the sponsorship and governance of public and private agencies and organizations. The National Council on Youth Sports estimates that as many as 46 million American youths participate in at least

---

Kinds of Sport Participation

It is useful to create broad categories of sport participation to better understand the different ways people relate to sport through their participation.

- *The recreational participant.* Although their participation may be frequent, recreational participants do not take part in formal competition in an institutionalized version of their sport. Examples are those who play in a pickup softball game, who play a weekly game of tennis, who take a ski vacation, or who play regular games of golf as members of a private club.

- *The amateur athlete.* Amateur athletes are regularly involved in formal competition governed by an official sport body but receive no monetary rewards. Rules are enforced and records are kept. Examples are high school athletes, golfers in sanctioned USGA events, softball players in a city league, or bowlers in a sanctioned corporate league.

- *The nonprofessional athlete.* This term has replaced the term amateur in Olympic rules. Nonprofessional athletes can make money, but it is typically kept in an account and drawn on for maintenance purposes. Examples are Olympic athletes, athletes training in the armed forces, and scholarship athletes in universities.

- *The professional athlete.* Professional athletes compete for profit or sign contracts for remuneration from a team. Examples are players in the NBA, Major League Baseball, and the Ladies Professional Golf Association.

Although boundaries between the categories are not always clear-cut, they do help us to understand how people relate to sport through their participation.

Some of the best sport is not formally organized.

one organized sport (that figure may include interscholastic participation), which means that about 65 percent of American children and youths participate in an organized sport (Eitzen & Sage, 2003). It is also estimated that 58 percent of those participants are in agency-sponsored programs, the largest of which is Little League baseball. Community recreation departments sponsor programs that account for about 36 percent of the participants, with the remaining 6 percent in private club programs. Girls' participation has increased markedly over the past two decades and now represents about 40 percent of the participation (Eitzen & Sage, 2003).

It is more difficult to estimate the level of participation in less organized and newer activities. For example, estimates are that activities such as snowboarding, in-line skating, treadmill exercise, and use of weights and resistance machines have experienced enormous growth since 1990, whereas participation in pickup softball and baseball has declined substantially (Sporting Goods Manufacturing Association, 2002).

Children are beginning to participate at younger and younger ages. Age-group gymnastics and swimming programs now enroll 3-year olds, and ice hockey, soccer, football and T-ball, among others, start with 4-year olds in many places. Many parents,

however, prefer that their children do not start at such an early age, which makes the average starting age closer to 10-years. Dropout rates for youths increase steadily from ages 11 to 18 years, with the percentage of dropouts higher for girls than for boys. Child and youth sport is full of controversy. How early should children begin? Why do so many youths drop out? Why aren't there more sport opportunities for youths outside the interscholastic programs? These issues will be addressed in Chapter 7.

Youth sport participation can be categorized as school-related or nonschool participation. Ewing and Seefeldt (1997) surveyed 8,000 youths and found that 55 percent had participated in a nonschool sport activity, with baseball, basketball, football, and soccer the most prevalent for boys, and swimming, softball, basketball, and volleyball the most popular among girls. Their survey also indicated that participation in school sport was only half that of nonschool sport, reflecting the *varsity model,* which provides decreasing opportunities from grades 8 through 12. Age 11 appears to represent the highest participation rates, and there is a steady decline from ages 11 to 18 years.

The Youth Sport Coalition of the National Association for Sport and Physical Education (NASPE) has developed a "Parent's Checklist for Quality Youth Sport Programs" (NASPE, 1995c), which provides a series of statements to help parents evaluate the developmental and educational benefits likely to accrue from children's and youths' participation in any sport program. The statements are organized into six areas: philosophy of the program, administration and organization of the program, coach qualifications and development, parental commitment toward child participation, children's readiness to participate, and safety. Ten statements appear in each area; the more statements a parent can check off, the greater is the possibility for a high-quality experience.

Duquin (1988) has suggested that child and youth sport programs will nurture healthy physical, psychological, and emotional growth and development if they

Organized sport begins early for many children.

- Are fun and enjoyable for the participant
- Provide a reasonably safe means for developing activity skills
- Foster moral sensitivity and caring
- Encourage taking pleasure in the body and in the beauty of movement skill
- Exercise a spirit of discovery, adventure, and creativity
- Provoke a commitment to lifelong involvement in activity
- Inspire a sense of community

The question sport educators must ask themselves is, What kind of child or youth sport program will achieve those characteristics?

In addition to formal child and youth sport programs, boys and girls enjoy enormous informal participation in sport. In my neighborhood, the current rage is roller hockey with in-line skates. From morning on, public basketball courts are filled with solitary players and with informal games. People of all ages toss around Frisbees in the autumn. There is no way to gauge the amount of formal participation or the role it plays in the development of youngsters. No doubt, some balance between informal and organized participation would be optimal for most youngsters.

Organization of Child and Youth Sport

Sport for children and youths in the United States has two distinct organizational features. First, sport for these age groups has developed without direction and influence from federal or state governments, unlike almost everywhere else in the developed world. Most sports for children and youths in this country are organized and funded through the private sector or through community agencies.

Some sports are highly institutionalized at the national level and are administered by national organizations, as is Little League baseball. Some religious organizations, such as the YMCA/YWCA and the CYO, sponsor child and youth sport through their local agencies. Many sport opportunities are developed and maintained through local efforts by parents and other interested community members, such as the soccer program described in Chapter 1. Many national service organizations, such as the Optimist and Kiwanis clubs, have traditions of sponsoring sport teams at the local level. There are also purely for-profit sport opportunities for children and youths, as in private gymnastic clubs or the increasingly popular summer sport camps.

Many of these child and youth sports have all the characteristics of highly institutionalized sport: uniforms, yearly schedules, spectators, records, and championships. Each is typically governed by a set of rules, although those rules often differ from area to area. Baseball leagues for children, for example, might have distinctive rules about pitching and mandatory playing time for all players, which differ from the rules for adult leagues. Soccer leagues might use different-sized fields and have different rules about playing time.

The second major organizational feature of child and youth sport in the United States is that it tends to be increasingly exclusionary as children become youths. For the 9- to 12-year-old child, there appears to be almost unlimited opportunity to learn sport and to compete in a variety of sports. For the 13- to 18-year-old boy or girl, however, those opportunities become substantially fewer. Sport for this age group is organized primarily through schools.

Interscholastic sport has become quite competitive; unless boys and girls are highly skilled, their chances of participating on a school team are not good.

It is the boy or girl who is not good enough to make the school team who seems to be excluded in America, thus making ours an exclusionary model of competition. Intramural opportunities within high schools are limited (and most often are not nearly as well organized or interesting as youth sport). Sport opportunities in the community are much more strongly oriented toward the younger child. So, for a 17-year-old who is not quite good enough to make the high school basketball team, there is little opportunity to continue to have meaningful sport experiences in basketball.

Those nations where sport for children and youth is organized through community or industries, or where there is a federal or state sport program, tend to be less exclusionary. In Australia, for example, a child who begins to compete in field hockey for a local club at age 8 years can, if desired, continue to compete in graded competition for that club throughout her or his lifetime. A 17-year-old who is not good enough to make the A team for the club will be able to compete on the B team or the C team.

Coaching for Child and Youth Sport

There are probably as many as 7.5 million youth sport coaches in North America, the vast majority of whom have had no formal instruction in the educational, developmental, and health aspects of coaching children and youth (Eitzen & Sage, 2003). A half-million more can be described as paid or professional coaches, typically working in for-fee sport clubs focused primarily on the development of elite athletes. In some sports, there are now *sport academies,* where youngsters can get top-level coaching and be with other young elite athletes as they live, train, compete, and go to school together. Many volunteer coaches played sports when they were younger, and many of them also watch a great deal of sport on television and in person, but that, of course, does not equip them with current knowl-

Coaches are fundamental to success in all sports.

edge from the fields of sport pedagogy, sport medicine, or sport psychology that would be useful in working with children and adolescents.

Again, the situation for coaching is different in nations where the government has played a stronger role in developing and administering child and youth sport. Canada, Great Britain, New Zealand, Australia, and other nations have developed coach-education programs with different levels of training necessary for positions at different levels of competition—from a beginning level, necessary to work with local children's teams, to the highest level, necessary to coach a state or national team. The coach-education materials are often developed in conjunction with national sport organizations and delivered through local recreation agencies. For example, a national volleyball organization might develop beginning coaching materials for volleyball, and local recreation agencies would use those materials to prepare volunteer coaches for youth volleyball.

In the United States, the American Sport Education Program (ASEP) is privately organized and marketed by Human Kinetics but is perhaps the closest to the models just described (Partlow, 1992). Started in the 1970s as the American Coaching Effectiveness Program, ASEP has trained well over 1 million coaches, parents, and administrators

---

TABLE 6.1   Courses and Programs Available in ASEP

Level One: Basic Education

A 3- to 5-hour course for volunteer coaches focusing on coaching principles, philosophy, and communication skills.

Level Two: Beyond the Basics

A 6-hour online course to teach coaches advanced methods and the "games approach" to instructing kids in sport skills and tactics.

Bronze-Level Certification

For coaches who complete the Coaching Principles course, the Sport First Aid course, and a sport-specific technique and tactics course. Bronze-Level certification is valid for 3 years and is renewable by completing the CPR component and one course at the Silver Level.

Silver-Level Certification
(available in 2004)

Advanced courses in sport physiology, sport psychology, mechanics of sport, and teaching sport skills. Sport-specific courses in advanced techniques and best practices of experienced coaches.

Gold-Level Certification
(available in 2005)

Advanced courses in sport sciences, conditioning, and instructional methods. Courses in risk management and social issues in sport.

ASEP also offers courses for administrators of community-based sport programs and administrators of school, Olympic, or sport club programs.

ASEP also offers educational materials for youth sport officials and a number of books, videos, and manuals for parents.

(www.asep.com). In 1990 the National Federation of State High School Associations joined with ASEP to offer coaching education for high school sport coaches. ASEP is now used in thirty four states, with over 200,000 school coaches trained. In 1994 ASEP expanded its mission to include educational programs for sport administrators of volunteer youth sport programs and also developed educational materials for parents. Organizations such as the YMCA and the Boys and Girls Clubs of America have adopted the Basic Education course for those who work in their sport programs. More than forty Olympic national governing bodies and sport organizations use ASEP materials in their coaching-education programs. Table 6.1 describes many of the programs now available through ASEP.

The nonprofit National Alliance for Youth Sports includes as one of its main programs the National Youth Sport Coaches Association (NYSCA), which has trained over 1.2 million coaches since its inception in 1981. Their program is offered through state offices and local/regional chapters. The program focuses on developmental and safety considerations, physiological and psychological concerns, and sport-coaching techniques. Participants must pass an exam on the materials they have covered and sign a pledge that they will uphold the association's Code of Ethics. The following box describes the National Alliance for Youth Sports in more detail.

INTERSCHOLASTIC SPORT

In the Constitution of the United States, education is specifically designated as a *state* function. Therefore, interscholastic sport is organized and regulated at the state level, with almost no federal-government involvement. Although the organization of school sport differs somewhat from state to state, the similarities in governance and structure

---

National Alliance for Youth Sports

Founded in 1981, the NAYS sponsors nine programs that educate volunteer coaches, parents, youth sport program administrators, and officials about their roles and responsibilities in youth sports. NAYS programs are provided at the local level through partnerships with community-based organizations.

- National Youth Sport Coaches Association trains volunteer coaches.
- National Youth Sports Officials Association trains volunteer youth sport officials.
- Academy for Youth Sport Administrators offers a 20-hour program to earn the Certified Youth Sports Administrator credential.
- National Clearinghouse for Youth Sports Information provides the public with access to a variety of materials pertaining to youth sports.

- Parents Association for Youth Sports provides materials and information to make parents aware of their roles and responsibilities in youth sports.
- Child Abuse and Youth Sports provides a comprehensive risk-management approach to building a protective shield around participants and programs.
- Hook a Kid on Golf™ helps communities develop comprehensive youth golf programs.
- Start Smart brings parents and children ages 3 and over together in an instructional program that helps parents learn how to teach their children.
- Kids on Target is a team-oriented program for archery for youngsters ages 10–14.

SOURCE: www.nays.org.

---

far outnumber the differences. Interscholastic sport occupies a place in the American sport culture that is unlike that in any other nation.

During the 2001–2 school year, 6,767,515 girls and boys participated in more than forty-five sports. Texas continues to have the most participants, followed by California and New York (see Table 6.2). It should be noted that many students participate in more than one sport and thus are double- or triple-counted. Participation of boys remained remarkably steady from 1971 through 2001, with fluctuations accounted for primarily by slight changes in total school enrollment. Participation of girls was only 294,915 in 1971 as compared with 3,666,917 boys. When Title IX became law in 1972, that picture began to change rapidly, and by 1977–78, participation by girls first topped the 2 million level. Participation among girls has increased not only in absolute numbers but also in relation to boys. The 2,806,998 count for 2001–2 was the largest ever for girls but still lagged behind boys' participation by

more than 1 million. If, however, one discounts the more than 1 million boys who participate in football where team size reaches forty to seventy players, sport participation by girls now nearly equals that of boys. It is fair to say that as a percentage of high school enrollment, sport participation has increased steadily across the past thirty years.

Basketball and track and field are the two most popular sports among girls (see Table 6.3), and football and basketball remain the most popular sports among boys. Volleyball has increased steadily as a participant sport for girls but does not come close to making the top ten for boys. The top ten sports have remained quite similar over the past decade.

Organization of Interschool Sport

Most states have adopted a system of competition in which the number of students in a school determines the classification within which the school competes (AAA, AA, and A; A, B, C, and D; or V, IV,

TABLE 6.2   Interschool Sport Participation by State, 2001–2002

Athletics Participation Survey Index

Rank	State	Total Number of Participants°	Rank	State	Total Number of Participants°	Rank	State	Total Number of Participants°
1.	Texas	773,850	18.	Indiana	136,837	35.	Arkansas	48,834
2.	California	656,245	19.	North Carolina	135,523	36.	Utah	46,489
3.	New York	338,248	20.	Colorado	111,580	37.	Idaho	45,967
4.	Illinois	301,626	21.	Kansas	98,261	38.	New Hampshire	40,664
5.	Michigan	301,196	22.	Maryland	94,173	39.	New Mexico	38,661
6.	Ohio	299,351	23.	Arizona	93,508	40.	West Virginia	36,813
7.	Pennsylvania	243,765	24.	Oregon	91,875	41.	Montana	35,389
8.	New Jersey	214,870	25.	Connecticut	89,944	42.	Nevada	33,910
9.	Florida	211,936	26.	Kentucky	86,404	43.	Hawaii	31,544
10.	Minnesota	211,693	27.	Louisiana	84,704	44.	South Dakota	29,860
11.	Massachusetts	193,880	28.	Tennessee	83,756	45.	North Dakota	29,321
12.	Wisconsin	191,425	29.	Alabama	82,716	46.	Vermont	25,495
13.	Missouri	157,815	30.	Mississippi	80,710	47.	Rhode Island	24,372
14.	Washington	153,487	31.	South Carolina	77,807	48.	Delaware	23,392
15.	Virginia	150,414	32.	Nebraska	77,649	49.	Alaska	18,883
16.	Georgia	148,063	33.	Oklahoma	66,858	50.	Wyoming	18,027
17.	Iowa	141,975	34.	Maine	53,766	51.	District of Columbia	3,984

° Reflects participation rate, i.e., individual who participated in two sports is counted twice, three sports—three times, etc.

Source: www.nfhs.org.

III, II, and I). **Interscholastic sport** is typically governed by a state agency, which in many states is *not* a government agency but, rather, a private corporation that schools join. For example, the Ohio High School Athletic Association (OHSAA) is a private organization to which Ohio high schools belong by virtue of paid membership. The OHSAA organizes and administers sports for the high schools that belong to the organization, including establishing rules for participation, length of season, starting times for practice; and conducting regional, district, and state championships in a variety of sports.

The financing of interscholastic sport also differs from state to state. In some states, interscholastic sport is considered to be a regular part of the educational program and is funded directly from tax revenues through regular school budgets. In other states, however, laws limit the amount of regularly

TABLE 6.3 Interschool Sport Participation, by Sport (2001–2 School Year)

Ten Most Popular Boys' Programs				
Sport		Participants		
1.	Basketball	17,135	1.	Football (11-player)	1,023,712
2.	Track and field (outdoor)	15,261	2.	Basketball	540,597
3.	Baseball	14,924	3.	Track and field (outdoor)	494,022
4.	Football (11-player)	13,509	4.	Baseball	451,674
5.	Golf	13,031	5.	Soccer	339,101
6.	Cross-country	12,456	6.	Wrestling	244,637
7.	Soccer	9,903	7.	Cross-country	190,993
8.	Wrestling	9,578	8.	Golf	163,299
9.	Tennis	9,365	9.	Tennis	139,498
10.	Swimming and diving	5,540	10.	Swimming	90,698

Ten Most Popular Girls' Programs				
Sport		Participants		
1.	Basketball (50/50)	16,851	1.	Basketball (50/50)	456,169
2.	Track and field (outdoor)	15,151	2.	Track and field (outdoor)	415,677
3.	Volleyball	14,083	3.	Volleyball	395,124
4.	Softball (fast pitch)	13,807	4.	Softball (fast pitch)	355,960
5.	Cross-country	11,976	5.	Soccer	295,265
6.	Tennis	9,378	6.	Cross-country	160,178
7.	Soccer	9,186	7.	Tennis	160,114
8.	Golf	7,754	8.	Swimming	141,218
9.	Swimming	5,935	9.	Competitive spirit squads	94,635
10.	Competitive spirit squads	4,245	10.	Field hockey	60,737

SOURCE: www.nfhs.org.

budgeted tax funds that may be spent on extracurricular activities. Interscholastic sport, as an extracurricular activity, then has partially to pay for itself through gate receipts and through fund-raising. It is in the latter area that high school booster clubs have developed; such clubs often provide substantial financial support for athletic departments.

The National Federation of State High School Associations is the national service and administrative organization for high school sport and fine arts as well as programs in speech, debate, and music. The mission of NFSHSA is to serve its fifty state high school athletic association members by providing leadership for and national coordination of the administration of high school sport in ways that improve the educational experience and reduce the risks of sport participation (www.nfhs.org). NFSHSA publishes rules for sixteen sports for boys' and girls' competition. Its 17,346 member high schools serve approximately 10 million girls and boys. NFSHSA has strong relationships with the National Federation of Coaches Associations, the National Athletic Administrators Association, and Human Kinetics, with whom it partners for the American Sport Education Program.

School Coaches

The number of coaches required to staff the 190,000-plus interscholastic sport teams in America each year is substantial (Stewart & Sweet, 1992). Since the enactment of Title IX, the need for coaches has increased significantly. In some sports, a variety of assistant coaches help the head coaches. Most high schools have at least varsity and reserve teams (the latter typically composed of freshmen and sophomores) in most sports.

The qualifications needed to coach these teams vary tremendously from state to state. Because our Constitution leaves the governance of education to the states, the methods for establishing and governing standards related to coaching in schools differ from state to state. Some states have no standards governing the hiring of coaches. In other states, the state boards of education set the standards. In still others, state activities associations set the standards.

Remember that we live in an era when sport has expanded markedly. Not only has access to sport been opened to girls in high schools, but since the early 1970s, most schools have also expanded the number of sports in their programs. In the early 1960s, because there were fewer sports and greatly restricted access for girls, fewer coaches were needed. Nearly all those coaches were certified teachers, and many of them were trained phys-

ical educators. Today, however, the situation has changed dramatically because not enough certified teachers are willing to coach.

School administrators have resorted to hiring coaches from outside the school, often community members interested in a particular sport but without formal preparation in teaching, physical education, or coaching. Many states have had to modify their coaching regulations to allow for the hiring of coaches whose qualifications often do not go beyond having played the sport themselves.

Some states still require all coaches to have a teaching certificate, whereas others require certification only for head coaches (Sisley & Weise, 1987). Very few states have strong coach-education requirements. In 1989 Colorado adopted a new coach-certification law with more stringent regulations (*CAHPERD Journal,* 1989). This law identified several avenues through which women and men could qualify for high school coaching positions, including a college major or minor in physical education or coaching, completion of a prescribed set of college coursework related to coaching, or completion of the leader level of the American Sport Education Program. The ASEP leader level is designed primarily for interscholastic coaching, as the volunteer level is designed chiefly for child and youth sport coaching. Coaching credentials can be renewed either through a successful performance evaluation or by completing continuing-education programs related to coaching.

The ASEP Basic Education course is part of the National Federation of Interscholastic Coaches Education Program (NFICEP) and has been endorsed by more than forty state athletic and educational agencies (Second Edition, 1992). A second coach-education program that has made important strides is the Program for Athletic Coaches Education (PACE), developed at the Institute for the Study of Youth Sports at Michigan State University (Seefeldt & Milligan, 1992). PACE is typically delivered through state organizations or universities. The coach-education course includes a basic text, an instructor's guide, a coach's guide, and videos that show simulated situations related to coaching.

In 1998 the California state legislature established the California High School Coaching and Training Program, which encourages schools to adopt local coaching guidelines, and established a matching-grant program to fund training programs for coaches. The act also established criteria for coach-education programs in California, which were based strongly on those developed in the American Sport Education Program Basic Education course for coaches.

The number of women coaching high school sports has declined dramatically since its high-water mark just after the passage of Title IX in 1972 (Pastore, 1994; Sisley & Capel, 1986). Several states have experimented with special programs to attract, train, and retain women in high school coaching positions (Hasbrook, 1987; Schafer, 1987), but the shortage continues. A 1988 Ohio study found that 33 percent of girls' teams had female head coaches, but a 1994 Illinois study found that only 25 percent of girls' teams had female coaches (Pastore, 1994).

In 1994 a national summit on coaching standards was convened by NASPE. LeRoy Walker, then president of the U.S. Olympic Committee, opened the summit by stating that "it is time to move the idea of national coaching standards 'off the back burner.' We need a framework that will guarantee us that there is at least a minimum level of competence among these coaches who are affecting the lives of our young people" (*NASPE News*, 1995c, p. 1).

Those national standards now exist (NASPE, 1995). Thirty-seven standards are grouped in eight domains, and appropriate competencies are identified to further define the meaning of each standard. The eight domains are

- Injury prevention, care, and management
- Risk management
- Growth, development, and learning
- Training, conditioning, and nutrition
- Social and psychological aspects of coaching
- Skills, tactics, and strategies
- Teaching and administration
- Professional preparation and development

These standards are not meant to be a certification program but instead were developed to help organizations and agencies that currently either work with coaches or certify them to develop programs and materials that will better serve the needs of coaches and the athletes who play for them. Many still argue, however, that there is a growing need for some kind of national certification program (Knoor, 1996).

The National Council for Accreditation of Coaching Education (NCACE) held its first meeting in the summer of 2000. The organization was formed by a variety of people interested in standardizing and improving coaching education at various levels. NCACE includes single-sport and multi-sport organizations, sport sciences and sport pedagogy organizations, as well as colleges/universities concerned about the availability of well-trained coaches at all levels of sport (NASPE News, Spring 2001). NCACE supports, facilitates the development of, and provides accreditation for coaching-education programs. It provides workshops that address the eight domains of the National Standards for Athletic Coaches (NASPE, 1995). NCACE sponsored a national coaching conference at Penn State University in June 2003, the theme of which was "Taking Coaching Education to Another Level: Giving Athletes the Edge."

COLLEGIATE SPORT PROGRAMS

Intercollegiate Sport

In the post–World War II era, when America became a major sport culture in the world, a significant factor in the overall development of sport was the substantial growth in intercollegiate sport. To be sure, America had a significant history in intercollegiate sport dating to the late nineteenth century, when student interest and pressure became so strong that universities began to incorporate sport

Football at all levels has become a major enterprise.

into their programs (see Chapters 2 and 3). Major intercollegiate rivalries had for years captured the interest of the entire nation—the Army–Notre Dame football game, for example. Between 1945 and 1960, intercollegiate sport still grew enormously in importance. It became more important as entertainment, more important economically, and more important on campus. The United States is still the only country in the world where sport and college or university education have become so completely linked.

Most colleges and universities offer extensive sport programs to their students. The advent of

Title IX provided the impetus for the phenomenal growth of intercollegiate sport for women in the 1970s. Many colleges and universities have joined with similar institutions in their region to form athletic conferences—the Big Ten, the Western Athletic Conference, and the Michigan Intercollegiate Athletic Association, for example. These athletic conferences govern issues such as eligibility and organize competition for the member institutions, including championships.

Nationally, college and university sport is governed by individual institutional membership in private organizations. The two organizations that dominate the governance of intercollegiate sport are the National Collegiate Athletic Association (NCAA) and the National Association of Intercollegiate Athletes (NAIA). As with child and youth sport, state and federal government have not become involved in the administration of college and university sport in America.

The NCAA has three main divisions, based on level of competition and rules regarding financial aid to athletes. Table 6.4 shows the number of member institutions in each division and the participation rates for female and male athletes. Division I is further subdivided into three divisions, again based on level of competition and rules for financial aid, but pertaining almost exclusively to football. Division I-A has 114 members, I-AA 122 members, and I-AAA 85 members. Division III is often re-

TABLE 6.4	NCAA Membership and Participation by Division			
Division	Number of Members	Women Participants	Men Participants	Total Participants
I (overall)	321	63,508	85,483	148,991
II	295	29,680	44,537	74,217
III	423	57,288	78,844	133,132
Total	1,039	150,476	208,864	356,340

SOURCE: www.ncaa.org.

ferred to as the "college" division and is defined by not allowing athletic scholarships rather than by size of school. Indeed, some universities in Division III actually have larger enrollments than some in Division I.

The NCAA conducts yearly championships in each division—nineteen in women's sports and twenty in men's sports. Nearly 100 athletic conferences are voting members of the NCAA, a major benefit of which is that conference champions automatically qualify for NCAA championship play.

In 1997 the NCAA completed a significant restructuring of its governance system. The restructuring gives each division greater autonomy and allows for more control over sport programs by the chief executive officers of the member schools, who are typically the presidents of the colleges and universities. An annual convention is held, at which all NCAA business is conducted. Each school and conference member has one vote on all issues before the convention.

The NAIA, which was formed in 1940, has over 500 institutional members. It organizes championships for thirteen sports in Divisions I and II. NAIA membership is divided into fourteen regions serving North American colleges and universities. Thirty athletic conferences have official affiliation with the NAIA. NAIA institutions are typically smaller colleges and universities. Although they do not attract the national attention that the NCAA does, they do provide organized intercollegiate sports competition for a large number of women and men.

There are a large number of 2-year colleges in the United States, many of which offer sport programs for their students. These institutions are organized and governed by the National Junior College Athletic Association (NJCAA), which both determines rules such as eligibility and organizes national championships.

Many people work professionally within intercollegiate sport—coaches, assistant coaches, athletic directors, sport information directors, sport business managers, sport trainers, sport-medicine experts. Only in the medical area—trainers and physicians—are there any specific certification requirements that define entrance into those professional roles.

Colleges and universities also have coach-education programs at both the undergraduate and the graduate levels (McMillin & Reffner, 1998). Nearly 200 such programs exist, 90 percent of them at the undergraduate level. The most common approach is to offer a minor in coaching education, from 12 to 33 semester credit hours. More than half the programs require a coaching internship. All programs require a course in the care and prevention of injury, and 80 percent require a further course in athletic training. More than twenty universities now offer an M.A. concentration in coaching education.

College Recreational Intramural Programs

In addition to intercollegiate sport, college and university programs of recreation and intramural sports have grown tremendously in the recent past. Many institutions, seeking to attract and retain students, have built new recreation facilities that have all the amenities of upscale private health and fitness clubs. Programs include all the traditional sport competitions, yearly membership sport clubs, special events (weekend three-on-three basketball tournaments, for example), regularly scheduled fitness and aerobics classes, and drop-in activity for both sport and fitness. Weight-training rooms are typically crowded from early morning until late at night. Pools are filled with recreational and fitness-oriented swimmers.

Many of these programs offer additional opportunities for faculty and for the families of students, staff, and faculty. Recently, recreation and intramural departments have entered the lucrative business of offering summer-camp programs for youths. Recreation and intramural departments are typically staffed by trained professionals and have development programs for student employees. Programs are funded through some combination of subsidies from the university, direct student fees, user fees, and facility rentals (Noyes, 1996).

Coaching Education within National Governing Bodies

The national governing bodies (NGBs) of most Olympic sports have developed their own coaching-education programs. Many of them use ASEP or a similar entry-level program as the beginning program but then advance to levels of accreditation that are more specific to the sport sponsored by the NGB. The program below is for USA Volleyball.

USA Volleyball Coaching Accreditation Program (CAP)

- Level 1: ASEP Coaching Principles, skills, games, drills, basic systems, and practice management. Candidate must pass test and sign coaching code of ethics statement.

- Level 2: Team systems, blocking and setting development, problem solving, and social issues. Candi-

date must attend or instruct one non-CAP volleyball clinic.

- Level 3: Instruction from peer coaches, critical thinking, outreach project.

- Level 4: Mentor with Cadre or National Team for one week. Candidate must complete three experiences from four categories of higher-level coaching and develop a publishable manuscript.

- Level 5: All current and previous national team coaches are considered honorary Level 5

Accreditation at most levels lasts for four years, during which time the candidate must advance to the next level or complete an accreditation-renewal course.

SOURCE: www.usavolleyball.org.

PROFESSIONAL SPORT

A main purpose of professional sport is to make money—professional sport is a business. The number of players involved in professional sport is remarkably small. The number of players in the NBA is only 250 to 300, whereas the number of boys competing in high school basketball in a given year is typically greater than 550,000. Nearly 400,000 girls participate in high school volleyball, but only a few compete in the Women's Professional Volleyball League. Looking at the figures from a different perspective, we can see that the odds for becoming a professional athlete are not good! There are about 3,000 professional athletes in the three major American professional sports for men—baseball, basketball, and football. Yet there are more than 110 million males in the country, which means that 1 out of every 42,000 makes it to the professional level. The number of players that can earn a good living from other sports is even less—the tennis

player or golfer ranked as 250 is not getting rich from sport.

It seems as though, every day, we read on the sport page about an athlete who has signed a lucrative professional contract. We must remember, however, that the wealth in professional sport is distributed unevenly among the athletes. A few make the headline money; the more typical athlete makes considerably less. It is also important to understand that being a professional athlete seldom amounts to having a career. Although a few athletes remain in their sport for 10 to 20 years, the average length of stay is much shorter: 4.3 years for football, 4.2 years for basketball, 6.5 years for baseball, and 4.8 years for hockey.

Although professional sport is not a realistic goal for most young men and women who compete in child, youth, interscholastic, and collegiate sport, the emergence of professional sport (and big-time intercollegiate sport) has been accompanied by the development of nonparticipant sport professions, many of which are reviewed in the final section of this chapter. Suffice it to say that an NBA team, with its eleven or twelve players, also has three coaches, at least one trainer, a general manager, and a publicity or promotion director, as well as assistant managerial and promotional staff; that is, the number of nonparticipant professionals is nearly equal to the number of participants!

Professional sport is organized and regulated through its parent organizations: NBA, National League, LPGA (Ladies Professional Golfers Association), National Hockey League (NHL), and so on. Most sports have commissioners who oversee the establishment and governance of standards and rules within the sport. Remember, however, that professional sport is a business. *Owners* exert the most influence on the governance of the sport, typically through an owners' council.

There are no formal qualifications for entrance into professional sport in most participant and nonparticipant roles. Concepts such as certification and training of personnel, which are so important to the future of youth and school sport, are not issues at the professional level.

ORGANIZED RECREATIONAL SPORT

The scope of organized recreational sport in the United States is enormous. By *organized,* I mean that a regular competition is organized and governed by a sponsoring agency, records are kept, and officials are provided to ensure appropriate play. Most organized recreational sport in the United States is sponsored by community recreation departments; businesses or industries; service clubs, such as the Kiwanis or Rotary; and private community organizations, typically started and maintained by interested parents.

The range of sport involvement at this level is as broad as sport itself—golf leagues, road races, fishing tournaments, baseball leagues, tennis tournaments, horseshoe leagues, and the like. We would also expect to find some major regional differences in organized recreational sport participation—

curling in the Dakotas, surfing in Southern California, cross-country skiing in New England. The major involvement in organized recreational sport, however, has been and continues to be in the dominant sports of basketball, touch football, volleyball, soccer, and, most of all, softball.

Here is a breakdown of the participation figures for the City of Columbus, Ohio, Parks and Recreation Department sports program in a recent year:

Softball	195 leagues	1,621 teams	29,000 players
Basketball	38 leagues	308 teams	4,600 players
Volleyball	38 leagues	376 teams	4,500 players
Football	7 leagues	68 teams	1,300 players
Soccer	4 leagues	32 teams	500 players

In all there were 12,177 games played in these various leagues, with 7,806 umpires, referees, and scorekeepers employed. There were, of course, similar kinds of programs in the many suburbs surrounding the city and active programs in the other cities, suburbs, and towns in the state—and all across the nation. This level of participation makes a mockery of accusations that we are a nation of spectators.

Different kinds of sporting interests are accommodated in organized recreation programs because the programs are most often sensitive to the needs and interests of those they serve. In the softball program alluded to previously, there are slow-pitch leagues for men, slow-pitch leagues for women, fast-pitch leagues for men, fast-pitch leagues for women, and *co-rec leagues,* where men and women compete together. These differentiations allow people to participate in a way that is most challenging and enjoyable to them. Some participate primarily as a *social* experience; others participate primarily as a *competitive* experience.

Similar kinds of organized recreational-sport programs are implemented in most colleges and universities. Students can participate in a wide variety of sport activities throughout the school year. As with community programs, college and university programs most often offer men's, women's, and co-rec competition.

An increasing amount of organized recreational sport is found in the private fitness-club industry. As part of their services to their members, clubs organize individual and team competition in a number of sports, most typically handball, racquetball, squash, tennis, and swimming.

Sport for People with Disabilities

One of the best features of recent sport history is the degree to which the benefits of sport participation have begun to be extended to people who, historically, have had difficulty finding ways to be involved in sport. I have mentioned many times the Title IX federal legislation, which opened the door to more equal opportunity in sport for girls and women. The next section considers the role of sport among older age groups. This section reviews sport opportunities for people with disabilities.

Should a physical or mental disability prohibit someone from participating in meaningful sport competition? No! Has it historically? Yes! Before World War II, there was virtually no opportunity for competitive sport participation for athletes with physical or mental disabilities (DePauw, 1984). Since then, we have made major progress. That progress is associated with three specific pieces of federal legislation:

1. Public Law 93-112 (Rehabilitation Act—1973) specified that equal opportunity and access must be provided for people with disabilities, including in physical education, intramurals, and athletics.

2. Public Law 94-142 (Education for All Handicapped Children Act—1975) required a free and appropriate public education, including instruction in physical education, in the least restrictive environment, for children with disabilities.

3. Public Law 95-606 (Amateur Sports Act—1978) specifically included people with disabilities within the province of the law.

4. Public Law 105–117 (Individuals with Disabilities Education Act of 1997) restructured IDEA to become the primary law guiding treatment of children and youth with disabilities in schools, including a requirement that they must have access to the general education curriculum.

The concern for people with disabilities (this term has recently been used in preference to the earlier term, *handicapped*) spread all the way to the United States Olympic Committee, which eventually provided leadership for the establishment of the Committee on Sports for the Disabled (COSD). The membership of COSD includes two representatives from each major national sport organization for athletes with disabilities, one of whom must be disabled (DePauw, 1984). COSD sponsors major national events such as the International Games for the Disabled, the World Wheelchair Games, and the Winter Games for the Disabled.

The many organizations that now support sport for people with disabilities are shown in Table 6.5. The development and spread of the movement in sport for people with disabilities not only has expanded the opportunities for a fuller life for the participants but also has served as a source of inspiration and motivation for countless others. In the summer of 2000, following the Olympic Games, the XI Paralympic Games were held in Sydney, Australia. Nearly 4,000 athletes from 122 countries participated, along with 2,300 team officials and 800 technical officials. A record number of tickets (1.2 million) were sold for the events. More than 300 Paralympic and world records were set. British wheelchair athlete Tanni Grey-Thompson crowned a distinguished career by winning gold medals in the 100M, 200M, 400M, and 800M races. Wheelchair rugby was a medal sport for the first time and became an instant crowd favorite. Paralympics is the term created to define the partnership between sport for people with spinal-cord injuries and the Olympics (Sherrill, 1993).

Perhaps the sport organization for people with disabilities that is most familiar to the general public is the Special Olympics, the sport program for mentally retarded people (Stevens, 1984). There are more than 20,000 community-oriented Special Olympics programs in the United States, operated primarily by an extensive volunteer organization of

TABLE 6.5   Sport Organizations for People with Disablities

American Athletic Association for the Deaf	National Foundation of Wheelchair Tennis
American Blind Bowling Association	National Wheelchair Basketball Association
American Wheelchair Bowling Association	National Wheelchair Marathon Association
American Wheelchair Pilots Association	National Wheelchair Racquetball Association
Amputee Sports Association	National Wheelchair Shooting Federation
Blind Outdoor Leisure Association	National Wheelchair Softball Association
Braille Sports Foundation	North American Riding for the Handicapped Association
Cerebral Palsy International Sports and Recreation Association	Paralyzed Veterans of America
Disabled Sportsmen of America	Skating Association for the Blind and Handicapped
Disabled Sports USA	Ski for Light, Inc.
Dwarf Athletic Association of America	Special Olympics International
Eastern Amputee Athletic Association	Tennis Association for the Mentally Retarded
52 Association for the Handicapped	U.S. Amputee Athletic Association
Goal Ball Championships	U.S. Association for Blind Athletes
Handicapped Scuba Association	U.S. Blind Golfer's Association
International Coordinating Committee of the World Sports Organization for the Disabled	U.S. Cerebral Palsy Athletic Association
International Foundation of Wheelchair Tennis	U.S. Deaf Skiers Association
International Paralympic Committee	U.S. Olympic Committee, Sports for the Disabled
International Sports Organization for the Disabled	U.S. Organization for Disabled Athletes
International Wheelchair Aviators	U.S. Quad Rugby Association
International Wheelchair Road Racers Club	Wheelchair Athletes of the USA
National Beep Baseball Association	Wheelchair Sports Federation

SOURCE: DePauw, 1984.

450,000 people who provide instruction and conduct competition in sixteen sports on a yearly basis. Any mentally retarded person above age 8 years may participate, and no person is considered too old or too disabled to have the opportunity to learn and compete in sport.

The **Special Olympics** program has developed a number of instructional programs, including books, films, and videos for use in training personnel to work with mentally retarded athletes. More than 24,000 people have completed training as officials, instructors, coaches, and event directors. The Special Olympics has become an international phenomenon since the mid-1970s, with the international games now a major sport spectacle.

A new effort of the Special Olympics movement is "**unified sports**" (Janes, 1995). The term *unified sports* refers to sporting events in which teams include athletes with and without mental retardation. Unified sports can be seen as a part of the larger movement toward inclusion, which is so prevalent in American schools (see Chapter 11). Unified sports have begun to spread at the local level through community recreation programs, Boys and Girls Clubs of America, and other local agencies. Unified sports also help schools meet the transition mandates required by the Individuals with Disabilities Education Act (IDEA).

The key legislative provision supporting increased access to sport for people with disabilities is Section 504 of the 1973 Rehabilitation Act (French, Henderson, Kinnison, & Sherrill, 1998). The language of this key provision states:

> No otherwise qualified handicapped individual in the United States, shall solely by reason of his handicap be excluded from participation in, be denied the benefits of, or be subjected to discrimination under any program of activity receiving Federal financial assistance or under any program or activity conducted by an Executive agency. (U.S. Congress, 1973)

The *otherwise qualified* phrase is legal terminology that means that the person has the skills or abilities to participate in the sport after reasonable accommodation has been made. As people with disabilities use Section 504 to challenge denial of access to participation in sport, more and more opportunities will open to them. A number of states are creating laws in this area that are even stricter than the federal law. When state and federal law conflict, the more stringent requirement is used.

Masters or Veterans Sport

The historical approach to sport and aging was simple: Young people compete, and older people watch. That too has changed. There is a growing movement for what, in the United States, is termed *masters sport* (in most of the world, the same movement is referred to as *veterans sport*). The general proposition underlying this movement is that men and women can continue to find meaningful competition in sport throughout their lifetimes.

Masters sport has become the major competitive outlet for people who want to devote more time to

training or to test themselves in a wider arena of competition than is available through organized recreational sport. Masters competition typically begins at age 40 years and is graded in 5-year age groups. At regional and national competitions, it is no longer unusual to find spirited competition in the 70- to 74-year age group.

Masters programs are most well developed in track and field, road racing, swimming, and bowling. There are more than 42,000 registered swimmers in the United States Masters Swimming organization (www.usms.org), which holds an annual convention and has a regular calendar of regional and national events. The World Association of Veteran Athletes (WAVA) was recently renamed the World Masters Athletics Association. The WAVA held its first world championships event in Toronto, Canada, in 1971 with 1,408 competitors. The most recent event was held in Brisbane, Australia, in 2001 with more than 6,000 athletes from seventy-nine countries competing. Competition is organized in 5-year age groups, starting with the 40–44 group and going up to the 95–99 group.

The World Masters Games is yet another age-group organization that holds regular world competitions. The first World Masters Games were held in Toronto, Canada, in 1985 with 8,000 athletes from sixty-one countries competing in twenty-two sports. The most recent games were held in Melbourne, Australia, in 2002 with 20,000 athletes competing in twenty-nine sports.

The involvement of adults and senior citizens in sport has led to the creation of statewide sport festivals, the first of which was held in New York in 1978. A state sport festival typically involves competition in a large number of Olympic, national, and local sports across all age ranges, but emphasizing adult and senior participation. Forty-four states have conducted state sport festivals over the past decade. These state games are good examples of the festive nature of sport competition, with goodwill and participation ranking as values equal to vigorous competition.

Like sport for people with disabilities, the growing availability of masters competition for older athletes not only enriches the lives of men and women who want to continue to train and compete in their sport but also serves as an important model for a healthy, active lifestyle, which has serious implications for fitness as well as for sport.

NONPARTICIPANT SPORT INVOLVEMENT

There are many ways to be involved in sport besides playing or coaching. As a sport becomes more highly institutionalized, a variety of roles are created that require professional expertise to be applied to the interests of the sport. Thus, sport vocations develop as a sport becomes more highly institutionalized. Organized sport at the local level, typically in communities, often operates primarily with part-time and volunteer help. To the extent that sport is more highly organized and more institutionalized, there is a need for full-time, professional services.

The following list of vocational opportunities is evidence of the diverse professional roles in the field of sport. Each listed vocation is followed by typical places of employment.

Athletic administration—high schools, colleges, pro teams, clubs

Sport administration—corporations, pro clubs, colleges

Sport leadership—recreation centers, industry, camps, churches, resorts, commercial centers

Sport broadcasting—radio, television stations

Sport journalism—newspapers, magazines, self-employed

Sport-facility design—corporations, government, self-employed

Sport camps—established camps, self-employed

Sport-facility management—government, pro teams, industry, universities

Sport medicine—hospitals, sport-medicine centers, universities, pro teams

Sport counseling—high school, colleges and universities, private practice

Athletic training—schools, universities, pro teams, sport-medicine centers

Sports officiating—schools, universities, pro teams, recreational programs

Sport psychologist—universities, pro teams, national teams

Sport scientist (physiology, biomechanics, etc.)—universities

Sport-equipment design—self-employed, industry

Sport studies (history, sociology, etc.)—universities

Sport fitness—universities, pro teams, national teams

Sport publicity—universities, pro teams

Sport promotion—universities, pro teams

Sport photography—newspapers, magazines, self-employed

Although many men and women earn their living within these vocations, this does not mean that they have been *specifically prepared* for that vocation. There are a few universities where a person can study sport photography, sport journalism, or sport broadcasting. The more typical route to these vocations is through the broader field of study: photography, journalism, or broadcasting. The physician specializing in sport medicine is exactly that—a *physician* who, after completing medical training, specialized in the application of medical science to sport.

In some of these vocational areas, one can study the vocation directly and proceed to work in that vocation. That would be true for sport psychology, the sport sciences, sport studies, and sport management and administration. Direct training in these fields, however, is not the only way to enter the vocation. Many sport psychologists were trained as psychologists and have a deep interest in sport. Many sport administrators were trained in business administration and have a deep interest in sport.

These are areas where direct training *is* available, but that training is not *necessary* to enter the vocation.

The vocation of athletic training is one of the few in the list where specific training is needed to enter the vocation—and it is difficult to enter the vocation without that training because of the certification needed to practice as an athletic trainer.

Thus, preparation for a career in a nonparticipant sport vocation, at the current stage of sport development in America, presents a flexible set of options. As sport becomes more highly institutionalized, we can expect that more specific preparation for nonparticipant vocational roles will be made available and that certification or licensing programs will be developed to ensure that people entering the vocational roles have the requisite skills and knowledge. Two such areas—sport management and administration and athletic training—are reviewed in this chapter. The sport sciences and sport studies are reviewed in Part 5.

Sport Management and Administration

One of the fastest-growing vocational specializations in sport, fitness, and physical education in recent years has been the area of **sport management** and administration. Sport-management programs currently attract large numbers of women and men who want a career in a sport-related field but have no interest in coaching or teaching. Many programs are now available. Some are undergraduate majors, providing a choice at that level for young men and women who traditionally might have majored in physical education. Other programs are at the master's-degree level, offering opportunity for further career development for students who have majored in physical education, business administration, or some other non–sport-related undergraduate subject.

The sport and activity industry can be divided into six segments (Miller, Stoldt, & Comfort, 2000). These are

- Professional sport entertainment (MLB, NFL, NASCAR, minor leagues, etc.)

- Amateur sport entertainment (college sport, high school sport, olympic-related events)
- Sport services (agents, event management, resorts, cruises, etc.)
- Sport and activity participation, for-profit (golf courses, bowling alleys, fitness centers, martial arts centers, etc.)
- Sport and activity goods (manufacturers, distributorships, retail, etc.)
- Sport and activity participation, nonprofit (parks and recreation, YMCA, hospital fitness, etc.)

The number of professional roles in these industry segments is quite varied and includes athletic directors, ticket agents, human resource managers, risk management, marketing, public relations, facility management, and financing/accounting. A facility manager, for example, might be employed by a university, a professional team, a community recreation department, or a resort hotel. Nearly all of these industry segments require marketing and publicity personnel. The nonprofit organizations almost always require professionals to direct and manage fund-raising.

The job opportunities are not evenly divided across the industry. Sporting goods and health and fitness management jobs appear to be most prevalent, with sports media and college athletics in the middle tier and professional sport and recreation administration in the lower tier (Miller, Stoldt, & Comfort, 2000).

In 1993 the National Association for Sport and Physical Education (NASPE) joined with the North American Society for Sport Management (NASSM) to develop competency standards for sport-management curricula at the undergraduate, master's, and doctoral levels. The core undergraduate curriculum for students in sport management includes ten competency areas: sociocultural dimensions of sport, management and leadership in sport, ethics in sport management, sport marketing, sport communications, sport finance, legal aspects of sport, economics of sport, sport governance, and a field experience in sport management. Each of these ten areas has required content that defines the minimum coverage to achieve the standard. The competency standards for the master's degree include nine areas, many of which are similar to the areas included in the undergraduate standards. Courses that fulfill these standards can be in the major department or in other departments, such as business, law, or economics.

More than 185 colleges and universities offer sport-management degrees (Miller, Stoldt, & Comfort, 2000). NASSM was founded in 1985 and has worked with NASPE to promote research, scholarship, and professional preparation in the field. Several years ago, NASSM instituted a program-approval process for undergraduate and master's programs in sport management. As of 2000, fourteen undergraduate and ten master's programs had received approval for their curricula. Currently, twenty-nine more programs are undergoing review. NASSM's official research journal is the *Journal of Sport Management,* which publishes theoretical and applied studies and articles related to sport, exercise, dance, and play.

Programs in sport management and administration often include an internship in which the student actually performs the skills necessary for the various roles. These may range from assisting an athletic director or working in a ticket office, to helping in the promotions department of a pro team. Sport management and administration programs are popular with young men and women who want a career in a sport-related vocation that is not directly in the coaching field.

Athletic Training

The most highly developed sport vocation is that of athletic trainer. The National Athletic Trainers' Association is one of the strongest of all the sport, fitness, and physical-education associations. Although athletic trainers are employed primarily by interscholastic, intercollegiate, and professional sport teams, they also find outlets for their professional services in sport medicine centers. A more detailed presentation of the purposes of **athletic training** and the requirements for certification can

Athletic trainers have become commonplace in high school and collegiate sports.

be found in Chapter 9 under the section Sports Medicine and the Rehabilitative Sciences.

Nonparticipant Sport Vocations: By Whom?

It would not be fair to complete this chapter without pointing out that the degree to which nonparticipant sport vocations are dominated by white males. The color barriers in professional and collegiate sport participation were broken several decades ago. Minority athletes now are highly visible in both collegiate and professional sport, *as participants.* Title IX more recently increased sport opportunities for girls and women, *as participants.* However, once we move beyond the roster of a team or the entries in a tournament, we much less often find minorities or women in coaching or administrative positions in sport.

When Title IX was passed in 1972, many women took coaching and administrative positions in newly expanded interscholastic and intercollegiate sport programs. In the 1980s, however, it became clear that the number of women in those roles had decreased substantially (Sisley & Capel, 1986). A recent longitudinal study at the collegiate level conducted by Vivian Acost and Linda Jean Carpenter (www.aahperd.org/nagws) shows some promising results for athletes and some disturbing results for coaching.

- All three NCAA divisions show an increased number of sports offered to women.
- The average number of women's teams per school is 8.34.
- In the last four years, 885 new teams have been added.
- There are 8,132 head coaching jobs for NCAA women's teams.
- We now have the lowest percentage of female head coaches in history (44%).
- Women filled only 10 percent of the 361 new positions in 2002.
- Division I programs are least likely to have female head administrators (8.4%).

Similar concerns have been expressed for women in officiating and in athletic administration at both collegiate and interscholastic levels.

In addition, low incidence of minority personnel in coaching and administrative positions has received substantial national publicity since the early 1990s. In response to media criticism, many professional leagues have developed specific recruitment and development programs to increase the number of minority persons in coaching and administrative positions.

Sport and Technology

Sport and technology have grown together since the early 1970s. Technology has been routinely used for years to improve athletic performance through computer simulations and comparison. The tech-

nology of strength development has changed the performance standards in most sports. Many elite athletes whose performance depends on optimum levels of strength and endurance are monitored daily through technology, and they adjust their workouts, sleep, and nutrition according to regular technological feedback from their bodily systems.

Newsgroups on the Internet and Web sites on the World Wide Web have created countless opportunities for gaining information about team and other sports. Professional basketball teams now typically have an assistant coach whose main role is to edit and splice video clips of offensive and defensive play for immediate feedback during half-time at games and for scouting in preparation for future play. Data on coaching behaviors are collected from laptop computers that can produce instant profiles for coaches and their athletes (Partridge & Franks, 1996).

For athlete recruitment, an "on line scouting network" (OSN) has been created for the World Wide Web (WWW; *Athletic Administrator,* 1996). High school athletes can register and create a comprehensive profile of their personal, academic, and athletic achievements, along with digitized photographs and digitized film clips. College recruiters and coaches can access the OSN through its Web site (http://www.osn.com) and can search the database according to different search criteria (e.g., geographical region, sport statistics, and type of sport). There is no telling how communications technologies will continue to influence sport: We can only be sure that they most certainly will exert a powerful influence.

Technology plays an increasingly important role in day-to-day coaching. For example, ARK Sports Technology has developed a portable digital video system for computers with sufficient hard-drive space to store an entire season's worth of game videos. Coaches can use this system in conjunction with the company's customized sport software to analyze and edit tapes for use with their athletes. The same firm has also developed scouting software, to be used with the video system, that allows coaches to both scout opposing teams and capture real-time video and statistics for their own team during practice or competition. The system can compile reports for team or player performance profiles, trend analyses for teams and players, and a host of sport-specific information (for example, serve, pass, set, attack, block, and defense statistics for volleyball). Although such systems are used mostly in elite sport at the moment, one can expect that they will become more readily available at all levels in the next decade.

The largest bibliographic database on sport is available through SPORTDiscus, developed by the Sport Information Research Centre (SIRC) in Canada (www.sportdiscus.com). SPORTDiscus contains more than 500,000 references, 20,000 theses and dissertations, and 10,000 Web site addresses. Each month SIRC examines more than 1,200 magazines and journals, from practical to scholarly, to compile references related to sport, sport medicine, physical fitness, sport administration, coaching, PE, sport law, physical therapy, and recreation. The system can be researched easily and quickly using key word indicators to guide the search. SPORTDiscus is often available through university libraries or through a variety of fee-based services.

SUMMARY

1. The sport culture of America is one of the most highly developed in the world. It extends from children's sport through age-group competition in masters-level sport.

2. All statistics—those on participation, attendance, money spent on leisure, coverage in the media, equipment, and cultural norms—indicate the growing size and importance of sport in American culture.

3. The idea that leisure abounds in contemporary American culture is a myth. Especially among the professional and business class—the group that is most involved in sport—much less leisure time is available than during most periods in history.

4. Sport participation can be classified as recreational, amateur, nonprofessional, and professional, with distinctions based on the degree of institutionalization of the sport involvement and the relationship of the involvement to monetary gain.

5. Participation in organized, nonschool sport for children and youths has grown substantially since the mid-1950s, with even stronger growth patterns for girls in the more recent past.

6. Organized sport for children begins as early as 3 years of age, with an average early-entry age of 5.8 years and an average entry age of 11 years.

7. Child and youth sport has developed in the United States almost entirely in the local government and private-community sectors, with major organizational entities at the state and national levels.

8. Child and youth sport tends to be exclusionary, in the sense that opportunity for participation decreases as young adolescents grow into their teens.

9. Coaching for child and youth sport is mostly volunteer, with little control or certification of people who coach.

10. Countries that have a stronger federal involvement in child and youth sport tend to have coach-certification programs at various levels.

11. Interscholastic sport is regulated at the state level and occupies a place in the American sport culture unlike that in any other nation, with more than 5 million boys and girls participating annually.

12. Most states have adopted a classification scheme that grades competition based on school enrollment. Financing differs from state to state, from full funding out of tax revenues to a model wherein most athletic funds have to be raised by boosters or earned in gate receipts.

13. Few states require any coaching certification beyond a valid teaching certificate; some states do not have any requirements; and only a few states require special certification in coaching.

14. Intercollegiate sport is primarily an American institution. Colleges and universities typically form leagues and affiliate voluntarily with a national governing organization, such as the NCAA or the NAIA.

15. College and university competition is classified by size of school and by the degree of funding available to athletes.

16. Professional sport actually involves a relatively small number of athletes, who typically have short careers and whose pay scales within a given sport are uneven.

17. Professional sport is organized through parent organizations typically run by a commissioner but with the real power retained by owners.

18. Organized recreational sport is implemented through recreation departments, businesses, service clubs, and private community organizations. The range and amount of participation are extremely diversified.

19. The enactment of federal legislation in the 1970s has greatly expanded the sport opportunities for people with disabilities. The scope of these people's sport involvement now rivals that of people without disabilities. The best-known example of these programs is the Special Olympics.

20. Masters sport is organized in 5-year age groups for people over age 40 years. It has recently experienced substantial growth, especially in road racing, track and field, and swimming.

21. With the institutionalization of sport in the twentieth century, a number of nonparticipant sport vocations developed, some of which require special preparation and certification.

22. Sport management and administration is the fastest-growing nonparticipant sport vocation. Many undergraduate and graduate programs are available throughout the country.

23. Athletic training is the most highly developed sport-related profession. Specific undergraduate and graduate programs lead to certification, which is typically necessary for entry into the vocation.

24. Nonparticipant sport vocations are dominated by white males; women and minorities continue to be underrepresented.

25. Technology has an impact on sport by providing more access to information and by offering highly sophisticated analysis of physiology, fitness, competitive strategy, and many other aspects of sport.

DISCUSSION QUESTIONS

1. In what ways do participating and spectating positively and negatively influence each other?

2. What would be the benefits and liabilities of increasing local, state, and federal government involvement in child and youth sport?

3. What would school sport be like if it were based on an inclusionary, rather than an exclusionary, model?

4. If a program for coaching certification were to be required, what criteria would you want coaches to meet?

5. What opportunities are available to athletes between the ages of 18 and 23 years to continue to develop in their sport if they do not go to college and are not skilled enough to be hired as professional athletes?

6. How should school sport be financed? How should recreational sport be financed?

7. How does the sport experience differ for (a) the athlete with a disability, (b) the masters athlete, (c) the scholarship athlete, and (d) the child athlete?

8. In what ways will the quality of preparation for nonparticipant vocations in sport be related to the future development of sport?

CHAPTER 7

Problems and Issues in Sport

My high school coach forced me to run intervals until I vomited. I did both, exceedingly well, and after graduation turned my back on running for more than a decade. Not much has changed. Too many high school coaches still follow the same prescriptions.

James C. McCullagh, Editor, *Runner's World*

My high school coach was short, white and out of shape— different than me. But he cared about me even though I wasn't the best player on our team. And it's a good thing too. Because nobody else was looking out for me then, and I needed his help more than once.

Former athlete and current school coach, from Coakley (1994, p. 189)

Sports teach, it is their nature. They teach fairness or cheating, teamwork or selfishness, compassion or coldness.

Wilfred Sheed, 1995

LEARNING OBJECTIVES

- To analyze the manner in which cooperation and competition are important to good sport participation
- To describe features and practices that provide developmentally appropriate competition
- To discuss major issues related to child and youth sport, interschool sport, and intercollegiate sport

- To analyze equity issues in sport at all levels
- To describe different sport systems and discuss how each one's goals, organization, and finance are related
- To describe myths related to sport participation and analyze their validity

Chapter 5 stressed the positive aspects of sport, the fundamental meanings of sport involvement, and the beauty that can be seen and experienced in sport participation. I argued that sport developed from play and was most meaningful when the sport experience was playful. Sport was also described as a natural religion highlighting excellence and competence, to which players and fans alike can become committed.

Chapter 6 emphasized the degree to which sport has become central to American culture in the past several generations and how it now extends from early childhood opportunities to masters sport. We also saw how sport has expanded to include greater participation by previously underrepresented populations: women, minorities, and people with disabling conditions.

The argument for the goodness and beauty of sport having been made, it is now time to examine the problems and issues that plague sport, that threaten to detract from and diminish its fundamental goodness and beauty. The task will not be difficult: The abundant and widespread problems have been widely publicized.

Many of the positive benefits of sport participation that historically have been claimed by sport enthusiasts have been questioned frequently and increasingly over the past several decades. In newspaper and magazine articles, in books, and on television, the problems in sport have been revealed and analyzed: drugs, abusive coaches, athletes who cheat to gain an advantage, crippling injuries, illegal payments, sexual abuse, gender inequities, racism, and others. If you are interested in sport, particularly if you are interested in a career in a sport-related profession, it is important that you understand these issues and problems, are acquainted with the facts surrounding them, and form a point of view that is professionally defensible and will help to make sport better. Sport experiences can be a positive influence on the development of young people. Sport can have positive effects on both adolescents and adults. But sport experiences can also be devastatingly injurious to young people, physically, psychologically, and emotionally, if handled irresponsibly. The adults who plan and implement sport programs for children and adults are the ones responsible for seeing that positive influences are more likely to occur than negative influences. If sport is to be a constructive experience for youths, it is the values, knowledge, and skills of the adults in charge that will determine that outcome.

All the contemporary scrutiny of sport—of sport's purposes and its accomplishments—has shown two things clearly: First, sport has become vitally important in the culture—unimportant issues do not attract that kind of attention. Second, there is an underside to sport to which we need to attend, lest the sport culture weaken. The purpose of this chapter is to review major issues and problems in sport, at all levels, with the main intention of identifying practices and programs that help to make sport better for participants and for the culture in general.

SPORT PROBLEMS OR GENERAL SOCIAL PROBLEMS?

There are many social problems in society, and there are many people who participate in sport. Inevitably, some sport participants fall prey to some of those social problems. A basketball player dies from a drug overdose. A football player is arrested for participating in a robbery. A tennis player is arrested for driving while intoxicated. A baseball player is sentenced to jail for failing to pay child support. Most of these stories are reported on the sport pages of our daily newspapers and in the sport segments of our daily television news shows. The question is, Are these sport stories or stories about social problems that happen to involve sport participants?

I contend that these stories are about pervasive social problems that happen to involve sport participants. Most of the evidence suggests that youths who participate in sport are *less likely* to be involved in such problems than their nonparticipating peers. In this chapter, I confine the discussion to problems that are specific to sport, while recognizing that all problems are interrelated at some level.

COOPERATION AND COMPETITION

A major criticism of sport at all levels is that it is too competitive. Every time a serious sport abuse occurs, someone is bound to suggest that sport should be *less* competitive or that *noncompetitive* games should replace sport activities. Because that criticism is made of all sport, from children's sport all the way to professional and Olympic sport, we deal with it first.

In Chapter 5, the concept of competition was considered at length. Competition, I argued, has meaning as a festival, as a striving for competence, and as rivalry. The rivalry in competition is seldom a zero-sum arrangement in which someone *has* to lose to the extent that someone else has won. Sports are games and contests in which there is competition. A noncompetitive sport should be a contradiction in terms. The concept of competition, in its *pure* sense, has a positive valence. Clearly, however, the goal of good, appropriate competition is not always realized.

What makes any competition *good*? First, it should manifest the characteristics of play. Competition should be even, voluntary, and strictly governed by rules. Perhaps most important, although competitors can strive seriously *within* the competition, the consequences of winning and losing *outside* the competition should not be important. Good competition is *good* primarily for the participants, not necessarily for the onlookers (parents, fans, the public).

What makes any competition *appropriate*? First, the rules must respect the developmental characteristics of the participants. So, too, must the equipment, the size of the field, and the length of the game or contest. Second, the psychological climate of the competition must be developmentally appropriate. No one expects a neighborhood adult-

league softball game to be a blood-and-guts setting. Why should a Little League football game be so?

In good, **appropriate competition,** participants are bound up in a cooperative effort. They learn as much about cooperation as they do about competition. Even in individual sports, the two competitors have to cooperate to have a good competition. In dual and team sports, the cooperation necessary to perform well is at least as obvious and important to the outcome as is the competition between opponents. A good individual performance in basketball does not make a good game, any more than a good performance by an actress makes a good play or a good performance by a violin section makes a good symphony.

Thus, cooperation among and between athletes is fundamental to good, appropriate competition. Furthermore, it is good, appropriate competition that is most satisfying to participants. Clearly, there *are* instances—far too many, in fact—where zero-sum competition is *imposed* on athletes. (I am convinced that athletes almost never *choose* to view their competition as zero-sum.) Here is what a former college football player said about his experience:

> The ceaseless . . . competition, with the serious consequences of failing, made for uneasy friendships and increasing isolation. Since we believed that the "winning–losing" distinction separated men from "others," we were put in a very uncomfortable bind. To be a winner meant to make some of our friends losers. . . . It was hard to escape the guilt. (Shaw, 1972, p. 67)

Imposing that kind of situation on a young man with an athletic scholarship is bad enough. Doing something similar to an 11-year-old boy or girl in children's sport is shamefully inappropriate.

Athletes, I believe, tend to react negatively to being put in that situation by friends, fans, parents, or coaches. Olympic high jumper Doug Nordquist showed the degree to which athletes often view competition in terms of performing well: "I train to jump high. Not to beat people, but to jump high" (Wiley, 1987, p. 52). At the 1984 Olympic Games in

Los Angeles, Nordquist jumped 7 feet, 6 inches, to earn a fifth-place finish. He wept afterward, but not because he did not win a medal.

> I always jumped because I could jump, not because I was obligated. All those people, the Olympic Games . . . it was unbelievable, just making the team. Then all the medal counts, the gold-or-nothing attitudes. It bothered me. I made seven-six. I waved. I was so happy to jump that high. I wanted to make sure people knew that I was proud to be fifth. (Wiley, 1987, p. 52)

Children do not like being put in zero-sum situations. Research on young athletes has shown that competence, affiliation, and fun are more important enduring motivations for their participation than is winning. If you listen to elite athletes talk about their competition, you are much more likely to hear about their hopes to perform well, or up to their capability, than about their wishes to win the competition. Children, youths, and elite athletes all try to win—that is one of the main purposes of the competition or contest. What is most important is that people who are in leadership positions with athletes do as much as possible to make sure that the competitions are good and appropriate for them. If that would happen more, the number of casualties of inappropriate competition would be reduced to near zero.

CHILD AND YOUTH SPORT

There are many critics of child and youth sport, some of whom would like to see organized sport abolished for children under a certain age (14 years, or 11 years, or 8 years, depending on the critic). Martens (1986) summarized the strengths of child and youth sport as follows:

1. Millions of children are playing and enjoying sport.

2. Diverse programs are available in many sports, at many skill levels, and for many age groups.

Children need appropriate coaching and supervision as they learn sport.

3. Sport is increasingly available to children regardless of race, gender, or socioeconomic status.

4. Sport is typically safe, with low injury rates compared with the rates in unorganized activity.

5. Sport is well funded, mostly on a voluntary basis.

6. Sport facilities are good to excellent.

The major problems and issues in child and youth sport result from the following:

1. Premature entry into organized sport (when children are too young)

2. Overuse injuries

3. Sports that are developmentally inappropriate

4. Specialization

5. Lack of training of coaches

6. Outside pressure to win from coaches and parents

7. Impact of sport on family life

8. Children and youths dropping out of sport programs

9. Unequal access based on socioeconomic status

We consider each of these problems in this section.

Premature Entry into Organized Sport

Most scientific experts (psychologists, pediatricians, etc.) suggest that children should not begin organized sport before the age of 8 years (Martens, 1986). That suggestion is based more on psychological than on physiological concerns. Children typically develop the ability to compare themselves with others in order to understand their own competence at about 5 or 6 years of age and learn competition as an individual social motivation around age 7 (Passer, 1986). Thus, the social and psychological abilities necessary to cooperate with teammates and to compete in games are typically underdeveloped in children before age 8.

This does not mean that younger children cannot participate in skill-oriented programs that have elements of loosely organized competition. It does mean, however, that persisting teams, standings, championships, won–loss records, and the like are inappropriate for young children because they are developmentally not ready for those adult-related features of sport. Many user-fee programs for young children and many recreational programs in communities have begun to recognize that young children need activity, and these programs are providing mostly noncompetitive, developmentally appropriate opportunities for activity.

Overuse Injuries

Many children now take part in sport quite early, and in some cases, such as gymnastics, they do it nearly year-round. *Overuse injuries* are caused by repeated stresses on joints or muscles from doing the same activities for long periods of time. The

---

What Kids Want to Tell Parents and Spectators

- Don't yell out instructions—then I can't concentrate on what the coach says.
- Don't put down the officials—that embarrasses me.
- Don't yell at me or the coach—that takes away from my fun.
- Don't put down my teammates—that hurts team spirit.
- Don't put down the other team—you're not being a good sport.
- Don't lose your temper—that embarrasses me too.
- Don't lecture me after the game—I've messed up, I already feel bad.
- Don't forget the things I did well—I'm proud of them.

- Don't forget it's just a game—I need to be reminded of that sometimes too.

Resources for Positive Spectating and Parenting in Sport

- Positive Coaching Alliance— www.positivecoach.org
- National Alliance for Youth Sports— www.nays.org
- Gatorade's "Playbook for Kids"— 1-877-PLAYKIDS
- Character Counts Sports— www.charactercounts.org
- The Center for Sports Parenting— www.sportsparenting.org
- Citizenship Through Sports— www.sportsmanship.org

SOURCE: Gatorade's "Playbook for Kids: A Parent's Guide to Help Kids Get the Most Out of Sports."

concern for children is particularly related to **epiphyseal injury.** As children develop, bone growth takes place through primary ossification in the bone center and secondary ossification at the end of the bone, a growth center termed the *epiphysis.* Eventually, in adolescence, the two loci for growth fuse, and the bone is fully developed. Before that time, however, injury at the epiphysis is serious because of the risk of permanent disability. A typical example is the increasing number of permanent wrist injuries among young gymnasts; similarly, injury to the tibial (lower-leg bone) physis may inhibit permanent bone growth. Both may lead to permanent anatomic change.

Sport participation for children and youths should be educational and should lead to a lifetime commitment to physical activity. Duquin (1998) has suggested that what she calls "sado-asceticism" has crept into child and youth sport too frequently. Too many adults proclaim a "no pain, no gain" ethic for practice, training, and participation. Duquin, however, argues that the wisdom of the body and the wisdom of childhood are to avoid pain, that "no pain is sane," and that children typically quit when they get hurt. The asceticism she describes as having crept into organized youth sport in recent years is to redefine pain as discomfort and to encourage young athletes to work through the "discomfort." As she so eloquently states: "Adults may choose to sacrifice their bodies for their perceptions of truth. In youth sport, the 'truths' are those of adults, the sacrificial bodies are those of children" (p. 35).

Developmentally Inappropriate Sport

To make sports most fun and useful for children and youths, we must modify them so that they are developmentally appropriate. There is seldom any situation in which children or youths should play the *parent* form of a game. The younger, less skilled, or less developed the participant, the more the game or contest needs to be modified to make it appropriate.

Modified games serve three important purposes. First, changes in rules, dimensions of playing

Swimmers sometimes train year-round from childhood through adolescence.

area, and equipment allow younger participants to develop skills more quickly and efficiently. Second, the changed game is more exciting, fun, and rewarding to the participants. Third, rules can be developed to ensure that all participants have equal opportunities to learn and play the sport.

There are endless ways to modify games to make them more developmentally appropriate for children—lowered baskets, smaller balls, smaller fields, simplified rules, reduced or eliminated contact, slightly deflated balls, friendly pitchers, and changed scoring rules, to mention a few. Rules demanding that all team members play an equal portion of the game ensure that all children profit equally from the experience.

As children gain skills and the ability to cooperate in more complex strategy play, games can change to approximate the adult form. This change must be gradual so that participants can continue to improve and to enjoy their participation.

Green (1997) described an alternative approach to sport for young children. A coed soccer program for young children had no formal competition, no league standings, no trophies, and no statistics. Play leaders led the coed play groups through a progression of soccer games over the course of the season. Each game emphasized one or more soccer skills and strategies while maximizing the number of times players touched the ball. There were no drills or scrimmages, just games. In this sense, the games became the teachers.

Research suggests that during informal, player-controlled games, children have four main interests (Coakley, 1994): (1) They like action, especially action leading to scoring; (2) they want personal involvement in the action; (3) they want a close score; and (4) they use games to reaffirm friendships. As sports become more institutionalized, games and competition become more adult controlled, and the children who play them become more concerned with game outcomes, what position they play, and the rules. Sport must bridge those two sets of interests by making sure that sport has action, that children have the opportunity to score often, that all children are involved, and that friendships among children are valued by the adults who control the sport experience. There is no need to romanticize informal play, since many not-so-good things happen in informal games, too. Nonetheless, children's sport must start as *children's* sport and gradually become more complex and formalized as children's play gradually changes to more adult forms of play.

Specialization

Not too many years ago, athletes did not often specialize in a sport until college; even at the collegiate level, many athletes participated in more than one sport. In high schools, many boys played on a different sport team during each of the three major seasons of the school year. (Girls typically did not have the opportunity, or they probably would have done so also!) What used to be common even 25 years ago is now rare. What is more common now is the *sport specialist,* the athlete who trains year-round for his or her sport. Is it the children and youths who want to specialize to this extent, or is it the parents and coaches who encourage them to do so?

Early specialization is now common in many sports. Gymnasts and swimmers train year-round from an early age. Ten-year-old hockey players play

ninety games in a season, and young figure skaters train 60 hours per week. The potential for overuse injuries in these situations is alarmingly high, and some of those injuries lead to permanent disabilities. In school sport, specialization has become common recently, primarily because of the advent of year-round strength training in some sports and year-round endurance training in others. Young athletes compete for their school, then compete in local or regional leagues in the off-season, and perhaps go to a specialized sport camp in the summer.

Not only do young athletes specialize in a single sport, but in some cases, they specialize in a single position within that sport; thus, a young boy might be solely a quarterback, with year-round training, camps, and the like; or a young girl might be an outside hitter in volleyball, following a similar year-round training and competition regimen (Gough, 1995). The better the athletes, the more likely they are to specialize. A primary liability of such specialization is the risk of burnout, a state where the athlete simply tires of doing the same thing over and over for years in a row. Is specialization inappropriate? For those who survive, there is little doubt that it breeds talented elite athletes. However, is the price paid by the many who drop out along the way worth the enhanced skill of the few who excel? There are few issues in child and youth sport about which there is more debate and for which there is less good evidence.

Lack of Adequate Training of Coaches

In the American system, child and youth sport coaches are almost always volunteers—and they almost always lack any specific training to coach children and youth. Research on volunteer coaches is sparse, but what has been done shows that they too often behave in ways that are not productive for young athletes—too much evaluation, too much criticism, too few supportive interactions (Eitzen & Sage, 2003). Research also shows that they can change (Smith, Smoll, & Curtis, 1978). Out of that research grew a model for preparing volunteer coaches called "Coach Effectiveness Training"

(Smoll, 1986), which has influenced most of the coaching-education programs now in use throughout the world. The philosophy of this program comprises four parts:

1. Winning is not everything, nor is it the only thing; that is, winning is an important goal, but not the *only* goal.

2. Failure is not the same as losing; therefore, losing does not need to imply personal failure in any way.

3. Success is not synonymous with winning; therefore, winning does not relate directly to a sense of personal triumph any more than losing relates to personal failure.

4. Success is found in striving for victory and is related to effort as much as or more than to the outcome of the contest or game.

That should stand in sharp contrast to the "winning is the only thing" ethic that seems to pervade so much of elite sport. Slogans such as "winning isn't everything, it is the only thing" are too common in sport and are wholly inappropriate for child and youth sport. Teaching research has shown for many years that patterns of negative interactions with, shaming of, and belittling of students are *always* associated with lessened achievement and lowered self-concepts (Siedentop & Tannehill, 2000).

There are good examples throughout the world—Australia and New Zealand being particularly exemplary—of efforts to better prepare volunteer coaches. The training need not be long and tedious. It should focus primarily on developmental considerations and appropriate ways to interact with children and youths so that their sport experience is positive. The American Sport Education Program (ASEP) has a Basic Education course for volunteer coaches. The YMCA now uses ASEP for all its volunteer coaches. The effort to provide reasonably qualified coaches for children and youths is far from being achieved. Thirty-three national sport governing agencies have endorsed the coaching guidelines developed by the Youth Sport Coalition of the Na-

tional Association for Sport and Physical Education (NASPE) but none *requires* its coaches to meet those guidelines (Siedentop, 1996c).

Outside Pressure to Win

Children and youths most often play hard to win—as they should. When the game or contest is over, however, they typically want to get on with whatever else is fun to do in their lives. Research (Orlick, 1986) indicates that children mention three things when asked what they would change about their sport experience. First, they all want to play—sitting around waiting to get into a game is not their idea of having a good time. Second, they want the sports to be modified so that they can play better. Third, they want less emphasis from outside on winning—which means they want to enjoy the fun of the competition without being hassled by coaches and parents.

The outside pressures probably account for the main reasons that children and youths drop out of sport. "Having fun" is the main reason children get involved in sport, and "lack of fun" is the main reason they cite for dropping out. As most other research confirms, children do not see winning as a primary benefit of sport participation, ranking it far behind fun, improved skills, being part of a team, staying in shape, and the challenge of competition (Eitzen & Sage, 2003). Children and youths who drop out of sport indicate that they might not have done so if practices had been more fun, coaches had understood them better, there had been less pressure, and there had been less conflict with other parts of their lives.

Nothing will diminish the playful nature of competition more than pressures that make winning a game or contest important *outside* the context of the game or contest. Parents and coaches too often want to replay games, talk about losses, and make all of that important after the game—in the locker room, at the dinner table, at the next practice. That imposes adult values on children—for whom they are inappropriate.

Impact of Sport on Family Life

During the years in which their young children participate in sport, many families have to totally readjust their lives (Harrington, 1998). That is particularly true for parents whose sons or daughters are skilled enough to make the "traveling" or "select" team. Participation costs can become substantial, especially for sports that require indoor facilities (winter soccer, ice hockey, etc.). Summer camps have become the norm rather than the exception. Some parents put 40,000 miles on the family car taking sons or daughters to away competitions. There are early mornings and late nights. The family seldom is able to have a meal together. Parents can get very intense about the participation and performance of their sons or daughters and their team. Although most parents willingly support all those endeavors because they believe them to be beneficial to the development of their children, there is no doubt that severe dislocation of family life can occur.

Dropping Out by Children and Youths

Although an estimated 20 million children and youths (ages 6–15 years) participate in organized sport outside school, about one third of those youngsters drop out of sport each year. The estimate may be a bit misleading because some boys and girls drop out of one sport but enter another; that is, they shift sports. Others may drop out for a time, then reenter. Regardless, the dropout percentage is far too high for activities that are thought to be educationally and developmentally appropriate.

Children and youths drop out of sport for a variety of reasons, including conflict of interest, in that they have something else to do; lack of success, improvement, or fun; overemphasis on winning and excessive pressures from parents or coaches; negative reactions to adults who coach them; and injuries. In most cases, youngsters become more likely to drop out when the disadvantages or negative aspects of their sport experience begin to outweigh the advantages or positive aspects of their

sport experience. What can be done? Clearly, attention needs to be paid to all the aforementioned reasons.

Unequal Access Based on Socioeconomic Status

Opportunity to participate in child and youth sport in the United States is not offered on a level playing field. Opportunity is strongly tilted toward the daughters and sons of the middle and upper socioeconomic classes. The Carnegie Council on Adolescent Development (1992) found that boys and girls from lower-social-status communities were seriously underserved in all forms of childhood and youth services, including sport opportunities. They concluded that "young adolescents who live in low-income neighborhoods are most likely to benefit from supportive youth development services; yet they are the very youth who have least access to such programs and organizations" (p. 12). The Center for the Study of Sport in Society at Northeastern University (www.sportinsociety.org) estimates that 15 percent of urban children and youths participate in youth sport programs, as compared with 85–90 percent of their suburban counterparts. That makes a mockery of the concept of a "level playing field" in child and youth development.

If we believe that appropriately planned and conducted sport experiences for children and youths are developmentally and educationally valuable, and the evidence strongly supports that belief, then we must all work to see that such experiences are available to all youngsters, whether they are rich or poor. (See the box on children's rights in sport on page 144.)

Aussie Sports: An Example of a National Program

As noted in Chapter 6, child and youth sport in America has developed without much involvement of the federal or state governments. Local government is sometimes involved through community recreation programs, but most child and youth sport operates out of the private sector. Other countries have taken a different approach, and it is

---

Children's Bill of Rights in Sport

Children in sport should have the right

- To participate regardless of ability level
- To participate at a level commensurate with their development
- To have qualified adult leadership
- To participate in safe and healthy environments

- To share in leadership and decision making
- To play as a child and not as an adult
- To receive proper preparation for participation
- To have equal opportunity to strive for success
- To be trained with dignity
- To have fun

SOURCE: Adapted from *Youth Sports Guide*, by J. Thomas, 1977; American Alliance for Health, Physical Education, Recreation and Dance.

---

useful to close this section by looking at one such program from Australia.

The **Aussie Sports** program is a comprehensive national program that offers all children, in their last 3 years of elementary school, a diversified and improved quality of sport participation. Aussie Sports was established in 1984 by the Australian Sports Commission, the Australian federal government's primary advisor on sport development. The stated goals of Aussie Sports are these:

1. To improve the quality, quantity, and variety of sport activities available to Australian children

2. To provide *all* children with the opportunity to participate in appropriate sport activities

3. To encourage participation and skill development in a variety of sports

4. To reduce the emphasis on winning at all costs and to promote enjoyment and good competition through participation in sport

5. To improve the quality of sport instruction available to Australian children

This national program has devised a series of *modified* sports that are taught to children. Parental and community involvement is encouraged and promoted. The program can be implemented at a school, through a community agency, or through a sport club. An awards scheme has been devised wherein children work toward a series of awards on the basis of participation rather than achievement,

but participation points can be earned only through organized and supervised practice sessions.

All schools, clubs, or agencies that participate in the program are eligible to receive a number of resources to help them implement the program, including an activities manual, a resource video, wall charts, logbooks, awards (certificates, badges, stickers, etc.), and medallions. An Aussie Sports Coaching Program has been initiated to help physical-education teachers, parents, and local volunteers to administer the program and to coach within it. The 4- to 6-hour coach-training program focuses on child development related to sport, safety, sport injuries, basic sport skills, the modified-game concept, and practice activities.

Aussie Sports has also created a series of *behavior codes* that provide fairly specific guidelines for all involved. Behavior codes exist for administrators, officials, coaches, parents, spectators, teachers, media, and players. The players' code of behavior shows the spirit of the program. (See the box on Aussie Sports.)

SCHOOL SPORT

Interscholastic sport for boys and girls is a major part of the American sport culture and provides a significant experience for many who take part in it. The large, diversified interscholastic sport program is unique to the American junior-high and high

---

Aussie Sports: Players' Code of Behavior

- Play for the fun of it, and not just to please parents and coaches.
- Play by the rules.
- Never argue with an official. If you disagree, have your captain or coach approach the official during a break or after a game.
- Control your temper. Verbal abuse of officials or other players, deliberate fouling or provoking an opponent, and throwing equipment are not acceptable or permitted in any sport.

- Work equally hard for yourself and for your team. Your team's performance will benefit, and so will you.
- Be a good sport. Cheer all good plays, whether they be by your team or by the other team.
- Treat all players as you would like to be treated. Do not interfere with, bully, or take unfair advantage of another player.
- Cooperate with your coach, teammates, and opponents. Without them, there would be no game.

SOURCE: Adapted from Australian Sports Commission, Canberra, Australia.

---

school model. Most high schools have teams at the junior varsity and varsity levels in a variety of sports. Larger schools, or schools in states where interschool sports are funded directly through the general budget, often have freshman, reserve (composed of mostly sophomore players), junior varsity, and varsity teams.

Many people are rightfully proud of the interscholastic sports model in the United States, the opportunities it provides youths to grow in a sport, and the cohesive force it creates in a school or community. *School spirit* is often shown in support for sport teams. In many communities throughout the nation, the high school team and its falling or rising fortunes provide a focal point around which the entire community coalesces. Like other parts of the sport culture, however, school sport is not without problems. We address those problems in this section.

The major problems and issues in interscholastic sport are as follows:

1. The exclusionary varsity model of interschool sport

2. Injuries in certain sports, especially football

3. Eligibility and pass-to-play rules

4. Specialization

5. Performance-enhancing supplements

6. The coach as teacher–coach

7. Parental pressures, especially via booster clubs

8. Pay-to-play plans

Exclusion and the Varsity Model

If you examine participation in child and youth sport in America, you see a triangle, with broad-based participation at the bottom (i.e., child and youth sport) and less participation in interscholastic sport (ages 14 to 18). As I have explained, sport for children is programmed primarily through community sources and is widely available. Sport for high school–aged youths is programmed mostly through the school and is *decreasingly* available as the youths get older. This tendency to make participation less available (or available only to the better players) is known as the **varsity model** of competition, and it is the dominant feature of American school sport.

Many children in communities across the nation play soccer or baseball when they are young, often continuing their competition until they are 12 or 13 years of age. Even small communities have a

The Benefits of Interscholastic Sport

As we examine problems in interscholastic sport, it is important to show that there is good evidence that school sport has benefits for many participants and the school.

- Better grades
- Better self-concept
- Higher educational aspirations
- Stronger sense of personal control
- More likely to eat healthy diet
- Less likely to used banned substances

There is also descriptive and anecdotal evidence that interschool sports can indeed create what we traditionally have called school spirit.

"Interschool sports competition, then, is a means of unifying the entire school. Different races, social classes, fraternities, teachers, school staff, and students unite in a common cause. . . . An athletic program sometimes keeps potentially hostile segments from fragmenting the school. The collective following of an athletic team can also lift morale, thereby serving to unify the school" (Eitzen & Sage, 2003, p. 93).

The high school varsity model produces elite athletes but excludes most students from the opportunity to participate.

soccer league or a Little League baseball competition involving many children. The same communities, however, each have only *one* school team—or perhaps one reserve team and one varsity team. What happens to the further participation of all of those soccer and baseball players? The answer in most communities is *very little*!

The nature of an *exclusionary* model of sport development is that the entire system acts to identify and eventually cater to the more highly skilled player. Those players who are excluded have few opportunities to continue to develop in a sport, at least not until they are old enough to take part in more adult-oriented recreational sport. Adolescence is the time when boys and girls develop many, varied interests. Thus, we should not expect that they all will want necessarily to continue to develop within a certain sport or to try a new one. The issue here is *opportunity*, and unless a child is good enough for a varsity team, she or he has little opportunity to continue to develop in a sport in the current varsity model.

This varsity system is different from the traditional European *club* system, where sport is programmed through community clubs and the opportunity to continue to learn and compete is routinely made available based on interest. If a soccer club or a baseball club has enough interest among a 14- to 18-year-old group, the A teams and B teams are organized, and competition is arranged. The club system is more *inclusionary*.

School Sport Injuries

In discussing children's sport earlier, I mentioned that injury rates are fairly low, compared with injury rates in unorganized activities. The same may be true for school sport, although accurate comparative data are difficult to obtain. High school sport in most places, however, is more highly specialized, with more rigorous training and competition than ever before. Inevitably, injuries occur.

The National Athletic Trainers' Association (www. nata.org) released the results of a 3-year study of injuries among high school athletes. Among their more interesting findings were these:

- More injuries occured in practice than during competitions.
- Football had the highest rate of injury; volleyball had the lowest.
- More than 73 percent of injuries restricted players fewer than eight days.
- The highest percentage of knee injuries occurred in girls' soccer, the lowest in baseball.
- Of the injuries requiring surgery, more than 60 percent were to the knee.

It is also clear that there are fewer injuries and reinjuries when schools employ a full-time athletic trainer (Rankin, 1989). The fact that more injuries occur in practice presents problems because medical care is less readily available than at games.

Preventive techniques are more widely available than ever, but it is uncertain how often they are employed. Many state high school athletic associations have created rules that are prevention oriented—for example, restrictions on what wrestlers can do to fit into a particular weight class and on what football teams can do on very hot, humid summer days.

School football injuries, however, remain a serious concern. Nearly 64 percent of high school football players will be injured sometime during the season, of which 37 percent will sideline the athlete temporarily (Rowe & Miller, 1991). Of even greater concern is that 43 percent of the injuries require surgery. Trends suggest that the number of injuries is lessening but that the incidence of *major* injuries—those that keep an athlete out of competition for at least 3 weeks—is increasing slightly (Dorsey, 1988).

In other sports, the injury problems are moderate and consist mainly of overuse injuries, especially in sports where athletes train year-round, thus subjecting certain joints and muscle groups to continuous stress. Increasingly, it appears that more knowledgeable coaches and athletic trainers are the best hope for future control of injuries. The National Athletic Trainers' Association estimates that fewer than 15 percent of the nation's high schools employ certified athletic trainers.

Eligibility and Pass-to-Play Rules

In almost all high schools, students have to meet eligibility standards to be on a school team. Many athletic-eligibility standards go well beyond criteria a student is required to meet to stay in school. In recent years, many states have instituted new *pass-to-play* eligibility standards, producing even more stringent requirements for athletes to maintain their eligibility.

In some cases, these more stringent eligibility standards have been legislated because of abuses in school sport. The issue is not whether abuses should be tolerated. The issue is how abuses should be remedied. The more fundamental issue in eligibility rules, however, has little to do with abuses. Instead, it has to do with one's basic view of the educational importance of school sport.

If school sport is an extracurricular activity, a privilege to be earned, then, clearly, eligibility rules are appropriate. If, however, school sport has basic educational value, then why deny the experience to anybody who is legitimately a student at a school? If being on a team provides an important set of experiences for personal and social development, then why should that opportunity for development be denied to some students?

As you can see, this argument is also related to the exclusionary issue discussed previously. The same logic prevails. If school sport is such a strong developmental experience for adolescent boys and girls, why not make it more widely available so that more students can benefit? It is true that there are important economic issues here also. Could we afford—or, more accurately, would we be willing to pay for—a greatly expanded school sport program? Despite the economic overtones, however, some

---

Ideas for Reforming High School Sport

Some high schools now play an almost national schedule. Coaches get shoe contracts. Games are televised. Players are recruited. Like college sports, high school sports are headed toward commercialization. What do you think of the following suggestions to reform high school sport?

- Schedule teams only in your own area.
- Eliminate postseason all-star games.
- Prohibit shoe companies and other corporate influences from compensating schools and coaches.
- Make eligibility rules academically defensible.

- Require coaches to be teachers having the same rights and responsibilities as other teachers.
- Develop sports programs that encourage participation by having more teams than just varsity and reserve.
- Allow students more direct involvement in decisions about their sport experience.
- Prohibit national televising of high school contests.

Which of those suggestions do you agree with? Which do you disagree with? What would you add to the reform list?

SOURCE: Adapted from Eitzen & Sage, 2003.

---

important philosophical issues are at stake in this debate.

Specialization

The problem of specialization was discussed in the section on child and youth sport. The issue is similar for school sport, with one added dimension. Athletes in high schools do specialize much more today than they did even as recently as the mid-1980s. Many athletes compete in one sport only and train for that sport in the off-season, sometimes attending a specialized summer camp. Sport specialization at the high school level seems to be related to two important developments in the American sport culture in recent years.

First, the value and importance of weight and endurance training has been widely recognized. For many school athletes, an off-season spent in the weight room is more important than is training for and competing in another sport. Many coaches promote this view—some directly demanding it, others more tacitly encouraging it. Second, many high school athletes have hopes for an athletic scholarship to a college or university. The number of

scholarships available has increased dramatically since the mid-1980s. To be as competitive as possible in the scholarship area, many high school athletes forgo multisport competition in favor of specialization.

Is specialization good or bad? As I said before, there are few issues in sport about which there is more heated debate—and for which there is less solid evidence. At this time, at least, the debate is more philosophical than scientific.

Performance-Enhancing Supplements

In the summer of 1998, Mark McGwire broke the single-season home-run record in Major League baseball and became the symbolic center of the debate surrounding the dietary supplement creatine. Creatine, which supposedly increases muscular performance in brief, high-intensity activities, is available over the counter and is now widely used by adolescent athletes. It is just one of a number of dietary supplements that are purported to enhance growth and improve athletic performance.

Creatine is produced naturally in the body; it can also be obtained from diet and stored in the body

(Bowers, 1999). Supplements are marketed on the basis that they can increase the availability of the substance to use in muscular performance. The effects, particularly the long-term effects of such supplements on young athletes, are largely unknown. Some experts feel that prolonged use may be related to kidney dysfunction. Creatine and most other supplements are not approved by the Food and Drug Administration (FDA) and are largely unregulated as to quality of the product.

In a sport environment where young athletes are striving to improve performance, hoping to get an athletic scholarship to college, and socialized into a view of sport that accepts the use of ergogenic aids in the form of nutritional supplements, it is no surprise that many young athletes use supplements. Coaches, athletic trainers, and parents need to play a stronger educational and supervisory role so that these young athletes do not use questionable aids that may prove harmful to them in the long run.

The School Coach as Teacher–Coach

In Chapter 6, details of coaching certification (or the lack thereof) were provided. In Chapter 13, the problem known as teacher–coach role conflict is addressed. That well-documented problem is straightforward. Men and women who fill both teaching and coaching roles over a period of years tend to spend more of their energies in coaching than they do in teaching because that is where the real and perceived rewards are found. The United States has chosen to program the largest part of its sport culture for adolescents through the school. That means, theoretically at least, that the coaches of school sport teams are *teachers*.

The involvement of *teachers* in *school* sport is no mere convenience or coincidence. An important philosophical issue is represented in that arrangement—namely, that sport is educational and should be conducted in an educationally sound manner. I have mentioned that few states require coaching certification and that many states do not require teaching credentials for their coaches. Thus, the philosophical principle underlying the system is not always followed.

In many school districts, coaching is compensated on a *supplemental* contract, a contract in addition to the regular contract for teaching. A teacher with 10 years' experience in a district might have a $40,000 regular teaching contract and a $3,000 supplemental contract for being the head basketball coach. The issue is clear: When a district hires a coach, should it hire the person *first* as a teacher and then as a coach, or should the person be hired *first* as a coach and then as a teacher of whatever subject can be found? Most school administrators, if asked that question, would agree to the former rather than the latter. Actual hiring practices, however, do not always reflect that choice.

Parental Pressures and Booster Clubs

Parents, coaches, and townspeople often care about the sport performance of local school teams and athletes in ways that *differ* from the ways that athletes care about them. Parents, coaches, and townspeople are adults, spectators, fans, and enthusiasts. The adolescent athletes are participants. The differences in points of view can sometimes create pressures that are counterproductive to the development of the athlete and of school sport in general.

Dress an adolescent in a uniform, have him or her play in front of spectators who include peers, parents, and friends, under the gaze of a coach who looms as an important person in the athlete's immediate future in the sport, with the results written about in school and local newspapers and talked about among people in the town—and what do you have? Pressure! That kind of pressure is often important to the development of the adolescent, important in a positive way. The major point here, however, is that it is a great deal of pressure, in and of itself. Additional pressure is unnecessary.

When parents put undue pressure on their sons and daughters, when coaches put too much pressure on their athletes, and when the expectations of administrators and parents put too much pressure on coaches, then the conditions are such that the sport experience can rapidly become less enjoyable

---

Parents and Coaches Out of Control!

On July 5, 2000, a parent watching his son at a youth hockey practice session assaulted the man supervising the practice and beat him so severely that he went into a coma and eventually died (Nack & Munson, 2000). That tragic event brought to the attention of the nation what appears to be widespread instances of parents and even coaches out of control in youth sport.

- In an Illinois state soccer playoff game, a coach is accused of striking a referee.
- In Florida, a parent walks out of the stands and head-butts a referee.
- In Pennsylvania, police are called to quell a riot involving fifty parents after a football game for 11- to 13-year-olds.
- In a California Little League baseball game, a man coaching his son's team assaults and beats the manager of the opposing team.

SOURCE: Meadows, 2000; Nack & Munson, 2002; Sutton, 2000.

- In Ohio, the father of a soccer player pleads no contest to the charge of assaulting a 14-year-old boy who had scuffled for the ball with the man's 14-year-old son.

Community and agency sport groups are beginning to take a more proactive stance to prevent such incidents. In Jupiter, Florida, for example, a community sport organization now requires that

- Parents take a class that includes a video on the responsibilities of parenting a young athlete.
- Parents sign a code of ethics pledging to behave at youth sport contests—if they don't sign, their kids don't play.
- Parent behavior be monitored at games. For a first offense, they review the video and sign another pledge.
- The parent and child are sent home after a second offense and not allowed to return.

---

and rewarding than it should be. In states where support for school sport has to come from booster clubs and gate receipts, the conditions that might create undue pressures on coaches, athletes, and programs are even more likely to occur.

Pay-to-Play Plans

School districts in many states have had enormous difficulties raising monies through local tax initiatives to fund the continuing expenses of education. As a result, many districts have begun to charge user fees for many extracurricular activities offered by the schools. *User fees* are a form of direct taxation; that is, those who use the services pay an additional tax for those privileges.

Pay-to-play plans have been declared illegal in California and New York, on the basis of the discriminatory effects of such plans; that is, students

who can't afford the fees should not be denied access to what is an approved school program (Swift, 1991). The National Federation of State High School Associations has also come out against such fees, arguing that interschool sport programs have documented educational value and that students should have access to them as part of the regular school program.

Still, pay-to-play plans are springing up all over the country. Often, the fees are relatively low, perhaps $35 to be on the high school volleyball team, and there are often discounts to families with several students involved. In Massachusetts, pay-to-play plans have become the norm. In some schools, students pay more than $150 per sport, with some fee-waiver or financial-aid provisions for families that cannot afford the fees. These pay-to-play fees generate up to $250,000 for the school athletic budget (Swift, 1991).

When a local district in my area raised fees to $225 per sport (Blackledge, 1994), the fees began to have serious impact on the programs; for example, in football, only 59 boys in this district's grades 9–12 came out for the team, whereas a comparable (size and socioeconomic status) neighboring district, with no fees, attracted 105 players in grades 9–12. Parents reported restricting their children to a choice of one sport per school year, rather than having the children compete in multiple sports in different seasons.

It is curious that pay-to-play programs have developed at the same time state courts all over the United States have begun to force states to fund schools more equitably—that is, to ensure that schools in financially strained districts have per-pupil budgets that are similar to those in schools in wealthy districts. The basis for such decisions is always a clause in a state constitution that ensures an equal and appropriate education to all children and youths in public schools. If pay-to-play plans become the norm, then it is certain that youths in financially strained districts will have fewer sport opportunities than their counterparts in wealthy districts, inferior equipment, and inferior training facilities and that their equipment and their training facilities will be inferior.

INTERCOLLEGIATE SPORT

Intercollegiate sport in the United States has become big business for some schools, especially in Division I schools in the NCAA. Yet big-time intercollegiate sport occupies an important niche in American sport culture. Events such as the Rose Bowl and the Final Four are truly national in scope. Intercollegiate sport provides a common ground of loyalty among alumni, students, and friends. Division I NCAA sport provides entertainment to millions via radio and television.

At the Division III level of the NCAA, thousands of student–athletes take part in competition that seems an appropriate extension of school sport. No scholarships are given for athletic prowess at this level. Athletes' commitments within and outside the boundaries of the season are more limited. There is less commercialism. Nobody expects the sports to pay for themselves.

Thus, when we talk about problems and issues in intercollegiate sport, we must keep in mind that there are major differences between big-time university sport and the kind of competition we might typically find at a local college. The major problems and issues in intercollegiate sport are the following:

1. Recruiting violations and pressures
2. Drugs used to enhance performance
3. Economic disparities among top powers
4. Economic pressure for winning
5. Treatment of athletes at the university

Recruiting Violations and Pressures

Each year, the NCAA puts several university athletic programs on *sanctions* because of recruiting violations. The recruiting of athletes to play on university teams is governed by rules established by the NCAA. The rules are intended to protect the athlete and to ensure reasonably equal competition among schools trying to influence young athletes to attend their universities.

What is sad and alarming about many recruiting violations is that they are done with the help and, in some cases, at the insistence of influential alumni and friends of the universities, who are often in positions of prestige, trust, and power within the community. Recruiting violations occur because the pressures to attract the best athletes are so strong. Those pressures are so strong because pressures to have a winning program are immense. The pressures to have a winning program exist because of economic factors, as well as because of the status that accrues to those associated with winning programs at universities—particularly alumni and friends of the university.

Coaches sometimes succumb to those pressures. In other situations, coaches sometimes initiate the cheating themselves because they want so badly to win or to advance their careers. Direct cash payments, cars, high-paying jobs that require little or no work, and sexual favors have all been used to lure young athletes.

Drugs That Enhance Performance

Drugs are a problem for many college-age youths. For athletes, however, there is a special set of problems that have to do with drugs taken to improve performance. Evidence (*USA Today,* November 11, 1988) indicates that the use of *anabolic steroids* (male hormones that help to increase strength and allow athletes to perform more work in training) has begun to show up even at the junior high school level! The use of these drugs in certain sports, such as track and field and football, is thought to be widespread at elite levels of competition.

Most of the increased size of weight-event athletes in track and field and of linemen in football is the result of more scientific application of weight-training principles. There is widespread fear, however, that some of it is also due to the regular use of anabolic steroids. Drug testing has become a major issue in the NCAA. Student athletes at NCAA championship events are regularly tested for drugs that might affect performance. The issue of drug testing has caused a national debate that still persists. The debate hinges on the right to privacy of the athlete (or the worker, if in a business) and whether such testing is constitutional under the U.S. Fourth Amendment prohibition against *unreasonable* search and seizure.

Economic Disparities among Top Powers

For a few universities, the sports of football and basketball generate most of the revenues that support all the rest of the sports in the program. The presence of 80,000 fans for every home football game, or of 15,000 for every home basketball game, means income for the athletic program. In addition, the monies earned from televised games or for bowl-game appearances can be even more important than the gate receipts. Nonetheless, the vast majority of NCAA Division I athletic programs do not even break even with their football and basketball programs, let alone provide support for other sports.

For big-time collegiate sport, the rule is that the rich tend to get richer. If you have a winning program and, for example, are consistently ranked in the top twenty in football or basketball, more fans come to your games, you are offered a large local television contract, you have more regional and national television appearances, and you play more postseason games. More people see your team play. More young athletes see your team play—and the better ones are easier to recruit as a result. Of course, some universities not in this inner circle would like to get in! The difficulties in doing so are enormous. Thus, the temptation is there to cheat in recruiting to overcome the natural advantage enjoyed by the established programs.

In professional football and basketball, there is a yearly player draft in which teams at the bottom of the yearly standings get to pick first, a system designed specifically to promote more even competition over time. No such system exists for university sport; so, over time, the same teams tend to dominate the top rankings. Remember, big-time sports are a losing proposition economically for most universities. Still, the temptations created by hoping to improve that situation are substantial.

Economic Pressure to Win

The economic disparities that exist in big-time collegiate sport produce strong pressures to win, simply because it is through winning over a period of years that university athletic programs either remain in the elite economic group or break into that group. The economic consequences of making it are substantial. Programs that do not make it still have to build stadiums, put Astroturf on their fields, build fancy scoreboards, and pay for equipping and training 100 football players. Without the economic power that accrues to the elite programs from gate receipts and television, these other institutions are

Learning to work together for a team goal is an important experience.

left with huge bills that they must pay from regular funds.

Of course, there are always the alumni and friends who would like the athletic program to be as good as those at the few universities with the largest gate receipts, television contracts, and visibility. The issue here is status. The combined pressures that result from the search for status and for economic gain through big-time collegiate sport are at the heart of most of the abuses within the system.

Treatment of the Student–Athlete

There are many student–athletes in sport programs in American colleges and universities who fit well the best possible image of how sport and academic life can be combined such that each is enriched by the other for a better total college experience. There are others, however, for whom the term *student–athlete* is badly misused. This is often not so much their fault as it is the fault of the institution that is *misusing* the young athlete.

What is the quality of life for an elite, scholarship athlete at a major university? Although there are surely as many answers to that question as there are individual athletes, there are some disturbing signs, to say the least. The NCAA commissioned a study of more than 4,000 athletes from forty-two Division I schools (Wrisberg, 1996). The major findings were as follows:

- Student athletes focus most of their attention on their sport. They miss more classes and

---

Do College Athletes Need a Bill of Rights?

Many people close to Division I college athletics believe that too many athletes are exploited and that a bill of rights is needed to protect their interests. How do you react to the following possible provisions of a bill of rights?

- The right to transfer to a different college without having to lose eligibility
- The right to a 4-year scholarship rather than one renewable at the discretion of the institution
- For those who compete for 3 years, the right to scholarship support until they graduate

- The same rights to protection from physical and mental abuse and the right of free speech that other university students have
- The right to consult with agents concerning their future in sports
- The right to be compensated for endorsements, speeches, and appearances
- The right to adequate insurance to totally cover current injuries and problems that arise from them

What can you add? What would you delete?

SOURCE: Adapted from Eitzen & Sage, 2003.

participate in fewer other university activities than their student peers.

- Basketball and football players perform less well than student peers on every measure of academic performance, even though there are substantial academic support services provided for them.

- Many suffer from frequent or chronic injuries and, despite better access to good health care, feel pressure to practice and perform in spite of injuries.

- Most elite-scholarship athletes suffer from chronic fatigue.

- These athletes tend to attribute actions to external influences more than do nonathletes; that is, they report less of a sense of personal control.

- These athletes report having little opportunity or time to participate in personal-development activities on campus.

The picture that emerges from this study "offers little evidence of a high level of life quality by any definition or measuring standard" (Wrisberg, 1996, p. 397). It should be noted that the NCAA has used the results of this study to foster changes in Division I athletic programs that are aimed at reversing these trends.

Some sport scholars have long argued that scholarship athletes are badly exploited by the system (Sack, 1977). Scholarship athletes can receive nothing more than tuition, room, board, fees, and books—at least, not legally. The total cost of this package differs, depending on the costs at the university, but even at the most expensive university, when one divides the number of hours of work that the athlete devotes to his or her sport by the total value of the scholarship, the pay per hour is low. Clearly, few athletes *feel* exploited. Most are happy to be where they are, and many feel extremely lucky to have been awarded the scholarship. The charge of exploitation comes from the huge financial rewards the institution can achieve, which are not shared in any way with the athlete.

EQUITY ISSUES IN SPORT

Many issues in sport have a central theme—*equity*. Historically, much of organized sport has been the special province of wealthy, white males. When the first Olympic Games were held in ancient Greece, the competition was available only to male citizens of the Greek city-states. Citizens were males of privilege. The menial labor of the day was done by slaves. Not only were women disallowed from competition—they could not even watch!

When the Olympic Games were reborn in 1896, the tradition had not changed very much. The new games were much like the old games, in that males dominated and wealth was assumed—the games were, after all, for *gentlemen* athletes. You were not a gentleman if you came from the working class or if you really trained hard for the competition. Much has changed since those days, particularly since the 1970s. Nonetheless, the traditions of inequity in sport still linger and need continually to be addressed. Women's issues and minority issues are two such areas.

Women's Issues

Access to training and competition in sport has historically been denied to women. The nineteenth-century "feminine virtues" of piety, purity, submissiveness, and domesticity were alien to sport competition. The philosophy of muscular Christianity from which twentieth-century sport and physical education emerged was, above all, a *masculine* philosophy. Clearly, those views have changed in recent years. The passage of Title IX made equity for girls and women in sport the law of the land. Since then, girls have had access to more sports, their participation has increased dramatically, and scholarships for them have become more widely available. Moreover, there have been some notable successes by women in elite and professional sport. In 1984 women were finally allowed to compete in the marathon at the Olympic Games, and Joan Benoit showed extraordinary athletic prowess in winning the event. In Barcelona, in

1992, it became clear that Jackie Joyner-Kersee was the greatest multievent track-and-field athlete of all time, regardless of gender.

In sport, compliance with Title IX focuses particularly on equal provision of equipment and supplies, practice and game times, travel, compensation of coaches, publicity, tutoring and other such services, locker rooms, medical and training facilities, housing and dining facilities, and financial aid (Fox, 1992). These are easily identifiable factors, and discrimination toward girls and women on the basis of these factors should be easily discernible. Yet, problems related to these factors still exist in many schools and universities. The more subtle forms of discrimination—negative stereotyping, poor media coverage, underrepresentation in coaching and administration, and lack of female role models—will be more difficult to confront and correct (Fox, 1992).

Title IX became law in 1972. After a brief period of increased opportunity for women in coaching and administrative positions, the 1980s saw a decrease in the percentage of women in those roles. In 1984 Grove City College in Pennsylvania brought suit, charging that since college athletic programs receive no direct federal support, Title IX did not apply to college athletics. The United States Supreme Court agreed. That decision led to a concerted lobbying effort in the U.S. Congress by advocates for women's sport and others interested in civil rights. Their efforts were rewarded when the Civil Rights Act of 1987 was passed, with much stronger provisions for Title IX (Motley & Levine, 2001). Thus, from the mid-1980s through the 1990s, we witnessed what might be called the first true "Title IX generation" of girl and women athletes. All fifty states offered state championships for girls' sports, and the NCAA sanctioned seventeen national championships for women.

Still, as shown in Chapter 6, recent data show that the percentage of women in coaching, administrative, and training positions remains low and shows few signs of improving dramatically in the near future. Women athletes receive only 30 percent of the scholarship dollars in intercollegiate

Girls and women continue to break down historical barriers in sport.

sport, 23 percent of the athletic operating budgets, 17 percent of the recruiting dollars, and 35 percent of the participation opportunities (Motley & Levine, 2001). Programs to attract, train, and place more female coaches have generally failed (Pastore, 1994), with the exception of a Colorado program that has increased the percentage of female coaches in school sport programs in that state. Male officials still dominate important women's sports such as basketball and softball (Casey, 1992). It is uncommon to see a woman as head athletic director at any level. Acosta and Carpenter (1994, pp. 117–118) have summarized the issues well:

> With the increase in women's participation in intercollegiate athletics has come a decrease in women's leadership opportunities at the administrative and coaching levels. If the women who currently enjoy collegiate athletics are to have the opportunity to remain in college athletics and exert leadership over the activities they enjoy, we must recognize the patterns of exclusion that presently exist in women's athletics and work to reverse this undesirable trend.

When interscholastic and intercollegiate sport budgets get tight, as they have in many places in recent years, it is now common to hear the requirements for gender equity in sports blamed for the reduced support for boys' and men's programs (Stourowsky, 1996). A men's volleyball program is eliminated at a university, and the reason given is the need to provide more support for the new women's tennis program—a zero-sum argument is forwarded suggesting that gains for women are only at the expense of men. This is what Sage (1987) and Stourowsky (1996) refer to as "blaming the victim" strategy; that is, the fault is found in the group that has the least amount of power while the focus is deflected from the main issue, which is providing resources that are sufficient and equitable.

Another barrier that girls and women are now contesting is the barrier to participation in contact sports such as football, wrestling, and ice hockey. Participation among high school girls in those three sports has increased steadily over the past several years. Although the presence of girls on boys' football teams is still reasonably rare (706 girls in 1998–99), more than 2,300 girls are on wrestling teams and more than 3,500 on ice-hockey teams (www.nfhs.org). This requires coaches to be educated and sensitive so that they can create conditions within the team that are supportive of girls' participation. Needless to say, it also confronts all the stereotypes that have hindered women's participation in sport.

What seems clear is that the status of women in sport will not improve without vigorous advocacy by sport and physical-education professionals. The National Association for Girls and Women in Sport (NAGWS) has adopted a strategic plan to remediate problems that exist for women because of unequal opportunity in sport and lack of compliance with Title IX (Hester & Dunaway, 1991). This plan includes advocacy for full participation both in athlete roles and in indirect roles in administration, training, officiating, and the like; recruitment, development, and promotion plans to help women assume leadership positions; and the initiation of new programs and enhancement of existing programs for females of all ages, races, economic levels, and ethnic origins.

Although the ideal of the athletic woman has become much more accepted today—even for substantial profit in advertising—the old conceptions linger in more subtle ways. We still hear male sports announcers describing a female athlete as "pretty,

---

The Three Point Test for Title IX Compliance

In 1979 compliance with Title IX was determined to be acceptable if institutions passed one of the three criteria listed below. In 1996 the Office of Civil Rights described the first criterion (the proportionality criterion) as the safest way for an institution to be in compliance.

1. The number of male and female athletes at a school must be in proportion to the overall student body. If women are half the school's population, half of its athletes should be women.

2. A school must demonstrate that it has increased opportunities for women, mostly by adding women's sports.

3. A school must continue to show that its existing athletic programs meet the interests of women on campus.

About one-third of schools that have had compliance complaints use the proportionality criterion to pass the inspection.

Few schools use the adding sports criterion to gain compliance.

Nearly two-thirds of schools use criterion three to show compliance.

The proportionality criterion continues to be the most controversial.

Source: Coffin, 2002.

too" when "prettiness" or "attractiveness" has nothing to do with the competition. (When is the last time you heard a male announcer talk about a handsome baseball or football player?) Recent research indicates that adults frown on girls' participation in activities considered to be normal for boys and that signs of assertiveness typically reinforced in young boys are often not accepted in young girls (Elias, 1983). All of this indicates that the nineteenth-century views still linger in many ways—and that as long as they do, equity for girls and women in sport will not be complete.

Minority Issues

If sport in America has been typically male-dominated, it has also been "lily white." Blacks and other minorities have always participated in sport but were denied access to mainstream sport competition in schools, universities, and professional sport. The *color barrier* in major professional sport was not broken until Jackie Robinson played for the Brooklyn Dodgers in 1947. The integration of top-level collegiate sport did not come until much later, especially in the South. Although integrated schools were first mandated in 1954 (*Brown v. Board of Education*), school sport was not fully integrated until lawsuits were decided during the civil rights movements of the 1960s and 1970s.

Today, black and Hispanic players are abundant in some professional sports—particularly baseball, football, and basketball. Yet it is still rare to see a minority athlete on the tennis court or on the professional golf circuit. Minority athletes have been traditionally stereotyped by position in many sports (Loy & McElvogue, 1981), and they are seriously underrepresented in coaching and administrative positions in all sports (Coakley, 1982).

Many coaches and athletic administrators are former players. It has been more than 50 years since the color barrier was broken in professional baseball and more than a quarter-century since the implementation of Title IX, but gender and race inequalities are still prevalent in hiring and promotion practices in both intercollegiate and professional sport. The Center for the Study of Sport in Society (www.sportinsociety.org) publishes a yearly "report card" on hiring and promotion practices. Here are a few highlights from the 1998 report card:

- Growth opportunities for women exceed those for people of color by significant numbers.

- The NBA has the best record for diversity in its administrative staff; Major League Soccer (MLS) has the best record for racial diversity and the NHL the best record for gender diversity.

- The percentage of black athletes decreased in all men's pro sports as well as in NCAA Division I sports. The percentage of Latino players in baseball reached an all-time high of 25 percent. Minority athletes in Division I reached an all-time high of 32.1 percent and women athletes an all-time high of 39 percent.

- The date for diversity among head coaches in pro sports and Division I continue to be bleak. Black coaches (5.8 percent) and other minority head coaches (2.1 percent) make up only 7.9 percent of head coaches in Division I. In the three major pro sports for men, there are only twelve minority head coaches. The percentage of women coaching women's teams was up to 43.7 percent. Universities continue to lag behind professional sport in the diversity of their head coaches.

- The diversity data among athletic directors are even worse, with only 3.2 percent black A.D.'s and 8.2 percent female A.D.'s.

Thus, at the top level of athletic management and at the top level of coaching in collegiate sport, minorities and women are seriously underrepresented. The organizations where women and minorities are best represented are the players' associations in professional sports.

As cities deteriorated economically in the 1980s and black professional athletes gained huge celebrity status, it became clear that for many black male youths in cities, a scholarship to play ball and the chance to make it big in professional sport had become a trap. Proportionately few athletes get scholarships and an even smaller proportion make it through to professional sport. The time and energy invested in preparing for sport has no doubt deterred many talented youths from preparing adequately for careers in business, education, law, and the like.

Sport participation has long been promoted as a vehicle for improving relationships among minority and majority students. Yet, to achieve that goal, minority students must be attracted to sport programs. Barriers to participation can be the high cost of equipment (financial), fear of medical exams or costs (medical/financial), fear of competition for some ethnic groups who value cooperation, and insufficient language skills (Olson, 1995). School districts that make an attempt to reduce these barriers are much more likely to attract more minority students.

Problems of race in sport tend to interact with problems that are socioeconomic in nature. The idea of "sport for all," an ethic of access and participation, is being achieved much less in cities than in suburbs, much less among nonwhite children and youths of color than among white children and youths, much less for the poor than for the wealthy. Although these issues represent problems that institutionalized sport can help to combat, it also needs to be recognized that the problems are manifestations of *structural* inequities in our society.

SPORT SYSTEMS

The sport system of the United States is composed of diverse elements: child and youth sport, school sport, university sport, professional sport, and recreational sport. Some features of this system are distinct in the world sports community. Nowhere is school or university sport as important to a sport culture as in the United States. Nowhere is government support for and regulation of sport less than in the United States. The combination of youth, school, and university sport that serves youths and young adults as they develop in sport is primarily an *exclusionary* model, one in which a few skilled sportspersons get to continue in the system, whereas those who are less skilled have little access to continued training and competition in their sport.

In most of the rest of the world, the overall sport system of countries is guided and funded by government. The **sport-club** system is the primary vehicle of training and competition from youth sport through to elite sport. Coaching is more often certified at all levels. Which system is the best? The question is relevant only if we have previously agreed to the purposes and goals the systems should serve. Sport systems serve different goals and reflect different political and economic systems. The systems thus are most often not directly comparable.

Alternative Goals for Sport Systems

What goals should a sport system serve? In what priority should those goals be arranged? These are useful questions to consider because there are real choices to be made as to how limited resources are allocated in sport.

To what extent should Olympic development programs dominate a sport system? Some countries keep national teams and athletes training year-round in a national training facility. Many countries have full-time national coaches. Should more resources be allocated to the continued training of elite athletes who are beyond their university years, especially in sports for which there is no way to earn a living in relation to those sports, or should resources be allocated more for increased participation at the recreational level?

Still another choice is whether to expand the opportunities for sport at the child and youth sport levels, providing better coaching and more developmentally appropriate sport forms, and extending

---

A More Inclusive Model for School Sport

Tawa High School in Wellington, New Zealand, is typical of involvement in school sport. In 2001 there were 1,170 students enrolled at Tawa HS. The school offered sports competition in ten sports.

In most sports, teams practiced on the average of twice per week and had a weekly competition on the weekend or after school. Coaches are teachers and volunteers from the community and are typically not paid for this service. National tournaments are held for most sports at the end of the season.

In 2001, 375 girls and 478 boys competed on at least one school sport team. That represents 68 per-

cent participation for girls and 75 percent for boys. The number of teams organized for competition depends on the number of students who wish to play. The more students show an interest, the more teams are organized.

This is *not* an elite development model. Elite sport development in New Zealand takes place in sport clubs outside school. It is a more educational model that allows more students to experience the value of interschool sport competition.

SOURCE: Peter Sharp, Hillary Commission, NZ.

---

those opportunities to *all* children rather than just to sons and daughters of the middle and upper classes. It would be nice if there were sufficient resources to do all the sport development implied in these questions. Resources are always limited, however, and choices must be made. What is interesting to consider in the United States is the means by which those choices are made. Do we need an overall national sport policy or a state-level policy? Instead, are we better off continuing to develop sport primarily through the private sector, with decisions made mostly on the basis of *consumer demands*?

Sport for All

One worldwide movement that might substantially influence the future directions of sport cultures is known as Sport for All. In 1966 the **Sport for All** movement was launched by the Council of Europe, an international organization founded after World War II to promote understanding and cooperation among nations. By 1976 the council had developed and examined the potential of a universal sport movement to the extent that it created a document

to outline the principles. The document—*On the Principles for a Policy of Sport for All*—had as its first principle the statement that "every individual shall have the right to participate in sport."

Sport for All is now an international movement in which broadly based sport participation is sponsored and funded by governments. The main goals of the Sport for All movement are clearly *participatory* at the broadest level. This movement is not directed toward elite athletes. By 1978 the Sport for All movement had become sufficiently well established that the General Conference of the United Nations Educational, Scientific and Cultural Organization (UNESCO) ratified an International Charter of Physical Education and Sport based on the Sport for All movement. Article 1 of the UNESCO charter is as follows:

Article 1: The practice of physical-education and sport is a fundamental right for all.
1.1 Every human being has a fundamental right of access to physical education and sport, which are essential for the full development of his personality. The freedom to develop physical, intellectual, and moral powers through physical education and sport must be

guaranteed both within the educational system and in other aspects of social life.

1.2 Everyone must have full opportunities in accordance with his national tradition of sport, for practicing physical education and sport, developing his physical fitness and attaining a level of achievement in sport which corresponds to his gifts.

1.3 Special opportunities must be made available for young people, including children of preschool age, for the aged and for the handicapped to develop their personalities to the fullest through physical education and sport programs suited to their requirements. (United Nations Educational, Scientific and Cultural Organization, *International Charter of Physical Education and Sport*)

The Sport for All movement has developed throughout the world under a number of different labels. In Norway, a program known as Trim was started; it was eventually adopted in Germany, Japan, the Netherlands, Sweden, and Switzerland. In Australia, the program is known as Life Be in It; in Mexico, it is Deportito; and in other places, it is Sportreal.

Sport in Perspective

In this chapter, we have focused on issues and problems in sport at all levels. To conclude the chapter, I need to remind you that in many instances sport is still just sport, an experience to be enjoyed and from which people derive substantial meaning for their lives. Sport does have problems. Sport can and often does provide substantial benefits to participants. In 1995 Nike (White & Sheets, 2001) developed a now famous television commercial featuring adolescent girls engaged in various sports. In each scene, a girl athlete began by speaking the same phrase, "If you let me play sports," which was followed by one of the following statements:

- I will like myself more
- I will have more self-confidence
- I will suffer less depression

- I will be 60 percent less likely to develop breast cancer
- I will be more likely to leave a man who beats me
- I will be less likely to get pregnant before I want to
- I will learn what it means to be strong

All these claims are backed by evidence, and the commercial was a powerful argument for increasing opportunities for girls in sport.

Compelling as the above argument is, we need to keep in mind that those are probably *not* the reasons girls want to play sports. Robin Marantz Henig is a writer from the pre–Title IX generation. Her daughter, Sam, is an athlete, and watching Sam and her teammates compete caused Ms. Henig to argue that although all those claims of benefits for girls are good and true, "sports is not birth control" (Henig, 1999). Because Ms. Henig was raised in a pre–Title IX era, she never came to view herself as an athlete, even though she was physically active. This is what she concluded as she watched her daughter compete:

> It is against this background that I find myself watching with great pleasure, as Sam plays basketball each winter—just as I love watching her play soccer in the fall and spring, and softball in the summer. I love the idea that she thinks of herself as an athlete and as a member of a team. When I join the other parents on those hard bleachers every Sunday afternoon of basketball season, we are all reveling in our daughters' freedom to dance a dance that was never really available to the mothers among us. Whether or not it keeps them out of harm's way, for these hours at least, basketball turns them into something quite remarkable: a group of graceful, agile, self-confident young women taking pride in their bodies, not for who or what they can attract, but for what they can accomplish.

The deepest meaning of sport is always in the moment. What the many moments do or do not do for any of us in other aspects of our lives is important, but it should never diminish our understanding or appreciation of sport as experience.

SUMMARY

1. Traditionally, sport enthusiasts have ascribed almost mystical and miraculous qualities to sport participation; more recently, many of these myths have been questioned seriously.

2. Cooperation among athletes is essential to high-quality sport and is a fundamental aspect of the sport experience.

3. Appropriate competition—developmentally sound and psychologically suited to the participants—should be the goal, rather than less competition or noncompetitive activities.

4. Children lack the social and psychological abilities to benefit from organized sport before age 8 years.

5. Epiphyseal injury due to year-round specialization or weight training is the most dangerous, common injury in children's sport.

6. Sport for children and youths needs to be developmentally appropriate; equipment, space, and rules should be modified accordingly.

7. Early specialization increases the risk of physical injury and psychological burnout.

8. Children and youths from relatively low socioeconomic areas have much less opportunity to participate in appropriately conducted sport, as compared with their wealthier peers.

9. Coaches in child and youth sport often behave in ways that are unproductive for player development, but evidence suggests that coaches can change easily once appropriate behaviors are made known to them, as is done in many coach-effectiveness training programs.

10. Children will play to win and then move on to the next interesting part of their daily life; inappropriate pressures to win are most often imposed by adults.

11. Aussie Sport is a national-level program aimed at improving the opportunity for good sport participation. It includes coaching programs, incentive schemes, modified games, and behavior codes for all people involved.

12. The large, diversified interscholastic sport program is unique to the American high school.

13. The interscholastic model is basically exclusionary, in that opportunities are available to fewer and fewer athletes as they advance. This model differs markedly from the European sport-club approach.

14. Injury in school sport is not a major problem, with the exception of injury in football. There, injury to the knee continues to be the biggest problem.

15. Eligibility for school sport continues to be a major issue. Legislation promoting pass-to-play practices is becoming more common.

16. Athletes tend to specialize more now than they did previously, with strength and endurance training occupying their off-season.

17. In most instances, school sport teams are coached by teachers; the problems associated with hiring teacher–coaches are substantial.

18. Pressure from parents and booster clubs is a potential source of problems for the adolescent athlete.

19. Pay-to-play plans are making access to interschool sport a socioeconomic issue.

20. Recruiting violations continue to be the major problem in intercollegiate sport, often resulting from economic pressures to win.

21. Performance-enhancing drugs have become a major problem in many sports.

22. Economic disparity among top powers and economic pressures to produce winning programs are responsible for many of the violations and abuses in intercollegiate sport.

23. Equity issues in sport are seen in the underrepresentation of women and minorities among athletes, coaches, and sport administrators. Furthermore, we are witnessing decreasing access

⟫ GET CONNECTED TO SPORT WEB SITES

Children and Youth Sport

National Alliance for Youth Sports www.nays.org
 The NAYS Web site will also connect you to
  National Youth Sport Coaches Association
  Parents Association for Youth Sports
  Academy for Youth Sports Administrators
  Start Smart Sports Development Program
  National Council on Youth Sports www.ncys.org
  National Youth Sports Safety Foundation www.nyssf.org
  Youth Sports Foundation www.youthsportsfoundation.com
  Center for Sports Parenting www.sportsparenting.org
  Institute for the Study of Youth Sports http://ed-web3.educ.msu.edu/ysi/
  Positive Coaching Alliance www.positivecoach.org
  Sport for All www.sportforall.net
  Character Counts Sports www.charactercounts.org
  Citizenship Through Sports www.sportsmanship.org
  American Sport Education Program www.asep.com
  Urban Youth Sports www.sportinsociety.org/uys.html

Interscholastic Sport

National Federation of State High School Associations www.nfhs.org
 Through the NFHS Web site, you can also connect to
  National Federation Coaches Association
  National Federation Officials Association
  National Federation Interscholastic Sport Association
  National Interscholastic Athletic Administrators Association
  NFHS Coaches Education Program

Intercollegiate Sport

National Collegiate Athletic Association www.ncaa.org
National Association of Intercollegiate Athletics www.naia.org
National Junior College Athletic Association www.njcaa.org
Canadian Interuniversity Athletic Union www.ciau.ca
National Association of Collegiate Directors of Athletics www.nacda.com
National Association of College Women Athletic Administrators www.nacwaa.org

Sport for People with Disabilities

American Association of Adapted Sports Programs www.aaasp.org
Special Olympics www.specialolympics.org
Athletes Helping Athletes www.athleteshelpathletes.com
Paralympics www.paralympic.org

(continued)

GET CONNECTED TO SPORT WEB SITES *(continued)*

Masters Sports

World Association of Veteran Athletes	www.wava.org
World Masters Games	www.worldmasters.org
United States Masters Swimming	www.usms.org
International Masters Games Association	www.imga-masters.com
Masters Track and Field	www.masterstrack.com

State Games and Sport Festivals

National Congress of State Games	www.stategames.org
Inner-City Games Foundation	www.innercitygames.org

Women in Sport

National Association for Girls and Women in Sport	www.aahperd.org/nagws
Women's Sports Foundation	www.womensportsfoundation.org
Women in Sports Careers Foundation	www.WiscFoundation.org
Empowering Women in Sports	www.feminist.org/research/sports2.html
Title IX—Equity Online	www.edc.org/womensEquity
Title IX—National Women's Law Center	www.nwlc.org>
Title IX—Office of Civil Rights	www.ed.gov/offices/OCR

Other Relevant Sites

Amateur Athletic Union	www.aausports.org
International Amateur Athletics Federation	www.iaaf.org
United States Olympic Committee	www.usoc.org
National Association of Sports Officials	www.naso.org
North American Society for Sport Management	www.nassm.org
Active Americans	www.activeusa.com
North American Society for Sport Management	www.nassm.org
European Association for Sport Management	www.unb.ca/sportmanagement/easm
National Association of Police Athletic Leagues	www.nationalpal.org

to sport in low-income areas, because of the shift of sport instruction and participation to the private sector.

24. Sport systems around the world differ markedly because they serve different goals, resulting in different resource allocation and different models for participation.

25. Sport for All is a worldwide movement aimed at increasing an entire population's participation in sport and fitness activities.

DISCUSSION QUESTIONS

1. In what ways can poor cooperation destroy competition? In what ways can inappropriate competition destroy cooperation?

2. Do the ways in which child and youth sport are practiced in your area reflect developmentally appropriate forms of competition?

3. What kind of coach-education program would you suggest for volunteer youth-sport coaches in a local recreation department?

4. Do eligibility rules for sport participation in school discriminate against less talented students?

5. How early should athletes specialize? What are the benefits and the problems of specialization at the high school level?

6. If you were making policy for the NCAA, what policies would you suggest for (a) drug abuse, (b) recruiting violations, and (c) academic progress of athletes?

7. How should youth and school sport be financed? What influences are exerted by differing approaches to financing sport?

8. Should America have a more developed national sport policy? Should it have a national sport system? How might such a system be structured?

PART THREE

Fitness

Chapter 8 Basic Concepts of Fitness

Chapter 9 Fitness Programs and Professions

Chapter 10 Problems and Issues in Fitness

The fitness and healthy lifestyle boom among adults in middle- and upper-income brackets is one of the major social phenomena in recent American history. Changes in diet and activity habits, along with a much greater understanding of the perils associated with inappropriate health habits such as smoking, poor diet, and inactivity, have produced an entirely new emphasis on lifestyle, of which physical activity, often in the form of moderate to vigorous exercise, is a fundamental part. Yet many physical-education and fitness professionals feel that too many children are unfit and that we are failing to identify and help children who are at risk for later health problems. Although the evidence base is thin and mixed, many experts believe that activity patterns developed in childhood strongly influence adult tendencies.

How much fitness is necessary? How much is too much? What levels of activity are necessary for good health? Can fitness be fun? What kinds of fitness programs for children and youths have been successful? Why has fitness become primarily a phenomenon involving young, upwardly mobile adults? The three chapters in Part 3 are designed to help you understand the fitness movement and to provide answers to these important questions.

CHAPTER **8**

Basic Concepts of Fitness

Scientists and doctors have known for years that substantial benefits can be gained from regular physical activity. The expanding and strengthening evidence on the relationship between physical activity and health necessitates the focus this report brings to this important public health challenge. Although the science of physical activity is a complex and still-developing field, we have today strong evidence to indicate that regular physical activity will provide clear and substantial health gains. In this sense, the report is more than a summary of the science—it is a national call to action.

Audrey Manley, Surgeon General
of the United States, 1996

LEARNING OBJECTIVES

- To discuss various approaches to defining fitness

- To distinguish between and explain health fitness and motor-performance fitness, as well as cosmetic fitness

- To discuss major concepts and issues in the dose–response debate

- To describe the health benefits of a physically active lifestyle

- To describe the social gradient in health and fitness and discuss its implications

- To describe fitness-training principles

- To describe and discuss differences among various kinds of fitness training

- To discuss major issues associated with the measurement of fitness

- To discuss major issues associated with the measurement of physical activity

In 1996 the U.S. Surgeon General issued a landmark report titled *Physical Activity and Health.* That report, as the quotation at the start of this chapter indicates, not only presented the most convincing case ever for the relationship between physical activity and health, but also served as a national call to action to increase physical activity among children, youths, and adults of all ages, especially among the many Americans who live essentially sedentary lives.

The relationship between physical activity and health has been known for some time, but we are now in the midst of a further evolution of our understanding of that relationship. For all of the twentieth century, physical education promoted physical fitness as a primary goal. Scientists, physicians, and health professionals came to adopt that view also, particularly as it relates to **hypokinetic diseases,** those ailments and problems that are not caught, as are infectious diseases, but instead develop through inappropriate diet, lack of exercise, and a generally sedentary lifestyle. Corbin and Lindsey (1983) referred to these as "hypokinetic diseases," meaning those caused by or related to a lack of appropriate physical activity. Illnesses that are typical of the hypokinetic or degenerative group are coronary artery disease, high blood pressure, lower-back pain, obesity, diabetes, and osteoporosis. Cardiovascular diseases have posed the largest and most serious health problems in modern life. That is why physical fitness and physical activity have become so important as our understanding of the prevention and remediation of those diseases increases.

> Regular physical activity, fitness, and exercise are critically important for the health and well being of people of all ages. Research has demonstrated that virtually all individuals can benefit from regular physical activity, whether they participate in vigorous exercise or some type of moderate health-enhancing physical activity. Regular physical activity has been shown to reduce the morbidity and mortality from many chronic diseases. Therefore, physical activity should be a priority for Americans of all ages. (U.S. Department of Health and Human Services, 2002)

As the preceding quotation indicates, regular physical activity has become a national priority. But, notice also that the start of the quotation specifies *physical activity, fitness, and exercise* as critically important. This chapter will help you to understand when the use of each of those terms is appropriate and especially the various meanings of the term *fitness.* We have been using that term in health and physical education for 100 years, but the meaning of the term has changed dramatically as our knowledge base has increased.

Many still use the term *fitness* in a global sense, encompassing physical, social, moral, mental, and spiritual fitness. Although that use of the term might be sufficient in everyday language, it is not specific enough to guide policy or programs. Others have said fitness is an adequate amount of strength and endurance to meet the needs of everyday life, but that too is very misleading. What are the needs of daily life? Whose life? Some women and men sit at a desk all day and watch TV in their leisure. They have enough strength and endurance to do that, but they are probably unfit.

When I was growing up, physical fitness was a list of characteristics including strength, endurance, flexibility, speed, accuracy, and power. Fitness tests had tasks to measure each of those, using chin-ups, pull-ups, push-ups, agility runs, squat thrusts, sprints, toe touches, and mile runs as test items. Such practices linger today even though our understanding of fitness has evolved markedly.

A CONTEMPORARY UNDERSTANDING OF FITNESS

Research in exercise science, medical sciences, and health has led to a changing concept of physical fitness—one that is not only more meaningful but also more useful in providing directions for sport, fitness, and physical-education professionals as they implement programs designed to help children, youths, and adults of all ages improve their fitness. The first step in this contemporary understanding

---

Key Definitions

- **Aerobic** The process of metabolizing body fuels through exercise in the presence of oxygen.

- **Anaerobic** The process of metabolizing body fuels through exercise without oxygen.

- **Body composition** The relative amounts of muscle, fat, bone, and other vital body parts.

- **Cardiovascular endurance** The ability of the circulatory and respiratory systems to supply fuel during sustained exercise.

- **Exercise** Leisure-time physical activity conducted with the intention of developing physical fitness.

- **Health** A state of being associated with freedom from disease and illness, including the positive component of wellness.

- **Healthy lifestyles** Presence of appropriate physical activity, nutrition, and stress management behavior patterns.

- **Hypokinetic diseases** Conditions related to physical inactivity or low levels of habitual activity.

- **Leisure activity** Physical activity undertaken during discretionary time.

- **Physical activity** Bodily movement that is produced by skeletal muscle and substantially increases energy expenditure.

- **Wellness** A state of positive biological and psychological health in the individual exemplified by quality of life and a sense of well-being.

Source: Corbin, Pangrazi, & Franks (2000) and Costill (1986).

---

was to recognize that fitness is not a single concept; indeed, there are different types of physical fitness (see Box above).

Fitness is currently viewed as a series of components, each of which is specific in its development and maintenance. Typically, fitness components are divided into two basic categories: those essentially related to health and those related to motor-skill performance (see Table 8.1). An additional category, cosmetic fitness, will also be considered because of its importance in the culture.

The distinction between these two categories of fitness is that the health-fitness components are related to a national public health agenda, whereas the motor-performance-fitness components are related to the performance of specific functional motor tasks. **Health fitness** is important in the prevention and remediation of disease and illness, both physical and mental. **Motor-performance fitness** is important in sport performance and in certain kinds of job performance that require physical skill and strength to do appropriately.

The components of health fitness are general in the sense that they apply to everybody and that each person should achieve and maintain certain levels of health fitness to stay as healthy as possible throughout a lifetime and to improve the quality of life. Motor-performance fitness, on the other hand, is more functional and specific. A football tackle, a sprinter, a tennis player, and a swimmer need different amounts of each of the motor-performance components. A certain combination of motor-performance-fitness components is *functionally* related to the goals of each activity. The strength and speed needed by a sprinter are different from the strength and speed needed by a football tackle or a tennis player—even though each performer, to improve her or his performance, needs strength and speed.

Health fitness is not, in its most important sense, related to shooting baskets more accurately or to jumping farther. It is related to living better, to being more resistant to diseases, and even, perhaps, to living longer.

Although historically an important competitive sport, running is often pursued now for its cardiovascular benefits.

The major difference in athletic performance today is increased levels of fitness.

Health fitness is an important component of **wellness,** which is often referred to now as the new overall goal for healthy individuals. Historically, health has been thought of primarily as the absence of disease and illness, but wellness adds a very strong positive component to the notion of health. Wellness is primarily about the decisions individuals and groups make about how they will lead their lives. Wellness is about achieving a high quality of life and a continuing sense of physical and psychological well-being (Fahey, Insel, & Roth, 2003).

Health Fitness

Health fitness is important for the prevention and remediation of hypokinetic degenerative diseases, the most serious of which—since the mid-1940s—have been those related to the heart and vascular systems. Medical, health, and fitness professionals refer to this problem of health fitness as the *cardiovascular plague.* A major step forward in the evolution of our understanding of health-related fitness came with increased evidence that regular **aerobic exercise,** which is sustained by oxygen, is very important. In 1968, Kenneth Cooper, in his book *Aerobics,* popularized this understanding of exercise

TABLE 8.1	Components of Health and Motor-Performance Fitness	
Health-Fitness Components	Motor-Performance Components
Body composition	Agility
Cardiovascular endurance and capacity	Balance
	Coordination
Flexibility	Power
Muscular endurance	Reaction time
Strength	Speed
	Strength

and introduced what would become a widely used standard term.

> To begin, it's necessary to recall that oxygen is the key to understanding what happens. Getting oxygen to the body tissue is the rock-bottom basis of conditioning, and it's convenient to think of the systems that process and deliver oxygen as one huge, magnificent, wondrous assembly line, complete with receiving lines to dispose of wastes, and the most beautiful engine ever conceived to keep all of it moving. (p. 87)

We have lived through 30 years of emphasis on aerobic exercise—road racing, marathons, triathlons, aerobics of all kinds (low-impact, water, etc.), cycling, and power walking. In that time, people have learned that regular aerobic exercise of the right intensity and duration can help to control weight, reduce the percentage of fat in body composition, improve circulatory function, control blood-glucose levels, increase insulin sensitivity, and reduce stress and depression (Blair, Kohl, & Powell, 1987; Fahey, Insel, & Roth, 2003).

Health-related fitness also focuses on strength and flexibility. Low-back pain and spinal disorders are the biggest cause of disability in the workforce (Pollock & Vincent, 1996). Osteoporosis, the degenerative disease characterized by lowered bone-mineral density, is among the most serious problems of older people, especially postmenopausal women. Weakness in the abdominal and back muscles and inadequate flexibility in the hamstring muscles are the main contributors to lower-back weakness and trauma. Lack of weight-bearing activity and muscular activity against resistance are major contributors to osteoporosis. These and many other medical problems can be improved through strength and flexibility training.

Physical activity in the form of resistance training has many benefits (Fahey, Insel, & Roth, 2003; Pollock & Vincent, 1996; Westcott, 1993). These include positive effects on bone-mineral density, body composition, muscular strength, glucose metabolism, serum lipids, maximal oxygen consumption, and basal metabolism. We have just begun to understand that resistance training, especially when done with lighter weight and increased repetitions, can improve aerobic capacity. Not only is metabolic rate increased during a strength workout, but also as a result, it is increased slightly throughout the day. Although our cultural perception of strength training is typically muscular young men in weight rooms, it is clear that regular resistance work is important for women and men, both young and old. Indeed, some regular resistance work is especially important as people get older.

Although the cardiovascular plague and reducing the incidence of heart disease through cardiovascular exercise dominated our attention in the 1970s and 1980s, it has become increasingly clear that there is also an epidemic of obesity and diabetes in the United States, among both children and adults (Mokad et al., 2001; Strauss & Pollock, 2001). Childhood obesity has increased by 50 percent in the last decade. In addition, the percentage of children who are overweight but not obese has increased over the last decade, and the rate of increase is higher for African American and Hispanic children and youths than for white children and youths (Ogden, Flegal, Carroll, & Johnson, 2002). Recent studies using weight and body mass index (rather than surveys where people "report" their weight) show that slightly more than 30 percent of adults are obese (Flegal, Carroll, Ogden, & Johnson, 2002). That is an increase from 22.9 percent in the early 1990s. Seventeen million Americans suffer from diabetes. Nearly 95 percent of them have Type II diabetes, which is associated with obesity and physical inactivity (U.S. Department of Health and Human Services, 2002). Both cardiovascular and strength-exercise programs can be effective in changing body composition to reduce body fatness to acceptable levels.

Flexibility is the ability of a joint to move through its full range of motion. Flexibility is important both to health fitness and to motor-performance fitness. Flexibility can be increased with a regular program of stretching; without such a program, flexibility tends to decrease. The main benefits of regular stretching include reduction of postexercise muscle soreness, relief of aches and pains, improved body position for better performance, maintenance of good posture, and relaxation (Fahey, Insel, & Roth, 2003).

What we commonly refer to as flexibility is **static flexibility,** the capacity to reach and maintain an extended position in a joint's range of motion. **Dynamic flexibility** is the capacity to move a joint quickly through its range of motion with little resistance. The structure of a joint, tightness of muscles, tendons, and ligaments around it, strength, and coordination all determine the degree of flexibility. Flexibility is dramatically important in improving low-back trauma at all ages and in helping older people maintain their capacity to move well and safely. Of course, flexibility is also very important in sport performance.

Motor-Performance Fitness

When people today talk about physical fitness, especially if they know what they are talking about, they are likely to mean health fitness. When someone asks, "Are you physically fit?" the question is probably about health fitness. Fitness classes are very likely to have a health-fitness focus these days. This does not mean that motor-performance fitness is not important—it simply means that it is different!

The purpose of motor-performance fitness is to perform a motor skill, typically a sport skill, better. Being well coordinated and very fast may help you perform certain sports better but will not affect your health much. Strength is a component of both health fitness and motor-performance fitness, so it may have some health benefits, even when done for the purpose of performing better in a sport. Still, strength training for health involves a program far different from that used in strength training to become a better outside hitter or pulling guard.

If jogging and aerobics are the most visible signs of health fitness, then activity in the weight room has become the most visible sign of motor-performance fitness. The most significant difference between athletes today and their counterparts of even only one generation ago is their strength. There can no longer be any doubt that strength plays a central role in sport performance at any level and in virtually every sport. Strength in motor-performance fitness is *functionally* related to a specific motor activity, such as strength to put a shot, to jump high, to hit a ball, or to pull an oar.

The *functional specificity* of motor-performance fitness means that a sprinter will have a vastly different training program from that of a wrestler, even though they each need to be strong. The same general principle of functional specificity holds true for the other components of motor-performance fitness also. You can improve your agility, power, balance, reaction time, speed, and coordination, but to do so, you must use training activities designed to be specific to the outcomes intended. For instance, a defensive back in football needs to be able to run backward quickly for short distances, a task for which the player can become more fit through specific training exercises.

COSMETIC FITNESS

It would be a mistake not to recognize that, for many people, youth and adult, looking good is an important outcome of fitness activities. One of the significant shifts in public perception over the past several decades is the change in what is considered to be an attractive physical appearance. It was not too many years ago that a man with well-defined muscular features was often described as "muscle-bound"—and was not necessarily admired for looking that way. If a girl or a woman had well-defined muscular features, she might have been socially ridiculed. Not so today!

Looking fit is in—and looking strong is an important part of looking fit. This is true for both men and women:

> Perhaps the most prevalent and least understood reason people train with weights is to add quality to their lives. Many people engage in strength training simply

because they look better and feel better when they do. They find the training process enjoyable, and the training product well worth the effort. For most people, controlled physical exertion is a satisfying experience, and increased muscle strength is a gratifying accomplishment. Something about becoming stronger enhances a person's self-image. (Westcott, 1982, p. 4)

If **cosmetic fitness** is not confused with health fitness, then it can be a positive addition to the overall fitness movement. The more our culture adopts an active lifestyle, the better off future generations will be. The outward appearance of a person is important—and maybe is particularly so to adolescents.

On the other hand, it is clear that television and print advertising has made the slim and athletic body shape the preferred one in order to sell products. The fact is that people come in all shapes; that is, genetic endowments determine their particular body shape, whether it be a slender, heavy, or more athletic build. Children, youths, and adults who do not fit the body shape advocated by advertising are at risk in what Australian physical educator Richard Tinning (1985) calls "the cult of slenderness." Cosmetic fitness is fine as long as it takes place in an educational environment where acceptance of different body shapes is the norm.

THE DOSE–RESPONSE DEBATE

Current investigations and discussions, referred to here as the "**dose–response debate,**" are about what is needed to generate the health benefits described in Table 8.2—that is, how much of what kind of activity, at what intensity, for how long, and how frequently (Pate, 1995). Put simply, what "dose" of exercise is necessary to achieve the beneficial health "responses"? The dose–response debate developed since the late 1980s, as a new, specialized field of scholarship called "exercise epidemiology" began to present evidence on the relationship of physical activity to all causes of mortality (Blair et al., 1989). Dividing activity patterns into five groups, from low activity to high activity,

researchers found that men in the least-fit category were 3.44 times more likely to die during the follow-up period than those in the most-fit category, and the least-fit women were 4.65 times more likely to die than the most-fit women (Blair, 1992). Figure 8.1 shows these data and indicates clearly that the most impressive improvements in mortality are between Groups 1 and 2—that is, between the least active group and the group that gets some activity regularly. There are some additional modest improvements as people move to the more and more active groups, but clearly the major problem is in the sedentary group and the major gain to be achieved is by modest increases in physical activity as part of lifestyle.

Several decades of research on aerobic fitness have established a dose formula for exercise prescription related to aerobic fitness, the most important ingredient in health-related fitness (Blair & Connelly, 1996). Most fitness professionals working in this current generation of emphasis on aerobic fitness have used a dose formula based on three factors: intensity, duration, and frequency, a formula approved by the American College of Sports Medicine as early as 1975.

Intensity is typically calculated by establishing a target heart rate. This is achieved by subtracting the person's age from 220 (a figure related to the maximum heart rate of a well-trained young person) and then taking 70 percent of that figure. (See the box on calculating your target heart rate.) Thus, if you are 20 years old, you would subtract 20 from 220 and multiply the result by 0.70 to get your target heart rate of 140 beats per minute. This would be the training intensity you would try to achieve to produce the optimum aerobic benefit.

Duration refers to the amount of time you can sustain aerobic exercise at your target heart rate. The important physiological adaptations that result from aerobic exercise are achieved by sustained exercise at the target heart rate. Put another way, if your target rate is 140 and you can achieve that by running 8-minute miles, then you will receive optimum aerobic benefit by sustaining that pace for longer and longer periods of time. If you increase

---

TABLE 8.2 Health Benefits Associated with Fitness and Physical Activity

High blood pressure. Regular physical activity prevents or delays the development of high blood pressure, and exercise reduces blood pressure for people with hypertension.

Cancer. Regular physical activity is associated with decreased risk of colon cancer and reduces the risk of cancer of the breast and reproductive organs in women.

Cardiovascular disease. Regular physical activity decreases the risk of cardiovascular disease in general and of coronary heart disease in particular.

Cognitive function. Exercise may be associated with small to moderate gains in cognitive functioning.

Immune function. Moderate endurance exercise boosts immune function. (Excessive endurance training suppresses immune function.)

Mental health. Physical activity relieves symptoms of depression and anxiety, improves mood, and may reduce the risk of developing depression.

Obesity. Physical activity favorably affects body-fat distribution, and low levels of activity contribute to the high prevalence of obesity in the United States.

Osteoarthritis. Regular physical activity is necessary for maintaining normal muscle strength, joint structure, and joint function.

Osteoporosis. Weight-bearing physical activity is essential for normal development and for achieving and maintaining peak bone mass in young adults. Regular activity may also reduce the risk of osteoporosis developing.

Overall mortality. Higher levels of physical activity are associated with lower mortality rates for both older and younger adults.

Quality of life. Physical activity appears to improve health-related quality of life by enhancing psychological well-being and self-esteem, and by improving physical functioning in people who have poor health.

SOURCE: Biddle, 1995; Fahey, Insel, & Roth, 2003; Shephard, 1995; U.S. Department of Health and Human Services, 1996.

---

the pace, say, to 7 minutes per mile, you will receive no added aerobic benefit; indeed, if the increased pace results in a decreased duration, then the aerobic benefit will be diminished.

The third variable is *frequency.* The importance of this variable directly relates to the need for bodily systems to recover and rebuild. Many joggers, cyclists, and swimmers work out every day. If their exercise intensity and duration are within their capabilities, their bodies will adapt and recover sufficiently to sustain daily workouts. Even so, those who train on a daily basis, even elite athletes, typically follow a hard–easy training program, wherein more-strenuous workout periods are followed by less-strenuous workout periods.

Thus, in this era of health fitness, it has become common to prescribe exercise based on the dose formula of three to five workouts per week at the target heart rate, with each workout sustained for a minimum of 20–30 minutes. Part of the success of this formula is that it clearly differs from the no-pain-no-gain myth of previous generations. If a person moves gradually into a program based on this dose–response formula, she or he can do so comfortably and without the fatigue, discomfort, or soreness often associated with high-intensity exercise.

The debate, which is the focus of this section, has developed because epidemiological research has shown that modest amounts of low- to moderate-

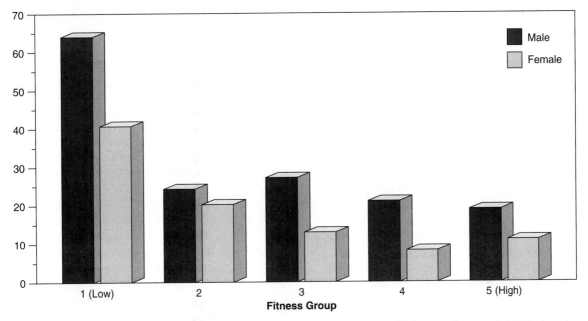

Figure 8.1   Age-adjusted death rates (all causes) per 10,000 person-years of follow-up for men (10,000+) and women (3,000+) in the Aerobics Center Longitudinal Study.

NOTE: Subjects were apparently healthy at baseline, physical fitness was assessed by maximal exercise testing on a treadmill, and the average length of follow-up was slightly more than eight years. Rates are based on 240 deaths in men and 43 deaths in women. Data for this figure were taken from Blair et al. (1989).

Calculating Your Target Heart-Rate Zone

Your target heart-rate zone should be between 65 and 90 percent of your maximum heart rate (MHR).

1. Estimate your MHR by subtracting your age from 220.
2. Multiply your MHR by 0.65 and by 0.90 to calculate your target heart-rate zone.

For example, a 21-year-old would calculate her target heart rate zone as follows:

MHR = 220 − 21 = 199 beats per minute (BPM)

Lower range of zone = 199 × 0.65 = 129 BPM

Upper range of zone = 199 × 0.90 = 179 BPM

Fitness benefits are gained when the heart rate stays within the parameters of the zone. Unfit people or people just starting an exercise program should use the lower end of the range for their threshold.

---

intensity physical activity result in substantial health benefits, and that this activity can be accumulated throughout the day in a variety of activities that are not typically thought of as fitness-training activities (Blair & Connelly, 1996). Remember, the data

in Figure 8.1, which have been replicated in a number of studies (Pate, 1995), show the most improvement between the least-active and the next group, which Blair and Connelly (1996) describe as the difference between being inactive (sedentary) and engaging in regular walking or recreational activity only.

The dose formula for exercise prescription that has developed from this research suggests that substantial health benefits will accrue to people who *accumulate* about 30 minutes of activity per day in 10-minute bouts doing activities at least equal to a brisk walk (Pangrazi, Corbin, & Welk, 1996). This dose formula was approved in 1996 by a consensus panel convened by the National Institutes of Health (*President's Council on Physical Fitness and Sports Newsletter,* 1996). Engaging in 30 minutes per day of moderate-intensity physical activity, in at least 10-minute bouts, accumulates 210 minutes per week, which is now the suggested baseline exercise prescription.

The prescription for children is about double that for adults. Children's physical activity (PA) is typically in short-duration bouts, which is appropriate to their developmental stage. Children naturally are active, then rest, and this natural approach should be encouraged (Pangrazi, Corbin, & Welk, 1996). In 1998 NASPE published its "Physical Activity Guidelines for Children," which suggested at least 60 minutes per day of PA of varying levels of intensity in bouts that last 10–15 minutes (Corbin & Pangrazi, 1998).

The current evidence relating physical activity to health and mortality variables has created a new sense of health-related activity, what many now refer to as moderate-to-vigorous physical activity (MVPA) (Simons-Morton, 1994). MVPA takes into account a broader range of physical activities than did health-related aerobic fitness, particularly activities that are near the moderate end of the range, such as brisk walking.

Which of the two dose formulas is correct? One appears to be anchored in the concept of fitness, albeit health-related fitness. The other is clearly anchored in health, particularly related to reductions in all causes of mortality. We have much to learn in both approaches, and a clear answer to the question is impossible at this time. Blair and Connelly (1996, p. 194), in reviewing studies from both traditions,

have suggested a holistic view that makes sense at this time.

> Most of these projects used the standard exercise prescription described by the ACSM as the training stimulus, although others have evaluated various combinations of frequency, intensity, and duration. It is still common, however, for scientists and clinicians to consider two somewhat competing views of the effects of physical activity: one on the role of physical activity in promoting health and the other on physical activity to improve fitness. We disagree with this approach of categorizing physical activity as contributing to health or fitness. We think physical activity works through multiple biological pathways to improve both health and function.

The Physical Activity Pyramid shown in Figure 8.2 reflects this holistic view. Some combination of strength training, flexibility work, aerobic conditioning, and MVPA is the way to achieve a level of PA that contributes significantly to health and well-being. The introduction of MVPA has opened up an entirely new realm of possibilities for lifespan engagement in PA that contributes to both the quality and the healthfulness of life.

THE SOCIAL GRADIENT IN HEALTH AND FITNESS

This review of basic concepts of fitness related to health would be incomplete without noting how social and economic status within a society affects health and longevity. We know that the proximal causes of degenerative diseases—commonly referred to as "risk factors"—are physical inactivity, smoking, a high-fat diet, and the like. These risk factors, however, are not distributed normally across populations within societies. The fact is that as people *move down* the social-class structure of developed nations, risk factors and health problems increase, resulting in increased mortality (Siedentop, 1996c).

This socioeconomic impact on health and fitness is what health epidemiologists refer to as the

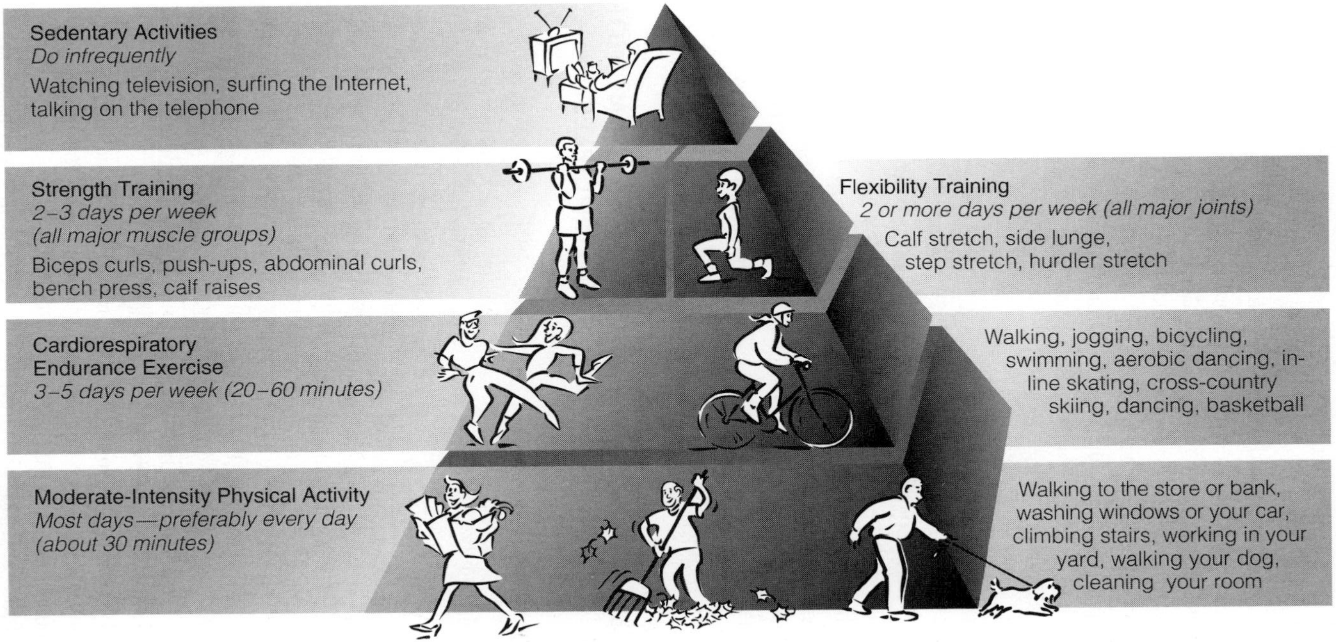
Sedentary Activities
Do infrequently
Watching television, surfing the Internet, talking on the telephone
Strength Training
2–3 days per week
(all major muscle groups)
Biceps curls, push-ups, abdominal curls, bench press, calf raises
Flexibility Training
2 or more days per week (all major joints)
Calf stretch, side lunge, step stretch, hurdler stretch
Cardiorespiratory
Endurance Exercise
3–5 days per week (20–60 minutes)
Walking, jogging, bicycling, swimming, aerobic dancing, in-line skating, cross-country skiing, dancing, basketball
Moderate-Intensity Physical Activity
Most days—preferably every day
(about 30 minutes)
Walking to the store or bank, washing windows or your car, climbing stairs, working in your yard, walking your dog, cleaning your room

Figure 8.2 The Physical Activity Pyramid.

SOURCE: Fahey, Insel, & Roth, 2003.

"**social gradient**" in health; that is, the health status of a particular class within a nation is typically better than that of the classes below it and worse than that of the classes above it (Hertzman, 1994). The social-gradient hypothesis argues that relative social and economic deprivation within societies accounts for better or poorer health. Hertzman (1994) suggested that "one's place in the social hierarchy and the experiences which follow from it appear to be powerful determinants of the length and healthfulness of life" (p. 169). Note that the term "determinants" is used purposely because that relative deprivation "influences life-style choices and differential access to high quality social environments" (Marmot, 1994, p. 213).

Traditionally, fitness has been viewed nearly totally as an *individual* responsibility (Tinning, 1990). When people are unfit or less fit than might be desirable, the less-than-optimally fit people get the blame for their condition. A socioecological view, on the other hand, looks to the social contexts within which people live their lives as partial explanations for their levels of health and fitness (Vertinsky, 1991, p. 83):

> Health is increasingly understood to be a social commodity, much like other social commodities such as housing and education. Some get more of it, some get less, and those at the top of the social stratification tend to do better than those at the bottom. Too many are, in current government parlance, underserved. For this reason, new strategies for empowerment, social support, and community-based services are advocated as broad and powerful strategies for health.

The **socioecological view** is supported by evidence showing that in nations where income inequality is less, life expectancy is higher (Wilkinson, 1994). Also, increases in life expectancy have been shown in countries that have reduced income inequality in the current generation.

People in lower socioeconomic groups have less access to nutritious food and to information about nutrition—and the foods high in fat are among the least expensive. Urban areas are in decay and are typically unsafe for outside physical activity. No infrastructure is available to support and sustain involvement in physical activity for children, youths, or adults. These are unhealthy settings (see Table 8.3). Although individual responsibility remains an important and compelling concept in the effort to improve the health and vitality of our nation, we must also realize that there are structural problems that have profound impact on individual motivation and responsibility.

If society is to become healthier and if a more fit citizenry can help to achieve that public health goal, then we need this new approach to understanding the social complexities of fitness and activity across the variety of groups within our society. We must view fitness as both an individual and a social issue—and we must attempt to develop a society in which more people have access to safe, affordable, and inclusive opportunities to pursue a physically active lifestyle.

FITNESS-TRAINING CONCEPTS AND PRINCIPLES

In the 1970s and 1980s aerobic exercise and cardiovascular health were the main emphasis in health fitness. We have already considered the notion of a cardiovascular heart-rate training zone and the frequency, intensity, and duration recommended for cardiovascular exercise. Muscle strength and flexibility were much less prominent in exercise prescriptions and discussions about the health benefits of regular exercise. Muscles make up more than 40 percent of body mass (Fahey, Insel, & Roth, 2003), and they are the place where a substantial portion of the metabolic-energy reactions in your body take place. This section will further consider some of the principles associated with aerobic activity and will also emphasize the principles and benefits associated with resistance training.

When you train properly, the muscles and the energy systems that fuel those muscles become more efficient and stronger. This is true whether

TABLE 8.3	The Prevalence of Obesity: Populations of Special Concern	
Group	Estimated Prevalence of Obesity°	*Healthy People 2010* Target
Children (age 6–11)	11%	5%
Adolescents (age 12–19)	10	5
Adults (age 20–74)	23	15
Men	20	15
Women	25	15
Low-income people	29	15
Mexican American women	35	15
Black women	38	15

°Children and adolescents are classified as obese if they have a BMI at or above the appropriate 95th percentile for body mass index (BMI); adults are classified as obese if they have a BMI of 30 or above.

SOURCE: *Healthy People 2010* (2nd ed.), Department of Health and Human Services. Washington, D.C.: DHHS, 2000.

the muscles in question are the heart and leg muscles of a marathon runner or the arm and shoulder muscles of a javelin thrower. In that sense, the basic mechanisms underlying fitness training are the same for health fitness, motor-performance fitness, and cosmetic fitness.

When you train appropriately, the muscular system *adapts* to the training stresses; that is, when the training *load* increases, muscles are stressed and they adapt and improve their function (Fahey, Insel, & Roth, 2003; Westcott, 1982). For aerobic fitness—or for endurance activities such as distance running, cross-country skiing, and cycling—it is important that individuals be able to use oxygen efficiently. That is why aerobic (with-oxygen) conditioning is so central to health fitness. To use oxygen efficiently, a person must have a fit heart muscle that is capable of pumping large amounts of blood. The blood, too, must be fit, in that it must be capable of carrying large quantities of oxygen (which it does through hemoglobin). The arteries must be

fit, in that they must be free from elements that prevent the flow of blood. Finally, the muscles to which the blood flows must be fit so that they are capable of using the oxygen brought by the blood to energize them for activity.

General Training Principles

The human body adapts to meet the demands that are placed upon it. Short-term adaptations, when done repeatedly, gradually translate into long-term improvements. The five main principles of fitness training are specificity, progressive overload, recovery time, intensity, and duration (Fahey, Insel, & Roth, 2003). **Specificity** means that to produce a desired effect, an exercise must be related to the fitness component in which improvement is sought; that is, if you want to improve aerobic conditioning, you have to do aerobic activities, and if you want to improve arm strength, you have to do exercises that focus on the muscles of the arms and shoulders.

Progressive overload means that the "load" or exercise chosen must be done at a level that produces a conditioning effect. If the exercise load is too light, it may maintain a fitness level but not increase that level. If the load is too great, it will limit the amount of exercise that can be done and risk injury. As you exercise within this appropriate zone, the **threshold** necessary to produce increasing effects will gradually rise; that is, you will need to use a progressively higher load to continue to improve fitness levels. There is a great deal of good literature that provides advice on gradually raising the exercise load and threshold to achieve continuing improvement, whether it is in aerobic conditioning or strength training. Unfortunately, too many people try to train by moving right to the upper edge of the exercise load they can handle. Too often, they are injured or burn out and subsequently neglect or even quit their fitness program. It is far better to establish long-term goals and use changes in exercise load that are easier to accommodate.

The third principle, **recovery time,** suggests that muscles need time to recover from an exercise bout before they are used again in similar activities. The muscular system needs time to adapt to training stresses, since the physiological and biochemical mechanisms responsible for fitness gains operate during the rest intervals between exercise bouts. The frequency with which one can exercise safely varies with the fitness component being developed and the level of fitness the person has in that component. After some beginning work, a person can generally do aerobic work every day if it is not an all-out effort. Most strength-training guides suggest that at least one day of rest be taken between periods of strength work on the same muscle groups.

Intensity refers to the "load" of an exercise bout. People who exercise often become very knowledgeable about appropriate intensities in their exercise program. Intensity in cardiovascular work refers primarily to heart rate during exercise. Intensity during strength training refers primarily to the level of resistance. Higher levels of fitness require greater intensity. Moderate-intensity exercise is sufficient for public health goals.

Duration refers to the length of an exercise bout. Obviously, intensity affects duration, in that higher exercise loads typically reduce duration. In strength training, duration typically refers to the number of repetitions and sets at any particular intensity. For health benefits, moderate-intensity and moderate-duration activities are wholly appropriate. For motor-performance-fitness goals, such as sport-performance improvements, higher levels of intensity and duration are typically required.

As we said at the start of this section, the body adapts to exercise stress and in so doing improves the components of fitness. It is just as true, however, that the body adapts to lack of exercise. Fitness gains that are not maintained through exercise will be lost. When a person stops exercising, it can be expected that 50 percent of whatever gains had been made will be lost in two months (Fahey, Insel, & Roth, 2003). Once a desired level of fitness is achieved, then a maintenance program can be developed to sustain those gains without increasing the exercise load.

These principles of training are relevant to health fitness, motor-performance fitness, and cosmetic fitness. Each should be applied somewhat differently, depending on what kind of fitness a person is trying to achieve.

Health-Fitness Training

People interested in health fitness typically engage in some form of aerobic training. The more faithfully they adhere to a workout schedule that represents the intensity, duration, and frequency required for cardiovascular improvements, the more likely they are to achieve those improvements. Other people prefer more moderate physical activity and perhaps walk for 30 minutes before or after dinner each night. Still others achieve their health-fitness goals through a form of workouts known as "interval training," in which more intense exercise periods are alternated with rest periods to allow for recovery.

The frequency of exercise patterns depends on which of these approaches people choose; that is, the moderate-activity approach typically requires daily exercise, whereas the continuous-aerobic and interval-aerobic approaches can achieve results with three to five workouts per week.

Current evidence for the long-term benefits of health fitness suggest that activity of moderate intensity is appropriate. The ethic of no pain, no gain is simply inappropriate when it comes to health-fitness development and maintenance. Indeed, if infrequent, high-intensity fitness activities are imposed on children and youths, as they often are during infrequent fitness-testing days in physical education, these children and youths are likely to become averse to involvement in fitness programs.

Continuous and Interval Training

Two kinds of aerobic training are used both for health-fitness purposes and by athletes training for endurance events: continuous and interval exercise. Walkers, joggers, and cyclists typically favor the continuous form of training, engaging in sustained exercise with their heart rate at or above the threshold level. More serious runners and many swimmers tend to favor interval training, wherein exercise bouts are interspersed with rest periods.

There is no doubt that both continuous training and interval training are sufficient to build and maintain high levels of health fitness. Disagreement over which is better arises when higher, competitive levels of cardiovascular fitness are needed for endurance events. Continuous exercise is probably the better form for beginners, simply because it is less intense and can be adjusted easily and done almost anyplace. **Interval training** tends to be more intense (i.e., intense exercise periods, followed by rest periods) and typically needs a measured distance to be done appropriately—for example, a 25-meter swimming pool or a 400-meter running track. The great value of interval training is that it allows you to do more work during any given exercise period because the exercise period can be more intense because it is followed by a rest period that allows for some recovery before the next exercise period begins.

The minimum continuous program for achieving and maintaining health fitness would involve exercising so as to lift the heart rate to the target threshold level and to maintain it there for 30 minutes (15 minutes would be an absolute minimum to achieve any training effect). This should be done three to five times per week. The same outcomes could be achieved through an interval program in which the trainee exercised at 80 percent of the maximum heart rate for a 2- or 3-minute period, then walked or did some mild jogging for the same length of time, then repeated the work–rest intervals.

Anaerobic Training

Anaerobic exercise is short-duration exercise completed without the aid of oxygen (which distinguishes it from aerobic exercise). Anaerobic exercise builds muscle mass. It has some health-related benefits, in that it positively affects resting metabolic rate, enhances bone density, and may contribute to long-term weight control (Gutin, Manos, & Strong, 1992). The main functional outcome of anaerobic exercise, however, is to move quickly and deliver great force, which is why anaerobic training is highly relevant to sprinters, wrestlers, football players, gymnasts, and other athletes who must move explosively or deliver a substantial amount of force in a short time.

The threshold for building and maintaining anaerobic fitness is much higher than that for aerobic training. Athletes must perform at near-maximum effort for short distances or time periods, then allow a sufficient rest for nearly complete recovery before repeating the effort. Thus, virtually all anaerobic training is of the interval variety, with much longer rest intervals than in aerobic training.

Strength Training

Strength training, the primary component of motor-performance fitness, is best done through some form of exercise against resistance, typically through weight training. In this form of fitness

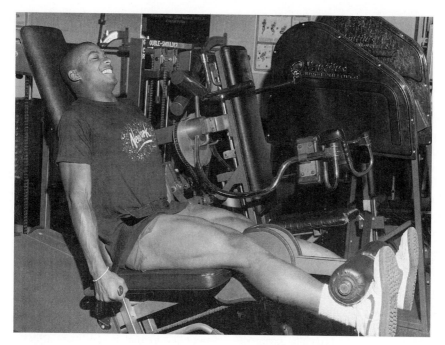

Strength training is often done on sophisticated weight machines.

training, there are four primary variables to be considered (Fahey, Insel, & Roth, 2003; Westcott, 1982):

1. Amount of resistance (weight) per lift
2. Number of repetitions of each lift (a set)
3. Number of sets per workout
4. Number of workouts per week

The phrase used most commonly among strength-training enthusiasts is *repetition maximums,* or *RMs;* for example, a "5RM" means a "five-repetition maximum," and "10RM" means a "ten-repetition maximum." Thus, a 5RM load is the most weight you could lift five times in succession, and a 10RM load is the most weight you could lift ten times in succession.

In strength training, there is a direct corollary to the aerobic–anaerobic distinction made earlier. To build muscle *endurance,* one would perform numerous repetitions against a fairly low resistance. To build muscle *strength,* one would perform few

repetitions against a much higher resistance. As in aerobic–anaerobic training, the results are highly specific to the nature of the exercise stress. The benefits of strength training are substantial (see Table 8.4).

Weight-training experts generally agree that weight loads at or exceeding 75 percent of one's maximum lifting capacity are most beneficial for developing and maintaining strength. (A 10RM weight load is generally thought to be about 75 percent of maximum for most individuals.) The five general training principles of specificity, progressive overload, recovery time, intensity, and duration apply to strength training just as they do to aerobic and anaerobic training. The application of those principles typically results in a program of weight training in which a person does five or six repetitions per set (against a 5RM to 6RM weight load), two to four sets per workout, and three workouts per week. As the person gets stronger, the weight load gradually is increased, even though the basic workout program remains the same.

TABLE 8.4 Physiological Changes and Benefits from Weight Training

Change	Benefits
Increased muscle mass°	Increased muscular strength Improved body composition Higher rate of metabolism Toned, health-looking muscles
Increased utilization of motor units during muscle contractions	Increased muscular strength and power
Improved coordination of motor units	Increased muscular strength and power
Increased strength of tendons, ligaments, and bones	Lower risk of injury to these tissues
Increased storage of fuel in muscles	Increased resistance to muscle fatigue
Increased size of fast-twitch muscle fibers (from a high-resistance program)	Increased muscular strength and power
Increased size of slow-twitch muscle fibers (from a high-repetition program)	Increased muscular endurance
Increased blood supply to muscles (from a high-repetition program)	Increased delivery of oxygen and nutrients Increased elimination of wastes
Biochemical improvements (for example, increased sensitivity to insulin)	Enhanced metabolic health
Improved blood fat levels	Reduced risk of heart disease

° Due to genetic and hormonal differences, men will build more muscle mass than women.

SOURCE: Fahey, Insel, & Roth, 2003.

The rest interval in resistance training is a function of the amount of resistance used. With less resistance—in a program to develop endurance and strength for purposes of wellness—a rest period of 1–3 minutes between sets is appropriate. For higher levels of resistance—to build maximum strength for some specific activity or for cosmetic purposes—a rest period of 3–5 minutes between sets is appropriate.

Weight training is among the most highly specific of all exercise programs. Specific muscles and specific muscle groups are stressed with each exercise done. Therefore, three additional training principles are particularly relevant to strength training (Fahey, Insel, & Roth, 2003; Westcott, 1982):

1. When lifting, a person should raise and lower the weight load in a slow and controlled manner so that the force is applied as consistently as possible throughout the movement.

2. The muscle or muscle group should be exercised through the full range of motion available at the particular joint, to avoid decreasing joint flexibility.

3. The strength program should avoid creating serious strength imbalances by exercising certain muscles or muscle groups and not those that are related to them. Balance of exercise is particularly important for *agonist–antagonist pairs* (muscles on either side of joints).

Resistance Training for Older People

You are never too old to start resistance training! In fact, resistance training is being shown to be of great benefit to older people. It is important for older people to retain their strength, but resistance training has other important benefits for them, too.

- Unless you maintain an exercise program, you tend to lose 5 pounds of muscle every decade in the older years.

SOURCE: Westcott & Baechle, 1998.

- As you lose muscle mass, your metabolic rate decreases and you burn fewer calories.
- Muscle mass can be added at any age through a regular program of resistance exercise.
- A modest but regular program adds muscle, reduces fat, and helps you lose weight even without reducing caloric intake.
- Resistance training also increases bone density and reduces the incidence of osteoporosis.

Strength training is done most often using either free weights or an exercise machine such as a Universal Gym or Nautilus equipment. Any of these approaches offers sufficient variety to exercise what most people consider to be the ten major targets for a complete program (chest, back, shoulders, triceps, biceps, quadriceps, hamstrings, lower legs, forearms, and neck). The degree to which each of those areas is included in a strength program, however, is highly specific to the desired outcomes of the program. Sprinters will have a strength program very different from that of discus throwers, and each of those will be substantially different from a program for basketball or volleyball players. You can be sure, however, that any athlete who is trying to get better at his or her sport will be involved in a strength-training program of some kind.

Flexibility

Physical activity is crucially important to maintaining good health. Activity requires movement. Movement is not possible without an adequate level of the fitness component commonly called *flexibility*. Flexibility refers to the property of body tissues that determines the range of motion achievable at a joint or a group of joints (Knudsen, Magnusson, & McHugh, 2000). *Static flexibility* refers to the linear or angular measurement of the limits of the range of motion at a joint. *Dynamic flexibility* refers to the rate of increase in tension in a relaxed muscle as it is stretched.

Increased flexibility allows for easier and more efficient performance of exercise activities. As we grow older, our flexibility decreases, and that inhibits our capacity to move efficiently. Most exercise programs now include regular flexibility work as a key component of a total program. Like other training modalities, flexibility work is also defined by frequency, intensity, and duration.

Flexibility work should be done at least 3 times per week after moderate or vigorous activity. Four to five stretches for each major muscle group are recommended, typically during the cooling-down period after exercise. Muscles should be slowly elongated and held for 30 seconds with low levels of force. Flexibility exercise before exercise, when muscles are not yet warmed up, is not recommended.

THE MEASUREMENT OF FITNESS

The measurement of fitness continues to be a source of considerable debate in the fitness and physical-education professions. The debate, of course, centers on the measurement of health fitness. Motor-performance fitness has only one meaningful measure, and that is the performance itself! If you are a basketball player, then strength training should help you to play basketball better—to rebound more strongly or shoot more accurately from a distance, or to play defense more aggressively. The fact that a basketball player can bench-press 200 pounds will not mean anything unless it translates directly into skills that improve his or her basketball game.

Likewise, there is no useful way to measure the effects of a strength program that is undertaken for cosmetic purposes. Do you think you look better? Do you feel better about yourself? Do other people think you look better? If so, then the program is a success.

In health fitness, however, the consequences of measurement are substantially more important and the strategies for measuring health fitness are considerably more varied, thus causing a certain amount of controversy. Two approaches dominate the current fitness-measurement scene: (1) fitness tests, and (2) direct measures of **cardiovascular fitness** and body composition.

Fitness testing is done frequently in school programs. A health-fitness test battery typically includes measures of body composition, back flexibility, abdominal strength, upper-body strength, and cardiovascular capacity. In the National Children and Youth Fitness Study II (Ross et al., 1987), these parameters were measured as follows:

- Body composition—triceps, subscapular and medial calf skinfolds
- Back flexibility—sit-and-reach test
- Abdominal strength—bent-knee sit-ups
- Upper-body strength—modified pull-ups
- Cardiovascular capacity—1-mile walk/run for children 8 years and older, ½-mile walk/run for children under age 8

This test is similar to a number of fitness tests currently used in fitness centers and schools. The two most widely used tests are the FITNESSGRAM® battery, developed at the Institute for Aerobics Re-

search, and the Physical Best battery developed by AAHPERD.

Fitness testing always involves the reporting of results. A measure is obtained from a test, and that measure must be interpreted and reported. The traditional method is to test a large number of subjects and then report *norm-referenced scores*—that is, a score that tells you where you stand relative to the performance of the larger group. If you are in the fiftieth percentile, then you are average for that group. A more recent approach has been to interpret and report scores based on criteria that are thought to produce a health benefit or indicate a reduced risk for a specific health problem, a method of scoring and reporting known as **criterion-referenced health (CRH) standards** (Corbin & Pangrazi, 1992).

Criterion-referenced standards have two distinct advantages. First, they assess fitness or physical activity against absolute standards that indicate minimum levels necessary to achieve health outcomes (Cureton, 1994). Second, they provide immediate diagnostic feedback about whether performance is adequate to promote health. Cureton (1994) argues that separate criterion-referenced standards should be used for physical fitness and physical activity and that children and youths should be encouraged to meet both sets of standards. There is also a strong consensus now that any award system associated with fitness or physical-activity programs should be related to criterion-referenced standards rather than norm-based performances.

Another possibility is to reduce standards to "zones of interpretation" (Whitehead, 1994). An *interpretation zone* allows people to use fitness-performance or physical-activity data to understand whether they are (a) at risk for hypokinetic disease, (b) at a level that will contribute to health, or (c) at a level necessary for some athletic performance. Figure 8.3 shows the differences among norm-referenced standards, criterion-referenced standards, and interpretation zones.

Fitness testing in hospitals or exercise-science laboratories typically focuses on cardiovascular functioning and body composition. The most com-

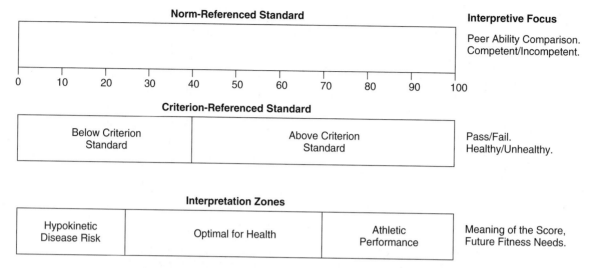

Figure 8.3   Three methods for interpreting the results of fitness assessments.
Source: Adapted from Whitehead, 1994.

mon form of cardiovascular-function testing is performed on a motor-driven treadmill. The maximal volume of oxygen (VO_2 max) that can be consumed by the body during exercise is measured; this value is considered by exercise scientists to be the best indicator of cardiovascular functioning (Costill, 1986). The treadmill can be finely calibrated for speed and grade (e.g., a 2 percent uphill grade) and the subject of the test is fitted with a mouthpiece through which she or he inhales and exhales, thus allowing her or his breath to be captured and analyzed. The speed of the treadmill is gradually increased until the person has given an all-out effort.

Clearly, the treadmill test is highly accurate and useful but also is comparatively expensive and time-consuming. Thus, tests such as the Harvard step test, the 12-minute run–walk, and the 1-mile run–walk are used as substitutes in school programs. This, in essence, is why mass fitness testing will always be controversial. The treadmill test is tightly controlled and yields many highly accurate data. The step test and the 12-minute run–walk test are much less tightly controlled and yield only one measure.

Body composition is also considered to be an important measure of health fitness. A high percentage of body fat relative to bone and muscle has been shown repeatedly to be a predictor of risk for a wide range of degenerative diseases (Ross & Pate, 1987). Body composition is a much better measure of health fitness than is body weight. Many people who begin to take part in health-fitness programs do not lose weight quickly. What happens is that the composition of their body changes as the percentage of fat decreases and the percentage of muscle increases—with weight staying level or reducing only slightly.

In fitness tests, technicians estimate body composition by taking skinfold measurements at two or three places (triceps, subscapular, and medial calf, in the National Children and Youth Fitness Study [NCYFS] II) and using the sum of these to estimate body fat. This method is relatively inexpensive and, if done carefully, can provide a sufficiently accurate gross measure of body composition to note changes that occur with training. Exercise-science laboratories, however, use a more accurate method of estimating body composition: hydrostatic or underwater weighing. Briefly, this method involves weighing

A bicycle ergometer test is one good way to measure cardiovascular function.

the body on land and under water to estimate body density. Fat is lighter per unit volume than is water (Costill, 1986) and, therefore, floats—people with a higher percentage of body fat have a lower density and therefore are good floaters.

Measuring MVPA

There are many problems associated with the measurement of physical activity, particularly moderate-to-vigorous physical activity (MVPA). For example, what activities count as "moderate" or as "vigorous"? One study might consider sustained walking moderate, and another study might label it vigorous. Walking, of course, can range from quite leisurely to intensely active (as in power or race walking). Researchers have had difficulty getting reliable data on the amount of time a person spends in MVPA (Lee & Paffenberger, 1996). Heart-rate monitors and accelerometers are two kinds of devices that have been used to provide more reliable information on MVPA (Beighle, Pangrazi, & Vin-

cent, 2001). Heart-rate monitors can be calibrated to estimate energy expenditure but tend to be influenced by factors such as age, mode of exercise, and body size. Accelerometers can store data that allow for assessment of the frequency, intensity, and duration of physical activity, and they are able to detect the intermittent activity of young children, which is an important variable in estimating MVPA. A major problem with accelerometers is that they are expensive. It appears now that the most cost-effective and widely accessible devices for measuring MVPA are pedometers, which measure the number of steps taken during activity. Although they are not sensitive to some forms of activity, such as cycling, they do allow for a valid assessment of the amount of daily activity. They are also very useful for teachers and parents who want to help children and youths develop active lifestyles. The goal for adults is typically set at 10,000 steps per day. It is also possible to calculate the number of calories expended each day from the step count. Pedometers are not overly expensive and can be used in a number of ways to help people learn more about the amount of activity they need and how they can get it through modest changes in their lifestyles.

Another promising method of informally measuring fitness is to estimate caloric expenditure of various activities. The unit of measurement used for this purpose is called a **MET**, or metabolic equivalent (Corbin & Pangrazi, 1996). METs are designed to estimate the metabolic cost of activity. One MET equals the number of calories expended at rest (resting metabolism). Activity that is twice that intensity measures 2 METs. Activities such as slow walking, slow stationary cycling, and bowling are typically 3 METs or less and are considered to be light activities. Activities that reach a level of 6 METs are labeled moderate, such as brisk walking, tennis, or mowing the lawn with a power mower. Activities that are 7 METs or higher are considered to be vigorous, such as jogging, fast cycling, mowing the lawn with a hand mower, and many sports.

AAHPERD has developed a functional fitness test for older adults (Darby & Temple, 1992). The tests measures agility, hip flexibility, muscular strength and endurance, coordination, and an endurance walk. The test is useful for formal programs in which adults seek to develop higher levels of cardiovascular fitness and also motor performance fitness that allows them to have greater flexibility and mobility.

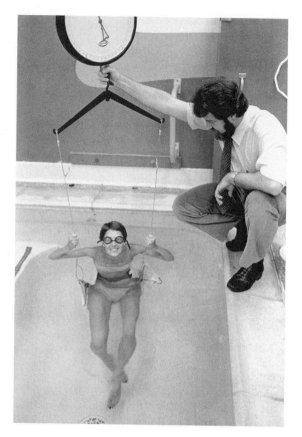

Hydrostatic weighing provides the most accurate estimate of body composition.

Informal Measurement of Fitness

Most adults are not interested in formal tests of fitness, although they do often want to monitor their fitness levels informally. This is particularly true for cardiovascular fitness. A simple way to do this is to regularly take your own heart rate during exercise and as you recover from exercise: Check your pulse rate, either at the carotid artery in the neck or at the radial artery in the wrist; count beats for 10, 20, or 30 seconds; multiply that total by 6, 3, or 2 to calculate the rate per minute at which your heart is beating.

As we saw earlier in this chapter, the method of calculating your target heart rate for maximum benefit in aerobic activity is to take a maximum heart rate of 220, subtract your age, and multiply by 0.65 and 0.90. Thus, if you are 35 years old, the lower range or your target rate zone would be $220 - 35 = 185 \times 0.65 = 120$. The upper range of your target heart rate zone would be $185 \times 0.90 = 167$. This is the threshold heart rate you would need to reach during exercise to gain maximum aerobic benefit. Figure 8.4 shows a target heart-range chart based on age and fitness level. It should be noted, however, that you can do aerobic exercise at a heart rate below the target rate and still gain substantial benefit.

Target Heart-Rate Range Chart
During exercise, the number of heartbeats in a 10-second interval should be counted. This chart should be used to determine whether the exercise heart rate is in the appropriate range for a given individual's age and fitness level.

Relative Fitness Level

Age	Low (60–70%)	Middle (70–80%)	High (80–90%)
20	20–23	23–26	26–29
25	19–22	22–25	25–28
30	19–22	22–25	25–28
35	18–21	21–24	24–27
40	18–21	21–24	24–27
45	17–20	20–23	23–26
50	17–20	20–23	23–26
55	16–19	19–22	22–25
60	16–19	19–22	22–25
65	16–18	18–21	21–24

Figure 8.4   Target heart rates based on age and fitness level.

SOURCE: Bryant & Peterson (1999), p. 31.

Another use of pulse rate as an informal measure is to assess your capacity to recover from exercise in which the pulse rate is elevated. The more-fit person will recover the resting pulse rate more quickly. People have different resting pulse rates. One way to calculate the resting pulse rate is to take it immediately upon awaking in the morning. If you keep a record of your morning resting pulse rate, you will be able to see clear signs of improvement in fitness as that pulse rate lowers. A second way is to take your normal resting pulse rate while standing before you begin to exercise. The time it takes to return to that rate after exercise is a good measure of fitness; that is, the more quickly you recover the preexercise heart rate, the better your fitness level.

Yet another way to monitor aerobic conditioning is to keep track of distance and time for the same kind of exercise. Thus, if you do brisk walking as a main aerobic exercise, you can walk measured distances and simply know the total time it took to complete the distance. Walking further in the same amount of time is a good measure of improved cardiovascular fitness.

The American College of Sports Medicine has estimated caloric cost of various activities based on the MET value of an activity and a person's body weight (Browder & Darby, 1998). Once those values are known, it is possible to calculate caloric cost per minute for each activity. Examples are about 100 calories expended per mile jogging and 80–90 calories per mile expended in brisk walking.

We should expect that further improvements will be made in measuring and monitoring MVPA. Fitness of all kinds has captured the attention of a large portion of the public, and the clear relationship between physical inactivity and a host of health problems will keep fitness high on the public-policy agenda for some time. How various forms of fitness and physical activity get done, where physical activity happens, and by whom programs are implemented is the focus of the next chapter.

SUMMARY

1. The health benefits of fitness and physical activity are better known now than ever before.

2. Early definitions of fitness were too broad and failed to distinguish between fitness characteristics related to health and those related to motor performance.

3. Current definitions of fitness distinguish between *health fitness,* with cardiovascular efficiency as the main component, and *motor-performance fitness,* with strength as the main component.

4. The major benefits of health fitness include a stronger heart, better circulatory function, increased oxygen-carrying capacity of the blood, more favorable body composition, and reduced levels of fat in the blood.

5. Motor-performance fitness relates directly to improved performance in physical skills.

6. Moderate and high levels of regular physical activity are associated with decreases in all causes of mortality and morbidity, as well as other health benefits.

7. The dose–response debate contrasts a view that is anchored in health-related fitness and cardiovascular functioning and a view that is anchored in health alone, particularly with regard to reductions in all causes of mortality.

8. Cosmetic fitness can be important to psychological well-being and is part of today's focus on an active, healthy lifestyle.

9. The social gradient in health and fitness reveals that socioeconomic status is strongly related to better or poorer health and fitness.

10. Muscles adapt to training by becoming more efficient and stronger, enabling people to do more intense or longer-duration work, or to do the same work with less effort.

11. Five general training principles for fitness are exercise specific to the fitness component where improvement is desired, progressive overload of the exercise stress, adequate recovery time between bouts, appropriate intensity within bouts, and appropriate length of the bout.

12. Health fitness is achieved through aerobic training with exercise bouts of sufficient intensity, duration, and frequency.

13. To improve and maintain aerobic fitness, a person must reach a threshold of training, sustain it for 15 to 20 minutes, and repeat this exercise three to five times per week.

14. Aerobic fitness can be achieved through continuous exercise at or just above the aerobic threshold or through interval training, in which shorter, more intense exercise bouts are interspersed with rest periods.

15. Anaerobic training requires nearly maximum effort for short periods, followed by long recovery periods.

16. Strength-training factors include the amount of resistance per lift, the number of repetitions per set, the number of sets per workout, and the number of workouts per week.

17. *Endurance* strength training uses lower resistances with more repetitions; *power* strength training uses higher resistances with fewer repetitions.

18. A typical power-strength training program involves five or six repetitions with a 5RM or 6RM workload, two to four sets per workout, and three workouts per week.

19. Additional weight-training principles include raising and lowering the weight load in a controlled manner, exercising muscle groups

through the full range of motion at a joint, and avoiding muscle imbalance by exercising muscle groups on both sides of a joint.

20. Motor-performance fitness is best measured through improved performance in the activity for which the fitness training is utilized.

21. Health fitness is measured typically through physical-fitness tests or through direct measures of cardiovascular functioning and body composition.

22. Criterion-referenced fitness standards have distinct advantages over norm-referenced standards, and zones of interpretation allow for people to understand their level of risk for hypokinetic disease.

23. The measurement of physical activity is highly dependent on self-reports, and there is no widespread agreement on what constitutes vigorous, as opposed to moderate, levels of activity.

DISCUSSION QUESTIONS

1. Should health fitness become a major, independent goal of school physical education? Why or why not?

2. To what extent are the differences in kinds of fitness misunderstood by the public? How can the public become better educated?

3. For which population groups might cosmetic fitness be more important than health fitness? How can that emphasis be changed? Should it be changed?

4. Give one example of how each of the five training principles is violated. Which principle is violated most often?

5. How can aerobic fitness be developed and maintained in everyday life? How can strength fitness be developed and maintained?

6. How fit are you? Answer in terms of your health, motor-performance, and cosmetic fitness. What factors in your life have contributed to your fitness or to your lack of fitness?

7. What fitness programs have you enrolled in? Which appealed to you? For what reasons? Which did not appeal to you? For what reasons?

8. To what extent do youths and adults suffer from the societal pressures to look fit?

9. How will the focus on moderate levels of physical activity affect fitness programs?

CHAPTER 9

Fitness Programs and Professions

Promotion of physical activity for children, adolescents, young adults, the middle-aged, and older adults is one of the most effective means of improving health and enhancing function and quality of life. All governments of the world should initiate policies to increase individual participation in physical activity by creating an environment that will encourage an acceptable level of physical activity in the whole population. This will require cooperation of governmental agencies, scientific and professional bodies, the private sector, and other community groups.

from Consensus Statement of the International Scientific Consensus Conference on Physical Activity, Health, and Well-Being, Quebec City, 1995

LEARNING OBJECTIVES

- To describe the purpose and goals of *Healthy People 2000* and outcomes related to those goals

- To describe fitness levels among children and youths

- To describe activity patterns among children and youths

- To describe fitness levels among adults

- To describe activity patterns among adults

- To describe and discuss school fitness and activity programs

- To describe AAHPERD efforts to promote fitness

- To describe and discuss worksite fitness programs

- To describe certification and preparation for fitness professions

In Chapter 8, we established the increasingly strong scientific evidence relating physical activity and fitness to positive health, mortality, and quality-of-life outcomes. We also indicated that motor-performance fitness has become increasingly important to success in sports and is important for quality-of-life outcomes among elderly people. It is also clear that many people engage in fitness activities to develop and maintain the kind of appearance that helps them to feel good about themselves. In this chapter, we will review information about fitness levels in the population, fitness programs, and career opportunities in the various professional fields that support the fitness movement.

From a national-policy perspective, it is clear that health fitness is the most important aspect of the entire fitness movement. The U.S. government has brought the issue to the nation's attention through a series of goals and reports that began in 1979 with the publication of *Healthy People: The Surgeon General's Report on Health Promotion and Disease Prevention.* That was followed in 1990 by *Healthy People 2000,* which established more than 300 health objectives in twenty-two priority areas, the first of which was "physical activity and fitness." Data related to achievement of the objectives are tracked and reported (Spain & Franks, 2001). No one thought that all the target goals could be reached in a single decade. One of the goals—increasing the number of worksite fitness programs—has been met, and we got close to meeting a few of the goals. For example, the death rate from coronary heart disease declined, nearly achieving the target goal; and 16 percent of people 18 and older engaged in vigorous PA 3 or more days per week for at least 20 minutes per session (target was 20%). For other goals, however, the picture was bleak. Overweight and obesity indicators rose rather than fell. The proportion of adolescents in grades 9–12 who participate in daily physical education fell precipitously (from 42% in 1991 to 27% in 1997; the target was 50%).

Early in 2000, *Healthy People 2010* was published, starting the second chapter in the nation's effort to become healthier. *Healthy People 2010* has two overarching goals: to increase the years of healthy life for all people and to eliminate health disparities based on race, gender, and income. HP 2010 has four primary enabling goals: to promote healthy behavior, to protect health, to achieve success in quality health care, and to strengthen community prevention. For our purposes, our main interest is goal 22: Improve health fitness and quality of life through daily physical activity. Table 9.1 describes that goal.

Nearly all states have now developed state-level healthy-people plans and programs. The only way to progress toward achievement of those goals is through widely accessible and inclusive programs with competent leadership. It is the purpose of this chapter to examine programs and the kinds of leadership that professionals bring to the fitness and physical-activity movements. In the following chapter, we will review problems and issues related to fitness and physical activity.

FITNESS LEVELS AMONG CHILDREN AND YOUTHS

In the mid-1950s, data from comparative fitness tests (Kraus & Hirschland, 1954) of European and American children set off the first large-scale, national children's fitness movement. Most tests and surveys of child and youth fitness since then have produced information that is discouraging, to say the least. The popular media have again focused attention on the low levels of fitness among children and youths. *U.S. News and World Report* (Levine, Wells, & Knopf, 1986) and *Time* magazine (Toufexis, 1986) featured stories on child and youth fitness, and the conclusions were gloomy indeed. The *Time* feature suggested that children were "getting an F for flabby."

It is difficult to make historical comparisons of child and youth fitness because fitness tests have historically emphasized motor-performance items rather than health-fitness items. Another complicating factor is the recent emphasis on the

TABLE 9.1 *Healthy People 2010* Goal 22 for Fitness and Physical Activity

22-1	Reduce the proportion of adults who engage in no leisure-time PA. (Baseline is 40% of adults 18 and older engaged in no leisure-time activity.) Target is 20%.
22-2	Increase the proportion of adults who engage regularly, preferably daily, in moderate PA for at least 30 minutes per day. (Baseline is 15% of adults 18 years and older who now engage at that level.) Target is 30%.
22-3	Increase the proportion of adults 18 years and older engaged in vigorous PA 3 or more days per week for 20 or more minutes per session. (Baseline is 23% of adults 18 years or older who now engage at that level.) Target is 30%.
22-4	Increase the proportion of adults who perform physical activities that enhance and maintain muscular strength and endurance. (Baseline is 18% of adults aged 18 and over who perform such activities 2 or more days per week.) Target is 30%.
22-5	Increase the proportion of adults who perform physical activities that enhance and maintain flexibility. (Baseline is 30% of adults aged 18 and older who do stretching activities regularly.) Target is 43%.
22-6	Increase the proportion of adolescents who engage in moderate PA for at least 30 minutes 5 days per week. (Baseline is 27% of students in grades 9–12 who engaged in moderate PA for at least 30 minutes on 5 of previous 7 days.) Target is 35%.
22-7	Increase the proportion of adolescents who engage in vigorous PA 3 or more days per week for 20 or more minutes per occasion. (Baseline is 65% of students in grades 9–12 who engaged in vigorous PA 3 or more days per week for 20 or more minutes per occasion.) Target is 85%.
22-8	Increase the proportion of public and private schools that require daily physical activity for all students. (Baseline is 17% for middle schools and 2% for high schools.) Targets are 25% for middle schools and 5% for high schools.
22-9	Increase the proportion of adolescents who participate in daily school physical education. (Baseline is 29% of students in grades 9–12 who participated in daily PE in 1999.) Target is 50%.
22-10	Increase the proportion of students in grades 9–12 who spend at least 50% of their school PE class time being physically active. (Baseline is 38% of students in grades 9–12.) Target is 50%.
22-11	Increase the proportion of adolescents who view television 2 or fewer hours on school days. (Baseline is 57% of students in grades 9–12 who viewed TV 2 or fewer hours.) Target is 75%.
22-12	Increase the proportion of public and private schools that provide access to their PA spaces for all people outside school hours. This is a developmental goal for which there is no baseline and no target.
22-13	Increase the proportion of worksites offering employer-sponsored PA and fitness programs. (Baseline is 46% of worksites with fifty or more employees that offered programs in 1999.) Target is 75%.
22-14	Increase the proportion of trips made by walking. (Baseline for trips of 1 mile or less is [a] 17% by adults and [b] 31% by children and adolescents.) Target is for 47% improvement for (a) and 68% improvement for (b).
22-15	Increase trips made by bicycling. (Baseline for [a] trips of 5 miles or less for adults is 0.6% and [b] trips by children and adolescents of 2 miles or less is 2.4%.) Targets are 2% for (a) and 5% for (b).

Source: Adapted from Spain & Franks, 2001; see also *Healthy People 2010: Physical Activity and Fitness;* President's Council on Physical Fitness and Sports; *Research Digest,* 3(13).

Fun and challenging physical activities are important for children.

accumulation of moderate-to-vigorous physical activity (MVPA), which is even more difficult to monitor and quantify, and still more difficult to compare with more traditional fitness measures, such as the 1-mile run.

In 1985 the results from the National Children and Youth Fitness Study (NCYFS I) were released. This nationwide study assessed the degree to which fifth- through twelfth-graders were fit and active. Because our understanding of what fitness is and of how it should be measured had improved greatly by the early 1980s, the NCYFS was the most rigorous study of youth fitness ever conducted in the United States. The investigators tested 8,800 boys and girls and completed surveys regarding the youths' activity habits.

The two results that are most alarming are the measure of **body composition** (skinfold test) and the cardiopulmonary measure (1-mile run–walk). The skinfold test data indicated that the average score for both boys and girls was in the moderately

high range, indicating some risk for problems associated with too much body fat. The average scores for the 1-mile run–walk showed that many girls did more walking than running and that many boys and girls could do no better than slowly jogging for that distance.

A similar fitness study (Milverstedt, 1988) in 1985, the National School Population Fitness Survey, examined a large number of elementary and secondary students on six fitness items and compared the results with national norms. Of the 9,678 boys tested, only 11 reached the eighty-fifth percentile on all six items! Thus, we should be concerned about not only the *average* scores on fitness tests but also the low number of high scores.

In 1987 the results of NCYFS II were released. This study examined the fitness levels and activity patterns of 6- to 9-year-old children (4,853 in the sample). The tests were similar to those in NCYFS I.

The low fitness scores were alarming, leading to the concerns voiced in the national media. The body-composition data indicated that the 6- to 9-year-olds in the study carried more body fat than did the children tested 20 years earlier (Ross & Pate, 1987). The general picture of these major, national tests seems clear. Children carry more body fat than is healthy. Children typically do not have well-developed cardiopulmonary capacity. Children, especially girls, perform poorly in tests of upper-body strength.

The general notion that children are not fit has been argued in both the professional and the popular literature since the 1970s. In the 1990s, the accuracy and fairness of that perception began to be questioned (Corbin & Pangrazi, 1992). Blair (1992) argued that we have been looking at the fitness data through the wrong set of lenses. He argues that physical activity that results in a particular level of energy expenditure per day is associated with important health benefits. (The figure is calculated to an energy expenditure of 3,000 calories per 1,000 grams of body weight per day, or 3Kcal/kg of body weight.) Blair recalculated the NCYFS II data and concluded that 77 percent of the boys and girls tested had met that standard, a finding that does not support the common perception of a nation of unfit children.

The effort to produce an accurate, reliable picture of the fitness levels of children and youths has also been hindered by the widespread use of norm-referenced scores to gauge fitness levels, a measurement problem discussed in Chapter 8. Recall that a norm-referenced score places any single child or youth in relation to all the other children or youths who took the tests when the norms were established. What do you know if you are a 12-year-old girl and you rank in the seventieth percentile on the 1-mile run? You know only that you ran a time that was faster than about 69 percent of those tested and slower than about 30 percent of those tested. It tells you nothing about whether the time you ran is a good indicator of your fitness level.

In most important tests, norm-referenced reporting has been replaced by criterion-referenced health (CRH) standards. CRH standards compare performances to criteria that indicate *potential risk,* where amounts of activity may be inadequate to contribute to health benefits. Thus, a performance score is immediately comparable to a standard related to health risks rather than to the performance of other children or youths.

Scientific evidence supporting the link between health-fitness or activity patterns and adult hypokinetic disease is not completely clear, but the likelihood of a strong link is becoming more widely accepted by scientists and other professionals (Ross & Pate, 1987). There is evidence (Pate, Trost, Dowda, et al., 1999) that children who are at risk on fitness measures in the fifth grade tend to remain at risk as seventh-graders. Likewise, children who do well in the fifth grade tend to do well in the seventh grade, suggesting that habits developed in childhood may tend to be sustained in the future.

It is obvious that the 1996 Surgeon General's report and other key documents, including *Healthy People 2010,* assume that childhood fitness and physical-activity measures are *predictive* of adolescent and adult patterns. Most health professionals believe that the prevention of hypokinetic disease begins in childhood.

These debates will continue, and their resolution is increasingly important to the nation's public health goals. Regardless of the resolution of the debate over the general state of child and youth fitness, there is common agreement that incidence of obesity is far too high in all subjects studied, that far too many children and youths are relatively inactive, and that many of them are at risk for later health problems. These children and youths can be identified, and there are intervention programs to help them (Bouchard, Shephard, & Stephens, 1993; Corbin, 2002; Sallis & McKenzie, 1991).

ACTIVITY PATTERNS AMONG CHILDREN AND YOUTHS

Participation in physical activity among children and youths is difficult to assess because information is typically obtained from self-reports, diaries, questionnaires, and reports from parents, and these reporting mechanisms often are not reliable. The NCYFS II survey found that nearly 85 percent of 6- to 9-year-old children participate in some activity through a community organization, typically public park and recreation programs, community-based sport programs, church programs, YMCA/YWCA programs, scouting groups, and private health clubs (Ross & Pate, 1987). The same survey found that children watch just over 2 hours per day of television during the week and 3.5 hours per day on weekends; these figures are substantially lower than those from many other national surveys.

The following conclusions can be reached regarding evidence of activity patterns among children and youths (American Sports Data, 1999; Rosenbaum & Leibel, 1989; Sallis, 1994; Sallis & McKenzie, 1991; U.S. Department of Health and Human Services, 1996):

1. The self-reports of children indicate that 90 percent or more are active at a level required for health benefits.

2. Studies monitoring the heart rates of children throughout the day show that most children

Children are more likely to be active if supported by their parents.

are sufficiently active to meet the ACSM (1990) recommendations for adult activity levels.

3. A large proportion of children do not get regular physical education from a specialist teacher.

4. When activity in physical-education classes is monitored, it is not uncommon for children to have as little as 2 minutes of vigorous activity in a 30-minute lesson.

5. More than 20 percent of American children and youths can be classified as obese. Girls are more likely to be obese than boys. African American and Hispanic children and youths are obese at nearly twice the rate of non-Hispanic whites.

6. Only about one half of American young people (ages 12–21 years) regularly participate in vigorous physical activity. One fourth report no vigorous physical activity.

7. Only 21.3 percent of all adolescents participate in school physical-education programs 1 or more days per week in their schools.

8. Data assessing *Healthy People 2000* goals show that 41 percent of ninth-graders participate in physical activity on a daily basis, but the figure declines to 13 percent by the twelfth grade.

9. About 50–60 percent of high school boys and 38–43 percent of high school girls participate on a school sport team each year. About 45 percent of boys and 25 percent of girls participate on sport teams run by nonschool organizations.

10. The participation data are all higher for males than for females. Because girls appear to be less active than boys, special programs may be needed to motivate and sustain their participation.

11. In the 1990s, the fastest-growing age group in frequent activity participation were children 6–11, and the steepest decline of all age groups was found in the 12–17 age bracket.

As children develop into their adolescent years, two things seem clear. Too many children reduce their physical activity substantially. It also appears that the "rich get richer and the poor get poorer," meaning that highly active children tend to develop habits that persist into adolescence, and those who are less active and less successful in physical activity tend to do less and less. This book has previously addressed the problem of the *varsity model* in American school sport, in which opportunities to participate decrease as youths grow older (see Chapter 7).

All evidence indicates that participation in sport and physical activity among youths reaches a peak at or about age 11 years and declines markedly through the teen years (Athletic Footwear Institute, 1990; Coakley, 1994; Sallis, 1994). In some cases, this decline occurs because opportunity to participate is reduced (e.g., the varsity model). In other cases, this decline is a reaction against how the sport is organized and conducted (many youths say it is no longer "fun"), and in still other cases, sport becomes less attractive when compared with other opportunities (work, dating, computers, etc.). It may be that some youths begin to participate in physical activities (recreational swimming, walking, or the like) that are not typically classified as sports and are difficult to monitor in terms of participation. Westcott (1992) has argued that youths are currently motivated by the adult model of fitness participation in clubs rather than by informal, recreational sports. Children are typically motivated by enjoyment, companionship, and adult approval of their activity participation. Adolescents are more likely to be motivated by seeking to influence their body shape, to control stress, to respond to peer influence, and to increase their sense of control over themselves and their lives. Attention to those factors is necessary to reduce the age-related decline in activity participation (Sallis, 1994).

Lack of participation among youths is a serious problem simply because the teen years are when adult habits begin to emerge. Because a large majority of children are active, adolescence must be the period most related to the high incidence of inactivity that is commonly found among adults. That relationship makes the reduction of physical activity among youths a major national problem, which must be solved if a healthier adult population is the goal.

FITNESS LEVELS AMONG ADULTS

It is difficult to obtain reliable and valid information about adult fitness levels. Whereas fitness testing of children and youths can be done in schools, no such opportunity exists for adults. Both public and private-sector agencies have tried to estimate levels of fitness and physical activity among adults, but these estimates come most frequently from surveys and questionnaires and are extremely variable: Some show that as much as 78 percent of the population has an active lifestyle, and others show that as little as 15 percent does (Blair, Kohl, & Powell, 1987). The best estimate we have is from the documentation for *Healthy People 2010* (see Figure 9.1), which shows estimated activity levels for women and men related to the 2010 goals.

American Sports Data (1999) has tracked adult activity patterns for more than a decade. Among their key findings are these:

- About one in five Americans is sufficiently active to gain health benefits, but 32 percent are not involved in fitness activities at all and an additional 22 percent are only minimally involved.

- In the 1990s, the number of adults in the 35–54 age range who maintained a regular fitness program increased from 4.7 million to 7.8 million; the number in the 55+ age group increased from 4 million to 4.5 million.

- The percentage of the adult population who participate regularly in sports remained unchanged during the 1990s.

- Health-club membership soared for all adult age groups; at the same time, the sales of home exercise equipment reached all-time highs.

- Activities that showed the largest gains in participation were fitness walking, free weights, and treadmills.

- In 1998, estimates were that 27.2 million females and 24.1 million males participated in fitness activities at least 100 times per year.

Another way to look at fitness levels among adults is to examine risk factors, those health-related problems that indicate a high degree of risk for cardiovascular disease (CVD). The data in Figure 9.2 show that inactivity is the most prevalent CVD risk factor. Current data suggest that inactive adults are twice as likely to die of CVD as are active adults (Sallis & McKenzie, 1991). These data support those fitness experts who are beginning to argue that activity levels rather than fitness-test data are the most important indicators for public health goals.

Those figures seem surprising in an era that has been described as a renaissance of fitness. There are two explanations for the difference between the *appearance* of a fitness boom and the *facts* about regular activity participation rates. First, the fitness boom is primarily a "yuppie" phenomenon; that is, it is primarily confined to young, middle- and upper-middle-class people, particularly professionals. Television and other forms of advertising cater to this group because its members have discretionary money to spend. Thus, all the slim, fit people we

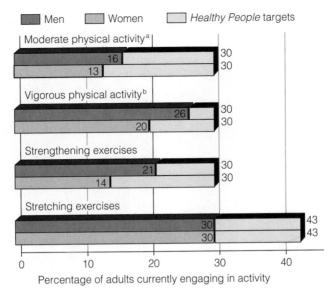

Figure 9.1 Current levels of physical activity among American adults

SOURCE: U.S. Department of Health and Human Services, 2000, *Healthy People 2010*, 2nd ed. Washington, D.C.: DHHS.

see on television tend to project a biased image of a fit nation.

Second, the image of an active lifestyle may be quite different from the reality of an active lifestyle. Although it is true that Americans are spending more on health-club memberships, home exercise equipment, and sports equipment, it is not clear that having access to facilities and equipment always results in more regular exercise patterns. Running shoes, for example, have become a fashion statement as much as a necessary item for frequent exercise.

What *is* clear is that more people of all age groups are becoming educated about health fitness and the importance of regular physical activity. There is no doubt that more adults now understand and believe that regular physical activity is an essential component of a healthy lifestyle. Still, it appears that the fitness boom of the mid- to late 1980s began to plateau in the 1990s, during which time

frequent fitness participation rates remained steady (American Sports Data, 1999). During the 1990s, the amount of money spent on fitness products also remained fairly steady.

What will adult participation in fitness and physical activity be like as we begin the new century? Obesity and coronary artery disease are still the primary killers of adults. The diets we consume have 30 percent more fat than did those of our grandparents (McNeill, 1987). These negative indicators are balanced by the very positive news that physical activity among children seems to have increased and that activity patterns among those aged 55 and older have also increased. This broadening of the fitness movement to include older Americans is an important trend, especially when one considers that the large segment of the population known as the "baby boomers" is beginning to move into that age group.

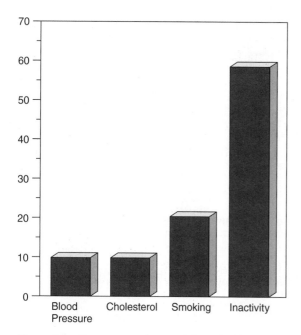

Figure 9.2   Percentage of U.S. adults with CVD risk factors.

NOTE: Risk factors are defined as: Blood Pressure = systolic blood pressure > 150 mm Hg, Cholesterol = total cholesterol > 268 mg/dl, Smoking = smoke at least one pack of cigarettes per day, Inactivity = less than 20 minutes of physical activity three times per week.

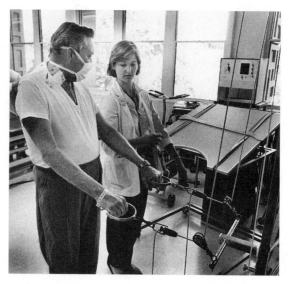

Exercise plays an important role in cardiac rehabilitation.

Mass exercise sessions take on the atmosphere of a festival.

FITNESS AND ACTIVITY PATTERNS AMONG OLDER ADULTS

No age group incurs greater public health costs than older citizens do. We live in a "graying America." Not only are baby boomers (those born between 1946 and 1964) entering the "senior citizen" age range, but it is also clear that they will live longer than previous generations (Mathieu, 1999). Not only has life expectancy increased steadily over the past 100 years, but also the fastest-growing age group in America are those 75 years and older.

All signs indicate that older citizens are becoming more active. Perhaps this is due to the increased knowledge that the benefits of regular physical activity to health and well-being are nowhere more clear than among older citizens (Mathieu, 1999). One study classified elderly walkers into three groups. The study showed that those in the least-active walking group were more than twice as likely as those in the other groups to suffer a heart attack or some other coronary event, even when differences in risk factors (such as age, hypertension, and cholesterol levels.) were taken into account (Physical Activity Today, 1999). Even for older people who have become sedentary and are seriously at risk for hypokinetic diseases of various kinds, the benefits of becoming more active are typically quick to appear and are tremendously important to improving lifestyle.

Thirty years ago, the common perception was that weight lifting was an activity for young men. No more! Resistance exercise may well be to the next generation what aerobic conditioning was to the previous one. The number of older citizens who regularly use strength equipment nearly doubled in the 1990s (American Sports Data, 1999). For older citizens to maintain their mobility and avoid the risk of broken bones associated with falling and osteoporosis, they must maintain an adequate level of muscular strength. Even terribly frail older adults can quickly realize important lifestyle gains through regular resistance exercise. And the increasing evidence that exercise is a good antidote to depression is especially important for older citizens, who suffer more frequently from this mental illness. All new evidence points to the conclusion that appropriate exercise can reduce and in some cases reverse the adverse effects of biological aging and also have significant psychological benefits (Duda, 1991; U.S. Department of Health and Human Services, 1996). Specifically, exercise can help to maintain peak bone mass during adulthood and can have important protective effects among the elderly by increasing muscle strength and balance. This is the classic use-it-or-lose-it syndrome. Bone cells respond to exercise by building greater bone mass, whereas lack of an exercise "load" (i.e., inactivity) results in a loss of bone mass.

All this good news needs to be tempered by a few sobering facts. Eighty-eight percent of those over 65 have at least one chronic health condition (National Blueprint on Physical Activity among Adults Age 50 and Older, 2000). Thirty-five to fifty percent of women over age 70 have difficulty with general mobility tasks such as walking a few blocks or climbing stairs in a home. Twenty-four percent of people over 50 who have hip fractures die within a year. Physical inactivity is not distributed evenly across the population. Inactivity is more frequent in lower-income groups and among minority populations.

Fitness and physical activity for seniors may be one of the most important research fields of the future. There is little doubt that it is already becoming an important new direction for fitness professionals. Little is known about how to work effectively with aging adults, where differences in fitness levels are marked and perceptions about the appropriateness of exercise differ. We must remember that most women and men who are now seniors grew up in an era when very little was known about the specific health benefits of exercise. We must also remember that there were strong cultural expectations that discouraged seniors from becoming and staying active, and those expectations were especially true for women.

FITNESS AND PA PROGRAMS FOR CHILDREN AND YOUTHS

Most parents would like their children to learn about fitness at school and develop and maintain an adequate level of fitness through school physical-education programs. The federal government agrees with that view, having cited fitness development and maintenance as a fundamental goal for the nation's elementary and secondary schools (Bennett, 1986). The Centers for Disease Control and Prevention (1997) developed the policy guidelines through which this agenda should be pursued. These guidelines for school and community programs to promote lifelong physical activity among young people are shown in Table 9.2. What will be clear as you review the guidelines is that the concept of "program" extends beyond physical-education classes to the entire school and out to the local community.

In 1998 the Council for Physical Education for Children (COPEC) published *Physical Activity*

TABLE 9.2 Youth Physical Activity (PA) Recommendations by the Centers for Disease Control

1. Establish *policies* that promote enjoyable, lifelong PA
   - Require daily physical education K–12
   - Require health education K–12
   - Commit adequate resources for PA instruction and programs
   - Hire professionally trained people
   - Require that PA programs meet the needs and interests of children

2. Provide physical and social *environments* that encourage PA
   - Provide access to safe spaces/facilities in school and community
   - Prevent PA-related injuries/illness
   - Provide time in the schoolday for unstructured PA (to accumulate a significant percentage of weekly PA requirements)
   - Do not use PA as punishment
   - Provide health promotion for school faculty

3. Implement planned and sequential *physical education (PE)* curricula that emphasize participation in PA and that encourage students to develop the knowledge, attitudes, motor skills, and confidence needed to adopt physically active lifestyles
   - Make PE curricula consistent with national standards
   - Impart knowledge of PA to students
   - Develop students' positive attitudes toward, motor skills for, and confidence in participating in PA
   - Promote participation in enjoyable PA in school, community, and home

4. Implement planned and sequential *health education (HE)* curricula that encourage students to develop the knowledge, attitudes, and behavioral skills needed to adopt physically active lifestyles
   - Make HE curricula consistent with national standards
   - Promote collaboration among PE, HE, and classroom teachers for PA instruction
   - Develop students' mastery of behavioral skills needed to adopt and maintain positive lifestyle behaviors

5. Provide *extracurricular PA programs* that meet students' needs and interests
   - Provide a diversity of developmentally appropriate PA programs for the largest number of students
   - Link students to community PA programs, and use community resources to support extracurricular PA programs

6. Include *parents and guardians* in PA instruction and extracurricular PA programs, and encourage them to support their children's participation in enjoyable PA
   - Encourage parents to advocate for high-quality PA instruction and programs for their children
   - Encourage parents to support their children's participation in appropriate, enjoyable PA
   - Motivate parents to be role models for PA and to plan family activities that include PA

7. Provide PE, HE, recreation, and health-care professionals with *training* that imparts the knowledge and skills needed to effectively promote PA among youths
   - Through higher education, provide preservice training for education, recreation, and health-care professionals
   - Teach educators how to deliver PE that provides a significant percentage of each student's weekly PA
   - Teach active learning strategies needed to develop knowledge about, attitudes toward, skills in, and confidence in PA

(continued)

TABLE 9.2   *(continued)*

- Create environments that enable youths to enjoy PA instruction and programs
- Qualify volunteers who coach sport and recreation programs for youths

8. Provide *health services* that assess PA among youths, reinforce PA among active youths, cousel inactive youths and refer them to PA programs, and advocate for PA instruction and programs for youths
   - Regularly assess PA, reinforce active youths, and refer inactive youths
   - Advocate for school and community PA instruction and programs

9. Provide a range of developmentally appropriate, noncompetitive *community sport and recreation programs* that are attractive to youths

10. Regularly *evaluate* school and community PA instruction, programs, and facilities
    - Conduct process evaluations to determine how policies, programs, and training are implemented
    - Conduct outcome evaluations to measure students' achievement of PA knowledge, behavioral skills, and motor skills

Physical activity recommendations: Adapted from *Guidelines for School and Community Programs to Promote Lifelong Physical Activity among Young People,* Centers for Disease Control and Prevention, Public Health Service, U.S. Department of Health and Human Services, 1997.

PA Guidelines for Toddlers and Preschoolers

In 2002 NASPE introduced physical-activity guidelines for children who have not yet reached school age. The guidelines suggest not only activity levels but also the kind of environment supportive of activity, and the individuals responsible for facilitating physical activity.

Guideline 1. Toddlers should accumulate at least 30 minutes daily of structured PA, preschoolers at least 60 minutes.

Guideline 2. Toddlers and preschoolers should engage in at least 60 minutes and up to several hours daily of unstructured PA.

Guideline 3. Toddlers should develop movement skills that are building blocks for more complex movement tasks, and preschoolers should develop competence in movement skills that build to more complex tasks.

Guideline 4. Toddlers and preschoolers should have indoor and outdoor areas that meet or exceed recommended safety standards for performing large-muscle activities.

Guideline 5. Individuals responsible for the well-being of toddlers and preschoolers should be aware of the importance of PA and facilitate the children's movement skills.

Source: *NASPE News,* Spring 2002.

---

for Children: A Statement of Guidelines, which suggested the following main principles:

- Elementary-aged children should accumulate at least 30–60 minutes a day of age- and developmentally appropriate activities.

- An accumulation of more than 60 minutes, and up to several hours per day, of appropriate activities is encouraged.

- Some of the daily activity should be in periods lasting 10–15 minutes or more and include moderate-to-vigorous activity.

- Extended periods of inactivity are inappropriate for children.

The guidelines also suggest that nonattached school time be used for physical activity and that activity at home and in the community be encouraged, making the document consistent with the CDC policy guidelines.

The fact is that what we typically consider the school physical-education program are the PE classes. Most elementary schoolchildren do not have daily PE classes; indeed, many of them have only 1 or 2 days per week of PE classes. Thus, it is not possible for the CDC or COPEC recommendations to be achieved through PE classes only. That is why the concept of a PE program needs to be expanded beyond the class schedule.

Following are examples of how creative and persevering physical educators have developed and sustained fitness and physical-activity programs in their schools. These examples should be considered together with the information on child and youth sport presented in Chapter 6 to form a comprehensive view of activity opportunities and programs.

1. *Schoolwide programs at the elementary level.* Some schools have adopted a schoolwide approach to programming for fitness. At a certain time of the day, for example, all classes might take a 15-minute jog or do various other kinds of aerobic activities.

2. *Fitness clubs.* At the elementary- and middle-school levels, many physical educators have successfully developed fitness clubs that provide incentives for students to engage regularly in fitness activities outside physical-education class time. For example, students might chart the course of a cross-country bicycle trip on a map by carefully keeping track of the miles they ride their bicycles each week.

3. *Fitness-remediation programs.* Some physical educators have focused on students who are particularly at risk in health fitness. After initial diagnosis with a health-fitness test, at-risk students and their families are informed of the problems, and the children are enrolled in a remedial program (Sie-

dentop, Mand, & Taggart, 1986). A special fitness class is developed for these students, and progress is monitored until the children have improved sufficiently to move out of the at-risk category.

4. *Home-based fitness programs.* It is essential to engage parents of at-risk children in the overall fitness program. The home-based fitness program (Taggart, Taggart, & Siedentop, 1986) is similar to the aforementioned remediation program. At-risk children are identified by testing. The children then enter into a contract with the teacher and with their parents. The contract calls for regular fitness activities at home, monitored by the parents. Individual improvement awards are determined by the parents and the children.

5. *Daily fitness programs.* Daily fitness first appeared on a national scale in Australia (Siedentop & Siedentop, 1985). *Daily fitness* is a program that separates fitness programming and goals from physical-education instruction. Each day, classroom teachers take 20 minutes to work with their children in aerobic activities. Fitness materials are provided, eliminating the need for extensive planning by the teacher. The children also get physical-education instruction, but the goals and activities of the two programs are kept separate.

6. *Fitness courses.* Many schools, particularly middle and high schools, have instituted a required fitness course, often at the ninth-grade level. The purpose of the course is to educate students about fitness, test them, help them to plan personal fitness programs, and teach them the kinds of activities in which to engage to maintain an adequate level of health fitness. The assumption is that, after completing the course, students will be more able and more likely to develop and maintain a personal fitness program.

7. *Fitness focus within physical-education classes.* Certain schools have combined the fitness-course approach with a recurring fitness theme throughout the physical-education program. In these programs, a certain portion of each physical-education lesson is devoted to health-fitness activity. The program is planned to meet the intensity, duration, and frequency criteria for health-fitness maintenance.

8. *Fitness elective courses.* Many high schools have started to offer a variety of fitness elective courses, ranging from aerobics to weight training to body shaping. These courses typically focus on the range of fitness outcomes—aerobic, motor performance, and cosmetic.

9. *Fitness centers.* Some middle- and high-schools have developed fitness centers that accommodate both classes and drop-in activities. Hoover High School in San Diego, California, operates a 2,800-square-foot fitness center (Samman, 1998) used for PE classes, sport teams, staff members, and the community. An after-school fitness club is open to all students.

10. *A complete high school fitness program.* Westcott (1992) described a high school in which physical education is required all 4 years, and a fitness focus defines the program. Students take a series of wellness courses, all of which have a fitness-related focus. They also choose from a series of activity courses that emphasize different approaches to fitness, including lifetime sports, fitness walking, aerobics, weight training, and the like.

11. *A state-requirement approach.* Florida requires all ninth-grade students to complete a semester of physical-education credit in personal fitness (Johnson & Harageones, 1994). A state syllabus has been prepared and staff development programs offered to teachers to help them prepare to teach the course, which involves both classroom and gymnasium sections. The course has three objectives: to develop a healthy level of fitness, to understand fitness concepts, and to understand the significance of lifestyle to health and fitness.

Comprehensive Schoolwide and Community-Linked Programs

The CDC guidelines indicate clearly that to serve fully the physical-activity needs of children and youths, educators must take a comprehensive approach that goes beyond regularly scheduled classes to build a total physical-education program. Several emerging models give us a glimpse of how more-comprehensive approaches can serve children and youths in ways that better achieve the CDC and COPEC goals.

1. *Kids Walk to School.* The U.S. Department of Health and Human Services has a guide to help schools and communities plan, implement, and assess programs to encourage children and youths to walk or cycle to school. In September of 2002, the Delaware state legislature passed a law creating a program to promote walking and cycling to school and funds to support school districts in developing the infrastructure to encourage walking and cycling.

2. *The Child and Adolescent Trial for Cardiovascular Health (CATCH).* CATCH program includes a PE curriculum emphasizing physical activity and skills, a classroom curriculum promoting cardiovascular health, a food-service intervention using the school cafeteria, an antismoking curriculum, and a home/family component. (McKenzie et al., 1996). CATCH was tested in ninety-six schools in four states over a 3-year period. Classroom teachers, PE teachers, cafeteria workers, and parents are part of this comprehensive approach.

3. *Districtwide Wellness Initiative.* Although school programs are effective, a districtwide emphasis on wellness can be even more powerful (Samman, 1998). The Escambia County Schools have a districtwide initiative that incorporates wellness throughout the curriculum and in the school environment; helps students, faculty, and staff to develop healthy lifestyles; forms partnerships with the community to promote wellness for students; and involves parents in developing student- and family-wellness activities. School and community facilities have been upgraded to provide a PA infrastructure, a wellness newsletter is published monthly, and an annual wellness fair is among many special events that include the total community.

4. *Community Sport and Recreation Center.* The community of Perry, Ohio, built a new high school that includes a comprehensive community sport and recreation center (Schmid, 1994b). This

---

Strength Training for Children

Children as young as 6 years of age have been shown to benefit from appropriately designed and monitored strength training. Previous concerns that early strength training had adverse affects on bone growth plates or produced hypertension have been discredited under conditions where the training approach is appropriately designed and monitored.

Indeed, the chances of preventing skeletal frailty in senior populations may be greatly enhanced by maximizing bone-mineral density among children through strength training and proper diet (especially calcium intake.)

Under appropriate supervision, children can use exercise machines, weighted balls, elastic tubes, and free weights to their benefit. Most experts agree that 1 to 3 sets of 6 to 15 repetitions 2 to 3 nonconsecutive days per week are appropriate. Focus should be on the upper body, lower body, and core (abdominal and back) musculature. Resistance should be light to begin with and increase only very gradually.

Each workout should be supervised and should be preceded by a thorough warm-up period.

SOURCE: Faigenbaum, 2001.

---

is a joint-use facility for students, faculty, staff, and community residents. The PE program and the sport teams use the facility, but it is also open 30 hours a week to students and residents for drop-in activity. The school district and the community share the cost of equipment, maintenance, and employee salaries.

5. *Collaboration for Intramural Sports and Fitness Programs.* The West Des Moines School District developed an intramural program for seventh- and eighth-graders in conjunction with a local YMCA and the city Parks and Recreation Department (Samman, 1998). Three junior high schools are served by an extensive program headed by school intramural directors assisted by YMCA and park-district personnel, who organize adult volunteers to serve as coaches, officials, and mentors. The program is jointly financed.

These programs provide models for other schools and districts to emulate. They show that the physical-activity and wellness needs of children and youths can be met, but only through a more expansive definition of what constitutes school physical education and only through collaboration with school personnel and community leaders.

AAHPERD Efforts to Promote Physical Activity and Fitness

AAHPERD, the main professional organization for sport, fitness, and physical-education professionals (now most commonly referred to as "the alliance"), has a long history of promoting physical fitness and continues to play a central role in national efforts to promote physical activity and fitness. AAHPERD has developed and promoted a series of fitness testing and motivational programs since the 1970s. In 1993 AAHPERD joined with the Cooper Institute for Aerobic Research (CIAR) in a partnership to develop educational materials, an assessment program, and an incentive program—which is called the "Physical Best-FITNESSGRAM®" program.

In 1999 AAHPERD joined the Cooper Institute and Human Kinetics Publishers to form the American Fitness Alliance (AFA) (www.americanfitness.net). The AFA produces a number of materials that are widely used in schools and elsewhere.

- *Physical Best* provides the educational component of a comprehensive health-related fitness-education program, providing curriculum materials, activity guides, and teacher certification.

- *FITNESSGRAM* test for evaluating K–12 students' physical fitness includes a test-administration manual, software, and related tools. The software includes an ACTIVITY GRAM option, which allows students to enter up to 3 days of physical-activity data and assess their own progress toward goals.

- *The Brockport Physical Fitness Test,* a national test developed especially for youths with disabilities, has features and tools similar to FITNESSGRAM.

- *FitSmart* test is designed to assess high school students' knowledge of concepts and principles of fitness. It includes a test manual and software.

- The *You Stay Active* recognition system is a program for setting goals and recognizing

achievement of those goals. It includes a manual and incentive awards.

In 1995 AAHPERD joined the ACSM and the American Heart Association (AHA) to form a National Coalition for Promoting Physical Activity (*Update,* 1995). The coalition will focus on communication and education about physical activity and its relation to health and will act as a physical-activity advocate to federal and state governments, concerning relevant policy and legislation; to corporations such as insurance companies, which might provide incentives for people to become and stay active; and to foundations that fund relevant research and development programs.

The alliance has also initiated, with the AHA, a program called Jump Rope for Heart. This program has both educational and fitness-development

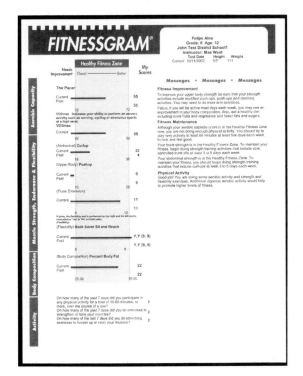

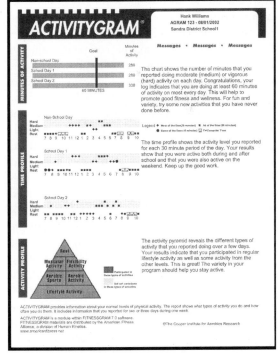

Example reports from a Fitnessgram and an Activitygram.

objectives. It also serves as a major fund-raiser for both the AHA and the AAHPERD. Children solicit pledges and then engage in continuous rope jumping to demonstrate the value of aerobic fitness activity, as well as to raise money.

In March 2001, NASPE launched a new program called *Sport for All,* intended to increase quality physical activity for children. The program includes three modules: SportFun for ages 3–5, SportPlay for ages 5–7, and SportSkill Basic for ages 8–10. Each module includes Activity Card Packets (available from Human Kinetics Publishers). Individuals can train as *Sport for All* program leaders through NASPE. *Sport for All* is intended to be used in camps, recreation centers, after-school programs, and day care centers.

WORKSITE FITNESS AND WELLNESS PROGRAMS

Worksite fitness and wellness programs have become common in the past 20 years. By 1992, 83 percent of companies with more than 750 employees had such programs. Smaller companies showed lower percentages, but worksites of all sizes showed marked increased over the 7-year period measured for assessment of *Healthy People 2000* goals. Companies develop and sustain worksite fitness and wellness programs because they reduce health-care costs, increase productivity of employees, and reduce absenteeism (www.fitwellinc.com). The combination of these factors results in a major benefit to the company compared with the costs incurred. The lesson is clear: Employees that are more fit and healthy work more productively, are absent less often, and cost companies less in insurance claims. The more risk factors employees have (smoking, high blood pressure, inactivity, and the like), the higher are the companies' medical costs—the costs for those with six or more risk factors are more than five times higher than the costs for those with no risk factors (Edington, 1993). Worksite fitness and wellness programs reduce many risk factors for employees who participate in them.

Strength training stations are increasingly common at worksites, schools, and other venues.

A worksite fitness and wellness program is typically made up of some combination of the following items (www.fitresource.com):

Fitness

- Personalized fitness programs
- Fitness testing
- Employee fitness facilities
- Organized classes and activities

Nutrition

- Healthy-heart programs
- Nutritional guidance
- Weight management

General Health

- Health-risk appraisal
- Healthy-back programs
- Blood pressure screening
- Cholesterol testing
- Smoking cessation
- Stress management
- Health-education programs

The Adolph Coors Company operates a wellness center that includes a gymnasium, a clinic, and a counseling center. Participation in the fitness program is voluntary, but workers who do take part receive a 5 percent reduction in their insurance payments. This form of *incentive* is common in worksite programs. Other companies, however, use a *disincentive* approach. Hershey's Food Corporation requires employees to pay an additional $30 a month for health insurance if they have high blood pressure, $10 a month if they have high cholesterol, $50 a month if they smoke, $10 a month if they are inactive, and $30 a month if they are overweight (Battagliola, 1993).

Other companies use different incentives, such as attractive workout facilities, organized company recreation programs, released time to participate in programs, and rewards for participation (T-shirts, duffel bags, and the like). Most companies and corporations of reasonable size employ adult-fitness professionals to administer their programs. Some companies charge a fee for the use of the fitness facilities, but the fee is typically much less than the cost of membership in a commercial fitness center, and the added benefit is that the company center is located at the workplace.

Facilities typically include an extensive workout center with resistance-training machines, free weights, treadmills, rowing machines, and stair climbers. They often include indoor running tracks and occasionally a gymnasium for activities such as volleyball and basketball. A health-assessment area is often adjacent to the workout spaces. Drop-in activity is encouraged and regularly scheduled sessions for aerobics or relaxation training are often available.

Although worksite fitness and wellness programs are becoming more widely available, it is not clear that the majority of employees participate, particularly on a regular basis. As health fitness has become a major issue in public health—and for corporations, too—the research field of exercise adherence has developed to investigate why people stay in fitness programs or leave them (Dishman, 1988). Lack of time, lack of suitable facilities, poor leadership, and inadequate programs are key reasons employees do not participate (Shephard, 1988). Personal factors such as income, education, perceived vulnerability, positive motivation, and strong sense of self-efficacy are positively related to participation (Landers, 1997).

Tenneco Corporation has been a leader in the worksite fitness movement since 1981 (Baun, 1995). Tenneco offers programs and facilities. They actively market their health-promotion programs to their own employees. They offer screening, assessment, support groups, counseling, and self-help programs. Programs offered are constantly monitored and changed, based on outcomes. Employees are regularly surveyed to gauge client satisfaction, as well as to identify new ways to involve employees and sustain their involvement. As with children's programs in schools, the multifactored approach appears to be necessary for success.

There are good reasons for worksites to involve themselves more in employee health-promotion and fitness programs. The savings in reduced absenteeism and health-related insurance costs are substantial. Also, a healthy and physically fit workforce is likely to be more productive and happier than a less fit or less healthy workforce. Although such outcomes are less direct and more difficult to measure, they may prove to be even more important than other benefits in the long run (Baun & Bernacki, 1988).

Informal Home-Based Fitness Activities

It is clear that many youths and adults exercise at home, or on their own, rather than through formal programs at specialized facilities. As the aerobics phenomenon grew in the 1980s, aerobics videotapes to use at home became big business. Jane Fonda's *Low-Impact Aerobics* video sold over 750,000 copies in one year in the mid-1980s. Magazines such as *Women's Sport & Fitness* were filled with articles on how to exercise at home, with many advertisers promoting their home fitness equipment. The athletic-shoe business, which had become the largest market in the sporting-goods area

---

Tech Support for Fitness Buffs

Many adult fitness buffs are drawn to technological support to record and assess their workout history and progress toward goals.

Typical of these is *Sport Brain*, a wearable personal fitness recorder that clips on to your waistband and records activities that cause your hips to move. *Sport Brain* is a pedometer that translates your activities into distance, calories burned, duration of the workout, pace, and the like, creating an online training log for you.

Activity data are sent through a SportPort transmitter, which connects to a regular phone line (no computer connection needed). The data are stored on a Web site that you can access to examine your fitness record.

SOURCE: www.sportbrain.com.

---

by the mid-1970s, became increasingly specialized, with shoes for running, court games, aerobics, cross-training, and walking.

Cycling for fitness and recreation provides another interesting look at how Americans do their fitness work. In 1970, 6.5 million bicycles were sold in the United States, with only 15 percent of the sales to adults (Wilson, 1977). By 1986 more than 12.3 million bicycles were sold, with well over 50 percent of the sales to adults. In the 1990s, road-bike and mountain-bike sales continued to grow, and stationary bicycles for indoor use became big business. In 1998, estimates were that 13.6 million adults regularly participated in outdoor fitness cycling and 30.8 million used stationary bicycles (American Sports Data, 1999).

The number of adults regularly involved in fitness activities leveled off in the 1990s, and their activity patterns changed (American Sports Data, 1999). Fitness walking increased somewhat, whereas running/jogging decreased and aerobic dancing stayed level. The largest increases in participation were in the area of resistance training: free weights, resistance machines, and multipurpose home gyms. The 1990s were clearly the "machine age" in fitness participation, with both cardiovascular equipment and resistance-training equipment showing marked increases in sales.

The design of new homes and remodeling of older homes began to accommodate this trend to-ward home fitness. Rooms were either designed or remodeled to house an array of machines and free weights. More expensive homes included very fancy and attractive home fitness centers, even indoor fitness pools that allow a person to swim in place against an adjustable current of water, a kind of aquatic treadmill. Technology, of course, made all these developments possible. Imagine yourself cycling on a wind trainer or a recumbent bicycle through exotic roads or trails viewed on a video screen, with sound effects and changes in pedal resistance corresponding to terrain changes—a truly virtual fitness experience.

Federal Efforts to Promote Fitness and Physical Activity

Historically, the federal government's concern with fitness has been in response to high rates of military draft rejects during wartime or in response to national health epidemics, such as the severe polio epidemic of 1916. In the mid-1950s, a "fitness crisis" occurred in the United States, the result of a series of tests showing that American children were much less fit than European children (see Chapter 3). In 1955 President Dwight Eisenhower, an avid golfer, convened a national conference of experts to examine fitness problems. Soon thereafter, the president suffered a heart attack, after which he spoke out even more vigorously about federal in-

This high-tech exercise system allows a person to swim in place against a current.

volvement in the nation's fitness. In 1956 an executive order created the President's Council on Youth Fitness, which, eventually, was to become the President's Council on Physical Fitness and Sport.

President John F. Kennedy continued this emphasis and published a much-discussed article in *Sports Illustrated* (1960) titled "The Soft American." Since then, the number of federal agencies involved in promoting and investigating fitness and physical activity has increased considerably. In 1978 the U.S. Department of Health, Education, and Welfare produced a major report that listed exercise as one of the twelve categories of behavior that are important determinants of health status (Blair, Kohl, & Powell, 1987). The federal government then established national objectives in the area of healthy lifestyle and fitness, known as the 1990 Objectives because they were articulated as goals to be met by the year 1990. Of the 226 specific objectives defined, 34 were related directly to physical fitness and health.

The President's Council on Physical Fitness and Sport (PCPFS) serves to encourage and motivate citizens of all ages to become physically active and to participate in sport. The PCPFS advises the president and the secretary of health and human services on how to encourage more Americans to be physically fit and active. The PCPFS consists of twenty members appointed by the president, and is currently headed by Lynn Swann, a former NFL great and TV commentator. The vice chair is Dr. Dot Richardson, an Olympic gold medalist in softball and an orthopedic surgeon.

The PCPFS collaborates with public and private-sector sponsors to conduct its programs and to produce public information materials. Among these programs and materials are the following:

- *The President's Challenge Physical Activity and Fitness Awards* program, a recognition program for school-aged children administered by teachers and others who work with youth
- *The Presidential Sports Award,* for Americans aged 6 and above who participate regularly in one of over sixty sports and fitness activities and who meet criteria defined by the governing body for each sport/activity

- *Web site* www.fitness.gov, a gateway Website to access programs and publications of the PCPFS
- *PCPFS Research Digest,* a quarterly publication, summarizing scientific research about topics related to physical activity and fitness
- *State Champion Award,* an annual award program for schools, conducted in collaboration with state departments of education
- *National School Demonstration Program,* conducted in coordination with state departments of education to recognize exemplary elementary, middle, and high school physical-education programs

Both the 1996 publication of the U.S. Surgeon General's *Report on Physical Activity and Health* and the 1997 recommendations from the CDC, which focused on policies and strategies for increasing physical activity and healthy lifestyles among children and youth, have placed the importance of fitness and physical activity more squarely in the public view than ever before. With increasing evidence of an obesity epidemic widely publicized, the campaign for activity and fitness has grown stronger and the federal government is increasingly involved. In 2000 the secretary of health and human services released *Promoting Better Health for Young People through Physical Activity and Sport.* This report included strategies for families, after-school programs, youth sports and recreation programs, and community support. It was followed in 2001 by *Increasing Physical Activity: A Report on Recommendations of the Task Force on Community Preventive Services* (Centers for Disease Control and Prevention, 2001). This report focused on the crucial roles that communities can play in supporting physical activity, including community campaigns, school physical education, and the creation of infrastructure to support activity.

In December 2000, the U.S. Congress passed the Physical Education for Progress (PEP) bill. The program awards grants to help initiate, expand, and improve physical-education programs for K–12 students. The legislation authorized $400 million over 5 years, starting with $5 million in fiscal year 2001, and was a major step forward in showing the commitment of the federal government.

Will these policies and programs help to improve the nation's fitness and physical activity? It is clear that the federal government is playing a proactive role in making the importance of activity clear. As we show in the next chapter, programs and infrastructures are needed, especially for those in the population who are most at risk. Now it remains to be seen if the infrastructure and the programs can be developed and sustained at the local level.

PHYSICAL-FITNESS INSTRUCTION: BY WHOM?

The material in this chapter makes it clear that physical fitness is pursued by people in many different places—schools, health spas, sport clubs, weight-training centers, YMCA/YWCA facilities, recreation centers, and homes. The number of health clubs in America has risen from 1,200 to more than 10,000 since the 1970s (Houlihan & De-Brock, 1991). Americans are said to spend more than $5 billion annually to keep fit! All those facilities and all those expenditures mean jobs for the fitness industry.

The difficulty in answering the question raised in this section—"by whom?"—is that there is no *national* certification for fitness instructors. Many organizations offer certification for various roles in the fitness professions, such as the American College of Sports Medicine, the Institute for Aerobics Research, the National Strength and Conditioning Association, the International Dance Exercise Association, and the Aerobics and Fitness Association of America. Many fitness centers now require certification as a condition of employment, and having certification certainly can be a factor in securing a job within the fitness industry. Still, there are fitness centers where fitness "leaders" and "advisors" have no certification.

Fitness programs in schools, of course, are planned and implemented by certified physical-education teachers. This, perhaps, is the most important reason for supporting the continued development and expansion of school fitness programs. Certified physical educators have typically taken courses in exercise science, conditioning, teaching methods, and the care and prevention of injuries—courses that are all relevant to planning and implementing fitness programs.

The fact remains that most fitness programs are organized and run outside schools and that most fitness instructors and leaders in those programs have little training. How is an out-of-shape adult to know whether what he or she is being asked to do by a fitness instructor in a local center is appropriate for his or her age and condition? Certainly, adults want to exercise in a way that provides no medical risk and also ensures that they reach their fitness goals quickly. That requires some expertise, which is what certification is meant to ensure. With the fitness industry growing so rapidly, it becomes increasingly important that people at all levels in the industry have specific training to do their jobs competently.

SPORT MEDICINE AND THE REHABILITATIVE SCIENCES

The material in this chapter and others makes it clear that sport and physical fitness are pursued by people of all ages and in many different venues—schools, health clubs, weight-training centers, parks, sports venues, and the like. Child and youth sport, interscholastic sport, collegiate sport, professional sport, and recreational sport have all experienced substantial growth in the past quarter-century. That growth has been accompanied by a parallel growth in the professions that serve these many participants, both by providing instruction about fitness and safety and by providing professional services in the care and prevention of sport- and fitness-related injuries.

Sport medicine is a generic term used to encompass many areas of specialization related to physical performance and injuries related to physical performance. The box "Sports Medicine—Professional Organizations" shows the major professional organizations that fall under the sport-medicine umbrella. Many of these organizations, and others that are more specialized, offer certification for various roles in the fitness profession, especially certification for providing different levels of instruction in fitness. These include the American College of Sports Medicine, the Institute for Aerobics Research, the National Strength and Conditioning Association, the Aerobics and Fitness Association of America, and the YMCA. Many fitness centers require certification as a condition of employment, but there are many fitness centers and fitness programs where "leaders" and "advisors" have no formal certification.

A sport-medicine team is required to provide health care to athletes and to those who are regularly involved in fitness work and may incur injuries. Key to this team are athletic trainers and physicians. Medical specialists who can often be found in sport-medicine centers include family-practice physicians, orthopedists, neurologists, internists, ophthalmologists, and pediatricians. One is also likely to find dentists, podiatrists, nutritionists, and physical therapists in some way related to the sport-medicine team. Nurses, physician's assistants, and other health-care professionals are also involved.

Athletic Training

The most highly developed sport vocation is that of athletic trainer. The National Athletic Trainers' Association is one of the strongest of all sport, fitness, and physical-education associations. The mission of NATA is "to enhance the quality of health care for athletes and those engaged in physical activity, and to advance the profession of athletic training through education and research in the prevention, evaluation, management and rehabilitation of injuries" (www.nata.org). Increasingly, where there

---

Sport Medicine—Professional Organizations

- *International Federation of Sports Medicine.* Created in 1928, this organization is made up of national sports-medicine associations from over 100 countries.

- *American Academy of Family Physicians.* Founded in 1947, AAFP promotes and maintains high-quality standards for more than 85,000 family practitioners. Many team physicians are members.

- *National Athletic Trainers' Association.* Founded in 1950, NATA is responsible for raising standards and developing this field. Currently, there are more than 27,000 members.

- *American College of Sports Medicine.* Founded in 1954, ACSM is a broadly based group that offers six different certifications and brings together experts from diverse fields.

- *American Orthopaedic Society for Sports Medicine.* Founded in 1972, AOSSM supports research in sport medicine and practices for sport and fitness programs.

- *National Strength and Conditioning Association.* Founded in 1978, NSCA provides certification and continuing education for its 14,500 members.

- *American Physical Therapy Association—Sports Physical Therapy Section.* Founded in 1981, this special section of APTA promotes prevention, recognition, and treatment of sport-related injuries.

- *American Academy of Pediatrics—Sports Committee.* The goal of this committee, which was organized in 1979, is to educate all physicians about the special needs of children who participate in sport.

---

are well-developed sport programs, you will find athletic trainers. More and more high schools and universities are hiring athletic trainers as full-time personnel. Athletic trainers work closely with sport physicians in the prevention and rehabilitation of sport-related injuries.

The chief function of NATA is to carefully supervise and control the certification of athletic trainers through its Board of Certification (NATABOC). NATA has traditionally approved two tracks toward certification: (1) completion of an approved athletic-training program of study in a college or university and (2) participation in an internship program in those colleges and universities that did not have a full program. In the 1990s, NATA moved away from the internship-only route and required that all newly certified trainers have completed a NATA-approved program of study. Even more recently, the NATA Board of Directors adopted a set of recommendations from the NATA Education Task Force, which included the primary provision that by 2004 all candidates must have a bachelor's degree and successfully complete an

accredited entry-level athletic-training education program to be eligible for NATABOC certification (NATA Education Task Force, 1997). Understanding that not all women and men decide to pursue a career in athletic training early in their undergraduate years, the task force also recommended that postbaccalaureate entry-level certification programs be established, possibly bundled as part of a master's degree. The task force also recommended the creation of a Certificate of Advanced Qualification (CAQ), recognizing the increasing specialization of the athletic-training job market.

As in sport management and administration, there are both undergraduate and graduate degree programs in **athletic training.** More than sixty-five colleges and universities offer such programs. The undergraduate requirements for athletic training are (1) a college degree with a teaching certificate; (2) completion of required courses in anatomy, physiology, exercise physiology, kinesiology, psychology, first aid, nutrition, health, and basic athletic training (various elective courses are also recommended); and (3) completion of 800 clinical-experience hours distributed over 2 academic years under supervision of a qualified clinical instructor in an acceptable clinical setting.

The graduate requirements, typically leading to a master's degree, are (1) a bachelor's degree from an accredited college or university; (2) completion of specific undergraduate requirements and clinical experience either before or during the degree program; (3) completion of specific courses in advanced athletic training, and advanced instruction in one or more of the foundational sciences; (4) a specified amount of elective work in a wide range of related areas; and (5) a minimum of 400 hours of clinical experience under the direction of a qualified clinical instructor in an acceptable clinical setting.

Once candidates have completed either the undergraduate or the graduate program successfully, they have to (1) present a Competency Evaluation Checklist from a certified athletic trainer, (2) present proof of certification in standard first aid and cardiopulmonary resuscitation (CPR), and (3) pass the NATA Certification Examination. Such persons then become Certified Athletic Trainers, a certification typically required for employment.

More high schools are hiring full-time athletic trainers, partially in response to the problems of liability and to research showing that the injury rate in schools without full-time trainers is much higher than in schools with such services (Rankin, 1989). Athletic training also used to be linked in most university training programs with teacher certification, but there appears to be a growing trend toward eliminating this linkage; that is, future trainers increasingly will be hired with the appropriate trainer qualifications but without teacher certification.

The employment potential for athletic trainers is good, and the profession they enter is obviously well controlled, perhaps being a model for other sport and fitness vocations to emulate. Specific skills are identified and specific programs are arranged to help young men and women acquire those skills. Meaningful, supervised experience is required. Then, entrance to the field is controlled by examination and presentation of a skills checklist.

ACSM FITNESS-INSTRUCTION CERTIFICATION

The mission of the American College of Sports Medicine (ACSM) is to promote and integrate scientific research, education, and practical applications of sport medicine and exercise science to maintain and enhance physical performance, fitness, health, and quality of life (www.acsm.org). ACSM is the nation's largest professional organization of exercise scientists, physicians, physiologists, physical educators, and fitness instructor/managers interested in the implementation of fitness programs.

ACSM offers different levels of certification within two specific tracks. The Health and Fitness certification track offers three certification levels for individuals who work in settings where the exercise participants are apparently healthy and exercising for health maintenance. The Clinical track offers three certifications for those who work with low to moderate-risk individuals or patients with acute or controlled diseases in hospital-based or medically supervised settings. Table 9.3 shows the purpose of and requirements for certification in each of these two tracks.

ACSM is also heavily involved in the continuing education of the professionals they serve. ACSM endorses more than 180 conferences a year in which those professionals can get continuing education credit or continuing medical education credit. Since most professional organizations now require a certain level of continuing education to maintain certification, these conferences are often heavily subscribed.

Strength and Conditioning Specialist Certification

The National Strength and Conditioning Association offers a Certified Strength and Conditioning Specialist (CSCS) certification program. The CSCS program was developed to identify individuals who have the knowledge and skills to design and implement safe and effective strength and conditioning

TABLE 9.3 ACSM Certification

Health and Fitness Track

ACSM Group Exercise Leader. Demonstrates techniques for safe, effective, sound methods of exercise in a group setting. Candidate must have (1) previous certification by an aerobic/dance exercise group (neither mail order nor correspondence) or (2) 250 hours of teaching experience in the exercise-leader field within a 2-year period. Candidate must also have current CPR certification and complete a written and practical exam.

ACSM Health/Fitness Instructor. Conducts fitness testing and designs and implements exercise programs for low to moderate-risk clients and for individuals with controlled diseases. Candidate must have a 2-year, 4-year, or master's degree in health-related field or 900 hours of practical experience in a fitness setting, and CPR certification.

ACSM Health/Fitness Director. Demonstrates administrative skills for health and fitness programs in corporate, commercial, or community settings in which low to moderate-risk clients participate in health education and fitness activities. Candidate must have a 2-year, 4-year, or master's degree in health-related field, 2 years full-time or 4,000 hours experience as a fitness manager or director, current ACSM H/F instructor certification, and CPR certification.

Clinical Track

ACSM Exercise Specialist. Demonstrates competence in graded exercise testing, exercise prescription and leadership, emergency procedures, counseling, and health education for people with low to moderate risk and for patients with known cardiovascular, pulmonary, or metabolic disease. Applicant must have a bachelor's degree in an allied health field, 600 hours of practical experience in a clinical setting, and Basic Life Support certification.

ACSM Program Director. Demonstrates administrative skills, develops and directs preventive and rehabilitative exercise programs, and provides education and risk-factor-modification programs for clinical populations. Candidate must have a post-baccalaureate degree in exercise science, medicine, or an allied health field, 2 years of clinical experience, 1 year of recent experience managing a clinical exercise program, current ACSM Exercise Specialist certification, and current Basic Life Support certification, and must complete a checklist to document administrative and clinical experience.

ACSM Registered Clinical Exercise Physiologist. Demonstrates exercise competencies in cardiovascular, pulmonary, metabolic, immunological, inflammatory, and neuromuscular areas with educational and clinical prerequisites. Candidate must have a graduate degree in exercise science, exercise physiology, or physiology, a minimum of 1,200 hours of relevant clinical experience, and experience providing clinical exercise services for patients with chronic diseases.

SOURCE: www.acsm.org.

programs. The association publishes a bimonthly journal, *Strength and Conditioning,* and a quarterly research journal, *Conditioning Research.*

Candidates must have at least a bachelor's degree or be currently enrolled as a college senior and have CPR certification at the time they register to take the certification exam. The exam has two parts: scientific foundations and practical applications. Candidates who pass the exam are required to earn six continuing-education credits (equal to 60 hours of study) over a 3-year period to maintain their certification.

In 2002 NSCA released new professional standards and guidelines for strength and conditioning specialists. The standards and guidelines document is designed to identify areas of liability exposure, increase safety standards, and decrease the likelihood of injuries that might lead to legal claims. The standards and guidelines concentrate on athletic preparticipation screening, personnel qualifications, program supervision, facility and equipment inspection, emergency planning and response, record keeping, youth participation, and the use of supplements, ergogenic aids, and drugs (NASPE News, 2002).

YMCA Fitness Instructor Certification

The YMCA has also developed a multilevel certification program for those who work in the many different fitness programs offered by the organization. Three certificates are offered:

1. *Basic fitness leader.* A candidate earns this certification by completing a 2-day workshop in which the fundamentals of exercise physiology, nutrition, liability, and the practical aspects of exercise leadership are taught. Candidates must have CPR certification. A practicum is included in the workshop.

2. *Fitness specialist.* A candidate earns this certification by completing a 1-week intensive course that includes all the fitness-leader objectives and more extensive training in exercise testing. Candidates must have CPR certification.

3. *Advanced exercise specialist.* The criteria for this certification are similar to those for the fitness-specialist certification but are more demanding.

The YMCA has many specialized fitness programs, such as the Healthy Back program, the Pulse program, and the Seniors program. Instructors and leaders in these programs typically achieve the basic fitness-leader certification and then receive more specific training to prepare them to provide leadership within the specialized program. Remember that a 1-week intensive workshop does not provide the level of preparation that a physical-education major receives during a 4-year college program.

Physical Therapy

One of the important careers in medical fields related to fitness and conditioning is physical therapy. As the population of developed nations ages, physical therapy (PT) will become an even more important career specialization. Physical therapists work in a variety of contexts, including rehabilitation, community health, industry, and sports. Although they often work as members of a health-care team in hospitals, they increasingly work in private PT practices, community and corporate health centers, sport facilities, rehabilitation centers, and the like. The American Physical Therapy Association is the main professional organization for PT (www. apta.org).

Physical therapists do therapeutic exercise, range-of-motion exercise, cardiovascular training, relaxation training, therapeutic massage, biofeedback, and a host of other therapies that help people recover from illness or injury. This is a highly specialized field requiring extensive training.

Most PT preparation and certification is done at the graduate-school level. To prepare for PT, undergraduates often major in one of the sciences; more and more, they are majoring in exercise science or kinesiology. Certification for PT is controlled at the state level, so students interested in a PT career should inquire at a university or the state licensing board about specific requirements. After graduating from an accredited PT program, candidates must pass a state-administered national exam.

Physical therapists can become certified as clinical specialists in seven areas: pediatrics, geriatrics, sports physical therapy, cardiopulmonary, clinical electrophysiology, neurology, and orthopedics.

Specialist certifications in these areas are controlled by the American Board of Physical Therapy Specialties.

Bachelor's Degree in Adult Fitness

There are many universities where it is now possible to obtain an undergraduate bachelor's degree in a fitness-related subject—adult fitness, corporate fitness, or fitness programming. There are also many universities where students can major in exercise science, but this undergraduate degree is more often designed to prepare students for entrance into graduate school than for employment in a professional role in the fitness world. (See Chapter 14 for a more complete description of the exercise-science degree.)

The nature of the requirements for the undergraduate degree in fitness differs somewhat at each university, depending on the emphasis within the program. The typical program includes core courses similar to those taken by other students studying for undergraduate degrees in physical education: foundations of physical education, exercise physiology, kinesiology, biomechanics, sport psychology, sport sociology, tests and measurements, and some activity-oriented courses such as aquatics, gymnastics, individual sports, and team sports.

Beyond this core, the fitness major takes further courses in exercise science, such as analysis of cardiopulmonary function and graded-exercise testing. In addition, the fitness major takes supportive scientific courses in areas such as nutrition and injury prevention/care. Because much fitness programming is done in the private sector, the fitness major is often likely to take courses focusing on the business aspects of fitness, such as marketing and administration. Often these courses are offered by a department of business administration.

The undergraduate fitness major should have intern experiences where knowledge and skill can be utilized and refined. These often take place in campus fitness programs but can also occur in local hospitals or fitness centers. This internship comes toward the end of the program and serves a function similar to student teaching in the teacher-certification program.

Many undergraduate fitness programs also encourage their students to achieve certification under the ACSM guidelines. In that way, the student graduates not only with a bachelor's degree in fitness but with certification as well. This student is equipped both to seek employment in the fitness field and to attend graduate school for further study and experience in the adult fitness field.

Master's Degree in Fitness

Master's-degree programs are widely available in a number of fitness-related areas: adult fitness, fitness programming, cardiac rehabilitation, strength development, fitness management, corporate fitness, and exercise physiology. The exact requirements for each degree depend on the specific focus for the master's program. Most programs include ACSM certification of one kind or another.

Although these degree programs differ in the specific course required for graduation, they do have much in common (Hall & Wilson, 1984). Because they are *graduate* programs, the entrance criteria are those common to the graduate program at the institution offering the degree. The criteria typically include at least a 2.75 to 3.00 undergraduate grade point average (GPA), a certain level of performance on the Graduate Record Examination (GRE) or a similar test, and a background in the core sciences related to fitness.

Specific prerequisites for entrance most often involve previous coursework in anatomy, physiology, and exercise physiology. Some programs also require coursework in chemistry, mathematics, physics, kinesiology, and measurement. Although being an undergraduate physical-education major is not often a prerequisite, many students applying for fitness-related master's programs have that background.

The degree programs themselves combine advanced coursework, acquisition of the technical skills associated with fitness (e.g., testing), practical experience within the program, and, often, an internship in an agency dealing with fitness (corporation, hospital, fitness center, etc.). Most programs take from 12 to 24 months to complete. In some programs, students must complete a thesis to graduate.

These programs require that candidates have a good background in science courses, and they emphasize the underlying scientific basis of fitness. A student who aspires to a career in a fitness-related profession should thus be sure to acquire the appropriate scientific expertise.

SUMMARY

1. It is clear that inactivity is a risk factor for hypokinetic disease.

2. Youth fitness testing indicates that boys and girls in the fifth through twelfth grades rank poorly in tests of body composition and cardiopulmonary efficiency.

3. Similar testing among children in the 6- to 9-year-old group indicates alarmingly high percentages of body fat and inadequate cardiopulmonary functioning.

4. Some experts feel that when activity is used rather than fitness testing, children and youths are more fit than reports indicate.

5. Research on activity patterns among children is uneven but indicates that too few get regular physical education and that those who do are less active within physical education than they should be.

6. Participation in sport declines dramatically as children approach adolescence.

7. There is often insufficient time within school physical-education classes to develop and maintain health fitness, which has led to a national movement to provide daily physical education that emphasizes health fitness.

8. A number of different effective fitness programs have been developed in school physical education, including schoolwide elementary programs, fitness clubs, remediation programs, home-based programs, daily fitness programs, fitness courses, and a strong fitness focus within the physical-education class.

9. The AAHPERD has promoted fitness strongly through testing and incentive programs such as the FITNESSGRAM® and Jump Rope for Heart.

10. Although reliable data on fitness levels of adults are difficult to obtain, the best estimates are that 20 percent of adults get sufficient health-fitness exercise, 40 percent get some but not sufficient benefits from exercise, and 40 percent are sedentary.

11. The recent fitness boom is mostly a young-adult, relatively upper-income phenomenon, in which the appearance of fitness participation seems more pervasive than is actual participation.

12. Surveys of activity patterns among adults and seniors indicate that exercise decreases with age and is relatively higher among males, in suburban communities, among professionals, among high school and college graduates, and among whites.

13. Most fitness professionals expect the fitness movement to continue to expand because of increased media exposure, discretionary income, acceptability among women, influence of elite sport, and emphasis within the health and medical professions.

14. Worksite fitness programs are becoming increasingly available but are still geared primarily to higher-level employees and are strongly influenced by the availability of facilities.

15. The federal government has become heavily involved in promoting health fitness and has developed specific objectives for the nation to achieve in the twenty-first century.

16. Most fitness programs are developed and led by uncertified personnel, although several organizations, such as the ACSM and the YMCA, have well-developed certification programs.

17. Many universities now offer bachelor's degrees in fitness-related subjects—adult fitness, fitness programming, or corporate fitness. These curricula typically require core coursework, special training in exercise science and testing, an internship, and some courses in business.

18. Many universities now offer master's-degree programs in fitness that combine advanced training in exercise science with training in the skills needed to work professionally within the fitness area. These programs typically require an internship and, sometimes, a thesis.

DISCUSSION QUESTIONS

1. Why is it that the fitness boom has been primarily a young-adult, upper-income phenomenon?

2. What can be done to promote regular fitness habits among children?

3. How fit are you? What either motivates you to maintain or prevents you from maintaining an adequate level of fitness?

4. What were fitness programs like when you were in elementary and high school? Were they effective?

5. What can communities do to promote fitness? Who should pay for community-based programs?

6. Why is it in the interest of corporations and businesses to promote fitness among their employees?

7. Will specializing in fitness become more of a profession, with increasing certification and preparation? Would such a trend be good?

CHAPTER **10**

Problems and Issues in Fitness

For years we have tried the same fitness philosophy; that is, trying to achieve fitness goals by compelling children to exercise. We should realize that it is time to try something different. As professional physical educators we must recognize that "getting children fit" (by itself) is not the answer if children and youth do not develop the lifetime habits of physical activity.

Charles Corbin, 1987, speaking of perennial
problems in the fitness curriculum

LEARNING OBJECTIVES

- To discuss the costs and the benefits to society of fitness and lack of fitness among various populations

- To analyze and discuss strategies that support or prevent the development of lifetime commitment to physical activity

- To discuss issues related to public information and misinformation about fitness

- To discuss equity issues in fitness and physical activity

- To describe issues related to certification for fitness professions

- To describe the role of fitness in an aging population.

- To describe and discuss the role of fitness in physical education

- To discuss research issues in fitness and physical activity

- To describe how a physical-activity infrastructure is related to physical-activity lifestyles

Physical fitness and physical activity of one kind or another have been and will continue to be of major importance to sport and to physical education. The previous two chapters have shown how important fitness and physical activity are to athletes and to the general public, including children, youths, adults, and older citizens. Each kind of fitness—health fitness, motor-performance fitness, and cosmetic fitness—has a different kind of importance.

Most clearly, health fitness is important to life itself, both to living well and to living free from degenerative disease. That kind of importance has both personal and social significance. Motor-performance fitness is important, too. For the high school volleyball player, jumping higher and hitting more strongly is of immediate short-term importance. The strength and endurance of an Olympic athlete are important not only to him or her but also to each of us who roots for the athlete and takes pride in his or her accomplishments. Cosmetic fitness has a different kind of importance; it enhances self-esteem and builds confidence, qualities that may be important to achievement in school, at work, and in social relationships. Therefore, although we tend to focus more on health fitness, we should not forget the importance of motor-performance and cosmetic fitness in the lives of people for whom those qualities are central to success.

In our graying society, life expectancy continues to lengthen with each generation, now over 75 years for males and over 80 years for females. A larger proportion of our population is retired, and that proportion will grow, relative to the working population, at least until the baby-boom generation is through its retirement years. Health-care costs for an aging population are extraordinary. Senior citizens who are healthy and fit not only lead higher-quality lives but also dramatically reduce national health-care costs. Most senior citizens, however, were raised and educated at a time when much less was known about fitness, and activity was considered to be something that young people did.

Few occupations in modern society require a high level of physical fitness. Some jobs—mail carrier, for example—tend to contribute to health-related fitness. The vast majority of modern occupations, however, do not contribute to health fitness but, instead, are dangerously sedentary. Most children do not grow up in rural areas where the local environment encourages them to run and climb regularly. Nor do they grow up on farms, where they might be required to help with chores that have a positive fitness component. They are more likely to grow up in cities and suburbs, where the environment demands little of them in the way of fitness. Most children and youths do not even walk to school. For many, the most compelling environmental stimuli—the television set and the computer—require them only to sit for many hours at a time.

The *requirements* of daily life in an urban, industrial society are insufficient to develop and maintain adequate levels of health fitness. If we are to develop and maintain fitness, we must do so purposely, through activities that are not part of our daily labor. The general nature of life in modern society poses important problems for developing and maintaining adequate levels of health fitness, and it is to those issues that we now turn.

THE COSTS OF INADEQUATE HEALTH FITNESS

Although fitness and health are typically seen as *individual* issues, there is no doubt that social and economic costs of inadequate fitness and health in the general population constitute a major *national* problem (see the box on chronic illness p. 223). Those costs now make up a substantial portion of the yearly gross national product and have contributed significantly to recent national deficits (Pritchard & Potter, 1990). The statistics on public costs related to health-fitness problems are staggering (Edington, 1993; Kaman, 1995; Pritchard & Potter, 1990; Teague & Mobily, 1983; Villeneuve, Weeks, & Schwied, 1983, www.fitwellinc.com).

- Absenteeism among less-fit employees is typically twice that of fit employees.

Chronic Illness Related to Sedentary Lifestyles in America

- 12.6 million people have coronary heart disease.
- 1.1 million people suffer a heart attack each year.
- 17 million people have diabetes. (90–95% of those have Type II.)
- 16 million people have "pre-diabetes."
- 107,000 people learn they have colon cancer each year.
- 300,000 people suffer from hip fractures each year.
- 50 million people have high blood pressure.
- Nearly 50 million adults (ages 20–74) are obese.
- An additional 58 million adults are overweight.

- 14–24 percent of all deaths are attributable to lifestyles that include physical inactivity and poor diet.

What Does It Cost?

- In the year 2004, $12.7 billion in direct and indirect medicare payments will go to diabetes treatment and services.
- The medical cost of overweight and obesity is estimated to be $117 billion.
- The estimated cost of treatment and services for heart disease is $183 billion, including $34.9 billion in medicare spending.

SOURCE: U.S. Department of Health and Human Services, 2002.

- Between 45 and 60 percent of employees have borderline-to-high cholesterol.
- Seriously overweight employees are nearly twice as likely to have expensive health claims as those at normal weight.
- Inactive employees have 30 percent more days in hospitals than do those who are physically active.
- General Motors spends more on employee health costs than it does to purchase steel for automobiles.
- Medical costs for people with six or more risk factors (smoking, drinking, inactivity, high blood pressure, etc.) are five times the cost for people with fewer risk factors.
- A one-pack-per-day smoker is estimated to cause his or her employer to pay nearly $1,000 per year in otherwise avoidable costs.
- Workers' compensation for low-back pain costs employers more than $400 million annually.

The list could go on and on. The point is that lack of adequate health fitness among students and workers is not simply an *individual* issue. The problem has *economic* and *social* implications that affect us all directly—in the pocketbook. The cost of health insurance goes up. Disbursements from public funds increase. Productivity goes down. We all pay for those, regardless of whether we are fit or unfit.

Moreover, the people who are often most at risk for health problems are those to whom fitness information and activity are least accessible—that is, the lower 25 percent socioeconomically. Viewing problems in health fitness as strictly a matter of individual responsibility is, in some cases, like blaming the victim. Although individual education and responsibility in fitness is important, we must recognize that the social structures of society also contribute to the problems and that solutions will not be achieved without addressing those structural inequities.

FITNESS BEHAVIOR: SHORT AND LONG TERM

There is no doubt that the public is becoming more aware of the importance of health-related fitness. Most current polls show that as many as 90 percent of Americans *believe* that regular exercise is important to health and well-being, but most Americans do not exercise regularly. Are you one of those?

A major issue in improving the health fitness of our society is determining how to confront this difference between belief and behavior. Why do people who *know* that regular exercise is important still fail to exercise regularly? Coming to grips with this problem and finding workable solutions to it may be the most important advancements of all.

The problem seems to stem from the fact that the positive, health-related *consequences* of regular involvement in appropriate aerobic activity are typically long term. The more *immediate* consequences of engaging in sufficiently intense aerobic activity are aversive to many people. Making the effort, getting out of breath, and sustaining exercise in that state all tend to be aversive to many people, especially those who go at it too vigorously at the outset and therefore also have to endure immediate postexercise fatigue and subsequent muscle soreness the next morning.

Health fitness requires exercise of sufficient intensity, duration, and frequency to develop and maintain adequate aerobic capacity. Thus, one not only has to get out and do the 30 minutes of aerobic work but also has to do it at a sufficient intensity (70 percent of maximum heart rate) to have it be beneficial. Furthermore, one has to do it three to five times per week—this week, next week, and the week after that. It seems so easy to skip a day if work piles up, if there is a good game on television, if there is a friend to see, if there is a test coming up, or if any other of a thousand good reasons not to exercise today occurs. The problem, of course, is that the same reasons will be there tomorrow—and the day after, too.

Using the physical-activity dose formula of 30 minutes per day of accumulated moderate-to-vigorous physical activity (MVPA) to total 210 minutes per week is an alternative road to the same goal. Brisk walking after dinner for 30–40 minutes a day, in addition to sound nutrition and absence of risk factors such as smoking, will lead to essentially the same health benefits as health-related fitness activities. Here, too, however, there has to be commitment to sustained involvement; that is, activity has to become a part of lifestyle.

From this rationale, it is clear that no satisfactory solution will be found to problems of inadequate health fitness among the public unless it involves a *change in lifestyle.* No quick-fix fitness program will be sustained. People need to make a commitment to lifelong fitness, and that will not happen unless that commitment is incorporated into a lifestyle.

Corbin (1987) has provided a model that involves what he terms *higher-order fitness objectives,* a model through which we can better understand the dimensions of fitness education that result in lifestyle changes (see Figure 10.1).

The model suggests that getting people to exercise is just a first step. Helping them to become fit is a second step, but it is *the* step at which most fitness programs stop. If fitness programs aim no higher than achieving an adequate level of fitness, they risk having the clients lose that level of fitness once the program is over. The Corbin model suggests that to develop a commitment to lifetime fitness, a program must help its clients (whether children in an elementary school or adults in a fitness center) establish personal patterns of exercising that fit their recreational interests and needs, as well as their physical makeup. Then the program must teach them how to evaluate their own fitness and how to solve problems related to fitness. To do this problem solving, the client must have a sound knowledge base related to fitness and must know a variety of ways to identify and remediate fitness problems.

Research is beginning to show that fitness programs that have this *lifestyle* emphasis tend to produce *commitment;* that is, those who complete such a program tend to think and behave differently *in the long term* (Rider & Johnson, 1986; Slava, Lau-

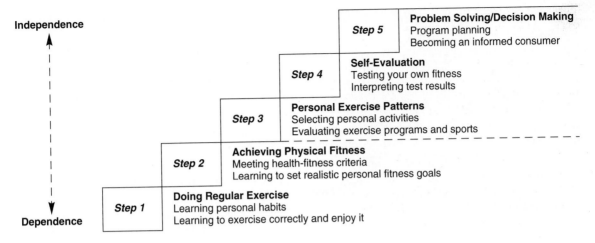

Figure 10.1   Stairway to lifetime fitness.

SOURCE: From *Fitness for life: Teachers annotated edition* (3rd ed), C. Corbin & R. Lindsey, 1993, Glenview, IL: Scott, Foresman.

rie, & Corbin, 1984). Programs that emphasize life-style not only teach people about fitness and help them to exercise regularly but also teach them self-testing skills, fitness-planning skills, consumer information, and related information, such as sound nutritional planning.

Motivation is, of course, the key to getting children, adolescents, and adults into activity programs and keeping them involved in those programs. It is clear that programs for children and adolescents must address three major motivations if those programs are to be successful (Weiss, 2000). First, boys and girls want to develop and demonstrate physical competence, through skills, fitness, or appearance. Second, they want to be accepted and supported within a peer social group, including appreciation and support from significant adults. Third, they want to have fun, which means that activity experiences have to be positive and that potentially negative aspects of the experience have to be minimized. Fitness experts, physical educators, recreation personnel, and sport coaches all need to keep those motivations in mind as they implement sport, recreation, and activity programs.

It would be interesting for you, along with classmates or other friends, to consider how the fitness programs you experienced as a student or an adult compare with what has just been described as a lifestyle approach to health fitness. What were they like? What effect do you think they had on your long-term commitment to fitness?

DEVELOPING A FITNESS-EDUCATED PUBLIC

A major step forward in any national effort to improve the health fitness of citizens will be taken when the general public becomes well educated about fitness issues. This means that the *average* person on the street will know about the different kinds of fitness, what needs to be done to develop and maintain health fitness, and what fitness products and services are appropriate to fitness goals. We are certainly a long way from being able to take that step forward.

Part of the problem associated with educating the public is that the popular media—through advertising and promotion of products—create false impressions that make it even harder for the general public to understand the *real* issues about fitness. Skinner (1988) has identified three general media-related problems:

Education must help people develop a serious lifetime commitment to personal fitness.

1. The media image of a fit person is typically someone who has a young, hard, thin, and beautiful body. That kind of body is neither necessary for health fitness nor attainable by most people, no matter what they might do!

2. The impression left by the media is that fitness miracles can occur quickly and often without any real effort on the part of the person undertaking the fitness program. The media goal seems to be to get people started in a program by buying products (a diet book, a workout video, a piece of exercise equipment). Whether you stay in that program is not the main interest of the company whose product is being promoted.

3. The media seem to create instant experts who have celebrity status but who may have no training in exercise science and who may actually know very little specific information about fitness. The amount of *misinformation* conveyed by these kinds of celebrities is often as harmful to the fitness movement as it is helpful.

Knowledge about fitness and fitness activities is fundamental to improving the nation's health. The amount of important fitness-related knowledge discovered in the exercise sciences over the past several decades is substantial—and research activity in the exercise sciences is so extensive at the moment that we can expect more knowledge in the near future.

This knowledge explosion related to fitness requires that sport, fitness, and physical-education

---

Walking toward a Healthier City

In April 2002, the city of Wheeling, West Virginia, began the "Wheeling Walks" campaign to encourage people of all ages to walk 30 minutes or more every day.

With a population of 35,000, Wheeling is considered to be a "walkable" city, with an 8-mile trail along the Ohio River, a 4-mile trail along Wheeling Creek, and ample sidewalks.

For 8 weeks, a public-information campaign was waged with television spots, cable spots, radio ads, and newspaper ads. The campaign sought to expose typical households to the TV messages fifty times over the 8 week period.

Researchers from West Virginia University surveyed residents and found that nearly 80 percent had seen the ads and could accurately describe the messages conveyed.

Researchers also did follow-up surveys and found that nearly 15 percent of residents who had reported being sedentary had become more active as a result of the campaign.

In September 2002, another series of "booster" ads was shown, and many community walking events were made available. The goal was to change the activity culture of everyday life.

SOURCE: *USA Today*, August 29, 2001, p. 7D.

professionals continually upgrade their own practices based on new knowledge and that they pass that knowledge on to those they serve. When professionals continue to use fitness-related practices that are contraindicated by current research, not only is the public poorly served but also the status of the professions suffers. For example, it is reasonably common to see fitness instructors, physical-education teachers, and coaches have their clients, students, or athletes doing straight-leg sit-ups, bent-leg sit-ups with hands behind the head, deep knee bends, or double leg lifts as strengthening exercises, even though each has been shown to be potentially dangerous, and for each, there is a safer substitute (Timmermans & Martin, 1987). The same is true for some popular stretching exercises—notably the hurdler's stretch, the quadriceps stretch, and the standing toe touch. How often do you do these exercises or stretches? How often do you see a sport, fitness, or physical-education professional have others do them?

Another good example of public miseducation is the degree to which people are *weight* conscious rather than *fat* conscious. People still gauge their fitness levels by stepping on a scale rather than by understanding their own body composition. When many people begin fitness programs, they expect to see their weight decrease immediately, and if it does not, they abandon the program. People beginning fitness programs, however, often lose fat and gain muscle without changing their weight at all! They are more fit, but the scale on which they weigh themselves cannot show them that fact. Therefore, educating people about body composition and providing low-cost, readily available tools for measuring their fat content will mark another step forward in the battle to improve the nation's fitness.

The communications technologies now available in the computer age make information much more accessible exactly when people need it. This does not suggest that there is not misinformation on the Internet but, rather, that people can gain access to information so much more readily, spontaneously asking questions and quickly receiving answers, thereby building their knowledge base about fitness and activity. The interactive nature of many information technologies is particularly well suited to reducing the amount of misinformation.

The major means by which the public will eventually become better educated about fitness are programs of health and physical education in schools. The American Public Health Association has long noted the importance of school programs, available to all children and youth.

> The school, as a social structure, provides an educational setting in which the total health of the child during the impressionable years is a priority concern. No other community setting even approximates the magnitude of the grades K–12 school education enterprise. . . . Thus, it seems that the school should be regarded as a . . . focal point to which health planning for all other community settings should relate. (McGinnis, Kanner, & DeGraw, 1991)

If school physical education continues to dwindle and private health clubs continue to grow, then future generations will learn about fitness and have access to fitness programs more and more as a result of the socioeconomic status of their parents. The fitness gap between rich and poor will grow. Fitness will continue to be seen primarily as an individual issue, even though the costs to the public of an unfit society will be enormous.

EQUITY ISSUES IN FITNESS AND ACTIVITY

Gender, race, and socioeconomic status are key factors in understanding differences in health, fitness, and activity participation in the United States. In nearly every data table presented in a 1996 U.S. Surgeon General's report (U.S. Health and Human Services, 1996), where data on participation in physical activity were differentiated on the basis of those factors, females were less active than males, blacks and Hispanics were less active than whites (although black males typically fared as well as white males, but black females fared much worse than did white females), and young people from lower-income families were less active than those from middle- and upper-income families. This reflects the social gradient in health and activity described in Chapter 8. To reiterate, socioeconomic groups are typically healthier than the groups below them and less healthy than the groups above them (Siedentop, 1996c).

Obesity and physical inactivity are more prevalent among females than among males, and especially among females of color. Throughout history, obesity has been a condition affecting the privileged; the rich were fat, and the poor were thin. Today, however, smoking, the consumption of refined foods and fat, and obesity are increasingly common as one moves down the socioeconomic class structure, particularly among females. There is no reason to suggest that this situation is based on genetic differences; indeed, the evidence supports the opposite view—namely, that the main determinants are environmental rather than genetic.

Physical activity and obesity are obviously related. Recent research has shown that minority children and youths are more at risk than whites, that girls are more at risk than boys, and that minority girls are the most at risk (Kimm et al., 2002; Strauss & Pollock, 2001). In the last decade of the twentieth century, overweight increased significantly among all children and youths, but the rate of increase among African American and Hispanic children was nearly twice that for whites. Research has also shown that participation in physical activity declines markedly among girls during adolescence, with the largest declines among black girls. From ages 8–9 to 18–19, the decline was 64 percent for white girls and 100 percent for minority girls. By the ages of 16 to 17, 31 percent of white girls and 56 percent of black girls reported no regular leisure time physical activity. The long-term health implications of these data for this age cohort of girls is substantial.

Only recently have fitness studies begun to focus on women's issues. Traditionally, most fitness research has been conducted on men (Wells, 1996). What is obvious is that the benefits of regular activity and a healthy lifestyle are as important for women as they are for men—perhaps more important than for men—particularly as they age. Exercise has been shown to reduce the risk of breast cancer (Physical Activity Today, 1996), and its benefits for combating problems associated with osteoporosis are well known. It is also clear that participation in physical activity and sport has important psychological and social, as well as physiological, benefits (Bunker, 1998). Research has shown that women are less active than men; that women of color are less active than white women; and that the incidence of inactivity is higher among those with less education (Wells, 1996). It becomes increasingly important that programs specifically designed to reach and assist those populations be developed and implemented.

Helping Young Girls Get and Stay Healthy

In 2002 the Department of Health and Human Services' Office on Women's Health launched a new Website (www.4girls.gov) to encourage adolescent girls to choose healthy behaviors.

Young girls (12–16), especially minority girls, are particularly at risk for physical inactivity and all the problems associated with inactivity.

One section of the Web site deals with being "Fit for Life," and provides girls with the tools to develop exercise plans that are safe, enjoyable, and long-lasting. That section also provides education about strength training, eating outside the home, and maintaining a healthy weight. A fitness questionnaire can be filled out to help girls understand their own needs.

The site also includes a parent/caregiver section that can be used to help address issues that face adolescent girls.

SOURCE: www.fitness.gov/4girls press release.html.

Residents of lower socioeconomic neighborhoods in urban areas are particularly at risk for health problems associated with physically inactive lifestyles. In urban areas, there is crime in the streets, high-density housing with few open spaces, working parents with little time for supervision of outdoor activity, relatively few recreation facilities, and little adult leadership (Sallis, 1994). The Carnegie Council on Adolescent Development (1992), in their landmark study of discretionary time among youths, concluded that "young adolescents who live in low-income neighborhoods are most likely to benefit from supportive youth development services; yet they are the very youth who have least access to such programs and organizations" (p. 12).

Opportunity for physical activity and fitness is not a level playing field in the United States. Those who have had restricted opportunity and support have become the most at risk for a number of health problems related to physical inactivity. Thus, whether one views this problem primarily as a social–moral issue or chiefly as a cost–benefit issue from the standpoint of health costs, the solution is the same—namely, to remove barriers and to target supportive programs at those among us whose opportunities have been most restricted. This is a *structural* problem requiring public policy and programs for its solution. Exhorting people to show more individual responsibility may be an element in this solution, but in and of themselves, such exhortations are unlikely to change anything.

CERTIFICATION OF FITNESS LEADERS

At the moment, most people who are in positions of leadership in adult-fitness groups are not certified in any way for that position. This is not to suggest that they are not competent in many cases. It only shows that the mechanisms are not present to *ensure* that exercise leaders have undergone a certain kind of training.

The number of different kinds of aerobic conditioning programs at the national level is substantial. In many cases, a person needs no specific certifica-

tion to put an advertisement in the paper or a sign in a window and to enroll people in aerobics classes. Many of these programs do certify their instructors, but the certification is sometimes available through the mail, and the requirements for obtaining it are minimal.

The physical-education teacher has a teaching certification in physical education, which almost always includes specific coursework in exercise physiology, first aid, the care and prevention of injuries, and often strength development and aerobic conditioning. The certification programs provided by the ACSM and the YMCA (see Chapter 9) are examples of other efforts to upgrade the qualifications of exercise leaders. Although those programs do not require preparation comparable to what a certified physical-education teacher has, they are a step in the right direction.

This problem of certification for exercise leaders is tied to the problem of public education about fitness. The more the public knows about fitness, the more likely people are to demand appropriate leadership in fitness classes and to be able to discriminate between good and bad practices. In the final analysis, an informed public might create such consumer awareness that inappropriate fitness leadership would be driven from the market. Still, requiring exercise leaders to obtain certification by an agency such as the ACSM would represent another major step forward in the fitness movement.

FITNESS TESTS OR ACTIVITY ESTIMATES?

As epidemiological data on exercise related to mortality have become available, it has become clear that inactivity is a serious risk factor but that moderate activity is nearly as valuable as a preventive measure as is vigorous activity (Blair, 1992). This has led some fitness experts to argue for measures of activity in children and youths as more valid estimates of health fitness than fitness tests themselves (Freedson & Rowland, 1992).

The notion is quite simple. A healthy lifestyle includes activity. Moderate activity is sufficient to serve public health goals, and many of the kinds of activities that people enjoy most are moderate in nature—that is, walking, recreational cycling, gardening, and the like. Earlier in this chapter, I argued that fitness education must focus on long-term goals and that changes in lifestyle are the main long-term outcomes. If that is so, then one must at least give serious consideration to the argument that measures of daily activity are, from this perspective, valid indicators of fitness.

In contrast to measures of activity, mass fitness testing with students competing against one another is typically counterproductive to fitness and activity goals. This does not mean that fitness testing has no place in school or agency programs. Pate (1994) has suggested the following guidelines for fitness testing:

- Testing should be used to identify at-risk children, but their privacy should be respected in both testing and remediation.

- Award systems should be based on criterion-referenced standards, not norm-based tables.

- Accumulated activity, as well as performance on fitness tests, should become part of the evaluation strategy with children and youths.

- Self-testing can reduce some of the unfortunate side effects of mass fitness testing in physical-education classes.

- The primary purposes of fitness testing should be diagnosis, providing feedback, setting goals, and charting improvements.

FITNESS AND AGING: CHANGING VIEWS AND EXPECTATIONS

The American population is graying! Not only are there more older citizens than ever before, but also our senior citizens have become one of our largest population groups. Every day, more than 4,000 Americans celebrate their sixty-fifth birthday. This population group has, traditionally, viewed vigorous physical activity as inappropriate. Increasingly, fitness for older Americans will become a major

Golf is growing in popularity as an activity for people of all ages.

issue in the sport, fitness, and physical-education professions.

The dimensions of the problems associated with an aging population are substantial. The post–65-year-old group will soon be the dominant social and political group in America. Most people who retire at age 60 or 62 can expect to spend 20 years or more in retirement. As of the year 2000, approximately 100,000 Americans were over the age of 100!

The most important issue resulting from all of this is not necessarily how to increase life expectancy further. Rather, it is how to help older citizens maintain their productive living capacity and better enjoy their later years. A pertinent corollary of this issue is reducing national health-care costs.

The benefits of activity in later years are beginning to be understood. Along with appropriate diet, exercise appears to be a key factor in controlling the effects of aging. It now seems that many of the so-called signs of aging (hearing loss, hair loss, reduced heart and lung function) are not as much signs of aging as they are signs of inactivity and poor nutrition (Kotulak & Gorner, 1992). Exercise programs do increase physical and physiological function among the elderly, thus having major effects on physiological aging and quality of life (Shephard, 1996). Quite elderly and even bed-ridden people have dramatically improved their physical status through planned exercise and nutrition interventions.

One of the most common ailments of senior citizens is depression of various kinds and intensities. The fact is that the declines that often accompany aging tend to produce depression and lower self-esteem. Recent studies (News, 2001), however, have shown that sedentary seniors who participate in regular physical-activity programs experience long-term psychological benefits. Even seniors suffering from major depressive disorder (MDD) who, as a treatment, participate in a 3-day-per week program of low-to-moderate-intensity aerobic activity show significant improvements, most to the point where MDD is no longer the diagnosis. Furthermore, these seniors are less likely to relapse than seniors who are treated with antidepressant medications. This is all more proof of the prophylactic and remedial benefits of regular activity.

Contemporary surveys of activity participation among the post–65-year-old age group are quite encouraging. It is clear that activities such as walking, cycling, aerobics, and calisthenics are popular with and doable by women and men in this age group. It is also clear that socioeconomic status is strongly related to activity in later years. Women and men who can afford to retire in retirement communities or care centers have access to planned activities and to easily accessible exercise facilities that cater to older adults.

On the other hand, once a person's habits and attitudes become ingrained through a lifestyle, they become difficult to change. Some research (*ARAPCS Newsletter*, 1986) shows that older adults have attitudes toward physical activity that make it highly unlikely that they will engage in appropriate fitness-related pursuits. Older adults tend (1) to have excessive fears about participation in activity, (2) to underestimate their physical capabilities, and (3) to overestimate the value of the light, infrequent activity in which they engage.

We are just now beginning to investigate and understand the problems associated with motivating older adults to incorporate regular physical activity into their lifestyles (Duda, 1991). Educating older people about the importance of physical activity must emphasize the personal meaning of the activity and the personal investment that the individual makes when entering an activity setting. It will take a great deal to overcome the traditional myth that people slow down because they get older. It appears that the opposite is more nearly true—that is, people get older because they slow down!

Our immediate needs are (1) better information among seniors about physical fitness in old age, (2) more programs that involve appropriate levels of aerobic activity for seniors, and (3) more publicity for senior role models whose vigorous activity involvement can encourage others to participate. It should be clear that there *are* many seniors who still exercise and even compete vigorously. Most local road races, for example, will have age-group competition at least through an over-60 class. The individuals competing in those classes may surprise you—both by how young and fit they look and by how fast they run.

In Melbourne, Australia, in 2002, more than 20,000 competitors took part in the Third World Masters Games. They competed in twenty-two sports, ranging from golf to cycling, from volleyball to softball, from judo to weight lifting. More than 30 percent of the competitors were over age 55! People such as these are not the norm. They do, however, give us a sense of what is possible—and it is clear that one of the major steps forward for the fitness of our aging population will be to change our common perceptions of what kind of activity is possible for older adults. Aside from enjoying themselves and their fellow competitors immensely, and participating in a great sport festival, what these athletes do for us is to provide a vision, a necessary vision if we are to achieve the major theme this text advocates: a lifespan commitment to sport, fitness, and physical education.

FITNESS ISSUES IN PHYSICAL EDUCATION

Most children first encounter physical fitness in their school physical-education program. These children will be in school for their formative years

Rollerblading is one of the most popular fitness activities among adolescents and adults.

of childhood and the crucial years of adolescence. Therefore, what their physical education classes teach them is likely to be of major importance in the formation of habits and attitudes that might last a lifetime.

The issues and problems associated with fitness programs within physical education are complex and not given to simple solutions. Nonetheless, to neglect them would be a serious mistake.

The degree to which physical fitness is attended to in school physical-education programs ranges from high to low. In some schools, physical fitness has completely taken over the physical-education curriculum, and traditional objectives such as sport-skill acquisition, game strategies, and social development are neglected entirely. In other programs, physical fitness is not attended to in any way that would allow for measurable gains in either health-related or motor-performance fitness. Perhaps the most typical approach is to have a fitness unit once per year.

Leaders in the fitness movement have been particularly critical of school physical-education programs. In 1986 Kenneth Cooper, the physician who made the nation aware of aerobics, commented that fitness among children was so poor that we may "see all the gains made against heart disease in the past 20 years wiped out in the next 20 years" (*ARAPCS Newsletter*, 1986, p. 4). More recent evidence estimating children's physical activity, rather than their performance of fitness tests, has reduced that concern but not changed that clear fact that too many

---

Children: Fit or Active?

Dr. Charles Corbin, a long-time leader in research and program development for physical fitness and physical activity, has said that "being active seems to be the ultimate goal" (Corbin, 2002, p. 34).

A focus on high levels of fitness with children may have some negative consequences:

- Loss of interest in physical activity because fitness tasks seem too distasteful

- Spending time in PE teaching to a fitness test on which children may be compared and graded

- Children losing confidence in themselves because they can't do certain fitness tasks

Some youngsters who have very adequate levels of fitness aren't very active! If they don't learn to be active as children, they will be less likely to be active as adults.

Some children who are adequately active may not score well on fitness tests. What happens if they get discouraged or if their own sense of themselves is impaired?

The "ultimate goal" Corbin refers to is a lifetime commitment to being physically active, and the surest way to achieve that goal is to focus on physical activity throughout childhood and adolescence.

Source: Adapted from Corbin, 2002.

School-based fitness programs must aim at developing lifetime habits of appropriate exercise.

children are obese and inactive and that during adolescence, many youths become much less active.

Many critics feel that the major problem is a lack of commitment to fitness in physical-education programs. Charles Corbin, a prominent researcher and spokesperson in physical education, has identified problems related to fitness in physical education and has offered some solutions. Corbin asks, "Would you buy a membership in a club which required you to wear a specific uniform, continually repeat activities you don't like, and required you to get showered and dressed in three minutes or less?" (Corbin, 1987, p. 52). The answer seems obvious.

One reaction to recent evidence on the relationship of physical activity to health has been to suggest that the "promotion of lifelong physical activity and fitness should be the primary goal of physical education" (Pate & Hohn, 1994). This goal would be accomplished through what Simons-Morton (1994) calls health-related physical education (HRPE). Such a program would emphasize children's fitness knowledge, attitudes, and practices by emphasizing participation in lifetime physical activities.

Physical educators and fitness professionals have also begun to argue for a fitness-club approach to high school physical-education classes (Berg, 1988; Siedentop & Locke, 1997; Westcott, 1992). The idea is that adolescents will relate better to an adult pattern of fitness involvement, for which the health/fitness club is the prototypic model. Also, fitness clubs eliminate some of the problems that seem to be endemic in school physical education; that is, they are bright, attractive, clean, and often quite social.

The physical-education profession has made many efforts to respond to criticisms and also to examine their own practices regarding fitness and physical activity. Some of the innovative steps forward are

- National incentive programs such as AAHPERD's Physical Best
- Special activity programs such as Jump Rope for Heart, Heart Smart, Moving Children, and the Healthy Children Project
- Continued efforts to lobby for high-quality, daily physical education
- Development of state requirements, such as the Florida legislation that requires a personal fitness course for all high school students (Harageones, 1987)
- Fitness emphases in total curriculum planning, such as the 4-year high school wellness program, emphasizing health-related fitness (Westcott, 1992).
- Special fitness-related opportunities in nonattached time for elementary students, such as a fitness-performance troupe (Steller, 1994), a schoolwide walking program (Weigle, 1994), and a series of daily all-school fitness breaks (Bradford-Krok, 1994).

Many physical educators believe that the major problem in achieving more in fitness and activity is the lack of time. If one looks at time only in terms of scheduled class time, the concern is well founded. Most elementary specialist teachers see children 1 or 2 days a week. Middle-school PE is often 3 days per week, and the norm for high school PE is 5 days per week for 1 year in the ninth grade. Physical educators need to expand

Sport Participation and Healthy Behaviors

A recent study of 14,221 female and male American high school students from three ethnic groups showed that sport participation among high school students is strong and that numerous positive health behaviors are associated with sport participation.

- 70 percent of males and 53 percent of female students reported participating on one or more sport teams.

- Sport participants were less likely to report not eating fruits or vegetables regularly.

- Sport participants were more likely to report participating in three or more vigorous physical-activity sessions in the past week.

- Female sport participants were less likely to report having sexual intercourse in the past three months.

- Both African American and Hispanic participants were somewhat less likely to be associated with positive health behaviors and somewhat more likely to be associated with negative health behaviors.

- Among males, sport participants across all three ethnic groups were less likely than nonparticipants to report cigarette smoking, illegal drug use, steroid use, or attempts to lose weight.

- Among females, sport participants across all three ethnic groups were less likely than nonparticipants to report cigarette smoking, illegal drug use, sexual intercourse, or contemplating or attempting suicide.

SOURCE: Pate, Trost, Levin, & Dowda, 2000.

their horizons beyond class schedules, especially through use of nonattached time and through establishing links with community programs (Siedentop, 1996c). Physical-education programs should include attractive, inclusive, invitational programs for children and youths in nonattached school time. School physical education should also be the place where children learn about community programs, are encouraged to participate, and are helped to gain access to those programs, especially those that are after-school, weekend, or summer programs.

The guidelines recommended by the Centers for Disease Control and Prevention (1997) clearly indicate that fitness and physical activity are *schoolwide* responsibilities (see Table 9.2). For children and youths to build habits that lead to a lifetime commitment to activity, we must develop activity as a *social norm* in the school. This can be done only if the entire school believes in and supports that norm, particularly through the development of attractive programs that include all children and youths. The

guidelines also suggest that the school is the hub of a school–family–community connection that supports physical activity for children and youths. In this sense, the physical education of children and youths becomes the responsibility of not only the PE teacher but also the other classroom teachers, the principal, the parents, and the community leaders.

RESEARCH ISSUES IN FITNESS AND PHYSICAL ACTIVITY

Although much has been learned about fitness and physical activity in the past several decades, there is much still to be learned. Some of these issues involve basic research, and others involve finding solutions to problems of delivery and exercise maintenance through applied research. Following are listed some of the more intriguing questions for research (Blair, Kohl, & Powell, 1987; U.S. Department of Health and Human Services, 1996):

- What is the relationship between exercise and the body's immune response system? Can exercise help to make us more resistant to infectious disease?

- What important features or combinations of features (intensity, duration, frequency, cumulation, type of activity) of physical activity are related to specific health benefits?

- What protective effects might physical activity have on lifestyle characteristics and disease-prevention behaviors?

- What type of exercise best preserves muscle strength and functional capacity among the elderly?

- What are the determinants of physical activity among various population subgroups (e.g., age, sex, race/ethnicity, socioeconomic status, geographic region)?

- What is the relationship between the amount and kind of physical-activity involvement in children and youths and their later adult habits?

- What interventions are most likely to promote adoption and maintenance of a physically active lifestyle at various stages of the life cycle?

As you can see, there is a great deal to be learned as we continue to know more, in order to be able to do more. Achieving a lifespan commitment to physical activity for a larger proportion of our population, regardless of age, sex, race/ethnicity, handicapping condition, or socioeconomic status remains the major problem to be solved.

TOWARD A PHYSICAL-ACTIVITY INFRASTRUCTURE FOR THE UNITED STATES

To solve the major problem described in this chapter, to substantially increase the percentage of citizens who value physical activity enough to voluntarily choose to be regularly active despite attractive alternatives to such activity, we need to move from a traditional focus on remediation to a focus on prevention. The goal of prevention will not be achieved if we focus solely on altering the risk status of individuals through smoking-cessation programs or activity-promotion ad campaigns. The best chance of establishing effective prevention of sedentary lifestyles is to develop and sustain attractive and inclusive physical activity infrastructures for children, youths, and adults (Siedentop, 1996c).

We all know that living well in modern society requires an infrastructure: roads, sewers, electric service, hospitals, schools, and the like. A physical-activity infrastructure includes facilities, spaces, and programs dedicated to physical activity. These need to be attractive, accessible, and safe to be well utilized. In their study of discretionary use of time among youths, the Carnegie Council on Adolescent Development (1992) suggested that "in a youth-centered America, every community would have a network of affordable, accessible, safe, and challenging opportunities that appeal to the diverse interests of young adolescents" (p. 77). We know that such an activity infrastructure is not equally accessible to all citizens of the United States.

The Atlanta–DeKalb Greenway Trail System— a 40-mile path for skaters, pedestrians, and cyclists—is a good example of a physical-activity infrastructure. The PATH Foundation, which is developing and supporting this initiative, plans to have 80 additional miles of trail system in place in Atlanta by the year 2005. Additional examples include school physical-education programs that have taken the responsibility to help students learn about, enroll in, and stay active in community programs; and community–school partnerships, where school facilities are used for physical activity in the early mornings, evenings, and weekends, and children and youths from local schools have access to these school community facilities. Also, as Lawson (1994) has argued, this activity infrastructure involves people, too; indeed, we need to reinvent a sense of community in which parents, schools, and community agencies invest more in their children, youths, adults, and senior citizens by providing competently staffed activity programs.

The districtwide wellness initiative described in Chapter 9 is a good example of a community building an infrastructure (e.g., people, programs, and facilities) to support fitness and wellness among students and adults (Samman, 1998). Wellness is incorporated throughout the school curriculum. Faculty, staff, students, and parents participate. School and community facilities and programs are interconnected. Eventually, an effort like this changes the *culture* of a community, so that youngsters are socialized into a school and community lifestyle that is active and healthy.

If we expect an increasing proportion of the next generation to value physical activity and to adopt a physically active lifestyle, then we must change the social context within which these young people de-

---

⟩ GET CONNECTED TO FITNESS WEB SITES

Fitness for Children and Youth

Healthy Schools	www.healthyschools.net
President's Council on Physical Fitness and Sports	www.fitness.gov
Project Fit America	www.projectfitamerica.org
Trim & Fit	www.tafisa.net/

Fitness for Adults

Worksite fitness programs	www.fitwellinc.com
Active America	www.activeusa.com
Fitness Resources	www.fitresource.com
Project Fit America	www.projectfitamerica.org
Senior Fitness Association	www.seniorfitness.net
Fifty-Plus Fitness Association	www.50plus.org

Fitness-Related Professions and Organizations

Healthy People 2010	www.health.gov/healthypeople
National Athletic Trainers' Association	www.nata.org
American Physical Therapy Association	www.apta.org
National Strength and Conditioning Association	www.nsca-lift.org
American College of Sports Medicine	www.acsm.org
American Council on Exercise	www.acefitness.org
American Occupational Therapy Association	www.aota.org
Fitness Management	www.fitnessworld.com
Cooper Institutue	www.cooperinst.org
President's Council on Physical Fitness and Sport	www.fitness.gov
Aerobics and Fitness Association of America	www.afaa.com
American Fitness Professionals & Associates	www.afpafitness.com
Aquatic Exercise Association	www.aeawave.com
National Association for Health and Fitness	www.physicalfitness.org
National Coalition for Promoting Physical Activity	www.ncppa.org
United States Water Fitness Association	www.uswfa.com
Canadian Fitness & Lifestyle Research Institute	www.cflri.ca/
Be Active America!	www.beactiveamerica.org

velop. We must also quickly begin to change the social context for exactly that portion of the population that is presently most at risk. This will require public-policy initiatives at the federal, state, and local levels. It will also require the commitment of professionals in the sport, fitness, and physical-education professions.

SUMMARY

1. Health, motor-performance, and cosmetic fitness are each important to individuals and to society. However, the demands of everyday modern life are typically insufficient for the development and maintenance of fitness.

2. The costs to society of inadequate health fitness are substantial; they include the costs of expensive health insurance, rehabilitation, reduced productivity, and lost workdays.

3. The immediate consequences of aerobic activity are often aversive, and the benefits are often delayed. To maintain health fitness, a person must make appropriate activity a regular part of her or his lifestyle.

4. Fitness programs that affect lifestyles incorporate education, activity, planning skills, and consumer information in a comprehensive effort to produce permanent changes in exercise behavior.

5. Media images of fitness are often misleading. A national fitness-education effort would help to curb the amount of fitness misinformation and help the public to make wiser choices about personal fitness.

6. The social gradient in health and activity results in highly inequitable access to activity programs and facilities.

7. Many exercise leaders have no certification. Others have only mail-order credentials. Certification, especially for adult-fitness leaders, would help to ensure that appropriate fitness testing and prescriptive programs are utilized.

8. The size of the senior population is growing, and seniors are living longer. Many seniors have many misconceptions about fitness and do not engage in activity that is as vigorous as it could be. Fitness in old age is important both for maintaining functional capacity and for improving quality of life.

9. Physical education has been strongly criticized for its lack of appropriate fitness programming, but fitness is just one of many objectives physical educators attempt to reach.

10. Fitness programs at the national, state, district, and local levels have been successful, but no single pattern has emerged. Lack of sufficient time for activities that meet minimum health-fitness requirements appears to be the biggest problem.

11. Health-related fitness among schoolchildren and youths will not be given appropriate attention until it becomes a schoolwide objective rather than an objective for physical educators alone.

12. Although substantial fitness research has been completed in the past several decades, much remains to be done, at both the basic and the applied levels.

13. To achieve national goals in health and physical activity, we must develop a physical activity infrastructure of accessible programs and facilities.

DISCUSSION QUESTIONS

1. Of what should fitness education consist if the goal is to incorporate regular fitness into the student's lifestyle?

2. Have the media helped or hurt the goals of fitness education? How could the media be used more effectively to promote those goals?

3. Should fitness be a required school subject? Should students have to meet fitness standards on a regular basis?

4. Should physical education have fitness as its most important goal? Why or why not?

5. How can fitness be made important for *all* segments of the national population? Will it remain a mostly upper-middle-class movement?

6. Could a program like Australia's daily fitness work in America? Could it work at the state level?

7. If the children of today are unfit, will the adults and seniors of tomorrow also be unfit?

PART FOUR

Physical Education

Chapter 11   Basic Concepts of Physical Education

Chapter 12   Physical-Education Programs and Professions

Chapter 13   Problems and Issues in Physical Education

Physical education has been an accepted part of the curriculum of American schools for about a century. Even in the midst of current educational reform, physical education is still described as a necessary subject that has the potential to contribute a great deal to the education of children and youths. Yet there is also a substantial amount of "fizz-ed bashing," both in the serious literature of education and in the popular media. Think for a moment about how the physical-education teacher is typically portrayed in contemporary films!

School is still one institution that touches us all—and that touches us at crucial periods of our development as individuals. It is vitally important that physical education thrive as a well-taught, well-accepted subject in our schools. What is physical education? What activities are acceptable? How can the subject be improved? What kinds of programs seem to work? The three chapters in Part 4 are designed to help you examine these issues and to reach conclusions that are informed by evidence and thoughtful argument.

CHAPTER **11**

Basic Concepts of Physical Education

Modern physical education with its emphasis upon education through the physical is based upon the biologic unity of mind and body. This view sees life as a totality. Correct in their appraisement that the cult of muscle is ludicrous, those who worship at the altar of mental development too frequently neglect the implications of unity. "Socrates with a headache" is always preferable to a brainless Hercules, but the modern spirit in physical education seeks the education of man through physical activities as one aspect of the social effort for human enlightenment.

Jesse Feiring Williams, 1930

LEARNING OBJECTIVES

- To discuss definitions of physical education

- To analyze education-through-the-physical and multiactivity programs

- To describe and discuss alternative curriculum influences

- To describe the development of and issues in adapted physical education

- To analyze the influences of liability and Title IX on physical education

- To formulate your own view on the central meaning and preferred focus of physical education

The one experience common to almost all people in this country is attending school during childhood. Not all of us went to the same kind of school. Differences in some cases are substantial. Nevertheless, we have all been students, and most of us have taken classes in good old "fizz ed." That experience no doubt partially shaped what each of us believes physical education to be, or what we think it should be. As you read this chapter, and study the basic concepts related to physical education, keep your own fizz-ed experience in mind, and use it as a standard against which to evaluate the ideas described here.

The theories presented may differ dramatically from the reality you experienced. That is all right. Educational theories are typically idealized models of the way things *could be* rather than descriptions of the way things are. Nonetheless, remember that without visions of how things could be, it would be difficult to improve education.

Introducing basic concepts of physical education is somewhat different from introducing basic concepts of sport and fitness. We can define cardiovascular fitness clearly, and we know what type of program and activities we would have to employ to achieve it. It is not possible to achieve that level of specificity when discussing physical education. Table 11.1 shows the National Association for Sport and Physical Education (NASPE) definition of a *physically educated person*. Table 11.2 shows the outcomes that demonstrate achievement of the qualities stated in the definition. Although the definition and the outcomes seem specific, there is little agreement within physical education about how to achieve them; thus, ideas about what physical education should be vary widely.

In this chapter, we present the major contemporary points of view about physical education with as little bias as possible so that you can decide which point of view seems most able to help children and youths become physically educated people. To understand these competing contemporary views, however, you should know some historical background, which is summarized in the box titled "Reminder."

EDUCATION THROUGH THE PHYSICAL

The most important model for physical education in the twentieth century was the **developmental model.** See Chapter 2 for a full explanation of the developmental model known as education

---

TABLE 11.1 Content Standards in Physical Education (NASPE, 1995b)

A physically educated person

1. Demonstrates competency in many movement forms and proficiency in a few movement forms.

2. Applies movement concepts and principles to the learning and development of motor skills.

3. Exhibits a physically active lifestyle.

4. Achieves and maintains a health-enhancing level of physical fitness.

5. Demonstrates responsible personal and social behavior in physical-activity settings.

6. Demonstrates understanding and respect for differences among people in physical-activity settings.

7. Understands that physical activity provides opportunities for enjoyment, challenge, self-expression, and social interaction.

Reprinted from *Moving into the Future: National Physical Education Standards: A Guide to Content and Assessment* with permission from the National Association for Sport and Physical Education (NASPE), 1900 Association Drive, Reston, VA 20191.

TABLE 11.2 NASPE Outcomes for the Physically Educated Person

NASPE Outcomes Project

The physically educated person

- *Has* learned skills necessary to perform a variety of physical activities
  1. ... moves using concepts of body awareness, space awareness, effort and relationships.
  2. ... demonstrates competence in a variety of manipulative, locomotor, and nonlocomotor skills.
  3. ... demonstrates competence in combinations of manipulative, locomotor, and nonlocomotor skills performed individually and with others.
  4. ... demonstrates competence in many different forms of physical activity.
  5. ... demonstrates proficiency in at least a few forms of physical activity.
  6. ... has learned how to learn new skills.

- *Is* physically fit
  7. ... assesses, achieves, and maintains physical fitness.
  8. ... designs safe, personal fitness programs in accordance with principles of training and conditioning.

- *Does* participate regularly in physical activity
  9. ... participates in health-enhancing physical activity at least three times a week.
  10. ... selects and regularly participates in lifetime physical activities.

- *Knows* the implications of and the benefits from involvement in physical activities
  11. ... identifies the benefits, costs, and obligations associated with regular participation in physical activity.
  12. ... recognizes the risk and safety factors associated with regular participation in physical activity.
  13. ... applies concepts and principles to the development of motor skills.
  14. ... understands that wellness involves more than being physically fit.
  15. ... knows the rules, strategies, and appropriate behaviors for selected physical activities.
  16. ... recognizes that participation in physical activity can lead to multicultural and international understanding.
  17. ... understands that physical activity provides the opportunity for enjoyment, self-expression, and communication.

- *Values* physical activity and its contributions to a healthful lifestyle
  18. ... appreciates the relationships with others that result from participation in physical activity.
  19. ... respects the role that regular physical activity plays in the pursuit of lifelong health and well-being.
  20. ... cherishes the feelings that result from regular participation in physical activity.

SOURCE: Adapted from NASPE (1992) outcomes. Reprinted with permission from *Definition and Outcomes of the Physically Educated Person,* National Association for Sport and Physical Education, 1900 Association Drive, Reston, VA 20191.

through the physical. This model was wholly consistent with progressive-education theory, which dominated ideas about schooling and learning in the first half of the twentieth century.

In 1910 Clark Hetherington earned the title of "father of modern physical education" with his landmark paper "Fundamental Education." Hetherington described both the scope and the categories of the *new* physical education.

This paper aims to describe the function and place of general neuromuscular activities, primarily play activities, in the educational process. ... To present the thesis four phases of the education process will be

---

Reminder
Historical Influences on the Development of Physical Education

1. Concerns about health and fitness and character development were at the heart of the early formal gymnastic systems. Concerns about fitness have occurred periodically as reactions to rejection of draftees for military service and epidemics such as polio.

2. Progressive-education theory focused on the development of the whole child and led to the developmental perspective known historically as education through the physical, which is still the most

widely accepted approach to articulating goals for physical education.

3. The continuing development of sport in the twentieth century merged with the developmental approach to make physical education largely a sport-based curriculum.

See Chapter 2 for a full discussion of these developments.

---

considered: organic education, psychomotor education, character education, and intellectual education. (Weston, 1962, p. 160)

Hetherington's four phases were to become the four primary objectives of the new physical education. Wherever education through the physical has been promoted and applied, chances are excellent that it has been explained and justified by reference to the fourfold objectives proposed originally by Hetherington. The four goals originally suggested by Hetherington began to shape the purposes of programs of physical education in schools, even to the extent that teachers were supposed to aim at some goal development in each phase during each lesson.

Although the goals have been defined somewhat differently by different leaders, those differences are minimal. Bucher's definitions of the four goals came nearly half a century after Hetherington's but were remarkably similar to the original concepts:

1. Physical development objective: The objective of physical development deals with the program of activities that builds physical power in an individual through the development of the various organic systems of the body.

2. Motor development objective: The motor development objective is concerned with making physical

movement useful and with as little expenditure of energy as possible and being proficient, graceful, and aesthetic in this movement.

3. Mental development objective: The mental development objective deals with the accumulation of a body of knowledge and the ability to think and to interpret this knowledge.

4. Social development objective: The social development objective is concerned with helping an individual in making personal adjustments, group adjustments, and adjustments as a member of society. (Bucher, 1964, p. 155)

A typical physical-education lesson included fitness, skill development, knowledge, and social development. Lesson plans organized around the four objectives quickly became the standard in the physical-education curriculum in schools.

A corollary feature of this developmental model for physical education was the establishment of the **multiactivity-program** approach to program design. For *full* development to be ensured, people believed, each child had to experience a *variety* of activities. Because physical education sought a diversity of physical, mental, and social goals, and because each child was unique in her or his own development, a wide variety of activities was needed to fulfill the promise of this developmental model;

Can physical education begin to engender the same enthusiasm among students that school sport does?

would experience a fairly large number of these activity units. The unit model with a multiactivity approach became the main distinguishing programmatic feature of education through the physical and today remains the dominant characteristic of American physical education.

In 1971 AAHPER launched the Physical Education Public Information (PEPI) project, designed to inform the public about the goals of physical education (Biles, 1971). PEPI's five primary concepts showed that Hetherington's four objectives were alive and well in physical education:

1. A physically educated person is one who has knowledge and skill concerning her or his body and how it works.

2. Physical education is health insurance.

3. Physical education can contribute to academic achievement.

4. A sound physical-education program contributes to development of a positive self-concept.

5. A sound physical-education program helps an individual to attain social skills.

Can you see Hetherington's influence? The language is different, but the emphasis on fitness, skill, knowledge, and social development remains.

NASPE'S MOVE TOWARD NATIONAL GOALS AND STANDARDS

In the 1990s, the National Association for Sport and Physical Education (NASPE), a main affiliate of AAHPERD, began to develop a set of national goals and standards for physical education. The first part of this initiative was called the "Outcomes Project," and it sought to answer the question "What should students know and be able to do as a result of physical education?" In 1992 NASPE published the outcomes statement shown in Table 11.2. The outcomes project, for the first time, provided a consensus statement that defined the physically educated person. The outcomes are divided into *has, is, does,*

team sports, individual sports, adventure activities, fitness activities, and dance all found acceptance within the multiactivity framework.

The multiactivity feature of the developmental model was officially sanctioned in 1927 by a national committee on curriculum development chaired by William Ralph La Porte. The results were published as a monograph, "The Physical Education Curriculum," in 1938 and eventually were revised through seven editions. This was as close to a *national* curriculum for physical education as we have ever come. The main feature of this curriculum was a *block* or *unit* approach to curriculum design. The ideal model proposed in the La Porte curriculum was units of instruction lasting for several weeks. Across a complete school year, students *knows,* and *values* categories, with twenty outcomes identified.

After the outcomes statement was published, NASPE formed a "Standards and Assessment Task Force" to develop content standards and assessment materials based on the outcomes document. The task force had two major purposes. The first purpose was to establish content standards for school physical-education programs that clearly identified what students should know and be able to do as a result of a high-quality, physical-education program (see Table 11.1). The second purpose was to establish teacher-friendly guidelines for assessment to allow for continuous evaluation of the degree to which students were progressing toward goals and the degree to which programs were effective.

The assessment portion of the document is written to be specific for each grade level, starting with kindergarten and proceeding every other school year until the twelfth grade (that is, grades 2, 4, 6, 8, 10, and 12). For each content standard, a description of purpose is provided, along with sample *benchmarks,* which are brief statements describing outcomes in performance terms. Then, examples and suggestions for how teachers might assess these performance outcomes are provided, along with criteria that define an adequate level of performance to meet the benchmark for that standard at that grade level.

An example of a kindergarten benchmark for the content standard "demonstrates competency in many movement forms and proficiency in a few" is that students can identify personal space, work in personal space, and move in general space during a lesson. An assessment might consist of a checklist on which a teacher records yes/no data in three columns, relating to (a) finding personal space when directed, (b) staying in or returning to personal space when directed during a lesson, and (c) moving in general space with an awareness of others so that space differences are maintained.

An example of a tenth-grade benchmark for the standard "exhibits a physically active lifestyle" is that students can analyze and evaluate a personal-fitness profile. An assessment might consist of a student portfolio in which students document their own activity record and their performances on relevant health-fitness test items, and compare them both with criterion-referenced standards to indicate potential risk or to analyze where they need improvement in their activity habits.

The outcomes and standards initiatives of NASPE were achieved through broad representation of physical-education professionals at all levels and throughout the United States. They represent the first truly national effort to begin to define what physical education can and should mean. It should be noted, however, that this initiative simply defines outcomes and standards and some means of assessing them. It does not prescribe or judge the effectiveness of specific physical-education activities, such as suggesting that volleyball is better or worse than hiking or rope climbing as a potential physical-education activity. Thus, it leaves fairly wide open the nature of what a physical-education program would look like from an activity point of view, or how the program is organized across the social year.

OTHER IMPORTANT CURRICULUM INFLUENCES

Views of what physical education *should be* always involve a philosophical point of view within which there is a strong value orientation (Jewett & Bain, 1985). The education-through-the-physical model starts with optimal individual development within a democratic social framework as its major value orientation and, from that, develops a set of goals and designs experiences to meet those goals (a process typically followed when developing a **curriculum**). The purpose of this section is to introduce some important curriculum models that were advocated in physical education in the second half of the twentieth century.

Movement Education

The strongest twentieth-century alternative to education through the physical was **movement education** (Jewett & Bain, 1985; Siedentop, 1980).

Children can help one another as they learn.

Movement education derives from a larger *human-movement* philosophy that has strongly influenced physical educators since the 1970s. Human movement, rather than fitness or sport, is seen as the common theme and central meaning of the profession. Important physical educators associated with this point of view have been Eleanor Metheny, Rosiland Cassidy, Lois Ellfeldt, Camille Brown, and Celeste Ulrich. The educational component of this philosophy—movement education—has been articulated and advocated by many prominent physical educators, among them Kate Barrett, Bette Logsdon, and George Graham.

The purposes of movement education are to teach the student to

1. Move skillfully, demonstrating versatile, effective, and efficient movement in situations requiring either planned or unplanned responses.

2. Become aware of the meaning, significance, feeling, and joy of movement as both a performer and an observer.

3. Gain and apply the knowledge that governs human movement. (Logsdon et al., 1977, p. 17)

Movement-education curricula are most commonly organized around three areas: educational dance, educational gymnastics, and educational games. Because human movement, rather than sport or fitness, defines the *content* of physical education, the units in a movement-education curriculum are defined by movement concepts. Thus, units on striking or absorbing force would appear, instead of units on basketball (as in a sport curriculum) or strength (as in a fitness curriculum).

Movement education has been innovative in both teaching method and curriculum design. Traditional teaching styles are replaced by ones that emphasize problem solving, guided discovery, exploration, acceptance, and success. Students are viewed as individual decision makers, and the teaching style is designed to create situations in which they can improve their abilities to make good decisions, with the final goal of achieving independence that will stay with them after schooling is finished. Eleanor Metheny clearly articulated the ultimate goal of movement education as physical education:

If we may define the *totally educated person* as one who has fully developed his ability to utilize constructively all of his potential capacities as a person in relation to the world in which he lives, then we may define the *physically educated person* as one who has developed the ability to utilize constructively all of his potential capacities for movement as a way of expressing, exploring, developing and interpreting himself and his relationship to the world he lives in. (Metheny, 1954, p. 27; emphasis in original)

Advocates and practitioners of the movement-education model tend to value the aesthetic dimension of physical education more highly than they do the competitive dimension. Competition is typically kept to a minimum in this approach. Children learn to value movement as much for its aesthetic and personal meaning as for its outcome in competition. Both the educational-gymnastics and the educational-games portions of the curriculum are less competitive than are their more traditional counterparts and tend to stress creativity and aesthetic enjoyment over objective performance.

Movement education has had an important influence on physical education for young children.

Most K–3 physical-education programs are now conceptualized using some variation of this model, often called *movement exploration* or *basic movement*. In some schools, this emphasis is carried through to the 4–6 program, focusing on educational gymnastics, educational dance, and educational games. Seldom, however, has this curriculum model been accepted beyond the elementary school.

Health-Related Physical Education

What would have been described as "fitness models" for physical-education curriculum in the late 1970s have coalesced into the health-related physical education (HRPE) movement (McKenzie & Sallis, 1996). Several fitness models have been described previously in this text, and many of them fit nicely into the **HRPE** model (see Chapter 9). The major purpose of HRPE is to influence students toward a physically active lifestyle that contributes to health and the prevention of hypokinetic disease. HRPE also includes a substantial knowledge component, so that students learn about the role of physical activity in achieving and maintaining a healthy lifestyle.

Textbooks that describe how to do HRPE appeared during the 1990s and have contributed to the spread of the model (Corbin & Lindsey, 1999; Pate & Hohn, 1994). A major feature of HRPE is that it is meant to be a comprehensive program, with some participation from and involvement by classroom teachers, school cafeteria personnel, and parents, as well as linkages with community programs. HRPE also often includes a health-education component, especially in the elementary and middle schools, where antismoking and anti-drug programs are included.

A major advantage of HRPE is that there have been several well-funded program trials of various kinds throughout the United States (McKenzie & Sallis, 1996). Examples of these are

- *Child and Adolescent Trial for Cardiovascular Health (CATCH)*—an HRPE intervention in the third to fifth grade in ninety-six schools nationwide (see Chapter 9)

- *Go for Health Program*—a Texas elementary-school program designed to produce changes in physical education, classroom health education, and school lunches (Simons-Morton, 1994)

- *Heart Smart*—a K–6 program in Louisiana that includes eating habits, exercise habits, and antidrug and antismoking programs, and that uses the Superkids–Superfit model for physical education (Virgilio & Berenson, 1988)

- *Know Your Body*—a classroom-based program focusing on diet, physical activity, and antismoking components in grades K–6

- *Sports, Play, and Active Recreation for Kids (SPARK)*—a California program for fourth- and fifth-grade physical education, focusing on promoting physical activity, both within and outside school, and including a self-management component through which children learn to monitor and manage their own physical activity (McKenzie & Sallis, 1996)

- *P.E.4LIFE*—a national nonprofit organization promoting middle and secondary school models to develop lifetime physical-activity habits and skills, and facilities looking more like fitness centers than like traditional PE gymnasiums (www.PE4life.org)

In many physical-education programs, physical fitness is still either a unit in the yearly activity plan or a small focus in each lesson throughout the year. Of course, the HRPE goals can be achieved by any program that (a) contributes to the amount of moderate-to-intense physical activity students get in physical education and (b) influences them to lead more physically active lives outside the physical-education setting. What HRPE has done is to take those as the primary goals and to focus on them through the entire physical-education program.

The Academic-Integration Model

In the 1960s and 1970s, the physical-education academic discipline of kinesiology emerged, extending and deepening the knowledge base in a number of areas related to sport, exercise, and physical education. In the 1980s, some high school physical-education programs moved to a *concepts curriculum* (Siedentop, Mand, & Taggart, 1986), in which knowledge from kinesiological studies was blended with activity, programs that split time between the classroom and the gymnasium. Lawson and Placek (1981, p. 6) defined this disciplinary model as "a unique blend of performance skills and experience in sport, exercise, dance, and contests with that knowledge about performance which is derived from the disciplinary foundations of the field."

In the 1980s, AAHPERD published a series of booklets titled *Basic Stuff,* which focused on important concepts in exercise physiology, kinesiology, motor learning, the psychosocial aspects of sport, motor development, and sport humanities. The purpose of the series was to provide teachers with information and strategies for incorporating disciplinary knowledge into their physical-education classes. The education-reform movement of the late 1980s and early 1990s further increased the pressure on physical educators to become more academic (Taylor & Chiogioji, 1987). A well-developed disciplinary knowledge model that persevered in maintaining a major commitment to physical activity was described by Vickers (1992).

The academic-discipline model of the 1980s has gradually given way to an emphasis on integration. The purpose of *integration* is to achieve a synthesis between traditionally diverse forms of knowledge (Placek, 1996). The integration model suggests that knowledge traditionally taught in the classroom be taught in physical education and that knowledge and skills traditionally taught in physical education be taught in the classroom; that is, the lines separating subject topics are blurred. A Russian folk dance might be taught during a fifth-grade social studies unit, biomechanical principles taught during a PE basketball unit, the early Olympic Games studied in a ninth-grade history class, or the social forces that make access to sport more or less likely based on income studied in a high school PE unit. Middle school, where integrated curricula are supposed to emerge, seems like the perfect school level for integrating PE with the rest of the school; yet,

Placek (1996) reported that most integrative curriculum work at the middle school has excluded physical education.

Placek (1996) suggests that an *internal integration* can take place with physical education and can provide a curriculum model for other disciplines to adopt. This is a contemporary version of the concepts curriculum mentioned earlier, with a new focus on thinking skills and personal/social development. This approach has been very popular and successful as an elective program in the eleventh and twelfth grades in Australia, New Zealand, and England (Macdonald & Leitch, 1994).

The *external integration model,* in which physical education is integrated with other classroom subjects, seems to be most popular at the elementary level, where such subjects as language arts can easily be integrated with physical education or where outdoor adventure skills can be combined with a focus on environmental education and nature study (Monroe, 1995). Integration has been a major goal of schools that reflect a common theme, in what are typically referred to as "magnet" or "alternative" schools. An excellent example was an alternative elementary school where adventure education was the integrating force for the entire school curriculum (Stroot, Carpenter, & Eisnagule, 1991).

The academic-integration model is widely heralded but too seldom seen in practice. Many teachers would like to work toward such a model, but the institutional barriers in traditional schools and the pressures of educational reform make it risky for many schools to attempt to build integrative curricula.

The Social-Development Model

One of the most important educational influences of the 1960s and 1970s was the humanistic-education movement. The integrating goals of the many diverse models that together constituted humanistic education were (a) treating students as individuals and (b) focusing primarily on personal growth and social development rather than on academic achievement. In physical education, this approach was articulated consistently by Donald

Hellison (1973, 1978, 1983). Although it is often referred to as the "humanistic" model for physical education (Jewett & Bain, 1985), it is described here as a **social-development model** because it has been most widely used for personal growth and social development, especially with troubled adolescent students.

The social-development model is designed to help young people cope better with a complex social world, to achieve a higher degree of control over their own lives, and to contribute more positively to the small social worlds of which they are a part. The medium through which these goals are

sought is physical education—the gymnasium, the weight room, and the playing field.

To achieve the goals of this curriculum model, Hellison (1995) has conceptualized a five-level progression of personal and social development (see Table 11.3). Level 1 focuses on respect for others, Level 2 on demonstrating effort within the class, Level 3 on self-direction as a learner and class member, Level 4 on helping others, and Level 5 on demonstrating those qualities outside the physical-education setting. The levels are viewed as a progression; that is, students have to learn how to control themselves and show respect for the rights

---

TABLE 11.3 Hellison's Responsibility-in-the-Gym Model

Major focus: Put kids first! Teachers have to care about students as whole persons. The teacher–student relationship is fundamentally important. Teachers have to respect students' struggles, individuality, and capacity for growth.

Purpose: To help students take responsibility for their own well-being and to be sensitive and responsive to the well-being of others.

Responsibility Levels	Instructor Values
1. Respect for others' rights and feelings – Control temper and mouth – Right to be included – Peaceful conflict resolution	Respect for students, equity, and empowerment
2. Effort – Explore effort and new tasks – Self-motivation – Learn persistence	Self-paced task mastery, task variation, competitive choices
3. Self-direction – Independence – Goal-setting progressions – Resisting peer pressure	Empowerment
4. Helping – Sensitivity and responsiveness – Leadership – Group welfare	Well-being of others
5. Outside the gym – Trying levels in other settings – Being a role model	Values transfer

SOURCE: Adapted from Hellison, 1995.

and feelings of their classmates before they can focus on self-motivation and persistence in the learning setting.

Activities are chosen for their capacity to help students learn about the behavioral characteristics needed at any particular level. Basketball, for example, is useful for Level 1 purposes because of the high level of interaction in the game and because there is only one ball for five players to share. Gymnastics are very useful at Level 2 for helping students to learn effort, self-motivation, and persistence. Individual fitness programs are useful at Level 3, since they help students learn how to set goals and behave independently in the learning setting.

The model also has a clear lesson format. Each class begins with a brief "awareness talk," the purpose of which is to teach the levels. The activity lesson itself occupies the bulk of the time and may use any number of teaching methods, depending on the level emphasized. As students progress in their personal and social responsibility, teaching tends to move from direct forms of instruction to more learner-directed forms of instruction, with increasing focus on individual and group decision making. After the activity session is finished, a brief group meeting is held to evaluate the day's lesson and solve problems that arose during the lesson. The lesson ends with a brief reflection time, during which students evaluate their own performance using the "levels" system.

As with other curriculum models, a particular kind of teaching is associated with the social-development model. The teacher is authentic and caring and can both tolerate student differences and be secure and firm enough to deal with them. The teaching methods used range from the traditional to the unconventional. Regardless of the teaching method, the teachers' interactions with students over time must show clearly the humanistic purposes of the model. Authoritarian teaching is viewed as counterproductive.

In the 1990s, problems associated with youths became a major issue in American life (Carnegie Council on Adolescent Development, 1992): vandalism, dropout rates, teen pregnancy, teen vio-

lence, teen drug use, and a host of other problems. Many physical educators who teach in urban schools, particularly middle and high schools, feel that cooperation, social development, and responsibility are more important outcomes than are skill and fitness (Ennis, Ross, & Chen, 1992). Hellison's (1990, 1995) recent work has focused on urban youths, particularly those who exhibit at-risk behaviors. The social-development model now is described as the "personal and social responsibility" model (Hellison, 1996). It is a well-tested model that has broad application and appeals greatly to many physical educators.

The Sport-Education Model

A more recent entry into the physical-education curriculum literature is **sport education** (Siedentop, 1994). This model defines the *content* of physical education as sport and describes ways that sport can be taught to all students within the context of physical education. Within this model, sport is defined as *playful competition*, thus deriving its main conceptual focus from what had been described in physical education as "play education" (Siedentop, 1980).

Sport education has five defining characteristics, which help to distinguish it from more traditional forms of physical education. First, sport typically is done in *seasons;* thus, in sport education, the yearly curriculum is divided into sport seasons, rather than into units. Second, in sport, players have *affiliation;* thus, in sport education, students become members of a team at the start of a season and retain that team affiliation throughout that sport season. Third, sport involves a *formal competition;* thus, in sport education, a season of competition is arranged at the beginning of a season—round-robin schedules, a series of dual meets, and so on. Fourth, it is in the nature of sport to determine a winner each season, which is accomplished through some kind of *culminating event;* thus, in sport education, a culminating event determines a champion for that season. Fifth, part of the meaning and interest in sport involves *records*—scoring averages, saves, turnovers, and so on; thus, in sport education,

The sport-education model aims to produce the intimacy among team members that seems common in school sport.

records are kept and published to enhance interest and to build traditions within the sport.

Sport education assumes that *good* competition is both fun and educationally useful. The sport-education model developed from the view that physical education was teaching sport but was doing so in ways that denied students access to the most important joys and lessons of organized sport competition. It also developed from the observation that only the more elite athletes in schools got the opportunity to compete on sport teams and that these benefits should be made more widely available to all students, regardless of talent.

Sport education, even though done in a regular class format, differs from traditional forms of physical education. At the start of a season, students are selected by or are assigned to teams. They practice as a team throughout the season and prepare for competition together. They then begin their competitive season, preparing for and playing the games or matches. Throughout this time, they strive to improve their performance, both individually and as a group. The teacher is much like a coach, although the model calls for student coaches to assume major responsibility for their teams (Siedentop, Mand, & Taggart, 1986). Daily lessons are divided between practice and competition, with more time devoted to the competition schedule as the season progresses.

The sport-education model also suggests that students learn the roles of coach, referee, and administrator. Students organize their teams, make substitutions, referee games, keep records, publish future schedules and recent results, and generally learn to administer their own teams and the details of that particular sport season. In this model, good sport behavior is not just a hoped-for outcome but also central to the purpose of the program. Students learn what it means to be a good competitor, how important the role of a good referee is, and how important honest and fair competition is to the sport experience.

The sport-education model has been used at all levels from third grade through high school (Bell, 1998; Jones & Ward, 1998; Siedentop, 1994). Teachers have found the model to be an excellent vehicle for helping students to assume more responsibility for their own sport involvement. The team-membership feature produces situations that require students to work together to achieve team goals. The various roles of sport education (coach, referee, scorer, trainer, statistician) require responsible performance for the season to move forward. Teachers also report that sport education produces excitement among students and encourages them to seek other sport opportunities outside the school (Grant, 1992).

The sport-education model can accommodate a host of activities other than traditional team and individual sports. For example, it has been used for a weight-lifting and strength-training course for high school girls (Sweeney, Tannehill, & Teeters, 1992) in which students were judged both on amounts lifted and on lifting techniques. It has also been used for dance "season" (Graves & Townsend, 2000), in which student teams learned and performed dances of the 1960s through the 1990s.

Sport education is now used widely in New Zealand and Australia, where reports from both teachers and students are promising and enthusiastic. Of special interest is the common finding that lower-skilled and typically nonparticipating students seem to gain the most from the sport-education model (Carlson, 1996; Siedentop, 1996a). Teachers feel that students improve their skills and their strategic play (Grant, 1992). Students report that they like learning from their peers, like the extended time in one activity, and relish the controlled competition (Alexander, 1994).

As sport education continued to spread in the mid- to late 1990s, it also began to be more thoroughly investigated. Many of the reports from students and teachers in earlier trials were verified through more focused investigations (Hastie, 1998a, 1998b). Not only does sport education provide typically nonparticipating and lower-skilled students a more equitable learning environment, but results also show that learning opportunities for all students are increased both in quality and in quantity. Social development, too, seems to be positively influenced as students learn to get along with one another on teams and as they work together toward team goals (Hastie & Sharpe, 1999). Articles showing teachers how to use the model at various grade levels have become more available (Alexander, Taggart, & Luckman, 1998; Bell, 1998; Jones & Ward, 1998; Mohr, Townsend, & Bulger, 2001; Siedentop, 1996a, 1998).

The Adventure-Education Approach

Two major trends together have led to the development of **adventure education** in physical education. First, the idea that adventure activities—particularly risk activities in the natural environment—have potential for education and

character development has grown consistently in educational philosophy throughout the twentieth century and into the twenty-first. Second, public interest in outdoor recreation has increased substantially in the past several decades. Taken together, these two trends have made it possible for physical educators to conceptualize and implement an adventure-education curriculum within physical education.

Adventure education often includes areas of interest such as wilderness sports and outdoor pursuits. Activities such as backpacking, kayaking, scuba diving, and caving take place in natural environments and often involve some risk. Adventure education includes not only these *natural* activities but also activities created for specific educational purposes. Thus, a high-ropes course or an initiatives course is designed and built so that students can experience the challenge inherent in the design. A *high-ropes course* is a series of obstacles that the student must overcome from 20 to 40 feet in the air, on ropes strung between trees in a wooded area. Although students are secured by a harness, there is no net underneath them as they climb, crawl, and jump through the ropes course. In *initiatives,* eight to twenty participants work together to solve an unusual task, such as how to get all members of a group over a 12-foot-high wall.

There are two sets of goals within adventure-education programs. The first set of goals is to gain skill, to participate safely, and to gain utmost satisfaction from participation—for example, to ski well enough to do it safely and to be excited about doing it again and again. These kinds of goals are quite traditional and are not unlike those in other physical-education curriculum models (Siedentop, Mand, & Taggart, 1986).

A second set of goals, however, has more to do with problem solving, self-concept, and personal growth. These goals are typically emphasized in the *adventure* portion of the program, in activities where obstacles are designed to produce some risk, with the assumption that the risk produces anxiety and stress for the participant. When the participant learns to deal with the stress and to overcome the

Adventure education, such as a high-ropes course, provides exciting challenges.

anxiety to solve the problem created by the obstacle, then personal growth is assumed to occur. Because this is often done within the context of a *group,* the interactions among members of the group also become an important educational focus.

Although adventure-education curricula can be pursued at school—for example, climbing walls in gyms or rappelling down the outside wall of the school building—they are more likely to take place away from the school. Thus, adventure education sometimes involves traveling away from school, spending an extended period of time together, sharing meals, and even staying overnight. The group fosters a sense of involvement and intimacy that is almost impossible to re-create in a regular class period in a school gymnasium.

The purposes of adventure education show both the similarities to and the differences from more traditional physical-education goals (Siedentop, Mand, & Taggart, 1986, p. 215):

1. To learn outdoor sports skills and enjoy the satisfaction of competence

2. To live within the limits of personal ability related to an activity and the environment

3. To find pleasure in accepting the challenge and risk of stressful physical activity

4. To learn mutual dependency of self and the natural world

5. To share this experience and learning with classmates and authority figures

Teaching within this model is obviously different from meeting classes at an appointed hour in a gymnasium. More time is needed. Instruction often takes place in small groups. Risk is involved, so safety becomes a paramount concern. Because travel and longer, more intimate time with students are often features of such programs, teachers must have skills for interacting with and guiding students in such situations. Also, particularly with wilderness sports, the teacher must have some substantial experience and skills in the activity being taught.

The Eclectic Curriculum

Although some schools have decided to adopt, in its entirety, one of the curriculum models we have described, it is far more common for schools to design an *eclectic* curriculum in which several models are featured. This mixture can be offered as units within a *required* program of physical education or as *elective* courses. Some high schools have chosen to designate parts of their curriculum as required and other parts as elective. A common model for schools is to require a fitness course for all students and then to allow students to choose electives to complete the physical-education requirements. The electives might include more fitness courses, adventure courses, sport courses, or social-development courses.

The physical-education curriculum in the elementary school and in the middle school is more often a standard program required of all students. Even here, however, it is increasingly common to find teachers or school districts arranging a yearly program that includes attention to fitness, sport development, social development, movement education, and adventure. Most often, these programs look very much like the multiactivity program described earlier; only the activities themselves sometimes differ. Some schools promote the fact that they offer a large number of activities within an eclectic model. However, offering a large variety of activities does not, in and of itself, ensure a good program. Quantity should not be confused with quality.

What Is the Subject Matter of Physical Education?

This chapter began with the assertion that it is more difficult to define *physical education* than to define either *sport* or *fitness*. The review of curricular options shows how valid that assertion is in contemporary physical education. Within these various curricula, one might see small children moving creatively to a poem, ninth-graders rappelling down the outside wall of their gymnasium, fifth-graders working hard as members of a soccer team engaged in a championship match, tenth-graders working out personal-fitness programs as part of a self-control exercise, eighth-graders estimating body composition through skinfold measurements as an exercise in an academic-discipline laboratory, and third-graders using different implements to hit different kinds of objects as part of a movement-education lesson on striking.

A stranger, viewing all such scenes and asking what is going on, might be told, "This is physical education!" If this stranger is middle-aged and has experienced a traditional form of physical education, it is easy to understand why she might ask, "What's going on?" It is also easy to see why the answer—"This is physical education!"—might be surprising: The activities look so different from the traditional stereotype of fizz ed.

Each curriculum model has a different view of the subject matter of physical education. What *is* physical education? Is it education in sport? Is it fitness education? Is it social development? Is it development through risk and adventure? Is it movement? Instead, is it all these things—and maybe more?

The problem with a broad conceptual definition of the subject matter—one encompassing all the models described—is that it becomes so loose almost nothing can be excluded. A subject matter so loosely defined that it excludes very little is inevitably going to include activities that are hardly useful or defensible by any criteria. The question then becomes, If physical education encompasses everything, can it ever stand for something specific and important? Before answering that question, I turn to two contemporary aspects of physical education: educating students with disabilities and responding to current issues such as state requirements, liability, and Title IX.

PHYSICAL EDUCATION FOR STUDENTS WITH DISABILITIES

There was a time, not too long ago, when the typical physical educator in the typical school never had a student with a disability. Most often, students with serious disabilities were not placed in regular schools. The field most commonly referred to as *adapted physical education* actually began during and shortly after World War II, when thousands of service personnel needed both rehabilitation from injuries and special activity programming in which they could enjoy leisure. The field grew slowly until the early 1970s, when it was spurred to further growth by an extraordinary series of federal laws (DePauw, 1996).

- 1968 PL 90-170, Elimination of Architectural Barriers Act
- 1973 PL 93-112, the Rehabilitation Act, prohibiting discrimination on the basis of disability
- 1975 PL 94-142, Education of All Handicapped Children Act, which requires a free and appropriate education for all children and youths with disabilities, including specifically physical education
- 1978 PL 95-606, Amateur Sports Act, which recognizes athletes with disabilities as part of the U.S. Olympic movement
- 1990 PL 101-476, Individuals with Disabilities Education Act (IDEA), extending provisions to young children and incorporating provisions of previous laws
- 1990 Americans with Disabilities Act, which extended the broad protection of the Civil Rights Act of 1964 to people with disabilities

The key legislation that catapulted adapted physical education into a new era was **PL 94-142,** simply because it singled out physical education and intramurals as important school activities and said that they must be available to students with special

The law requires that *all* children with disabilities receive an appropriate physical education.

needs. Another key provision of 94-142 was the notion of placing students in the *least restrictive environment* (LRE) to meet their needs and making every effort to see they eventually became *mainstreamed* into regular classrooms if those classrooms met the provisions as the LRE.

The field of adapted physical education encompasses three main types of programs: adapted, corrective, and developmental (Jansma & French, 1994). An *adapted program* focuses on the modification of regular activities to enable individuals with disabilities to participate safely and successfully. A *corrective program* focuses on the rehabilitation of functional postural and body-mechanics deficiencies. A *developmental program* focuses on basic fitness and motor-skill training to raise students' skills and abilities to the point where they can participate with peers.

In the 1990s, the concept of **inclusion** became a central theme and rallying point among many who support the rights of students with disabilities. Inclusion means that all students are educated in one educational system and that all students with disabilities should be in regular classrooms. Inclusion now stands as an alternative philosophy to the LRE approach, but it needs to be pointed out that LRE is the law. Although there are many arguments pro and con about inclusion, proponents tend to rest their case on the ethical issue that any segregation of students with disabilities is inherently unequal (Paul & Cartledge, 1996).

Nonetheless, we now have a field called "adapted physical education" with strong programs in schools and agencies. We also have several generations of professional physical educators trained specifically in adapted physical education. They have their own association within AAHPERD, their own journal, and specific graduate programs at the M.A. and Ph.D. levels, to train future adapted-physical-education specialists.

State Requirements for Physical Education

There is no federal law that requires physical education to be taught in schools. States vary widely in the degree to which they mandate physical education as part of the state education system (*NASPE News,* Fall 2001). States typically set *minimum standards* for physical education, but individual school districts interpret those standards somewhat differently and, of course, can exceed them if they so desire and have the resources to do so. Some states delegate authority for what is taught in schools to the local school districts.

The objectives for physical education in the federal policy described in *Healthy People 2010* (U.S. Public Health Service, 2000) include the following:

- Increase the proportion of the nation's public and private schools that require daily physical education

- Increase the proportion of adolescents who participate in daily school physical education

- Increase the proportion of adolescents who spend at least 50 percent of school physical-education class being physically active

State laws and guidelines supporting physical education at the elementary level are typically weak; for example, many specify a minimum number of minutes per week in physical education but do not specify what counts as "physical education." In many places, recess is counted toward meeting the minimum standard. This is especially true for districts that do not employ physical-education specialist teachers but, rather, leave the responsibility to already overburdened classroom teachers. Fewer than half the children in the United States get physical education from a specialist teacher (Siedentop & Locke, 1997), even though federal reports on elementary education have strongly supported the improvement of physical education (Bennett, 1986).

At middle-school and high-school levels, standards are often a bit stronger, typically specified in "units." (Carnegie units are the standard way of designating course requirements in high school—for example, one unit of American history, one unit of physical education.) Sadly, there are many ways that local districts "get around" the requirements. In some districts and states, students can get credit for the physical-education requirement by participating in interscholastic sports, marching band, or ROTC (*NASPE News,* 1998). Approximately 25 percent of high schools have physical-education requirements that extend beyond 1 year. This is particularly disturbing because in the crucial years of adolescence, when health and activity habits are being formed, students have limited access to physical-education programs.

It is fair to say that over the past several decades, states have tended to water down their requirements for physical education, despite the vocal opposition of physical-education and health professionals. Some state associations have been successful in defeating the passage of legislation to reduce

2001 Shape of the Nation Report Highlights

- Forty eight states mandate physical education, but many require only that PE be provided and leave content and format to individual school districts.

- Illinois is the only state that requires daily physical education, but a recent "waiver" law allows exemptions and there are no time or content guidelines for the mandates.

- Alabama requires daily PE for all K–8 students.

- State requirements for elementary PE range from 30 to 150 minutes per week. (NASPE recommends 150 minutes per week.)

- At middle school level, mandates range from 80 to 225 minutes per week. (NASPE recommends 225 minutes per week.)

- Most high school requirements are for one year and are most typically fulfilled at the ninth-grade level.

- One "unit" is required in eighteen states, two units are required in six states, and four units are required in two states.

- Sixty percent of the states require a grade for PE and include it in the grade point average. Three states do not include PE in the grade point average, and eight states leave the decision to local districts.

- Forty-two percent of the states do not allow any substitutions for PE, and 58 percent of the states do allow substitutions (marching band, ROTC, etc.).

- Forty-four states either have developed or are in process of developing state standards for PE content.

SOURCE: Data from *2001 Shape of the Nation Report,* National Association for Sport and Physical Education, Reston, VA: National Association for Sport and Physical Education, 2002.

requirements, with the result that "holding the line" is seen as a victory. In 2002, in response to the national concern about obesity among children and youth, the state of Texas, which had eliminated mandatory elementary physical education a decade earlier, reinstated the 135-minute-per-week requirement—a real victory (News, 2002). In summary, there is little evidence that the nation is on target to achieve the national goals by 2010.

NASPE commissioned a national survey of physical-education requirements that has been reported in a *Shape of the Nation Survey* (2002). This significant report also includes related information from the *School Health Policies and Program Study* (2000) and the *Youth Risk Behavior Surveillance* (1999). The most significant results of that survey are shown in the "2001 Shape of the Nation Report" box.

Physical education grew tremendously in the United States during that time when professional groups and associations persuaded state legislators to pass laws in support of required physical education (see Chapter 2). The current era can be characterized as a fight to maintain those gains. Any honest appraisal of the past several decades, however, leads to the conclusion that the fight is gradually being lost.

Recent federal efforts to promote high-quality daily physical education might mark the beginning of a new era. Some federal reports on education, such as *First Lessons: A Report on Elementary Education in America* (Bennett, 1986), have strongly supported the improvement of physical education. The suggested improvements, however, would require stronger state legislation to be implemented. Hence, the amount of physical education experienced by K–12 students in American schools is not significant. Moreover, instructional practices within physical education often minimize the amount of activity involvement among students.

Liability

We live in an era when citizens have become increasingly assertive about prosecuting in courts of law to maintain their rights. In no area has this trend had greater visibility than in liability. Doctors spend enormous amounts of money on malpractice insurance because of the number of suits brought against them—suits in which patients try to hold them *liable* for alleged inappropriate or negligent practice of medical skills.

This era of **liability** has recently reached education and, more specifically, has affected physical education. In the 1970s, it would have been fairly common to find a trampoline being used in a school gymnasium. Today, it is almost impossible to find one in schools. Why? There are simply too many safety issues that might lead to liability litigation for the teacher and school to risk using the trampoline or to risk even having one in the facility.

This contemporary concern with liability has a strong, positive side. Doctors, lawyers, businesspeople and teachers all tend to be more conscious of safety in what they do. They plan activities more carefully and check equipment more often. They supervise activities more closely and more often make sure that students, clients, or patients are ready for whatever they might be asked to do. Those are all benefits of this focus on liability.

There is a negative side also. Activities sometimes are not used because of perceived liability issues. Rappelling and rock climbing, when done properly, are safe activities. Yet they are often not done because of the fear of liability. Teachers are discouraged from being innovative with equipment because they are more likely to be held liable for an injury sustained on homemade equipment than for one acquired with manufactured equipment. It is clear that liability has affected what is done, and

how it is done, in physical education. It will be interesting to continue to monitor the influence of legal liability in the years ahead.

Title IX

Perhaps the most profound influence on physical education since the 1970s was the adoption of Title IX of the Education Amendments of 1972. The major provision of Title IX was that no person would be denied access to participation based on sex in any educational program receiving federal financial assistance. Nearly every school in America receives some form of federal assistance, so all physical education and sport programs came under the aegis of Title IX.

In physical education, the most important specific influences of Title IX were (1) coeducational classes, (2) assignment of teachers according to skill rather than gender, (3) grouping based on ability rather than on gender, and (4) equal access for boys and girls to the entire physical-education curriculum. Physical education does not have a particularly admirable history with respect to discrimination based on gender. Girls have been systematically denied access to learning and participating in most sports. Women teachers have not been able to teach those activities for which they are best prepared. Facilities and equipment have not been shared equally. Thus, overcoming those traditional forms of discrimination has not been easy for many professionals who had become accustomed to them. These issues are considered more fully in Chapter 13.

In 1992 Title IX was 20 years old. Clearly, some important gains have been made, particularly in the areas of more school and intercollegiate sport opportunities for girls and women, more equity in interschool and intercollegiate budgets, and the like. In other areas, the results have been disappointing, particularly in the relatively low number of female coaches, the inability to secure fair representation in athletic-administration positions, and continued underrepresentation in officiating, training, and media positions (Fox, 1992).

In physical education, the effects of Title IX are very unclear. There has been an alarming reduction in the percentage of female teachers in high school physical education (Hulstrand, 1990). In our own research (Siedentop & O'Sullivan, 1992), we found female secondary physical educators to be marginalized by male colleagues in their own departments—and we found girls to get fewer opportunities in physical education and to like it less than do boys. The coeducational provisions of Title IX are routinely ignored in some schools. On the other hand, there are physical-education programs where girls and boys learn and participate together, where all activities are available regardless of gender, and where teaching assignments are made on the basis of competence and interest, rather than gender.

Title IX has both legal and moral implications. The legal implications are fairly clear and, if enforced, will make important differences. The moral implications are, in the long run, more profound. It is one thing to do something—for example, to make traditional single-sex classes such as swimming open to boys and girls—because there is a legal mandate to do so. It is another thing to do it because it is viewed as the *right* thing to do. The activity undertaken reluctantly, with a great deal of lingering prejudice, is counterproductive to the intent of the legislation. The same activity, done positively, promotes individual and social development. We have come a long way toward meeting the letter of the law but perhaps have not yet met the spirit of Title IX.

DOES PHYSICAL EDUCATION HAVE A CENTRAL MEANING?

What does *physical education* mean? How should this field's content be defined? Is it human movement? Is it play? Is it fitness? Is it sport? Is it social development? Is it risk and adventure? Is it general human development? Instead, is it all of these things together? What follows are scenes we might see in physical education today:

- Young children move to the sounds of a drum, each carrying a scarf. They change directions and change the level of their bodies as they move. The teacher, holding the drum, encourages them, from time to time, or gives them new directions in the form of a problem question, but does not tell them what to do.

- A coed group of ninth-graders works in a well-equipped Nautilus training room. They work in pairs, each carrying a chart on a clipboard. The teacher moves about, interacting with each pair, but provides no group cues or directions. Students move from machine to machine periodically.

- A group of 55 seventh-graders is receiving instruction from a teacher. The students are scattered in groups of 4 or 5 around a large gymnasium. Each group has a ball. The teacher gives instructions to the group, then signals for the group to begin practice. During practice, the teacher moves about, mostly watching to see that things are going smoothly. After several minutes, the teacher signals for attention, gives some feedback on what she has seen, then gives new instructions for a slightly different task.

- Fifth-graders enter the gym and move into one of six areas to begin a group practice on soccer warm-up drills. At a signal, the groups form into teams. One member of each group leaves to pick up materials while two other members put on referee shirts. Shortly, three small-sided soccer games begin, with students acting as referees and coaches. On the gym wall, there is a soccer-season schedule and the standings for this soccer league. After 5 minutes, the game ends; within 3 minutes, a new game has begun, involving similar teams but made up of different children.

- Twenty-four helmet-wearing seventh-graders have harnesses around their waists. They stand beneath a clearing in a woods and look up to see a ropes course 40 feet above their heads, with different configurations of wood and rope at different places on the course. Their teacher is giving them instructions on belaying techniques, safety, and appropriate procedures for moving through the ropes course.

- A teacher sits with a group of ninth- and tenth-graders at the start of a lesson, describing what will be done that day. The teacher solicits comments on the students' feelings about their progress, talking about individual growth and responsibility. There is talk about levels, and students learn that today is a fitness day, when they will work on their individually developed programs.

- A group of eleventh-graders have toured community health and fitness facilities as part of their assignment in physical education. They also have monitored their own activity and nutritional intake for 6 weeks. Based on their own data and what is available in the community, they each plan a comprehensive health-fitness plan for themselves, which they can easily do within their own community. They include their plans in a portfolio they are building for evaluating their eleventh-grade physical-education experience.

All those scenes are part of physical education by today's standards. You should recognize in them the various models described in this chapter. Although they all are legitimate physical-education models, it is unclear that any central theme or concept underlies the different approaches. They appear, as a group of educational models, to fit most clearly under the developmental model that has historically been the most widely adopted model for physical education. In this model, the *activities* themselves are not as important as *what they are used to accomplish,* which is why this model has always been referred to as *education through the physical.*

The focus of this chapter has been physical education *in schools.* As the following chapter shows, however, physical education can and does occur in settings other than schools, and it does so increasingly in current times. Are the concepts and curricular models presented in this chapter actually implemented in physical-education programs? Where are these programs conducted? Who leads them? These issues are explored in the next chapter.

SUMMARY

1. No single definition of *physical education* has gained widespread acceptance in contemporary professional circles.

2. Education through the physical was the dominant curricular philosophy for the first half of the twentieth century.

3. The fourfold objectives of physical development—physical development, motor development, mental development, and social development—have dominated thinking in physical education for most of this century.

4. The multiactivity curriculum and the associated unit model for organizing activities became the standard for planning in physical education.

5. Since the late 1960s, movement education has become the strongest alternative interpretation of physical education, espousing a different way of defining content and a different teaching process.

6. Health-related physical education has developed as a response to public health concerns.

7. The academic-integration approach focuses on the emerging knowledge base in the subdisciplines of physical education. It has gained strength recently because of the emphasis on academic excellence in schools.

8. The social-development model grew out of the humanistic-education movement and has

emerged as a distinctive curricular option with a focused purpose.

9. The sport-education model is an inclusive approach to sport; it emphasizes appropriate competition and learning about multiple roles within sport.

10. Adventure education uses risk and challenge to develop personal and social skills through a variety of natural and contrived activities.

11. Most physical-education programs are conceptualized as an eclectic model that combines the approaches described in this chapter.

12. State requirements for physical education differ markedly and heavily influence physical-education programs in schools.

13. Concerns over liability have changed what activities are included in a curriculum, how those activities are taught, and what equipment is used.

14. Title IX has opened access for girls and women to sport and physical education.

15. Adapted physical education has developed into a specialized area, which now focuses on inclusion.

16. It is still not clear what the central focus of physical education is.

DISCUSSION QUESTIONS

1. To what extent was your school program rooted in the education-through-the-physical philosophy? What were its main features?

2. Is the multiactivity approach useful? Can any real objectives be accomplished with short-term units? Is the variety engendered by this approach appropriate?

3. Which of the newer curriculum models most appeals to you? Which least appeals to you?

4. What are the requirements for physical education in your state? Did your school's program exceed them?

5. What was PE like in your high school? Were the classes coed? Did boys and girls like or dislike it equally?

6. What kind of PE experience would adolescents have to have in order to influence their lifestyle choices about physical activity and health?

7. What do you believe should be the central focus of physical education at elementary-school, middle-school, and high-school levels? Can you develop a definition of physical education that accurately reflects that perspective?

CHAPTER **12**

Physical-Education Programs and Professions

Whereas a high quality daily physical education for all children in kindergarten through grade 12 is an essential part of a comprehensive education: Now, therefore, be it resolved by the House of Representatives (the Senate concurring), that the Congress encourages State and local governments and local education agencies to provide high quality daily physical education programs for all children in kindergarten through grade 12.

House Concurrent Resolution 97, One Hundredth Congress

LEARNING OBJECTIVES

- To discuss the narrow and broad views of physical education
- To discuss the effects of and prospects for high-quality, daily physical education
- To describe exemplary programs for a variety of curricular models
- To discuss the roles played by a physical educator

- To describe various certification models
- To describe the NASPE national standards for beginning teachers
- To describe how certification for adapted physical education is achieved

Physical education is best known as a subject offered in schools. Most people who prepare to become physical-education teachers complete a curriculum that culminates with not only a degree but also a teaching certificate. Does physical education take place *only* in schools? Here again, as we indicated at the beginning of Chapter 11, a problem of definition arises. If physical education is limited, *by definition,* to activities that occur in schools, then how do we describe programs that look similar to physical education in schools but are conducted in other places? All the curriculum models described in Chapter 11 could easily be implemented in places other than schools.

Adventure education is often done in summer camps and by private agencies such as Outward Bound. Fitness programs are conducted in health centers, spas, and family centers such as the YMCA and the YWCA. Children and youths learn and participate in sport (i.e., they become *educated* in sport) in community programs. Movement skills can be learned in preschools, gymnastic academies, and dance studios. Sport and fitness programs with strong social-development goals can be found in church camps, Police Athletic League programs, and family centers such as a Jewish Community Center. Are these all physical education?

How you answer that question will reflect how narrow or broad is your concept of physical education and of how it affects the lives of children and youths. Most professionals tend to take the broader rather than the narrower perspective. Certainly, if you are serious about the notion of a *lifespan* physical education—as advocated in Chapter 1—then the broader perspective is necessary.

Obviously, school physical education is important. School is still the one institution in our culture that touches the lives of virtually all children and youths. It is the institution to which we have delegated a primary responsibility for passing on the best of our culture and for trying constantly to improve the culture. You do not have to be rich to go to school, nor do you have to have special talents to take part in the school curriculum. If the goal of

physical education for all—another position advocated in Chapter 1—is ever realized, then the school will have played the most important role in achieving it.

In 1987 a resolution was introduced in the U.S. Senate to encourage state and local governments to provide a high-quality, daily physical-education program for children and youths from kindergarten through the twelfth grade (see Table 12.1). Can you imagine the impact of such an ideal? Every day, from kindergarten through twelfth grade, students would get a high-quality lesson in physical education. If the average school year has 150 days of instruction and the average length of a lesson is 30 minutes, each child would receive more than 75 hours of instruction in physical education per year. After 13 years, each student would have had nearly 1,000 hours of high-quality physical-education instruction.

What wondrous things might be accomplished if that could be achieved! Is it too much to expect or even to hope for? Not if you consider how much time is spent on sport for the more talented students. During a typical season, a high school basketball player attends team practices 2 or 3 hours per day, 5 days a week for nearly 5 months. That amounts to approximately 275 hours of practice per season, not counting games. If the player is active for 4 years in high school, he or she will accumulate nearly 1,100 hours of practice. Thus, in 4 years, a varsity-level basketball player will spend more time in practice (with a much lower teacher–student ratio, better equipment, and better facilities) than will a student in physical education throughout his or her educational career *even under optimal circumstances*!

It is difficult to imagine achieving the ideal of daily, high-quality physical education in schools when the curriculum is already so crowded and demands for higher performance in reading, mathematics, and computer literacy dominate education-reform discussions. It may be that the only way to find the time necessary for daily, high-quality physical education is to explore nonattached school time (recess, before school, intramurals, etc.) or, even

TABLE 12.1   Resolution Supporting Daily Physical Education: House Congressional Resolution 97–in the House of Representatives Concurrent Resolution

To encourage State and local governments and local educational agencies to provide high quality daily physical education programs for all children in kindergarten through grade 12.

Whereas physical education is essential to the development of growing children;

Whereas physical education helps improve the overall health of children by improving their cardiovascular endurance, muscular strength and power, and flexibility, and by enhancing weight regulation, bone development, posture, skillful moving, active lifestyle habits, and constructive use of leisure time;

Whereas physical education increases children's mental alertness, academic performance, readiness to learn, and enthusiasm for learning;

Whereas physical education helps improve the self-esteem, interpersonal relationships, responsible behavior, and independence of children;

Whereas children who participate in high quality daily physical education programs tend to be more healthy and physically fit;

Whereas physically fit adults have significantly reduced risk factor for heart attacks and strokes;

Whereas the Surgeon General, in Objectives for the Nation, recommends increasing the number of school-mandated physical education programs that focus on health-related physical fitness;

Whereas the Secretary of Education in First Lessons—A Report on Elementary Education in America, recognized that elementary schools have a special mandate to provide elementary school children with the knowledge, habits, and attitudes that will equip the children for a fit and healthy life; and

Whereas a high quality daily physical education program for all children in kindergarten through grade 12 is an essential part of a comprehensive education: Now, therefore, be it

Resolved by the House of Representatives (the Senate concurring), That the Congress encourages State and local governments and local educational agencies to provide high quality daily physical education programs for all children in kindergarten through grade 12.

more important, to investigate physical-education programming in the after-school and evening hours, or even on weekends. That would mean extending our concept of physical education to community programs rather than thinking about it only as a school-based program. That should be kept in mind as we review programs and professional preparation in this chapter.

EXEMPLARY PHYSICAL-EDUCATION PROGRAMS

As the next chapter shows clearly, there are substantial problems in contemporary physical education. In this chapter, however, we focus on programs that accomplish their goals. The programs described are real, and each typically represents

one or several of the physical-education models described in Chapter 11.

A Comprehensive Health-Related Elementary-School Model

Health-related physical education has developed in the wake of evidence strongly supportive of the health benefits of a physically active lifestyle in a time when health costs to the nation have become a major political issue. Virgilio (1996) has described a comprehensive healthy-lifestyles elementary program that grew from his work in developing the national Heart-Smart fitness program (Virgilio & Berenson, 1988). A comprehensive model recognizes that children are unlikely to get sufficient physical activity in the time allotted to physical education in the elementary-school curriculum. The emphasis in this model is placed "on learning motor skills and participating in sport to stay physically active and develop lifelong movement skills" (Virgilio, 1996, p. 4). This physical-education program emphasizes learning lifelong skills and participating in high amounts of regular physical activity, utilizing many of the materials and programs from the Heart-Smart program. According to this model, children develop their own personalized fitness portfolio, which they carry with them through their elementary years.

In addition, the model stresses a strong parent-education component, using newsletters, parent seminars, progress reports, parent–teacher conferences, PTA demonstrations, and a parent resource room. The progress reports include summaries of the child's fitness progress, physical-activity levels, and recommended areas for improvement. The parent resource room contains videos, computer software, cookbooks, cassettes, and educational games that parents can check out and use at home with their children. The model also involves parents in extending and improving participation in physical activity at school in nonattached time. Parents serve as aides in classes, monitor playground activity, help to build or repair equipment, and participate in a committee that serves as an advocacy group for the goals of the program.

A home-based activity program is also a component of the model. Families are encouraged to commit to a family contract to exercise together, using a specific, family-developed schedule. Parents assist children in their fitness homework—for example, developing a fitness trail through their neighborhood and using it regularly. Parents are also encouraged to develop summer activity packets, which include activity plans, reading lists, games, and opportunities in the community. The nutrition component of the program is also extended to the home through the parent newsletter and through family activities designed to improve the nutritional content of family meals.

Classroom teachers include health, nutrition, and cardiovascular fitness in the classroom curric-

Classes that are well organized and managed result in more activity.

ula. They are also asked to ensure that the children in their classes get at least 30 minutes per week of physical activity, excluding physical education and recess time. The school cafeteria is also a component of the program. The parent committee meets with the school-lunch staff to ensure that school meals have reduced sodium, fat, and sugar levels. Cafeterias are decorated to promote healthy choices in food selection. If there is a school snack service, the service is encouraged to stock relatively healthy snack foods.

The physical-education teacher, in conjunction with the parent committee, seeks to develop links with community agencies that offer physical-activity programs for children. Efforts are made to get children into after-school activity programs, and if none exist in the community, to develop such a program at the school site. Special projects such as youth sport fairs and community health fairs are developed. The entire effort is designed to affect lifestyle choices, and the total environment of the child—school, home, and community—is enlisted in that effort.

Preschool Programs

We are just beginning to witness the development of a new physical-education industry for preschool children. This industry, at present, exists exclusively in the private sector. Programs provide child care, as well as exercise, motor-development, and social-development activities for young children. At present, they cater to those parents who have sufficient disposable income to afford them. They have names like "Gymboree," "Playorena," and "Babycise" (Kantrowitz & Joseph, 1986). There is a great deal of controversy about such programs because so little is known about the effects of early physical-activity programs on very young children.

A High School Lifetime Physical-Activity Program

Lake Park High School has adopted a lifetime physical-activity focus for its high school program. Their philosophy states: "In order to live longer and to be as functional and independent as possible in the future, our students need to be able to assess their own health and make a plan to maintain and/or improve it" (www.lphs.dupage.k12.us/acd dept/pe/philosophy.htm). Students are continually involved with self-assessment and problem-solving situations. They learn how to set goals, monitor progress, and make changes to achieve their goals. They learn not only about health and fitness but also about how to manage and change their own behaviors in activity, diet, safety, and stress management.

The Lake Park program offers introductory courses in physical education and health education in the ninth and tenth grades and then offers a series of courses including dance, cross-training, personal wellness, team activities, leadership fitness training, strength and conditioning, and strength training in the eleventh and twelfth grades.

This program is highly consistent with the current emphasis in physical education on preparing students to take active control of their health and physical activity as they move into adulthood.

An Upper-Elementary Sport-Education Program

The upper-grades curriculum at Olde Sawmill Elementary School is based on the sport-education model described in Chapter 11 (Darnell, 1994). In

grades 4–6, the curriculum is sport oriented. Students are placed on teams at the start of the school year and remain with their teams throughout the year as they work for points toward an all-sport award. Students select a name for the team and team colors. Captains and assistants are assigned and selected for each new sport season. A schedule of competition is arranged for each season.

Each day that the students have physical education, they do everything as members of their team. When they enter the gym, they have an assigned space where team members do their warm-ups together, led by their team captain. A period of skill practice follows, with captains again leading their teams through the assigned drills. As the season progresses, less time is allocated for team skill practice and more time is allocated for games.

In each sport season, students are players, coaches, referees, or scorekeepers. Simple records are kept for each game performance. Short-duration, small-sided games are used for team sport competition. Teams can earn points toward an overall championship in a number of ways, including winning games, practicing as a team at recess, behaving as good sportpersons, passing the knowledge tests, and exhibiting leadership.

In the soccer season, each class typically has three or four teams. Captains lead teams during the class and administer schedules and assignments between class sessions. The soccer season begins with a 2 v 2 (two players versus two players) round-robin competition in which games last 4 minutes. Captains must assign players from their team for each of the 2 v 2 games. Students not playing at any given time are involved as either referees or scorekeepers. Captains must have all these assignments completed and written out before the class begins.

After the 2 v 2 round-robin competition is completed, a 4 v 4 (four players versus four players) round-robin competition begins. Here the game is more complex, requiring more teamwork and careful execution of skills. Again, captains make all assignments, and all students are involved in some capacity during each game. At the end of the soccer season, an overall soccer champion is named for each class, based on points accumulated during game and practice time, as well as by good sportspersonship. At the end of the season, intramural time is used for interclass games at the same grade level.

The gymnastic season is done differently but still teaches gymnastics primarily as a competitive sport. The first part of the season focuses on compulsory competition, in which each team member must learn and perform a group of gymnastic skills. Students warm up and practice each day as a team, with captains not only leading during class but also handling administrative duties between classes. As part of learning the skills, students are also taught how to judge the performance of those skills. The compulsory competition is a routine involving the activities being practiced. Students choose routines at three levels of difficulty. They then make up their own routine, following the guidelines for their level of difficulty.

Compulsory competition takes place over a number of class sessions, with students acting as judges. Students earn points, based on performance within their own level of difficulty. The team championship is determined by total points won in competition and for practicing.

An optional competition follows the compulsory part of the season. Now students choose one event in which to practice and compete. Each day there is opportunity to practice and to take part in at least one optional competition. Again, coaches have administered the assignment of students to events and have determined when each will compete. All individual performances count toward a team total. Students act as judges for the optional performances also. At the end of the gymnastic season, interclass competitions are arranged during intramural time. At the end of the season, an overall champion is determined, individual awards are presented for each event, and awards for sportspersonship and coaching are also presented.

By the end of a school year, all students will have learned to be a coach, a referee, a judge, a scorekeeper, and a record keeper. They no doubt will have been on some teams that lost, some that won, and some that finished toward the middle. They will

have learned and experienced what makes any sport a sport and how the sport can be enjoyed from various perspectives.

A High School Personal-Growth Curriculum

Students at Gregory Heights and Jefferson High Schools (Hellison, 1983) take part in a personal-growth curriculum based on Hellison's (1978) social-development model for physical education. Progress through the curriculum is based on levels, which are often defined similarly to those shown in Figure 12.1.

Each week is divided into three parts: 2 days of skill development and play, 2 days of fitness activities, and 1 day of activities designed to facilitate sharing and cooperation. Issues of self-control, cooperation, and responsibility are constantly kept to the forefront of the class, through either activities or group discussion. Every incentive is provided for students to take greater responsibility for themselves, in their own behavior within class and in their physical-education curriculum.

Strategies such as personal contracting are often used in the fitness portion so that students can set goals, monitor progress, and experience the relationship between consequences and effort. Cooperative games and risk activities are often used for the day devoted to sharing and cooperation. Students are asked to keep a daily journal, which is used to communicate with the teacher also.

As students begin to achieve Level 3, responsibility, they take over more and more direction for their own physical-education experience, planning fitness programs, choosing activities, and charting future directions. Teaching strategies used by teachers in this model are highly interactional. Teachers provide the opportunity for students to negotiate programs, attendance, and grades, thus providing necessary practice in negotiation skills. Teachers do a large amount of personal counseling and occasionally use direct confrontational procedures when these seem appropriate.

Although fitness and skill outcomes may be achieved in this model, they clearly are not what is

Name _____   Adviser _____

Social Development Levels Checklist

Definitions of Ratings	Period	Student Rating/Date	Teacher Rating/Date	Comments
0 Little self-control Not involved Uses putdowns Irresponsible Disruptive	1			
	2			
1 Under control, not involved Not participating Not prepared Nonproductive	3			
	4			
2 Under control, involved **when teacher-directed** Frequently off task Needs prompting Needs frequent reminders	5			
	6			
3 Self-responsibility Works independently Self-motivated Positive attitude	7			
	8			
4 Self-responsibility and caring Cares about others Involved with others Sensitive to needs of others	Adv.			

Figure 12.1   Checklist for social development

SOURCE: Jeff Walsh, Gregory Heights School, Portland, Oregon.

most important in it. Success for this model is achieved when students learn and display responsibility, begin to cooperate, are more willing to share, and, eventually, demonstrate to their classmates that they care and are willing to help.

An Elementary Adventure Program

A portion of the physical-education curriculum at the Worthington Hills Elementary School focuses on adventure activities (Moore, 1986). Students learn sports and engage in fitness activities, just as many other children in elementary physical-education programs do, but what makes this program special is the manner in which risk, adventure, and cooperation are woven into the curriculum throughout the school year.

The regular activity program includes elements of adventure and cooperation throughout the year. For example, team sports are always introduced initially through cooperative games—for example, in volleyball, two teams work together to try to keep the ball in play. Skill instruction and practice for activities such as archery and orienteering are also done as part of the regular school curriculum.

For several weeks during the school year, special adventure activities become the focus of the curriculum. Climbing and rappelling are two skills learned by all students. The gymnasium contains three indoor climbing walls: a horizontal climbing course that traverses 60 feet along one wall and two vertical climbing courses of differing levels of difficulty. There are also several rappelling stations throughout the gymnasium. Each course has been attractively decorated, with the help of the art teacher, to look like a mountainous challenge. Climbing and rappelling are technical skills that have a strong element of perceived risk and challenge. (The tasks, in fact, are very low in actual risk when done properly.) Students are encouraged to extend themselves, improve their skills, and take new risks. Students reaching the top of one vertical course—where a snowy peak has been painted—can sign their names. At the top of another course, they can honk a horn while touching the golden egg depicted at the top of the beanstalk course.

Students get more opportunity to practice those and other adventure skills in the intramurals program. A final component of the adventure curriculum is a series of field trips. Sixth-graders go on a 3-day camping trip, in which the adventure curriculum learned indoors is extended to natural settings. In addition, there are several 1-day trips to a nearby adventure center, where students participate in a high-ropes course, group-initiatives courses, field archery, and orienteering, thus extending to a wooded, natural setting the skills learned originally at the school.

The goals and objectives of the adventure program described here have much in common with those of the social-development program described earlier. Both are concerned primarily with personal growth, cooperation, sharing, and responsibility. They differ primarily in the means through which those goals are achieved.

A High School Fitness Emphasis

At Needham High School, students are required to complete 16 quarters of physical education across their 4-year program (Westcott, 1992). The program's emphasis is on physical fitness from a personal perspective involving individual goals and lifestyle outcomes. The core of the program is a 6-quarter series of wellness courses, ranging from fundamentals of fitness to nutrition to stress management. These courses involve extensive classroom work, as well as activity involvement.

Needham students are also required to choose three fitness courses from a range of activity options, including aerobics, cross-training, fitness games, stretching, and weight training. The third set of requirements is in the lifetime sport category, again with an option to choose from a variety of offerings, including archery, badminton, golf, jazz dance, tennis, and volleyball. The final 4 quarters of required physical education may be chosen from any of the three main areas: wellness, fitness, and lifetime sports.

All 1,000+ students at Needham High School get an individual fitness evaluation each year, focusing on the health-fitness factors of cardiovascular endurance, muscular endurance, muscular strength, flexibility, and body composition. Students receive a cumulative computer printout of their evaluation, with specific information related to strengths and weaknesses.

The physical-education staff at Needham has worked diligently over a period of years to write grants to obtain the necessary activity equipment, testing equipment, and educational materials to run this exemplary program. Students leave the program knowing a great deal about fitness and their own strengths and weaknesses related to fitness. They also have had an excellent opportunity to develop lifestyle skills and commitments that will lead to a long-term commitment to personal health fitness.

A Research-Based National Elementary Program

Project SPARK (Sports, Play, and Active Recreation for Kids) originated as a five-year national research study funded by the National Institutes of Health. Following the research phase, the program focused on dissemination through a nonprofit organization housed at San Diego State University (www.foundation.sdsu.edu/projects/spark/index). SPARK offers elementary-school physical-education curricula, staff development, and follow-up support to school districts, elementary physical-education specialist teachers, and classroom teachers nationwide. SPARK was validated by the National Diffusion Network of the U.S. Department of Education as an "Exemplary Program."

The program has several major goals. The first is to prepare children to be physically active through an emphasis on skills and play, along with learning how to manage their own behavior. SPARK also organizes lessons so that students are physically active a large percentage of class time. SPARK also works with the school food service and classroom teachers to provide support for students to be active and make healthy choices in nutrition.

SPARK offers specific support for physical education in grades K–2 and grades 3–6, along with two levels of self-management (grades 4/5 and 5/6). They also provide support for after-school programs and nonattached time in the school day through their Active Recreation program.

Project SPARK is unique among physical-education programs in that it is based on extensive research that shows improvement in physical activity, fitness, academic achievement, motor-skill development, student enjoyment, improvement in body composition, and teacher acceptance of the program.

An Early-Elementary Movement Program

A class of first-graders at Maryland Avenue School is spread out across the gymnasium space. Each student has a small racquet and a foam ball. The teacher periodically asks the students to try a new way to strike the ball with the racquet, most often in the form of a question: "Can you keep the ball up in front of you by hitting it softly?" A student occasionally loses control of his or her ball but retrieves it without interfering with the activity of classmates. It gradually becomes clear that the progression of activities is leading toward the development of striking skills that will be useful later in sports such as tennis, badminton, softball, hockey, and lacrosse. With each series of questions asked by the teacher, the children are carefully guided toward forehand, backhand, overhand, and underhand striking pat-

Basic skills are important early learning experiences.

terns. The children do not know—or care, for that matter—that eventually this will all lead somewhere. They are obviously enjoying the activity for what it is at the moment. There is no competition among the children. The learning is success oriented. The children often have to make decisions about what they will do in response to the prompts and questions from the teacher.

Movement education uses movement skills, rather than traditional sport skills, as organizing centers for activity. The children in this program will have units in striking, throwing/tossing, catching, and dodging. Later, in upper-elementary grades, they will use these skills in the more conventional games that dominate the curriculum.

Movement-education curricula are most often divided into the areas of educational games, educational gymnastics, and educational dance. The themes from which curricular units are developed are movement themes rather than sport themes. In the educational-gymnastics portion of the curriculum, children will have lessons that focus on balance, transferring weight, hanging and swinging, bearing weight on different body parts, and locomotion—both on the feet and on different body parts. Small apparatuses—such as boxes, benches, balance beams, bars, ropes, rings, and inclined planks—will be used as aids in exploring movement possibilities.

This approach to physical education stresses the cognitive involvement of children, the development of positive self-concepts, and the establishment of a broad repertoire of movement skills (Siedentop, Herkowitz, & Rink, 1984).

A Comprehensive High School Program

The Louisiana School for Math, Science, and the Arts (Dugas, 1994) offers a comprehensive program of fitness, leisure, and sport activities. All students participate in a fitness course similar to others described in this chapter. The remainder of the program is elective. Each semester, students can choose from fitness activities such as weight training and aerobic dance; leisure activities such as canoeing, swimming, and sailing; and sport activities such as volleyball, fencing, golf, and soccer.

The sport component within the curriculum is done in the sport-education model. Each semester is divided into two seasons. Students can elect an individual sport or a team sport each new season. Students become members of a team immediately and take part in the season, much as an athlete would on an interschool team. In addition, as a requirement in each sport course, students keep records, manage schedules, and arrange for publicity. The physical-education department publishes a weekly sport newsletter listing the competitions for the week, the leading performers for the past week, and the standings in the various individual and team competitions.

This curriculum has something for every student in the school. Students must acquire sound knowledge of fitness but then are allowed to pursue their own interests in leisure, fitness, or sport activities.

The "New PE" at Middle School

Madison Junior High School is recognized nationally as a leader in developing a new approach to physical education that emphasizes preparing students for lifetime health and physical activity. Featured nationally on CNN and in *USA Today,* the program has influenced the direction of physical education in many parts of the nation. The Madison program (www.ncusd203.org/madison) was built on a limited set of clear goals (lifetime activity, understanding and being able to monitor and direct your own efforts), an innovative change in physical-education facilities, and a dramatic increase in the use of technology to support program goals.

Students at Madison have physical education 5 days a week. One day is spent in the "health club" working on cardiovascular and strength machines. (The health club looks much more like a community health/fitness center than it does a sport training facility, which is a real clue as to what the goals are all about.) A second day is spent doing the weekly cardio run/walk. The other 3 days are spent in activities such as rollerblading, using the climbing wall, or participating in individual or team sports.

Technology is ever present. Students wear heart-rate monitors when working in the health club or doing their weekly cardio walk/run. In the autumn and again in the spring, they test and record their progress at a series of computer-aided fitness test stations. These stations measure flexibility, blood pressure, body composition, upper body strength, and cardiovascular performance.

In 2001 the school district entered into a partnership with P.E.4LIFE, a national nonprofit organization dedicated to promoting quality physical-education programs nationally to create the P.E.4LIFE Institute so that teachers, administrators, and community representatives can attend programs where they can learn how to develop and sustain "New PE" approaches (www.PE4life.org).

A High School Program Emphasizing Community Linkages

Seattle's twenty-five high schools have embarked on a curriculum-development initiative to add interesting, challenging activities to their curricula and to do so by partnering with community, professional, and private-sector sport organizations (Turner, 1995). Each of the high schools was challenged to add a new alternative activity to its traditional list

P.E.4LIFE
Madison Junior High School

Student Body Pledge

I pledge to do my best and participate in daily physical education.

I will use these skills to improve my physical and emotional health.

I will encourage others to enjoy and get involved with physical education.

I will ask my parents to get involved with my fitness and support me in these efforts.

I will also try hard to reach my potential and have fun.

I know physical activity can help stregthen my mind and body.

I will promote daily physical activity to my friends and family.

SOURCE: Madison Junior High School, www.ncusd203.org/madison.

of offerings. Most of those alternative activities required partnering with a local agency or a national organization. For example, they have taken advantage of the U.S. Tennis Association's program of equipment, assemblies, and instruction, as well as the "First Swing" golf program sponsored by the Professional Golfers Association. Locally, the Seattle Fire Department paramedics have taught CPR classes, and the Seattle Parks and Recreation Department, in cooperation with U.S. Rowing, has provided free rowing instruction. An added benefit of these efforts is the knowledge students gain about where activities are done in the community, along with the skills to take part in them. The partnering allows for use of equipment and expertise that no single school could possibly afford.

A Districtwide Wellness Initiative

The Escambia County schools have a districtwide wellness initiative that links school efforts to those in the community and among families (Samman, 1998). The program incorporates wellness throughout the K–12 curriculum and in the school environment. Programs were developed for faculty and staff as well as students. Partnerships with the community were formed to make it easier for students to get into activity programs. Parents were educated and encouraged to develop family wellness programs. Each school has a wellness team, composed of administrators, school nurses, cafeteria managers, building janitors, classroom teachers, physical-education teachers, parents, and community representatives.

School and community facilities and programs were improved—walking paths, exercise classes after work, an annual wellness fair, and special events. Each student develops an individual wellness plan that focuses on nutrition and physical activity. Parents meet with their children and the school wellness team to design summer family wellness programs. Local hospitals and health agencies participate in school programs and extend their services to students and their families. This kind of comprehensive effort is exactly what the CDC guidelines suggest is needed to truly influence the lifestyle habits of children and youths.

A State Wellness Curriculum for High Schools

Kansas has created the *Physical Dimensions* curriculum for high schools. The development of this physical activity and wellness curriculum was funded through the Kansas Health Foundation and aims to help adolescents build healthy lifestyles. The curriculum includes three dimensions: health-related fitness, lifetime physical activity, and health/wellness concepts (see the box on the following page). Students receive three weeks of instruction in each of the three dimensions every nine weeks. Students who successfully complete the curriculum receive a certificate of achievement (the High School Ph.D.).

What Makes These Programs Work?

The physical-education programs described in this section are not necessarily unique. There are many good programs in many places. Those described here represent different approaches to physical education, approaches that reflect the various models described in Chapter 11. What properties do they share? Are there features or characteristics common to all of these programs?

My own experience with reviewing these programs and many others (Siedentop, 1987) is that they do have several common characteristics. First, in each program, a physical educator or a group of physical educators exerted substantial leadership to get the program started and to maintain it until it was sufficiently established.

Second, although each of these programs is obviously different, each stands for something *specific*. In each program, there is a main theme or focus—fitness, sport education, adventure, movement, personal growth, and so on. Good comprehensive programs tend to be either of two types. Either they have a main theme, which runs through the program, as does the Needham High School program, or they join two or three main themes, as does the program at the Louisiana School for Math, Science, and the Arts.

Third, the programs not only look exciting but also, by all reports, tend to *be* exciting for the students who participate in them. Clearly, the teachers who have created and maintained them are excited about what they did. This excitement reflects a sense of purpose and a set of expectations that are no doubt communicated in many ways to students, fellow teachers, administrators, and parents.

Fourth, very few of the teachers who were responsible for these programs had major commitments in coaching interscholastic teams. The problem of role conflict that is suggested by this fact is reviewed in Chapter 13.

TECHNOLOGY IN PHYSICAL EDUCATION

Technology has made strong contributions to improving physical education in schools. Although too many schools cannot afford the kinds of technology described in this section, it is important to note how it is being used to improve the learning experience for students. Examples of technology in physical education are everywhere:

- Heart monitors enable students to track exercise patterns. The data can be downloaded into computers, where they can be displayed graphically and used by students and teachers (Hinson, 1994). See the "New PE" middle school model on page 272.

- Students and teachers use the Internet to take part in newsgroups that address needs and interests related to physical activity and teaching (LaMaster, 1996).

- Teachers have access to a number of Websites that can help them with lesson planning, assessment, promoting their program, and other issues. See PE Central Website on page 277 (Figure 12.2).

- An online technology newsletter for K–12 physical education keeps students and teachers up to date with the latest developments in the use of technology in physical education. See www.pesoftware.com/news.

- The Kinesiology Department at California State University at Northridge offers an online master's specialization program in *Technology and Physical Education*.

- Students and staff at Fargo, North Dakota public schools get a complete fitness evaluation two times a year using the TriFIT 600

The Kansas Physical Dimensions HS Curriculum

Dimensions

One	Two	Three
Health-Related Fitness	Lifetime Physical Activity	Health/Wellness Concepts and Skills

Outcomes

• Knowledge and skills to enhance cardiorespiratory endurance, muscular strength and endurance, flexibility, and body composition	• Skills development • Fitness reinforcement • Participation in a variety of physical activities with lifelong significance	• Analysis of health issues impacting youth and adults • Assessment of own health behaviors • Personal and social skills development to enhance health

Achieved through

• Aerobics • Walking/Jogging • Strength and Conditioning • Orienteering	• Rhythms • Tennis • Golf • Badminton • Swimming • Volleyball	• Nutritional and weight management • Stress management • Personal safety and conflict resolution • Preventing pregnancy, STDs, and HIV

Lifetime Wellness

This course is designed to provide young adults with the knowledge and skills needed to engage in a physically-active, healthy lifestyle throughout life. Three areas of focus in the course include:

1. Health-Related Fitness
2. Lifetime Physical Activity
3. Health/Wellness Concepts and Skills. The curriculum consists of four, three-week segments for each area. Students receive three weeks of instruction in each of three areas every nine weeks.

Course Outcomes

As a result of participation in this course, students will be able to:

1. Interpret personal health/fitness status in order to design, implement and evaluate a personal health/fitness plan to develop and maintain a physically active, healthy lifestyle.
2. Analyze current health issues impacting youth and adults.
3. Demonstrate effective use of personal and social skills to enhance health/fitness behavior.
4. Develop the motor competency to utilize a variety of physical activities to engage in a healthy lifestyle.
5. Display consideration and respect for differences among various individuals.

Being on a team is often a positive developmental experience for adolescents.

System, a portable fitness evaluation system (www.fargo.k12.nd.us/schools/Agassiz/PE/ Mauch/TriFit).

- Pedometers are widely used to count steps per day in fitness evaluation. Students wear the pedometers throughout the day and compare their activity with national standards.
- Teacher educators and staff-development leaders use videotapes to help prospective and practicing teachers improve their practice by analyzing tapes (Everhart & Turner, 1995).

A number of software programs are available for use in physical education and by physical-education teachers. Teachers have access to software programs that can be used for such teaching purposes as grading, banner and sign making, awards, and yearly calendars (Wilkinson, Hillier, & Harrison, 1998). Teachers can also use software programs to plan and analyze student learning activities, such as workout programs, cardiovascular evaluation, health-risk appraisal, and diet analysis.

Tutorials for fitness, interactive software for sport instruction, educational games, simulations for fitness and sport, and laboratory exercises for health and fitness are available directly for student use. Through these software programs, students can play a virtual racquetball game, learn how the heart works, or learn rules of and strategies for a variety of sports.

Telecommunications can also be utilized to enhance instruction and expand the student experience in physical education. Physical-education listservs can be created for each class or for a school physical-education program. This allows for e-mail messages to be sent and received. Bulletin boards are electronic message systems by which individuals can post and read messages. Chat rooms can be created so that students may discuss issues related to their class work. Web pages can be created for physical-education programs to allow communication to students, parents, and the community. Links from Web pages can allow direct access to resources needed by students and their parents.

Technology can also be used to extend physical education in interesting ways. During the recent winter and summer Olympics, many PE classes in the United States linked up with classes in the host countries to discuss issues involving the games. A junior high school in Nebraska used e-mail to organize a track meet involving seventeen schools around the world; the schools conducted similar meets and compared times, distances, and heights for each event. Overall results and standings were distributed to each school (Mills, 1997).

Using the Web has become second nature to most students and teachers. Key Websites are listed throughout this text. A primary example of the success of Websites in physical education is *Physical Education Central,* developed under the leadership of George Graham and Mark Manross at Virginia Tech (see Figure 12.2). This comprehensive Website includes pages for students, teachers, parents, administrators, and other professionals. The most popular sections of this Website are lesson ideas, assessment ideas, top Websites, the job center, and adapted physical education. It also includes links to other important sites, which is typical of how the Web works. In a recent 6-month period, PE Central averaged 60,918 unique visitors, many of whom no doubt visited the site frequently. In that same time period, more than 2.3 million pages of the site were

E-cards   **Jobs**   **Contact Us**   **Newsletter**   **PEC Store**

PE CENTRAL

The Premier Web Site for Health & Physical Educators

Search

LOG IT Record your Activity Steps & Miles

Walk Across the USA

Register Now!

WIN PRIZES! Kids Quiz!

Welcome to the premier Web site for health and physical education teachers, parents, and students. Our goal is to provide the latest information about developmentally appropriate physical education programs for children and youth. We encourage you to submit your own lesson ideas which are reviewed by our editorial team. Information about who we are and our awards and honors are available. Last update: 3-29-03.

Founding Sponsor

FLAGHOUSE.

Submit Your Ideas Now!
Free Equipment for Publishing on PE Central

Equipment Specials!   *Adapted Specials!*

ORDER A FLAGHOUSE CATALOG

SHOP PE Central!

New!

Dance Lesson Idea Books

PEC Partners

● **Lesson Ideas**
PreK-12 Health/PE, Integrated
Search All Lessons, Submit a Lesson...

● **Assessment Ideas**
Paper & Pencil, Alternative (rubrics)...

● **Adapted Physical Education**
FAQ's, IEP Info, Activity adaptations...

● **Preschool Physical Education**
Lesson ideas, Articles, Equipment, FAQ's...

● **Creating a Positive Learning Climate**
Classroom management info, Lesson ideas, FAQ's...

● **Professional Information**
Defending PE, Research, PEP Bill...

● **Instructional Resources**
Fitness testing, Interactive learning sites...

● **PE Central Store**
PEC Books & Curriculums, Videos, Apparel...
FREE Shipping & Handling

Books: Dance Lesson Ideas | Field Day Ideas

● **PEC Store**
PEC Books & Curriculums, Videos, Apparel...
FREE Shipping & Handling

● **Books & Music**
PE Books/Music from **Amazon.com**...

● **Health & PE Products**
Products for PE programs, Advertising Rates...

● **Best Practices Program**
Special events, Fitness nights, What's New...

● **Top Web Sites**
PE People/Programs, Dance, Fitness, Sports...

● **Log It**
Log your steps/miles, Walk across USA...

● **The Pedometry Site**
Pedometer info, lesson ideas, Lot It...

Figure 12.2 PE Central's Website: home page.

Initial page of the PE Central Web site sponsored by Virginia Tech Health and Physical Education Program (image used by permission of the authors).

accessed. A list of key physical-education Websites can be found on page 300.

THE PHYSICAL-EDUCATION TEACHER

Physical education in schools is taught by trained professionals who hold certificates indicating that they have passed the requirements to be licensed as teachers in their states. Many certified physical-education teachers also gain employment teaching in YMCAs/YWCAs, health spas, community or recreation centers, and private sport clubs. You do not *have* to be certified to teach physical education in those settings, but a teacher certificate is often an advantage in competing for those jobs.

Schools are required to hire people who are certified in the subject matter they will teach. Although school districts in some states have some limited discretion to hire noncertified personnel on a short-term basis, in the long run, the only way to teach in schools is to be a certified teacher. How you acquire certification is described in the next section.

What Do Physical-Education Teachers Do?

The most obvious duty of physical-education teachers is to teach, but that is not all they do! Professional teachers occupy a number of important roles that require skilled performance to fulfill their professional obligations (Siedentop, 1991; Siedentop, Herkowitz, & Rink, 1984; Siedentop & Tannehill, 2000):

- Teachers *plan* lessons, units, and whole curricula. They also plan for equipment replacement and facility utilization, as well as for field trips and special events.

- Teachers *manage* not only groups of students but also the use of parent volunteers, teaching aides, student helpers, equipment inventories, and the like.

- Teachers *collaborate* with other teachers, school administrators, parents, activity profes-

sionals in the community, and university faculty members.

- Teachers continue their *professional development* through journals, conferences, staff-development programs, and professional contacts at other schools and in the community.

- Teachers *counsel* students, not only in regard to the goals of physical education, but also in regard to family issues and personal matters.

- Teachers *represent* their schools, the physical-education profession, and the teaching profession in general. They are expected to be knowledgeable and to behave in ways consistent with a professional role.

Together, these roles constitute professional life. If teachers aspire to achieve more respect for their professional status, then they have to be willing to accept the extra obligations that professionals typically carry. That means not only doing the primary job of instruction as well as possible but also attending to and performing well in these other important roles.

A Day in the Life of Two Teachers

Jay is an elementary-physical-education specialist. He leaves his house at 7:20 each morning for the half-hour drive to the neighboring suburb where he teaches. When he arrives, he posts a list of things for his gym helpers to do when they come in; then he heads for his three-times-per-week 8:00 A.M. conference to work on individual education plans (IEPs) for students with disabilities. Following the meeting, he grabs a quick cup of coffee in the teachers' lounge before heading to the gym to make sure the equipment has been set up properly. He does a last-moment check of his lesson plans for the day and chats with the gym helpers, who are just finishing their tasks.

His first class will arrive at 9:10, and he will have four consecutive 35-minute classes this morning. When one class leaves the gym, the next is waiting at the door with their teacher. At 11:30, he ends his morning classes but moves directly to early lunch duty, where he monitors students in the school cafeteria. At the second lunch period, he eats his own lunch in the teachers' lounge, usually more quickly than he should because the noon hour is when he has managed to squeeze in some intramural time for his students.

After intramural time, he has a planning period of 35 minutes—his only one during the week. Then, he sees three more classes before the gym helpers arrive at 3:30 to put away equipment and to prepare for the next day. Jay does some paperwork related to the day's lessons, checks in the office for any school messages or mail, stops to talk with the first-grade teacher, and then heads home at 4:15 P.M., where he does more school planning before he has dinner.

Joan leaves her home at 7:00 each morning for the short drive to the high school where she teaches and coaches. The school enrollment has grown, so classes now begin at 7:30. She has a planning period during the first period, but she is expected to be in her office when school officially begins at 7:30. She will teach six classes today, supervising the locker room before and after each class. Two of her classes will have a fitness orientation, three will be on soccer, and one is a special elective class she started on weight training for females. She has some lunch-supervision duties but manages to spend a pleasant 45 minutes in the teachers' lounge having lunch herself and chatting with her colleagues. Her last 50-minute class is over at 3:00, and she has half an hour to prepare for her basketball practice.

The season has just started, so, when practice is over at 5:30, she grabs a quick dinner on her way to scout the team that her school will play against the next weekend. She finally returns home at 9:30 P.M., works on her practice plans for the next day, and organizes the scouting information she gathered at the opponents' game. She will need to be up at 6:15 the next morning, to be at school by 7:30, to go through the routine again.

Only those who have taught or have observed a teacher for a full day can appreciate the intensity of these schedules. The coaching added to the full day of teaching extends the intensity longer in the day. When you teach and coach, you are *responsible* for the students in your care. If you try hard to do a good job of teaching and coaching, you are busy interacting with your students/players most of the time you are with them. All in all, the job of physical-education teacher is a demanding one that is often seriously underappreciated.

PREPARING TO BECOME A PHYSICAL-EDUCATION TEACHER

As stated earlier in this chapter, the primary way to become a physical-education teacher is to attend a college or university and to enter a teacher-preparation program. Some states have experimented with *alternative* routes to certification for teaching, but these all involve college graduation and, eventually at least, some specific teacher preparation. The purpose of this section is to describe the different ways in which teachers are prepared.

Because the U.S. Constitution leaves the responsibility for education to the states, the *rules* for teacher certification are made by state legislatures. Teacher education in the United States takes place almost exclusively at colleges and universities. Programs of teacher education in colleges and universities must adhere to *standards* that are devised by state legislatures or state departments of education.

Differences among States

Because states differ markedly in their approach to teacher certification, what a student has to do to become certified as a physical-education teacher differs dramatically from state to state. Here are some of the ways in which states differ:

1. *Level of certification.* The three main kinds of certification in physical education are K–12, which allows you to teach at any grade level; K–6, which specializes training and restricts teaching to the elementary school; and 7–12, which specializes training and restricts teaching to the middle and secondary schools. Relatively few states have K–6 certification, whereas K–12 is the certification most commonly received by graduating physical-education majors.

2. *Number of teaching specialties.* States with many small, rural schools tend to require more than one teaching major, or a teaching major with one or two teaching minors. Thus, the newly graduated teacher is certified in more than one teaching area (e.g., physical education and history; or physical education, general science, and health). This enables principals in small schools to utilize staff more effectively. In states with more consolidation and larger school districts, the trend has been toward certification in only one subject area.

3. *Amount of field experience.* There has been a strong trend in teacher education over the past several decades to increase the amount of contact that teacher candidates have with schools and students. This is typically done through what is called **field** or *school-based* **experience.** These experiences range from observation through full-scale teaching. Some states require extensive amounts of field experience before candidates start their official student teaching. Other states require none. Thus, first-year teachers may differ dramatically in the amount of teaching experience they have received in their preparation programs.

The actual curriculum that teacher candidates receive differs, depending on how the state in which they prepare creates standards reflecting the differences we have described. A student in a state that emphasizes K–12 certification, and that requires two teaching majors but no field experience before student teaching, receives a preparation very different from that of a student in another state who is working toward a K–6 certificate, where only physical education as a teaching area is required and where there is a strong emphasis on field experience. What does your state require or al-

low? How do its requirements differ from those of neighboring states? What do you think would be the best approach to preparing teachers in your state? These are all interesting questions, discussion of which will quickly get you deeply involved in feelings about and points of view relative to teacher education.

National Standards for Beginning Physical-Education Teachers

In 1995 NASPE published the first national standards for beginning physical-education teachers (NASPE, 1995b). A representative task force of physical-education teachers and teacher educators created the standards, disseminated them widely to various professional audiences, and achieved consensus on the final product. Standards for teachers are a major aspect of recent educational reform, which aims to improve both the initial preparation of teachers and their continuing professional development (that is, the National Board for Professional Teaching Standards and the National Council on Educational Standards and Testing).

The NASPE standards for beginning physical-education teachers were designed to reflect the NASPE content standards for K–12 curricula and the NASPE student outcomes (see Tables 11.1 and 11.2 in Chapter 11). Thus, the outcomes that define the physically educated person are closely aligned with the standards for preparing beginning teachers of physical education. The NASPE teacher standards are shown in Table 12.2. For each standard, the NASPE document suggests a series of *dispositions,* which describe the attitudes, beliefs, and assumptions about teaching and learning that underlie the standard as a basis for professional practice. The document also lists specific *knowledge* and *performance descriptors,* which provide concrete guides for what has to be done to demonstrate the standard.

For example, for Standard 2, one of the dispositions is that the teacher "appreciates individual variations in growth and development and is committed

---

TABLE 12.2   NAPSE Beginning Physical-Education Teacher Standards

Standard 1—Content Knowledge

The teacher understands physical-education content, disciplinary concepts, and tools of inquiry related to the development of a physically educated person.

Standard 2—Growth and Development

The teacher understands how individuals learn and develop and can provide opportunities that support their physical, cognitive, social, and emotional development.

Standard 3—Diverse Learners

The teacher understands how individuals differ in their approaches to learning and creates appropriate instruction adapted to diverse learners.

Standard 4—Management and Motivation

The teacher uses an understanding of individual and group motivation and behavior to create a learning environment that encourages positive social interaction, active engagement in learning, and self-motivation.

Standard 5—Communication

The teacher uses knowledge of effective verbal, nonverbal, and media communication techniques to foster inquiry, collaboration, and engagement in physical-activity settings.

Standard 6—Planning and Instruction

The teacher plans and implements a variety of developmentally appropriate instructional strategies to develop physically educated individuals.

Standard 7—Learner Assessment

The teacher understands and uses formal and informal assessment strategies to foster physical, cognitive, social, and emotional development of learners through physical activity.

Standard 8—Reflection

The teacher is a reflective practitioner who evaluates the effects of his or her actions on others and seeks opportunities to grow professionally.

Standard 9—Collaboration

The teacher fosters relationships with colleagues, parents/guardians, and community agencies to support learners' growth and well-being.

SOURCE: NASPE standards for beginning physical education teachers, adapted from National Association for Sport and Education, 1995b. Reprinted from *Moving into the Future: National Physical Education Standards: A Guide to Content and Assessment* with permission from the National Association for Sport and Physical Education (NASPE), 1900 Association Drive, Reston, VA 20191.

---

to helping learners become competent and self-confident" (NASPE, 1995b, p. 9). A knowledge indicator associated with that disposition is for the teacher to have knowledge of "physical, cognitive, and emotional development and their influence on learning and how to address these factors when making instructional decisions" (p. 9). A performance indicator related to the disposition is that the teacher "assesses individual and group performance in order to design safe instruction that meets learner developmental needs in the physical, cognitive, social, and emotional domains" (p. 9).

These standards can be used by state and national accrediting review teams to assess the degree to which any college or university program meets the needs of beginning teachers. Inevitably, in this process, programs of teacher preparation will change, so that content and experiences more closely match the intended knowledge and performance indicators described in the standards.

Certification for Teaching Adapted Physical Education

The Individuals with Disabilities Education Act (IDEA) mandates that children and youths with disabilities receive physical-education services and specially designed services (adapted physical education) from qualified personnel; however, the law does not specify what is meant by "qualified." Some states have interpreted the law to mean that teachers are certified in physical education, whereas others are more lenient and interpret the law to mean that personnel have teaching certificates in any field. Those states that have developed special requirements for adapted-physical-education teachers typically do so as an add-on validation or endorsement to a previously earned teaching certificate.

Fourteen states currently offer a validation/endorsement in adapted physical education. The National Consortium for Physical Education and Recreation for Individuals with Disabilities (NCPERID) has developed national standards through a federally funded project under the leadership of Luke Kelly at the University of Virginia (NCPERID, 1995). A national certification examination has been developed based on those standards, and NCPERID has begun to administer the exam nationally. It is hoped that the national certification exam will serve as a motivation and resource for states that have not yet developed a validation/endorsement program.

The programs described in this chapter show that physical education can be done well and can contribute significantly to the education of all children and youths. Nonetheless, physical education in schools is beset by problems and controversial, unresolved issues. Those problems and issues are explored in the next chapter.

SUMMARY

1. Although a broad view of physical education takes into account all the settings in which people learn, practice, and enjoy sport and fitness activities, the school is still the setting where physical education can best serve the majority of people.

2. High-quality daily physical education for all students is a hope for the future. It is necessary if we are to achieve fully the goals of physical education.

3. High-quality programs can and do exist with a broad range of curricular approaches, including fitness, comprehensive-skill-grouped, sport-education, personal-growth, adventure-education, movement-education, and comprehensive elective programs.

4. Characteristics of exemplary programs are leadership by a qualified physical educator, a specific programmatic theme, a sense of excitement, and a teacher whose main interest is this program (as opposed to coaching).

5. Physical-education teachers earn certificates in the state in which they graduate from an approved teacher-education program.

6. The physical-education teacher plays a number of diverse roles, including planner, manager, colleague, member of a profession, counselor, and representative of the school and school district.

7. Teachers lead intense daily lives in schools, teaching and supervising students. After-school coaching responsibilities can increase the length of the school day.

8. States provide different levels of certification, the most common being K–12, K–6, and 7–12.

9. NASPE's national standards for beginning teachers provide a mechanism for improving the quality of teacher preparation in physical education.

DISCUSSION QUESTIONS

1. What staff and facilities would an elementary school with 400 students require to implement a daily physical-education program? What would a high school with 1,000 students require?

2. Which exemplary program did you like most? Why? Which did you like least? Why?

3. Are there programs in your region that you think are exemplary? Which of the characteristics described in the chapter, if any, do they manifest?

4. Do you know people who are now teacher–coaches? Are their professional lives like those of the teachers described in the chapter? What roles do they occupy?

5. What certification is available in your state? If you are certified in your state, where else does that certification allow you to teach?

6. How does your preparation program compare with the NASPE standards?

CHAPTER **13**

Problems and Issues in Physical Education

In the United States, physical education in schools continues, along with art and music, to be disposable: embraced when budgets are full and public outcries loud, restricted when money is scarce. Currently, finances are strained in most states, but the recognition of the value and importance of physical activity has never been higher. It is an interesting period in school physical education K–12 in the United States.

George Graham, 1990

LEARNING OBJECTIVES

- To analyze issues related to time allotment, specialist teachers, and facilities in elementary physical education

- To analyze issues related to class size, heterogeneity of skill levels, and coed teaching in secondary physical education

- To evaluate issues related to role conflict and role strain

- To discuss the role of physical education as a school subject

- To discuss the problems associated with and prospects for a national curriculum

- To analyze equity and liability issues in teaching

- To describe good and bad competition

- To discuss the role of physical education in lifespan involvement in physical activity

This chapter addresses major problems and issues in physical education. Chapters 11 and 12 presented models for contemporary physical education and examples of those models in action in school programs. Those chapters focused on what physical education *can be,* then provided examples of places where those goals and aspirations are being achieved. With the context of good models and exemplary programs in mind, it is now useful to turn to some of the continuing problems that plague physical education. Certainly, as we discussed in Chapter 12, physical education does occur in places other than school. This chapter, however, focuses on the special problems of school physical education. For issues and problems associated with physical education programs in the community and private sectors, review Chapters 7 and 10.

This chapter first discusses problems in elementary- , middle- , and secondary-school physical education, then considers general problems that cut across the K–12 spectrum.

ISSUES IN ELEMENTARY-SCHOOL PHYSICAL EDUCATION

Most experts who write about the elementary school consider regular physical education to be essential to achieving the goals of elementary education. There is a clear understanding that habits of participation and fitness develop in childhood. Most evidence suggests that if children become obese, unfit, and inactive in childhood, they will remain so throughout their adolescence and adulthood (Dishman, 1989). The major concerns and issues in elementary physical education are time, specialist teachers, facilities, developmentally appropriate practices, and curricula.

Time

Time is clearly the biggest issue for most professionals associated with elementary physical education. Accomplishing the goals of a high-quality physical-education program for children requires time. We know that improvement in skills and an understanding of tactical play in games requires repeated practice under good conditions—and practice takes time! Time for elementary physical education varies widely within states and across states. In some places, children get a physical-education period every day; in other places, they get it once per week. In some places, there is a specialist physical-education teacher; in other places, physical education is taught by the classroom teacher. In many suburban districts that have adequate funding for schools, elementary physical education often involves two 35-minute lessons per week.

Results of surveys purporting to assess how much time children spend in physical education are not always reliable because those responding often (a) count recess as physical education or (b) describe what is *supposed to be* done, by state or district rule, rather than what is *actually* done. This is especially true for districts and states where there are few specialist physical-education teachers in elementary schools.

Education reform in the United States is emphasizing reading, mathematics, science, and computer literacy. Under pressure to find more time for those subjects, teachers, curriculum directors, and principals too often find that time by reducing or eliminating art, music, and physical-education programs. There is compelling evidence (Sallis et al., 1999; Trudeau et al., 1998) that time spent in physical education does not decrease learning in other school subjects. Indeed, there is substantial thought that regular physical activity during the school day actually enhances student performance.

There is growing awareness that the physical-activity needs of children, and their development as physically educated people (as NASPE defines this), cannot be met without devoting more time to physical education. Evidence that the amount of physical activity within physical-education classes falls well below the levels suggested in *Healthy People 2000* makes this concern even more acute. The additional time needed is most likely to be found outside the regular school schedule—that is, nonattached time during the school day, after-school time, and weekend and summer time. Inevitably, if physical education is to find time outside the regular school schedule, it must do so by linking with community physical-activity and sport programs for children. Some examples of how this can be done were presented in Chapter 12.

Elementary Specialist Teachers

The traditional elementary school is organized around the *self-contained classroom,* in which one teacher provides instruction in all the subjects. Over the years, specialist teachers have begun to relieve the classroom teacher of some of the instructional responsibilities in areas such as physical education, art, and music. Most states now certify specialist teachers in those areas.

States that have laws requiring physical-education instruction in the elementary school seldom specify that the instruction has to be done by a specialist teacher. However, the National Children and Youth Fitness Study II found that 83 percent of the children in grades 1–4 who were tested in the study had physical education at least once per week from a specialist teacher. That finding is higher than are most estimates. Regardless of what the actual percentage might be, it is clear that many school districts hire elementary physical-education specialists even though they are not required by law to do so.

The issue here is clear. Most classroom teachers have had only one course in physical-education methods as part of their teacher preparation. They are not well prepared to teach physical education. The demands on their curricular time increase year by year. They cannot possibly do all the things expected of them—and physical education is too often the subject that gets left out. The physical-education specialist has extensive training to do the job and has that job as his or her sole teaching interest. Children clearly benefit more from specialist teaching than from physical-education instruction given by the classroom teacher.

In many school districts, elementary physical-education specialists travel from school to school, often serving three or four schools each week. The specialist teacher teaches one lesson per week, and the classroom teacher follows up with a second and perhaps a third lesson that week. The specialist teacher is often responsible for providing lesson plans for the classroom teacher that build on what was taught during the specialist's one lesson with the children. Being a traveling specialist is a difficult job. Continuity is hard to achieve. The specialist sometimes does not feel that he or she is a member of any single school faculty. It is clear that elementary physical education will take a major step forward when *each* school has at least one specialist physical educator.

School districts that want children to have a daily period of physical education have one to three

---

Preparing Classroom Teachers to Teach Elementary PE

Classroom teachers can do a good job teaching elementary physical education, *but they have to have better preparation to do so!*

Research shows that a 2-year program to help classroom teachers in fourth and fifth grades teach the Project SPARK model (a physical-activity and student self-management focus) was successful.

Teachers were more willing to teach PE 3 days a week and felt more confident when they did so.

One of the teachers had the following comment: "At the beginning of last year, when you said, 'You're going to teach your own PE and you're going to do it three times a week.' I would have said, 'I'd rather chew on some aluminum foil!'"

Source: Faucette, Nugent, Sallis, & McKenzie, 2002.

full-time specialist physical educators in each elementary school. The benefits of such an arrangement are clear. The school district obviously values physical education. Groups of specialist teachers can work together, each teaching in those activities for which he or she is best prepared. That this situation might someday become the norm for elementary schools everywhere is the hope behind the movement for high-quality, daily physical education.

Facilities

Have you seen a well-designed, fully equipped elementary-school gymnasium? What a bright, joyful, interesting place it is! How clearly it contributes to the potential of a program to accomplish programmatic goals! Yet many children do not have the benefit of instruction within such a facility. In temperate climates, nearly 80 percent of elementary physical education is taught outside, on a school playground (Ross et al., 1987). Even in cold climates, many children study physical education in a multipurpose room or an auditorium, not in a gymnasium.

The facilities for physical education obviously affect what can be taught (choice of activities) and how it will be taught (teaching method). This is not to suggest that high-quality physical education cannot occur in an elementary school without a real physical-education facility. Of course it can! The issue here is providing appropriate facilities and equipment so that teachers can help children to achieve the full range of benefits within a subject matter such as physical education.

Developmentally Appropriate Practices

Those who have studied effective elementary-physical-education specialists have come away in awe of the manner in which they provide interesting, innovative, and **developmentally appropriate** experiences for a variety of children—some more skilled than others, some more fit than others,

Are parachute activities appropriate for physical education?

some more interested than others (Rauschenbach, 1992; Siedentop, 1989). In its continuing efforts to promote high-quality physical education for children, the Council on Physical Education for Children (COPEC), an affiliate of NASPE, published its position statement on "Developmentally Appropriate Physical Education Practices for Children" (NASPE, 1992).

COPEC has identified appropriate and inappropriate practices for twenty-six components in an elementary physical-education program. Some components—such as curriculum, cognitive development, and affective development—are broad and are intended to be general guidelines. Other components—such as using fitness activities as punishment, forming teams, and measuring success rates—are quite specific. In each case, COPEC has provided a statement identifying appropriate practice and a companion statement identifying inappropriate practice.

School principals, parents, and policymakers can use the COPEC document as they evaluate and plan for elementary physical education. Teaching professionals also find the document beneficial as they attempt to continue to provide high-quality physical education for children.

Curricula

Another major area of disagreement among physical-education professionals is the question of what constitutes the best model for elementary physical education. The debate here is between advocates of the movement-education model and those who want a more traditional, broadly based physical-education program. This debate is typically conducted *within* the profession, with laypeople not usually aware of the heated differences of opinion that can surround such issues.

Nearly every professional agrees that physical education for young children should not consist of highly specific skill practice and competitive games; that is, it should be a real physical education for *children* rather than a watered-down version of varsity sport. However, should it be fitness, skills, and games made developmentally appropriate to children, or should it be something entirely different, such as the kind of curriculum advocated by movement educators? That is the focus of the debate.

The movement educators see traditional elementary physical-education curricula as too competitive, too oriented toward specific skill development, lacking in creativity, and potentially damaging to the child's developing self-concept. They advocate an approach that is more aesthetically oriented, focusing on a child's individual talents, with a more creative approach to teaching.

The traditionalists (this term is not meant to be pejorative) see movement education as too fluffy—it does not lead to anything, it is difficult to teach, and it has no clear outcomes. They argue that children can learn sport skills, participate in fitness activities, and begin to experience the dynamics of group activities in developmentally appropriate ways, leading up to the time when sport and fitness will be the main focus of the curriculum.

This kind of professional debate is not won in any real sense of settling the issue. Most elementary physical-education specialists are free to develop their own programs, choosing between these alternatives and often using some elements from each to build their own unique approach.

ISSUES IN SECONDARY-SCHOOL PHYSICAL EDUCATION

Concern about the quality and viability of physical education in many high schools has been expressed consistently in the professional literature and at conferences for the past 15 years. One article calls high school PE an "endangered species" that will likely fail if it continues on its present course (Siedentop, 1987). Another talks about the "decline and fall of physical education" (Hoffman, 1987). Although many remain optimistic about elementary physical education, we should all be concerned about why high school physical education appears to be so devalued by students. Possible explanations are explored in this section.

Busy, Happy, and Good

In 1983 Judith Placek investigated how teachers conceptualized successful teaching in secondary physical education. In the article reporting her findings, she coined a phrase that has become famous in the profession: She found that most teachers thought that keeping students "busy, happy, and good" (Placek, 1983) was the main gauge of their own success. If students are well behaved, fairly active in class, and reasonably happy, then teachers feel they have been successful. But what about significant learning? What about students getting excited about performing better or becoming more fit? As Griffey (1987, p. 21) argued, "The sense of mastering something important is denied most students in secondary physical education programs in this country." When students are busy, happy, and good, school administrators are usually quite satisfied. One of the keys to solving this problem is for school administrators to show more interest in a physical-education program focused on important learning outcomes. Instead, too many high school classes can be honestly described as supervised recreation.

Multiactivity Curriculum

Many people who have assessed the problems of secondary physical education agree that the multiactivity curriculum contributes to the general lack of outcomes. Many high school programs comprise a series of short-term units covering a wide variety of activities. (See Chapter 3 for the history of the multiactivity approach.) However, can 3- to 7-day units provide sufficient in-depth learning to produce lasting outcomes? Taylor and Chiogioji give an answer with which most experts would agree:

> The generally accepted goals of physical education are to promote physical fitness, self-esteem, and cognitive and social development. However, the practice—the proliferation of and emphasis on teaching too many activities in too short a time—has made these goals more difficult to attain. The smorgasbord approach of requiring team sports, individual sports, dance, physical fitness activities, all within the space of one school year lessens those students' opportunities to master any one activity through which they can meet the stated goals. (Taylor & Chiogioji, 1987, p. 22)

Providing accurate feedback on students' performance is an important teaching skill.

Improvement, achievement, and mastery are themes that are neither readily apparent in multiactivity programs nor likely in programs that focus on keeping students busy, happy, and good.

There clearly *are* excellent high school physical-education programs. It is interesting to note that some people believe that a dominant characteristic of such programs is that they have a main curricular theme:

> The (good) programs stood for something specific. We learned about good fitness programs, good social development programs, and good adventure programs. Each of the programs had a main focus that defined and identified the program. While many of these programs were multidimensional, each had a main theme that dominated the curriculum. (Siedentop, 1987, p. 25)

Main-theme curricula allow students to focus for longer periods of time on mastering content. Examples of main-theme curricula for developmental physical education, adventure education, sport education, fitness and wellness, and integrated physical education can be found in Siedentop and Tannehill (2000). There is evidence from high school reform models that a more focused curriculum improves student interest and achievement; thus, it may provide one way that high school physical education can rescue itself from its current troubles.

Difficult Teaching Situations

If high school physical education is in trouble, certainly part of the reason is the difficult situation many of its teachers face. The difficulties involve combinations of class size and heterogeneity of skill levels, as well as coed participation (addressed in the next section). In some schools, it is not uncommon to find fifty to seventy students in a physical-education class, although classes in, say, English or algebra are considerably smaller. With that many students, there are always problems of classroom management, equipment, and space. Good teaching can be done in such situations, but it is difficult.

A second factor is the marked heterogeneity of the skill levels of a typical secondary physical-education class. Varsity-level athletes are scheduled in the same class as inexperienced, unskilled students. Whereas algebra teachers or chemistry teachers can expect their students to have a basic level of skill and understanding, physical educators have no such luxury. Physical educators must often accommodate enormously diverse levels of skills and interests in any given class, which makes effective teaching difficult. In programs where students *elect* classes and in programs where classes are based on progressions in skill (e.g., Tennis I, Tennis II), this major problem is reduced substantially. The high school program described in Chapter 12 used a fitness-skill testing procedure to place students in classes that were developmentally appropriate for them. Practices such as those enhance the quality of experience for the student and allow teachers to teach more effectively.

Coed activity presents both opportunities and problems.

Coed Participation

Traditionally, boys and girls have been taught in separate classes in secondary physical education. When I was going to high school, before Title IX, it was generally known that the girls' PE classes were better taught and more interesting than the boys' classes. Title IX made coeducational classes mandatory, except in rare instances. It is true that in many places girls had less access to instruction, time, and equipment in physical education than did boys. It is not entirely clear that in the 31 years since Title IX this particular provision of the law has "worked" as well as many hoped it would.

The assumption of Title IX was that sex-integrated classes would lead to more sex-equitable classes. Some coed classes surely do meet that assumption. Others do not. Some studies have shown that lower-skilled girls are often marginalized in coed physical-education classes (Scraton, 1990; Siedentop & O'Sullivan, 1992). Recently, a study of adolescent girls in physical education found that many of them disliked their PE classes intensely

and tried to find ways to avoid them (Olafson, 2002). Coed teaching is often difficult for teachers because of the wide range of abilities they encounter, especially when invasion games are the focus of the curriculum, reflecting, no doubt, a history of girls having less opportunity to learn to excel in invasion games (basketball, soccer, touch football, etc.).

The issue of coed or sex-segregated physical education has also been addressed in other parts of the world. In England, as a result of extensive study of girls' participation in high school physical education, Scraton (1990) recommended that a girls-centered physical education be developed that emphasized physicality, consciousness raising, and confidence building in physical-activity settings. Scraton believes in the ultimate value of coed physical education but believes also that in most current situations, a girls-centered approach will increase the likelihood that young women will benefit from subsequent coed participation.

Australia developed a national policy for junior sport that speaks specifically to coed participation (Australian Sports Commission, 1994, p. 11)

Physical differences between girls and boys under the age of 12 are generally considered irrelevant to sporting ability. However, socialization may—and often does—prevent girls from developing sporting competencies equal to those of boys. Current evidence suggests that skill development in mixed groups is generally appropriate, but that competition should remain single-sex until it can be shown that girls will not be disadvantaged in mixed-sex contests.

The Australian policy provides a middle ground—that is, coed participation in skill development but separation for competition.

Most physical-education teachers have found that coed classes are fine for sports such as archery, bowling, and skiing. Where most problems develop are in invasion games such as touch football, basketball, and soccer. In many cases, some team and contact sports have been dropped from the curriculum to accommodate coed teaching (Geadelmann, 1981). Remember, this debate is not about the goal, which is a gender-equitable physical education. Rather, it is about the means to achieve that goal.

Treaner and her colleagues (1998) studied perceptions of coed physical education among middle school students. Forty percent of boys and 33 percent of girls preferred same-sex classes, and 27 percent of boys and 30 percent of girls preferred a coed class structure. Both boys and girls reported that they performed skills better, played team sports better, and received more learning opportunities in same-sex classes. Boys tended to like physical education more than girls, and that difference increased from the sixth to the eighth grade. The study was possible because teachers had become frustrated by the challenges of teaching coed classes and wanted to experiment to see what differences occurred.

The difficulties in teaching coeducational physical education can be reduced substantially by planning programs and scheduling students in ways that will help to group students (girls and boys) of like interests and abilities together in physical education. This will make it easier for teachers to plan and conduct lessons and will make it easier for students to profit from those lessons.

It is clear that many women and men become physical-education teachers partially, if not mostly, because they want to coach (Stroot, Collier, O'Sullivan, & England, 1994; Templin, Sparkes, Grant, & Schemmp, 1994). Thus, the potential for role conflict exists from the outset of their careers. Not surprisingly, therefore, there is evidence that some women and men who teach and coach suffer from **role conflict** (Chu, 1981; Locke & Massengale, 1978). Teaching is one role. Coaching is another role. Performing in both roles can produce role conflict and role strain. *Role conflict* exists when there are incompatible expectations for the different roles—for example, high expectations for coaching and lower expectations for teaching. *Role strain* exists when total role demands require more time and energy than a person has to give. The daily schedule, in and of itself, is sufficient to produce role strain over time. Role conflict also builds gradually, especially for head coaches, because the coaching role receives more attention than the teaching role, the expectations are higher, and the immediate rewards are greater. Coaching performance is very public and under the regular scrutiny of parents, administrators, and the community. Teaching is very private in comparison.

When role strain occurs, something eventually has to give. In some cases, the most likely casualty is quality teaching, thus producing the stereotype of the teacher-coach who throws out the balls and sits on the sidelines working on coaching plans. That stereotype, however, is not inevitable! O'Connor and Macdonald (2002) found that some teacher/coaches manage the issues quite well and actually enjoy the dual responsibilities, and they particularly like the differences in the student/teacher relationships in the two settings. There is also some evidence that some high school physical-education teachers seek out responsibilities in school sport because it provides more challenge and satisfaction than they find in their teaching (O'Sullivan, Siedentop, & Tannehill, 1994).

There is no simple solution to this problem. Some people have suggested that coaching become part of the teaching assignment, thus allowing coaches to have a much lighter teaching load during their seasons. Some school administrators prefer to hire coaches who are classroom teachers, as opposed to physical education teachers, thus avoiding this problem, or, perhaps, shifting it to another group of people. Still others have suggested that a second teaching staff should be employed. Those people would begin their work in midafternoon and would continue through the evening hours, staffing recreational and community programs in schools, as well as coaching. If secondary-school physical education is to thrive, this problem must be solved.

Rethinking Secondary Physical Education

Recently, there has been widespread discussion and debate about the possibility of rethinking how secondary physical education is conceptualized and delivered to youths (Locke, 1992; Siedentop, 1992; Vickers, 1992). These discussions have proceeded on the assumption that in many places, high school physical education is sufficiently dysfunctional that it needs to be replaced rather than repaired—completely reinvented rather than improved.

Fortunately, there is evidence that such change can take place—and some interesting models are beginning to emerge. In New Zealand, more than 150 high schools have replaced a traditional multiactivity approach with the sport-education model in a drastically revised tenth-grade program (Grant, 1992). In Florida, a required fitness semester is followed by semester-long courses in a variety of activities (Graham, 1990). In many places, there have been experiments with health/fitness clubs in high schools, using an adult model of participation rather than the more compliance-oriented, regularly scheduled model common to most schools (Cohen, 1991). In other schools, physical educators have adopted a total-fitness perspective, similar to

the Needham High School program described in the previous chapter (Westcott, 1992).

What is most needed at the moment is a better understanding of how such innovative programs get started and how they are sustained. They are exciting. They give us all hope for the future. Unfortunately, they too often have a way of not outliving the creative people who developed them.

Physical Education in Urban High Schools

Urban high schools often present difficult teaching situations. Physical-education facilities are typically old and inadequate, and class sizes are large. Many urban youths grow up in relative poverty and fail to develop healthy behaviors with regard to physical activity and good nutrition.

Urban play environments are inadequate, and those that do exist are typically unsupervised (Knop, Tannehill, & O'Sullivan, 2001). They are also typically dominated by skilled adolescent boys to the disadvantage of all others. Violence and the fear of violence too often pervade the lives of these adolescent boys and girls. For physical education to be successful in such settings, it must create trust through both sensitive curricular choices and appropriate teaching tactics, build and sustain a sense of community so students know they are cared for and feel some responsibility for the group, and find multiple ways for students to be successful (Knop, 1998).

Two successful models for urban high school youth are worth noting. The first is the social-development model created by Don Hellison (1995, 1996), which is described in Chapter 11. This model has been applied successfully in a number of urban high schools using very different curricular approaches but maintaining the focus on the development of personal responsibility. A second model is the "sport for peace" curriculum (Ennis, Satina, & Solomon, 1999). This is a variation of the sport-education model described in Chapter 11, but with a strong focus on conflict resolution and good decision making during the sport season.

Physical education has much to offer in the form of positive youth development and physical fitness, both of which are important to the future of urban youth. Unfortunately, most urban schools are under extreme pressure to raise test scores in math, reading, and science, so most of their energies go to those parts of the curriculum.

The Intramural Program

Intramural activity is typically defined as activity beyond the regular instructional program but confined within the school. The traditional model for portraying the relationships among instructional physical education, intramurals, and interscholastic sport is a pyramid (see Figure 13.1). The base of the pyramid is the instructional physical-education program, which reaches all the students. The second tier in the pyramid is the intramural program, which provides activity opportunities for students who are interested in extending their skills and engaging in more competitive situations. The top of the pyramid reaches fewer students but is intended for those who are especially talented, providing them more practice and competitive opportunities. In the best of all

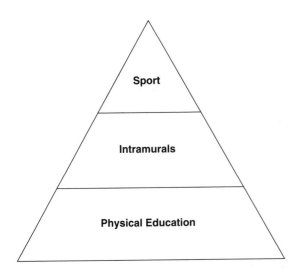

Figure 13.1 Traditional pyramid model for physical-education programs.

worlds, **intramurals** would occupy a place of major importance in the school day. Many students would participate. A wide variety of activities would be available. Students could extend and refine the skills learned in the instructional program. Students could have an important competitive experience without making the daily commitment necessary to be on an interscholastic team. That ideal is seldom achieved. In fact, in many schools, the intramural program is virtually nonexistent, thus eliminating a major component in any complete physical-education program.

Intramurals suffer from a number of problems. Schools often do not have the resources to hire personnel to administer and conduct these programs. Teachers, with full class loads, are often not enthusiastic about the extra burden imposed by such an assignment. Facilities used in the instructional program are often taken over immediately after school by the sport teams. Students find it difficult to go home and then return to school for intramurals.

Where intramurals are an integral part of the total physical-education program, they are often popular among students, with high rates of enthusiastic participation. When they are conducted in poor facilities at inopportune times, with little care and attention from staff, they tend to be poorly attended, often so much so that they are eliminated because of lack of student interest.

The immense popularity of intramurals in colleges and universities and the equally strong success of community recreation programs suggest strongly that boys and girls will take advantage of recreational sport and fitness opportunities that are available in reasonable facilities at reasonable times with reasonably competent staff. Intramurals have much to offer the secondary physical-education program and deserve to be done well.

GENERAL PROBLEMS IN PHYSICAL EDUCATION

Some problems in physical education cut across the K–12 spectrum. Although they may not manifest themselves in exactly the same ways for the elementary specialist as for the high school physical educator, they are nonetheless endemic to the teaching of physical education in schools. These include general issues, such as being accepted as a basic subject, articulating goals and outcomes to the public, and defining the curriculum. They also include more specific teaching issues, such as liability, mainstreaming, sex equity, and the changing nature of urban schools.

Can Physical Education Be a "Basic" Subject?

Many professional leaders believe that the underlying problem in school physical education is the field's lack of acceptance as a fundamentally important subject for children and youths. To be sure, *some* amount of physical education is required in most states, but we are a long way from the ideal of high-quality, daily physical education from kindergarten through twelfth grade.

Is physical education as basic to the education of children and youths as are mathematics and reading? If you, a preservice professional physical educator, do not believe that physical education is basic, then it is not surprising that the public does not believe that it is either. Physical educators need to *believe* that fitness is fundamental to a healthy lifestyle, that meaningful involvement in leisure is fundamental to a well-lived life, and that sport is an important activity throughout life.

Because physical education is so seldom seen as basic to the school curriculum, it often has to fight for its continued existence. State regulations requiring physical education have been reduced. Support for physical education often crumbles at the first sign of financial problems in a local school district.

A major contributing factor to this fundamental problem for physical education is that the Western traditions of education define the most important school subjects as those affecting the mind. The *dualistic* traditions in Western education are deeply ingrained in our culture and still affect what we do today. Mind is too often separated from body, with education of the whole person neglected in favor of subjects that emphasize cognition.

Educational philosophies change slowly. Someday, perhaps, physical education will be central to the education of children and youths, considered to be every bit as important as daily instruction in mathematics, literature, and social studies. If that day is to come, physical education will have to *learn* its way into a more central role in elementary- and secondary-school curricula.

Assessment

Many physical educators have to regularly report grades. In some school districts, there is a grading format that must be followed and gives guidance to the physical educator. In other districts, physical-education teachers devise their own grading schemes and are only required to turn in grades at the end of each grading period. The "busy, happy, and good" approach described earlier in this chapter sometimes results in grading on the basis of attendance, dress, and participation; that is, to earn the top grade, students have to have good attendance, be dressed for class, and participate in activities with no serious behavior problems. Whether they actually know more or get better at an activity does not factor into the grade. Some teachers add "effort" to their grading scheme to differentiate between students who participate minimally and those who participate enthusiastically. In some districts, physical education may still be graded pass/fail, which strengthens the tendency to use attendance, dress, and participation as grading criteria.

At the national level, NASPE has made a substantial effort to define the attributes of a physically educated person and to develop content standards for physical-education programs (see Chapter 11). NASPE has also placed great importance on *assessing* student progress toward meeting content standards. Assessment refers to "tasks and settings where students are given opportunities to demonstrate their knowledge, skill, understanding, and application of content" (Siedentop & Tannehill, 2000, p. 178–179). Assessment is mostly about supporting and encouraging learning and growth, although it is clear that the results of assessments would provide a solid basis for grades also.

Physical-education teachers who utilize assessment do so primarily to motivate students and to help them to learn more. They use skill tests, rating scales, checklists, portfolios, journals, written tests, and observations of game play to develop assessment profiles of their students. Some assessments are *formative;* that is, they are intended to provide feedback on developing skills, knowledge, and tactics. Other assessments are *summative;* that is, they provide a final judgment on outcomes achieved at the end of a unit.

The main issue here is that it is hard to imagine how physical education can be taken seriously as an important school subject if there is no evidence that students have achieved valuable learning goals. If students know that their grades are based on attendance, dress, and participation, they will show up for class, be appropriately dressed, and put forth only as much effort as is necessary to get by. Only those few who are self-motivated in a particular unit will try hard to get better at the activity. Moving to a more assessment-based instructional format will require a major shift in the culture of school physical education.

Outcomes and Credibility with the Public

Teaching more carefully and more intensively to achieve outcomes is the big first step that physical education must take if it is to become better established in the school curriculum. Once that is being more obviously accomplished, then those outcomes must be communicated to parents and educational administrators. Communication *is* important, but effective communication must be preceded by a clearer sense of mission and a clearer achievement of objectives.

> Have we been poor salespeople? Have we failed to provide students with opportunities to master skilled movement? Have we failed to bring the spirit of play into their lives and help them to understand that play is central to all human creativity and thought? Have we failed to help students understand the principles of fitness and to guide them to make healthy lifestyle choices? Have we failed to educate them to be good sportspersons and to understand what sport should be? Have we failed to give them an appreciation of dance and the power of human movement as a communication device? Have we sold them, their parents, school boards, or administrators on the matter of our very important, and unique, contribution to education? We have not been reflective enough about our mission, and that has cost us dearly. (Griffey, 1987, p. 21)

I am convinced that these failures underlie all the problems in school physical education. Class size, poor facilities, lack of support from administrators, role conflict between teaching and coaching, and not enough time to teach the subject matter well have all had their genesis in the frequent undervaluing of physical education as a school subject. To become more highly valued, physical education must achieve more visible outcomes and communicate the achievement of those outcomes to its important constituencies—students, parents, educational administrators, and legislators.

Should School Physical Education Have a National Curriculum?

The previous two chapters have shown clearly that physical-education curricula differ markedly from place to place. There are several appealing models for physical education (see Chapter 11), and there is evidence that these models can translate into effective school programs (see Chapter 12). Yet the issues considered in this chapter reveal that physical education, as a school subject, is in trouble in many ways. One problem is that there is no common understanding of what physical education should be and what students who study it in school should achieve. This has led to suggestions that there should be a *national curriculum* in physical education.

The idea of a national curriculum sparks debate among physical educators (Berg, 1988). Proponents see such a curriculum as providing a badly needed common foundation for skill, knowledge, and fitness. The common foundation would ensure that students would experience the kinds of activities that would lead to goal achievement; yet, it would also be sufficiently flexible to allow for local and regional influences.

The opponents of a national curriculum cite a number of concerns. First, many people fear that a national curriculum would fail to consider local needs and interests. Second, they fear that it would stifle the creativity that leads to new, valuable program ideas. Third, they fear that a national curriculum would comprise only sport and games because that has been the dominant curricular approach in recent times.

Mullan (1986) has suggested that a better solution to current problems would be to develop from four to six curricular models, perhaps similar to those described in Chapter 11. School districts could choose from among these approved curricular models, thus satisfying local interests and needs. The benefit of having districts choose from among curricular models is clear. It would require each district to conduct a serious discussion about which goals in physical education are *most* important, then would allow for the adoption of a curriculum designed to achieve those goals.

Liability

Physical-education teachers who approach teaching tasks carelessly are jeopardizing their careers. Students may be injured in a class left momentarily unattended. Students may be asked to do activities for which they have had insufficient progressive lead-up activities. Equipment designed and manufactured for one purpose may be used for a different purpose. Children may be hurt in floor hockey because rules of participation about "high sticking" were not made clear and firmly enforced. In recent years, each of these situations has resulted in a liability suit.

Not too long ago, it was common to see students in physical education getting instruction on a trampoline. No more! Trampolines sometimes result in injury. Injured students, and their parents, began to sue teachers and school boards. So often did courts hold teachers and school boards *liable* for negligence in the use of the trampoline that this piece of equipment began to disappear from physical education.

Legal liability has become a fact of daily life for physical educators in the past several decades. Physical education often involves activities in which there is some risk to students. Teachers need to be aware of the risks involved and to take proper precautions to safeguard students from those risks. If those precautions are taken, then teachers have acted as *reasonable, prudent* people, minimizing any chance that a court will find them negligent.

In one sense, the entire era of liability and its rash of *malpractice* suits has greatly improved professional practice in a number of areas, teaching included: Teachers pay more attention to the procedures they develop and supervise students more carefully. They plan activities and relate them to the curriculum syllabus more thoughtfully. They think about safety when designing instruction. They are more sensitive to the skills students bring to an activity, and they try to build on those skills. They keep equipment in better repair and use it only for the purposes for which it was manufactured. If a teacher fails to do any of those things, and if it can be shown that an injury resulted from that omission, then the teacher may be considered to have been *negligent* in his or her professional duties.

The main negative effect of the era of liability is that some teachers choose not to do certain activities because of *perceived* liability risks. Typical of those activities is the adventure curriculum described in Chapter 11. Most adventure programs operate safely, with few student injuries—often fewer than are sustained in a regular physical-education program. With proper equipment and instruction, adventure activities can be undertaken without undue concern about liability issues. Yet, because they appear to be riskier than typical activities, some teachers shy away from incorporating them within the curriculum.

Gender Equity

Physical education does not have an admirable history of giving equal opportunity and access to girls and women. As we have discussed many times, the

Education Amendments of 1972 included a section commonly referred to as Title IX, a federal antidiscrimination law that guarantees equal opportunity for girls and women. Nowhere has Title IX been more clearly applicable than in physical education and sport.

Title IX made it illegal to discriminate on the basis of sex in areas such as scheduling, teaching assignments, budgeting, and use of facilities. Coeducational teaching became the norm rather than the exception. Students were required to be grouped by ability rather than by gender. Requiring different activities for girls and boys was not permitted, and rules had to be applied equally to both sexes.

Why was Title IX so badly needed in physical education and sport? The answer is straightforward: Physical education and sport had long histories of inequity as regards girls' and women's participation. The following illustration (based on a real experience) makes the point.

It is midautumn. The next physical-education unit for the fifth- and sixth-graders is about to begin. The unit is flag football. The teacher describes to the students what will happen. Players will be placed on teams. They can choose a team name and make up some of their own plays. Skills of centering, catching, throwing, dodging, and blocking will be practiced. A tournament will be held. The *boys* will be divided into four teams. The *girls* will be organized into cheerleading groups!

The messages of this kind of teaching are clear. Football is clearly a *boys'* sport—fast, rough, competitive. *Girls* can occupy only a supportive, nonparticipant role in such sports. The instruction and practice will be aimed toward the boys. The girls can have *fun* doing their cheers.

Although those kinds of procedures are strictly forbidden under Title IX, they still go on in some places. The discriminatory practices may be more subtle than those in the vignette, but they exist. The fact is that physical education has been a place where gender stereotypes have traditionally been reinforced.

The issues surrounding coed classes in physical education, described earlier in this chapter, are a part of this picture. If girls had better opportunity and support in elementary physical education and in children's sport, perhaps coed teaching in high school would be less an issue than it is today. The fact remains, however, that many high school girls get less opportunity than boys, enjoy physical education less, and are more often bored by it (Knoppers, 1988; Siedentop & O'Sullivan, 1992; Vertinsky, 1992).

Teachers are responsible for developing an equitable learning environment in their classes. Research has shown that in many classes, girls do not have equal opportunities to interact with the teacher and to learn (Davis, 1999). Awareness of equity issues is the first challenge, since teachers are frequently unaware that they are treating girls and boys differently. Teachers are also responsible for seeing that students treat one another respectfully and are committed to a fair learning environment. They must teach students specifically how to apply the concepts of respect and fairness in a physical-education class, and then must support students when they make that application so that such behavior becomes the norm in the class.

The problems secondary physical education has encountered over the past several decades—reduced requirements, disaffected students, and generally bad press—will not be resolved unless and until physical education becomes a place where girls are treated justly, where their opportunities to learn and grow are equal to those of boys, and where their own interests and needs are taken into account in both curriculum and instruction. Physical educators, male and female, have a responsibility to help boys and girls overcome gender stereotypes that exist in society and to provide an equitable physical education for all students.

Skill Equity

Another problem that occurs frequently in physical education is the inability to provide equitable learning experiences for less-skilled children and youths. Evidence suggests that less-skilled students typically get fewer opportunities to respond and have less success than do their more-skilled peers (Siedentop, 1991). When games are played, the

Children can help one another learn if they are taught how to do it appropriately.

less-skilled students sometimes get few real opportunities to take part in meaningful play. It is also clear that peers value competence in physical activity and sport; that is, one way in which children and youths can achieve better status among their peers is to be perceived as physically competent (Evans & Roberts, 1987).

Low-skilled students often don't try. They tend to have negative expectations for themselves because of their lack of success in physical education (Portman, 1995) and because they have received little assistance from the teacher or their classmates. They also are often the object of ridicule from classmates and criticism from teachers. It is no wonder that students like these try to find excuses to avoid participation or to be absent from physical education. The only fair description of what has happened to them is physical *mis*education.

Physical educators have the responsibility to provide equitable learning experiences for all children, regardless of skill level. Indeed, it is obvious that helping a less-skilled student to improve in ways that are recognized by peers not only is important in the physical domain but also produces benefits in the social and emotional domains.

Procedures for modifying activities to make them developmentally appropriate are available in our professional literature (NASPE, 1992; Siedentop, 1991). Physical educators must renew their commitments to helping less-skilled students experience success and improve in ways that contribute to the development of lifespan activity habits.

Good and Bad Competition

A continuing concern within physical education is the proper role and level of competition. Many of the abuses associated with organized sport (see Chapter 7) are assumed to be the result of an overemphasis on competition, of a win-at-all-costs perspective. It is not uncommon for physical educators to advocate reducing competition, to replace competitive activities with cooperative activities, and to modify competitive activities in ways that reduce competitiveness. In its most extreme form, this kind of criticism within the physical-education profession suggests that competitive activities are harmful for children.

The issue can be viewed from another perspective (Siedentop, Mand, & Taggart, 1986). The issue is not whether competition is all good or all bad but, rather, how we can eliminate *bad* competition and emphasize *good* competition. Good competition creates a *festival* atmosphere, with all the attendant traditions, rituals, and celebrations. Good competition creates a *forum* within which children and youths can test themselves against accepted standards of excellence. Good competition involves *rivalry,* but never the kind of rivalry in which one side can win only to the extent that the other side loses. Good competition also means *striving* within the rules and traditions to make the best effort possible—and then, when the competition is over, understanding that the winning or losing has little meaning outside the competition itself.

Bad competition, on the other hand, should be eliminated. Using the rules to gain an advantage, assuming that the only way to win is to have the best score, disregarding the traditions and rituals of the activity, and letting the outcomes affect the participants after the competition is over are all indications of inappropriate competition. Students in physical education should learn the differences between good and bad competition. The only way they can do this is to have these things pointed out to them as they experience good competition.

PHYSICAL EDUCATION IN THE SPORT/FITNESS CULTURE

One of the most intriguing, and disturbing, issues facing physical education is the apparent lack of interest in and support for physical education as a school subject at exactly that point in our history when fitness and sport seem to be more popular than ever. Expenditures for fitness and sport in the private sector have increased steadily since the mid-1960s. The sport and fitness industries are booming, to say the least. Parents spend substantial amounts of money on lessons, clubs, and camps for their children—and a great deal of time and energy supporting community groups that sponsor sport and fitness activities for children and youths. Participation has increased, spending is up, and interest is higher than ever before.

How can school physical education be in decline in this era when fitness and sport are so popular? How can school physical education suffer from lack of support when the support is so willingly provided in the private sector? These serious and disturbing questions deserve to be carefully considered. There are no easy answers, to be sure, but the fact remains that school is the one institution that touches the lives of *all* children and youths. The same cannot be said for the community sport program, and most certainly not for the elite, private sport/fitness club.

Is school physical education an endangered species? Will it survive in this era of popular support for fitness and sport? If it is to survive and even to grow, what do we need to do to change how it is conceptualized and taught? How physical-education professionals answer the third question may indeed determine the answer to the first and second questions.

School physical education should provide the foundation from which community and private-sector physical education grows and prospers. School physical education should provide children with the basic skills, understandings, and attitudes to engage in lifespan sport, fitness, and physical education. There is strong evidence, presented in Parts 2 and 3, that interest in sport and fitness among children and youth is substantial. The three chapters in this part have provided evidence from real programs that sport and fitness in school physical education can also be well done and engage the interest and enthusiasm of children and youths.

Expanding the Responsibility for Healthy Lifestyles

In October 2002, a national "Healthy Schools Summit" was held in Washington, D.C. Designed to bring together the nation's leading education and children's health and nutrition organizations, the purpose of the Summit was to improve kids' health and educational performance through better nutrition and physical activity in schools.

The assumption of this Summit was that the *responsibility* for developing healthy lifestyles in children belongs not only to physical-education teachers but also to the entire school and to families and the community as they connect with the school.

The Summit focused on the obesity epidemic, on making nutrition and physical activity a priority for the whole school community, on marketing better nutrition and physical activity to kids, on how to fund change, on coalition building, and on family and community involvement.

This is exactly the kind of total effort that is needed to achieve real gains in the health and well-being of children.

Source: www.actionforhealthykids.org.

⊃ **GET CONNECTED TO PHYSICAL EDUCATION WEB SITES**

Teaching and Curriculum

PE Central	www.pecentral.org
PE Links 4U	www.pelinks4u.org
P.E.4Life	www.pe4life.org
PE Zone	www.reach.usf.edu/~pezone
Action for Healthy Kids	www.actionforhealthykids.org
SPARK Physical Education	www.foundation.sdsu.edu/projects/spark.index.html
PE Teacher	www.peteacher.info
PE Digest	www.pedigest.com
Hot P.E.	www.hotpe.com
Sports Media	www.sports-media.org

Adapted Physical Education

Physical Activity for All	www.usf.edu/pafa
Adapted PE National Standards Project	www.teach.virginia.edu/go/apens
National Center on Physical Activity & Disability	www.ncpad.org
Motor Opportunities Via Education (Move)	www.move-international.org
National Consortium on PE and Recreation for Individuals with Disabilities	www.ncperid.usf.edu/index.html
American Association of Adapted Sports Programs	www.aaasp.org
Individuals with Disabilities Education Act (IDEA)	www.ed.gov/offices/osers/idea/index.html
Special Olympics	www.specialolympics.org

General Organizations and Associations

AAHPERD	www.aahperd.org
National Association for Sport and PE	www.aahperd.org/naspe
Society of State Directors of HPER	www.thesociety.org
National Board of Professional Teaching Standards	www.nbpts.org
Association for Supervision and Curriculum Development	www.ascd.org
International Council of HPERD	www.ichperd.org
Canadian Association of HPERD	www.capherd.ca/

These goals, however, are not accomplished often enough. If lifespan sport, fitness, and physical education are to become more of a reality in the future, then school physical education must begin to achieve its goals more completely.

SUMMARY

1. In elementary physical education, time allotted is often insufficient to achieve fitness and other instructional goals.

2. Two few schools require that elementary physical-education specialists be hired, and classroom teachers often do not actively teach physical education.

3. Facilities for elementary physical education are often inadequate, which can hamper program development.

4. Within the profession, there is disagreement about the nature of elementary physical education.

5. Too many secondary physical educators are content to keep their students busy, happy, and good, instead of focusing on learning and achievement.

6. The multiactivity program does not allow enough time in any one activity to realize important goals.

7. Large class size, heterogeneity of skill levels within a class, and the demands for coeducational teaching have all made it more difficult to teach secondary physical education.

8. The dual demands of teaching and coaching often produce role strain and role conflict, with the result that teaching is sometimes relegated to a lesser status.

9. Intramurals should occupy a central place in the activity opportunities for high school youths, but time, facilities, and staffing problems often cause them to be minimally important.

10. Many people believe that physical education has not yet been accepted as a subject of basic importance in the school curriculum.

11. Credibility can be earned only when real outcomes are achieved in physical-education programs and are then communicated effectively to the public.

12. There is current debate about the possibility of a national curriculum for physical education, or of a series of national curricular models from which school districts might choose.

13. Liability concerns have prompted teachers to pay more attention to instruction, curriculum, and supervision and have also resulted in some activities being deleted from the curriculum.

14. Physical education has a poor history regarding equity for girls; Title IX has begun to remedy that history of discrimination.

15. Skill equity requires that less-skilled students get equal opportunity and experience success.

16. There are important differences between good competition and bad competition, and these differences should be taught to students in physical education.

17. It is disturbing that physical education seems to be suffering during an era in which sport and fitness have assumed major cultural importance.

18. School physical education should provide the foundation for lifespan involvement in sport, fitness, and physical education, but to do so, it must begin to achieve its goals more completely.

DISCUSSION QUESTIONS

1. Were you taught by an elementary physical-education specialist? What was your elementary-school physical-education program like?

2. What was your high school physical-education program like? Were you kept busy, happy, and good?

3. What would an ideal elementary or secondary program be like? What facilities would be needed? What teacher–student ratio would be adequate?

4. Did your high school have intramurals? If so, what were they like? What role should intramurals play, relative to the instructional and interschool-sport programs?

5. What credibility did the physical-education program have in the schools you attended, among students and among teachers?

6. Should we have a national physical-education curriculum? Why or why not? If we were to have one, what should it include?

7. How were equity issues handled in schools you attended? Did girls have equal access to facilities? Did they receive equal funding?

8. Why do you think that physical education is suffering during a time when fitness and sport are booming? How can that be changed?

PART FIVE

The Scholarly Study of Sport, Fitness, and Physical Education

Chapter 14   Exercise Physiology

Chapter 15   Kinesiology and Biomechanics

Chapter 16   Motor Behavior

Chapter 17   Sport Sociology

Chapter 18   Sport and Exercise Psychology

Chapter 19   Sport Pedagogy

Chapter 20   The Sport Humanities

The recent history of sport, fitness, and physical education has been dominated by a tremendous surge of interest in scholarly study within these fields. The subdiscipline movement of the past three decades has created a group of scientific and scholarly disciplines in which the main focus is on research and on the generation of theory related to sport, fitness, and physical education. Accompanying the development of these areas of inquiry have been new literature, new scholarly journals, and new scientific organizations. The subdiscipline movement has also resulted in new graduate programs and a changed undergraduate curriculum.

It is important that people who aspire to a professional role in sport, fitness, and physical education understand the development and contribution of each of these scholarly fields. It is also quite possible that many readers will see one of these areas as the appropriate goal for their own lifework. These seven chapters provide information that serves both of those purposes.

CHAPTER 14

Exercise Physiology

Physiology of exercise is the oldest academic study area in physical education. The concerns today are longstanding; they still originate from questions about how the body responds to the physical stress of exercise. But, while the basic quest remains the same, the techniques and the technology of investigation are remarkably different—far more sophisticated than early researchers could probably have imagined. In addition, the concerns have now expanded to include areas of human function once reserved only for medicine.

Robert Gensemer, in *Physical Education: Perspectives, Inquiry, Applications,* 1985

LEARNING OBJECTIVES

- To explain how exercise physiology emerged and what its traditional focus has been

- To describe recent changes in that traditional focus

- To explain the influence of George Fitz on the field of exercise physiology

- To discuss the clinical and scientific fields now included under the umbrella field of exercise physiology

- To evaluate the questions researchers in the field attempt to answer

- To describe what an exercise physiologist does

- To describe the preparation for clinical and scientific careers in exercise physiology

- To discuss current problems and issues in the field

Early physical education was preoccupied with health and fitness (see Chapter 2). Many of the great, early leaders in our profession were trained initially as medical doctors. The European systems of gymnastics that were imported into America, and the American systems that were developed to compete with the European systems, focused primarily on the development of fitness through vigorous exercise. It is not surprising, therefore, that many of the early scientific endeavors in our profession focused on exercise and fitness. Indeed, our primary scientific tradition has been the measurement and promotion of physical fitness. This tradition has developed into a formidable science, known most widely as *exercise physiology.*

People today, young and old alike, are more knowledgeable about exercise physiology than about any other of the sport and physical-education sciences. Since the early 1970s, adults have shown an extraordinary explosion of interest in health and fitness. Evidence of this interest is everywhere: joggers, health spas, exercise centers, aerobics, television exercise shows, popular books about exercise and health, and a national concern about the health aspects of fitness. (See Chapters 8, 9, and 10 for a full treatment of these phenomena.)

The important concepts that derive from exercise physiology are now understood by many laypeople. Language that just a generation ago would have been known only to specially trained professionals is now used commonly as a part of everyday discourse—terms such as *aerobic, resting heart rate, training effect, cardiovascular,* and *cholesterol* are all used with some accuracy in everyday language. More than ever, people are interested in *knowing* the results of the latest research about exercise and health.

Public health has become a national social and political issue. Physical inactivity is now strongly established as a major risk factor for all causes of mortality and is related to a number of health problems that together are referred to as degenerative diseases. The publication of the U.S. Surgeon General's report on *Physical Activity and Health* (U.S. Department of Health and Human Services, 1996) has placed exercise physiology research and professions more clearly in the limelight than ever before.

Exercise physiology was at the forefront of research on fitness and performance for all of the twentieth century. Results from this research field dramatically changed some common practices that were based on completely erroneous understandings, bordering on myths. For example, it was not very long ago that athletes were not allowed to drink water on hot days during practice, that girls were not allowed to compete in vigorous sports because of their supposedly weaker constitutions, that swimmers were cautioned not to work with weights, or that endurance work for children was prohibited for fear of developing what was then called the athlete's heart. Today, the athlete's heart is considered positively rather than negatively, women run marathons brilliantly, swimmers regularly lift weights as part of their training, and water is drunk in abundance at all practices and competitions where heat is a problem. Exercise physiology has made a difference!

Exercise physiology is now the largest and most popular subdiscipline of physical education. Much of the research conducted in this area is of great interest to scientists, professionals, and laypeople alike. Some typical questions investigated in exercise physiology are as follows:

- How can exercise prevent or retard the aging process?
- Can exercisers load up their muscles through diet to produce fuels used for short-duration, high-intensity exercise?
- How do muscle cells adapt to increasingly high exercise workloads?
- How do various energy systems contribute to performance?
- What levels of aerobic exercise are optimal for maintenance of cardiovascular health?
- How does heat (or cold) affect muscular performance?

- How does lung volume change as a function of exercise?
- How do different nutrients affect sustained exercise performance?
- At what age should children begin to engage in endurance exercise?

The answers to some of these questions are of interest primarily to exercise scientists, who then must translate their meaning for practical activity and communicate that practical meaning to professionals and to the public. The answers to other questions are of immediate concern to people in the fitness, sport, and physical-education professions. The answers to still other questions are of immediate interest to individuals concerned about their own health and to parents concerned about the development of their children. Thus, exercise physiology speaks to a scientific community, to a professional audience, and to the general public.

Definition of Exercise Physiology as a Field of Study

Physiology is the study of the functioning of plants and animals, and of the activities by which life is maintained and reproduced, including the functioning of and interrelationships among cells, tissues, organs, and systems such as the nervous and circulatory systems. *Exercise physiology* is the "study of acute physiological responses to physical activity and changes in physiological responses to chronic physical activity" (Haymes, 2000, p. 383).

There are two primary goals for exercise physiology (Brooks, 1994) and, therefore, two branches of the subdiscipline. One goal is to use exercise to further our understanding of human physiology. Those who focus on this first goal tend to be basic scientists. Historically, this area has focused primarily on (1) how oxygen is utilized in the cardiovascular system and (2) what metabolic responses to exercise and training are—for example, exercise metabolism (Brooks, 1987). More recently, exercise biochemistry has emerged as a specialization within

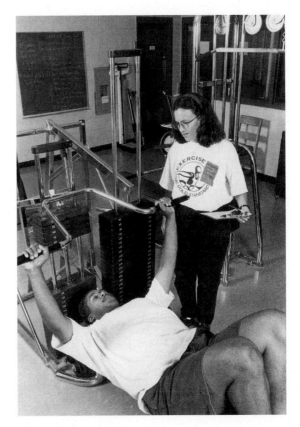

A thorough knowledge of exercise science leads to better exercise prescriptions.

the basic field. This new area of study was made possible by the development of the muscle-biopsy needle in Sweden in 1996 (Haymes, 2000), which allows investigators to study energy sources, muscle mitochondria, and muscle-fiber types.

The other goal is to use physiology to understand human exercise. Those who focus on the second goal tend to be applied scientists. Applied-exercise physiologists use physiology to understand aerobic exercise, strength development, sport performance, physical fitness, and the health benefits of physical activity. The field of **cardiac rehabilitation** is a more recent development from the applied side of exercise physiology. Cardiac rehabilitation involves the assessment of cardiovascular functioning and prescriptive work in preventing cardiovascular trauma or rehabilitating people who have experienced cardiac problems.

Exercise physiology is a disciplinary field of study that provides the main focus for academic programs in exercise science. Exercise science has become a broad umbrella under which several applied fields have developed, such as athletic training, adult fitness, corporate wellness, and strength training. Exercise science is increasingly a favored course of study for students who seek application to graduate programs in physical therapy. Thus, programs in exercise science have attracted the interest of women and men who are seriously interested in a professional career in the fitness and rehabilitation fields. Chapter 9 provided information on several of these fields and how one prepares to enter them.

DEVELOPMENT OF EXERCISE PHYSIOLOGY

In the latter part of the nineteenth century, various European and American gymnastic systems of exercise battled for supremacy in the then-developing field of American physical education. Many claims were made for each system, and, as the battle escalated when curricular adoptions in schools were at stake, the claims tended to become more outlandish. Into this battle stepped a physician who, at the young age of 37, was the president of the department of physical education of the National Education Association (Gerber, 1971). His name was George W. Fitz, and he is rightly described as the *father of exercise physiology.*

Fitz had been speaking out for some time against claims that could not be substantiated by research. In 1892, at the age of 32, Fitz addressed the problem clearly in a speech given at the Association for the Advancement of Physical Education convention.

What right have we to theories? Physiology has not reached the point where they can say deductively that

this should be so and that otherwise. . . . To claim any system is based upon physiological grounds, then, is not justified. . . . As physiologists, we should study the conditions under which the exercises are done and the results of these exercises upon the system. . . . What we want is the clear scientific study of the physiology; the exercise, whether presented in one form or another. (cited in Gerber, 1971, p. 302)

Fitz earned his medical degree from Harvard Medical School, where he was no doubt influenced by Dudley Allen Sargent, a legend in American physical education, who was then director of the Hemenway gymnasium at Harvard. It was at Harvard that Fitz began the first exercise-physiology research laboratory in physical education, which quickly became a fundamental part of America's first degree program in physical education, the Bachelor of Science in Anatomy, Physiology, and Physical Training (Gerber, 1971).

Brooks (1987) suggests that by the 1920s and 1930s, *muscle and exercise physiology* were virtually synonymous with *physiology and biochemistry.* The tradition begun by Fitz at Harvard continued and was strengthened. By the late 1930s and 1940s, the Harvard Fatigue Laboratory had become the world's major site for exercise-physiology research and the primary model for the development of other laboratories in America and throughout the world.

In the post–World War II period, when physical education expanded rapidly in colleges and universities, exercise physiology became firmly entrenched as the scientific cornerstone of the field. In 1954 the American College of Sports Medicine (ACSM) was formed, linking the scientific endeavors within physical education with those in the larger medical and scientific communities. Many exercise-physiology textbooks were published, laboratories were built, and the study of exercise physiology became the main scientific focus of graduate study in physical education. The *Research Quarterly of Exercise and Sport* was a main outlet for research in this area until more recently, when more specialized journals began to appear, such as the *American Journal of Sports Medicine, Medicine and Science in Sports and Exercise,* the *International Journal of Sports Medicine,* and *The Physician and Sports Medicine.*

In the recent explosion of interest in fitness and healthy lifestyles, exercise physiology not only has commanded a role of central importance but also has become fertile ground on which a number of more applied, professional endeavors have developed. Adult fitness, athletic training, and strength development have all emerged as serious professional fields in their own right. These professional fields draw much of their knowledge base from exercise physiology and are often housed, along with cardiac rehabilitation, within exercise physiology in college and university departments.

As the role of exercise has become better understood, exercise physiologists have been able to attract substantial amounts of research monies to expand further the knowledge base in this area. Thus, in many instances, the exercise-physiology programs within physical-education departments have had the most success in securing research funding, increasing both the stature of the field within physical education and the number of graduate students who can be supported.

The substantial amount of interest in the field and the growing number of professional roles that derive from a study of exercise physiology have led to the development of undergraduate majors. Sometimes, these are majors in exercise science, with a primary emphasis on scientific training. In other cases, they are majors in adult fitness, with a primary emphasis on professional preparation. In still other cases, there is a common core, with different tracks leading to the more scientific (research) specializations and to the more professional (applied) specializations.

CURRENT STATUS OF EXERCISE PHYSIOLOGY

To say that exercise physiology is alive and well is to make an understatement. Exercise physiology has been and continues to be the most popular

and well known of the physical-education subdisciplines. Interest in health and fitness among the adult population has never been higher in America than it is today. Many adults participate regularly in some fitness-related activity. The markets for fitness-related shoes, clothing, and equipment have prompted the development of an entire new industry. What all this means is that a cultural climate has been created within which the scientific study of exercise is a valued activity.

Although it is probable that more people are knowledgeable about exercise than they are about any other sport-science area, it is also true that myths still abound, that improper exercise habits persist, and that a great deal of research and education is still needed. Too many people still believe that *spot reducing* is possible (i.e., that weight can be lost in particular areas by use of heat or belts), that running faster rather than farther is the better approach to cardiovascular fitness, and that weight lost through perspiration (such as in a steam bath or a sauna) is permanent rather than temporary, fat rather than water.

There certainly is *no* area in the physical-education subdisciplines where a popular literature (as opposed to a technical, scientific literature) exists to the same extent as in exercise and fitness. Much of the popular literature focuses on various self-proclaimed miracle approaches to diet and weight loss, but increasingly, there is a corresponding focus on exercise, too. Bicycling, cross-country skiing, jogging, and walking are all fine aerobic activities, and each has a popular literature available. For example, in most bookstores, you can find popular books that describe where to find good jogging or walking routes when you travel on vacation or business. There are also books describing bicycling routes that you can explore locally or as a vacation enterprise.

The extraordinary increase in sales of fitness equipment since the mid-1980s is also evidence of the current high status of this field. Although the increased interest in fitness might understandably result in increased sales of running shoes or bicycles, it is the rapidly increasing sales of fitness equipment that is in many ways most remarkable. Weight-training systems, Nautilus equipment, rowing machines, bicycle trainers, and even complete home gyms are no longer uncommon.

This increased interest among the adult population, however, shows little evidence of spilling over to benefit children and youths. There is still a great concern in our society over the fitness levels of children and youths. Most laypeople and professionals feel that children and youths are seriously unfit, even though a debate has begun among exercise physiologists over such claims (see Chapters 9 and 10).

Our knowledge about the amount and type of fitness activity necessary to enhance life is changing. A new, specialized field of exercise physiology, referred to as **exercise epidemiology,** has emerged. People in this field study the relationships between activity patterns and mortality. We are also in a period when the study of how exercise, or the lack thereof, affects aging is of great interest. This interest is due to findings suggesting that many typical signs of aging may be attributable to poor nutrition and lack of activity rather than to merely getting older.

The increased cultural attention to health and fitness is also apparent in the growth of interest in exercise physiology, both in the scientific study of basic exercise phenomena and in the clinical applications of that knowledge. In the scientific study of basic exercise phenomena, the areas studied and the typical kinds of questions asked within them are shown in Table 14.1.

As mentioned previously, exercise physiology has become the ground on which a number of clinical, professional areas have developed. Cardiac rehabilitation, adult fitness, strength training, and athletic training are the most frequently cited clinical subdisciplines of exercise science. These areas have developed sufficiently to have their own professional organizations, journals, textbooks, and training programs. In some cases, certification is necessary to practice in these subdisciplines. Some of these fields may be categorized as "clinical exercise." The clinical-exercise fields use the information developed from basic exercise research and also have specific areas of study, as shown in Table 14.2.

Because not one of the questions in either of the tables has been answered fully, it is easy to see why research in basic and clinical-exercise physiology continues to be important. The successful results of exercise-physiology research over the past several decades have begun to change the way in which many people protect their health through exercise. People are beginning to appreciate how exercise can be used as both a preventive and a rehabilitative instrument in the treatment of various kinds of medical problems. Obviously, much remains to be done.

What Do Exercise Physiologists Do?

Exercise physiologists are involved in research, teaching, and clinical service. In a narrow sense, the field of exercise physiology is confined mostly to colleges, universities, and laboratories. Exercise physiologists can be found in departments of sport sciences, physical education, physiology, cardiology, general medicine, and veterinary medicine. They teach courses in exercise science, conduct research, train graduate students, and provide clinical services to an increasingly large number of diverse populations, ranging from elite athletes to patients who have had heart attacks.

In smaller departments, exercise physiologists typically focus on one of the three major approaches to exercise physiology: traditional cardiovascular and metabolic exercise physiology, exercise biochemistry, or applied exercise physiology, related to cardiac rehabilitation, athletic training, adult fitness, and the like. In larger departments, it is not uncommon to find all three represented. Funding sources tend to drive much of the research focus of a department. Thus, if a department attracts chronic-disease funding, chronic disease becomes the focus. If it attracts funds to do epidemiological research, then that becomes the focus. If it relies on tuition from large numbers of undergraduate and graduate students, it is more likely to focus

TABLE 14.1	Areas of Study in Basic Exercise Science
Area	Typical Questions Asked
Environmental effects on exercise	How does altitude affect exercise functions?
	What kinds of pollutants most affect exercise functions?
	What are the regulatory responses to exercise under conditions of high heat and humidity?
Disease and health	How does exercise affect diseases such as diabetes, coronary artery disease, or cancer?
	How is exercise related to blood pressure, appetite control, insulin sensitivity, and blood clotting?
Cardiovascular system	How is blood flow regulated during exercise?
	How is breathing regulated during exercise?
	What factors limit aerobic capacity?
	How do anaerobic and aerobic systems function under different exercise stresses?
Exercise biochemistry	How is glucose homeostasis maintained during exercise?
	How does exercise affect the aging process?
	How does exercise affect obesity?
Ergogenic aids	How does creatine supplementation affect strength development?
	How does preexercise carbohydrate loading affect cycling performance?

Source: Adapted from Brooks, 1987, and Blair et al., 1987.

on career choices, such as athletic training and cardiac rehabilitation.

Students who study exercise physiology at the master's-degree level are likely headed to one of the exercise and fitness professions and will be employed as athletic trainers, personal trainers, cardiac rehabilitation workers, leaders of work-site fitness programs, strength and conditioning coaches. These fields are very popular with young women and men today, and exercise physiology is the foundation science for their professional work.

Thus, an exercise physiologist might test an elite athlete on a treadmill, obtain a muscle biopsy, analyze oxygen-consumption data with the help of a computer, direct a patient through a graded test on a bicycle ergometer, lecture an undergraduate class on basic cardiovascular functions, conduct an advanced seminar on recent research, or administer a large-scale fitness program.

If we view exercise physiology as a ground on which the fitness professions grow, then our description of what exercise professionals do expands greatly. Athletic trainers have their own certification system and work with teams at all levels, in both preventive work and rehabilitation from injury. Cardiac rehabilitation has also become a strong specialization, with professionals often working in hospitals or in other medical facilities. Strength-training professionals do both testing and rehabilitative work, often on referral of patients

TABLE 14.2	Areas of Study in Clinical-Exercise Science
Area	Typical Questions Asked
Rehabilitation	What factors influence the exercise progression for patients who have had a heart attack?
	How can a muscle be best rehabilitated after trauma?
	What role does exercise play in treating depression?
Prevention	What level of fitness is needed to lower cardiovascular risk?
	How does exercise relate to regulation of diseases such as diabetes?
	What level of fitness is needed to resist the onset of high blood pressure?
	How is children's fitness related to problems in their later years?
Age-related	At what age should children begin fitness training?
	How can exercise programs increase the quality of life for older people?
	What role does exercise play in changes that occur in adolescence?
	How can exercise deter traditional signs of aging?

from orthopedic physicians and podiatrists (trained to specialize in problems of the foot). An adult-fitness professional typically has responsibilities for developing, implementing, and evaluating programs of fitness that are primarily preventive in nature. Such professionals are employed at health centers, private fitness clubs, and private corporations that seek to improve the fitness of their workers and to reduce the costs of insurance benefits paid out when employees suffer from disease and trauma related to inactivity.

How Does a Person Prepare to Be an Exercise Physiologist or a Fitness Specialist?

Exercise physiology, as a research and teaching field, is a graduate-training specialization, typically within a physical-education or sport-science department. Requirements for entry into graduate programs in basic exercise physiology increasingly include substantial coursework in chemistry and biochemistry. The typical undergraduate physical-education major, with a teacher-preparation emphasis, is no longer a direct path to graduate programs in exercise physiology. The many exercise-science under-

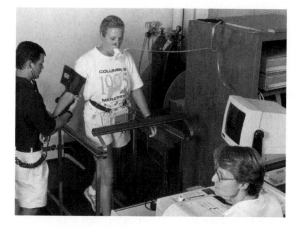

Exercise testing is an important step both in research and for prescriptive programs.

graduate programs no doubt provide more direct access to the graduate specialization.

Students with majors in exercise science, physiology, and biochemistry might all be likely candidates for doctoral programs in exercise physiology. The doctorate is a requirement if you wish to pursue a career in colleges and universities or in a laboratory setting as an exercise scientist. Doctoral training emphasizes the underlying disciplines of cardiology, physiology, biochemistry, and molecular biology, along with specific coursework in exercise physiology, laboratory techniques needed for fitness assessment (e.g., underwater weighing for body composition and treadmill testing for aerobic capacity), and substantial coursework in statistics and research methods. Applied work, such as in cardiac rehabilitation and adult fitness, is also often included.

There are master's-degree programs in exercise physiology, but these more typically prepare students for applied work as exercise specialists, as exercise technicians, or in professional programs such as cardiac rehabilitation or adult fitness. Many of these emerging professional areas have certification requirements.

CURRENT ISSUES AND PROBLEMS IN EXERCISE PHYSIOLOGY

As in most fields that have a basic and an applied focus, the issues and problems of exercise physiology tend to be distributed between those related to the basic scientific investigation of exercise-related phenomena and the practical problems associated with clinical practice. Professionals in the clinical practice of exercise physiology do more applied research and would like the help of their more basic-oriented scientific colleagues to answer questions of immediate, applied significance. The basic researchers, on the other hand, feel strongly that theoretically oriented research pays higher dividends in the long run because it tends to focus on underlying mechanisms rather than on applied problems.

Another issue emerging within exercise science is the increasingly clear need for interdisciplinary approaches to investigate more fully problems in exercise and sport. Since the mid-1960s, scholars and researchers in physical education have become more and more specialized in their graduate preparation and in their own fields. Now, it appears, there is recognition that to investigate and understand sport phenomena, we may require knowledge and techniques from several sport sciences—exercise

physiology, biomechanics, and motor control, for example. In the near future, we might see a more concerted effort to prepare graduate students more completely in the sport sciences rather than narrowly in one field of study. If this begins to happen, undergraduate sport-science specializations will quickly follow.

Physical educator Janet Harris (1992) has argued that exercise physiology has largely ignored the social and political problems in which the field is embedded. In Chapter 8, the newer *socioecological* view of health and fitness was described, a view that focuses not only on individual responsibility for health and fitness but also on the social, political, and economic structures that prevent portions of the population from gaining access to information, facilities, and programs related to fitness and health. The fact is that a person's fitness status is related to her or his socioeconomic status and that solving national problems related to fitness requires sensitivity to sociopolitical issues and programs designed to resolve sociopolitical problems.

The current emphasis on accumulations of moderate-to-intense physical activity and the clear evidence that many children and adolescents are not getting sufficient activity have created the need for exercise physiologists to collaborate with physical and health educators to experiment with intervention programs designed to change exercise and nutrition *habits*. This current public health need may reverse a trend toward isolation and specialization that developed since the early 1970s within exercise physiology.

Another issue relates to the increased job market for people who apply knowledge of exercise physiology clinically in treating groups and individuals. Should these people be licensed? Currently, the field is dominated by older professional groups, such as physical therapists and occupational therapists, but the need may soon arise for a specialization licensing in clinical exercise physiology.

The American College of Sports Medicine is the main professional and scientific association for this field, but it has grown large, primarily because of the emergence of public interest in exercise and fitness. Large professional organizations can exert substantial power and can guide public policy, but they also become so diverse in their membership that the specific needs of exercise physiologists may get less attention.

The many important issues related to exercise, physical activity, and fitness were reviewed in Chapter 10. Needless to say, this is an active field with an important future, one that is exciting and attracts the interest of many talented women and men.

SUMMARY

1. Exercise physiology emerged from the medical and gymnastic beginnings of American physical education and developed as the dominant scientific enterprise within the field.

2. Traditionally, exercise physiology was focused on oxygen utilization during cardiovascular exercise and metabolic responses to exercise and training.

3. More recently, exercise biochemistry has emerged as an important focus, and several clinical fields, such as cardiac rehabilitation, have also developed.

4. George Fitz, known as the father of exercise physiology, started the first major exercise-science laboratory at Harvard University.

5. The exercise sciences have grown rapidly in recent years, because of the tremendous increase in the general public's interest in health and fitness.

6. Exercise physiology has become a ground on which the basic, scientific study of exercise and the clinical, professional applications of exercise have arisen.

7. Exercise science is the largest and strongest of the physical-education subdisciplines, both in its scientific and clinical endeavors and in its general, popular appeal.

8. Exercise physiologists teach, conduct research, and provide clinical service to diverse populations, ranging from elite athletes to cardiac patients to people with disabilities.

9. Exercise physiology as a scientific endeavor requires a doctoral degree and is housed in universities or private laboratories.

10. Exercise physiology, in its clinical forms (cardiac rehabilitation, adult fitness, strength training, athletic training), often requires a master's degree. Work is available in a large variety of school, community, and private-sector positions.

11. Current problems in the field include debates about the relative worth of basic and applied research, the increasing need for interdisciplinary cooperation in the sport sciences, and the degree to which the field is becoming divorced from its roots in physical education.

DISCUSSION QUESTIONS

1. Why has exercise physiology always been—and why does it remain—the most important scientific field in physical education?

2. To what extent are the clinical and research endeavors within the field different? Do they attract different kinds of people?

3. What clinical job opportunities exist in your area for someone trained in the general field of exercise physiology?

4. What options exist for you in local or regional universities for clinical or research training in this field?

5. Have you visited or worked in an exercise physiology laboratory? What kinds of things go on there?

CHAPTER 15

Kinesiology and Biomechanics

Biomechanical analysis is the wave of the future in professional and world-class amateur sports. An individual athlete is videotaped in performance; his movements are broken down and mathematically analyzed by computer; the results are compared with a predetermined computer simulation based in part on measurements of the athlete's physical characteristics; flaws in the athlete's technique, ways in which he can improve his effectiveness, can then be identified.

Physicist Peter Brancazio, in *Sport Science*, 1984

LEARNING OBJECTIVES

- To differentiate the field of kinesiology from that of biomechanics

- To describe the various fields using information from kinesiology or biomechanics

- To discuss the issues researched within these fields

- To describe the techniques used to research these issues

- To describe the preparation for entering the fields

- To discuss current problems and issues in the fields

Professionals in sport, fitness, and physical education have always been interested in how the body moves and in how more efficient and effective movement can be brought about. Sometimes, the goal is primarily educational, as when a physical-education teacher helps children to learn fundamental motor skills, such as jumping and throwing. At other times, the goal is primarily competitive, as when a coach seeks to improve the technique of a hurdler in order to improve the athlete's speed. At still other times, the goal is safety, as when a fitness instructor demonstrates proper lifting technique. Regardless of the specific goal, in each of these situations, the professional in charge would have to know a great deal about how the body is structured, how it moves, and what principles can be utilized to increase movement effectiveness. These areas constitute the realms of kinesiology and biomechanics.

The term **kinesiology** has a broad meaning, in that it has become the most common umbrella term used to describe the discipline devoted to the study of physical activity. As shown in Chapter 3, Kinesiology (I shall use the uppercase spelling to denote the broad meaning) was officially adopted as the appropriate name for the discipline by the American Academy of Physical Education in the 1990s, when it changed its name to the American Academy of Kinesiology and Physical Education. Part Five of this text is devoted to describing the various subdisciplines that fall under this umbrella, which includes experiential knowledge, theoretical knowledge, and professional-practice knowledge (Hoffman & Harris, 2000). The term *kinesiology* has also historically been used to refer to the study of how the muscular system moves the bony structure of the body; indeed, most undergraduate programs in physical education, sport sciences, exercise science, or Kinesiology require at least one course in kinesiology. *Biomechanics* is the science that applies the mechanical principles of physics and engineering to the investigation of human movement and the structure and function of the human body (Simpson, 2000). Together, kinesiology and biomechanics form an increasingly important Kinesiology subdiscipline, which attracts the interests of scientists from diverse areas and which has many practical applications in the worlds of sport, fitness, and physical education.

Sometimes, biomechanical analysis *follows* advances made by athletes, providing an explanation for and an understanding of newly introduced techniques. The best modern example is the high-jump style popularized by Dick Fosbury in the mid-1960s. Fosbury won the Gold Medal at the 1968 Olympic Games in Mexico City and changed the course of high jumping with his flop style. Within 10 years, virtually all high jumpers in the world had switched from roll styles to the flop style. Biomechanists provided the explanations of why this new style was more effective.

In other cases, however, kinesiology and biomechanics have *led* changes in technique. The best example here is in swimming, where over a period of years in the 1960s and 1970s, kinesiologists working with elite-level coaches determined that the traditional method of the arm pull in crawl swimming, based on drag forces for producing propulsion, was not as biomechanically efficient as an arm pull that produced lift forces (Adrian, 1983). The primary figure in this revolution in swimming was James Councilman of Indiana University, a swim coach with an excellent background in physical education. Again, within 10 years, virtually every swim coach in the world had changed the techniques taught to swimmers in crawl events. This was an example of scientific investigation leading changes in practice, rather than providing explanations of changes in practice brought about through innovations by athletes.

Kinesiology and biomechanics are important sport sciences because they are so fundamental to the work of sport, fitness, and physical-education professionals, and to that of other sport scientists. In areas as diverse as fitness, rehabilitation, equipment design, physical therapy, injury prevention, basic motor education, and improved sport performance, kinesiology and biomechanics have an im-

Knowledge from biomechanics has revolutionized swim instruction and coaching.

portant role to play. The kinds of questions asked in this subdiscipline show how both scientists and practitioners might find the answers interesting and useful in their work:

- How are muscle forces summated to produce power in the golf swing?
- How can joint flexibility be increased for rehabilitative purposes?
- What movement patterns do elite-level volleyball players use for spiking?
- What kind of shoe support can be developed to counter foot problems in distance running?
- How can tennis rackets be changed to produce better control?
- Which baseball hitting technique is best for a singles hitter? Which is best for a power hitter?
- How does muscle use in throwing change as children develop skill?

The answers to those questions, and to others like them, have traditionally been based on experience, on opinion, and, far too often, on unwarranted assumptions and beliefs. A *scientific* answer to those questions comes only from improvements

in scientific methodology that allows research to examine the issues systematically. Those scientifically derived answers can then form the primary information on which a sport, fitness, or physical-education professional bases judgments for intervention with clients, students, and athletes.

DEFINITION OF KINESIOLOGY AND BIOMECHANICS AS FIELDS OF STUDY

As mentioned previously, *kinesiology* is the study of human motion, more specifically the study of how the muscles move the bony structure of the body. The human body consists of a bony structure—its anatomy—connected at the joints and moved and supported by muscles and tendons. The motions of which humans are capable are determined by the nature of the joints and of the muscles that move the bony structure at the joints. The knee joint, for example, is effective in flexion and extension movements, whereas the shoulder is effective at rotational movements.

To understand human motion, we must have a complete command of the various actions of different joints and the muscles that contract and relax to move the bony structure at those joints. Thus, kinesiology has traditionally been the course within which students have learned to identify the actions of joints and the muscles that cause those actions. This kind of knowledge is fundamental to the practice of a profession such as *physical therapy,* where a practitioner might have to provide graded exercise to restore the full range of motion at a shoulder joint following an injury sustained by a patient.

The study of kinesiology is often organized by joints or groups of joints in the same anatomical region of the body and subclassified by the type of movement at the joint. Thus, a primary grouping might include the foot and ankle, the knee, the hips and pelvic girdle, the spinal column, the elbow and wrist, and the shoulder girdle. The movements possible at each of these joints are determined by the nature of the joint and by the positions of the

Physical Principles Applicable to Biomechanical Analysis

Motion

Linear displacement, velocity, acceleration
Angular displacement, velocity, acceleration
Free-falling objects
Path of projectiles—parabolic, curvilinear

Force

Weight and mass
Newton's laws of motion (inertia, acceleration, reaction)
Gravity
Friction
Momentum, transfer, conservation
Leverage
Moment of inertia

Work and Energy

Work
Power
Potential, kinetic, and rotational energy

Aerodynamics

Projection angle
Flight velocity
Spin
Air resistance, wind, air density, shape of projectile

Landing and Striking

Angle of incidence and rebound
Shape of striking surface
Elasticity, rebound, and dissipation of force
Surface friction and resiliency

Hydrodynamics

Buoyancy
Surface area for propulsive force
Water resistance

SOURCE: Adapted from Singer, 1976, p. 225.

muscles around the joint. Some of these movement possibilities are *abduction* and *adduction* (movement *away from* and *toward* the midline of the body), flexion and extension, pronation and supination, inversion and eversion, medial and lateral rotation, and elevation and depression. This approach to the study of human motion is often referred to as *anatomical kinesiology.*

Biomechanics, often referred to as *mechanical kinesiology,* is the study of human motion from the standpoint of physics. In most cases, the study of kinesiology precedes the study of biomechanics because it is easier to understand the influence of various forces on human motion if you have a thorough knowledge of the motions of which the body is capable. *Mechanics* is the area of physics that studies how forces, both internal and external, affect the

motions of objects, animate or inanimate (Brancazio, 1984). Biomechanics regards human motion from this mechanical point of view, in which the body is divided into a collection of segments (shoulder, arm, wrist, etc.) connected to one another at the joints and moved by both muscular forces and externally applied forces. Biomechanics has developed into a highly sophisticated research field.

The idea is to study the human body in action as it goes through some particular movement—swinging a golf club or throwing a javelin, for instance—in order to isolate the various individual motions that make up the activity, to measure the speeds of body segments and the forces that act on them, and in general to acquire accurate data on all aspects of the movement. The analysis can become quite complex—the golf swing, for example, involves nearly a hundred different forces acting on thirteen body segments—so sophisticated research equipment is a virtual necessity. (Brancazio, 1984, p. 18)

Biomechanists study how physical principles affect human motion and performance. If a subject uses an implement (tennis racquet, javelin, etc.) or has to strike or receive an object (kick a football, head a soccer ball, etc.), then the implement and the object also become part of the biomechanical analysis. The accompanying box contains a partial list of important physical principles that have been applied directly to the analysis of sport skills.

The fields of kinesiology and biomechanics form a coherent whole that represents a fundamental aspect of the emerging sport sciences. Not only are these fields important in their own right, but also they are increasingly being utilized by researchers in other sport sciences in attempts to provide a more integrated investigation of sport and fitness phenomena.

DEVELOPMENT OF KINESIOLOGY AND BIOMECHANICS

Kinesiology has been a traditional scientific field of study in physical education, along with anatomy, physiology, and measurement. These subjects formed the core scientific training of physical educators during that time when health, fitness, recreation, and sport professionals all were educated under the umbrella of physical education. Historically, kinesiology has focused primarily on anatomical and structural issues, with less focus on the mechanical factors that influence movement. To the degree that mechanical factors were considered, they were investigated within the kinesiology course.

Biomechanics, as a specialized field of study, began to emerge in the mid-1960s as part of the development of the subdisciplines of physical education. Biomechanics developed as an international field of investigation. The First International Seminar on Biomechanics was held in Switzerland in 1967, followed by similar meetings in Holland in 1969, Rome in 1971, and the United States at Pennsylvania State University in 1973. Research journals in medicine, engineering, sports, and exercise began to review biomechanics research (Adrian, 1983).

During the late 1960s and 1970s, growth was rapid. The International Society of Biomechanics was founded, as was the American Society of Biomechanics, which also began to publish a new journal, the *Journal of Biomechanics.* Kinesiology texts had long been available in physical education, but the 1960s and 1970s witnessed the publication of a number of basic biomechanics textbooks as well as specialized biomechanical books. Two of the earliest and most influential were Councilman's (1968) *The Science of Swimming* and Dyson's (1964) *The Mechanics of Athletics.*

In the 1980s, there was sufficient research and development to warrant the formation of specialized organizations devoted to sport biomechanics. The International Society of Biomechanics in Sport was formed in 1982. Researchers and scholars in physics, many of them amateur athletes themselves, have begun to show interest in applying their knowledge of physics to sport. Many articles have appeared in the *American Journal of Physics*, a respected journal devoted to applications of physics in cultural life (Brancazio, 1984).

As do other subdisciplinary fields, biomechanics has both research and clinical subfields, and there is often a circular relationship between the two; that is, problems identified in the field are investigated and research findings are put to use in the field. This circularity, and the entire field of biomechanics, was greatly enhanced with the initiation in 1982 of the Elite Athlete Project sponsored by the U.S. Olympic Committee (Hay, 1991). The research and clinical activity spurred by the project has helped to improve both research and methods and the delivery of services to athletes and coaches.

Biomechanics developed out of the traditional field of kinesiology. Recently, biomechanics has come to dominate the field. It is becoming more and more common for the field to be referred to as *sport biomechanics*. We can expect that label and the focus it implies to continue to dominate research and application.

CURRENT SCOPE OF KINESIOLOGY AND BIOMECHANICS

Kinesiology and biomechanics are firmly rooted in the emerging sport sciences. The explosion of interest in sport and fitness in the recent past has greatly increased interest in the work of biomechanics. Although technique has always been considered important in teaching and coaching, it is only recently that professionals and laypeople alike have become more knowledgeable and sophisticated about the mechanical aspects of technique and have learned how physical principles can be used to explain and improve performance.

There has also been a steady improvement of equipment, much of which is directly traceable to a better understanding of biomechanics. Pole vaulters continue to vault higher as poles provide more thrust and as the vaulters accommodate their technique to the new mechanical demands of the poles. Tennis players have been able to control their games better with bigger racquets. Distance runners avoid injury by wearing better-designed shoes.

Biomechanical research is carried out utilizing a number of technical methods. High-speed photography has been a major tool in the development of biomechanics research methods. Whereas a standard movie camera records images at the rate of eighteen frames per second, specialized cameras can operate at thousands of frames per second, thus apparently slowing down the motion to the point where it can be analyzed in great detail.

Electromyography (EMG), a technique for recording the electrical impulses within muscles, has also been a favored research method. The impulses are translated into graphs or other representations so that the functions of muscles can be analyzed and compared. This kind of information can

Computer-enhanced performance images can be used to analyze skills.

be used in many ways. For example, athletes have a certain rhythm to their performances that is detectable through EMG recordings. When they hit a slump, this is reflected by changes in their EMG patterns.

Transducers are used in clinical strength-measuring devices to quantify the force a subject can exert. Transducers are used in *force platforms* to assist in the measurement of force exerted by a performer. This kind of knowledge is used to evaluate footwear and is also useful in human-gait analysis (Simpson, 2000). Pressure devices are also placed in shoe inserts to provide analysis of pressures placed on the foot during human motion. This kind of research is often a prelude to producing an *orthotic* (special shoe insert) that can provide correction and relief both to athletes and to individuals who experience foot problems because of structural or muscular abnormalities.

Technology has affected all the sport sciences, but none more profoundly than sport biomechanics. Combinations of video, analog, and computer technology allow for viewing and analyzing the movement of athletes (www.peakfperform.com). Software programs calculate accurate kinematic measurements of linear and angular displacements, velocities, and accelerations that are necessary to analyze and improve technique. Movements can be viewed in two- or three-dimensional space. These technologies, of course, are also useful for the medical professions and for the media industries. The more general field that has developed from these technologies is referred to as "motion analysis."

A major focus in biomechanics has been the use of *profiles* to enhance performance of athletes. High-speed videography captures the performance of a skilled athlete, and biomechanists use *kinematics* (the measurement of location, velocity, and acceleration) to produce a profile of the performance. The characteristics that define the skilled performance can then be taught to less-skilled athletes as a way of improving their performances. Profiling is also used to help patients or people with disabilities to learn movement patterns that are associated with the biomechanical patterns of the general population (Simpson, 2000).

Light-emitting-diode (LED) systems have in many cases replaced film and video as the preferred motion-analysis methodology in the biomechanics laboratory. LED systems produce three-dimensional coordinates that can be entered directly into computer software programs. Force platforms have been used both in the laboratory for basic research and in clinical practice—for example, in analyzing and improving weight-lifting performance and in helping discus throwers to improve their performances.

Quantitative biomechanical analysis utilizing these sophisticated techniques dominates the research field. Such methods are also being used more frequently as training aids for elite athletes. However, the ordinary coach or teacher has to depend more on *qualitative* biomechanical analysis if she or he is to provide the necessary help for students and athletes as they attempt to improve their performances. The regular, accurate application of biomechanical analysis in the gymnasium and on the playing fields remains the most important step forward to be made by the coaching and teaching

Qualitative skill feedback depends on a teacher's knowledge of the skill.

professions. If this important step is to be accomplished, the field must be approached in terms of what physical educator Shirl Hoffman (1977) called a **"pedagogical kinesiology"**—that is, an approach to biomechanics that emphasizes the recognition of the critical elements and common errors in sport skill performance as it occurs in practical situations. Teachers and coaches must be able to *see* critical elements of sport skill performance as it occurs, to *detect* common errors being made, and to *respond* to the performer with accurate, relevant feedback.

Although sport biomechanics is emerging as an important sport science, this does not mean that sport is the sole or even the most important field of application for biomechanics knowledge. Areas such as physical therapy, occupational therapy, adapted physical education, and rehabilitative medicine have all utilized new knowledge from biomechanics directly in their professional practices. The major areas of study within kinesiology and biomechanics and the typical questions asked within them show the diversity of application within these fields (see Table 15.1).

The subdisciplines of kinesiology and biomechanics have a bright future, not only because they

TABLE 15.1   Areas of Study within Kinesiology and Biomechanics

Area	Typical Questions Asked
Kinesiology	How does the wrist joint move when baseball pitchers throw curve balls?
	How does muscle potential differ in middle- and long-distance running?
	What range of motion should be achieved in rehabilitation of the knee after surgery?
	How do kicking motions change as children develop?
Quantitative biomechanics	How do forces summate most efficiently to produce maximum performance in the discus throw?
	What variables influence human tolerance to externally imposed stress, such as occur in football tackling?
	What are the performance patterns of world-class spikers in volleyball?
Qualitative biomechanics	What are the critical performance elements of various sport skills?
	What are the most common errors made at various developmental stages in acquiring a sport skill?
	How can these critical elements and common errors be taught to teachers and coaches?
Equipment analysis	What is the optimal design of a golf club?
	How can shoes better prevent overpronation in running?
	What materials can best absorb shock in contact sports where protective gear is worn?

have the ability to contribute important information to sport, fitness, and physical-education professionals, but also because they have a strong potential for contributing to areas such as medicine, rehabilitation, child development, and gerontology. In the field of sport equipment, too, we can expect continuing improvement based partially on contributions made by sport biomechanists.

What Do Kinesiologists and Biomechanists Do?

Kinesiologists and biomechanists work primarily in academic positions in colleges and universities, although there are increasing employment opportunities in the private sector, particularly in the equipment industries. In the academic world, these specialists are most often found in departments of physical education or sport science.

As do all academicians, kinesiologists and biomechanists teach, do research, and provide service to various constituencies. Much of the research is highly theoretical and has no immediate practical application. Some of the research, however, is designed to provide immediate answers to practical problems in sport and fitness.

The fields have become very technical, and biomechanics laboratories can cost a great deal to build. Kinesiologists and biomechanists who find work in the private sector are more typically involved in the practical problems of product design, testing, and evaluating. In some countries, sport biomechanists are finding employment with national sport teams or at national training centers, where their work focuses mostly on helping elite athletes to improve their performances.

How Does a Person Prepare to Be a Kinesiologist or a Biomechanist?

Specialization in these fields is almost exclusively at the graduate level of university training. Undergraduate degrees are not available in these areas. The master's degree may provide a beginning study of these fields but in and of itself does not qualify a person for employment as a kinesiologist or a biomechanist. The doctorate is the main training degree for these fields.

The most typical background of people entering these fields is physical education or one of the emerging sport-science undergraduate degrees, although undergraduate training in physics is not unheard of. The graduate degree in kinesiology/biomechanics typically includes substantial training in engineering, physics, and related scientific fields; mastery of laboratory and equipment techniques; extensive preparation in research methods and statistics; and some experience in related sport-science fields. Because mathematical modeling, especially as used in developing hypothetical performance profiles based on a large number of variables, appears to be an important technique of the future, students in these areas probably will be required to master advanced mathematics.

CURRENT ISSUES IN KINESIOLOGY AND BIOMECHANICS

The major issues within kinesiology and biomechanics are similar to those in other sport sciences. A continuing debate exists concerning the relative contributions made by quantitative analysis and qualitative analysis. The debate tends to be joined over the question of which approach should be emphasized in the typical undergraduate course for physical-education majors who are preparing to teach. Many professionally-oriented people believe that the undergraduate course should emphasize qualitative techniques on a sport-by-sport basis. Others favor the teaching of principles that then can be applied to many sports. Still others favor the teaching of beginning quantitative techniques, because that approach is the dominant research approach within the field.

These fields, as described earlier, have contributed research and information that is valuable to a variety of fields outside sport and physical education. Biomechanists often receive research monies from sources with concerns that are not at all related to sport and physical education. Thus, there is some danger that kinesiologists and biomechanists will become more and more distanced from sport and physical education.

SUMMARY

1. *Kinesiology* is the study of human motion; more specifically, it examines how the muscles move the bony structure of the body.

2. *Biomechanics* is the study of the human body as a mechanical system, utilizing principles drawn from the discipline of physics.

3. Kinesiology/biomechanics sometimes follows sport innovation, as in the Fosbury flop, and sometimes leads sport innovation, as in the crawl swimming technique.

4. Knowledge from kinesiology/biomechanics is used in a variety of areas other than sport, including physical therapy, occupational therapy, equipment design, rehabilitation, basic motor education, and fitness.

5. Kinesiology has been a traditional area of study in physical education, whereas biomechanics developed in the 1960s as part of the physical-education subdiscipline movement.

6. Biomechanics has become the dominant area within the field. It is also called "sport biomechanics."

7. Biomechanists use high-speed photography, electromyography, and computer analysis as basic research methods.

8. Quantitative biomechanics is distinguished from qualitative biomechanics, which involves on-the-spot analysis of performance with resultant feedback to performers.

9. Kinesiologists/biomechanists typically work in universities as faculty, although some private-sector jobs exist, particularly in equipment design and testing.

10. Kinesiology/biomechanics is almost exclusively a graduate-level specialization in physical-education or sport-science departments, with most work at the doctoral level.

11. Major issues in kinesiology/biomechanics include whether emphasis should be on quantitative or qualitative methods in undergraduate courses in teacher preparation, and to what degree the field is becoming distanced from its roots in physical education.

DISCUSSION QUESTIONS

1. In what sports has biomechanics most contributed to improvements in technique or equipment?

2. Does a typical physical-education major provide the right background for graduate study in biomechanics?

3. What questions might a biomechanist be able to answer regarding a sport you know well?

4. Where in your region can biomechanics/kinesiology be studied as a graduate specialization?

5. Can biomechanics/kinesiology contribute as much to child and youth sport as it has to elite sport? Give examples of research that you think could be helpful.

CHAPTER **16**

Motor Behavior

Improving skill means that the performance of any motor task becomes more efficient, thereby reducing the time taken to complete the task and the level of effort required. This increased level of skillfulness could also mean more enjoyment and satisfaction for the performer by increasing the ease with which the task can be completed or by allowing new, more complex skills to be attempted. If by understanding the processes that govern the control of movement we can show the way for all individuals to improve their ability to perform the myriad of motor tasks that they confront, then we can claim to have made a real contribution to improving the quality of life within our society.

Robert Kerr, in *Psychomotor Learning,* 1982

LEARNING OBJECTIVES

- To differentiate among the fields of motor learning, control, and development

- To discuss the various ways information from these fields is used

- To describe the questions researched in these fields

- To describe the preparation for entering the fields

- To analyze current problems and issues in the fields

Motor behavior is the subdiscipline of Kinesiology that focuses on how motor skills are acquired and controlled across the lifespan (Thomas & Thomas, 2000). This subdiscipline comprises three fields, which are distinct but highly related. **Motor learning** focuses on how motor skills are learned, particularly the conditions under which practice leads to improvement. **Motor control** focuses on the "neural, physical, and behavioral aspects of movement" (Schmidt, 1988, p. 17). **Motor development** is the specialized aspect of the subdiscipline that focuses on how the acquisition, improvement, and control of motor skills change and vary across the lifespan.

People who practice in the sport, fitness, and physical-education professions have always been centrally concerned with helping people acquire and improve motor skills. Because a major portion of motor-skill learning occurs from infancy through adolescence, these same professionals have a keen interest in the developmental stages humans go through and how those affect motor learning, control, and performance. Faced with an aging population over the past half-century, professionals have also become increasingly concerned with motor-skill issues in older citizens.

Although most readers of this text will be particularly interested in how these areas relate to sport-skill acquisition and performance, we should also be aware that there is great interest in how youngsters hold a pencil while learning to write, how a dentist learns to control a drill while looking in a mirror, how students learn to type using a computer keyboard, or how pilots learn to fly airplanes (Thomas & Thomas, 2002). Motor behavior, therefore, is concerned with a whole range of physical activities that have implications for healthy development and work, as well as sport and recreation.

Motor learning and control have formed a clear family of scientific interests since the early 1970s. Researchers in motor learning seek to understand the processes through which motor skills are developed and the factors that facilitate or inhibit skill development (Shea, Shebilske, & Worchel, 1993).

Under what conditions do children best acquire sport skills?

Researchers in motor control seek to understand how motor skills are actually executed and what factors lead to the breakdown of such skills. Motor development might be thought of as a first cousin. Researchers in motor development seek to understand the hereditary basis of motor development and the environmental factors that facilitate or inhibit such development.

How do children and youths learn motor skills? How are those skills executed? How do developmental processes interact with the learning and performance of motor skills? These are the questions that tend to make these scientific disciplines a family. The questions are particularly important in three developmental stages: childhood, adolescence, and old age. It is easy to recognize the importance of an integrated understanding of how children develop and execute motor skills, and what factors facilitate or inhibit skill development and execution, but it is becoming increasingly important to understand how the process of aging affects motor-skill development and performance.

Professionals in sport, fitness, and physical education share a common interest in motor-skill performance and learning. Learning to perform motor skills well is prerequisite to achieving goals in all three areas. Can the child learn to skip, jump, and throw overhand? Will the adolescent student learn how to lift the weight bar properly? Can the basketball player learn appropriate defensive technique? Will the students be able to master the two-hand backhand shot in tennis? How will the students' performance capabilities change as they move through puberty? At what age can a young child begin to learn sport skills? How can an inappropriate technique be replaced with a more appropriate one? These questions are at the heart of the day-to-day life of professionals in sport, fitness, and physical education.

Researchers in motor learning, motor control, and motor development work to provide good answers to these practical questions, as well as to develop and refine theories within their fields. As with many fields, the link between theory and practice is not always strong or direct, a concern that periodically resurfaces within both the practitioner and the researcher communities. Nonetheless, the motor-learning, -control, and -development subdisciplines of physical education have grown and prospered since the early 1970s and are now firmly rooted within the sport, fitness, and physical-education sciences.

Motor learning and motor control tend to make up two branches of the traditional field of motor-skill acquisition. Motor development has had a separate history but remains linked to motor learning and control in fundamental ways. The kinds of questions asked within each of these three areas are obviously interrelated:

Good physical education presents challenges that lead to real accomplishments.

- Should practice trials be massed together or spaced over time?
- How does the quality of information in knowledge of results affect skill acquisition?
- How does a performer plan a complex, coordinated skill response?
- What stages does a child go through in learning to run?
- How does eye–hand coordination develop in children?
- Can mentally rehearsing a skill enhance performance?
- How can practice conditions best prepare an athlete for game play?
- How do performers visually track objects so as to catch or hit them?
- Are there gender differences in learning and performing skills?

To the extent that there may be definitive answers to those and other questions, the professional basis of teaching and coaching will be greatly enhanced. These areas have become part of the coursework typically done by teachers and coaches working toward certification—and it is easy to see why.

DEFINITION OF MOTOR BEHAVIOR AS A FIELD OF STUDY

Motor learning, control, and development have their historical roots in the discipline of psychology, defined broadly as the study of human behavior and development. Traditionally, psychology has been concerned with the effects of both heredity and environment on human development and behavior. The effects of the environment typically fall under the study of *learning,* which can be defined as a relatively permanent change in performance resulting from experience or practice (Kerr, 1982). Sport, fitness, and physical education are concerned primarily, but not exclusively, with the acquisition and refinement of motor or physical skills, defined as muscular actions directed toward the achievement of a goal. *Motor learning,* therefore, is a relatively permanent change in the performance of a motor skill, resulting from experience or practice. The motor skill can be as basic as a young child learning to climb and as complex as a highly trained basketball player performing intricate maneuvers in a constantly changing game.

Most motor-skill tasks initially involve perception of an object, especially visual perception (as in hitting a ball or striking an object). Thus, interest in perception accompanied the development of interest in skill acquisition. In fact, in many places, the field is referred to as *perceptual–motor learning.* The interest in the perceptual aspects of motor-skill learning and performance continue to the present day.

As psychology developed in the mid–twentieth century, it turned more and more of its attention to the underlying mechanisms associated with human behavior and development. Researchers in sport, fitness, and physical education began to focus on the processes underlying movement and skill performance. A major focus in this area is how the nervous system controls the muscular system to produce skilled movement. This focus has resulted in a strong emphasis on the cognitive basis of motor skill, and on how the underlying cognitive processes are organized and used to control skilled movement. This relatively more recent area is referred to as *motor control.* The emphasis here is still on learning, but more so on the underlying processes that accompany learning.

The field of motor development focuses on how the learning and performing of motor skills changes across the lifespan. Within motor development are both the study of how heredity influences motor development and performance and the study of how differences in motor development and performance may be explained among age groups. Motor development has roots in developmental psychology and child development. Researchers in motor development have been vitally interested in young children and their stages of development and in how growth and maturation affect motor-skill acquisition and performance.

Motor learning and motor control are fairly narrow fields of specialization, conducted almost exclusively in universities in departments of physical education, sport science, or psychology. There are no direct, applied motor-learning practitioners. Indirectly, of course, teachers and coaches represent the applied practice of motor learning.

In motor development, the link between research and practical use of that research is closer. Elementary physical-education teachers, preschool specialists, and, increasingly, infant-stimulation specialists all directly apply knowledge generated in the research field of motor development. Motor-development knowledge is also of great importance to the professional in adapted physical education. Often, behavioral deficits of disabling conditions involve development delays in motor patterns. Thus, the adapted-physical-education specialist teaches basic motor patterns to individuals with disabilities.

Knowledge from motor development is used widely in the entire field of early childhood development. During infancy and early childhood, a child's mental, physical, social, and emotional development are intimately related to and dramatically grounded in movement. A child's exploration of his or her world and the child's sensory development all depend on movement. Thus, cognitive and emotional development are intimately related to motor development in these early stages.

> The early childhood years, from birth to approximately seven, should be filled with exciting and challenging movement experiences. During this time children master hundreds of new motor skills: these movement experiences are the basis of all learning and constitute the child's first language. (Boucher, 1988, p. 42)

The rapid increase of participation in child and youth sport has also captured the attention of motor-development specialists. Even more recently, there have been attempts to develop systematic skill- and fitness-development programs for infants. Here, too, motor-development specialists have much to do in investigating such efforts and much to say about appropriate practices that respect what is known about developmental stages.

DEVELOPMENT OF MOTOR BEHAVIOR

Psychology developed as a science in the late nineteenth century. Early in its development, researchers explored the learning of motor skills. Sometimes, using infrahuman subjects such as chimpanzees, psychologists did basic research on learning, using motor-skill acquisition as the focus. In other instances, such as the early studies of the acquisition of telegraphy skills using Morse code, there was a direct, applied interest in motor skills.

When physical education developed as a full-fledged professional field in the early twentieth century, researchers began to show interest in how motor skills were learned and how the various developmental stages affected skill performance and fitness. Concepts such as general motor ability (GMA) were developed, researched, and widely discussed. Early research by physical educators often tried to relate general motor ability to motor-skill acquisition, much in the same way as educators attempted to link the intelligence-quotient (IQ) measure with learning in schools (Sage, 1984). The major publishing outlet for this work was the *Research Quarterly*.

The period of most important growth for the field of motor learning was during and just after World War II. During that time, government agencies funded many projects aimed at better understanding of and training in a wide range of perceptual and motor skills. Those important wartime tasks had to do with sighting and identifying enemy planes at great distances, tracking quickly moving objects so as to shoot at them, operating the controls of airplanes, and designing display panels that would provide the necessary cues and information for quick, dependable responses from pilots, navigators, and gunners (Sage, 1984).

When physical-education departments grew rapidly during the baby-boom era, motor learning had already become a standard subject of study for the preparation of teachers in the field. When the discipline of kinesiology was created in the 1960s (see Chapter 3), motor behavior emerged as one of its subdisciplinary areas. During that period, motor-learning research was oriented primarily toward task problems and environmental variables, such as massed versus distributed practice schedules, the type and amount of feedback provided a learner, and motivational variables. Two new journals, *Perceptual and Motor Skills* and the *Journal of Motor Behavior*, became primary outlets for research in the field.

During the 1970s, however, many researchers began to show interest in the underlying *processes* that accompany the more visible task attributes of motor learning. That was the beginning of the area now referred to as *motor control*. Rather than manipulate environmental variables, such as feedback, to investigate their effects on the task performance, motor-control researchers began to look instead at the underlying cognitive processes and at the nervous system's interaction with the muscular system to produce skilled movement.

To investigate aspects of motor control, researchers needed to extend their work beyond the traditional boundaries of psychology. Fields such as neuropsychology, neurophysiology, cognitive psychology, biomechanics, and computer science all contributed to the emerging field of motor control (Christina, 1987). Today, the fields of motor learning and motor control are equal partners in the general area of perceptual–motor development.

Motor learning and sport psychology emerged together as subdisciplines in physical education. The first American organization embracing these two areas was the North American Society for the Psychology of Sport and Physical Activity (NASPSPA). Both areas looked to psychology as a parent discipline, so it was not surprising that they linked together organizationally. NASPSPA still exists as a coalition of motor-learning and sport-psychology specialists, even though the two areas have become distinct subdisciplines with their own organizations and journals.

Motor development is the study of motor growth and performance changes that are due to heredity rather than to environmental influences. Motor development has always been a special area within developmental psychology. As physical education grew into a specialized, professional field in the early twentieth century, motor development slowly emerged as a focus within the field. Motor development often divides into strongly related fields: (1) growth and (2) perceptual–motor development. Issues surrounding physical and motor growth have long held the interest of researchers from a number of fields. Longitudinal studies of growth and development are among the most famous and important in twentieth-century psychological and educational research. Following in that tradition, physical educators conducted similar studies. For example, the Wisconsin Growth Study focused on annual measurement of a variety of anthropometric, strength, and motor-performance items for boys and girls from ages 7 through 12 years; also, the Medford,

Oregon, Boys Study followed a group of boys from ages 7 through 18 years (Clarke, 1986).

In addition to examining physical characteristics associated with development, researchers and practitioners have been interested in developing motor behavior, such as walking, climbing, jumping, throwing and catching. As physical education for elementary-school children became more available through specialist teachers, this aspect of the motor-development field became extremely important to practitioners, spurring new interest in the field.

Early-childhood education and elementary education did not develop as distinguishable fields until the end of the nineteenth century. Only in the twentieth century did people generally recognize childhood as a unique stage, asserting that children are not miniature adults. As children grow, develop, and learn, they need to be treated in ways that respect their changing developmental status. Teachers, coaches, and child-care workers need to know how best to help young children to acquire and refine skills and to build and maintain fitness. It is at this nexus that the fields of motor learning, motor control, and motor development come together to form a coherent subdisciplinary focus within physical education.

CURRENT STATUS OF MOTOR BEHAVIOR

Motor learning, control, and development are now distinct subject areas within the broad spectrum of the sport and physical-education sciences. Most teacher-certification programs in physical education require at least one course in motor learning and one in motor development. Motor control is typically treated within the motor-learning course. At the graduate level, motor learning, motor control, and motor development have emerged as distinct areas of specialization, especially at the doctoral level.

Motor learning and motor control have developed into highly specialized research fields with strong ties to experimental psychology and neuropsychology. The links between research in these areas and the practices of teaching and coaching have weakened considerably since the mid-1980s. (See discussion of this issue later in this chapter.) Motor development, on the other hand, has strong, direct links to the practices of early-childhood education, elementary physical education, and adapted physical education. Much has been learned about the advantages of early-childhood education and the influence that early learning has on behavior throughout life. Many fitness problems among adults, for example, are traceable to problems that developed and habits that were established during early childhood. These links between experiences in childhood and lifestyles as adults have fostered growing interest in motor development.

Parents concerned about the early development of their children have also shown increased interest in popular literature on motor and physical devel-opment. As with all areas of popular interest, there is a high risk of fads and misinformation. Thus, researchers and professionals in motor development also have a strong interest in disseminating accurate public information, especially as it relates to proposed programs of infant stimulation and early-childhood motor and fitness training.

The major areas of study within motor learning, control, and development are broadly based. Some of those areas and associated typical questions are shown in Table 16.1. As the fields of motor learning, control, and development grow and mature, we should expect that they will be able to speak to wider audiences. Many of the topics shown in Table 16.1 are of interest to groups other than sport, fitness, and physical-education professionals. For example, the areas of physical rehabilitation, gerontology, architecture, industrial technology, and early-childhood education all might have reason to seek answers to

TABLE 16.1 Areas of Study within Motor Behavior	
Area	Typical Questions Asked
Motor learning	How do the frequency and timing of feedback influence skill acquisition and maintenance?
	How does skill performance change as it becomes more automatic?
	How does fatigue interfere with performance and learning?
	How does aging affect memory in motor-skill learning and performance?
Motor control	What series of cognitive steps does a beginner go through when acquiring a skill?
	How does the plan for executing a skill change from beginning to advanced levels of performance?
	What is the nature of the human information-processing system that stores and retrieves information for use in skill performance?
	How are verbal instructions for skill learning translated into images used by performers?
Motor development	At what age can a child safely benefit from cardiovascular training?
	What developmental stages do children go through as they learn to throw, catch, and strike objects?
	At what age or developmental status can young learners use mature motor forms?
	How is early motor stimulation related to the development of intelligence and thinking?

problems that fall within the scope of the motor-learning, motor-control, and motor-development subdisciplines. Professionals in physical rehabilitation need to understand motor-control information as they seek to help people regain full use of limbs and motor functioning. Gerontologists need to know how memory and motor-skill performance change in older people. The architect needs the motor-development specialist to design appropriate play spaces, and the industrial technologist needs him or her to develop play equipment.

The field of motor development may be beginning a period of substantial growth. Issues surrounding child care and early-childhood education are emerging important political forces in America. We should expect that by 2005 or so, major legislation supporting child care and early-childhood education will be enacted at both the federal and the state levels. When that happens, the expertise and information available in motor development will be widely sought, new programs will develop, and many new people will be attracted to the field.

What Do Specialists in Motor Behavior Do?

Motor-learning and motor-control specialists work almost exclusively in academic positions in universities, usually in sport-science, physical-education, or psychology departments. Motor-development specialists are mainly employed in universities too, in similar departments, but there are increasing opportunities for them in private industry and in child care and early-childhood education.

Motor-learning and motor-control specialists typically teach and do research, performing little direct clinical application of their expertise. Motor-development specialists teach, do research, and provide clinical services through infant and early-childhood motor-development programs. Since the mid-1980s, motor-development specialists have also become more involved in areas such as playground safety, playground design, and play-equipment design. It is also increasingly common to find university faculty positions that require expertise in both motor development and elementary physical edu-

cation. Most students who seek advanced degrees specializing in elementary physical education or teacher education have cognate training in motor development.

How Does a Person Prepare to Be a Specialist in Motor Behavior?

Specializations in any of these three areas are not typically available at the undergraduate level. Some master's-degree programs do provide specialization in these areas, but it is much more common for such specialization to occur only at the doctoral level.

There are two paths to specialization in motor learning and motor control: the path through physical-education or sport-science undergraduate preparation, and the path through preparation in psychology. Graduate specializations in these areas are available in both sport-science and psychology departments in many universities. The degrees are similar in that they require substantial in-depth study of psychology, statistics, and research design. The degrees differ in the amount of work demanded in related sport-science areas.

Motor development is more typically a specialization in graduate programs of physical education. It sometimes has a pedagogical emphasis and sometimes a sport-science emphasis. Graduate study in the area requires substantial coursework in related areas such as psychology, neuropsychology, physical anthropology, research methods, and statistics. Although they are now frequent, we should expect that more professionally oriented master's-degree programs in motor development will emerge as programs in child care and early-childhood education develop nationally.

CURRENT ISSUES AND PROBLEMS IN MOTOR BEHAVIOR

Within any scientific discipline, there are numerous issues and problems relating to questions of theoretical and methodological importance. These problems, however, are seldom of interest to people who are not members of the discipline. From a broad perspective, one major issue has always been present in motor learning: the relationship between research in motor learning and control and the practices of teaching and coaching.

Motor learning developed in physical education with a strong link to psychology. Most of the language and concepts of early motor learning were drawn from psychology. As the field developed, it turned quickly to psychology for its theoretical directions, its concepts, and the language it used to discuss issues. From the inception of the field as a subdiscipline, questions were raised about its relevance to teaching and coaching. Responding to a research paper in 1969, psychologist Robert Simon spoke directly to the issue:

> Certainly we know quite a lot about information feedback, and certainly Bilodeau and Jones know more than most of us. And, yet, if I try to look at their paper through the eyes of a physical education teacher or coach, I find very little there which I would be able to apply in teaching someone a particular athletic skill. (cited in Smith, 1970, pp. 24–25)

Five years later, in 1975, the same problem was addressed by motor-learning expert Robert Wilberg, who suggested that the field had completely lost track of its professional counterparts in physical education and sport and that the language of motor learning had become "so filled with 'jargon' that the less well informed professional members have no idea about what we are doing, what we are saying, and where we are going" (Wilberg, 1975, p. 215).

As research and theory in motor learning and control have grown more sophisticated, the problem of application to sport coaching and physical-education teaching has grown more rather than less severe. Recently, however, motor-learning scholars are beginning to rethink their relationship to sport and physical education, not only because of the problem of applying the findings from their research, but also because they recognize that in sport and physical education, they may be able to build better theories. In 1987 Christina criticized the view that good science always proceeds from theory to practice, rather than the relationship being bidirectional:

> Allowing this kind of thinking to guide our research efforts these past 15 years, we have suppressed applied research . . . and isolated it from basic research. . . . This is truly unfortunate because, by suppressing applied research, we have not only ignored its potential for helping practitioners find solutions to their practical problems but have overlooked the special potential it has for assisting basic research in its attempt to build a body of theory-based motor learning knowledge. (Christina, 1987, p. 36)

A corollary to this is a debate that has gone on within this subdiscipline since the mid-1980s: whether there should be more applied research in motor behavior (Thomas & Thomas, 2002). Most research has been done in laboratories to enable investigators to control conditions such as subjects, treatments, and measurement protocols. Applied research is much less easy to control; therefore, results may be more ambiguous. Christina (1989) provided a summary of this debate and suggested solutions. It would appear that the favored approach now is to develop principles in the laboratory setting, then test them in applied settings.

The debate within motor learning and motor development—and between these fields and sport pedagogy—is valuable. A 1990 (Volume 42) issue of *Quest* was devoted to the debate, which at times becomes quite heated as proponents of various positions prosecute their cases. Professional and scholarly debates such as these, however, are simply part of how academic life is lived and how knowledge advances. It is important that these fields coalesce in the future and work together on common problems.

In the field of motor development, debate continues concerning the degree to which heredity or environment can be linked to developmental changes. The nature–nurture question is difficult to answer satisfactorily; in trying to answer it, however, researchers and practitioners have found many effective new ways to help children develop more completely.

We should expect that, in the future, the field of motor development will focus more on aging populations, where decrements in motor performance will become the main focus. What causes these decrements to happen? How can they be forestalled? These are important questions in a nation where the aging population continues to grow both because of new members and because of longer lifespans.

SUMMARY

1. *Motor learning* is the study of how changes in motor performance are acquired as the result of experience and practice.

2. *Motor control* is the study of how the nervous system controls the muscular system and of the cognitive processes underlying motor-skill acquisition.

3. *Motor development* is the study of motor-growth and motor-performance changes that occur across the lifespan, with a special focus on growth and maturation and developmental stages.

4. The theory–practice linkages are much stronger in motor development than in motor learning or motor control.

5. Motor learning and motor development have long histories within physical education, whereas motor control emerged in the era of the physical-education subdisciplines.

6. Research and training monies made available during World War II greatly increased the attention to perceptual–motor learning and training.

7. Knowledge from these three areas is used widely in fields outside sport, fitness, and physical education, including physical therapy, gerontology, architecture, industrial technology, and early-childhood education.

8. Motor-learning and motor-control specialists work almost exclusively in universities as professors, mostly in departments of physical education and occasionally in departments of psychology.

9. Motor-development specialists work in universities in specialized areas or within teacher-education faculties; they also can find work in the private sector, especially in equipment design.

10. Preparation for these areas is done at the doctoral level in departments of physical education, sport science, or psychology.

11. The theory–practice gap in motor learning and control has widened; this gap is the major issue in the field.

12. In motor-development research, the nature–nurture issue continues to be debated.

13. We can expect that the study of motor development will contribute substantially to gerontology.

DISCUSSION QUESTIONS

1. Which of these fields is most relevant to physical education? Which is most relevant to sport? Which is most relevant to fitness?

2. What kind of background best suits a person who wishes to enter graduate study in these fields?

3. If you were having a difficult time teaching a motor skill to a young child, which of these fields would provide helpful information?

4. Where in your region can these fields be studied as graduate specializations?

5. In what ways might these fields become more important as lifespan involvement of the general public becomes more of a reality? How might infants and the aged lead different lifestyles, compared with the lifestyles that are common among most adults today?

CHAPTER 17

Sport Sociology

Despite the magnitude of the public's commitment to sport, as a social phenomenon it has received little serious study. The ubiquitous presence of sports has largely been taken for granted by social scientists and physical educators alike. A clear description, let alone explanation of this social force, is largely nonexistent. Many of its manifest and most of its latent functions have been ignored. For the physical educator, sport provides a medium for pursuing educational goals. For almost anyone else it probably serves quite different purposes. In neither case is its social significance understood. Therefore, we urge the development of a "sociology of sport" as a division of an academic discipline.

Gerald Kenyon and John Loy, in their landmark article "Toward a Sociology of Sport," which appeared in 1965

LEARNING OBJECTIVES

- To define the field of sport sociology
- To differentiate among play, games, and sport
- To discuss the questions studied in this field
- To describe how information from this field is used

- To describe the preparation for entering this field
- To discuss current problems and issues in this field

You probably grew up with an interest in sport and tend to take sport for granted. Sport is a basic part of your life, and you would have difficulty imagining what everyday life would be like without it. Most people in Western industrialized societies take sport for granted. It is just *there,* part of the fabric of daily, weekly, and seasonal life. As sport sociologist Ricky Gruneau has explained, sport is to be lived and enjoyed but not often analyzed.

> They (People in Western societies) live in a world where exposure to sport in one form or another is inescapable, but they rarely question sport's existence or see it posing problems which require anything more than superficial explanations. Sport is something that may be enjoyed, played, worked at, discussed or even disliked, but it is not something that is systematically analyzed, criticized or understood in its broader context. (Gruneau, 1976, p. 8)

Even in academic communities, this lack of interest in the deeper meanings of sport has been the norm. From time to time, scholars have attempted to examine and analyze sport, but those rare efforts have not been well received in academic communities and are virtually unknown to the public.

In the 1960s and 1970s, this traditional neglect of sport as a subject of inquiry and analysis began to change. One development that brought about this change was the emergence of the field of sport sociology. In the 1960s and 1970s, scholars within physical education and sociology began to ask questions using the research strategies of sociology. The questions in the realm of sport sociology are often of substantial interest not only to specialists but also, increasingly, to sport fans.

- Does participation in sport build character?
- Do minority athletes become more fully integrated into the dominant culture than do their nonathlete peers?
- How are children socialized through sport?
- How does the structure of professional sport affect participation?
- How does television affect sport institutions?

Cultural differences in sport are topics for sport sociologists.

- How do various sport subcultures differ?
- How has increased sport opportunity affected the social and economic status of women?

The answers to questions such as these are of interest both to sport sociologists and to coaches, administrators, parents, and teachers, among others. As the disciplines of physical education and sport emerged in the 1960s, sport sociology quickly became one of their most important components.

DEFINITION OF SPORT SOCIOLOGY AS A FIELD OF STUDY

Sociology is a discipline that focuses primarily on social organization, social practices, and social behavior. Sociology has been an accepted scientific discipline for more than 100 years. *Sport sociology* focuses on the "shared beliefs and social practices that constitute specific forms of physical activity (e.g., sport, exercise)" (Harris, 2000, p. 209). Sport sociologists examine basic social units, such as individuals, groups, institutions, societies, and cultures. They also examine social processes, such as socialization, social control, stratification, social conflict, and social changes (McPherson, 1981).

The subdiscipline of sport sociology has historically focused primarily on sport, but more recently there has been a growing interest in social phenomena in the area of exercise, particularly how society views and influences perceptions of the body and how it should look. Thus, it is not uncommon for sport sociologists to consider the fitness room or the health club, not just the playing field or the coaching office, as a place to do research.

Sport sociologists conduct their investigations in the real worlds of sport and exercise. They don't study player–coach relations or aerobic exercise in a laboratory but, rather, in the places where those things occur in society. They do so through surveys, interviews, thematic analysis of materials such as newspapers or the content of television coverage of sport, long-term observation in places where sport and exercise occur (called ethnography), theoretical analysis of trends in society, and historical analysis of changes in trends (Harris, 2000).

Sport sociology is typically defined, analyzed, and investigated within those definitional boundaries. Yet there is a broader sense of sport sociology, too. In the twentieth century, people recognized that sport is fundamental to the cultural fabric of organized, industrialized societies. Thus, not only was a sociology of sport created, but sport also was recognized more frequently in the larger analyses of basic social processes. In other words, sport not only became the main focus of a group of scholars known as sport sociologists but also began to be mentioned as an important factor when sociologists investigated and explained fundamental cultural processes. For example, in the twentieth century, world-famous sociologists such as Thorstein Veblen, George Herbert Mead, Max Weber, and David Reisman included sport as part of their general theories of culture. Sport is simply too important to be ignored in analyses of culture, and most scholars have come to recognize that fact.

Sport sociology, therefore, is typically defined within boundaries that derive from the parent discipline of sociology; however, laypeople's interest in topics that would typically fall within the parameters of sport sociology develops from the experience of sport, both as participants and as spectators.

As sport becomes more highly institutionalized, does it lose its playfulness?

People recognize that sport is a social phenomenon and that it is part of a society—not a hypothetical society, but a particular society. Thus, to understand high school football in Texas or ice hockey in Minnesota or ocean sports in Australia, one has to understand them in the context of the particular culture.

Although the term *sport* is used in the label of this subdiscipline, the actual focus of study is considerably broader than laypeople might assume. In fact, sport sociologists have been among the leaders, along with sport philosophers, in helping to clarify a group of related terms that, together, better define this area of interest: *play, games,* and *sport.*

The concept of *play* is of major importance in sport sociology, as it is in a number of related fields. What is play? How does it relate to games and sport? Most experts use the work of the Dutch scholar Johan Huizinga as a starting place for defining this concept. Huizinga argued that play is a fundamental impulse in human behavior.

Summing up the formal characteristics of play we might call it a free activity standing quite consciously outside "ordinary" life as being "not serious," but at the same time absorbing the player intensely and utterly. It is an activity connected with no material interest, and no profit can be gained by it. It proceeds within its own proper boundaries of time and space according to fixed rules and in an orderly manner. (Huizinga, 1962, p. 13)

Child's play is typically spontaneous, carefree, loose, and changeable; it is governed by rules, albeit rules that the children constantly change. Adult play, on the other hand, is more typically rule governed and requires more preparation and training.

Games are structured, organized, rule-governed forms of play that have a specific purpose and a means for attaining that purpose. French sociologist Roger Caillois (1961) developed a model for games that is widely used in sport sociology and based on the fundamental playful motivation in the game. He recognized (a) *competitive games,* such as football, chess, and racing; (b) *games of chance,* such as roulette, poker, lotteries, and betting; (c) *games involving mimicry or pretense,* such as theater, imitations, and the wearing of masks; and (d) *games that stress vertigo,* such as skiing and playing on a teeter-totter. Games can be loosely organized and flexible, with rules changing often, or they can become more institutionalized, with rules generally adhered to by all players.

Sport is typically seen as a physically active, competitive game that has become highly institutionalized. Sport has rules, histories, records, and governing bodies. Sports are games and can be participated in playfully—thus the relationship among these three concepts. Gruneau (1976) has placed these concepts on a continuum that helps to show the definitional relationships among them (see Figure 17.1).

How the play, games, and sport of a culture affect the participants and the culture are the main topics that define sport sociology.

DEVELOPMENT OF SPORT SOCIOLOGY

Sport sociology was one of the earliest subdisciplines to emerge during the 1950s through the 1970s, when the discipline of physical education began. There was limited interest in the sociological

Figure 17.1   Relations among play, games, and sport
SOURCE: Adapted from Gruneau, 1976.

aspects of sport before that time, and there were a few publications of note, but the topic of sport was hardly of main interest in sociology. Sport sociologist George Sage (1979) reported that in surveys undertaken by the American Sociological Association in 1950 and again in 1959, so few sociologists listed sport as an area of teaching or research that it was not classified as a topic in that field.

By the 1970s, however, all that had begun to change. The International Committee on Sport Sociology had formed in 1964; by 1968 it had acquired representatives from twenty-seven countries. International conferences were held, attracting the interest of both sociologists and physical educators. The *International Review of Sport Sociology* began in 1966, later to become a quarterly journal in 1973. In 1968 the Big Ten Symposium on Sport Sociology was held; in 1969 an initial, major textbook appeared: Loy and Kenyon's *Sport, Culture, and Society.*

The sociology of sport started quickly and attracted many adherents. Early leaders in the field were typically sociologists with an interest in sport or physical educators trained in departments with strong science emphases (McPherson, 1981). In the 1970s, courses in sport sociology appeared in most universities, and specialized graduate training programs developed in a few. The second generation of sport sociologists prepared primarily in those young programs. The programs, housed almost exclusively in physical-education departments, required much

American football is not the only popular form of football in the world.

coursework in the cognate areas of sociology and social psychology. In the early and middle 1970s, the number of books published in the area increased, and several important journals began—namely, the *Review of Sport and Leisure,* the *Journal of Sport and Social Issues, Leisure Sciences,* and the *Journal of Sport Behavior.*

In the 1970s, the social dimensions of sport became, for the first time in America, a topic of considerable interest to the general public. Popular magazines, such as *Sports Illustrated,* published features on problems and issues in sport—for example, on gambling, on the plight of the black athlete, and on recruiting violations in collegiate sport. Popular books by and about athletes and sport began not only to be published but also to sell—Pete Axthelm's (1970) *The City Game,* David Meggyesy's (1971) *Out of Their League,* Harry Edwards's (1969) *The Revolt of the Black Athlete,* Larry Merchant's (1971) *And Every Day You Take Another Bite,* Don Schollander's (1971) *Deep Water,* and Glenn Dickey's (1974) *The Jock Empire,* to name a few. In 1976 the noted American author James Michener wrote a social critique of sport entitled *Sports in America,* indicating clearly the degree to which sport had become of interest to the general public.

This explosion of interest in sport as a topic for social analysis created a vast literature and a climate within which sport sociology prospered as an academic field of study in the late 1970s and early 1980s. AAHPERD formed a Sport Sociology Academy, national and international scientific congresses always include sections related to this area, and publishing opportunities continue to expand. Sport sociology remains today a vital part of the sport sciences.

CURRENT STATUS OF SPORT SOCIOLOGY

Sport sociology has emerged as a social science of sport. Some undergraduate programs in physical education (or kinesiology) require at least one course in this area, although it might be a sport-and-social-issues class rather than one defined by the discipline itself. Most programs believe that because sport plays an important role in culture, students need to understand how people are socialized in and through sport, how sport affects culture, and how an understanding of sport sociology can inform disciplinary education in kinesiology and professional practice in physical education. Specialization in sport sociology is typically limited to graduate programs, mostly at the doctoral level. A major concern among sport sociologists today is the dwindling job market for Ph.D.'s who specialize in this field and what that means for the future of sport sociology in undergraduate programs.

Problems in sport, and the public's awareness of those problems, increased markedly during the 1990s. People are genuinely concerned about issues such as the overemphasis on winning in youth sport, the forces that produce anorexia among too many young female athletes, the use of steroids to build strength, the use of drugs among professionals in sport, the recruiting scandals in collegiate sport, and the lack of minority representation in sport management. Clearly, these problems can be analyzed in a number of ways through the sport sciences, and sociological analysis is one way that seems most important to many interested sportspersons.

Since the early 1990s, a number of prominent sport sociologists have been influenced by the emergence of **critical theory,** a viewpoint that focuses on structural inequities in society and works to eliminate them through action-oriented programs known as *praxis.* Sage (1991), for example, has argued that the enhancement of performance among elite athletes has largely ignored the athlete and his or her own life agendas. Harris (1991) has offered a series of suggestions as to how the sport-training fields can be more sensitive to athletes by examining the social and ethical issues within which training and competition decisions are made.

The major areas of study within sport sociology have remained fairly consistent throughout the years. A list of those areas of study and of the typical related questions is shown in Table 17.1.

Research and commentary in the area of sport sociology have made sportspersons and the public more aware of important issues in sport that reflect societal concerns in areas such as discrimination and socialization. The average sportswriter or sport commentator today is more sensitive to these issues than were his or her colleagues of the previous gen-

TABLE 17.1 Areas of Study within Sport Sociology	
Area	Typical Questions Asked
Social class and sport involvement	How does social class affect sport participation?
	How does sport participation affect social mobility?
	How are social class and spectating related?
Team dynamics	How is team cohesiveness related to success?
	How are coach–player relationships related to player success and satisfaction?
	What are the characteristics of leadership on teams?
Sport and education	What role does sport play in school dynamics?
	Are school athletes better students than their peers are?
	To what extent do athletes get preferential academic treatment?
Sport and social processes	How do integrated sport teams affect player relationships and team success?
	How is spectating affected by economic swings?
	How do different sports socialize children differently?
Sport and social problems	How is aggressiveness treated in different sports?
	To what extent can sport participation decrease delinquency?
	Do professional sports stack athletes in positions by race?
Gender relations and sport	How does sport influence our views of male and female bodies?
	How do the media portray female bodies in sport?
	How does sport socialize boys and girls differently?
Global/national relations?	To what extent is there a global sport culture emerging?
	How does sport change national identity?

eration. Teachers and parents are also more knowledgeable about sport involvement, from both positive and negative points of view.

Sport sociologists make an important contribution by "taking on" issues that are controversial and getting to the root of certain problems of social organization and social identity in modern cultures. Their consistent attempts to analyze issues such as gender relations, racial discrimination, ethnicity, and social and personal views of exercise and the body have resulted in a deeper understanding of these important issues and an increased willingness to discuss them. Inevitably, much of this research and commentary deals with societal inequities that are rooted in differences of race, ethnicity, gender, and wealth. In one sense, it is fair to say that the field of sport sociology has acted as a "conscience" for the discipline of Kinesiology.

There is still much work to do. We see physical violence among the parents of youth-sport participants. We live with the commercialization of sport at many levels. The mass media covers sport and exercise more than ever, and we need examination of that coverage. As children's and youth sport continues to grow, we need to better understand how sport contributes to the positive or negative socialization of children.

What Do Sport Sociologists Do?

Sport sociologists are almost always employed in academic positions in colleges and universities. Thus, their primary job obligations are in teaching, research, and service within the university and surrounding communities, and in the professional worlds that define their academic interests. Sport sociologists are most often housed in departments of physical education, of sport sciences, or of sociology. If the departments have graduate programs, the faculty members are more likely to be regularly engaged in research and publication, with correspondingly lighter teaching responsibilities.

Sport sociologists often do field-based research, examining from different perspectives what is happening in various kinds of sport settings. Researchers tend to specialize in areas within the field,

defined either by the kind of problem in which they are most interested (e.g., the economics of professional sport and how it affects decisions about players) or by the kind of sport in which they are most interested (e.g., community-based youth sport or school sport). There is, however, no clinical application of sport sociology as there is in consulting sport psychology, where the specialist might work directly with individual athletes or teams.

How Does a Person Prepare to Be a Sport Sociologist?

There appear to be two paths to becoming a sport sociologist, but the paths seem to be closer together now than in the past. First, you can major in physical education or sport studies and go on to graduate school in a department that has a sport-sociology specialization. Second, you can major in sociology and seek graduate training in that area, but in a department that has a strong sport-sociology component. Of course, the two approaches can be mixed; for example, you could major in sociology and do graduate work in a sport-sociology area in physical education. It is unlikely, however, that graduate departments of sociology would accept students whose undergraduate major was in physical education.

Doctoral training will necessarily include a strong concentration of coursework in sociology, specialized coursework in sport sociology, and extensive preparation in research methods common to the social sciences. Employment after graduation will be almost exclusively in a college or university department, often teaching a variety of courses, but specializing in sport sociology.

CURRENT ISSUES AND PROBLEMS IN SPORT SOCIOLOGY

As with most other specialized fields, the problems and issues confronting sport sociology fall into two groups, those within the field and those between the field and its publics. Within the field of sport sociology, several persistent issues continue to be debated—namely, the degree to which scholarship can or should be value free, the degree to which research can or should be objective, the degree to which sport sociology should focus on basic research or applied research, and the combination of sport sociology and sport psychology.

From the beginning, many sport sociologists have suggested that research and scholarship within the field should be *value free*. Pioneering sport sociologists Gerald Kenyon and John Loy, in an important and influential early article, emphasized that scholarship in this new field should be fundamentally different from the professional tradition in physical education from which it developed: "The sport sociologist is neither a spreader of gospel nor an evangelist for exercise. His function is not to shape attitudes but to describe and explain them" (Kenyon & Loy, 1965, p. 38). This position, which reflects the traditional posture of scientific inquiry, has been questioned seriously by other scholars in the field (Sage, 1979), who suggest that all methods and positions have value implications and that these should be dealt with specifically, rather than the ability to achieve value-free research being assumed. General points of view within sociology tend to have strong political overtones, and these quasipolitical viewpoints often supersede the more theoretical and research-oriented questions being debated.

A companion issue to the value-free question is the degree to which social phenomena—the basic stuff of sport sociology—can be investigated objectively, using methods common to the natural sciences. A large portion of sport-sociology research has been conducted using methods similar to those of the natural sciences, but many people within the field question this approach and prefer to use methods that respond more to the subjectivity they believe characterizes human behavior. Some people think that the natural-science methods used for studying the physiology of sport or kinesiology are not appropriate for sociological analysis, whereas others believe that more subjective methods produce data and results that lack objectivity.

A third issue within the field is the extent to which sport sociology should be theory oriented or action oriented. In traditional academic life, it has been sufficient to produce knowledge and build theory. More recently, however, a number of approaches have emerged, the most prominent being *critical theory*, which emphasizes action and change in the social structures of society to bring about a more equitable and humane society. This debate affects both what is studied in the field and what is done with the results of research.

A related question, more typical of other fields, is whether sport sociologists should investigate research questions that arise systematically from theory or whether they should answer questions that arise from the practice of sport. Both types of research occur, of course, and each has its own particular value. The issue is one of emphasis. Traditionally, in most universities and scholarly fields, the emphasis has been on theoretically derived research rather than on practical research.

The problems and issues for sport sociology that tend to exist between the field and its many constituents (e.g., coaches, physical educators, sport commentators, sport journalists) have to do with problems in sport rather than in theory. The expectation here is that the sport sociologist will act as a social critic and even a social reformer. The many problems of youth sport, school sport, university sport, and professional sport (see Chapter 7 for a discussion of these problems) are of substantial interest to both the sport sociologists and the professional groups that might use their work. Therefore, these professional groups look to sport sociology for viewpoints and even answers to problems that are sometimes complex. This tends to create conflict within the academic field of sport sociology, where roles are seen differently and answers are not viewed in the same manner as they are in professional fields.

Sport sociology has expanded its focus into the social dimensions of exercise and fitness, and this represents a positive direction for research and understanding. The psychology of sport and exercise and the sociology of sport and exercise are often combined in the work of many professors. This has led to a hybrid field commonly referred to as "psych-soc." Many college and university departments are too small to hire specialized faculty in each of these fields, so that often a single faculty member has to teach in both areas. Often, they find that the two areas have much in common and that students are interested in the blending of the two fields in their coursework.

SUMMARY

1. Serious analysis and explanation of sport is a recent phenomenon, both in academic circles and in the world of sport.

2. *Sport sociology* seeks an understanding of basic social units and social processes in a variety of sport settings.

3. During the 1990s, sport not only was more completely analyzed within sport sociology but also was utilized by sociologists to explain and understand general cultural life.

4. *Sport, play,* and *games* are related constructs within sport sociology.

5. *Play* is activity that is voluntary, separate, uncertain, economically unproductive, and rule governed.

6. *Games* are structured, organized, rule-governed forms of play.

7. *Sports* are physically active, competitive games that have become institutionalized.

8. Sport sociology developed as a physical-education subdiscipline in the 1960s and 1970s.

9. A substantial, popular sport literature appeared in the 1970s, which helped to bring problems and issues in sport to the attention of the general public.

10. Sport sociologists typically are employed in universities, where they teach, do research, and provide related professional service.

11. Preparation for a career in sport sociology is completed at the doctoral level. Students may have either a physical-education or a sociology background.

12. Current issues within sport sociology are the degree to which scholarship can or should be value free, the degree to which investigations can or should be objective, and the degree to which investigations should be theory oriented or action oriented.

DISCUSSION QUESTIONS

1. To what extent are sportswriters and sport commentators in the popular media educated in sport sociology? Should they be knowledgeable in this area?

2. Why is it important to relate sport to culture and to examine the various ways culture influences sport?

3. Why is there neither a sociology of fitness nor a sociology of physical education?

4. Where in your region can you study sport sociology as a graduate area of specialization?

5. What are five questions about sport (or about fitness or physical education) that you believe merit attention within this field?

CHAPTER 18

Sport and Exercise Psychology

All types of physical activity involve a mental or psychological component as well as the more obvious physical component. This psychological component of physical activity is the focus of study in psychology of sport and exercise. Specifically, sport and exercise psychology focuses on the mental and behavioral processes of humans as they engage in physical activity.

Robin S. Vealey in *Introduction to Kinesiology*

LEARNING OBJECTIVES

- To define sport and exercise psychology
- To differentiate between the academic role and the consulting role
- To identify and discuss the questions researched in sport and exercise psychology
- To describe how consulting sport and exercise psychology is practiced
- To describe the preparation for entering this field
- To discuss current problems and issues in the field

Myths and superstitions about sport and exercise performance almost always have a psychological basis: A male player shaves his head before every contest as long as the team continues to win; a weight lifter trains by rotating through the workout in exactly the same pattern each day; sportscasters attribute changes in the ebb and flow of a contest to the teams being "up" or "down" or to the "momentum" having shifted.

Research and common sense agree that athletes and exercisers perform best when they are in an optimal performance zone, but how do they get there? What psychological strategies are helpful in achieving and sustaining peak performance? Sport and exercise psychology has been an active research field since the early 1970s. The field has also developed a substantial *consulting* capacity to individuals and teams. Its findings and techniques are even becoming better known to the general public through popular books that are meant to help weekend golfers or age-group swimmers. Indeed, much of what has been developed in sport and exercise psychology is also proving useful in the world of work as corporations and businesses try to help employees work better as teams or deal with stresses that inevitably accompany pressure situations, as they do in sport. Issues such as the following are of common interest to many:

- What is the optimal relationship between "getting up" (arousal) and performance?
- What techniques best help athletes to concentrate?
- How can *choking* (being so gripped with fear that performance falters) be treated?
- How can imagery be utilized to improve performance?
- What strategies are best to help injured players cope with rehabilitation?
- What effects does good sport and exercise performance have on self-esteem?

Both laypeople and professionals in physical education, sport, and exercise have long been interested in answers to questions like these. Many coaches, athletes, and trainers believe that the psychological aspects of training and competition are as important as the physical aspects. It is no surprise, therefore, that sport and exercise psychology has grown into one of the most popular of the subdisciplines of Kinesiology. We should also note that the knowledge and strategies developed in sport and exercise psychology have many applications other than elite sport. The elementary physical educator, the fitness trainer, the youth-sport coach, and a host of others deal with the psychological issues of their students, clients, or players.

DEFINITION OF SPORT AND EXERCISE PSYCHOLOGY AS A FIELD OF STUDY

Broadly speaking, *psychology* is the study of human behavior. A dominant focus of psychology has been the mental aspects of behavior; indeed, the field of *cognitive* psychology has become a strong subfield of the general field of psychology. Sport psychology is the application of psychology to issues and problems in the world of sport. A companion field, exercise psychology, has developed and is devoted to issues and problems in the fields of fitness, exercise, and physical activity.

The manner in which sport psychology and exercise psychology have developed indicates that there are two major approaches to the fields: the academic study of sport and exercise psychology and how the knowledge from the fields can be applied to those who are engaged in sport and exercise, typically through a consultant relationship. Psychologists who complete rigorous preparation programs in clinical psychology are licensed by states to do clinical practice in the field of psychology. Sport and exercise psychologists, on the other hand, are not licensed but in some cases can earn certification. Thus, it is appropriate to describe theirs as a consultant role rather than a clinical-practice role. The distinction is important. Certified sport psychologists can help athletes learn to do mental rehearsal, visualization, and goal setting, but when they encounter issues such as eating disorders or substance abuse, they should usually refer athletes to a physician or a licensed psychologist for other professional assistance.

The consulting sport psychologist uses psychological interventions to improve the performance of athletes and to increase their psychological well-being. Many national, international, professional, and collegiate sport programs now employ full-time staff sport psychologists, and many others retain sport psychologists on part-time consulting contracts. A national team in track and field, for example, might travel to an international competition with coaches, managers, trainers, strength specialists, a sport-medicine physician, and a sport psychologist. Some licensed clinical psychologists become sport psychologists. Sport psychologists may be trained originally in counseling psychology, but many are prepared in sport psychology and work in a consulting relationship with the team and athletes.

Some sport psychologists tend to focus primarily on the mental aspects of sport performance. They use imagery, mental rehearsal, and other such techniques with athletes. Other sport psychologists prefer to deal directly with the behavior of athletes, using techniques from the field of applied behavior analysis. These consultants focus on actual physical rehearsals, behavior-shaping strategies, and behavior-modification approaches. Many, of course, use techniques from both perspectives.

Successful coaches often have strong psychological skills.

In the 1990s, sport psychology and exercise psychology began to come together. This convergence will eventually result in changes in both curricula and clinical experiences in graduate programs, emphasizing health- and medicine-related topics, in addition to the more traditional sport-related topics. Given the current importance of public health policy and agendas in the nation, it will not be surprising if exercise psychology becomes more dominant as a potential professional field for those seeking ways to combine their interests in psychology and in physical activity.

In one sense, the academic and consulting approaches to sport psychology should work together, with each informing the other. One group is interested in *why people behave as they do* in sport settings. The other group is interested in *helping people to behave more effectively* in sport settings. There is no doubt that the two groups interact, often productively. As this chapter later shows, however, there is also tension between the two groups and concern that their interactions are not always as productive as they could be.

DEVELOPMENT OF SPORT PSYCHOLOGY

In 1925 the University of Illinois hired Coleman Griffith, a psychologist, to help coaches improve the performance of their players (Williams & Straub, 2001). Griffith wrote *Psychology of Coaching* in 1926 and *Psychology of Athletics* in 1928. He is rightfully considered to be the grandfather of sport psychology in America. Between that time and the 1960s, however, very little occurred to develop the field. The early history of sport psychology is closely related to that of motor learning (see Chapter 16), because people with a background in psychology could understand work in each of those developing fields. Whereas in Europe the two are still tightly intertwined, in the United States they have become distinct subdisciplines.

We could argue that the field of sport psychology was born in Rome in 1965 at the first International Congress of Sport Psychology, held just after the Rome Olympic Games. It was for purposes of organizing and administering that congress that the ISSP was founded. Three years later, the membership of the ISSP had reached 1,400 representing forty-seven nations (Antonelli, 1970).

The 1968 Olympic Games were held in Mexico City. Because of political and civil strife in Mexico at that time, it was decided that the second International Congress of Sport Psychology should be held in the United States, in Washington, D.C. To organize that meeting, the North American Society for the Psychology of Sport and Physical Activity (NASPSPA) was formed. This organization embraced the then still intimately related subdisciplines of motor learning and sport psychology.

The formation of NASPSPA marked the emergence of the first generation of sport psychologists in North America (Harris, 1987). Most of the professionals who were responsible for developing this field held doctoral degrees in physical education but had special interests in psychology and motor performance. Many of them had taken psychology courses as part of their doctoral training. It was this group that began to develop courses, and later programs, of sport psychology in North American universities.

In 1969 the Canadian Society for Psychomotor Learning and Sport Psychology (CSPLSP) was founded. The early members of NASPSPA and CSPLSP were primarily responsible for the development of the sport and exercise psychology research base and also for helping it to grow as a significant subdiscipline (Williams & Straub, 2001). In the 1970s, graduate students were able to prepare in emerging sport psychology programs at a number of universities in North America. By the 1980s, sport and exercise psychology had become very popular as a graduate specialization and undergraduate students were able to take courses in the field, both in physical-education departments and in psychology departments.

In 1985 the Association for the Advancement of Applied Sport Psychology (AAASP) was formed to promote applied research and to advance the idea of establishing qualifications and certification for sport psychologists (Williams & Straub, 2001). Another significant milestone in the development of the field came in 1987, when the large and influential American Psychological Association created Division 47, devoted to sport psychology. In 1991 AAASP created criteria for minimum professional training (see the box on page 352). Preparation to be a sport psychologist is strictly at the graduate level, and programs are now available in a number of universities. Students who meet the AAASP criteria and successfully undergo an extensive review process can be designated as "Certified Sport Psychology Consultant." Those with such certification and membership in AAASP and APA are approved to work with Olympic athletes and national teams and are listed on the U.S. Olympic Committee registry.

In the 1980s, *exercise psychology* developed as a companion field to sport psychology. The main focus of exercise psychology is to explain the "antecedents and consequences of exercise behavior" (Dishman & Buckworth, 2001). With the enormous interest in public health generated by the Surgeon General's report (see Chapters 1 and 8), it is no surprise that academics and professionals in the field of psychology would want to investigate both the conditions under which people do or do not exercise regularly and the effects that physical activity has on psychological well-being. Dishman and Buckworth (2001) suggest that research currently coalesces in four areas; exercise and mental health, anxiety and depression, sleep, and self-esteem. We should expect that sport psychology and exercise psychology will converge to a certain extent and that both graduate school curricula and clinical experiences will change as a result to accommodate interests in both areas.

At the university level, sport and exercise psychology is still a *graduate* enterprise. Although undergraduate courses exist in many programs, it is not possible to specialize in sport and exercise psychology at the undergraduate level. Increasingly, graduate specialization in sport and exercise psychology tends to blur the lines between psychology and physical-education departments. At this point,

it is unclear where the sport and exercise psychologist of the future will be trained. The choice of department probably will hinge on the future of certification and licensing in sport and exercise psychology—issues that are addressed later in this chapter.

CURRENT STATUS OF SPORT AND EXERCISE PSYCHOLOGY

Sport and exercise psychology is a healthy field with a bright future. The emerging coupling of sport psychology and exercise psychology should serve to enhance that future and make the field even more attractive for both research and clinical practice. Still, that coupling has not yet been realized in many places, so the field is still described here primarily in terms of its sport-related focus.

There is no doubt that the field currently divides between people who *study* the psychological aspects of sport performance and people who *work with athletes* in the capacity of sport psychologists. The former are *academic sport psychologists,* the latter are *consulting sport psychologists.* A person does not have to be exclusively one or the other. Many sport psychologists work directly with athletes and still contribute to the emerging knowledge base through their research and scholarship.

Academic Sport Psychology

No field can develop and improve without an expanding knowledge base that is built on sound research and constantly improved theories. The development of a knowledge base through research and the continued refinement of theory are the province of the academic sport psychologist. This work is done predominantly in university settings in departments of physical education or of psychology.

Sport psychologist Dan Landers (1983) has argued that research in sport psychology can be divided into three stages. The first stage (1950 to 1965) was dominated by research on how the personalities of athletes related to performance. Ques-

TABLE 18.1 Topic Areas and Questions in Sport Psychology	
Topic Areas	Typical Questions Asked
Psychophysiological approaches	Can teaching cognitive skills to athletes help them to regulate physiological responses?
	What happens physiologically during mental-imagery practice?
	What physiological effects does anxiety have on novice and expert performers?
Psychobiological approaches	What causes a person to feel good during exercise?
	What occurs physiologically during the "runner's high"?
	Can sport exercise help to replace chemical dependency?
Self-regulation	Can athletes learn to be aware of and to control their internal systems?
	Can stress be controlled and used to improve performance?
Social psychology	What factors control role modeling in sport?
	How are cooperation and aggression related?
Exercise psychology	How does strength training affect body image and self-concept?
	Are exercise programs an effective intervention for people experiencing depression?

tions such as the following were researched: Do elite athletes have personalities different from those of average athletes? Do athletes in contact sports have personality traits different from those of athletes in noncontact sports? Can a winning personality be identified?

The second stage (1966 to 1976) was dominated by the borrowing of then-current theories from mainstream psychology, to test them in the sport setting; by the development of interactional approaches; and by the formulation of operant-conditioning models for sport. The third stage (1976 to the present) has focused more on developing information and theory directly derived from sport and on developing and refining psychological skills and strategies to enhance sport performance. Table 18.1 shows the topic areas and typical questions that are being investigated in academic sport psychology.

People who practice sport psychology by working directly with athletes or teams most often inte-grate their research with that practice. Thus, the kinds of problems addressed in practice-oriented research in sport psychology typically derive from the techniques used by psychologists. These techniques and strategies are described in Table 18.2.

Both academic and practice-oriented sport psychology have established themselves within the emerging sport sciences. Both have a bright future, both in integrative work with other sport sciences and in work directly related to the improvement of sport performance.

What Do Sport and Exercise Psychologists Do?

People who pursue academic sport psychology typically are employed in university programs, particularly those with graduate concentrations in this field. They teach classes in sport psychology, conduct research, and supervise graduate students. They may also, of course, practice sport psychology by working with teams or individual athletes.

Athletes need different types of precompetition preparation.

Since the 1970s, it has become increasingly clear that sport psychologists can help teams and individuals to improve their performance. Thus, professional teams and athletes, as well as national and international amateur teams and athletes, have employed people who can provide those services. When a national team travels, a practicing sport psychologist is likely to accompany it.

The consulting sport psychologist often fills two roles, although the roles can be filled by different individuals. One role utilizes psychological strategies with athletes to improve performance directly —the *performance-enhancement role.* Within this role, the sport psychologist might teach the athlete to relax during competition, to overcome a competitive fear, to cope with competitive stresses, or mentally to rehearse positive performances.

The second role, the *counseling role,* is less direct; it involves counseling athletes to help them to overcome problems, to adjust to situations, and to deal with stresses in their lives. Counseling an athlete to help that person adjust to and cope with a personal problem might affect her or his performance, but the relationship is indirect. Working with an injured athlete to help him or her adjust to not being able to regain the same competitive edge is another example of the counseling function of the sport psychologist.

In these two primary roles, the consulting sport psychologist focuses on distinct areas of assistance to coaches and athletes. One area is the immediate improvement of performance—for instance, by using mental imagery just before competition. A second area is helping athletes cope with the pressures of competition—for instance, using one of several relaxation strategies. A third area is assistance with injury rehabilitation, helping athletes to deal with both physical rehabilitation and the psychological stresses of not being able to participate. A more general focus is working with teams on general mental and behavioral preparation for a season of competition. The sport psychologist might also work with teams to improve communication among teammates and to resolve conflicts among players and between players and coaches.

Table 18.2 shows the kinds of psychological interventions in sport psychology, with descriptions and examples of each. These techniques have typically been well researched and have been shown to have significant effects with athletes.

The consulting sport psychologist can also collect information and offer advice on how to improve the use of time in practice, how to help individual athletes to improve skills, and how to motivate individuals and groups through individual and group behavior-modification strategies.

The counseling function of the consulting sport psychologist is less well documented in the sport-psychology literature. There is, of course, substantial information about counseling strategies and their effects in the *counseling-psychology* literature, but few studies have been conducted with

TABLE 18.2	Psychological Interventions Used with Athletes
Intervention	Description and Examples of Use
Relaxation training	Teach athletes to feel tension in muscles and to learn how to control release of tension. *Example:* Relax between events
Cue-controlled relaxation	Tie relaxation strategy to a word cue; allows the athlete to say the word to him- or herself to induce relaxation. *Examples:* Preparation for diving, free-throw shooting, putting in golf
Desensitization	Gradually reduce anxiety caused in specific competitive situations by teaching athlete to relax while imaging a series of increasingly aversive competitive situations. *Examples:* Fear of hitting head on platform in a back dive; fear associated with heights in climbing
Mental imaging	Teach athletes to rehearse mentally successful performance just before beginning the performance. *Examples:* High jump, swim races, wrestling
Coping strategies	Predict what events might intrude in preperformance time and during performance, and help athlete to develop and rehearse behavioral strategies to cope with and overcome those incidents. *Examples:* Rehearsing the specific procedures to follow when going to compete in a foreign land—how to cope with language, security, time, and food incidents; practicing what to do during an event if certain situations arise
Covert modeling	Teach athlete to imagine a model doing a particular performance as a means to help the athlete acquire that skill or ability. *Example:* Helping an athlete become more competitive in tense situations

teams or with individual athletes. Athletes are often young people who are going through important developmental stages within their own lives. This means they must cope with stresses related to family, school, work, and relationships, as well as those related to being athletes. Sport psychologists can often function as counselors to help athletes deal with these personal problems, thus allowing the athletes to devote their full attention to the athletic performance.

A second area for the counseling function is enhancing the relationships among athletes on a team and between athletes and their coaches. Here, too, the sport psychologist can fulfill an important counseling function. First, the sport psychologist can observe interpersonal situations that seem to be developing inappropriately and can intervene carefully to alter those situations before they become problems. Second, once problems do arise, the sport psychologist can counsel athletes, suggest solutions, and provide support for the parties involved.

How Does a Person Prepare to Be a Sport Psychologist?

There are three primary paths that can lead to a career in sport psychology: graduate training in sport psychology, training in clinical psychology, and training in counseling psychology. Currently, no special license or certification is needed to practice sport psychology. The Psychological Advisory Committee of the United States Olympic Committee has defined minimum educational and experiential requirements for people working with Olympic teams in the capacity of sport psychologist (Feltz, 1987). The United States Olympic Committee guidelines reflect credentials for applied sport psychology developed by the Association for the Advancement of Applied Sport Psychology (AAASP) and membership in the American Psychological Association (see the box below).

The vast majority of academic and consulting sport psychologists have doctoral degrees. Thus, the path to a career in sport psychology almost always involves acquiring a doctorate. In a survey, Feltz (1987) reported that most sport-psychology doctoral programs are in departments of physical education (even though the name of the department might be more clearly associated with the sport sciences). Students who enter sport-psychology doctoral programs in such departments but do not have a background in physical education typically are required to address their deficiencies in that field. However, Feltz also reported in the same survey that sport-psychology concentrations were beginning to appear in psychology departments.

Regardless of the department granting the doctorate, the student typically takes a large number of courses in psychology and in research methods. Increasingly, clinical experiences are part of the program requirements for the doctorate with an emphasis in sport psychology. Almost all programs that have sport psychology as the main emphasis are preparing students for a career in academic sport psychology, which is typically pursued by becoming a member of a university department.

Students who aspire to a career in sport and exercise psychology and think that they will work with a professional or national team probably have unrealistic expectations (Williams & Straub, 2001). However, there is some possibility that those trained in sport and exercise psychology will find employment in expanding sport-medicine clinics or in the corporate world. When you have acquired skills and understandings in team building, stress management, coping, and decision making under pressure, you have a capacity that can be utilized in the corporate world and in working with a team of other professionals on the staff of a sport-medicine clinic. A tracking study (Andersen et al., 1997) found that 59 percent of sport-and-exercise-psychology graduates held positions in university departments, 13 percent were in private practice, 9 percent were in research, and the remainder were

---

AAASP Criteria for Professional Training

A doctoral degree from an accredited institution of higher education and knowledge of:

1. Scientific and professional ethics and standards

2. Sport psychology subdisciplines of intervention/performance enhancement, health/exercise psychology, and social psychology

3. Biomechanical and/or physiological bases of sport

4. Historical, philosophical, social, or motor-behavior bases of sport

5. Psychopathology and its assessment

6. Basic skills in counseling

7. Skills and techniques within sport or exercise

8. Skills in research design and statistics, and psychological assessment

9. Biological bases of behavior

10. Cognitive bases of behavior

11. Social bases of behavior

12. Individual behavior

SOURCE: www.aaasponline.org.

spread among student services, teaching/coaching, and business.

The American Association of State Psychology Boards has recommended minimum standards for all doctoral programs in psychology. These standards include 3 years of full-time graduate study, with at least 1 year of continuous full-time residency at the university. The standards recommend that candidates receive a minimum of 6 semester hours of credit in each of four substantive areas: the biological bases of behavior, the cognitive–affective bases of behavior, the social bases of behavior, and individual differences. In addition, candidates are expected to master areas such as statistics, research design, professional ethics, psychometrics, and history of psychology.

The other two paths to sport psychology are through specific doctoral programs in clinical psychology or counseling psychology. All states have laws governing the certification or licensing of psychologists who provide psychological services to clients for a fee within those states. Thus, the exact provisions of a degree in clinical or counseling psychology are typically determined by state licensing and certification rules. Clinical and counseling psychologists receive a great deal of supervised practice as part of their preparation. They learn to do the things described in Table 18.2. If they have a background in or an interest in sport, they can apply those skills with teams or individual athletes. Psychologists associated with the growing field of sport medicine and housed in a sport-medicine facility are most often licensed clinical or counseling psychologists.

CURRENT ISSUES AND PROBLEMS IN SPORT PSYCHOLOGY

The two main issues in sport psychology currently are the split between academic and consulting sport psychologists and the related issue of licensing. In the mid-1980s, a definite split occurred in American sport psychology. Concerns were expressed that sport psychology had become too academic, too theory oriented, and not sufficiently grounded in the practice of sport. In 1985 the AAASP, was started; shortly thereafter, a new journal, the *Journal of Applied Sport Psychology,* appeared. As in many other fields, people who practiced sport psychology were concerned that their academic counterparts were not studying events and phenomena that would prove to be directly useful in their practices.

Within academic sport psychology, this general concern is also debated strongly. The issue tends to be the degree to which academic sport psychology should utilize theory and research from the parent discipline of psychology, as opposed to developing its own theory and research from the field of sport.

Since the late 1980s, sport psychology has moved to more applied work. Having firmly established their field as an academic subdiscipline, many sport psychologists have engaged in more practice-oriented research and have devoted more time to clinical services. This has resulted in increased tensions between those who have taken this route and those who believe that the theoretical research base of the field should remain the primary focus.

A consensus seems to be emerging within sport psychology that the field needs to be more firmly anchored in the sport and exercise sciences. This trend toward embedding sport psychology more firmly in the sport and exercise sciences will be further enhanced by the emergence of exercise psychology as a companion field. Indeed, the funds available for exercise-psychology research and the demand for professionals in exercise psychology will probably soon outpace the funding availability and job demands for sport psychologists, resulting in pressures to bring the two fields together. We can expect that the future sport and exercise psychologist will be more broadly prepared in areas such as nutrition, exercise physiology, and sport biomechanics.

The need for broader preparation relates closely to the issue of licensing and certification, which is typical of any newly emerging field in which specialized skills are offered to clients, often for a fee, in the hope of improving some aspect of the clients' lives. How can clients be protected from less-than-well-prepared people taking advantage of them?

What recourse does a client have if he or she is inappropriately treated? These kinds of questions are answered much more easily if the practitioner involved has had to pass a licensing or certification test, thus establishing minimum competency to practice within a field.

On the other hand, the tradition in European sport psychology is to teach these psychological skills directly to coaches—and it is the coaches who apply the skills to teams and athletes. There is no doubt that coaches can learn these techniques and can utilize them with athletes.

As sport psychology has emerged, the athletes and institutions that have felt the need to receive psychological services have tended to be in the elite category—professional golfers, Olympic-level teams, professional teams, and the like. These athletes and institutions have the resources to employ sport psychologists. Because of this financial incentive, many sport psychologists, and subsequently the field itself, have tended to focus on elite performance (Gill, 1991). There has been increasing debate within the field on this issue, with arguments that sport psychology needs to focus more on the individual athlete's total well-being than on performance enhancement and more on children and youths, or recreational participants, than on elite athletes.

When Davis Love III broke through to win his first major golf championship, one of the first people to whom he publicly expressed gratitude while holding the trophy on the eighteenth green was his sport psychologist, Dr. Robert Rotella—so important has sport psychology consulting become to many elite athletes. Many amateur sportspersons also want this assistance, and a ready market has developed to satisfy them, mostly in the form of magazine articles, books, and audiotapes.

Another important issue for the future of the field is the degree to which evidence supports claims that sport-and-exercise-psychology interventions are actually responsible for performance gains and other important outcomes. Recent reviews have shown that in forty five studies employing sport-and-exercise-psychology interven-

tions and training programs to enhance performance in competitive sport settings, 85 percent have found positive performance outcomes (Weinberg & Williams, 2001). What appears to be important in the successful studies is that the intervention must be individualized and systematic, carried out over time, as part of a total package. These very positive findings give strength to the further development of the field.

SUMMARY

1. *Sport psychology* is the study of human behavior in sport settings, with an emphasis on the mental aspects of behavior.

2. The two major subgroups are the academic study of sport psychology and the consulting practice of sport psychology.

3. Sport psychologists are not as yet licensed and have a variety of backgrounds, including physical education, sport science, counseling psychology, and clinical psychology.

4. Some sport psychologists focus primarily on the mental aspects of sport performance, whereas others focus more broadly on the psychological aspects of all behavior in sport settings.

5. Sport psychology developed as a distinct field during the era of growth of the physical-education subdisciplines.

6. Academic sport psychology focuses on research and the development of theory, whereas consulting sport psychology focuses on working directly with athletes to improve sport performance or athlete well-being.

7. Consulting sport psychologists have a repertoire of research-tested psychological interventions for working with athletes and teams.

8. The counseling function of sport psychology is less well documented but is becoming more important.

9. Paths to careers in sport psychology are graduate training in sport psychology, training in clinical psychology, and training in counseling psychology.

10. Career work in sport psychology requires a doctoral degree; licensing of sport psychologists probably will be required in the future.

11. Recently, a split has occurred within sport psychology. A new organization and journal have been developed for people whose primary interest is in consulting sport psychology directly with athletes.

12. Issues in the field include debates about whether licensing should be required, whether psychological work with athletes should be done by coaches or by specialists in sport psychology, whether the field should be more firmly anchored in the sport sciences, and whether it should focus less on elite athletes and more on the developmental needs of boys and girls in sport.

13. Sport psychology and exercise psychology are coming together as a combined field, resulting in changes in curriculum and clinical experiences.

DISCUSSION QUESTIONS

1. How will consulting psychology eventually provide for interscholastic, youth, and child sport the services it now provides for elite and professional sport?

2. Will athletes eventually learn psychological skills, just as they learn the physical skills of their sports?

3. Why is there no psychology of fitness?

4. Which clinical-intervention technique seems most important to you? Explain your answer.

5. What psychological issues in sport do you believe merit attention?

CHAPTER 19

Sport Pedagogy

Teaching makes only the difference it can make; it is not magic. Teaching is vital because it is the only factor we can really do much about in the short run. It is impossible to change a student's heredity, and socioeconomic conditions change only slowly over generations. The quality of teaching, on the other hand, can make an immediate difference. . . . A small but substantial portion of what any student achieves in the gymnasium is a consequence of what we do as teachers. It is now possible to find out which behaviors are effective and how they work. It is possible to learn from teaching.

Lawrence Locke, in *Learning from Teaching*, 1979

LEARNING OBJECTIVES

- To define the scope of the field of sport pedagogy

- To differentiate between issues in curriculum and those in instruction

- To describe the development of the field and its institutional affiliations

- To describe the preparation to enter the field

- To discuss problems and issues in the field

People are not born with sport skills. They may be genetically equipped to be stronger, taller, or faster, but those qualities in and of themselves will not allow them to be successful in sport. Somewhere, sometime, they must *learn* sport skills and the sport strategies that result in satisfactory participation in sport and competitive success. In most cases, young people learn sport skills and sport strategies from people who are designated to teach those things—physical-education teachers and coaches. Virtually all cultures, once they get beyond the subsistence stage of development, consider sport and physical education to be sufficiently important that they arrange programs for the young people in the culture to acquire the skills and strategies of sport in their childhood and youth, and to improve those sport skills through practice and competition.

In most school systems, the areas of sport and fitness are considered to be of such importance that special courses are arranged and people with special credentials are employed to teach within those courses. The course of study is most often called "physical education," and the person designated to teach it is a physical educator.

The general field within which all this happens is **sport pedagogy.** In the United States, this field is also termed *teacher education* or *curriculum and instruction.* The questions that are the province of sport pedagogy are of obvious importance to all people in the sport-and-fitness culture who teach or coach:

- What are the most effective teaching techniques?
- What interpersonal coaching skills should coaches acquire?
- What activities should be in the school physical-education curriculum?
- Should youth-sport coaches be certified?
- How can large groups of students be managed effectively?
- How can fitness be integrated into the school curriculum?

- What should be the content of a teacher-education program in physical education?

These questions have been studied and debated within professional physical education for more than 100 years. Answers to them continue to be refined and are of obvious importance to the culture of sport and fitness. Since the early 1980s, these questions have become more the special province of sport pedagogy as it has emerged as a full-fledged member of the sport and exercise sciences.

DEFINITION OF SPORT PEDAGOGY AS A FIELD OF STUDY

Sport pedagogy is the study of the processes of teaching and coaching, of the outcomes of such endeavors, and of the content of fitness, physical-education, and sport-education programs. *Sport pedagogy* is a term used widely in international physical education and sport sciences. This label tends to restrict the field's scope to school programs of physical education, teaching within school programs, and the content of the programs themselves. In most of the world outside the United States, coaching in the community or in clubs and teaching physical education in schools are considered to be part of the same total endeavor. Thus, the field of sport pedagogy, as it is defined internationally, encompasses both school programs of physical education and community-based and club programs of sport and fitness. The term *sport pedagogy* is beginning to be used more frequently in the United States and appears to be the term that will define this field in the future. Therefore, it is the term used to define and describe the field in this chapter.

Sport pedagogy is a broad field concerned with the content, processes, and outcomes of sport, fitness, and physical-education programs in schools, community programs, and clubs. The term **pedagogy,** of course, refers to teaching but should be taken in its broadest context; for example, it encompasses not just the *act* of teaching, however important that is, but also the development of an instructional program, the plan for the implementation of that program, and an assessment of the outcomes of the program. The term *sport* should also be taken broadly, to include not only competitive sport but also leisure activities and fitness. This is how the term *sport* is used in most of the world, and it is the same broad meaning that underlies the *Sport for All* movements prevalent throughout the world.

One of the best reasons to use the term *sport pedagogy* rather than *teacher education* is that the former clearly encompasses both teaching in schools and teaching and coaching in community and club programs. As we saw in Chapter 1, individuals now have the opportunity for lifelong involvement in sport, fitness, and physical education. They can learn for a lifetime, participate in many ways, and compete for a lifetime if that is their desire. If sport pedagogy is restricted solely to what goes on in school programs of physical education, then it will have defined itself far too narrowly.

The youth-sport coach in charge of 22 players in a community-based program faces many of the same problems and needs many of the same skills as does the middle school physical-education teacher in charge of a class of 28 seventh-graders. There are differences, to be sure! Some of those differences are important and need to be studied and documented carefully. Nonetheless, the similarities are more striking than the differences. Both people need to teach skills, to organize large groups of children, to plan a seasonal program, and to be prepared for each lesson or practice session. Both are concerned with the development of their students or players in ways that go beyond the outcome of any lesson or practice, beyond the score of any competition. It is fair to say that both are involved in sport pedagogy!

Sport pedagogy typically divides into two main areas: instruction and curriculum. The teaching-versus-coaching distinction, with a somewhat different emphasis within each field, tends to cut across those two areas, as does the setting within which the activity takes place—for example, school, community, sport club, or industry. Within sport pedagogy, there are people whose main task is to do research about instruction or curriculum, to pro-

Plastic pipe javelins allow the learning of important track-and-field skills.

vide knowledge about current practices, and to investigate potentially better practices. These sport pedagogists are involved in the *creation* of the new knowledge that helps us to understand and improve the field. Other people, the practitioners of sport pedagogy, are charged with the responsibility to use the knowledge discovered in sport-pedagogy research in other sport-science fields, to provide the best sport and fitness programs possible for children, youths, and adults in schools, communities, and clubs.

The field of *instruction* within sport pedagogy examines issues such as planning, teacher–student interaction skills, the activities of students or players that contribute to learning, the assessment of performance and learning, the comparison of different teaching or coaching methods, and the management and discipline issues associated with teaching and coaching. Most of the research in instruction is done by faculty members in universities, typically those involved in programs in which teachers and coaches are prepared and certified—for example, in departments of physical education.

The field of *curriculum* within sport pedagogy focuses more on the content of programs, the goals to which programs are or should be devoted, the manner in which programs are implemented, and

Mainstreaming children with disabilities in physical education requires sound pedagogical skills.

the outcomes achieved within programs, especially as they relate to program goals. Some work within curriculum is highly theoretical, focusing on models for physical-education and sport programs. Other work is highly practical, focusing on what actually goes on in programs and how consistently programs achieve their stated goals.

The fields of instruction and curriculum are, of course, not totally separate. People with primary interests in instruction also are interested in curriculum, and vice versa. Those people who actually practice sport pedagogy—teachers and coaches—have a vital interest in both areas; for them, the distinctions between the two fields are not so clear-cut.

DEVELOPMENT OF SPORT PEDAGOGY

Sport pedagogy is the youngest of the sport sciences. The emergence of a discipline of physical education in the 1960s and 1970s was in many ways a reaction to the low status of teacher-education programs in physical education in those days (see Chapter 3). Many education professionals and university administrators had become concerned about the perceived low quality of university education departments. Teacher-education programs were often viewed as being of low quality, as lacking a research foundation, and as being out of step with the directions of a modern university.

In physical education, areas such as sport psychology and sport sociology began to emerge as scholarly areas. Faculty members who were interested in those areas wanted to align themselves with the values and practices found in the parent disciplines (i.e., psychology and sociology) rather than with those found in education and physical-education departments. Thus, in the early days of the development of the subdisciplines of physical education, there was much heated debate about the perceived low quality of teacher-education programs in physical education.

In this sense, sport pedagogy developed partially as a reaction to the development of subdisciplines such as sport sociology and sport biomechanics. Before the 1970s, virtually every physical educator who held a doctoral degree considered himself or herself to be a teacher educator! That was true simply because the major mission—and, in many cases, the sole mission—of most undergraduate programs in physical education was to prepare teachers. In the 1970s, all that changed.

Not only did the development of subdisciplines in physical education change the manner in which people and programs were defined, but also an impending oversupply of teachers in schools caused physical-education departments to experiment with *alternative career programs* for their students. Whereas before the 1970s, almost all undergraduate physical-education majors were preparing to teach, during the 1970s, programs developed in areas such as sport management, adult fitness, sport journalism, and sport studies. This specialization occurred at the graduate level in the form of the subdisciplines and at the undergraduate level in the form of alternative career programs. Eventually, teacher education became more specialized, too.

The beginning of a distinct field of sport pedagogy can be traced to the development of specialized graduate-training programs at a few universities. These universities were most often ones where the physical-education department was either embedded within or had close ties to a good college of education. Specialized courses in teaching and teacher-education research became more prevalent. Graduate students and their professors began to involve themselves more deliberately in the various teaching-research movements that were developing in general education. As graduates from these programs began to be employed in other colleges and universities, they argued for and eventually developed teacher-education programs that more closely reflected the emerging knowledge base from teaching and teacher-education research.

Unlike most of the other subdisciplines, sport pedagogy has not developed its own national organization. Professionals interested in sport pedagogy have tended to maintain affiliations with the major national physical-education organization, AAHPERD. AAHPERD has several member organizations within which sport pedagogy has been able to play an important role: NASPE, the Council of Physical Education for Children (COPEC), and the Curriculum and Instruction Academy.

An important milestone in the development of sport pedagogy as a specialized area was reached when the *Journal of Teaching in Physical Education* (*JTPE*) was first published in 1981. This journal publishes research and commentary on topics in instruction and curriculum in physical education.

Since the mid-1980s, sport pedagogy has grown rapidly, holding a number of specialized conferences. It is regularly included as one of the sections at Olympic Scientific Congresses. Internationally, sport pedagogy is well represented by an International Committee of Sport Pedagogy, jointly sponsored by four major international organizations: the Association Internationale d'Education Superior d'Education Physique (AIESEP), the Federation Internationale d'Education Physique (FIEP), the International Association of Physical Education and Sport for Girls and Women (IAPESGW), and the International Society on Comparative Physical Education and Sport (ISCPES). Each of these organizations publishes newsletters and sponsors conferences in which sport pedagogy is a major focus.

Research in sport pedagogy has begun to change the content of textbooks used in teacher-education programs in physical education. When we compare recent texts with those of a generation ago, it is clear that issues such as classroom management, discipline, and instruction are handled differently. Those differences most often represent knowledge gained from research and scholarship within sport pedagogy.

Sport pedagogy has also begun to contribute to the growing coach-certification movement (see Chapter 6). Several of the most prominent coach-education programs include coursework in such areas as teaching, interaction skills, and time management—all pedagogical functions fulfilled by coaches. Although there has been less research on coaches than on physical-education teachers, it is likely that the coach-education movement will motivate an increased interest in coaching research. The obvious place for this research to begin is in sport-pedagogy programs.

CURRENT STATUS OF SPORT PEDAGOGY

During the 1970s and early 1980s, school enrollments dropped and a serious oversupply of teachers resulted. Jobs in teaching were scarce. Enrollments in teacher-education programs at universities were reduced drastically. Subsequently, there were few jobs for young professionals newly qualified as specialists in sport pedagogy. All of that has begun to change. Many faculty members who joined the university ranks in the 1960s, during the major expansion period in American educational history, are now reaching retirement age, and we are now beginning another period of expansion in school enrollments. The demand for teachers has risen each year during the 1990s. Enrollments in teacher-education programs have increased.

Thus, the need for new teacher-education faculty at the university level has increased. When a teacher-education position is created, or a position becomes vacant upon the retirement of the incumbent, the job description is likely to be specialized

TABLE 19.1 Areas of Study within Sport Pedagogy	
Area	Typical Questions Asked
Teacher behavior	What kinds of feedback do teachers provide?
	Do elementary teachers behave differently than secondary teachers?
	How much time do teachers spend in various teaching activities?
	How does the behavior of teachers differ from that of coaches?
Student behavior	Do students enjoy and value physical education?
	How do students spend their time in classes?
	How many good learning opportunities does a highly or poorly skilled student get during a class?
	How do children behave in youth sport?
Teacher effectiveness	What differentiates effective from ineffective teachers and coaches?
	What teaching methods are most effective?
	How do teachers cope with the problems encountered during their first year?
	What characteristics make a coach effective?
Teacher issues	To what extent is there role conflict in individuals who both teach and coach?
	How do teachers cope with burnout?
	What goals do teachers have for their students?
Curriculum	What is the ideal physical-education curriculum?
	How do teachers' values affect curriculum decisions?
	To what extent do teachers achieve their goals?
	How can fitness best be programmed?
	What outcomes occur in youth-sport programs?

in the area of sport pedagogy. Research and scholarship in sport pedagogy continue to develop. The general areas most often investigated and the typical questions asked are listed in Table 19.1.

The success of sport-pedagogy research and the dissemination of research findings, particularly in textbooks, have begun to change the content of teacher- and coach-preparation programs, the content of in-service education for practicing teachers, and, subsequently, the manner in which physical educators and coaches teach and coach. The area of classroom management has been greatly influenced by this body of knowledge. Teachers and coaches now know more about developing managerial routines, keeping managerial time short, developing clear rules and consequences for breaking rules, and using positive interactional strategies to support appropriate student or player behavior.

Instructional strategies have also been influenced. Teachers and coaches are more aware of the definition and progression of instructional tasks, the quality of learner responses, and the specificity of the feedback provided. They understand more clearly how important it is to provide for as many good learner responses as possible in each lesson or practice. The old phrase "practice makes perfect" is more clearly understood as "good practice makes perfect."

Work in the area of curriculum has also progressed rapidly. Whereas physical education 30 years ago would have looked similar from school to school, it is more likely to look distinctive today, as a variety of new curriculum models have appeared. Chapter 12 described a number of these newer curriculum models, including adventure education, social-development physical education, sport education, fitness education, movement education, and the more traditional multiactivity program.

What Do Sport Pedagogists Do?

People who describe themselves as sport pedagogists are almost always employed as teacher educators in departments of physical education. They occupy a variety of roles in teacher-education programs. These roles may include (a) teaching sport skills to physical-education majors, (b) teaching various methods classes (e.g., elementary physical-education methods, secondary-school physical-education methods), (c) organizing and supervising on-campus clinical experiences for preservice teachers, (d) organizing and supervising field-based experiences for preservice teachers, (e) supervising student teachers, and (f) teaching other courses related to teacher preparation in physical education.

The job market for doctoral graduates of sport-pedagogy programs has been very robust for a number of years and promises to be so for the foreseeable future. There are probably more university jobs in sport pedagogy than in any of the other subdiscipline fields. This is true because school enrollments continue to be strong and many of the teachers who came into K–12 teaching in the baby-boom era are now retiring. Thus, many K–12 jobs are available; and that tends to attract more young women and men to teacher-education programs at colleges and universities.

If the department has a graduate program, sport-pedagogy personnel may be called on to provide courses and experiences at the master's-degree level for area teachers who want to upgrade their qualifications and to teach courses and direct research at the doctoral level if there is a specialization in sport pedagogy at that university. In addition, as university faculty members, they take part in professional activities at the local, state, regional, and national levels and engage in scholarly activities, such as publishing journal articles and books.

Equipment should be modified to be developmentally appropriate for instruction and practice.

How Does a Person Prepare to Be a Sport Pedagogist?

Sport pedagogy is currently a doctoral specialization in a number of universities. Men and women enrolled in such programs are mostly preparing to become faculty members in colleges and universities, although some seek employment in K–12 schools as department directors, curriculum directors for school districts, or supervisors of physical education for school districts. An undergraduate degree in physical education and teaching certification are almost always required for entry into such doctoral programs. Most doctoral programs also require that the applicant have teaching experience; 3 years is the usual requirement.

People who specialize in sport pedagogy take courses in education research, teacher education, supervision, instructional design, and instructional theory. They often take many hours of coursework in education departments, pursuing their cognate interests. They also most often take a series of research courses. Often, they specialize in either elementary physical education or secondary physical education. The fields of motor development and adapted physical education are closely related to sport pedagogy. Thus, students pursuing degrees in any of these fields are likely to gain experience in the other fields, as well.

CURRENT ISSUES AND PROBLEMS IN SPORT PEDAGOGY

Many of the major concerns within sport pedagogy are reflections of major concerns with the general fields of physical education and coaching. (See Chapters 7, 10, and 13 for complete descriptions of problem areas.) For instance, should there be a national physical-education curriculum? How can teacher–coach role conflict be lessened? How can schools develop effective fitness programs without taking all their allotted instructional time to do so? What can be done to prevent teachers from burning out or to help those who have burned out?

How can youth-sport coaches be better prepared to deal effectively with young athletes? What activities should be included in a modern secondary-school physical-education program? These are typical questions debated within physical education, fitness, and youth sport; they are also widely discussed in sport pedagogy.

In addition, there are questions more specific to the field of sport pedagogy, many of which relate to the preparation of teachers because teacher education is a primary mission of sport pedagogy. For example, how much sport-skill training should prospective teachers have? Should sport-skill training be oriented to performance, to learning about the activity, or to learning how to teach the activity? How can teaching skills be acquired most effectively and efficiently? Are on-campus clinical experiences as effective as off-campus field experiences? How should field-based teaching be supervised?

There are parallel issues in the field of instruction. How can teachers best plan for high-quality learning experiences despite the diversity of talents within a typical school class? How should tasks be sequenced within a lesson and throughout a unit? How can teachers best communicate tasks to students? What motivational strategies work best to get students more completely involved in physical education? As research and scholarship within this young discipline become more sophisticated, some of these questions will be answered, and new questions will arise.

Sport pedagogy resides in areas traditionally referred to as teacher education. The link between the health and vitality of teacher-education programs in colleges and universities and the health and vitality of school physical-education programs is weak, at best. Teacher educators in physical education have seldom felt responsible for the quality of school programs. It is not uncommon to hear teacher educators talk about improvements in their programs at the same time they bemoan the lack of exemplary local school programs to use for their field experiences and student-teaching assignments. Siedentop and Locke (1997) argue that the bottom-line criterion for judging the success of teacher-education programs is that they contribute directly to the development, maintenance, and dissemination of high-quality school physical-education programs. This is certainly not the mainstream view but is an issue worthy of debate.

A major problem within sport pedagogy in America is the uncertain future of the undergraduate program in teacher education in physical education. Part of the most recent educational-reform movement has focused on the level at which teachers should be trained. The argument typically is stated as follows: "American teachers do not know their subject matters well enough and are not sufficiently well educated in the liberal arts. Therefore, at the undergraduate level, prospective teachers should receive a strong liberal-arts preparation and a strong subject-matter preparation. The *professional* training to become a teacher should take place after the baccalaureate degree has been earned." Thus, since the mid-1980s, most educational-reform documents have called for postbaccalaureate teacher education.

A major issue in teacher preparation in physical education is the nature of the "content" that is learned by students who desire to teach K–12 physical education. Research in education has shown consistently that *content knowledge* is a crucial component of effective teaching. For example, there is general consensus that part of the explanation for the poor performance of American students in international studies of mathematics learning is that American teachers do not have sufficient knowledge of mathematics. A prospective math teacher should have thorough knowledge of mathematics. A prospective history teacher should have a thorough knowledge of history. But what should a prospective physical educator have a thorough knowledge of? Some say it should be knowledge of the subdisciplines described in Part Five of this text. What is taught in K–12 physical education, however, is not biomechanics or exercise psychology or sport literature, even if knowledge of those fields might help the physical educator be a better teacher. What are taught are motor skills, exercise

patterns, sport skills, and tactical skills. The curriculum is typically defined not by subdisciplines but by adventure activities, dance, sports, and exercise. This is not to suggest that much of the knowledge generated by the subdisciplines is not useful for teacher preparation. It is! The issue here is how the teacher-preparation curriculum is defined and what balance there is between learning about and how to do sport, exercise, games, and dance and the underlying knowledge from the subdisciplines.

SUMMARY

1. *Sport pedagogy* is the international label for the field known in the United States as teacher education or curriculum and instruction.

2. *Sport pedagogy* is the study of the processes of teaching and coaching, of the outcomes of such endeavors, and of the content of fitness, physical-education, and sport programs.

3. Sport pedagogy encompasses both teaching in schools and teaching and coaching in community and club programs.

4. Sport pedagogy typically is divided into the fields of instruction and curriculum.

5. Sport pedagogy is the most recent sport-related subdiscipline to develop, growing out of dissatisfaction with traditional programs of teacher education.

6. Sport pedagogy has national affiliations with AAHPERD and strong international representation from several organizations represented on the International Committee of Sport Pedagogy.

7. Research from sport pedagogy has begun to change the content of teacher- and coach-preparation programs.

8. Sport pedagogists are typically employed in universities; a doctoral degree and teaching experience are the primary qualifications.

9. Recent reform movements in teacher education have called for a shift to postbaccalaureate prep-

aration. It is not clear how physical educators can implement this model.

DISCUSSION QUESTIONS

1. Why is *sport pedagogy* a more inclusive label than is *teacher education*?

2. Can sport pedagogy eventually include coach education, as well as teacher education? Should it?

3. What was different (from other subdisciplines) about the development of sport pedagogy as a specialized field?

4. Judging from your own teaching and coaching experience, on what kinds of questions or problems do you think sport pedagogy should focus?

5. Should teacher education be taught at the graduate level, or should it remain an undergraduate program? Explain your answer.

CHAPTER 20

The Sport Humanities

The sport experience defies precise description. Nevertheless, attempts at description can be facilitated by discussing the setting, citing the critical elements, and probing the broader meaning of a given sport experience. The potential significance of the sport experience can be found primarily in the fact that we learn through experiences. In the case of sport, there is the possibility of learning about oneself, learning more about others, and acquiring a better understanding of life itself.

Harold VanderZwaag and Thomas Sheehan,
in *Introduction to Sport Studies*, 1978

LEARNING OBJECTIVES

- To distinguish among sport history, sport philosophy, and sport literature

- To distinguish between first- and second-order questions in philosophy

- To describe the various approaches to sport history

- To discuss the scope of sport literature

- To describe the development and institutional affiliations of these fields

- To describe the preparation to enter these fields

- To discuss problems and issues in these fields

When *Chariots of Fire* won the Academy Award for Best Picture of 1981, it became clear that the old argument—that sport was not suitable for popular and serious literary consideration—was no longer true. The film was a historical study of athletes competing in the Olympic Games in track and field in the early part of the twentieth century. Major philosophical themes—such as fair play, amateur versus professional, and the meaning of competition—were woven throughout the story. It was a *good* story, well acted, and enjoyable to all who viewed it. For people involved in the sport, fitness, and physical-education professions, it not only was enjoyable as theater but also was a literary vehicle through which sport could be examined historically and philosophically. The film is a good example of the contemporary impact of the **sport humanities.**

Nearly everyone who has participated in a fitness, sport, or physical-education program has at some point wondered about the field's meaning. Why do people do these activities? From where do these activities come? How do games develop, and why are people devoted to them? Why is sport "this way" rather than some "other way"? Most people who participate in or enjoy watching sport have a deep interest in it that goes beyond the competition itself. Many are concerned about some of the problems and excesses associated with sport, from children's involvement to the most elite levels. What is fair in sport? What are appropriate practices? Many of these kinds of questions are addressed in the sport humanities.

The fields of sport history, sport philosophy, and sport literature constitute the sport humanities. The *humanities,* as a general field, include those branches of learning concerned directly with human thought and relations. In general education, the humanities include literature, philosophy, the fine arts, and history. The study of the historical and philosophical aspects of sport, fitness, and physical education has a long tradition within professional physical education. The study of sport literature as an organized field is much more recent. Because the roots of these three areas are to be found in humanistic studies, rather than in the sciences, they are treated together in this chapter.

The term *sport* is used here to describe these fields because it is the word used increasingly by people within the fields. Both physical education and fitness have also been the focus of philosophical and historical study, and they still are. In recent years, however, the organizational and scholarly focus of study in history and philosophy has been on sport. Sport literature, a more recent addition, has never had the broader focus that might include aspects of physical education and fitness, too.

The full development of the sport humanities seems to have accompanied the explosion of interest in sport within Western culture generally and American culture in particular that started in the early 1970s. The degree to which sport is now a part of everyday life is truly extraordinary. Fifteen to 20 percent of newspaper space is devoted to sport information. Endless hours of television coverage are provided. Sport has become part of nightly local television newscasts. International events such as the Olympics occupy the major share of television for extended periods. A major national event such as the Super Bowl or NCAA basketball finals seems to bring the nation to a halt. The sport and fitness magazine sections in bookstores are likely to be among the largest, with specialized magazines in a large number of sport and fitness activities, as well as comprehensive, weekly coverage in magazines such as *Sports Illustrated.* More people spend more money and more time on sport- and fitness-related activities than ever before in history. It is no surprise, then, that the philosophical, historical, and literary aspects of sport have also prospered in this era. Because sport seems to affect so many people, and in often so fundamental a way, it is highly appropriate that philosophical, historical, and literary investigations have been undertaken to help us understand what all of this means, from both an individual and a collective point of view.

Although the search for understanding that derives from philosophy, history, and literature somewhat differs across these fields, the questions each considers not only cut across the three areas but also interest the general public:

- How have sport and religion affected each other?
- How and for what reasons has youth sport developed?
- What changes have occurred in opportunities for girls and women?
- What has been the sport experience for African Americans?
- What values does professional sport promote?
- In what ways can competition be understood?
- What does *fair play* mean? What should it mean?
- In what ways is sport portrayed in films?
- How has the sport hero been treated in novels?

DEFINITION OF THE SPORT HUMANITIES AS FIELDS OF STUDY

The sport humanities comprise three related fields, each of which has its own organizational structure, its own methodologies, and its own scholarly literature. *History,* as a field of study, is more than just descriptions of past events:

> Although when we use the word history we instinctively think of the past, this is an error, for history is actually a bridge connecting the past with the present, and pointing the road to the future. (Nevins, 1962, p. 14)

History, therefore, not only chronicles the past but also interprets the past, relates the past to the present, and provides guidelines as to what might be expected or what courses might be taken in the future.

Sport history tends to separate into two categories based on the goals of the scholar conducting the investigation. One approach is to identify and describe patterns of change and stability in sport in particular societies or cultures during specific time periods (Harris, 2000). The second is to not only identify and describe patterns but also analyze them in terms of their relationships and the events that influenced the patterns. This is essentially the same distinction made by Adelman (1969), who separated sport history into narrative-descriptive history and interpretive-comparative history.

Some history books are written for popular consumption and may be read widely. An example is John Feingold's *A Season on the Brink,* a chronicle of one season of Indiana basketball and Coach Bob Knight. Some are written for a much more narrow audience and are more scholarly in nature. A classic example is H. A. Harris's *Greek Athletes and Athletics,* which is the most authoritative source of information about sport in ancient Greece and what purposes it served. College textbooks in both sport history and sport philosophy are available, and sometimes these are combined—for example, in a course on the history and philosophy of sport.

As sport was taken more seriously by the general public, books about sport were also more seriously written and found acceptance in the general literary culture. Two shining examples of quality literature in sport history are Roger Kahn's poignant history of the fates of the 1958 Brooklyn Dodgers in *The Boys of Summer* and David Halberstam's chronicle of elite rowers preparing for the Olympic games in *The Amateurs.*

Philosophy is a formal field of study that includes four main areas. *Metaphysics* is the branch of philosophy that addresses questions about the nature of reality. *Axiology* is the study of values. How knowledge is acquired is the field of *epistemology,* and how ideas are related composes the study of *logic.* Many people, however, are interested in what are popularly called "philosophical issues," although these differ from the concerns of formal philosophy.

Bressan and Pieter (1985) have referred to this distinction as "first-order" and "second-order" philosophy. Philosophy as a *first-order activity* is a discipline with a unique set of problems that are classified within the four primary philosophical branches and several subdisciplines. Philosophers have specific methodologies by which to investigate those problems. Like other disciplines, philosophical investigation is highly technical and has a language and a concept system that people must master to take part in the discipline. Philosophy as a *second-order activity,* however, includes thinking creatively and logically about problems that belong to areas outside philosophy itself. Virtually every professional person in sport, fitness, and physical education has a philosophical point of view about what he or she does, and for what reasons.

Thus, in a more ordinary sense, philosophy deals with issues such as goals and objectives, values, codes of right and wrong conduct, and explanations for why and how things are done as they are. These widespread philosophical concerns among practicing professionals tend to fall into three areas, which are also categories for more formal philosophical research. *Speculative philosophy* focuses on arguments that extend beyond the limits of scientific or factual knowledge. An example of a question of this type is, What are the origins of play, and how does play relate to elite sport? *Normative philosophy* focuses on general value-based principles that provide guidelines for behavior in practical activities. An example of a question of this type is, By what rules of fair play should good sportspersons abide during competition? The third area is *analytic philosophy,* which deals with the clarification of words and concepts. An example of this type is, What various meanings does the term *fitness* have in current popular and scientific literature?

Harris (2000) suggests that the first goal of philosophy of sport is to clarify thinking about sport, play, games and dance, including the relationship between body and mind. The second goal, she argues, is to encourage people to use their insights about sport and the relationship between body and mind to improve people's lives. The first goal is consistent with most views of the purpose of philosophy of sport, but the second moves into actually using insights to improve sport and the lives of people involved with sport. The idea that philosophers of sport, and those who use the literature of the phi-losophy of sport, would engage in activities directly intended to improve sport and the sport experience is very close to the *critical theory* branch of sport sociology, where programs designed to improve the sport experience are referred to as *praxis* (see Chapter 17, p. 000).

There has always been a literature of philosophy in the field of physical education because most of the great early leaders wrote books that had strong philosophical overtones—J. B. Nash, Jesse Feiring Williams, Clark Hetherington, and Rosalind Cassidy among the first generation of great twentieth-century leaders and Eleanor Metheny and Delbert Obertueffer among the midcentury leaders. In the past 25 years, there has been a very strong literature in the philosophy of sport. Some books, such as Howard Slusher's *Man, Sport and Existence,* have been read mostly within the profession. Others, such as Paul Weiss's *Sport: A Philosophical Inquiry* and Michael Novak's *The Joy of Sports,* were written by people outside the field of sport philosophy and have been widely read both within the profession and by the general public. When famous and serious people take sport seriously and write about it, the public listens. Such was the case when A. Bartlett Giamatti, former president of Yale University and commissioner of Major League Baseball wrote *Take Time for Paradise,* a philosophical and historical analysis of sport and play.

Literature, in the sense used here, refers to prose, poetry, and films that have a permanent value because of their excellence of form, their emotional effect, and their ability to provide insights about the human condition. Literature, in this sense, has literary value and is often contrasted with scientific writing, ordinary newswriting, and general nonfiction writing, such as in textbooks. Sport literature is a recent and welcome addition to the sport humanities. It has arisen as a field because of the marked increase, since the early 1970s, in serious literary work that focuses specifically on sport or using sport themes as vehicles through which to examine basic human dilemmas and situations. This field does focus almost exclusively on sport, with little attention to fitness or physical education.

Sport literature is dominated by sport fiction, with a lesser emphasis on sport poetry. Increasingly, films that are about sport, or that use sport as a theme to examine important human questions, have been included within sport literature. Some film scripts have been adapted from novels, such as Bernard Malamud's *The Natural*, Mark Harris's *Bang the Drum Slowly*, and Pete Gent's *North Dallas Forty*. A few novels that have sport as a main theme or context have achieved critical acclaim *and* have become best-sellers—John Updike's *Rabbit Run* is perhaps the best example. Many more novels, although not achieving best-seller status, have received good critical reviews and have sold moderately well. Good examples are W. P. Kinsella's *Shoeless Joe*, Eric Rolfe Greenberg's *The Celebrant*, and Tom McNab's *Flannagan's Run*.

Of course, a number of books have been written about celebrities and sport teams. Each new hero or heroine, each new big winner, and each new major championship team seems to precipitate a large number of books, often ghostwritten or written in collaboration with a local sportswriter. Many of these books sell well, but they are very seldom considered to have literary merit in the sense defined here. They constitute the fringe of sport literature yet are nonetheless an important vehicle through which sport is interpreted and made available to the public.

Sport films are becoming more and more popular and are likely to increase in importance in the field of sport literature. Historically, most films in which sport was a main theme could not be described as taking sport seriously or making a serious comment about sport and its role in the lives of women and men. In the past 20 years, however, sport films that have been very good entertainment have also made serious statements about sport. Primary examples are *Bull Durham, Field of Dreams,* and *A League of Their Own,* just to mention a few in which baseball was the sport focus. *Field of Dreams* had a strong philosophical focus, and *A League of Their Own* had more of a historical focus. Recently, *The Legend of Bagger Vance*, a philosophical treatise about golf and the game of life, found success both as a novel and as a popular film.

Many books and films have tried to unravel the deep meaning of sport.

DEVELOPMENT OF THE SPORT HUMANITIES

Within the profession of physical education, during its development as a field from 1850 to 1950, the history and philosophy of physical education were always areas of interest to professionals. Chapter 4 reviewed the changing historical philosophies that accompanied the development of American physical education. At least one course in these areas has typically been included in teacher-training programs. Many of the most important early leaders in the field were best known for their contributions to a developing philosophy of physical education (using the term *philosophy* here in its broadest, professional sense).

The fields of sport history, sport philosophy, and sport literature are of more recent origin, being part of the general trend toward a discipline of physical education. (See Chapter 3 for a historical overview of this movement.) Historical interests in sport and physical education coalesced formally in 1973 with the first meeting of the National Society for Sport History (NSSH). This organization publishes the *Journal of Sport History;* that publication and the *Canadian Journal of History of Sport and Physical Education* have become the main publishing outlets for scholars working in the field.

Sport historian Marvin Eyler (1965) suggested that the field of sport history would develop through three periods: the *awakening period,* the *fledgling period,* and the *approbatory period.* It seems clear that the field has been through the awakening period and is now in the fledgling period. The final period, characterized by a rich and full body of knowledge covering the major periods of history and the full range of sports, and utilizing the interpretive–comparative approach, is still to come.

Although philosophy, in the general sense, has always been important within physical education, there is little evidence that academic philosophers took sport seriously until the 1970s. As the physical-education subdisciplines developed, it was logical that a philosophy group would form—and it did. In 1973, at the annual meeting of the American Philosophical Association, a group of philosophers interested in sport joined with a group of physical-education specialists interested in philosophy to form the Philosophic Society for the Study of Sport (PSSS). The first president of PSSS was Paul Weiss, then Sterling professor of philosophy at Yale University. The society published its first issue of the *Journal of the Philosophic Society for the Study of Sport* in 1974.

The marriage of sport and philosophy represented by the formation of PSSS has had both benefits and liabilities. Sport philosophers who work within this organization and publish articles in its journal have tended to approach philosophy as a first-order activity. Membership in the society numbers only 100 (Kleinman, 1987). Each year, however, more than 2,000 members of AAHPERD indicate an interest in philosophical issues by affili-

ating with the Philosophy of Sport and Physical Education Academy, a subgroup within AAHPERD. The vast majority of these professionals are interested in philosophy as a second-order activity, using it to examine issues in sport, fitness, and physical education. As is discussed later in this chapter, this difference in interest has resulted in a discontinuity between people who study philosophy and professionals who have a philosophical interest in current issues.

The field of sport literature did not emerge until the 1980s. Physical-education faculty members and professors of English joined to form the Sport Literature Association (SLA) in 1982. In the autumn of 1983, the first issue of *Arete: The Journal of Sport Literature* appeared. In the summer of 1984, the association held its first meetings. The SLA continues to be a joint venture of professionals in physical education and in English. Its major focus has been and continues to be sport, with only minor attention paid to either physical education or fitness.

CURRENT STATUS OF THE SPORT HUMANITIES

The sport humanities continue to make important contributions to our understanding of sport, fitness, and physical education. However, changes in direction in undergraduate and graduate preparation in physical education have constrained the growth of these fields. During the late 1970s and early 1980s, the demand for teachers for our nation's schools fell quickly as school enrollments dropped. That caused a reduction of interest in teacher-education programs in general and in physical-education programs in particular because physical education was one of the school subjects for which there was a serious oversupply of teachers. As applications to teacher-education programs dwindled, many college and university departments of physical education began to look for different curricula to attract students.

One model with which several universities experimented was a new undergraduate major in *sport studies.* This major had a strong emphasis in

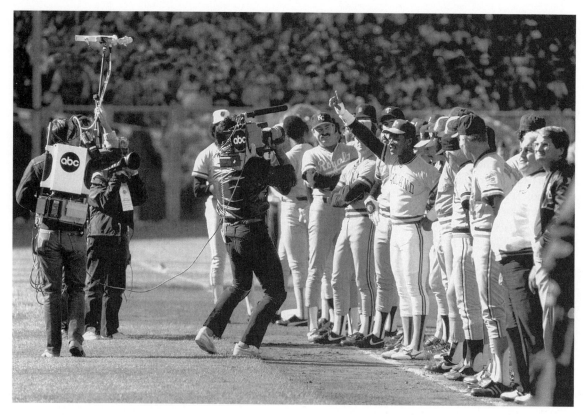

Television has influenced sport markedly.

the sport humanities but did not specifically prepare students for jobs. It was more of a liberal-arts approach—and it did not fare too well. Many other universities began to experiment with alternative career curricula such as sport journalism, but these tended to be too narrow, with few jobs awaiting graduates. The only new curricula, other than teacher education, to survive widely have been those in adult fitness and sport management, each of which tends to be vocationally oriented.

Thus, the sport humanities have not grown because there are few programs that emphasize them, and the trend has been toward vocationally oriented programs rather than toward those emphasizing a liberal-arts approach. Because people who specialize in the sport humanities tend to be em-

ployed almost exclusively as college and university faculty, and because there has been no strong need for more professors in these areas in undergraduate programs, the number of universities offering graduate specializations has not grown.

We have not yet seen the day when an undergraduate degree in some sport-related field is considered to be useful and interesting in and of itself, without its being vocationally oriented or leading directly to a job in an established market. Some members of the sport, fitness, and physical-education professions believe that such a degree would be popular with and attractive to students seeking an interesting undergraduate curriculum as they grow and develop. Almost all believe that sport, taken broadly, is worth studying in its own right! Therefore, it is conceivable that an undergraduate liberal-arts degree in sport studies might develop in the future.

Unfortunately, however, there is little evidence that the sport humanities are gaining ground as a coherent field of study in which people prepare at the graduate level to become teachers and researchers. This is not to suggest that the topics covered in sport humanities have not gained ground. Many sport-oriented humanities courses have developed in college and university curricula, but they typically are dispersed in the departments belonging to the parent disciplines—that is, sport-literature courses in English departments, sport-history courses in history departments, and sport-philosophy courses in philosophy departments. These are typically taught by people trained specifically in the parent discipline who happen also to have a strong interest in sport. Thus, the sport humanities have become a dispersed discipline, loosely held together by some common journals and associations but without a firm structural base in the university. Regardless, the serious study of sport from a humanities perspective continues to grow. The major areas of study and the associated typical questions are shown in Table 20.1.

Because sport and fitness have come to occupy an increasingly central role in our culture, it is important that we try harder to investigate, debate, and eventually understand what that role means, how it came about, and how we—as sport, fitness, and physical-education professionals—fit into the picture. Investigations in the sport humanities can help us to focus on and clarify these issues. We cannot afford to misunderstand our history. We cannot afford to neglect the philosophical issues that

TABLE 20.1	Areas of Study in the Sport Humanities
Area	Typical Questions Asked
Sport history	What causes certain sports to be more or less popular at certain times?
	How has sport been changed by television?
	How has Title IX changed participation by girls?
	How is sport changing as a social force in culture?
	How did the Olympics change in the twentieth century?
Sport philosophy	Does competition mean something different to spectator and competitor?
	How is the play element in sport changed as the sport competition becomes more highly organized?
	How does feminist philosophy interpret sport?
	What should "fair play" mean in elite sport?
	How do coach and athlete philosophies differ?
Sport literature	How are coaches portrayed in films emphasizing sport?
	How is the "sport hero past his or her prime" treated in sport fiction?
	How are failure and success treated in sport novels?
	What ideas and values are being expressed in sport poems?
	What role does sport play in fiction that focuses on adolescent development?

surround our professional work. We can be sensitized to these issues through film, fiction, and poetry. The potential of the sport humanities is strong.

It is through the sport humanities that much of what we do as professionals is interpreted to the general public. Think of some of the films about students of high school age involved in sport or about elite-level sportspersons (examples of such films are *Hoosiers, Bull Durham, Chariots of Fire, The Natural, Any Given Sunday,* and *Everybody's All American*). How were the coaches portrayed? Were they caring, bright, enthusiastic, and hardworking, or were they insensitive, dull, and lazy? To what extent is the film characterization true of our profession?

Many people preparing to enter the sport, fitness, and physical-education profession find it difficult to understand why they should study the sport humanities. Issues of historical, philosophical, or literary merit seem often not to be immediately relevant to their preparation—but that view is shortsighted. Study within the sport humanities not only stimulates interest but also promotes one's ability to think critically about the work one does, and it extends one's appreciation for the importance and complexity of that work.

What Do Sport-Humanities Specialists Do?

People who work in the fields of sport history, sport philosophy, and sport literature are usually employed in academic positions in colleges and universities. They are either in departments of physical education (or departments of sport science and sport studies) or in departments of history, philosophy, or English. During the 1990s, it became much more common for faculties in the main areas of history, philosophy, and literature to choose sport as a field for investigation. Thus, membership in organizations supporting these fields tends to be made up of people both within and outside physical education.

As academics, such people typically teach, do research, and engage in service related to their discipline. Because the sport humanities are small

Gender issues in sport represent an active field of study in the sport humanities.

areas in most departments, people are not likely to be able to teach only specialized courses. Usually, they have to teach a range of sport-humanity courses in a physical-education department, or, if they are in a history, philosophy, or literature department, they have to teach regular courses in addition to courses in their specialized interest. Only in physical-education departments with doctoral-level concentrations in one of these areas would a faculty member be able to teach only courses in his or her area of specialization.

How Does a Person Prepare to Be a Sport-Humanities Specialist?

As with the other subdisciplinary specializations we have reviewed, there are two paths to becoming a sport historian, a sport philosopher, or a sport-literature specialist. One is the path through physical education, starting as an undergraduate and proceeding through graduate study in the specialization within a physical-education department. The second path is through a major in history, philosophy, or literature.

A few people have tried to mix those two paths. Some sport historians, for example, have majored in physical education as undergraduates but then done graduate work in a history department. Oc-

The role of the sport hero is a research topic in the sport humanities.

casionally, a doctoral student in sport philosophy in a physical-education department will have completed undergraduate preparation in a philosophy department. Those are the exceptions rather than the norm, however.

To become an academic specialist in any of these areas, a person must earn the doctoral degree first. Few colleges and universities are willing to employ in academic roles people who do not have a doctoral degree. Doctoral training will necessarily include a strong concentration in the parent area— history, philosophy, or literature. It will also include coursework, seminars, and research in the specialized area.

CURRENT ISSUES AND PROBLEMS IN THE SPORT HUMANITIES

There is little doubt that the main problem within the sport humanities is that they are too small and are not sufficiently represented in undergraduate and graduate curricula in teacher education and the sport sciences. There are too few graduate programs emphasizing the sport humanities. This underrepresentation creates a situation where

the fields are in constant jeopardy of losing more courses, more faculty, and, subsequently, more graduate programs. With the current focus on the sport sciences, it has been difficult for people in the sport humanities to hold their own in terms of faculty positions, budgets, and courses.

A second area of concern is related to the first. There is a widespread belief among specialists in the sport humanities that sportswriters and sport commentators in newspapers, magazines, radio, and television are often ignorant of the historical, philosophical, and literary issues that surround the sport events they report and comment on. You no doubt watch the sport news on a local television station from time to time. How well educated in the sport humanities do you think the local television sport reporter is? How educated is the local sportswriter?

The concern here is that these people provide the commentary on and interpretation of sports, sport events, and athletes to the general public. When they comment on an event, the behavior of an athlete, or the importance of what has happened in sport, we would hope that their commentary would be informed by some specific knowledge of sport history, sport philosophy, or sport literature. However, how often is their commentary so informed? "Seldom" is probably the fair answer.

A special problem in sport philosophy does not appear to be relevant to sport history or sport literature. Kleinman has suggested that sport philosophers have tended strongly to pursue academic philosophy—the first-order approach described earlier in the chapter—rather than to speak to second-order issues of general concern to professionals who practice in sport, fitness, and physical education. He believes that their work is in danger of becoming irrelevant to the sport profession.

> Yet, large numbers of people, whom I suspect know nothing of language analysis, formal logic, and hermeneutics (the concerns of contemporary professional philosophers) continue to be interested in philosophic matters: the classic existential questions of truth, beauty, right and wrong, and the nature of good. Their "silent scream" should be telling our sport

GET CONNECTED TO KINESIOLOGICAL DISCIPLINE WEB SITES

Exercise Physiology

American College of Sports Medicine	www.acsm.org
American Medical Society for Sports Medicine	www.amssm.org
American Orthopaedic Society for Sports Medicine	www.sportsmed.org
American Osteopathic Academy of Sports Medicine	www.aoasm.org
International Federation of Sports Medicine	www.fims.org
American Sports Medicine Institute	www.asmi.org
Gatorade Sports Science Institute	www.gssiweb.com
Institute for Preventive Sports Medicine	www.ipsm.org
SportsDoc Online	www.medfacts.com/sprtsdoc.htm
SportsMedicine.com	www.sportsmedicine.com
The Physician and Sports Medicine Online	www.physsportsmed.com
American Society of Exercise Physiologists	www.cces.ca/
British Association of Sport and Exercise Sciences	www.bases.org.uk

Kinesiology and Biomechanics

American Society of Biomechanics	www.asb-biomech.org
International Society of Biomechanics	www.isbweb.org
International Society of Biomechanics in Sports	www.uni-stuttgart.de/External/isbs
International Sports Engineering Association	www.sorts-engineering.co.uk
Biomechanics Magazine	www.biomech.com

Motor Behavior

Canadian Society for Psychomotor Learning and Sport Psychology	www.scapps.org

Sport Sociology

American Sociological Association	www.asanet.org
North American Society for the Sociology of Sport	www.nasss.org
Center for the Study of Sport in Society	www.sportinsociety.org
Centre for Research on Sport and Society	www.le.ac.uk/crss
Sociology of Sport Online	www.otago.ac.nz/sosol/home.htm
International Sociology of Sport Association	http://u2.u-strasbg.fr/issa/

Sport and Exercise Psychology

Association for the Advancement of Applied Sport Psychology	www.aaasponline.org
Exercise and Sport Psychology—APA Division 47	www.psyc.unt.edu/apadiv47
International Society for Mental Training and Excellence	www.coach.ca/ismte
International Society for Sport Psychology	www.fitinfotech.com/ISSP
North American Society for Psychology of Sport and Physical Activity	www.naspspa.org
Athletic Insight	www.athleticinsight.com
Mental Skills	www.mentalskills.co.uk
Sport Psychology, Ltd.	www.sportpsychology.co.uk

(continued)

⟳ **GET CONNECTED TO KINESIOLOGICAL DISCIPLINE WEB SITES** *(continued)*

Sport Pedagogy

National Association for Sport and Physical Education   www.aahperd.org/naspe/
National Board for Professional Teaching Standards   www.nbpts.org
International Association of Physical Education in
   Higher Education (AIESEP)   www.zinman.macam98.ac.il/aiesep
American Educational Research Association   www.aera.org

Sport Humanities

Sports Ethics Institute   www.sportsethicsinstitute.org
International Association of Sports Law   www.iasl.org
International Society for the History of Physical Education and Sport   www.2.umist.ac.uk/sport/ishpes.html
North American Society for Sport History   www.nassh.org
International Society for Comparative Physical Education and Sport   www.iscpes.uwo.ca/
British Society of Sport History   www2.umist.ac.uk/sport/index2.html
International Society of Olympic Historians   www.olykamp.org.isoh
Sport Literature Association   www.etsu.edu/english/aethlon.htm
Sport Literature   www2.h-net.msu.edu/'arete/

---

and physical education philosophers something. It is a loud and clear message that, while philosophers continue to play their word games, the world is passing them by. They and their activities are regarded by their professional practitioners as irrelevant and meaningless. (Kleinman, 1987, p. 112)

The fact that the work of professional philosophy specialists may be in danger of becoming irrelevant to professional life *does not* suggest that interest in philosophical issues is waning. Quite the contrary! Many of the problems of youth sport, substance abuse in sport, unequal competition, use of athletes for inappropriate purposes, the role of women in sport, the length of practice seasons, the purposes of school physical education, and the role of fitness in a healthy life all have strong philosophical overtones that *are* being addressed.

A final problem transcends all three of the specializations in the sport humanities. Each of these specializations has tended to focus more and more exclusively on sport. Fitness and physical education get only cursory treatment, if any. The names of the specializations clearly show their main interest—sport. It will be interesting to see whether this narrow focus continues or whether there is some broadening of focus to include the related areas of fitness and physical education.

SUMMARY

1. Sport humanities include the fields of sport history, sport philosophy, and sport literature.

2. The *sport humanities* are concerned with human thought and relations in the context of sport.

3. *Sport history* describes the past in relation to sport, interprets it, relates it to the present, and provides guidelines about the future.

4. Sport history typically falls into the categories of narrative-descriptive history and interpretive-comparative history.

5. *Sport philosophy* can be *first-order philosophy*, dealing with metaphysics, axiology, epistemology, and logic; or it can be *second-order*

philosophy, dealing with professional issues from a philosophical perspective.

6. Sport literature includes fiction, poetry, and films that have permanent value because of their excellence of form, emotional effect, and insights about the human condition.

7. The philosophical and historical foci in sport, fitness, and physical education have long traditions; sport literature is a more recent addition.

8. Each of the three branches has its own organizational affiliation and its own literature.

9. The marked increase in sport interest since the early 1970s has been accompanied by a popular literature and an increase in serious films about sport, as well as a similar increase in academic study of sport within the sport humanities.

10. Faculty members in history, philosophy, and literature have joined with faculty members in physical education to form the nucleus for the sport humanities.

11. Paths to careers in the sport humanities are through academic preparation, typically at the doctoral level, either in physical education or in the parent disciplines of history, philosophy, or literature.

12. Two problematic issues in the field are the relatively small sizes of the areas, with associated problems of limited resources, and the degree to which popular-media sport commentators are ill informed about the knowledge base in the sport humanities.

13. Sport philosophy as an academic study has tended to focus narrowly on first-order philosophy, whereas many professionals are interested in second-order philosophical issues associated with their work.

14. To date, these areas have focused almost exclusively on sport, with less attention paid to fitness or physical education.

DISCUSSION QUESTIONS

1. Why have sport films become so popular? What does this popularity indicate regarding the importance of these fields?

2. Do coaches typically have a real philosophy of the sport they coach? Do you?

3. What books about sport have you read? How would you classify those books?

4. What do you know about the history of sport? How would a knowledge of sport history help you as a coach or a sport administrator?

5. Why is there no comparable interest in the history or philosophy of fitness or of physical education?

PART SIX

Future Problems and Prospects

Chapter 21 Relationships to Allied Fields

Chapter 22 Sport, Fitness, and Physical Education in the Twenty-First Century: Themes Defining Our Present and Future

At the beginning of the twentieth century, sport, fitness, and physical education were in many respects indistinguishable from health, recreation, and dance. All of these endeavors coexisted comfortably under the umbrella of the emerging physical-education profession. However, the subsequent development of these fields has been toward specialization and a separate identity. Each now has its own professional goals, organizations, literature, and certification. The person who is interested in activity and leisure, for whatever purposes, is not likely to make these distinctions.

What do the fields of health, recreation, and dance do? How are they allied to sport, fitness, and physical education? What does all of this mean for our future? What needs to be done in the future to ensure that appropriate services are provided to people? The two chapters in Part 6 are designed both to provide insights that help you answer those questions and to challenge you to think carefully about important issues in our future.

CHAPTER **21**

Relationships to Allied Fields

The time has come to address the problem of the splintering of the discipline of human development into minor professional fiefdoms. The splintering of physical education, health education, and recreation, and sometimes their further separation into narrow specialties, is harming the development of the activity and leisure industry.

Michael Ellis, 1988

LEARNING OBJECTIVES

- To distinguish among the fields of health, recreation, and dance

- To discuss the scope of the leisure-services industry

- To discuss the scope of the health-enhancement industry

- To describe the occupational prospects in these fields

- To discuss the scope of dance education

- To describe the preparation to enter these fields

- To discuss problems and issues within these fields

At the beginning of the twentieth century, a number of emerging professional fields came together under the umbrella of physical education. (See Chapter 2 for a history of this period.) Three of those fields were *recreation, health,* and *dance.* During the time that these fields developed, there were no sharp distinctions among them, and professionals often worked within several of the areas. During the period of emergence, training as a physical educator included a broad preparation that allowed people to work in any of the fields under the physical-education umbrella. Even today, AAHPERD attempts to preserve that tradition through its alliance of professional organizations. From one perspective, recreation, health, and dance have achieved success in developing as distinct professional areas, with their own certifications, their own professional literatures, their own specialized research fields, and their own constituencies.

Recreation, health, and dance have made significant progress as independent fields. People who prepare for professional work within these fields frequently specialize to the point where they have little contact with the larger physical-education field from which they emerged in the 1940s. As Ellis (1988) has argued, it is less clear that those who seek activity, leisure, or health services recognize these specializations as distinct.

> The professions of health, education, physical education, and recreation, however, remain inextricably linked. All of them develop and deliver services that are part of the total health package. All contribute to the constructive use of leisure. If the boundaries between them are difficult for the professionals themselves to draw, they are impossible for the client. The client's body has multiple needs and possibilities, but the client lives and experiences these needs, and the connections between them, as a whole. (Ellis, 1988, pp. 5–6)

It can be further argued that most of the significant problems related to leisure, health, and activity cannot be solved except through collaboration by professionals within these fields. For example, the most successful interventions on the health and activity status of children have been achieved through elementary-school programs in which physical educators, health educators, school food-service workers, and classroom teachers collaborate. Thus, as the separate professions of recreation, health, and dance are described in this chapter, please keep in mind that, for most consumers of these services, the separation is not apparent. Among professionals themselves, there is growing recognition that these separations need to be decreased.

RECREATION

What is increasingly referred to as the *recreation and leisure-services industry* is a huge national industry, providing enormous and varied career opportunities for women and men. This industry includes sports and games, travel and tourism, hobbies and the arts, various kinds of entertainment (theme parks, etc.), fitness pursuits, and outdoor activities, as well as traditional recreation providers such as the YMCA, the YWCA, community recreation departments in towns and cities, state recreation departments, and federal parks and recreation (Kraus, 2002). Annual expenditures for recreation range from the U.S. Commerce Department's estimate of over $490 billion (U.S. Census Bureau, 2000, p. 253) to as high as a trillion dollars a year.

Recreation providers are private and public, commercial and nonprofit. Together they constitute an enormous job market and create an increasing need for well-prepared professionals who seek a career in the industry. This diverse job market is best seen by perusing *Careers in Recreation* (American Association for Leisure and Recreation, 2000), which describes more than 25 types of positions. Among them are jobs in municipal and community recreation programs, at ski resorts, at theme parks, at tennis clubs, at family recreation

Worthy use of leisure is a lifetime issue.

centers, in conservation areas, in state and national parks, at corporate recreation centers, at armed-services recreation centers, in university recreation and intramural programs, in camps of every imaginable variety, in therapeutic recreation programs, and in a host of other agencies for which recreation is a key component—YMCA, YWCA, Boy Scouts, Girls Scouts, 4-H, Police Athletic League, Boys and Girls Clubs, and so on. As this industry developed during and after World War II, it moved from a base of primarily public and service-organization offerings with many volunteer workers to a base of commercial/private/municipal services with paid workers.

Recreation has been defined as activities or experiences chosen voluntarily and done during leisure time for the satisfaction they provide the individuals and groups involved (Colfer et al., 1986). The worthy use of leisure time by citizens has been a national concern since the cardinal principles of education were enumerated in 1918. An active, healthy leisure life is thought to have restorative power and is considered to be a necessary part of an overall high-quality lifestyle.

As a profession develops, more professional preparation is required for entry into its ranks, of-ten through programs that must meet certification standards of one kind or another. The professional preparation of recreation and leisure-services personnel started after the 1930s (McLean et al., 1988). Yet, in this short time, a number of specializations have developed, and certifications for entry into professional roles are much more common. In the 1960s, a person would have been prepared as a general recreation specialist; today she or he is more likely to focus specifically on one aspect of the recreation and leisure-services industry—parks, resource management, recreation-program management, recreation and park administration, therapeutic recreation, outdoor recreation, camping, school recreation, youth-agency recreation, recreation-sport management, aging, corrections, commercial tourism, recreational planning, environmental interpretation, or research (McLean et al., 1988). Estimates in the 1980s indicated that as many as 550 institutions of higher education offered a curriculum that prepared students to enter the recreation and leisure-services industry (McLean et al., 1988).

A number of professional organizations exist within the field of recreation. The largest of these, the National Recreation and Park Association (NRPA), was formed in 1966. This association was created specifically to provide for a unified recreation profession and was formed by the merging of five professional groups: the American Recreation Society, the American Institute of Park Executives, the American Association of Zoological Parks and Aquariums, the National Conference on State Parks, and the National Recreation Association (McLean et al., 1988). The NRPA has an active citizen component, in which laypeople interact with professionals to establish goals and programs. The organization serves its members in many ways, through research, dissemination of program information, professional development, legislative policy information, field services to local groups, and publications, including three major journals: *Parks and Recreation, Journal of Leisure Research,* and *Therapeutic Recreation Journal.*

Other professional organizations that serve this area directly are the American Association for Leisure and Recreation, which is the member organization for recreation in AAHPERD; the World Leisure and Recreation Association, which promotes professional interests at the international level; and the American Camping Association, which for many years has promoted camping as an educational and recreational experience for children and adults.

Kraus (2002) has identified ten distinct areas of professional recreation service and employment.

1. *Public recreation and park agencies.* These are tax-supported and publicly regulated units, ranging in size from local recreation and park units to major national agencies such as the National Park Service, the National Forest Service, and the Bureau of Land Management. Together they employ hundreds of thousands of administrators, program directors, facility planners, and other specialists.

2. *Nonprofit organizations.* Voluntary community agencies, both religious and secular, provide a range of services, including recreation. Although many of these depend on volunteers, they increasingly employ paid professionals to manage and provide services. For example, the Boys and Girls Clubs serve 3 million youth members in 2,260 club locations with nearly 10,000 full-time professional staff.

3. *Commercial recreation.* These "for-profit" enterprises range from small local putt-putt golf to large corporations who franchise chains of fitness clubs or family play centers. Larger enterprises typically employ recreation professionals for program, marketing, and management positions.

4. *Therapeutic recreation.* This increasingly clinical field works with disabled or ill people in hospitals, long-term care settings, special schools, and rehabilitation clinics. Certification requirements and other issues in this field are the province of the National Therapeutic Recreation Society and the American Therapeutic Recreation Association.

5. *Armed-forces recreation.* Key elements on military bases in the United States and throughout the world are "morale, welfare, and recreation" programs, ranging from organized sport programs to crafts and hobbies. The Armed Forces Recreation Society is the primary group promoting and improving military recreation.

6. *Employee services and recreation.* Large corporations and businesses typically sponsor programs for their employees and often their families. These programs range from traditional recreation opportunities to fitness and stress management. Included within this group would be the large and growing worksite fitness movement.

7. *Private-membership groups.* This group ranges from private country clubs with golf, tennis, swimming, and fitness facilities to housing and condominium associations that include recreation facilities to help attract buyers to their developments. Sun City, a retirement community near Phoenix, Arizona, offers its 46,000 residents a large variety of recreation opportunities in seven large recreation centers.

8. *Campus recreation.* Colleges and universities have invested enormous sums of money to upgrade their recreation facilities, programs, and staffs. These are ways to attract students, keep them in school, and encourage them to stay on campus on weekends.

9. *Sport management.* This rapidly growing field includes a large number of professional roles in the public and private sectors. More than 200 colleges and universities offer degree programs in this field. (See Chapter 6 for a full description of career opportunities and degree requirements.)

10. *Travel, tourism, and hospitality.* This very large field offers opportunities that range from cruise-ship and tour programs to resorts and theme parks. The size of the field has led to an expansion of undergraduate and graduate degree programs in travel and tourism, often located in departments or colleges of business.

Leisure and recreation have become big businesses, so it is not surprising that the for-profit commercial enterprises have grown very rapidly in recent years. There is also increasing evidence that historically public and not-for-profit enterprises (city recreation departments, YMCAs, etc.) are now creating partnerships to better serve the large demands for recreation services. The latest entry into the leisure field is electronic entertainment, which ranges in complexity from video games for home computers to video-game arcades to highly sophisticated virtual-reality experiences—for example, in skiing or golf.

The number of different occupations needed to keep the recreation and leisure-services industry going is staggering. Not all these occupations require *specialized* preparation, but many of them do. The trend in the recreation professions, as in any other professional group, is toward certification and licensing; typically, state legislation establishes the criteria for the certification. Thus far, recreation has not achieved widespread certification status, although that is clearly the direction being taken within the profession. An intermediate step is *accreditation,* an approach in which institutions that train personnel have their programs approved by an autonomous body. Accreditation provides assurance to the public that personnel have competencies that ensure safety and appropriate programming for recreation services. Program accreditation now exists widely in the recreation and leisure-services professions.

The prospects for the recreation and leisure-services field are virtually limitless. Recreation is what Dunn (1986a) has described as America's "giant opportunity." As life in the modern age becomes more complex, stresses seem to increase, even to the extent that *stress management* has become a specialized field that tends to bring together the recreation and health professions.

This *restorative* goal for recreation will, however, be increasingly balanced by a newer view that sees recreation as a positive, preventive activity, as seen in the growing wellness movements in health. Corporations have begun to recognize that a healthy employee who has an active and satisfying leisure life is a more productive employee. Preparation for leisure continues to be recognized as a goal in school programs. Recreation for the increasingly large segment of the population in retirement is a growing field, filled with bright prospects and perplexing problems. Recreation for people with disabilities, for both regular and therapeutic purposes, is also a growing field. It is no wonder that recreation specialists view the next few decades as being filled with possibilities.

> The years ahead are years of opportunity. They may become the golden years of the first 100 years of the recreation movement. The profession has great responsibilities and opportunities. It will be an interesting period professionally because of growth, greater professional recognition, and the universal acceptance that recreation is inherent in all phases of community, family, and individual living. (Jack, 1985, p. 98)

A major issue in recreation now and for the future will be the reduction and elimination of constraints that interfere with access to and involvement in recreation (Henderson & Bialeschki, 1991). Historically, we have tended to think of constraints as limited time because of work and other obligations, inadequate skills for participation, insufficient discretionary monies, poor facilities, and the like. Although those remain important, it is now clear that issues such as gender, age, disability, and socioeconomic status are also serious constraints (Cordes & Ibrahim, 2003). Of particular concern are the problems of adequate recreation for urban children, youths, and adults who live in

Many kinds of competition engage us in our leisure time.

relative poverty, especially compared with the typically abundant recreation opportunities in the suburbs. Inner-city communities have less public recreation land, fewer recreation staff, and minimal community volunteer support, and must contend with the threat of gangs and violence (Cordes & Ibrahim, 2003, p. 275).

These inner-city problems led Kraus (1995) to argue that the growth of commercial recreation and the explosion of private-membership recreation groups, located primarily around city beltways and in suburbs, have divided American society into leisure haves and have-nots. Recreation is quickly becoming privatized. It is now common in residential development for a development area to feature its own recreation facilities, for which homeowners pay a yearly fee; programs are available only to those who live within the development.

Another key issue is that by the year 2020, more than 20 percent of the population will be over 65 years of age, living longer, living healthier, and more in need of quality leisure and recreation experiences. Older people have traditionally been raised to think that active recreation is not something to aspire to, but it is clear that their attitudes are changing dramatically. We can expect that when the baby-boomers reach the 65-and-beyond age group, they will fully expect to remain active and to participate in recreation activities.

Recreation has always been closely allied to sport, fitness, and physical education. Historically, the fields had similar beginnings and strong relationships in programs and personnel. In the past several decades, however, each has tended to become more specialized, and interrelationships among the allied fields have weakened. That issue is addressed in the following chapter. Suffice it to say that if lifespan sport, fitness, and physical education is to become more of a reality for a larger percentage of the population, interrelationships among the fields will need to develop and strengthen.

HEALTH

It must be evident and convincing to the average citizen and community leaders, including politicians, that the strength of the nation rests upon the health of its people; that the future of the health of the people depends to a large extent on what is done to pro mote, improve, and preserve the health of school and college-age children and youth. (Johns, 1985, p. 105)

The healthy lifestyle is in! Americans, especially those in the middle- and upper-income brackets, have taken health more seriously in the past several decades than they ever did before. The health professions have gradually shifted from a primarily remedial or medical approach to a primarily preventive or wellness approach. Whereas remediating or preventing sickness and disease characterized the main agenda of the health professions early in the twentieth century, the notion of living well increasingly shared that agenda at century's end. Americans are living longer, and the senior population is becoming a strong political and social force in American society. For these senior citizens, access to health care and a healthy lifestyle have become important issues.

Traditionally, the primary focus of the health professions has been the education of children and youths. Thus, it is health education that has, historically, been the strongest force in the emerging health professions. Since the mid-1980s, however, that tradition has been modified substantially. We have witnessed the growth of the **health-enhancement industry** and an explosion of in-

terest in health-related issues pertinent to people of all ages.

Lifestyle decisions concerning nutrition, drugs, safety, activity, stress management, and other related areas have been clearly identified as major influences on health and disease. The people's health needs are met by a complex web of service delivery systems—hospitals, clinics, health centers, counseling centers, fitness programs, advertising, health clubs—designed to enhance health as well as to eliminate disease. These systems exist in both the public and private sectors of our economy. They are created by individual action, by businesses for profit, by philanthropic organizations, and by the government. They employ a very large number of people and consume an enormous proportion of the nation's wealth even as they contribute to it. Together, they are known as the *health enhancement industry,* and they share a simple, common goal: improving people's health. (Ellis, 1988, p. 4)

When we consider the health needs of individuals, we most commonly think about the medical profession. Yet many health professionals work outside the area of direct medical care, such as is provided in hospitals. They work both in the public sector, through community and government programs, and, increasingly, in the private sector, through a host of entrepreneurial and corporate programs.

One way to understand the broad parameters of the health-enhancement industry is to consider the many topics and issues that are now addressed within the field of health and health education: family living, sexuality, substance abuse, personal health, nutrition, weight control, first aid and safety, consumer health protection, and interpersonal relationships. Since the 1960s or so, these topical fields have been brought together under the concept of **wellness,** which conveys the broader meaning of a positive, vigorous, healthy lifestyle.

Healthy People 2010 now charts the course for health promotion and health education. The two main goals of HP2010 are to increase the years of healthy life for all people and to eliminate health disparities based on race, gender, and income. (See Chapter 9 for further details.) HP2010 created a set of leading health indicators that are intended to make the importance of health promotion more easily understandable to a wide audience. The indicators were chosen for their ability to motivate action, the availability of data to measure their progress, and their relevance as broad public health issues. These indicators are

- Physical activity
- Overweight and obesity
- Tobacco use
- Substance abuse
- Mental health
- Injury and violence
- Environmental quality
- Immunization
- Access to health care

Data on progress for all the 28 focus areas of HP2010 and the 467 objectives embedded in those areas are available through DATA2010, an interactive database system accessible through the National Center for Health Statistics Web site.

The services of the health-enhancement industry are delivered to people through five major components: school health education, government and community health programs, nonprofit health organizations, worksite health programs, and private-sector entrepreneurial programs. Health education has been historically linked with physical education and has long been an accepted part of the K–12 school curriculum. Originally referred to most commonly as *hygiene*, the school health-education program has grown steadily more important and increasingly separate from physical education. Many states have enacted laws requiring that health education be taught in schools, often specifying the grade levels at which it must be taught and the amount of time or the number of units to be devoted to it.

Health education in schools is likely to become increasingly important as more of the nation's wealth is devoted to health care and maintenance.

Family-oriented activities are important to the wellness movement.

School is still the only societal institution that reaches most children and youths; therefore, it makes sense for most health promotion and education for children and youths to be programmed through schools. Six categories of behaviors are strongly related to mortality and morbidity statistics, thus warranting attention in school health education and promotion (Kahn et al., 1995):

1. Behaviors that contribute to injuries, such as carrying weapons or not wearing seat belts

2. Tobacco use (smoking or chewing)

3. Alcohol and other drug use

4. Sexual behaviors that contribute to sexually transmitted diseases and unintended pregnancies

5. Poor dietary habits

6. Physical inactivity

Most of these behaviors are established during late childhood and early youth, thus making them relevant targets for school-based interventions.

School health education and community health have, traditionally, been the two general areas of preparation for health professionals. Government and community health programs are varied in nature and widespread, ranging from direct intervention, such as in school lunch and breakfast programs, to educational efforts, such as the development of literature on subjects such as prenatal care. Most state, county, and municipal governments have agencies devoted to health care and education. At the federal level, the Department of Health and Human Services is a huge organization, the director of which serves on the U.S. president's cabinet. It is now common for city governments to develop senior-citizen centers where issues of health and recreation are dealt with through both education and direct intervention.

Nonprofit health organizations have become increasingly active in the health-enhancement industry—the American Heart Association and the Lung Association are two good examples. The main purposes of nonprofit health associations are to generate financial support for research and program development in the particular areas they serve, to educate the public about the central issues surrounding their focus, and to influence people to lead healthier lifestyles. Thus, these organizations not only solicit funds and produce educational materials but also promote healthy behavior. The American Heart Association sponsors competitive road races, fun runs, and walkathons, and the Lung Association each year sponsors the "Great American Smoke-Out," encouraging smokers to quit smoking. Perhaps most important, these organizations fund substantial research.

As with the leisure-services industry, strong contemporary growth in the health-enhancement industry has occurred in the corporate and private sectors. The field of **worksite health promotion** has developed and promises to become an even more important sector of this industry.

In the next twenty years, as we evolve toward a more health- and leisure-centered society, we should not be surprised to find the workplace become a major provider of health, recreation, and fitness. . . . Moreover, an increasing number of employers are moving to an enlightened and comprehensive approach which enhances life quality of the employee and his/her family. "State of the art" corporate programs now offer sports, recreation, and primary prevention programs. Even small firms without facilities are contracting with neighborhood golf, tennis, and health clubs to give employees access to programs at reduced or no cost. (Fain, 1983, pp. 32–33)

The number of companies providing formal programs of worksite health promotion has increased steadily since the early 1970s. Of the many objectives in *Healthy People 2000,* the goal for increase in worksite health and fitness programs was the only one to achieve the recommended improvement. The incidence of such programs increased from 2.5 percent in 1979 to 85 percent in 2000. Unfortunately, estimates also suggest that no more than 20 percent of eligible workers take part, and only half of those remain active in the program over time (Shephard, 1988).

Companies provide worksite health programs for a variety of reasons, not the least of which is increased worker productivity, which increases profit margins. The costs of poor health among employees are incurred in high absenteeism, reduced productivity, reduced morale, and increased costs of worker compensation (Villeneuve, Weeks, & Schwied, 1983). The cost of health insurance is now a major factor in overall company costs, and reducing that cost item is perhaps the quickest way for companies to increase their profitability. Many firms have not only introduced health and recreation programs for employees but also pay end-of-year bonuses to employees who remain healthy—for example, those who are not often absent and who do not present claims on the employee health-insurance program.

Health enhancement in the private sector has become big business, with big profits to be made by entrepreneurs who cater effectively to the increasing demands of Americans for health-related activities, literature, and programs. Many of the private-sector programs described in Chapters 6 and 9 would qualify as health-enhancement efforts. The scope of the private-sector health industry is large, and its parameters are difficult to define. It is not unusual to see health-food or nutritional-supplement stores in shopping malls. The exercise-equipment industry is growing rapidly. Health clubs are now a common sight in many areas. Counseling for substance abuse, interpersonal relationships, marital discord, nutrition, and weight control is widely available in the private sector. Massage therapists advertise their skills mostly on the basis of health benefits. The health sections of bookstores are large and filled with self-help books, ranging from the latest fad diet to self-concept improvement to family relations.

The private sector of the health-enhancement industry is largely unregulated. Although many health professionals do have certifications and licenses, many do not. Most states allow people who have *not* completed a certified program or earned a license to continue to advertise their services as "counselors" or "specialists." Although many counselors are, in fact, either clinical psychologists or psychological counselors, which guarantees their training, many have no such preparation. Many consumers are anxious for quick results and are looking for miracle programs to improve their lives. This combination of loosely regulated services and consumers who are anxious to improve but are not always well informed about the services has resulted in a certain amount of quackery in the private-sector health-enhancement industry.

School health educators are certified and licensed to teach in the same way as all teachers are: They complete an approved program of teacher education at a university or college, one that meets the standards established by the state. Health educators are typically certified as K–12 specialist teachers. There is no certification in community health programs, although many colleges and universities have undergraduate-degree specializations in community health. A graduate degree, the Master of Public Health (M.P.H.), is a widely sought and highly valued degree in the health professions. Criteria for accreditation of M.P.H. programs have been established by the Council on Education for Public Health.

A host of more specific certifications exist in some parts of the health-enhancement industry. In the fitness area, the ACSM has a series of certifications, and institutions such as the YMCA are increasingly involved in training and certifying people who work within their fitness programs. Most states have laws regulating the training of clinical psychologists and psychological counselors, many of whom practice within the health field. Massage therapists typically have a license that guarantees they have had a certain amount of training.

There are more than 300 professional preparation programs for health educators (Cissell, 1992). The task of creating and enforcing credentialing for such a diverse profession is substantial. Beginning in 1992, the National Commissions for Health Education Credentialing required professionals to complete an approved health-education program to become eligible to take an examination to become a certified health-education specialist. Because the health-education field is so diverse, with individuals working in schools, communities, industry, and government, the direction of preparation for health specialists has been toward skills related to interaction processes between health professionals and their clients.

The contemporary emergence of healthy lifestyle management as a positive force represents a major shift in perception among the public. The *possibility* and the *desirability* of involving individuals in the development and maintenance of a healthy lifestyle represent an important new value in American life. On the other hand, this revolution is mostly confined to young people with middle or high income levels. There is little evidence that people in lower income brackets with little discretionary income have become involved in the wellness movement. The evidence on fitness levels and eating habits of children is so alarming that we cannot fairly say that this revolution is being passed on to the next generation.

Still, there is hope! Fewer people smoke. Smoking is prohibited in many transportation, office, commercial, and restaurant settings, making it more difficult for people who want to smoke to find a place where they are allowed to smoke. Although too many teens begin to smoke, and smoking, like many health-related behaviors, appears to be strongly related to social class, the nation has made important progress in this health-related behavior.

It appears that more people are exercising and have become more conscious of the nutritional values of the foods they eat regularly. The advertising industry has obviously made the healthy person the centerpiece of advertisements selling a variety of products. People are portrayed as fit, active, and concerned about the health value of their lifestyles. Good information relative to the health benefits and liabilities of an increasing number of products, programs, and activities is now widely available.

In 1979 the United States Surgeon General pointed out that a few relatively simple decisions, controlled by individuals, can result in dramatic improvements in people's health. An individual can greatly reduce his or her risk for degenerative disease by making the right personal decisions about smoking, alcohol use, diet, exercise, seat-belt use, and periodic screening for major diseases (Richmond, 1979). The individual benefits with a greatly reduced probability of early morbidity and mortality; the nation benefits through greatly reduced health costs and a more productive citizenry. The goal of the health professions must be to encourage the public to make these personal positive lifestyle decisions. Through HP2000 and HP2010, the public-policy apparatus of the federal government has clearly moved to promote health goals and

programs. These filter down through state government to local government. The private sector also has a role in policy development to support healthy lifestyles, examples of which are prohibition of smoking in restaurants and workplaces, better nutrition in school and worksite cafeterias, reductions in insurance premiums based on health behaviors, and the increase in worksite health-promotion programs. It is an exciting time to be a health educator or a health-promotion professional.

DANCE

> The movement for serious dance education is ripe. Unified efforts can produce significant results in placing dance education in schools throughout America. Students deserve to be exposed to the beauty, joy, symbology, and expression that dance affords. Through the study of dance, students appreciate how we are tied to a continuous line of man's history and how cultures past and present have danced in ritual, in celebration, and in efforts to establish social interaction. (McLaughlin, 1988, p. 60)

Dance seems to be a significant human activity in virtually every culture known. Dance can be a cultural art form, as are modern dance and ballet. Dance can be strongly educational, as are the creative-dance movement in schools and the educational dance portions of movement-education curricula. Dance can be utilized as a means of expression, as when it is used as therapy. Dance has also become an important fitness activity; the growing aerobic-dance movement is an example.

Dance has always been an expression of the popular culture. What we now study as folk dance involves the popular forms of dancing from other cultures in other times. The traditional folk dance of the westward expansion of the United States was the square dance. Ballroom dancing has been a popular form of social dance for many years and is still taught, in both schools and the private sector. The jitterbug and swing were the popular dance forms of several generations ago, and dancing to

Dance traditions are important in almost every known culture.

rock-and-roll music was the folk dance of the sixties generation. Popular films such as *Footloose* and *Dirty Dancing* focused on the power of popular dance in the lives of young people.

The inclusion of dance in the physical education of children and youths is a product of the twentieth century. Margaret H'Doubler of the University of Wisconsin is generally credited with establishing dance as part of the school physical-education curriculum (Hayes, 1980). As physical education became a required subject in many states in the 1920s, dance was introduced into school programs. Within physical education, however, dance became severely restricted. As elementary physical education grew and prospered, many physical-education teachers included units on creative dance in their

programs. Units on folk dance were also taught, often with the help of the specialist music teacher. In middle schools and high schools, folk-dance units were common, but specialized teaching of jazz dance and ballet was infrequent, mostly elective, and mostly chosen by girls. Dance educators believe strongly that this typical scenario makes it impossible for any student to receive an education in dance (Posey, 1988). If young girls or boys wanted specific training in jazz, modern, or ballet dancing, they had to go to the private sector, where dance schools have catered to those needs.

Physical educators often are required to take one or two dance courses as part of their certification programs. Many, however, do not like dance themselves, have insufficient training in it, and exclude it from their school programs if they have a choice. Thus, dance education in many places disappeared or was severely restricted to a unit on square dance.

In the 1970s, that picture began to change (McLaughlin, 1988). Dance, as an important cultural art form, began to be rediscovered. Established dance companies were revitalized. Important new companies were developed. Experimental forms of modern dance were well received. A growing national interest in dance precipitated renewed interest among children and youths. The federal and state governments made more money available to promote dance and dance education.

In the educational-reform climate of the 1980s and 1990s, arts education became a focus of school curriculum reform—and dance education became part of an integrated-arts approach in many elementary and middle schools. Physical education has played only a minor role in this new integrated-arts approach to school curricula. Schools and communities have begun to work together to bring dancers and other community artists into the schools.

Perhaps, of all the activity connected with the reform of arts education, the movement toward collaborative ventures has been the most productive resource for the improvement of how the arts are taught in local communities around the country. These collaborative ventures, involving schools, art specialists, artists, cultural institutions, institutions of higher education, and the arts provider organizations, have yielded significant results in communities where they have occurred. These communities have garnered increased advocacy for the arts in school, have enacted arts education policies leading to curriculum development, and have witnessed increased numbers of artist residencies and relationships with cultural facilities. (McLaughlin, 1988, p. 39)

Another significant development in arts education is the emergence of a movement known as **discipline-based arts education** (Posey, 1988). This movement focuses on art as technique—on learning to dance—but also has an equal emphasis on understanding the arts, on becoming an educated, literate consumer of the arts, and on being part of a knowledgeable arts audience. New curricula have been developed that stress the audience or consumer role in dance education. Students learn not only how to dance but also how to create dances, how to make decisions about what they see in dance, and how to enjoy dance as a member of a dance audience (Allen, 1988).

Dance is one of the best vehicles for achieving goals in multicultural education, which is important and popular in many schools and agencies. For instance, dance, music, storytelling, and festivals are ways in which we come to understand both our own culture and other cultures (Monroe, 1995). The "Full-house Children's Dance Company" of St. Cloud, Minnesota, is a good example. By creating a multiracial dance company of children and by exploring cultural differences through dance, this company has contributed to significant social change in its local area (Leigh, 1994).

Many colleges and universities offer majors or minors in dance. Many of these departments are oriented toward performance and focus on preparing dancers for professional work as members of dance companies. Ballet and modern dance remain the two strongest dance forms in college and university departments. Few states offer teaching certification in dance. Thus, dance education is still embedded primarily within physical education. Although movement education and the emerging integrated-arts approach have made dance more important in elementary-school curricula, it is still viewed primarily as another activity unit in most school programs where it is taught by the physical educator. More intense and specific dance education takes place in the private sector, in dance schools. No certification is necessary, however, to teach dance in the private sector.

When the AAHPER was reorganized in 1974 to become the alliance, the Dance Division of the old AAHPER became the National Dance Association in the new alliance. In 1980 dance was added to the alliance name, which became AAHPERD. A "D" was also added to the major journal of the alliance, which became *JOPERD*. The National Dance Association continued to be an active member of the alliance and has worked hard to develop curricula and educational materials to foster the growth of dance education in schools.

ALLIED OR INTEGRATED?

Recreation, health, and dance are still nominally integrated with sport, fitness, and physical education. The AAHPERD umbrella still exists, with each of these fields having major organizational representation within the alliance. Yet it is equally clear that each has established itself as an independent field, with its own organizations and literature. Recreation has increasingly aligned itself with other aspects of the emerging leisure industry. Health has increasingly aligned itself with other allied medical fields. Dance has increasingly found a home with music and art, within a unified- or integrated-arts perspective.

In one sense, the explosion of knowledge and interest in these various fields has required their development as independent professional areas. In 1900 it was possible for one person to acquire the basic knowledge, understanding, and skills to perform professionally as a physical educator, recreation educator, health educator, and dance educator. That is no longer true. Physical education has moved well beyond its limited gymnastics origins.

⊃ **GET CONNECTED TO ALLIED FIELD WEB SITES**

Recreation

American Association for Leisure and Recreation	www.aahperd.org/aalr
American Trails	www.americantrails.org
American Hiking Society	www.americanhiking.org
American Recreation Coalition	www.funoutdoors.com
American Therapeutic Recreation Association	www.atra-tr.org
National Recreation and Park Association	www.nrpa.org
Therapeutic Recreation	www.recreationtherapy.com
Wilderness Education Association	www.weainfo.org
League of American Bicyclists	www.bikeleague.org

Health

American Association for Health Education	www.aahperd.org/aahe
American College Health Association	www.acha.org
American Public Health Association	www.apha.org
American School Health Association	www.ascha.org
Department of Health and Human Services	www.os.dhhs.gov
National Institutes of Health	www.nih.gov
Society of Public Health Education	www.sophe.org
Health Education Professional Resources	www.nyu.edu/education/hepr
National Education Association—Health Information Network	www.neahin.org
Action for Health Kids	www.actionforhealthykids.org

Dance

National Dance Association	www.aahperd.org/nda
Folk Dance Association	www.folkdancing.org
American Dance Therapy Association	www.adta.org
Dance Vision	www.dancevision.com
DanceDanceDance	www.dancedancedance.com

Recreation has become a multidimensional enterprise. The field of health has moved well beyond its historic emphasis on hygiene. Dance has also become a multifaceted discipline. It seems unlikely that any curriculum could be developed to prepare professionals to function well in each of the three areas. Thus, it seems unlikely that the course of specialized development of these separate fields will reverse itself in the near future. Yet it also seems clear that some new integrative efforts will have to be made to satisfy the growing demand of people in the private sector for services that cut across these increasingly separate fields. That issue is discussed further in the next chapter.

SUMMARY

1. Recreation, health, and dance developed under the umbrella of the emerging physical-education profession early in the twentieth century. They have more recently become independent fields, with their own associations, literature, and constituencies.

2. The fields are linked but separate. The separations often are not noticed by clients but are rigidly adhered to by professionals.

3. The recreation and leisure-services industry is broadly based, with a number of specializations and professional organizations.

4. Recreation programs are delivered through government agencies, voluntary organizations, private-membership groups, and commercial enterprises.

5. The number of occupations available in the recreation and leisure-services industry is large. Only a few such positions require certification or accreditation.

6. The future prospects of this industry are limitless, especially in areas providing services for older citizens and people with disabilities.

7. The health professions have moved from a remedial to a wellness approach, with the focus shifting from children and youths to lifespan health and lifestyle education.

8. The health-enhancement industry is broadly based. It is delivered through five major components: school health education, government and community health programs, nonprofit health organizations, worksite health programs, and private-sector entrepreneurial programs.

9. Whereas school health professionals are certified, many of the professional occupations within the health-enhancement industry require no certification, especially those within the private-sector entrepreneurial programs.

10. Although the healthy-lifestyle revolution is confined primarily to adults in the middle- and upper-income brackets, there is increasing evidence that more people are responding to health information with changes in behavior.

11. Dance education has played a relatively minor role in school programs and has been offered more by the private sector. It has, however, received markedly increased attention since the 1970s, because of a general resurgence of interest in dance.

12. In the educational-reform climate of the 1980s and 1990s, dance received renewed curricular attention as part of arts education.

13. The discipline-based arts-education movement focuses not only on technique but also on understanding and appreciating art forms from the perspective of the viewer or audience.

14. Few states certify dance educators, and none requires that a person have a license to practice as a dance instructor in the private sector.

15. Recreation, health, and dance have become increasingly independent fields yet are still allied with AAHPERD.

DISCUSSION QUESTIONS

1. What are the prospects of unification between (a) health, recreation, and dance, and (b) sport, fitness, and physical education?

2. Is there a chance that health, recreation, and dance will grow so strongly that they gradually will encompass sport, fitness, and physical education? Explain your answer.

3. In your local area, what are examples of how health and leisure services are delivered to diverse populations?

4. Why has dance splintered from physical education in so many places? Who teaches dance in schools in your area—a physical-education teacher, a music teacher, a dance teacher, or someone else?

5. What do you see as the main components of a lifestyle education? Who would deliver these components? Where would they be delivered?

CHAPTER 22

Sport, Fitness, and Physical Education in the Twenty-First Century: Themes Defining Our Present and Future

My contention . . . is that we in health, physical education, recreation, and dance—that centaur known as HPERD—desperately need to widen and scrub off the windows through which we view the world. My belief is that our vision is too narrow and blurred, leaving us muddle-headed and exposed to the sharp edges of professional life.

John Burt, 1987

LEARNING OBJECTIVES

- To analyze issues and problems within and between the specialized professional and scientific groups

- To analyze problems between these groups and larger societal interests

- To analyze issues related to equity that cut across these professional groups

- To discuss public and private concerns about how sport, fitness, and physical education are delivered

- To evaluate unification and fragmentation as they relate to the future needs of lifespan involvement

The twenty-first century is here. Sport, fitness, and physical education traveled a long way in the twentieth century. In 1900 school physical education consisted largely of formal gymnastics. Physical fitness was a topic unknown to most people. School sport was virtually nonexistent. Intercollegiate and professional sport were in their infancies. Public health concerns centered primarily on infectious, rather than degenerative, diseases. Should the same amount of progress occur in the next 100 years, it is hard to imagine what sport, fitness, and physical education might look like in the early twenty-second century. We can, however, look carefully at the major themes that appear to be most salient for understanding the foreseeable future. How the issues and problems embedded within those themes develop and are resolved will determine the course of events for sport, fitness, and physical education for the first part of the twenty-first century.

The purpose of this chapter is to address the important common themes that have been identified throughout the text, to examine them critically, and to allow you to form a point of view regarding each of them. In each of the themes, I will take a clear position and provide an argument to support that position. You may disagree partially or wholly with some or all of these positions. That's fine! I want you to make your own argument, to form your own opinion on these issues. In Part 1 of the text, I argued that the ability to reflect critically on important issues is the hallmark of a professional. A professional philosophy is not an opinion but, rather, a coherent, defensible way of looking at your professional world and making judgments as to future directions.

I began this text by arguing that the dominant characteristic of the era we live in is the possibility and desirability of lifespan involvement in sport, fitness, and physical education. Will that *possibility* become more of a *probability* during the twenty-first century? Will that *possibility* be available to all or just to some? What do we need to do *now* so that sport, fitness, and physical education will be more available to more people with higher-quality services? How do we engage more of the population in lifelong learning related to physical activity? How do we educate children and youths so that they value physical activity enough to make it part of their adult lifestyle? These are the important questions that the themes identified in this chapter are meant to inform. The themes explored are (1) meeting the public health challenge, (2) distributing sport, fitness, and physical education more equitably, (3) focusing on new populations, (4) gender equity in sport, fitness, and physical education, (5) the need for development of after-school programs for children and youths, (6) collaboration between disciplines and professions, (7) the activity and leisure industries, (8) the movement toward an expanded physical education, (9) the movement toward an inclusive rather than exclusionary sport culture, and (10) wellness as the center of lifestyle education.

THEME 1: MEETING THE PUBLIC HEALTH CHALLENGE

Since the late 1980s, the harmful effects of inactivity among the population have been documented scientifically. Engaging in regular physical activity has a host of health benefits, which in turn are strongly related to reducing the proportion of the nation's wealth that is spent on health care. The 1996 U.S. Surgeon General's report clearly established the public health importance of regular physical activity and further established national policy related to improving the physical-activity involvement of children, youths, and adults.

Most of our professional efforts have been directed toward changing individuals' behavior related to risk factors such as smoking, consumption of fatty foods, and physical inactivity. Our most typical strategy has been to offer risk-factor education and intervention programs aimed at individuals: smoking cessation, nutrition education, be-active ad campaigns, and the like. We have done much less to influence public policy in ways that might produce more systemic changes, particularly in influencing policy that is directed toward the establishment and maintenance of physical-activity infrastructures, such as parks, facilities, bike trails, and activity programs.

Health, physical-education, recreation, and fitness professionals are now trained mostly in specialized programs. Although that enables them to be prepared at greater depth and breadth, it comes with a cost—namely, that they are less aware of one another's goals and problems and are less able to work together effectively. There is no doubt anymore that effective programs that will contribute to achieving the goals of *Healthy People 2010* require a broadly based, integrated approach. School personnel do not work with community professionals often enough to extend and sustain health and activity programs for youngsters. Exercise scientists know a great deal about the health benefits of activity but less about how to get people active and keep them active. To meet the public health challenge, we must create groups of specialized professionals who can combine their talents and knowledge to build and sustain programs that work.

It is clear that healthy lifestyles in general and physical activity in particular are not distributed equally throughout the population (Siedentop, 1996c), what health epidemiologists have called the social gradient in health (see Chapter 8). Evidence shows that the health status of a particular socioeconomic class within a nation is typically better than that of classes below it and worse than that of classes above it (Hertzman, 1994). There is some evidence that in nations where socioeconomic distances have been reduced, relevant health-marker variables have improved (Wilkinson, 1994). These facts are clearly recognized now in federal health policy. One of the two overarching goals of HP2010 is to eliminate health disparities based on race, gender, and socioeconomic status. This will be an enormously difficult task and will require strong and creative collaborations among the various health, fitness, recreation, and physical-education professions.

THEME 2: DISTRIBUTING OPPORTUNITY MORE EQUITABLY

The public health challenge described in Theme 1 is not the only reason to hope that sport, fitness, and physical education will be distributed more equitably in the future. Adults who participate in all the various forms of physical activity—climb mountains, square-dance regularly as part of a social club, play golf each weekend in the same foursome, take long bike rides into the country, regularly compete in weekend distance-running events, or play in recreational volleyball leagues, for example—do so for many reasons, most of which have little to do with public health goals. The social and personal benefits of regular engagement in sport, recreation, or physical activity are tremendously important to what people think is meaningful in their lives. The question remains, however, if the experiences are so important for so many reasons, should more people have a chance to take part?

This theme relates directly to Theme 7 because the provision of health, activity, and leisure services

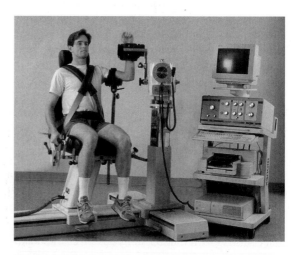

Exercise technology takes the guesswork out of exercise prescription.

has increasingly been catered to by the private sector since the mid-1970s. This private-sector leisure-services industry is driven primarily by consumers who have discretionary income to spend on these services. The industry hardly touches the low-income families who live in the United States, who now represent 25–40 percent of the population. This is particularly true for programs aimed at children and youths; indeed, the children and youths who could most benefit from structured activity programs are the least likely to have access to them (Carnegie Council on Adolescent Development, 1992). Recreator Diana Dunn's description of this dilemma for recreation is equally true for sport, fitness, and physical education:

> If there is an overarching goal for American recreation in the last years of this century, it is the frustratingly familiar but increasingly urgent challenge to balance the continuum of available recreation opportunities to achieve social, political, and economic justice for both the haves and have-nots of America, wherever this dichotomy appears or however it is defined. (Dunn, 1986a, p. 35)

There are only two ways in which this problem can be addressed. One is to work within the political system to distribute income more equitably among people in America. This would require re-distributing income through income-tax revisions and changing somewhat the economic structure of our society. There is little evidence that this will happen in the near future. A second solution is to work to have sport, fitness, and physical education distributed more through the *public* sector—through programs in schools, community recreation centers, public senior centers, and some form of publicly supported child care for infants and preschoolers.

A clear trend since the 1950s has been the **privatization** of leisure, recreation, sport, and fitness (Ellis, 1988; Kraus, 2002). User fees and pay-to-play plans have become more the norm than the exception. Public expenditures on sport, recreation, and fitness have decreased as this privatization has grad-

Will women finally achieve equal opportunity in sport?

ually spread. The real action in the sport, fitness, and leisure worlds is in the private sector.

If this trend continues, it seems clear that access to opportunity in sport, fitness, and physical education will increasingly be tied to wealth. I believe the trend needs to be reversed. As a nation, we have to be willing to tax ourselves to ensure that *all* citizens have access to opportunity in sport, fitness, and physical education. This issue will become increasingly important as child care becomes more common and as the importance of fitness and physical education of young children is more clearly recognized. Should a young boy or girl be denied appropriate developmental care and experience because he or she was born to a poor family?

THEME 3: FOCUSING ON NEW POPULATIONS

Sport, fitness, and physical education have tended to focus primarily on children and youths. School physical-education programs, youth sport, inter-school sport, and youth recreation have dominated the preparation of professionals in these areas and, subsequently, how these professionals plan and implement programs. The focus of our professions needs to extend in both directions, down below the kindergarten to infant and early-childhood programs, and up from college physical education and sport to adult activity and leisure, all the way to planning and implementing programs for senior citizens.

Two important trends mandate this expanded focus. First, it is becoming increasingly clear that early intervention and education in childhood is appropriate both from an educational point of view and, particularly, from an economic point of view. Young children can be more easily educated and more easily directed with respect to lifestyle than can adults, and at considerably less cost. Fitness and leisure habits are ingrained early in childhood, and once ingrained, they become difficult to change. Because adult habits are difficult to change, it tends to cost more to change them than to educate children to form good habits early. The saving to the nation in health costs and medical expenditures of a fitter, more active citizenry would be enormous.

The focus on children as a new population is made more difficult by the fact that children are the new poor in the United States. Estimates suggest that 30 percent of U.S. children live in poverty, representing a segment of the childhood population that is most at risk for health problems. These children and their parents and other caregivers have little access to health-care, nutrition-counseling, or physical-activity programs. They are most affected by the inequitable distribution of sport, fitness, and physical education, described in Theme 2.

The second trend is equally clear. The average age of Americans is increasing. The baby boomers who so greatly expanded the school system in the

Eastern forms of exercise have a strong mental and spiritual component.

1960s and 1970s are now entering their middle age and represent the largest age group in the population. Americans are also living longer. Thus, the older population groups represent major economic and political power. Their needs and interests in sport, fitness, and physical education must be taken into account.

An expanded focus for professional programs in sport, fitness, and physical education requires knowledge and skills different from those traditionally included in professional preparation programs. We know a great deal about how to organize, teach, manage, and motivate captive children and youths in the context of schools. The typical sport, fitness, and physical-education professional knows much less about, and has fewer skills relative to, young children or older adults.

It also appears that much of the programming for these new population groups will take place in the private rather than the public sector, most typically in situations where consumers pay for services. This, too, means professionals will need knowledge and skills that are not typically included in current professional-preparation programs. Unless sport, fitness, and physical-education programs expand to include the knowledge and skills that allow people to work effectively with the younger and older population groups, the market extending services to these groups will be captured by other people who are so trained.

THEME 4: GENDER EQUITY IN SPORT, FITNESS, AND PHYSICAL EDUCATION

In 1900 women could not vote. Being active and fit, or engaging in vigorous sport, was inconsistent with then-male-dominated views of femininity. Today's culture is different. When the American women won the world soccer championship, the entire nation celebrated. In 2002 Title IX became 30 years old. The high school and intercollegiate participation data shown in Chapter 6 clearly indicate progress. Still, there is much to be done before gender equity is fully realized. Girls and women athletes still struggle in many places for an equal share of facilities and budget. Female coaches are seriously underrepresented in coaching and administrative positions. Old stereotypes too often linger.

Cultures tend to change slowly. Practices in and attitudes toward sport, fitness, and physical education have traditionally been shaped by males—they have typically been sexist. The male-dominated belief system has shaped a series of myths that have served to exclude girls and women from opportunity to participate (Coakley, 1994). These myths include prohibitions against strenuous activity because of supposed resulting problems in childbearing, damage to reproductive organs, and menstrual problems, because women were thought to have more fragile bone structures, because muscle development was deemed unattractive in women, because women were believed to be unable to perform endurance activities, and, most of all, because there was a perceived general threat to femininity for girls and women who actively involve themselves in fitness and sport. These socially invented myths served to deter young girls from becoming involved in sport and fitness, and habits developed young tend to persist in adulthood.

Ellis (1988) suggested that the activity and **leisure-services industry** is strongly influenced by the increased economic power of women in contemporary culture. He is optimistic about the future:

> However, the changes we have seen in sex roles have not been just economic. During the last two decades women have insisted upon, and have been granted, a fuller participation in all facets of American life. In sport, politics, and management particularly, and to a lesser degree in the male-dominated areas of trucking, maintenance, and construction, women have joined in and demonstrated clearly that they are equally capable. The process has not run its course, but it is clear that our society will continue to evolve in the direction that welcomes women into all areas of endeavor and achievement and breaks down sex-role stereotyping. (Ellis, 1988, p. 24)

I wish I could be as optimistic, but, at least as regards the near future, I am not. Sex stereotyping in sport, fitness, and physical education begins in families and neighborhoods and is often reinforced in schools. The power structures in the educational, political, and economic sectors of our society are still male dominated. Girls and women not only need equal opportunity and access to sport, fitness, and physical education but also need open, visible support for exploring their potential in these areas. Prejudices in these areas still run deep. Legislation such as Title IX is extremely important in the public, legal arena, but the moral imperative to rid our culture of these prejudices is much more profound and considerably more difficult to achieve. Professionals in sport, fitness, and physical education need to be advocates for girls and women.

THEME 5: CHILD AND YOUTH DEVELOPMENT: THE AFTER-SCHOOL HOURS

The responsibility for child and youth development has traditionally resided nearly solely in families. Currently, however, that responsibility is shared with day-care, preschool, school, and community agencies and programs. There are 39 million children between the ages of 5 and 14 in the United States. In most two-parent households, both parents work. Three of four mothers with school-aged children work, two-thirds of them full-time (Executive Summary, 1999). During the after-school hours, rates of juvenile crime triple, and many unsupervised youngsters experiment with alcohol, tobacco, drugs, and sex.

It is clear that children and youths have better developmental opportunities if they are in after-school programs supervised by caring adults. The sport, fitness, and physical-education professions have much to offer in this area, as do the health, recreation, and dance professions. Of particular importance is the need to develop after-school programs for children and youths at risk for academic or social failure (Witt & Baker, 1997). There is ample evidence that organized academic, recreation, and sport programs for children and youths are useful in helping them to progress toward becoming competent adults. Younger children and those in areas of poverty seem to gain the most from such programs, perhaps because they have less access to them. Teens who regularly engage in after-school programs achieve better academically and are less likely to engage in risky behavior than their peers who are not in such programs.

This national problem, however, cannot be solved by any single profession working alone. It is clear that collaborations between schools, community agencies, city government, and the private sector are necessary to develop and sustain successful programs. At the moment, it would be inaccurate to describe the United States as either a child-centered or a youth-centered nation. We need to make an investment in our children and youth, both in regard to their physical health and well-being and in regard to their personal and social development. Few national problems provide more opportunity for the sport, fitness, and physical-education professions to offer solutions.

THEME 6: COLLABORATION BETWEEN DISCIPLINES AND PROFESSIONS

Chapter 3 described the emergence of the disciplines now subsumed most commonly under the umbrella of kinesiology. Before the mid-1960s, the parent discipline of physical education spawned a family of emerging professions in health, recreation, sport, and fitness. The emergence of academic disciplines created tremendous growth of knowledge, detailed in Part 5 of this text. The sad part of this era of differentiation between the emerging disciplines and their older professional cousins was a series of family wars in colleges and universities, where the various familial groups competed to define the primary mission of departments, with all the accompanying issues of budgetary control and faculty divisions associated with control over the mission of the department. The literature of that 25-year split is filled with debates for and against both sides.

Although it is clear that the remnants of that split and the ensuing debates live on, it is even more clear that to address the major issues of the twenty-first century, scholars and professionals must work together. Evidence of the need to work together is found throughout this text. The evidence supporting the relationship of regular physical activity to a host of health benefits and to increased lifespan itself has been the most important catalyst for bringing scholars and professionals together to meet the challenge of the public health mandate, which is the topic of Theme 1 in this chapter.

There is still much to learn about physical activity and how it works its magic on the systems of the body to produce health benefits, and researchers will continue to investigate those unknowns, but it is clear now that getting people engaged in activity and maintaining that engagement throughout the lifespan is the key area about which we know very little and within which the results have been so disappointing. Education and activity programs can be viewed as interventions, meant to influence people in the short and long terms. To seriously study such interventions and to come to understand the short- and long-term outcomes of various kinds of educational and activity interventions will require the collaboration of scholarly researchers and professionals in the field.

There is also evidence that the age of hyperspecialization in both the academic disciplines and the professions may have outlived its usefulness. Most intervention programs focus on nutrition *and* exercise. Effective school programs must *link* children and youths to community programs. Effective educational programs focus on physical activity *and* health issues. All of this suggests a more broadly prepared scholar or professional, one who can work across contexts to achieve various goals. Especially on the professional side, it is clear that activity professionals are part of a larger human-services profession; that physical activity always takes place in the context of home, school, and community; and that to understand and effectively influence children and youths, the larger context must be considered, or the intervention is unlikely to have lasting impact.

THEME 7: THE ACTIVITY AND LEISURE INDUSTRIES

Ellis (1988) has argued convincingly that activity and leisure services are being provided more and more in the *private* sector and that increasingly, it is the adult client who pays for those services directly. The activity and leisure-services industry is made up of sections of the health-enhancement industry and sections of the leisure-services industry (see Figure 22.1). The defining characteristic of this new industry is activity, for both health and leisure purposes.

There is little doubt that this industry is *happening now*. Professionals in sport, fitness, and physical education who ignore it do so at risk of losing their influence and of losing substantial sources of income. At present, this industry is largely *unregulated,* except insofar as clients decide what pro-

How early should sport-specific training begin?

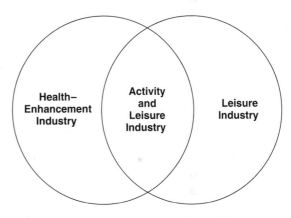

Figure 22.1   Relationship among the health-enhancement, activity and leisure, and leisure industries
SOURCE: Ellis, 1988, p. 5.

grams they will support. This is a market-driven industry. It is easy to make money in it, but it is also easy to fail. We can expect more and more competition within this industry because of the substantial amounts of money being spent on health- and leisure-related activity.

Except for programs in adult fitness and sport management, and some in recreation, the sport, fitness, and physical-education professions have not responded quickly to the emergence of this new industry. The professions still prepare people more for the public sector and for occupations for which certification or accreditation is necessary.

We need to be in this industry! It seems to me that people in sport, fitness, and physical education have a professional responsibility to help shape the quality and direction of this industry. We cannot afford to stand on the sidelines and make snide remarks about the poor quality of an aerobics program, the lack of qualifications of a person directing a seniors' program, or the questionable activities being used in an infant program. As long as the industry remains unregulated, there will be fads and a fair amount of quackery in it. People who are prepared with the knowledge and skill to provide appropriate activity programs for infants, children, youths, adults, and seniors not only have a professional obligation to help make this industry as good as it can be but also have the expertise to compete, especially as citizens become better informed about the differences between good and bad programs.

THEME 8: TOWARD AN EXPANDED PHYSICAL EDUCATION

Physical education will remain a largely ineffective educational intervention as long as it is conceptualized as a school subject that is pursued in small bits of time in a regular school day and school week. Many of the effective physical-education programs described in this text have taken a much more expanded view of what the subject is and when children and youths are involved in the subject. Effective programs seem to break out of the box in which they have been confined—namely, as a school subject that meets in the elementary school for typically no more than two 30-minute periods per week or in the high school for a daily period of 50 minutes for 2 semesters in the ninth grade.

Effective programs find ways to get students physically active in nonattached school time and in out-of-school discretionary time. They do this by building links to the community and to the home, and then by developing programs that encourage and reward children and youths for becoming involved and staying involved in activity programs of a formal and informal nature in the community and at home. The physical educator of the future will not only see these linkages as opportunities but also will indeed see them as fundamental to developing and maintaining a dynamic physical-education program.

The school will be seen as the hub of the developmental triangle—home, school, community—in which children and youths learn and grow. This is not to suggest that PE classes will be a thing of the past. There is certainly an important role for physical education to play in the regular school curriculum, but to the extent that it is confined solely to that curriculum and attended in classes that meet between 8:00 A.M. and 3:00 P.M., it will surely continue to be largely ineffectual in its influence. Some of the main responsibilities for physical educators should include providing activity programs at recess, at lunchtime, and in after-school time; building links to community activity programs and then helping children and youths learn about them and gain access to them; building enduring links to parents and providing parents with information and equipment to pursue physical-activity interests in the family; and providing drop-in activity in attractive, inclusive programs.

This may require that some physical educators come to work at midday and stay through to early evening, especially in areas where the incidence of latchkey families is high and certainly in all areas where community-based youth programming is weak. It certainly will require that physical educators be prepared differently, prepared to develop relationships with community agencies and programs, and with parents, too.

Fortunately, we are beginning to see evidence of school–community linkages to promote physical activity and health among children and youth. Several of these were described in Chapter 12. They often involve local recreation departments, local hospitals, and local child- and youth-sport programs.

We also see fitness linkages beginning to develop, such as walk-or-ride-to-school programs. Together these begin to show what has been described in this text as an *infrastructure* to support physical activity and health—people, programs, and facilities collaborating to provide opportunities to children, youths, and adults.

THEME 9: TOWARD AN INCLUSIVE RATHER THAN EXCLUSIONARY SPORT CULTURE

Clearly, the American sport culture has developed remarkably in this century. Chapters 5 through 7 described that culture, its scope, and some of its problems. There are no signs that the public's attraction to sport is waning. To the contrary, many commentators see the nation as increasingly involved in sport: "Richer and with more leisure time than ever, the U.S. has truly become a sport-crazy nation. In every age group, in every region, in every walk of life, a passion for athletics is blossoming" (Maloney, 1984, p. 23).

The sport culture, as it is currently constituted, is exclusionary in its developmental stages. Youth sport is widespread (see Chapter 6), and school sport is healthy. Yet, as children grow into their adolescence, there is less and less opportunity for them to continue to develop in organized, competitive sport. This is the varsity model that was adopted long ago in America and continues to dominate the developmental aspects of our sport culture. For adolescents and young adults who are not skilled enough to make the varsity teams, little is available in the way of organized sport through which they can continue to develop and compete. The emergence of the masters sport movement (see Chapter 6) indicates that many women and men would like to continue sport involvement beyond their young-adult years.

In New Zealand high schools, it is not uncommon to find ten or fifteen basketball teams for boys and also for girls. The squads are smaller than in American schools, and they typically practice only

Many new sports involve risk and are competed in individually.

2 days per week and have one game per week. The squads are all graded by ability, so that as players improve they move up in the squad hierarchy. What this means is that probably ten times more boys and girls get the opportunity to represent their high school in basketball competition. I was in a New Zealand girls' high school one day a few years ago on what I learned was their badminton-competition day. The school had fourteen teams competing that day against a neighboring high school. Each team had three singles players and a doubles team, so that ninety girls were competing for that high school. In this model, nobody gets cut. If interest among students increases, more teams are created. This is a different model. It certainly does not do as well as the American model in preparing elite

athletes, but it does allow for much greater participation in organized school sport.

Much of the sport culture outside schools is becoming more inclusionary. Recreation and sport clubs often try to attract more participants. Since their programs are often fee-based, it is in the interest of the sponsoring group to attract more players. More adults are continuing their participation beyond their young-adult years. To be sure, this is a loosely coupled infrastructure, but at least it is a beginning.

THEME 10: WELLNESS AS THE CENTER OF LIFESTYLE EDUCATION

The concept of wellness was introduced in Chapter 1, and its philosophical and historical roots were described in Chapter 4. To reiterate, wellness is about getting and staying well—healthy and active. It is a *proactive* concept and movement rather than a reaction to illness or disease. Noted physical educator Celeste Ulrich was prophetic when in 1976 she described wellness as a "macrocosmic concept of fitness" (Ulrich, 1976, p.151). Wellness is a valuable concept because it brings together the areas of nutrition, physical activity, psychological well-being, and stress management. Wellness is about *managing* your own lifestyle, hence the increasing use of the term *lifestyle management* as a descriptor for the effort to take control of your own well-being.

To achieve wellness, educational programs must focus on behavior change, not just information. Clearly, the school, the community, and the family must work together to form what has been appropriately called the *developmental triangle*. Knowledge about nutrition, physical activity, and stress management is important, but there must be an accompanying effort to influence the development of appropriate behaviors and habits. It is tremendously important that the behaviors that represent wellness be taught and reinforced in a number of different settings if they are to become part of a young person's lifestyle. This means that the col-

laborations referred to in Theme 6 must be taken seriously.

Wellness stresses the importance of lifestyle and encompasses work, leisure, and personal relationships. Wellness is viewed as a positive value with a primary emphasis on personal development. There is also widespread agreement that adoption of such a lifestyle by a larger percentage of the population can increase the productivity of workplaces and reduce the staggering costs of health and medical care. This is clearly why wellness has been so readily accepted by industry, as demonstrated by the development of worksite fitness programs (see Chapter 9).

Wellness cannot be viewed solely as an individual concern. Our nation has public health goals (Sallis & McKenzie, 1991) that should alert us to the important *collective* interest we have in wellness. The new socioecological view of health and fitness (see Chapter 8) suggests that wellness proponents need to examine the social structures that tend to prevent certain groups from gaining access to information, facilities, and programs that could improve their health and fitness. The costs of health care alone should motivate all of us to consider the wellness of all citizens, not just our own!

There is also great need for consumer education as regards the wellness movement:

> Quackery abounds in the wellness marketplace, from the media hype concerning sauna belts and sauna suits to vitamins and protein supplements. Exercise is big business. Again, profit is dictating practice. The public needs to be educated concerning what is being delivered at the health spa and its contribution to healthy living. Many health spas are an extension of the same process that resulted in our adverse life-style changes. Few contribute to anything other than the cosmetic appearance of being well; they simply pamper us in a luxurious surrounding. (McNeill, 1987, p. 93)

Any notion as pervasive and important as wellness is bound to create the situation health educator Alexander McNeill described. I believe that wellness can become a positive force in lifestyle education, but I believe that it requires solid education with good, accurate information and a stronger focus on behavior change, rather than information alone. Lifestyle education needs to begin with very young children and is most important in elementary and middle school, when habits form and children adopt activity patterns that often last a lifetime.

SUMMARY

1. The public health challenge to achieve a healthier citizenry and reduce the nation's health costs will require cooperation among specialized professional and disciplinary groups.

2. Distributing sport, fitness, and physical education more equitably is made more difficult by the trend toward privatization.

3. Young children and older citizens represent new populations traditionally not addressed by the sport, fitness, and physical-education professions, yet these age groups represent important populations with unique problems, especially children in poverty.

4. Gender equity in sport, fitness, and physical education needs to be promoted, not only through legal means, but also actively through education that breaks down stereotypes that have effectively prohibited girls and women from having equal opportunities.

5. Programs for children and youths in the after-school hours need to be developed and staffed by caring adults. Few national problems provide more opportunity for the sport, fitness, and physical-education professions to offer solutions.

6. Academicians and professionals must collaborate more closely to solve the complex problems that threaten public health, sport, and physical education, and it appears that recent trends toward specialization have hindered such collaboration.

7. An activity and leisure-services industry has emerged. We need to respond to it by creating new programs that combine knowledge and skill from health, recreation, and physical education.

8. It will be difficult for physical education to grow and prosper if it is confined to being a class subject within the school day. Ways of expanding opportunity and involvement for children and youths in nonattached time at school, in the community, and at home must become the focus of physical education.

9. The sport culture needs to develop new forms for children and youths that are inclusionary rather than exclusionary and that promote lifespan involvement in competitive and recreational activity.

10. Wellness can become the foundational concept undergirding lifespan sport, fitness, and physical education. Children need to start at an early age to attend educationally sound programs that emphasize behavior change.

DISCUSSION QUESTIONS

1. What school, home, and community interventions, taken together or separately, would increase the likelihood of achieving public health goals in the next generation?

2. What can be done to make the sport culture in your area less exclusionary and more lifespan oriented?

3. Can activity opportunities throughout the lifespan be equitable and accessible if they are provided primarily through the private sector?

4. What does school physical education have to do to survive and prosper by the year 2020?

5. How will technology improve the activity lives of people? What are the risks that technology will worsen the inactivity problems so prevalent today?

6. Choose a specific activity problem in the area in which you live. How can the activity disciplines and the activity professions collaborate to solve the problem? What does each bring to the potential solution?

7. How can we integrate our efforts in schools, communities, and households to promote and sustain a more active citizenry?

8. When should wellness education begin? What might it look like for a first-grader, an eighth-grader, and a senior in high school?

9. Should activity be available through publicly supported programs to all income groups, or should we adopt more of a pay-as-you-go philosophy, where user fees fund programs?

Glossary

academic discipline   A theoretically grounded body of knowledge in which extensions of that knowledge are pursued for their own worth.

academic-integration model   The movement to integrate traditional classroom subjects into physical-education instruction and, reciprocally, to integrate physical-education subjects into classroom instruction.

adventure education   The use of risk activities, especially in the out-of-doors, to achieve goals of physical education.

aerobic exercise   Any low-intensity exercise in which oxygen is utilized.

aerobics   A form of exercise designed to produce cardiovascular health benefits.

alternative sport   New sport forms that appeal to youths and young adults; also referred to as *extreme games* or *risk sports*.

anaerobic exercise   An oxygenless process of metabolizing body fuels through exercise.

appropriate competition   Competition that is developmentally sound and psychologically suited to participants.

Arnoldism   The British educational philosophy in which physical activity and sport have a central role in developing physical strength, patriotism, moral courage, and intellectual independence.

athletic training   The profession that provides for prevention, care, and rehabilitation of sport injuries.

Aussie Sports   The Australian national program of modified sports, with emphasis on developmentally appropriate participation.

biomechanics   The study of the human body as a mechanical system, utilizing principles drawn from physics.

body composition   The percentage of body fat relative to bone, muscle, and other tissue.

Boston conference   The historic 1885 meeting of physical-education leaders that marked the beginning of American physical education.

cardiac rehabilitation   The assessment, rehabilitation, and prevention of further damage to patients who have suffered cardiovascular trauma.

cardiovascular fitness   The particular fitness of the heart, circulatory system, and lungs that allows people to sustain effort for periods of time.

club sport   A nonexclusionary organizational model of sport participation, common in Europe.

competition   A coming-together in a festive atmosphere to test competence within a defined set of rules in which various forms of rivalry exist.

cosmetic fitness   The use of physical activity to improve appearance.

criterion-referenced health (CRH) standards   A method of reporting and interpreting fitness-test scores, based on criteria sufficient to produce a health benefit or indicate a reduced risk for a specific health problem.

critical theory   Contemporary analysis of structural inequities in society and action oriented to combat them.

curriculum   The goals of an educational program and the activities through which those goals are achieved.

developmentally appropriate   Describes activities and experiences that take into account the developmental level of the child.

developmental physical education   A dominant twentieth-century approach, in which physical activity is used to achieve physical, mental, and social outcomes.

discipline-based arts education   The movement in art education that emphasizes understanding and appreciation, as well as performance.

dose-response debate   The debate focusing on the type, duration, frequency, and intensity of physical activity related to health outcomes.

duration   The "length" of an exercise bout; e.g., the number of repetitions in strength training or the amount of time in cardiovascular training.

dynamic flexibility   The capacity to move a joint quickly through its range of motion.

education through the physical   A dominant twentieth-century philosophy in which physical activity is used to reach goals in fitness, skill, knowledge, and character.

epiphyseal injuries   Trauma to the epiphysis, the growth center at the end of each bone; common in youth sport.

exercise epidemiology   The field of study that assesses relationships between physical activity and mortality.

exercise physiology   The study of bodily systems and their reactions to the stress of exercise.

fair play   The tradition from British sport that to play the game well is to play hard, play fair, be courteous, and not allow the outcome of the game to influence behavior once the contest is concluded; modernized in fair-play programs throughout the world.

field experience   The development of professional skills and knowledge through practice in an applied setting.

fitness   Optimal condition or functioning of the body; health-related fitness, motor-performance fitness, and cosmetic fitness are the three major kinds of fitness.

flexibility   Ability of a joint to move through its full range of motion.

formal gymnastic systems   The programs of group and individual gymnastics and exercises that formed the core of the physical-education curriculum in the nineteenth century.

form sports   Sports, such as gymnastics, where the physical form of the performance determines the winner.

games   A form of playful, rule-governed competition in which outcomes are determined by skill, strategy, or chance.

health-enhancement industry   The delivery of health and wellness programs through public- and private-sector programs.

health fitness   Fitness that reduces the risk of degenerative diseases.

health-related physical education (HRPE)   The movement to emphasize health outcomes as the main outcomes for school physical-education programs and to adjust program components to achieve those outcomes.

humanistic philosophies   Contemporary views stressing self-development, self-growth, and interpersonal relations.

hypokinetic diseases   Those degenerative diseases for which health fitness reduces the likelihood of developing severe forms of the ailments.

inclusion   The movement to have all students with disabilities mainstreamed into regular classes, and the philosophy supporting that strategy.

intensity   The "load" of an exercise bout; e.g., the level of resistance in strength training and the heart rate during cardiovascular training.

intercollegiate sport   The system and organization of sport between colleges and universities.

interscholastic sport   The system and organization of sport between schools.

interval training   A workout system in which high-intensity work periods are interspersed with rest periods for recovery.

intramurals   A program of formal and informal exercise and sport activity within a school.

kinesiology   In its narrow sense, the subdiscipline that studies human motion—more specifically, of how the muscles move the bony structure of the body; and in its broader sense, the current preferred name for the total discipline of sport and exercise.

leisure   An attitude of freedom from the demands of ordinary life, an activity that is freely chosen, or discretionary time left over after work, family, and personal-maintenance commitments are fulfilled.

leisure-services industry   The provision of leisure activity through the public and private sectors.

liability   Legal responsibility-liability issues tend to be related to promotion of safety and to avoidance of negligence in professional practice.

lifespan involvement   The possibility and desirability of fitness and recreational physical activity from infancy to old age.

lifetime sports   Those sport activities for which ample recreational outlets are available in the culture.

marathon   A 26.2-mile race.

masters athletics   Organized competition for people over age 40, in 5-year increments.

MET   Unit of measurement to estimate the cost of metabolic activity during exercise, with one MET equaling the number of calories expended at rest.

modified game or sport   A game or sport that has been changed to be developmentally appropriate for players.

motor control   Nervous-system control of the muscular system; its study includes investigation of the cognitive processes underlying motor-skill acquisition.

motor development   The motor-growth and -performance changes due to heredity rather than environmental influences.

motor learning   The changes in motor performance related to experience and practice.

motor-performance fitness   Fitness that contributes to improved performance in physical skills.

movement education The educational component of the human-movement philosophy in which curricula are organized around educational dance, educational gymnastics, and educational games.

multiactivity curriculum The traditional model in physical education, with a variety of short-duration activity units.

muscular Christianity The philosophy that reconciled physical activity and sport with the theologies of Protestant churches in the mid-nineteenth century.

MVPA Moderate-to-vigorous physical activity, which, when accumulated 30 minutes per day and 210 minutes per week, is related to health benefits and increased life expectancy.

new physical education The sport-games-fitness curriculum based on progressive-educational theory, which emerged early in the twentieth century.

pay-to-play plans Charging fees for participation in interscholastic sport programs.

pedagogical kinesiology The qualitative analysis of sport performance, especially that done in applied settings for purposes of providing feedback.

pedagogy The art and science of teaching.

physical-activity infrastructure The combination of facilities and programs that support and sustain people in their physical-activity pursuits.

physical education Programs related to physical fitness, motor-skill development, social development, and knowledge—especially K-12 programs.

play Activity that is free, separate, uncertain, economically unproductive, and either rule governed or make-believe.

play education A contemporary philosophy of physical education in which purposes are related to successful participation in playful motor activities.

primary rules The rules that identify how a game is played and how winning is achieved.

privatization The trend over several generations for sport, fitness, and leisure services to be in the private rather than the public sector.

progressive-education theory A twentieth-century philosophy that subscribed to a holistic view of children and that viewed school as a microcosm of life.

progressive overload The principle that conditioning improves when the exercise load is gradually raised but still stays within an appropriate zone for safety.

Public Law 94-142 The legislation that mandated equal access and opportunity for people with disabilities, especially in education.

recovery time Optimal time for the muscular system to recover from and adapt to exercise stresses so as to be able to maintain a progressive training regimen.

role conflict The stress created when a person must perform in two different roles that have competing demands; teaching and coaching are often two such roles.

secondary rules The rules of games that can be modified without changing the essence of the game.

skinfold measure Measurement used for the estimation of body fat. A fold of skin is measured with a pair of calipers.

social-development model A contemporary physical-education model in which social responsibility and growth are primary goals.

social gradient The recognition that socioeconomic status is a contextual determinant of health and mortality.

socioecological view of fitness The view that social and economic structures in society affect the degree to which people have access to information about fitness and opportunity for involvement in fitness activities.

Special Olympics A national and international movement to provide sport experiences and competitions for people with mental disabilities.

specificity To produce a desired effect, an exercise must be related to the fitness component in which improvement is sought.

sport Institutionalized games and activities in which outcomes are determined by physical skill, prowess, and strategy.

sport aesthetics The study of sport as an art form.

sport education A contemporary physical-education model in which the goal is to produce competent, literate, and enthusiastic sportspersons.

sport ethics The study of values in and through sport.

sport for all A worldwide movement to encourage sport and exercise participation by all age groups.

sport history The description and interpretation of sport in the past, as it relates to the present and future of sport.

sport humanities The historical, philosophical, and literary study of sport.

sport literature Fiction, poetry, and films about sport, which have permanent value because of their form, emotional effects, or ability to provide insights about sport.

sport management A vocational/professional field encompassing most nonparticipant roles in institutionalized sport.

sport medicine   The medical field concerned with the prevention, treatment, and rehabilitation of sport injuries and with sport performance.

sport pedagogy   The study of the processes of teaching and coaching, the outcomes of such endeavors, and the content of fitness, physical-education, and sport-education programs.

sport philosophy   The study of values, knowledge, the relationships of ideas, and the nature of reality in sport.

sport psychology   The study of behavioral and psychological issues and problems in sport.

sport sociology   The study of social structure, social patterns, and social organization of groups engaged in sport.

static flexibility   The capacity to reach and maintain an extended position in a joint's range of motion.

strength training   Exercise against resistance; resistance, repetitions, and number of workouts per week are manipulated to allow progressive, goal-directed development.

subdiscipline   In this text, each of the various areas of scientific and scholarly study of sport and exercise.

Title IX   Federal legislation that mandated equal access for girls and women in schools supported by federal funds.

training principles   The relationships among overload, progression, and recovery periods that allow a person to gradually build strength or endurance.

training threshold   The amount of exercise stress necessary to produce a training effect (improvement).

triathlon   A race composed of swimming, cycling, and running phases.

unified sports   Sport competitions in which people with disabling conditions compete along with people without those conditions.

varsity model   An exclusionary model of sport involvement common to American high school and intercollegiate practices.

wellness   A proactive view of health in which people strive to develop a lifestyle that results in positive physical, mental, and emotional health.

worksite health promotion   A system of programs to prevent degenerative illness and promote wellness, implemented where people work.

zero-sum competition   A form of competition in which whatever is gained by one competitor must necessarily be lost by the other competitor.

Bibliography

Acosta, R., & Carpenter, L. (1992). As the years go by: Coaching opportunities in the 1990s. *Journal of Physical Education, Recreation, and Dance, 63*(3), 36–41.

———. (1994). The status of women in intercollegiate athletics. In S. Birrell & C. Cole (Eds.), *Women, sport and culture* (pp. 111–118). Champaign, IL: Human Kinetics.

Adelman, M. (1969). The role of the sports historian. *Quest, 12,* 61–65.

Adrian, M. (1983). Biomechanics: Theory into practice. *Proceedings of the National Association for Physical Education in Higher Education, 4,* 37–50. Champaign, IL: Human Kinetics.

Albany Times Union. (1992, July 22). Empire State Games special section.

Alderman, R., & Wood, N. (1976). An analysis of incentive motivation in young Canadian athletes. *Canadian Journal of Sport Sciences, 1*(2), 169–176.

Alexander, K. (1994). Developing sport education in Western Australia. *Aussie Sport Action, 5*(1), 8–9.

Alexander K., Taggart, A., & Luckman, J. (1988). The sport education crusade down under. *Journal of Physical Education, Recreation, and Dance, 69*(4), 21–23.

Allen, B. (1988). Teaching training and discipline-based dance education. *Journal of Physical Education, Recreation, and Dance, 59*(9), 65–69.

Almond, L. (1983). Reflecting on themes: A games classification. *Bulletin of Physical Education, 19*(1), 33–36.

———. (1986a). Primary and secondary rules in games. In R. Thorpe, D. Bunker, & L. Almond (Eds.), *Rethinking games teaching.* London: Esmonde Publications.

American College of Sports Medicine. (1990). The recommended quantity and quality of exercise for developing and maintaining cardiorespiratory and muscular fitness in healthy adults. *Medicine and Science in Sports and Exercise, 22,* 265–274.

American Sports Data. (1999). *Tracking the fitness movement.* North Palm Beach, FL: Fitness Products Council.

Anderrson, M., Williams, J., Aldridge, T. & Taylor, T. (1997). Tracking the training and careers of graduates of advanced degree programs in sport psychology, 1989–1994. *The Sport Psychologist, 11,* 326–344.

Antonelli, F. (1970). Opening address. In G. Kenyon (Ed.), *Contemporary psychology of sport* (pp. 3–9). Chicago: The Athletic Institute.

ARAPCS Newsletter. (1986). Our kids are out of shape, getting flabby. *ARAPCS Newsletter, 3*(1), 4.

Arnheim, D., & Prentice, W. (2000). *Principles of athletic training* (10th ed.). New York: McGraw-Hill.

Athletic Footwear Institute. (1990). *American youth and sports participation.* North Palm Beach, FL: Athletic Footwear Institute.

Australian Sports Commission. (1994). *National junior sport policy.* Canberra, Australia.

Battagliola, M. (1993). Indian industries takes aim at employee health. *Business and Health, 11,* 12.

Baun, W. (1995). Culture change in worksite health promotion. In D. Dejoy & M. Wilson (Eds.), *Critical issues in worksite health promotion.* Boston: Allyn & Bacon.

Baun, W., & Bernacki, E. (1988). Who are corporate exercisers and what motivates them? In R. Dishman (Ed.), *Exercise adherence* (pp. 321–348). Champaign, IL: Human Kinetics.

Baun, W., & Landgreen, M. (1983). Tenneco health and fitness. *Journal of Physical Education, Recreation, and Dance, 54*(8), 40–41.

Becker, D. (1996, January 18). More women athletes head for Atlanta. *USA Today,* p. 12C.

Beighle, A., Pangrazi, R., & Vincent, S. (2001). Pedometers, physical activity and accountability. *Journal of Physical Education, Recreation, and Dance. 72*(9), 16–19, 36.

Bell, C. (1998). Sport education in the elementary school. *Journal of Physical Education, Recreation, and Dance, 69*(5), 36–39.

Bennett, W. (1986). *First lessons: A report on elementary education in America.* Washington, DC: U.S. Department of Education.

Berg, K. (1988). A national curriculum in physical education. *Journal of Physical Education, Recreation, and Dance,* 59(8), 70–75.

Biddle, S. (1995). Exercise and psychosocial health. *Research Quarterly for Exercise and Sport,* 66(4), 292–297.

Biles, F. (1971). The physical education public information project. *Journal of Health, Physical Education, and Recreation,* 41(7), 53–55.

Blackledge, S. (1994, October 7). Pay-to-play takes toll at Big Walnut. *The Columbus Dispatch,* D-1.

Blair, S. (1992). Are American children and youth fit? The need for better data. *Research Quarterly for Exercise and Sport,* 63(2), 120–123.

Blair, S., & Connelly, J. (1996). How much physical activity should we do? The case for moderate amounts and intensities of physical activity. *Research Quarterly for Exercise and Sport,* 67(2), 193–205.

Blair, S., Kohl, H., III, Paffenbarger, R., Jr., Cooper, K., & Gibbons, L. (1989). Physical fitness and all-cause mortality: A prospective study of healthy men and women. *Journal of the American Medical Association,* 239-240, 262.

Blair, S., Kohl, H., & Powell, K. (1987). Physical activity, physical fitness, exercise, and the public's health. *The Academy Papers,* 20, 53–69.

Block, M. (1995). Americans with disabilities act: Its impact on youth sports. *Journal of Physical Education, Recreation, and Dance,* 66(5), 28–32.

Bookwalter, K., & Vander-Zwaag, H. (1969). *Foundations and principles of physical education.* Philadelphia: W. B. Saunders.

Bouchard, C., Shephard, R., & Stephens, T. (1993). *Physical activity, fitness and health: Consensus statement.* Champaign, IL: Human Kinetics.

Boucher, A. (1988). Good beginnings. *Journal of Physical Education, Recreation, and Dance,* 59(7), 42.

Bowerman, W., & Harris, W. (1967). *Jogging.* New York: Grosset & Dunlap.

Bowers, C. (1999). The creatine debate. *Strategies,* 12(6), 5–8.

Bradford-Krok, B. (1994). Citrus county fitness break: Funding and developing fitness videotapes. In R. Pate & D. Hohn (Eds.), *Health and fitness through physical education* (pp. 205–210). Champaign, IL: Human Kinetics.

Bradley, B. (1998). *Values of the game.* New York: Artisan.

Brancazio, P. (1984). *Sport science: Physical laws and optimum performance.* New York: Simon & Schuster.

Bressan, E., & Pieter, W. (1985). Philosophic process and the study of human moving. *Quest,* 37(1), 1–15.

Brooks, G. (1987). The exercise physiology paradigm in contemporary biology: To molbiol or not to molbiol—that is the question. *Quest,* 39(3), 231–242.

———. (1994). 40 years of progress: Basic exercise physiology. In 40th Anniversary lectures. Indianapolis, IN: American College of Sports Medicine.

Browder, K., & Darby, L. (1998). Individualizing exercise: some biomechanical and physiological reminders. *Journal of Physical Education, Recreation, and Dance,* 69(4), 35–44.

Bryant, C., & Peterson, J. (1999) Prescribing exercise for healthy adults, *Journal of Physical Education, Recreation, and Dance,* 70(6), 31.

Bucher, C. (1964). *Foundations of physical education* (4th ed.). St. Louis: Mosby.

Buckworth, J. & Dishman, R. (2001). Exercise psychology. In J. Williams (Ed.), *Applied sport psychology* (4th ed., pp. 497–518). Mountain View, CA: Mayfield.

Bunker, L. (1998). Psycho-physiological contributions of physical activity and sports for girls. *President's Council on Physical Fitness and Sports Research Digest,* 3(1), 1–6.

CAHPERD Journal. (1989). Coaching certification law. *Colorado Association for Health, Physical Education, Recreation, and Dance,* 15(3), 14.

Caillois, R. (1961). *Man, play and games.* New York: Free Press of Glencoe.

Caldwell, S. (1966). Conceptions of physical education in twentieth century America: Rosalind Cassidy. Doctoral dissertation, University of Southern California, Los Angeles.

Carlisle, R. (1974). Physical education and aesthetics. In H. Whiting & D. Masterson (Eds.), *Readings in the aesthetics of sport* (pp. 21–32). London: Lepus Books.

Carlson, T. (1996). "Now I think I can." The reaction of eight low-skilled students to sport education. *ACHPER Healthy Lifestyles Journal,* 42(4), 6–8.

Carnegie Council on Adolescent Development. (1992). *A matter of time: Risk and opportunity in the nonschool hours.* New York: Carnegie Corporation.

Casey, A. (1992). Title IX and women officials: How have they been affected? *Journal of Physical Education, Recreation, and Dance,* 63(3), 45–47.

Centers for Disease Control and Prevention. (2001). Increasing physical activity: A report on recommendations of the Task Force on Community Preventive Services. MMWR 2001, 50 (No. RR-18), 1–14.

Christina, R. (1987). Motor learning: Future lines of research. *The Academy Papers*, 20, 26–41.

———. (1989). Whatever happened to applied research in motor learning? In J. Skinner, et al. (Eds.), *Future directions for exercise science and sport research* (pp. 411–422). Champaign, IL: Human Kinetics.

Chu, D. (1981). Functional myths of educational organizations: College as career training and the relationship of formal title to actual duties on secondary school employment. In V. Crafts (Ed.), *Proceedings of the National Association for Physical Education in Higher Education* (pp. 36–46). Champaign, IL: Human Kinetics.

Cissell, W. (1992). Health educators as professionals in the year 2000: A prediction. *Journal of Physical Education, Recreation, and Dance*, 63(5), 27.

Clarke, D. (1986). Children and the research process. *The Academy Papers*, 19, 9–13.

Coakley, J. (1982). *Sport in society* (2nd ed.). St. Louis: Mosby.

———. (1994). *Sport and society: Issues and controversies* (5th ed.). St. Louis, MO: Mosby.

Coffin, J. (2002, September 9). Football a focal point in the Title IX debate. *Golfweek*, 22.

Cohen, A. (1991). The children's crusade: In pursuit of youth fitness. *Athletic Business*, 15(10), 24–28.

———. (1995). Fitness equipment: The next generation. *Athletic Business*, 19(3), 26–36.

Colfer, G., Hamilton, K., Magill, R., & Hamilton, B. (1986). *Contemporary physical education*. Dubuque, IA: Wm. C. Brown.

Columbus Dispatch. (1988, November 16). Gayle's school teaches fitness. *Columbus Dispatch*, p. B-3.

Cooper, K. (1968). *Aerobics*. New York: Bantam Books.

Corbin, C. (1981). First things first, but don't stop there. *Journal of Physical Education, Recreation, and Dance*, 52, 36–38.

———. (1987). Physical fitness in the K–12 curriculum: Some defensive solutions to perennial problems. *Journal of Physical Education, Recreation, and Dance*, 58(7), 49–54.

———. (2002). Physical activity for everyone: What every physical educator should know about promoting lifelong physical activity. *Quest*, 21(2), 128–144.

Corbin, C., Dowell, L., Lindsey, R., & Tolson, H. (1974). *Concepts in physical education* (2nd ed.). Dubuque, IA: Wm. C. Brown.

Corbin, C., & Lindsey, R. (1983). *Fitness for life*. Glenview, IL: Scott, Foresman.

———. (1999). *Concepts of physical fitness*, (10th Ed.). New York: McGraw.

Corbin, C., & Pangrazi, R. (1992). Are American children and youth fit? *Research Quarterly for Exercise and Sport*, 63(2), 96–106.

———. (1996). How much PA is enough? *Journal of Physical Education, Recreation, and Dance*, 67(4), 33–37.

———. (1998). *Physical activity for children: A statement of guidelines*. Reston, VA: NASPE Publications.

Corbin, C., Pangrazi, R., & Franks, B.D. (2000). Definitions: Health, fitness, and physical activity. President's Council on Physical Fitness and Sport. *Research Digest*, 3(9), 1–8.

Cordes, K., & Ibrahim, H. (2003). *Applications in recreation and leisure* (3rd ed.). Boston: McGraw-Hill.

Costill, D. (1986). *Inside running: Basics of sport physiology*. Indianapolis: Benchmark Press.

Councilman, J. (1968). *The science of swimming*. Englewood Cliffs, NJ: Prentice-Hall.

Cremin, L. (1961). *The transformation of the school: Progressivism in American education*. New York: Knopf.

Cureton, K. (1994). Physical fitness and activity standards for youth. In R. Pate & D. Hohn (Eds.), *Health and fitness through physical education* (pp. 129–136). Champaign, IL: Human Kinetics.

Darby, L., & Temple, I. (1992). A research project that combines research, teaching and service. *Journal of Physical Education, Recreation, and Dance*, 63(8), 65–67.

Darnell, J. (1994). Sport education in the elementary curriculum. In D. Siedentop (Ed.), *Sport education in physical education*. Champaign, IL: Human Kinetics.

Davis K. (1999). Giving women a chance to learn: Gender equity principles for HPERD classes. *Journal of Physical Education, Recreation, and Dance*, 70(4), 13–14.

De Grazia, S. (1962). *Of time, work and leisure*. New York: Twentieth Century Fund.

DePauw, K. (1984). Commitment and challenges. *Journal of Physical Education, Recreation, and Dance*, 55(2), 34–35.

———. (1996). Students with disabilities in physical education. In S. Silverman & C. Ennis (Eds.), *Student learning in physical education: Applying research to enhance instruction* (pp. 101–124). Champaign, IL: Human Kinetics.

Dishman, R. (Ed.). (1988). *Exercise adherence.* Champaign, IL: Human Kinetics.

———. (1989). Determinants of physical activity and exercise for persons 65 years of age or older. *The Academy Papers, 22,* 140–162.

Dorsey, V. (1988, January 22). Fewer high school players hurt, but major injuries up. *USA Today,* 10C.

Duda, J. (1991). Motivating older adults for physical activity: It's never too late. *Journal of Physical Education, Recreation, and Dance, 62*(7), 44–48.

Dugas, D. (1994). Sport education in the secondary curriculum. In D. Siedentop, *Sport Education: Quality PE through positive sport experiences* (pp. 105–112). Champaign, IL: Human Kinetics.

Dulles, F. R. (1940). *America learns to play.* New York: Appleton-Century.

Dunn, D. (1986a). An introduction. *Journal of Physical Education, Recreation, and Dance, 57*(8), 34–35.

———. (1986b). Professionalism and human resources. *Journal of Physical Education, Recreation, and Dance, 57*(8), 50–53.

Duquin, M. (1988). Gender and youth sport: Reflections on old and new fictions. In F. Smoll, R. Magill, & M. Ash (Eds.), *Children in sport* (pp. 31–41). Champaign, IL: Human Kinetics.

Dyson, G. (1964). *The mechanics of athletics.* London: University of London Press.

Earls, N. (1981). Distinctive teachers' personal qualities, perceptions of teacher education and the realities of teaching. *Journal of Teaching in Physical Education, 1*(1), 59–70.

Edington, D. (1993, January 27). Worksite wellness update. Presentation at Ohio State University School of Health, Physical Education and Recreation.

Edlin, G., & Golanty, E. (1982). *Health and wellness.* Boston: Science Books International.

Eitzen, S., & Sage, G. (2003). *Sociology of North American sport* (7th ed.). Boston: McGraw-Hill.

Elias, M. (1983, November 17). We frown on girls who play rough. *USA Today,* p. 1A.

Elliot, R. (1974). Aesthetics and sport. In H. Whiting & D. Masterson (Eds.), *Readings in the aesthetics of sport* (pp. 107–116). London: LePus Books.

Ellis, M. (1988). *The business of physical education.* Champaign, IL: Human Kinetics.

Ennis, C., Ross, J., & Chen, A. (1992). The role of value orientations in curricular decision making: A rationale for teachers' goals and expectations. *Research Quarterly for Exercise and Sport, 63*(1), 38–47.

Ennis, C., Satina, B., & Solomon, M. (1999). Creating a sense of family in urban schools using the 'sport for peace' curriculum. *Research Quarterly for Exercise and Sport, 70*(3), 273–285.

Evans, J., & Roberts, G. (1987). Physical competence and the development of peer relations. *Quest, 39*(1), 23–35.

Everhart, B., & Turner, E. (1995). Computer feedback for improved teacher training. *Journal of Physical Education, Recreation, and Dance, 66*(9), 57–60.

Ewing, M., & Seefeldt, V. (1997). Youth sports in America: An overview. *President's Council on Physical Fitness and Sports Research Digest. 2*(11), 1–12.

Executive Summary. (1999). When school is out. *The Future of Children, 9*(2), 1–4.

Eyler, M. (1965). Sport historians. *Proceedings of the National College Physical Education Association for Men,* 57–60.

Fahey, T., Insel, P., & Roth, W. (1999). *Fit and well* (3rd ed.). Mountain, View, CA: Mayfield.

Fahey, Insel & Roth, 2003.

Faigenbaum, A. (2001). Strength training and children's health. *Journal of Physical Education, Recreation and Dance, 72*(3), 24–30.

Fain, G. (1983). Introduction. *Journal of Physical Education, Recreation, and Dance, 54*(8), 32–33.

Faucette, N., Nugent, P., Sallis, J., & McKenzie, T. (2002). "I'd rather chew on aluminum foil." Overcoming classroom teachers' resistance to teaching physical education. *Journal of Teaching in Physical Education, 21*(3), 287–308.

Feltz, D. (1987). The future of graduate education in sport and exercise science: A sport psychology perspective. *Quest, 39*(2), 217–222.

Flegal, K., Carroll, M., Ogden, C., & Johnson, C. (2002). Prevalence and trends in obesity among US adults, 1999–2000. *Journal of the American Medical Association, 288:* 1723–1727.

Fox, C. (1992). Title IX at twenty. *Journal of Physical Education, Recreation, and Dance, 63*(3), 33–35.

Fraleigh, W. (1985). Why the good foul is not good. In D. Vanderwerken & S. Wertz (Eds.), *Sport: Inside out* (pp. 462–466). Fort Worth: Texas Christian University Press.

Freedson, P., & Rowland, T. (1992). Youth activity versus youth fitness: Let's redirect our efforts. *Research Quarterly for Exercise and Sport, 63*(2), 133–136.

Freeman, W. (1982). *Physical education and sport in a changing society* (2nd ed.). Minneapolis: Burgess.

French, R., Henderson, H., Kinnison, L., & Sherrill, C. (1998). Revisiting section 504, Physical Education and Sport. *Journal of Physical Education, Recreation, and Dance, 69*(7), 57–64.

Geadelman, P. (1981). Co-educational physical education: For better or worse. *NASSP Bulletin,* 65, 91–95.

Gensemer, R. (1985). *Physical education: Perspectives, inquiry, applications.* Philadelphia: Saunders College Publishing.

Gerber, E . (1971). *Innovators and institutions in physical education.* Philadelphia: Lea & Febiger.

———. (1974). *The American woman in sport.* Reading, MA: Addison-Wesley.

Giamatti, A. B. (1989). *Take time for paradise.* New York: Summit Books.

Gill, D. (1991). Social psychological contributions to performance enhancement. *The Academy Papers,* 25, 117–121.

Gober, B., & Franks, B. (1988). The physical and fitness education of young children. *Journal of Physical Education, Recreation, and Dance, 59*(7), 57–61.

Goetzel, R., Sepulveda, M., Knight, K., Eisen, M., Wade, B., Wong, C., & Fielding, N. (1994). Association of IBM's "A plan for life" health promotion program with changes in employees' health risk status. *American College of Occupational and Environmental Medicine,* 36, 1005–1009.

Gorman, J., & Calhoun, K. (1994). *The name of the game: The business of sports.* New York: Wiley.

Gough, D. (1995). Specialization in youth sport. *Coaching Clinic, 34*(3), 5–6.

Graham, G. (1990). Physical education in U.S. schools, K–12. *Journal of Physical Education, Recreation, and Dance, 61*(2), 35–39.

Grant, B. (1992). Integrating sport into the physical education curriculum in New Zealand secondary schools. *Quest, 44*(3), 304–316.

Graves, M., & Townsend, J. (2000). Applying the sport education curriculum model to dance. *Journal of Physical Education, Recreation, and Dance, 71*(8), 50–54.

Green, J. (1997). Action research in youth soccer: Assessing the acceptability of an alternative program. *Journal of Sport Management,* 11, 29–44.

Griffey, D. (1987). Trouble for sure: A crisis perhaps. *Journal of Physical Education, Recreation, and Dance, 58*(2), 20–21.

Gruneau, R. (1976). Sport as an area of sociological study: An introduction to major themes and perspectives. In R. Gruneau & J. Albinson (Eds.), *Canadian sport: Sociological perspectives* (pp. 3–7). Reading, MA: Addison-Wesley.

Gutin, B., Manos, T., & Strong, W. (1992). Defining health and fitness: First step toward establishing children's fitness standards. *Research Quarterly for Exercise and Sport, 63*(2), 128–132.

Hall, L., & Wilson, P. (1984). Industrial fitness, adult fitness, and cardiac rehabilitation graduate programs. *Journal of Physical Education, Recreation, and Dance, 55*(3), 40–44.

Harageones, M. (1987). Impact of educational reform: The quality of Florida's high school physical education programs. *Journal of Physical Education, Recreation, and Dance, 58*(6), 52–54.

Harrington, M. (1998, April 27). Families driven to keep competitive in sports. *USA Today,* 6D.

Harris, D. (1987). Frontiers in psychology of exercise and sport. *The Academy Papers,* 20, 42–52.

Harris, J. (1991). Modifying the performance enhancement ethos: Disciplinary and professional implications. *The Academy Papers,* 25, 96–103.

———. (1992, April). Using kinesiology: A comparison of applied veins in the subdisciplines. Amy Morris Homans Lecture, National Convention of the American Alliance for Health, Physical Education, Recreation, and Dance, Indianapolis.

———. (2000). *Sociology of physical activity.* In S. Hoffman & J. Harris, (Eds.) pp. 207–240. Champaign, IL: Human Kinetics.

Hasbrook, C. (1987). Interscholastic coaching and officiating: Programs designed to increase the number of women involved. *Journal of Physical Education, Recreation, and Dance, 58*(2), 35.

Hastie, P. (1998a). The participation and perception of girls during a unit of sport education. *Journal of Teaching in Physical Education, 18*(2), 157–171.

———. (1998b). Applied benefits of the sport education model. *Journal of Physical Education, Recreation, and Dance, 69*(4), 24–26.

Hastie, P., & Sharpe, T. (1999). Effects of a sport education curriculum on the positive social behaviors of at-risk rural adolescent boys. *Journal of Education for Students Placed at Risk,* 4, 417–430.

Hay, J. (1991). Reaction to performance feedback: Advances in biomechanics. *Quest*, 25, 33–37.

Hayes, E. (1980). History of dance in the Alliance. *Journal of Physical Education, Recreation, and Dance*, 51(5), 32.

Haymes, E. (2000). Physiology of physical activity. In S. Hoffman & J. Harris (Eds.) *Introduction to Kinesiology* (pp. 381–412). Champaign, IL: Human Kinetics.

Hellison, D. (1973). *Humanistic physical education*. Englewood Cliffs, NJ: Prentice-Hall.

———. (1978). *Beyond balls and bats: Alienated youth in the gym*. Washington, DC: AAHPERD.

———. (1983). Teaching self responsibility (and more). *Journal of Physical Education, Recreation, and Dance*, 54(7), 23.

———. (1984). *Goals and strategies for teaching physical education*. Champaign, IL: Human Kinetics.

———. (1990). Teaching PE to at-risk youth in Chicago: A model. *Journal of Physical Education, Recreation, and Dance*, 61(6), 38–39.

———. (1995). *Teaching responsibility through physical activity*. Champaign, IL: Human Kinetics.

———. (1996). Teaching personal and social responsibility in physical education. In S. Silverman & C. Ennis (Eds.), *Student learning in physical education: Applying research to enhance instruction* (pp. 269–286). Champaign, IL: Human Kinetics.

Henderson, K., & Bialeschki, M. (1991). Girls' and women's recreation programming: Constraints and opportunities. *Journal of Physical Education, Recreation, and Dance*, 62(1), 55–58.

Henig, R. (1999, January 21). Girls enjoy sports—isn't that enough? *USA Today*, 15A.

Henry, F. (1964). Physical education: An academic discipline. *Journal of Health, Physical Education, and Recreation*, 37(7), 32–33.

Hertzman, C. (1994). The lifelong impact of childhood experiences: A population health perspective. *Daedalus*, 123(4), 167–180.

Hester, D., & Dunaway, D. (1991). NAGWS: Paths to advocacy, recruitment, and enhancement. *Journal of Physical Education, Recreation, and Dance*, 62(3), 30–31.

Hetherington, C. (1910). Fundamental education. *American Physical Education Review*, 15, 629–635.

Hinson, C. (1994). Pulse power: A heart physiology program for children. *Journal of Physical Education, Recreation and Dance*, 65(1), 62–68.

Hoffman, S. (1977). Toward a pedagogical kinesiology. *Quest*, 28, 38–48.

———. (1987). Dreaming the impossible dream: The decline and fall of physical education. In J. Massengale (Ed.), *Trends toward the future in physical education* (pp. 121–135). Champaign, IL: Human Kinetics.

Hoffman, S., & Harris, J. (2000). Discovering the field of physical activity. In S. Hoffman & J. Harris (Eds.), *Introduction to kinesiology* (pp. 1–33). Champaign, IL: Human Kinetics.

Houlihan, S., & DeBrock, L. (1991). Economics in sport. In B. Parkhouse (Ed.), *The management of sport* (pp. 198–209). St. Louis: Mosby.

Huizinga, J. (1962). *Homo ludens: A study of the play element in culture*. Boston: Beacon Press.

Hulstrand, B. (1990). Women in high school PE teaching positions: Diminishing in number. *Journal of Physical Education, Recreation, and Dance*, 61(9), 19–21.

Jack, H. (1985). Division of recreation. *Journal of Physical Education, Recreation, and Dance*, 56(4), 97–98.

Janes, M. (1995). Unified sports gains momentum at '95 World Games. *Exceptional Children*, 25(6), 56–57.

Jansma, P., & French, R. (1994). *Special physical education*. Englewood Cliffs, NJ: Prentice-Hall.

Jewett, A., & Bain, L. (1985). *The curriculum process in physical education*. Dubuque, IA: Wm. C. Brown.

Johns, E. (1985). Division of health education. *Journal of Physical Education, Recreation, and Dance*, 56(4), 105–106.

Johnson, D., & Harageones, E. (1994). A health fitness course in secondary physical education: The Florida experience. In R. Pate & D. Hohn (Eds.), *Health and fitness through physical education* (pp. 165–176). Champaign: IL: Human Kinetics.

Jones, D., & Ward, P. (1998). Changing the face of secondary physical education through sport education. *Journal of Physical Education, Recreation, and Dance*, 69(5), 40–44.

Kahn, L., Collins, J., Pateman, B., Small, M., Ross, J., & Kolbe, L. (1995). The School Health Policies and Programs Study (SHPPS): Rationale for a nationwide status report on school health programs. *Journal of School Health*, 65(8), 291–302.

Kaman, R. (1995). Costs and benefits of corporate health promotion. *Fitness in Business*, 5, 39–44.

Kantrowitz, B., & Joseph, N. (1986, May 26). Building baby biceps. *Newsweek*, 79.

Karvonen, M. (1996). Physical activity for a healthy life. *Research Quarterly for Exercise and Sport*, 67(2), 209–212.

Keating, J. (1973). The ethics of competition and its relation to some moral problems in athletics. In R. Osterhoudt (Ed.), *The philosophy of sport* (pp.157–175). Springfield, IL: Charles Thomas.

Kenyon, G., & Loy, J. (1965) . Toward a sociology of sport. *Journal of Health, Physical Education, and Recreation,* 36, 24–25, 68–69.

Kerr, R. (1982). *Psychomotor learning.* Philadelphia: Saunders.

Kimm, S., Glynn, N., Kriska, A., Barton, B., Kronsberg, S., Daniels, S., Crawford, P., Sabry, Z., & Liu, K. (2002). Decline in physical activity in black girls and white girls during adolescence. *New England Journal of Medicine,* 347(10), 709–715.

Kirchner, G. (1970). *Introduction to human movement.* Dubuque, IA: Wm. C. Brown.

Kleinman, S. (1987). On the edge (of oblivion). *American Academy of Physical Education Papers,* 20, 109–114.

Knoppers, A. (1988). Equity for excellence in physical education. *Journal of Physical Education, Recreation, and Dance,* 59(6), 54–58.

Knoor, J. (1996). The need to rethink coaching certification. *Coach and Athletic Director,* 65(6), 4–6.

Knop, N. (1998). Reconstructing physical education in an urban secondary school to create a more democratic environment. Teaching as praxis. Unpublished doctoral dissertation, Ohio State University, Columbus.

Knop, N., Tannehill, D., & O'Sullivan, M. (2001). Making a difference for urban youth. *Journal of Physical Education, Recreation, and Dance,* 72(7), 38–44.

Knudson, D., Magnusson, P., & McHugh, M. (2000). Current issues in flexibility fitness. *Research Digest* 3(10), 1–8. President's Council on Physical Fitness and Sport.

Kotulak, R., & Gorner, P. (1992, January 12). Diet, fitness proven keys to long life. *Columbus Dispatch,* p. 6F.

Kraus, H., & Hirschland, R. (1954). Minimum muscular fitness tests in school children. *Research Quarterly,* 25, 178–185.

Kraus, R. (1995). Play's new identity: Big business. *Journal of Physical Education, Recreation, and Dance,* 66(8), 36–40.

———. (2002). Careers in recreation: Expanding horizons. *Journal of Physical Education, Recreation, and Dance,* 73(5), 46–49, 54.

LaMaster, K. (1996). Go on-line: Get new ideas from newsgroups. *Strategies,* 9(5), 18–20.

Landers, D. (1983). Whatever happened to theory testing in sport psychology? *Journal of Sport Psychology,* 5(2), 135–151.

———. (1997). The influence of exercise on mental health. *President's Council on Physical Fitness and Sport Research Digest,* 2(12), 1–8.

Lawson, H. (1994). Toward healthy learners, schools, and communities. *Journal of Teacher Education,* 45(1), 62–70.

Lawson, H., & Placek, J. (1981). *Physical education in the secondary schools: Curricular alternatives.* Boston: Allyn & Bacon.

Lee, I.-M., & Paffenbarger, R., Jr. (1996). How much physical activity is optimal for health? Methodological considerations. *Research Quarterly for Exercise and Sport,* 67(2), 206–208.

Lee, M., & Bennett, B. (1985a). 1885–1900: A time of gymnastics and measurement. *Journal of Physical Education, Recreation, and Dance,* 56(4), 19–26.

———. (1985b). 1930–1945: A time for affiliation and research. *Journal of Physical Education, Recreation, and Dance,* 56(4), 43–51.

Leigh, D. (1994). Dance for social change. *Journal of Physical Education, Recreation, and Dance,* 65(5), 39–43.

Leonard, F., & Affleck, G. (1947). *A guide to the history of physical education.* Philadelphia: Lea & Febiger.

Leonard, G. (1974). *The ultimate athlete.* New York: Viking Press.

Levine, A., Wells, S., & Knopf, C. (1986, August 11). New rules of exercise. *U.S. News and World Report,* 52–56.

Lister, V. (1993, December 9). More opportunities open, but roadblocks still there. *USA Today,* p. 9C.

Locke, L. (1992) . Changing secondary school physical education. *Quest,* 44(3), 361–372.

Locke, L., & Massengale, J. (1978). Role conflict in teacher/coaches. *Research Quarterly,* 49(2), 162–174.

Logsdon, B., Barrett, K., Broer, M., McKee, R., & Ammongs, M. (1977). *Physical education for children: A focus on the teaching process.* Philadelphia: Lea & Febiger.

Lowe, B. (1977). *The beauty of sport: A cross-disciplinary inquiry.* Englewood Cliffs, NJ: Prentice-Hall.

Loy, J. (1969). The nature of sport: A definitional effort. In J. Loy & G. Kenyon (Eds.), *Sport, culture and society* (pp. 23–32). New York: Macmillan.

Loy, J., & McElvogue, J. (1981). Racial segregation in American sport. In J. Loy, G. Kenyon, & B. McPherson (Eds.), *Sport, culture and society: A reader on the sociology of sport* (pp. 103–116). Philadelphia: Lea & Febiger.

Lucas, J., & Smith, R. (1978). *Saga of American sport.* Philadelphia: Lea & Febiger.

Macdonald, D., & Leitch, S. (1994). Praxis in PE: The senior physical education syllabus on trial. *New Zealand Journal of Physical Education, 27*(2), 17–21.

Maloney, L. (1984, August 13). Sports crazy Americans. *U.S. News & World Report, 23.*

Marmot, M. (1994). Social differentials within and between populations. *Daedalus, 123*(4), 197–216.

Martens, R. (1986). Youth sport in the USA. In M. Weiss & D. Gould (Eds.), *Sport for children and youths* (pp. 27–33). Champaign, IL: Human Kinetics.

Mathieu, M. (1999). The surgeon general's report on leisure services for older adults. *Journal of Physical Education, Recreation, and Dance, 70*(3), 28–31.

McCloy, C. H. (1936). How about some muscle? *Journal of Health and Physical Education, 3*(4), 22–24.

McCubbin J., & Zittel, L. (1991). PL 99–457: What the law is all about. *Journal of Physical Education, Recreation, and Dance, 62*(6), 35–37, 47.

McGinnis, J., Kanner, L., & DeGraw, C. (1991). Physical education's role in achieving national health objectives. *Research Quarterly for Exercise and Sport, 62*(2), 138–142.

McKenzie, T., Nader, P., Strikmiller, P., Yang, M., Stone, E., Perry, C., Taylor, W., Epping, J., Feldman, H., Luepker, R., & Kelder, S. (1996). School physical education: Effect of the child and adolescent trial for cardiovascular health. *Preventive Medicine, 25*(4), 423–431.

McKenzie, T., & Sallis, J. (1996). Physical activity, fitness, and health-related physical education. In S. Silverman & C. Ennis (Eds.), *Student learning in physical education: Applying research to enhance learning* (pp. 223–246). Champaign: IL: Human Kinetics.

McLaughlin, J. (1988) . A stepchild comes of age. *Journal of Physical Education, Recreation, and Dance, 59*(9), 58–60.

McLean, J., Peterson, J., & Martin, W. (1988). *Recreation and leisure: The changing scene* (4th ed.). New York: Macmillan.

McMillin C., & Reffner, C. (1998). *Directory of College and University Coaching Education Programs.* Morgantown, WV: Fitness Information Technology.

McNeill, A. (1987). Wellness programs and their influence on professional preparation. In J. Massengale (Ed.), *Trends toward the future in physical education* (pp. 89–94). Champaign, IL: Human Kinetics.

McPherson, B. (1981). Past, present and future perspectives for research in sport sociology. In J. Loy, G. Kenyon, & B. McPherson (Eds.), *Sport, culture and society: A reader on the sociology of sport* (pp. 10–22) Philadelphia: Lea & Febiger.

Meadows, K. (2003, February 16). Parents have to play nice before kids can play sports. *Columbus Dispatch,* p. D1.

Metheny, E. (1954). The third dimension in physical education. *Journal of Health, Physical Education and Recreation, 24*(3), 27.

———. (1970). The excellence of Patroclus. In H. Slusher & A. Lockhart (Eds.), *Anthology of contemporary readings: An introduction to physical education* (pp. 63–66). Dubuque, IA: Wm. C. Brown.

Mihalich, J. (1982). *Sports and athletics: Philosophy in action.* Totowa, NJ: Littlefield, Adams.

Miller, L., Stoldt, G., & Comfort, G. (2000) Sport management professions. In S. Hoffman & J. Harris (Eds.), *Intoduction to kinesiology.* (pp. 525–552). Champaign, IL: Human Kinetics.

Mills, B. (1997). Opening the gymnasium to the World Wide Web. *Journal of Physical Education, Recreation, and Dance, 68*(8), 17–19.

Milverstedt, F. (1988). Are kids really so out of shape? *Athletic Business, 12*(1).

Mohr, D., Townsend, J., & Bulger, S. (2001). A pedagogical approach to sport education season planning. *Journal of Physical Education, Recreation, and Dance, 72*(9), 37–46.

Mokdad, A., Bowman, B., Ford, E., Vinicor, F., Marks, J. & Koplan, J. (2001). The continuing epidemics of obesity and diabetes in the United States. *JAMA, 286*(10), 1195–1120.

Monroe, J. (1995). Developing cultural awareness through play. *Journal of Physical Education, Recreation, and Dance, 66*(8), 24–27.

Moore, G. (1986). Elementary physical education: Involving outdoor adventure activities. *Journal of Physical Education, Recreation, and Dance, 57*(5), 61–63.

Morrow, J., & Gill, D. (Eds.) (1995). The academy papers: The role of physical activity in fitness and health. *Quest, 47*(3).

Motley, M., & Lavine, M. (2001). Century marathon: A race for equality in girls' and women's sports. *Journal of Physical Education, Recreation, and Dance, 72*(6), 56–59.

Mullan, M. (1986). Issues. *Journal of Physical Education, Recreation, and Dance, 57*(6), 18.

Nack, W., & Munson, L., (2000). Out of control *Sports Illustrated*, 93(4), 86–95.

Naisbitt, J. (1983). *Megatrends: Ten new directions transforming our lives*. New York: Warner Books.

NASPE News. (1994, Summer). National summit on coaching standards, *NASPE News*, 39, 1, 9.

———. (1998, Winter). Shape of the Nation Report, *NASPE News*, 50, 1, 14.

———. (2001a, Fall). Latest Shape of the Nation to be released. *NASPE News*, **58**(5), 1.

———. (2001b, Spring). Quality sports begin with quality coaches. *NASPE News*, **56**(6), 1.

———. (2002, Spring). Standards developed for strength and conditioning professionals. *NASPE News*. (60), 6.

National Association for Sport and Physical Education. (1992). *Developmentally appropriate physical education practices for children*. Washington, DC: AAHPERD.

———. (1995). *National Standards for Athletic Coaches*. Washington, AAHPERD.

———. (1995a). *Moving into the future: National standards for physical education*. St. Louis: Mosby

———. (1995b). *National standards for beginning physical education teachers*. Reston, VA: NASPE.

———. (1995c). *Parent's checklist for quality youth sport programs*. Reston, VA: NASPE.

———. (2002). *2001 Shape of the Nation Report*. Reston, VA: American Alliance for Health, Physical Education, Recreation, and Dance.

National Blueprint on Physical Activity Among Adults Age 50 and Older (2000). Princeton, NJ: Robert Wood Johnson Foundation.

National Consortium for Physical Education and Recreation for Individuals with Disabilities. (1995). *Adapted physical education national standards*. Champaign, IL: Human Kinetics.

Nevins, A. (1962). *The gateway to history*. Garden City, NY: Anchor Books.

Newell, K. (1990a). Physical education in higher education: Chaos out of order. *Quest*, 42(3), 227–242.

———. (1990b). Kinesiology: The label for the study of physical activity in higher education. *Quest*, 42(3), 269–278.

News. (2001). Active seniors less susceptible to depression. *Journal of Physical Education, Recreation, and Dance*, 72(1), 9–10.

———. (2002). Texas reinstates physical education. *Journal of Physical Education, Recreation, and Dance*, 73(5), 5.

Newsletter. (1996). NIH panel links activity to improved cardiovascular health. Washington, DC: President's Council on Physical Fitness and Sports, 96(1), 6.

Novak, M. (1976). *The joy of sports*. New York: Basic Books.

Noyes, B. (1996). The program. *Athletic Business*, 20(4), 29–35.

O'Connor, A., & Macdonald, D. (2002). Up close and personal on physical education teachers' identity: Is conflict an issue? *Sport, Education and Society*, 7(1), 37–54.

Ogden, C., Flegal, K., Carroll, M., & Johnson, C. (2002). Prevalence and trends in overweight among US children and adolescents, 1999–2000. *Journal of the American Medical Association*, 288, 1728–1732.

Olafson, L. (2002). "I hate Phys. Ed.": Adolescent girls talk about physical education. *The Physical Educator*, 59, 67–74.

Olsen, E. (1986). Your number's up. *The Runner*, 8(8), 40–47.

Olson, J. (1995). Sports participation: Efforts to involve minorities, females prove fruitful in Madison schools. *Interscholastic Athletic Administration*, 22(2), 4–5.

Orlick, T. (1977). Cooperative games. *Journal of Physical Education, Recreation, and Dance*, 48(7), 33–36.

———. (1986). Evolution in children's sport. In M. Weiss & D. Gould (Eds.), *Sport for children and youths* (pp. 169–178). Champaign, IL: Human Kinetics

O'Sullivan, M., Siedentop, D., & Tannehill, D. (1994). Breaking out: Codependency of high school physical education, 13, 421–428.

Pacific Mutual Insurance Co. (1978). *Health maintenance* (Survey conducted by Louis Harris and Associates, Inc.). San Francisco: Author.

Page, C. (1969). Reaction to Stone. In G. Kenyon (Ed.), *Aspects of contemporary sport sociology* (pp. 17–19). Chicago: The Athletic Institute.

Pangrazi, R., Corbin, C., & Welk, G. (1996). Physical activity for children and youth. *Journal of Physical Education, Recreation, and Dance*, 67(4), 38–43.

Partlow, K. (1992). American Coaching Effectiveness Program (ACEP): Educating America's coaches. *Journal of Physical Education, Recreation, and Dance*, 63(7), 36–39.

Partridge, D., & Franks, I. (1996). Analyzing and modifying coaching behaviors by means of computer assisted observation. *The Physical Educator*, 53(1), 8–23.

Passer, M. (1986). A psychological perspective. In M. Weiss & D. Gould (Eds.), *Sport for children and youths* (pp. 55–58). Champaign, IL: Human Kinetics.

Pastore, D. (1994). Strategies for retaining female high school head coaches: A survey of administrators and coaches. *Journal of Sport and Social Issues*, 17(2).

Pate, R. (1994). Fitness testing: Current approaches and purposes in physical education. In R. Pate & D. Hohn (Eds.). *Health and Fitness through Physical Education* (pp. 119–128). Champaign, IL: Human Kinetics.

———. (1995). Physical activity and health: Dose–response issues. *Research Quarterly for Exercise and Sport*, 66(4), 313–317.

Pate, R., & Hohn, D. (1994). A contemporary mission for physical education. In R. Pate & D. Hohn (Eds.). *Health and fitness through physical education* (pp. 1–8). Champaign, IL: Human Kinetics.

Pate, R., Trost, S., Dowda, M., Ott. A., Ward, D., Saunders, R., & Felton, G. (1999). Tracking of physical activity, physical inactivity, and health related physical fitness in rural youth. *Pediatric Exercise Science*, 11, 364–376.

Pate, R., Trost, S., Levin, S., & Dowda, M. (2000). Sports participation and health-related behaviors. *Archives of Pediatric Adolescent Medicine*, 154, September, 904–911.

Paul, P., & Cartledge, G. (1996). Inclusive schools—the continuing debate. *Theory into Practice*, 35(1), 2–3.

Physical Activity Today. (1996). Exercise shown to lower breast cancer risk! *Physical Activity Today*, 2(1), 1.

Physical Activity Today. (1999). Elderly walkers miles ahead of inactive peers. *Physical Activity Today*, 5(3), 1.

Pifer, S. (1987). Secondary physical education: A new design. *Journal of Physical Education, Recreation, and Dance*, 58(6), 50–51.

Placek, J. (1983). Concepts of success in teaching: Busy, happy and good? In T. Templin & J. Olson (Eds.), *Teaching in physical education* (pp. 46–56). Champaign, IL: Human Kinetics.

———. (1996). Integration as a curriculum model in physical education: Possibilities and problems. In S. Silverman & C. Ennis (Eds.), *Student learning in physical education: Applying research to enhance learning* (pp. 287–312). Champaign, IL: Human Kinetics.

Pollock, M., & Vincent, K. (1996). Resistance training for health. *Research Digest*. Washington, DC: President's Council on Physical Fitness and Sports Research Digest, 1–6.

Portman, P. (1995). Who is having fun in physical education classes? Experiences of sixth-grade students in elementary and middle schools. *Journal of Teaching in Physical Education*, 14, 445–453.

Posey, E. (1988). Discipline-based arts education: Developing a dance curriculum. *Journal of Physical Education, Recreation, and Dance*, 59(9), 61–64.

President's Council on Physical Fitness and Sport Newsletter (1973, May). National adult physical fitness survey. *Newsletter*, 1–27.

Pritchard, R., & Potter, G. (Eds.) (1990). *Fitness, Inc.: A guide to corporate health and wellness programs.* Homewood, IL: Dow-Jones-Irwin.

Quain, R. (1990). Community based sport. In J. Parks & B. Zanger (Eds.), *Sport and fitness management* (pp. 57–62). Champaign, IL: Human Kinetics.

Rankin, J. (1989). Athletic trainer education: New directions. *Journal of Physical Education, Recreation, and Dance*, 60(6), 68–71.

Rarick, L. (1967). The domain of physical education as a discipline. *Quest*, 9, 50–59.

Rauschenbach, J. (1992). Case studies of elementary physical education specialists. Unpublished doctoral dissertation, Ohio State University, Columbus.

Richmond, J. (1979). *Healthy people: The surgeon general's report on health promotion and disease prevention* (DHEW Publication No. 79–55071). Washington, DC: U.S. Government Printing Office.

Rider, R., & Johnson, D. (1986). Effects of Florida's personal fitness course on cognitive, attitudinal, and physical fitness measures of secondary school students: A pilot study. *Perceptual and Motor Skills*, 62(2), 548550.

Robert Wood Johnson Foundation. (2001). *National blueprint on physical activity among adults age 50 and older,* Princeton, NJ: Robert Wood Johnson Foundation.

Rosenbaum, M., & Leibel, R. (1989). Obesity in childhood. *Pediatric Review*, 11(2), 43–55.

Ross, J., Delpy, L., Christenson, G., Gold, R., & Damberg, C. (1987). Study procedures and quality control. *Journal of Physical Education, Recreation, and Dance*, 58(9), 57–62.

Ross, J., & Pate, R. (1987). A summary of findings. *Journal of Physical Education, Recreation, and Dance*, 58(9), 51–56.

Rowe, P. J., & Miller, L. (1991). Treating high school sports injuries: Are coaches/trainers competent? *Journal of Physical Education, Recreation, and Dance*, 62(1), 49–54.

Sack, A. (1977). Big time college football: Whose free ride? *Quest*, 27, 87–96.

Sage, G. (1979). The current status and trends of sport sociology. In M. Krotee (Ed.), *The dimensions of sport sociology.* West Point, NY: Leisure Press.

———. (1984). *Motor learning and control: A neuropsychological approach.* Dubuque, IA: Wm. C. Brown.

———. (1987). Pursuit of knowledge in sociology of sport: Issues and prospects. *Quest,* 39(3), 255–281.

———. (1991). Beyond enhancing performance in sport:Toward empowerment and transformation. *The Academy Papers,* 25, 85–95.

Sallis, J. (1994). Determinants of physical activity behavior in children. In R. Pate & D. Hohn (Eds.), *Health and fitness through physical education* (pp. 31–44). Champaign, IL: Human Kinetics.

Sallis, J., & McKenzie, T. (1991). Physical education's role in public health. *Research Quarterly for Exercise and Sport,* 62(2), 124–137.

Sallis, J., McKenzie, T., Kolody, B., Lewis, M., Marshall, S., & Rosengard, P. (1999). Effects of health-related physical education on academic achievement: Project SPARK. *Research Quarterly for Exercise and Sport,* 70, 127–134.

Samman, P. (1998). *Active youth: Ideas for implementing the CDC physical activity promotion guidelines.* Champaign: IL: Human Kinetics.

Schafer, S. (1987). Sport needs you. The Colorado model. *Journal of Physical Education, Recreation, and Dance,* 58(2), 44–47.

Schiller, F. (1910). Letters upon the aesthetic education of man. In C. Eliot (Ed.), *The Harvard Classics* (Vol. 32). New York: P. F. Collier & Son.

Schmid, S. (1994a). Campus showpiece. *Athletic Business,* 18(1), 47–50.

———. (1994b). Community asset. *Athletic Business,* 18(3), 20.

Schmidt, R. (1988). *Motor control and learning: A behavioral emphasis* (2nd ed.). Champaign, IL: Human Kinetics.

Schor, J. (1991). *The overworked American: The unexpected decline of leisure.* New York: Basic Books.

Scott, J. (1974). Sport and the radical chic. In G. McGlynn (Ed.), *Issues in physical education and sport* (pp. 155–162). Palo Alto, CA: National Press.

Scraton, S. (1990). *Shaping up to womanhood: Gender and girls' physical education.* Buckingham, England: Open University Press.

Seefeldt, V., & Milligan, M. (1992). Program for Athletic Coaches Education (PACE): Educating America's public and private school coaches. *Journal of Physical Education, Recreation, and Dance,* 63(7), 46–49.

Shaw, G. (1972). *Meat on the hoof: The hidden world of Texas football.* New York: St. Martin's Press.

Shea, C., Shebilske, W., & Worchel, S. (1993). *Motor learning and control.* Englewood Cliffs, NJ: Prentice-Hall.

Sheed, W. (1995, Winter). Why sports matter. *Wilson Quarterly,* 11–25.

Sheehan, G. (1982). Viewpoint. *Runner's World,* 27(7), 14.

Shephard, R. (1988). Exercise adherence in corporate settings: Personal traits and program barriers. In R. Dishman (Ed.), *Exercise adherence* (pp. 305–319). Champaign, IL: Human Kinetics.

———. (1995). Physical activity, health, and well-being at different life stages. *Research Quarterly for Exercise and Sport,* 66(4), 298–302.

———. (1996). Habitual physical activity and quality of life. *Quest,* 48(3), 354–365.

Sherman, N. (2001). Tracking the long-term benefits of physical education. *Journal of Physical Education, Recreation, and Dance,* 72(3), 5.

Sherrill, C. (1993). *Adapted physical activity, recreation, and sport* (4th ed.), Dubuque, IA: Brown & Benchmark.

Siedentop, D. (1972). *Physical education: Introductory analysis.* Dubuque, IA: Wm. C. Brown.

———. (1976). *Physical education: Introductory analysis* (2nd ed.). Dubuque, IA: Wm. C. Brown.

———. (1980). *Physical education: Introductory analysis* (3rd ed.). Dubuque, IA: Wm. C. Brown.

———. (1981, August). Must competition be a zero-sum game? *The School Administrator,* 38, 11.

———. (1987). High school physical education: Still an endangered species. *Journal of Physical Education, Recreation, and Dance,* 58(2), 24–25.

———. (1989). The elementary specialist study. *Journal of Teaching in Physical Education,* 8(3), 187–270.

———. (1990). Commentary: The world according to Newell. *Quest,* 42(3), 315–322.

———. (1991). *Developing teaching skills in physical education* (3rd ed.). Mountain View, CA: Mayfield.

———. (1992). Thinking differently about secondary physical education. *Journal of Physical Education, Recreation, and Dance,* 63(7), 69–73.

———. (1994). *Sport education: Quality PE through positive sport experiences.* Champaign, IL: Human Kinetics.

———. (1996a). Physical education and education reform: The case for sport education. In S. Silverman & C. Ennis (Eds.), *Student learning in physical education: Applying research to enhance instruction* (pp. 247–268). Champaign, IL: Human Kinetics.

———. (1996b). Sport education: A curricular success story. *Teaching Secondary Physical Education, 2*(3), 8–9.

———. (1996c). Valuing the physically active life: Contemporary and future directions. *Quest, 48*(3), 266–274.

———. (1998). What is sport education and how does it work? *Journal of Physical Education, Recreation, and Dance, 69*(4), 18–20.

Siedentop, D., Herkowitz, J., & Rink, J. (1984). *Elementary physical education methods.* Englewood Cliffs, NJ: Prentice-Hall.

Siedentop, D., & Locke, L. (1997). Making a difference for physical education: What professors and practitioners must build together. *Journal of Physical Education, Recreation, and Dance. 68*(4), 25–33.

Siedentop, D., Mand, C., & Taggart, A. (1986). *Physical education: Teaching and curriculum strategies for grades 5–12.* Palo Alto, CA: Mayfield.

Siedentop, D., & O'Sullivan, M. (1992). Preface. *Quest, 44*(3), 285–286.

Siedentop, D., & Siedentop, B. (1985). Daily fitness in Australia. *Journal of Physical Education, Recreation, and Dance, 56*(2), 41–43.

Siedentop, D., & Tannehill, D. (2000). *Developing teaching skills in physical education* (4th ed.). Mountain View, CA: Mayfield.

Simons-Morton, B. (1994). Implementing health-related physical education. In R. Pate & D. Hohn (Eds.). *Health and fitness through physical education* (pp. 137–146). Champaign, IL: Human Kinetics.

Simpson, K. (2000). Biomechanics of physical activity. In S. Hoffman & J. Harris (Eds.), *Introduction to kinesiology* (pp. 353–380). Champaign, IL: Human Kinetics.

Singer, R. (Ed.). (1976). *Physical education: Foundations.* New York: Holt, Rinehart, and Winston.

Sisley, B., & Capel, S. (1986). High school coaching: Filled with gender differences. *Journal of Physical Education, Recreation, and Dance, 57*(3), 39–44.

Sisley, B., & Weise, D. (1987). Current status: Requirements for interscholastic coaches. *Journal of Physical Education, Recreation, and Dance, 58*(7), 73–85.

Skidelsky, R. (1969). *English progressive schools.* Middlesex, England: Penguin Books.

Skinner, J. (1988). The fitness industry. *The Academy Papers, 21,* 67–72.

Slava, S., Laurie, D., & Corbin, C. (1984). The long-term effects of a conceptual physical education program. *Research Quarterly for Exercise and Sport, 55*(2), 161–165.

Smith, C. (1992a, August 16). Equality's hurdles. *New York Times,* Sports Pages, 27.

———. (1992b, August 16). Too few changes since Campanis. *New York Times,* Sports Pages, 27–28.

Smith, L. (Ed.). (1970). *Psychology of motor learning.* Chicago: The Athletic Institute.

Smith, R., Smoll, F., & Curtis, B. (1978). Coaching behaviors in Little League baseball. In F. Smoll & R. Smith (Eds.), *Psychological perspectives in youth sports* (pp. 173–201). Washington, DC: Hemisphere.

Smoll, F. (1986). Stress reduction strategies in youth sport. In M. Weiss & D. Gould (Eds.), *Sport for children and youths* (pp. 127–136). Champaign, IL: Human Kinetics.

Spain, C., & Franks, D. (2001). Healthy people 2010: Physical activity and fitness. *Research Digest, 3*(13), 1–12. President's Council on Physical Fitness and Sports.

Sparkes, A. (1991). Alternative visions of health-related fitness: An exploration of problem-setting and its consequences. In N. Armstrong & A. Sparkes (Eds.), *lssues in physical education* (pp. 204–227). London: Caswell Educational Limited.

Spears, B., & Swanson, R. (1978). *History of sport and physical activity in the United States.* Dubuque, IA: Wm. C. Brown.

Sporting Goods Manufacturing Association. (2002). *Youth sport participation trends.* www.sgma.com.

Steller, J. (1994). The physical education performance troupe: A skill and fitness approach. In R. Pate & D. Hohn (Eds.). *Health and fitness through physical education* (pp. 191–196). Champaign, IL: Human Kinetics.

Stevens, J. (1984). Special Olympics. *Journal of Physical Education, Recreation, and Dance, 55*(2), 42–43.

Stewart, C., & Sweet, L. (1992). Professional preparation of high school coaches: The problem continues. *Journal of Physical Education, Recreation, and Dance, 63*(6), 75–79.

Stourowsky, E. (1996). Blaming the victim: Resistance in the battle over gender equity in intercollegiate athletics. *Journal of Sport and Social Issues, 20*(2).

Strauss, R. & Pollock H. (2001). Epidemic increase in childhood overweight, 1986–1998. *JAMA, 286*(22), 2845–2848.

Stroot, S., Carpenter, M., & Eisengale, K. (1991). Focus of physical education: Academic and physical excellence at Westgate Alternative School. *Journal of Physical Education, Recreation, and Dance, 62*(7), 49–53.

Stroot, S., Collier, C., O'Sullivan, M., & England, K. (1994). Hoops and hurdles: Workplace conditions in secondary physical education. *Journal of Teaching in Physical Education, 13*, 342–360.

Struna, N. (1991). Further reactions to Newell: Chaos is wonderful! *Quest, 43*(2), 230–235.

Suits, B. (1976). What is a game? *Philosophy of Science, 34*, 148–156.

Sutton, A. (2000, May 19). Parents out of control *Chicago Tribune,* Internet Edition, www.chicagosports.com.

Sutton, W. (1984). Family involvement in youth sports: An examination of the YMCA Y-winners philosophy. *Journal of Physical Education, Recreation, and Dance, 55*(8), 59–60.

Sweeney, J., Tannehill, D., & Teeters, L. (1992). Team up for fitness. *Strategies, 5*(6), 20–23.

Swift, E. M. (1991). Why Johnny can't play. *Sports Illustrated,* 60–72.

Taggart, A., Taggart, J., & Siedentop, D. (1986). Effects of a home-based activity program. *Behavior Modification, 10*(4), 41–52.

Taylor, J., & Chiogioji, E. (1987). Implications of educational reform on high school programs. *Journal of Physical Education, Recreation, and Dance, 58*(2), 22–23.

Teague, M., & Mobily, K. (1983). Rustproofing people: Corporate recreation programs in perspective. *Journal of Physical Education, Recreation, and Dance, 54*(8), 42–44.

Templin, T., Sparkes, A., Grant, B., & Schemmp, P. (1994). Matching the self: The paradoxical case and life history of a late career teacher/coach, *Journal of Teaching in Physical Education, 13*, 274–294.

Thomas, J., & Thomas, K. (2000). Motor behavior. In S. Hoffman & J. Harris (Eds.), *Introduction to kinesiology* (pp. 243–281). Champaign, IL: Human Kinetics.

Timmermans, H., & Martin, M. (1987). Top ten potentially dangerous exercises. *Journal of Physical Education, Recreation, and Dance, 58*(6), 29–31.

Tinning, R. (1985). Physical education and the cult of slenderness. *ACHPER National Journal, 1*(7), 10–13.

———. (1990). *Ideology and physical education.* Geelong, Australia: Deaking University.

Toufexis, A. (1986, July 21). Putting on the Ritz at the Y. *Time,* 65.

Treanor, L., Graber, K., Housner, L., & Wiegand, R. (1998). Middle school students' perceptions of coeducational and same-sex physical education classes. *Journal of Teaching in Physical Education, 18*, 43–56.

Trudeau, F., Laurencelle, L., Tremblay, J., Rajic, M., & Shephard, R. (1998). A long-term follow-up of participants in the Trois-Riviers semi-longitudinal study of growth and development. *Pediatric Exercise Science, 10*, 366–377.

Turner, B. (1995). No more ifs, ands, or buts. *Teaching High School Physical Education, 1*(4), 11.

Ulrich, C. (1976). A ball of gold. In C. Ulrich (Ed.), *To seek and find* (pp. 150–160). Washington, DC: AAHPERD.

Update. (1995, July/September), AAHPERD, ACSM, AHA collaborate to launch national coalition for promoting physical activity. *American Alliance for Health, Physical Education, Recreation, and Dance, 1.*

USA Today. (1988, November 11). Anabolic steroids. *USA Today,* p. 1C.

U.S. Census Bureau. (2000). *Statistical abstract of the United States.* Washington, DC.

U.S. Department of Health and Human Services. (1996). *Physical activity and health: A report of the surgeon general.* Atlanta: U.S. Department of Health and Human Services, Centers for Disease Control and Prevention, National Center for Chronic Disease Prevention and Health Promotion.

———. (2000). *Healthy People 2010.* Washington, D.C: U.S. Government Printing Office.

———. (2000). *Promoting better health for young people through physical activity and sports,* Washington, DC.: U.S. Government Printing Office.

———. (2002). Physical activity fundamental to preventing disease. Washington, D.C.: U.S. Department of Health and Human Services, Government Printing Office.

U.S. Public Health Service. (1991). *Healthy people 2000: National health promotion and disease objectives* (DHHS Publication No. [PHS] 91–50212). Washington, DC: U.S. Government Printing Office.

U.S. Public Health Service, 2001.

U.S. Public Law 93-112. (1973). *Rehabilitation Act.*

Vernon, J. (1980). Effects of vaulter and pole parameters on performance. In J. Cooper & B. Haven (Eds.), *Proceedings of the Biomechanics Symposium.* Indianapolis: Indiana State Board of Health.

Vertinsky, P. (1991). Science, social science, and the "hunger for wonders" in physical education: Moving toward a future healthy society. *The Academy Papers,* 24, 70 88.

―――. (1992). Reclaiming space, revisioning the body: The quest for gender-sensitive physical education. *Quest,* 44(3), 373–397.

Vickers, J. (1992). While Rome burns: Meeting the challenge of the second wave of the reform movement in education. *Journal of Physical Education, Recreation, and Dance,* 63(7), 80–87.

Villeneuve, K., Weeks, D., & Schwied, M. (1983). Employee fitness: The bottom line. *Journal of Physical Education, Recreation, and Dance,* 54(8), 35–36.

Virgilio, S. (1996). A home, school, and community model for promoting healthy lifestyles. *Teaching Elementary Physical Education,* 7(1), 4–7.

Virgilio, S., & Berenson, G. (1988). SuperKids–SuperFit: A comprehensive fitness intervention model for elementary schools. *Journal of Physical Education, Recreation, and Dance,* 59(8), 19–25.

Weigle, S. (1994). A walking program in your school? Practice tips to make it work. In R. Pate & D. Hohn (Eds.). *Health and fitness through physical education* (pp. 201–204). Champaign, IL: Human Kinetics.

Weinberg, R., & Williams, J. (2001). Integrating and implementing a psychological skills training program. In J. Williams (Ed.), *Applied sport psychology* (4th ed., pp. 347–377). Mountain View, CA: Mayfield.

Weiss, M. (2000). Motivating kids in physical activity. *Research Digest,* 3(11), 1–8. President's Council on Physical Fitness and Sports.

Weiss, P. (1969). *Sport: A philosophic inquiry.* Carbondale, IL: Southern Illinois Press.

Wells, C. (1996). Physical activity and women's health. *Physical Activity and Fitness Research Digest,* 2(5), 1–6.

Wessell, J., & Zittel, L. (1995). Smart start. *Adapted Physical Activity Newsletter,* 1(1), 1–2.

Westcott, W. (1982). *Strength fitness.* Boston: Allyn & Bacon.

―――. (1992). High school physical education: A fitness professional's perspective. *Quest,* 44(3), 342–351.

―――. (1993). *Be strong: Strength training for muscular fitness for men and women.* Dubuque, IA: Brown & Benchmark.

Westcott, W. & Baechle, T. (1998). Strength training past 50. Champaign, IL: Human Kinetics.

Weston, A. (1962). *The making of American physical education.* New York: Appleton-Century-Crofts.

White, E., & Sheets, C. (2001). If you let them play, they will. *Journal of Physical Education, Recreation, and Dance,* 72(4), 27–28, 33.

Whitehead, J. (1994). Enhancing fitness and activity motivation in children. In R. Pate & D. Hohn (Eds.), *Health and fitness through physical education* (pp. 81–90). Champaign, IL: Human Kinetics.

Wilberg, R. (1975). The direction and definition of a field. In *Trabajos científicos* (Vol. 3). Madrid: Instituto Nacional de Education Fisica.

Wiley, R. (1987, July 21). A man of bars and measures. *Sports Illustrated,* 50–53.

Wilkinson, C., Hillier, R., & Harrison, J. (1998). Improving the computer literacy of preservice teachers. *Journal of Physical Education, Recreation, and Dance.* 69(5), 10–13.

Wilkinson, R. (1994). The epidemiological transition: From material scarcity to social disadvantage? *Daedalus,* 123(4), 61–78.

Williams, J., & Straub, W. (2001). Sport psychology: Past, present, future. In. J. Williams (Ed.), *Applied sport psychology* (4th ed., pp. 1–12). Mountain View, CA: Mayfield.

Williams, J. F. (1930). Education through the physical. *Journal of Higher Education,* 1, 279–282.

Wilson, W. (1977). Social discontent and the growth of wilderness sport in America: 1965–1974. *Quest,* 27, 54–60.

Witt, P., & Baker, D. (1997). Developing after-school programs for youth in high risk environments. *Journal of Physical Education, Recreation, and Dance,* 68(9), 18–20.

Wrisberg, C. (1996). Quality of life for male and female athletes. *Quest,* 48(3), 392–408.

Zeigler, E. (1962). A history of professional preparation for physical education (1861–1961). In *Professional preparation in health education, physical education, and recreation education* (pp. 116–133). Washington DC: AAHPERD.

―――. (1979). A history of physical education and sport. Englewood Cliffs, NJ: Prentice-Hall.

Credits

PHOTO CREDITS

Chapter 1 p. 7, © Sam Forencich; p. 8, © Corbis; p. 9 (top), © Ohio State University; p. 9 (bottom), © Sam Forencich; p. 10, © Ohio State University; p. 12, © Ohio State University; p. 15, © Ohio State University. *Chapter 2* p. 25, © Ohio State University Archives; p. 30, © Ohio State University Archives; p. 32 (left), © Ohio State University Archives; p. 32 (right), photograph by Katherine Elizabeth McClellan, Smith College Archives; p. 35, © Ohio State University Archives; p. 38, © Bettman/CORBIS. *Chapter 3* p. 54, © PhotoDisc; p. 58, © PhotoDisc; p. 60, © Ohio State University. *Chapter 4* p. 72, © PhotoDisc; p. 73, © Digital Vision; p. 77, © Sam Forencich; p. 81, © Daryl Siedentop; p. 83, © PhotoDisc. *Chapter 5* p. 90, © PhotoDisc; p. 95, from Prentice, W. E., *Get Fit, Stay Fit*, 2nd ed., © 2001 McGraw-Hill, by permission of the author; p. 99, © PhotoDisc; p. 105, © Sam Forencich; p. 106, © Wayne Glusker Photography. *Chapter 6* p. 113, © Ohio State University; p. 114, © PhotoDisc; p. 115, © Ohio State University; p. 122, © PhotoDisc; p. 131, from Arnheim, D. D., and Prentice, W. E., *Principles of Athletic Training*, 11th ed., © 2003 McGraw-Hill, by permission of the author. *Chapter 7* p. 138, © Ohio State University; p. 140, © PhotoDisc; p. 146, © PhotoDisc; p. 153, © Ohio State University; p. 155, © Ohio State University. *Chapter 8* p. 170 (left), © Ohio State University; p. 170 (right), © PhotoDisc; p. 182, © Daryl Siedentop; p. 187, © Daryl Siedentop; p. 188, © Daryl Siedentop. *Chapter 9* p. 195, © Daryl Siedentop; p. 197, © Digital Vision; p. 200 (bottom), © Ohio State University; p. 200 (top), © Sam Forencich; p. 207, © 1999, The Cooper Institute for Aerobics Research, Dallas, Texas; p. 208, © Ohio State University; p. 211, © SwimEx, Inc. *Chapter 10* p. 226, © PhotoDisc; p. 230, © Ohio State University; p. 232, © Ohio State University; p. 233, © Ohio State University. *Chapter 11* p. 245, © PhotoDisc; p. 247, © Ohio State University; p. 252, © PhotoDisc; p. 254, © Daryl Siedentop; p. 256 © Digital Vision. *Chapter 12* p. 266, © Ohio State University; p. 271, © Ohio State University; p. 276, © PhotoDisc. *Chapter 13* p. 287, © Ohio State University; p. 289, © Daryl Siedentop; p. 290, © Daryl Siedentop; p. 298, © Wayne Glusker. *Chapter 14* p. 307, © Ohio State University; p. 312, © Ohio State University. *Chapter 15* p. 317, © PhotoDisc; p. 321, © Daryl Siedentop. *Chapter 16* p. 326, © Sam Forencich; p. 327, © Daryl Siedentop. *Chapter 17* p. 336, © Ohio State University; p. 337, © PhotoDisc; p. 339, © PhotoDisc. *Chapter 18* p. 346, © Sam Forencich; p. 350, © PhotoDisc. *Chapter 19* p. 358, © Ohio State University; p. 359, © Sam Forencich; p. 363, © Daryl Siedentop. *Chapter 20* p. 370, © PhotoDisc; p. 372, © Sam Forencich; p. 374, © Ohio State University; p. 375, © PhotoDisc. *Chapter 21* p. 383, © Ohio State University; p. 386, © Sam Forencich; p. 388, © PhotoDisc; p. 392, © Digital Vision. *Chapter 22* p. 398, from Arnheim, D. D., and Prentice, W. E., *Principles of Athletic Training*, 11th ed., © 2003 McGraw-Hill, by permission of the author; p. 399, © PhotoDisc; p. 400, © Ohio State University; p. 403, © PhotoDisc; p. 405, © PhotoDisc.

TEXT CREDITS

Fig. 8.2, p. 177, from Fahey, T., Insel, P., and Roth, W., *Core Concepts and Labs in Fitness and Wellness*, 5th ed., © 2003 McGraw-Hill. Fig. 8.4, p. 189, used with permission from the *Journal of Physical Education, Recreation, and Dance*, 70(6), p. 31, a publication of the American Alliance for Health, Physical Education, Recreation, and Dance, 1900 Association Drive, Reston, VA 20191. Figure 9.1, p. 199, U.S. Department of Health and Human Services, 2000, *Healthy People 2010*, 2nd ed., Washington, D.C.: DHHS. Figure 9.2, p. 200, adapted with permission from *Research Quarterly for Exercise Science and Sport*, 62(2), 1991, p. 124–137, a publication of the American Alliance for Health, Physical Education, Recreation, and Dance, 1900 Association Drive, Reston, VA 20191. Table 11.1, p. 242, reprinted from *Moving into the Future: National Physical Education Standards: A Guide*

Index

AAALF. *See* American Association for Active Lifestyles and Fitness

AAFP. *See* American Academy of Family Physicians

AAHE. *See* American Association for Health Education

AAHPE. *See* American Association for Health and Physical Education (AAHPE)

AAHPER. *See* American Association for Health, Physical Education, and Recreation (AAHPER)

AAHPERD. *See* American Alliance for Health, Physical Education, Recreation, and Dance

AAKPE. *See* American Academy of Kinesiology and Physical Education

AALR. *See* American Association for Leisure and Recreation

AAPE. *See* American Academy of Physical Education; Association for the Advancement of Physical Education

abduction, 318

academic discipline movement, 60–64

academic-integration model, 248–249

academic sport psychologists, 348
   preparation to become, 351–353
   what they do, 349–351

academic sport psychology, 348–349

Academy for Youth Sport Administrators (ACYSA), 117

Academy Papers, The, 40

accelerometers, 187

access
   equity and, 43
   unequal, 143

accreditation, 385

Acost, Vivian, 132

ACSM. See American College of Sports Medicine

activity. *See* physical activity

activity estimates, fitness tests vs., 229–230

ACTIVITY GRAM, 207

activity industry, 403–404

activity patterns. *See also* children and youths
   five groups of, 173

activity, as theme for the future, 403–404

adapted physical education, 256, 257
   certification for teaching, 282
   Web sites about, 300

adapted program, 256

adduction, 318

Adelphi Academy, 23–24

Adelphi Conference of 1885, 24

administration
   athletic, 129–131
   sport, 129–131
   women in, 155

Adolescence (Hall), 39

Adolph Coors Company, 16–17, 209

adults
   child's play and adult's play, 94–95, 338
   emphasis shift from youths to, 18
   fitness levels among, 198–200
   fitness Web sites, 236
   focusing on, 400
   levels of physical activity among, 199
   obesity in, 18
   statewide sport festivals, 128
   young. *See* young adults

advanced exercise specialist (YMCA), 217

adventure education, 81
   as curriculum influence, 253–255
   elementary-school level, 269–270
   in school physical education, 60
   in summer camps, 264

adventure skills, 8

aerobic, defined, 169

aerobic exercise
   central to health fitness, 179
   duration of, 173–174
   emphasis on, 170–171
   era of, 58–59
   frequency of, 174
   intensity of, 173

Aerobics and Fitness Association of America, certification, 212, 213

Aerobics (Cooper), 170–171
aerobics era, 58–59, 61
aesthetics. *See also* beauty in sport; sport aesthetics
    of form sports, 104
    quality of, in other sports, 104–106
AFA. *See* American Fitness Alliance
affiliation, in sport education, 251
African Americans. *See also* black people; minorities;
    minority issues; race
    overweight, 171
    post-World War I era athletes, 41
    sport programs, 41
age
    breakdown of stereotypes, 18
    fitness and, 230–231
    lifespan physical activity not limited by, 5
    recreation and, 386
agility, 170
aging
    depression with, 231
    fitness and, 230–231
    resistance training and, 184
agonist-antagonist pairs, 183–184
AHA. *See* American Heart Association
allied fields, 381
    allied or integrated, 393–394
    dance, 391–393
    health, 387–391
    recreation, 382–387
    Web sites about, 394
alternative career programs, 359
alternative schools, 249
alternative sport, 83
amateur athlete, 112
Amateur Athletic Union, 72
amateurism, 71–72
Amateur Softball Association, 48
amateur sport entertainment, 130
Amateur Sports Act (1978), 126, 256
Amateurs, The (Halberstam), 102, 368
American Academy of Family Physicians (AAFP), 214
American Academy of Kinesiology and Physical Educa-
    tion (AAKPE), 63, 316
American Academy of Pediatrics—Sports Committee,
    214
American Academy of Physical Education (AAPE), 63,
    316
    formation of, 40
American Academy of Sports Medicine, 61

American Alliance for Health, Physical Education, Rec-
    reation, and Dance (AAHPERD), 23, 41
    alliance of professional organizations, 382
    Basic Stuff, 249
    Dance Division, 393
    efforts to promote physical activity and fitness, 206–
    208
    fitness tests, 185, 188
    mission, purposes, associations, and districts, 62–63
    Philosophy of Sport and Physical Education Academy,
    371
    Physical Best, 233
    Physical Best battery, 185
    Physical Best program, 206, 233
    professional organization evolution toward, 40–41
    recreation and, 384
    sport pedagogy and, 360
    Sport Sociology Academy, 339
    subject matter definition of, 60
    as umbrella association, 62
American Association for Active Lifestyles and Fitness
    (AAALF), 63
American Association for Health and Physical Educa-
    tion (AAHPE), 41, 50
American Association for Health Education (AAHE), 63
American Association for Health, Physical Education,
    and Recreation (AAHPER), 49
    in Depression era, 49
    name changes and, 41, 49
    National Dance Association, 393
    Physical Education Public Information (PEPI) proj-
    ect, 245
    professional conferences of, 55
American Association for Leisure and Recreation
    (AALR), 63, 384
American Association of State Psychology Boards, 353
American Association of Zoological Parks and Aquari-
    ums, 383
American Board of Physical Therapy Specialties, 218
American Camping Association, 384
American Civil War, 24
American Coaching Effectiveness Program, 115–116
American College of Sports Medicine (ACSM), 189, 214
    certification programs, 213, 216, 229
    certification titles (table), 216
    conferences, 215
    exercise physiology, 313
    fitness-instruction certification, 215–219
    instructor certification, 212

links of, 308
mission of, 215
American Fitness Alliance (AFA), 206–207
American Folk Dance Society, 39
American Heart Association (AHA), 207, 389
American Institute of Park Executives, 383
American Journal of Physics, 319
American Journal of Sports Medicine, 308
American Orthopaedic Society for Sports Medicine
    (AOSSM), 214
American Philosophical Association, 62, 371
American physical education. *See* Physical education,
    beginning of
American Physical Education Association (APEA), 41,
    43, 47, 49, 50
American Physical Therapy Association, 214, 217
American Psychological Association, Division 47, 348,
    349
American Public Health Association, 227
American Recreation Society, 383
American Sport Education Program (ASEP), 115–116,
    120, 142
    Basic Education course, 120, 121, 142
    courses and programs available in, 116
American Sports Data, 198
Americans with Disabilities Act (1990), 256
American Therapeutic Recreation Association, 384
American Tobacco Company, 37
Amherst College, 24, 25, 32
anabolic steroids, 152
anaerobic
    defined, 169
    training, 181
analytic philosophy, 369
anatomical kinesiology, 318
Anderson, William G., 23–24, 33
And Every Day You Take Another Bite (Merchant),
    339
anthropometrics, 33
Any Given Sunday, 102, 374
AOSSM. See American Orthopaedic Society for Sports
    Medicine
APEA. *See* American Physical Education Association
Applied Anatomy and Kinesiology (Bowen), 39
appropriate competition, 137
APTA. *See* American Physical Therapy Association
architects, 332
arete, 23
Arete: The Journal of Sport Literature, 371

ARK Sports Technology, 132
armed-forces recreation, 384
Armed Forces Recreation Society, 384
Arnoldism, 70, 72, 107
Arnold, Thomas, 70
arts education, discipline-based, 393
asceticism, 140
ASEP. *See* American Sport Education Program
assessment, 294–295
Association for the Advancement of Applied Sport Psy-
    chology (AAASP), 347
    criteria for professional training, 352
Association for the Advancement of Physical Education
    (AAPE), 24, 41, 308
Association Internationale d'Education Superior d'Edu-
    cation Physique (AIESEP), 360
associations, Web sites about, 300
athletes
    amateur, 58, 112
    child, specialization of, 141
    elite, 58
    kinds of, 112
    minority, 157–158
    nonprofessional, 112
    open competition and, 58
    professional, 112
    psychological interventions used with, 350–351
    scholarships for, 53
    student, treatment of, 153–154
    as subjects for artists, 103–104
athletic administration, 129
athletic associations, 36
athletic clubs, multipurpose, 14–15
Athletic Conference of American College Women, 37
athletic conferences, beginning of, 37
Athletic Congress, 100
Athletics for Athletes (Scott), 79
athletic training, 129, 131
    degree and certification programs, 213–219
    women and, 154–155
Atlanta-DeKalb-Greenway Trail System, 235
Aussie sports program, 143–144
Australian policy on coed participation, 291
axiology, 106, 368
Axthelm, Pete, 339

baby boom generation, 52, 56
    academic-discipline movement and, 61
    health care costs for, 222

baby boom generation (*continued*)
   influence of, on culture, 84
   movement into older adult category, 199
   as a new population for sport, fitness, and physical
     education, 400
   youth sport and, 53
Babycise, 267
bachelor's degree, in adult fitness, 218
balance, 170, 201
Bancroft, Jessie, 43
Bang the Drum Slowly (Harris), 102, 370
Bannister, Roger, 100
Barrett, Kate, 247
baseball
   Brooklyn Dodgers, 157, 368
   Cincinnati Red Stockings, 34
   first intercollegiate game, 24
   first truly national sport, 34
   Little League, 49, 53, 112, 113, 114
   Major League, 53, 148
Basedow, Johann Bernhard, 74
basic fitness leader (YMCA), 217
Basic Life Support certification (ACSM), 216
basic movement, 248
Basic Stuff (AAHPERD), 249
basketball
   H-O-R-S-E tournament, 10
   invention of, 35
"battle of the systems," 29–34, 33, 47
Beamon, Bob, 100
beauty in sport, 103–106. *See also* aesthetics; sport
   aesthetics
Beck, Charles, 25, 30
Beecher, Catherine, 24, 25
Beecher, Henry Ward, 24
Beecher system, 25, 31–32
behavior codes (Aussie sports program), 144, 145
benchmarks, 246
Benoit, Joan, 154–155
Berenson, Senda, 32, 35
bibliographic database, 133
Big Sky State Games, 17
Big Ten, 37, 122
Big Ten Symposium on Sport Sociology, 338
biomechanics, 61, 129
   areas of study within, 322
   current issues in, 323
   current scope of, 320–323
   defined, 316–317

   development of, 319–320
   as a field of study, 317–319
   as an important sport science, 316–317
   physical principles of, 318
   Web sites about, 376
biomechanists
   preparation to become, 323
   research grants for, 323
   what they do, 322–323
black athletes, 57, 157–158
black people. *See also* African Americans; minorities;
   minority issues; race
   access and equity, 43
   discrimination against, 56
   equity issues in fitness and activity, 227–229
   in today's professional sports, 157
Blakie, William, 24
block approach to curriculum design, 50, 245
"blue book," 55
Bluegrass State Games, 17
bodily control, 6
body composition, 170, 186, 195
   defined, 169
booster clubs, 9, 149–150
Boston Conference (1889), 33–34
Boston Normal Institute for Physical Education, 32
Boston Normal School, 31
Bowen, William, 39
Boys Club, 116, 383, 384
Boys Clubs of America, 128
Boy Scouts, 49, 383
Boys of Summer, The (Kahn), 368
Boys Study (Medford Oregon), 330
Brace Motor Ability Test, 43
Bradley, Bill, 105
Brancazio, Peter, 315
Breaks of the Game, The (Halberstam), 102
British ideals, 71–72
British tradition, fair play and, 106–107
broadcasting, sport. *See* sport broadcasting
Brockport Physical Fitness Test, 207
Brockport State Normal School, 43
Brooklyn Dodgers, 157, 368
Brown, Camille, 247
Brown v. Board of Education (1954), 56, 157
Bull Durham, 102, 370, 374
Burchenal, Elizabeth, 43
Burdick, William, 40
Bureau of Land Management, 384

Burt, John, 396

"busy, happy, and good" approach, 288, 294

Caillois, Roger, 93, 94, 338

California High School Coaching and Training Program, 121

camping movement, 39

camps. *See* sport camps

campus recreation, 384

Canadian Journal of History of Sport and Physical Education, 371

Canadian Society for Psychomotor Learning and Sport Psychology (CSPLSP), 347

cancer, 174

CAQ. *See* Certificate of Advanced Qualification

cardiac rehabilitation, 307–308

Cardinal Principles of Education, 40

cardiopulmonary measure, 195

cardiorespiratory endurance, 177

cardiovascular disease (CVD), 168, 174, 198

cardiovascular endurance, 169, 170

cardiovascular fitness, 185

cardiovascular plague, 170, 171

Careers in Recreation, 382

Carnegie Council on Adolescent Development, 143, 229, 235

Carnegie Report (1929), 48

Carpenter, Linda Jean, 132

Carson, Rachel, 56

Cassidy, Rosiland, 38–39, 42, 60, 61, 76, 77, 247, 369

Catholic Youth Organization (CYO), 49, 76, 114

Celebrant, The (Rolfe), 370

Center for Sports Parenting, 139

Center for the Study of Sport in Society, 143

   report card on hiring and promotion practices, 157

Centers for Disease Control and Prevention, 201, 234

Certificate of Advanced Qualification (CAQ), 214

certification, 217–218

   adapted physical education, 282

   American College of Sports Medicine, 215, 216

   athletic trainers, 213–219

   bachelor's degree in adult fitness, 218

   dance exercise, 393

   of fitness leaders, 229

   levels of, 279–280

   master's degree in fitness, 218–219

   physical-education teachers, 279–282

   physical fitness instructor, 212–213

   physical therapist, 217–218

   school health educators, 390

   sport psychologists, 345–347

   strength and conditioning specialist, 215–217

   YMCA fitness instructor, 217

Certified Athletic Trainers, 215

Certified Strength and Conditioning Specialist (CSCS), 215–217

Chamberlin, Wilt, 100

Champion, Aaron, 34

chance elements, 95

chance, games of, 338

Character Counts Sports, 139

character education

   models, 81

   through physical challenge, 72–73

Chariots of Fire, 102, 367, 374

Chicago World's Fair (1893), 22, 37–38

Child Abuse and Youth Sports, 117

Child and Adolescent Trial for Cardiovascular Health, The (CATCH), 205, 248

child and youth development, as theme for the future, 401–402

child and youth sport, 112–113. *See also* youth sport

   Aussie sports example, 143–144

   Children's Bill of Rights in Sports, 144

   coaching for, 115–116

   developmentally inappropriate sport, 140–141

   dropping out, 143

   impact on family life, 143

   lack of adequate training of coaches, 141–142

   organization of, 114–115

   outside pressure to win, 142

   overuse injuries, 139–140

   premature entry into, 139

   problems in, 138–144

   school-related or nonschool, 113

   socioeconomic status, 143

   specialization, 141

   strengths of, 138

   Web sites about, 162

   what kids want to tell parents and spectators, 139

children. *See also* child and youth sport; children and youths; youth sport

   dislike of zero-sum situations, 138

   early motor-activity programs, 6

   elementary physical education, 7–8

   fitness levels among, 193, 195–196

   focusing on, 400

   importance of physical activity for, 17

children (*continued*)
   main interests for games, 141
   negative consequences of high levels of fitness, 232
   as a new population for sport, fitness, and physical education, 400
   obesity in, 18
   overweight, 171
   play of, and adult play, 94–95
   preschool physical-activity programs, 6
   Rousseau's argument about, 74
   sport opportunity for, 6–7
   strength training for, 206
children and youths, 264; *See also* child and youth sport; children; youth sport
   AAHPERD efforts to promote physical activity and fitness, 206–208
   activity patterns among, 196–198
   after-school hours, 401–402
   comprehensive schoolwide and community-linked programs, 205–206
   development—after-school hours, 401–402
   fitness and physical activity programs for, 201–208
   fitness levels among, 193, 195–196
   fitness Web sites, 236
   low fitness scores, 195–196
Children's Bill of Rights in Sports, 144
choking, 345
chronic illnesses, sedentary lifestyle and, 223
CIAR. *See* Cooper Institute for Aerobic Research
Cincinnati, Ohio, 25
Cincinnati Red Stockings, 34
Citizenship Through Sports, 139
City Game, The (Axthelm), 339
Civilian Conservation Corps (CCC), 47, 49
Civil Rights Act, 56
   1987, 155
civil rights movement, 56, 57
Civil War, 24
climbing, in elementary adventure program, 253, 269–270
clinical-exercise science, areas of study in, 312
clubs
   athletic, multipurpose, 14–15
   sport, 15
club-sport movement, 158
"Coach Effectiveness Training," 141–142
coaches. *See also* school coaches
   depiction in films, 374
   lack of adequate training of, 141–142

coaching
   for child and youth sport, 115–116
   education, with national governing bodies, 124
   technology and, 132–133
   women in, high school, 121
Cobb, Ty, 40
codification of rules, 99
coed participation, in secondary-school programs, 290–292
cognitive function, 174
cognitive psychology, 345
Cold War superpowers, 53
collaboration between disciplines and professions, as theme for the future, 402–403
Collaboration for Intramural Sports and Fitness Programs, 206
collective responsibility, 83
college campus, sport on (1852–1900), 35–36
College of Physical Education Association, 50
college recreational intramural programs, 123
college recruiting, on line scouting network, 132
college sports, chronology of, 35–36
collegiate sport programs
   intercollegiate sport, 121–123
   recreational intramural programs, 123
color barrier, 157
Columbia University, 43, 74
commentators, sport. *See* sport commentators
commercial recreation, 384, 385
commercial recreation enterprises. *See* leisure-services industries
Committee on Sports for the Disabled (COSD), 126
communication, effect of, on sport, fitness, and physical education, 28–29
community recreation, for young adults, 11–12
Community Sport and Recreation Center, 205–206
competition
   appropriate, 137
   beauty in, 105
   festival nature of, 97
   formal, in sport education, 251
   forum for competence, 97
   games and, 95, 338
   good, 252
   good and bad, 137, 298–299
   open, 58
   playful, 251
   in sport and games, 97–98

as sport problem, 137–138
zero-sum, 97
competitive games, 95, 338
comprehensive schoolwide and community-linked programs, 205–206
computer simulations, 132
concepts curriculum, 249
Conditioning Research, 216
Conduct of Life, The (Emerson), 70
consolidation, time line for, 51
consulting sport psychologists, 346, 348, 350, 352
continuous training, 181
cooperation
    competition vs., 137–138
    in elementary adventure programs, 269
Cooper Institute for Aerobic Research (CIAR), 206
Cooper, Kenneth, 59, 170–171, 232
coordination, 170
COPEC. *See* Council for Physical Education for Children
coping strategies, 351
Corbin, Charles, 221, 232–233
Corbin model, 224
Cornell University, 43
coronary artery disease, 199
corrective program, 256
COSD. *See* Committee on Sports for the Disabled
cosmetic fitness, 172–173
costs, of inadequate health fitness, 222–223
Coubertin, Baron Pierre de, 33, 35, 71–72
Council for Physical Education for Children (COPEC), 201–202, 287, 360
Councilman, James, 316
Council on Education for Public Health, 390
counseling. *See* sport psychology
Course in Calisthenics for Young Ladies, A (Beecher), 24
court games, 96
covert modeling, 351
Cozens' Tests for General Athletic Ability, 43
creatine, 148–149
criterion-referenced health (CRH) standards, 185, 196
critical theory movement (1990s), 80, 340, 369
CSCS. *See* Certified Strength and Conditioning Specialist
cue-controlled relaxation, 351
culminating event, in sport education, 251
"cult of slenderness," 173
culture
    gender issues and, 401
    sport/fitness, 299–300

curriculum, 246. *See also* physical-education program; sport pedagogy
    block or unit approach, 50, 245
    eclectic, 255
    elementary school, 288
    important influences, 246–255
    instruction and (sport pedagogy), 357
    main-theme, 289
    multiactivity, 289
    national, 295
    Physical Dimensions curriculum for high schools (Kansas), 273–274
    physical-education, 50
    process of developing, 246
    "sport for peace" model, 292
    sport pedagogy, 361
    state wellness for high schools, 273–274
    Web sites about, 300
Curriculum and Instruction Academy, 360
CYO. *See* Catholic Youth Organization

daily fitness programs, 204
dance, 39, 391–392
    as multicultural education, 393
    Web sites about, 394
Dark Ages, 23
Darwin, Charles, 29
Darwinism, 73
Das Kapital (Marx), 29
DATA2010, 388
Deep Water (Schollander), 79, 339
degenerative diseases, 168, 170
Dempsey, Jack, 41
Department of Health and Human Services, 389
desensitization, 351
"Developmentally Appropriate Physical Education Practices for Children," 287
developmentally appropriate practices, 287
developmental model, 242–245
developmental program, 256–257
development triangle, 406–407
Dewey, John, 39, 50, 73–75
diabetes, 18, 168, 171
Dickey, Glenn, 79, 339
diet
    fat content in, 199
    inappropriate, 168
    poor, 389
    in schools, 266

diet (*continued*)
  worksite fitness and wellness programs and, 208
dietary supplement, creatine, 148–149
DiMaggio, Joe, 100
Dio Lewis system, 32
Dirty Dancing, 392
disabilities, people with. *See* people with disabilities
discipline-based arts education, 393
discipline of physical education, 59, 61
diseases
  degenerative, 168, 170
  hypokinetic, 168
disincentive approach, 209
Districtwide Wellness Initiative, 205
diversity in sports. *See also* African Americans; black people; gender equality; minorities; minority issues; race; women
  NBA, NHL, and MLS, 157
Division of Physical Fitness, 55
dose-response debate, 173–176
dressage, 9
dropping out of sports, 143
"Ds, five," 82
dualistic traditions in Western education, 294
Duff, James, 55
Dunn, Diana, 399
duration, 173–174, 180
dynamic flexibility, 172, 184

eclectic curriculum, 255
economic disparities
  children and youth sport, 150–151
  fitness and activity, 222–223
  health and fitness, 176, 178
  intercollegiate sports, 152
economic pressure to win, 152–153
Ederle, Gertrude, 41
Education Amendments of 1972 (Title IX), 296–297
Education for All Handicapped Children Act (1975), 126, 256
education, effect of, on sport, fitness, and physical education, 29
education, physical. *See* physical education
education-reform movement, 249
education through the physical, 41–42, 47, 242–245, 261
Edwards, Harry, 339
Eisenhower, Dwight, 55, 210–211

Electromyography (EMG), 320
elementary physical education, 7–8
elementary-school programs
  adventure program, 269–270
  comprehensive health-related model, 265–266
  curricula, 288
  developmentally appropriate practices, 287
  early-elementary movement program, 271–272
  facilities for, 287
  fitness programs in, 201–208
  health-related model, 265–266
  issues in, 285–288
  movement program, 271–272
  research-based national program, 270–271
  specialist teachers, 286–287
  time issue, 285–286
  upper, sport-education, 267–268
eligibility, rules for school sport, 147–148
Elimination of Architectural Barriers Act (1968), 256
Elite Athlete Project, 319
elite athletes, 58, 138
Elite sport development (New Zealand), 159
Ellfeldt, Lois, 247
Ellis, Michael, 381
Emerson, Ralph Waldo, 69–70
Emile (Rousseau), 74
Empire State Games, 17
employee services and recreation, 384
endurance, 182
environmental movement, 57
epiphyseal injury, 140
epistemology, 368
equitable distribution, as theme for the future, 398–399
equity, access and, 43
equity issues. *See also* gender equity; skill equity
  in fitness and activity, 227–229
  minority issues, 154–158, 227–228
  socioeconomic status, 229
  women's issues, 154–158, 228
Escambia County Schools, 205, 273
ethics, 106. *See also* sport ethics
Europe. *See also* gymnastic systems
  club system, 146
  influence of, on new physical education and progressive education, 74–75
  nationalism in, 68
  Sport for All, 159–160
European club system, 146
Everybody's All American, 374

exclusion, 114–115, 405–406
exclusionary model
    inclusive, rather than, in sport culture, 405–406
    nature of, 146
    in sport systems, 158–159
    varsity model and, 145–146
exercise
    aerobic, 170–171, 173–176
    anaerobic, 169, 181
    decline of religious opposition to, 28
    defined, 169
    resistance, 31
exercise epidemiology, 310
exercise physiologists
    preparation to become, 312–313
    what they do, 310–312
exercise physiology, 61, 305
    current status, 309–310
    defined, 307
    development of, 308–309
    as a field of study, 307–308
    issues and problems, 313–314
    questions investigated in, 305–306
    Web sites about, 376
exercise psychology, 345–347, 349–353. See also sport
        psychology
    Web sites, 376
exercise science. See also exercise physiology
        kinesiology
    areas of study in, 311
    laboratories, 185–187
exercise specialist (ACSM), 216
Expeditionary Learning Outward Bound, 73
expedition concept, 81
experience, 280
experiential education, 81
external integration model, 249
extreme games, 83
eye-foot coordination, 6
eye-hand coordination, 6
Eyler, Marvin, 371

facilities. See also settings
    different kinds, 14–17
    elementary-school programs, 287
    in elementary schools, 287
faculty control, 47
    national intercollegiate system and, 36–37
faculty psychology, 30

fair play, 71. See also sportsmanship
    British tradition and, 106–107
    concept of, 106–107
    philosophy of, 106–107
family life, impact of sport on, 143
fans, 103
federal government
    Depression-era intervention of, 49
    disability laws, 256
    fitness promotion by, 210–212
Federation Internationale d'Education Physique
        (FIEP), 360
Feingold, John, 368
femininity, ideals of, 70–71
festivals
    atmosphere, 298
    nature of competition, 97
    sport/games, 17
    statewide, 128
    Web sites about, 163
field experience, 280
field games, 96
Field of Dreams, 102, 370
FIEP. See Federation Internationale d'Education
        Physique
films. See also sport films
    dance, 392
    sport, 102, 370, 374
Final Four, 90, 151
First International Seminar on Biomechanics, 319
First Lessons: A Report on Elementary Education in
        America, 258
first-order philosophy, 368–369
"First Swing" golf program, 273
Fisher Act (1961), 61
"Fit by Five," 6
"Fit for Life," 228
fitness. See also fitness training; health fitness
    access and equity, 43
    aerobics era, 58–59
    aging and, 230–231
    arguments for (McCloy), 50
    basic concepts, 167–191
    cardiovascular, 185
    communication, effect on, 28–29
    contemporary understanding, 168–172
    cosmetic, 172–173
    defined, 168–170
    distributing, more equitably, 398–399

fitness (*continued*)
    dose-response debate, 173–176, 177
    education, effect on, 29
    education through the physical, 41–42
    equity issues in, 227–229
    facilities, 12–13
    as fashionable, 59
    federal efforts to promote, 210–212
    gender equity in, 401
    Great Depression era (1930–1940), 48–50
    health, 170–172
    health benefits, 174
    heritage of, 23–24
    immigration, effect on, 28
    industrialization, effect on, 28
    informal measurement of, 188–190
    intellectual climate, effect on, 29
    key definitions, 169
    levels of. *See* fitness levels
    lifetime, stairway to, 225
    measurement of, 184–190
    mid-1950s and on, 56–60
    misinformation about, 226
    motor performance, 169
    motor-performance fitness, 172
    new populations, 400–401
    new settings for, 14–17
    objectives of, 42
    philosophical forces in, since 1950, 77–84
    post-World War I era, 42–43
    post-World War II era, 52–56
    renaissance, 58–59, 61, 82–84
    research issues in, 234–235
    scientific understanding of, 19
    social gradient in, 176, 178
    target heart-rate zone, 175
    transportation, effect on, 28–29
    underlying philosophy, 82
    urbanization, effect on, 28
    vocation in sport, 129–130
    Web sites about, 236
    World War II era, 50–52
fitness assessments, 186
fitness behavior, 224–225
fitness programs for children and youth, 201–206
fitness crisis, 55–56
fitness-educated public, 225–227
fitness facilities. *See* sport facility
FITNESSGRAM®, 8, 185, 207

fitness issues, in physical education, 231–234
fitness leaders, 212, 213
    certification, 229
fitness levels
    among adults, 198–200
    among older adults, 200–201
    children and youths, 193, 195–196
fitness programs, 264
    AAHPERD, 206–208
    for children and youths, 201–208
    children and youths, 201–208
    daily, 204
    informal home-based, 204, 209–210
    schoolwide and community-linked, 205–206
    types of, in schools, 204–205
    worksite wellness and, 208–209
    YMCA specialized, 217
fitness-remediation programs, 204
fitness specialist (YMCA), 217
fitness testing
    activity estimates vs., 229–230
    in hospitals or exercise-science laboratories, 185–187
    for older adults, 188
    in school programs, 185
fitness training, 178
    anaerobic training, 181
    continuous and interval training, 181
    five main principles, 179–180
    flexibility, 184
    general principles, 179–180
    health-fitness training, 180–181
    muscle systems and, 178–179
    resistance training, for older people, 184
    strength training, 181–184
FitSmart test, 207
Fitz, George W., 308
"five Ds," 82
Flannagan's Run (McNab), 370
flexibility, 170, 171–172, 184
    training for, 177
Follen, Charles, 25, 30
Fonda, Jane, *Low-Impact Aerobics* video, 209
Food and Drug Administration (FDA), 149
Footloose, 392
force platforms, 320
Forest Service, 49
formal competition, in sport education, 251
formative assessments, 295
form sports, aesthetics of, 104

Fosbury, Dick, 316
foundations courses, 59
4-H, 383
Fraleigh, Warren, 78
Frank Merriwell sagas, 71
frequency, 174
Freud, Sigmund, 29
Frisbee, 96, 114
Froebel, Friedrich, 74–75
Full-house Children's Dance Company, 393
functional specificity, 172
"Fundamental Education" (Hetherington), 41–42, 243
future, themes defining the
    activity and leisure industries, 403–404
    child and youth development, 401–402
    collaboration between disciplines and professions,
        402–403
    equitable distribution, 398–399
    expanded physical education, 404–405
    gender equity, 401
    inclusive sport culture, 405–406
    new populations, 400–401
    public health challenge, 397–398
    wellness, as center of lifestyle education, 406

games
    of chance, 338
    children's main interest for, 141
    classification of, 96
    competition in, 97–98, 97–98
    competitive, 338
    court, 96
    defined, 95, 338
    festivals, sport and, 17
    field, 96
    knowledge of, 96–97
    mimicry or pretense, 338
    modified, 140–141, 140–141
    nature of, rules and, 107–108
    noncompetitive, 95
    play, sports and, relations among (figure), 338
    primary rules, 96
    secondary rules, 96
    state, Web sites about, 163
    target, 96
    types, defined, 338
    vertigo and, 338
Gatorade's "Playbook for Kids," 139
Gehrig, Lou, 41

gender
    breakdown of stereotypes, 18
    equity issues, 227–229
    lifespan physical activity not limited by, 5
gender equity, 296–297, 401
    in the future, 401
    NHL and, 157
    physical education and, 296–297
General Conference of the United Nations Educational,
        Scientific and Cultural Organization (UNESCO),
        159–160
General Electric Corporation, 17
general motor ability (GMA), 329
General Motors, 223
general play, 42
Gensemer, Robert, 305
Gent, Pete, 370
German Gymnastics (Jahn), 30
German system, 25, 29, 30, 32, 34, 68
gerontologists, 332
Giamatti, A. Bartlett, 89, 91, 369
G. I. Bill, 52
Girls Club, 116, 383, 384
Girls Clubs of America, 128
Girl Scouts, 49, 383
girls' sport programs, 70–71
GNSP. *See* gross national sport product
Go for Health Program, 248
golf, 41, 53–54, 125, 273
Gordonstoun School, 72
government. *See also* federal government
    publications on the Web, 394
    state requirements for physical education, 257–259
Graham, George, 247, 276, 284
Grange, Red, 41
"Great American Smoke-Out," 389
Great Depression era (1930–1940), 47–50
Greece, ancient. *See also* Olympic Games
    athletes as subjects for artists, 103
    gymnasiums in, 23
    importance of sport in, 90
Greek Athletes and Athletics (Harris), 368
Greenberg, Eric Rolfe, 370
Gregory Heights High School, 268–269
Grey-Thompson, Tanni, 126
Griffith, Coleman, 347
gross national sport product (GNSP), 111
group exercise leader (ACSM), 216
Grove City College, 155

Gruneau, Ricky, 336, 338
Gulick, Luther Halsey, 38–39, 40, 42, 43
Gymboree, 267
gymnasiums
    in ancient Greece, 23
    home, 16
gymnastic philosophies, 68
gymnastics, 26
    Lewis system of, 32
    medical, 31
    scientific understanding of, 33
    Swedish system, 33
    systems of (1885 to 1900), 29–34, 47
    in upper-elementary sport-education program, 267–
        268
Gymnastics Monthly and Journal of Physical Culture
    (Lewis), 32

Hahn, Kurt, 72
Halberstam, David, 102, 368
Hall, G. Stanley, 38–39
Hampton Institute, 43
Hanna, Delphine, 40, 43
harmony, 104
Harris, H. A., 368
Harris, Janet, 313
Harris, Mark, 102, 370
Harris, William, 33
Hartford Seminary for Girls, 31
Hartwell, Edward, 31, 33
Harvard College, 24, 25, 26, 30, 31
Harvard Fatigue Laboratory, 308
Harvard Medical School, 308
Harvard University, 33, 37
H'Doubler, Margaret, 41, 392
Head Start, 6
health
    components of, 170
    defined, 169
    delivery of industry services, 388
    education in schools, 388–389
    "five Ds," 82
    health-enhancement industries, 387
    Industrial Revolution and, 39
    lifestyle management, 390–391
    nonprofit organizations, 389
    poor, costs of, 389–390
    private-sector, 390
    professional preparation, 390
    school health educators, 390
    social gradient in, 176, 178
    traditional definitions related to illness, 82
    Web sites about, 394
    wellness and, 82, 387–388
    worksite programs, 389–390
health-enhancement industries, 63–64, 387, 403–404
health fitness, 169–172
    aerobic exercise, 170–171
    importance of, 222
    inadequate, costs of, 222–223
    training, 180–181
health/fitness director (ACSM), 216
health/fitness instructor (ACSM), 216
health-fitness training. *See* fitness training
health-related physical education (HRPE) movement,
    248
Healthy Children Project, 233
healthy lifestyle management, 406
healthy lifestyles, defined, 169
Healthy People 2000, 4, 83, 193, 197, 285, 389, 391
Healthy People 2010, 4, 83, 193, 196, 198, 257, 387–388,
    391, 398
    Goal 22 for Fitness and Physical Activity, 194
*Healthy People: The Surgeon General's Report on
    Health Promotion and Disease Prevention*, 193
"Healthy Schools Summit," 299
heart rate
    monitors, 187
    target, 175
    zone, 175, 189
Heart Smart program, 233, 248, 265
Hellison, Donald, 79, 80, 249–250
    responsibility-in-the-gym model, 250
    social-development model, 292
Hemenway Gymnasium, 26, 31, 33, 308
Hemenway, Mary, 31, 33
Henig, Robin Marantz, 160
Henry, Franklin, 46, 60–61
Hershey's Food Corporation, 17, 209
Hetherington, Clark, 38–39, 40, 41–42, 74, 76, 243–
    244, 369
high blood pressure, 174
higher-order fitness objectives, 224
high-ropes course, 253
high school. *See* high-school programs; physical educa-
    tion programs; secondary school programs
high-school programs. *See also* secondary-school
    programs
    comprehensive, 272
    emphasizing community linkages, 272–273

fitness emphasis, 270
ideas for reforming, 148
interschool sport programs, 8–9
lifetime physical-activity, 267
personal-growth curriculum, 268–269
state wellness curriculum, 273–274
urban, 292–293
Hirschland, Ruth, 55
Hispanics, 57, 157–158
equity issues in fitness and activity, 227–229
overweight, 171
in today's professional sports, 157
history. *See* sport humanities
Hitchcock, Edward, 24, 25, 32–33, 42
Hitchcock system, 32–33
Hoffman, Shirl, 321
Hogan, Ben, 53
Hogan, James, 37
holistic view, 74
Homans, Amy Morris, 31, 33, 43
home-based fitness activities, 209–210
home gymnasiums, 16
Homer, 50
Hook a Kid on Golf™, 117
Hoosiers, 374
H-O-R-S-E tournament, 10
hospitality, 385
House Concurrent Resolution 97 (1987), 4, 263, 264–265
Howard University, 43
How to Grow Strong and How to Stay So (Blakie), 24
HRPE. *See* health-related physical education movement
Huizinga, Johan, 93, 337–338
human-gait analysis, 320
humanistic education, 249–251
humanistic philosophies, 79–80
Humanistic Physical Education (Hellison), 79
humanistic psychology, 79
humanities. *See* sport humanities
Human Kinetics, 115, 120
Human Kinetics Publishers, 206
human motion, 317
human movement philosophy, 77–79, 247
hydrostatic (underwater) weighing, 186–187
hygiene, 388
hypokinetic diseases, 168, 170
defined, 169

IAPESGW. *See* International Association of Physical Education and Sport for Girls and Women

IBM Corporation, 16–17
IDEA. *See* Individuals with Disabilities Education Act
immigration, effect of, on sport and fitness, 28
immune function, 174
incentive, 209, 233
inclusion, 257
as theme for the future, 405–406
inclusionary model, 146
inclusive model for school sport, 159
Increasing Physical Activity: A Report on Recommendations to the Task Force on Community Preventive Services, 212
Indianapolis 500, 40
Indiana University, 316
individual responsibility, 178
Individuals with Disabilities Education Act (IDEA, 1997, 126, 128, 256, 282
industrialization, effect of, on sport, fitness, and physical education, 28
Industrial Revolution, 39, 67–68
inequitable distribution. *See also* equity issues
as theme for the future, 398–399
informal measurement of fitness, 188–190
information, readily available, 19
injuries
children and, 139–140
epiphyseal, 140
overuse, 139–140
school sport, 146–147
Institute for Aerobics Research, 185
certification, 213
instructor certification, 212
Institute for the Study of Youth Sports (Michigan State University), 120
institutionalization of sport, 34, 96–97, 98–102
codification of rules, 99
genesis of sports organizations, 99–100
importance of records, 100–101
in progress, 101
public nature of, 101–102
role of referee, 99
integration, 157
of knowledge, 249
model, 157
intellectual climate, effect of, on sport, fitness, and physical education, 29
intensity, 173, 180
Intercollegiate Conference of Faculty Representatives, 37

intercollegiate sport, 121–123, 151–154
  early abuses in, 36, 37
  economic disparities, 152
  economic pressure to win, 152–153
  faculty control of,, 36–37
  national, beginning of, 36–37
  performance-enhancing drugs, 152
  recruiting violations and pressures, 151–152
  treatment of the student-athlete, 153–154
  Web sites about, 162
  women and, 37
internal integration, 249
internal integration model, 294
International Association of Physical Education and
    Sport for Girls and Women (IAPESGW), 360
International Charter of Physical Education and Sport,
    159–160, 159–160
International Committee of Sport Pedagogy, 360
International Committee on Sport Sociology, 338
International Conference on Education (1893), 73
International Congress of Sport Psychology, 347
International Congress on Education, 22, 37–38
International Dance Exercise Association, instructor
    certification, 212
International Federation of Sports Medicine, 214
International Games for the Disabled, 126
International Journal of Sports Medicine, 309
International Review of Sport Sociology, 338
International Society of Biomechanics, 319
International Society of Biomechanics in Sport, 319
International Society on Comparative Physical Educa-
    tion and Sport (ISCPES), 360
International Training School of the YMCA, 25
Internet, 132. *See also* World Wide Web; Web sites
interpretation zone, 185
interscholastic sport, 116. *See also* school sport
  benefits of, 146
  financing of, 118–119
  organization of, 117–120
  participation by sport, 119
  participation by state, 118
  school coaches, 120–121
  Web sites about, 162
interschool sport programs, 8–9
interval training, 180, 181
intramural programs, 39–40
  college recreational, 123
  in secondary physical education, 293
Introduction to Kinesiology (Vealey), 344

Introduction to Sport Studies (VanderZwaag and
    Sheehan), 366
invasion or territory games, 96
ISCPES. *See* International Society on Comparative
    Physical Education and Sport
issues and problems in sport
  child and youth sport, 138–144
  cooperation and competition, 137–138
  equity issues, 154–158
  intercollegiate sport, 151–154
  school sport, 144–151
  sport problems or social problems?, 136–137
  sport systems, 158–160

Jahn, Friedrich Ludwig, 30, 31, 68, 74
James, Henry, 71
Jefferson High School, 268–269
Jeffries, Jim, 40
Jewish Community Centers, 264
Jock Empire, The (Dickey), 79, 339
Jocks, The (Shector), 79
Johns Hopkins University, 73
Johnson, Jack, 40
Johnson, Michael, 100
JOHPER. *See Journal of Health, Physical Education,
    and Recreation*
joints
  dynamic flexibility, 184
  kinesiology and, 317
  static flexibility, 184
Jones, Bobby, 41
JOPERD, 393
journalism. *See* sport journalism
Journal of Applied Sport Psychology, 353
Journal of Biomechanics, 319
Journal of Health and Physical Education, 47
*Journal of Health, Physical Education, and Recreation
    (JOHPER),* 55, 60
Journal of Leisure Research, 383
Journal of Motor Behavior, 61, 329
Journal of Sport and Social Issues, 339
Journal of Sport Behavior, 339
Journal of Sport History, 62, 371
Journal of Sport Management, 131
Journal of Sport Psychology, 61
Journal of Teaching in Physical Education (JTPE), 62,
    360
*Journal of the Philosophic Society for the Study of
    Sport,* 62, 371

Joyner-Kersee, Jackie, 155
Joy of Sports, The (Novak), 91, 369
Jump Rope for Heart, 207–208, 233

Kahn, Roger, 368
Kansas Health Federation, 273–274, 275
Kelly, John, 55
Kelly, Luke, 282
Kennedy, John F., 55, 211
Kentucky Derby, 54
Kenyon, Gerald, 335, 342
Kerr, Robert, 325
Kids on Target, 117
Kids Walk to School, 205
Kilpatrick, William Heard, 39
kindergarten, creation of the word, 75
kinematics, 321
kinesiologists
    preparation to become, 323
    what they do, 322–323
kinesiology, 341
    areas of study within, 322
    current issues in, 323
    current scope of, 320–323
    defined, 316–317
    development of, 319–320
    as a field of study, 317–319
    as an important sport science, 316–317
    Web sites about, 376
Kinesiology Academy, 62
King, Billie Jean, 54
King, Martin Luther, Jr., 56
Kingsley, Charles, 70
Kinsella, W. P., 102, 370
Knight, Bob, 368
Know Your body program, 248
Kraus, Hans, 55
Kraus-Weber tests, 55, 58

Laban, Rudolph, 77
Ladies Professional Golfers Association (LPGA), 112, 125
Lake Park High School, 267
Landers, Dan, 348–349
La Porte model, 50, 54
La Porte, William Ralph, 50, 245
leadership. *See* sport leadership
League of Their Own, A, 102, 370
learning, 328

Learning from Teaching (Locke), 356
least restrictive environment (LRE), 256–257
Lee, Mabel, 47
Legend of Bagger Vance, The, 102, 370
Leiber, Francis, 30
leisure, 92–93
leisure activity, defined, 169
leisure industry, as theme for the future, 403–404
leisure myth, 111–112
Leisure Sciences, 339
leisure-services industries, 63–64
    electronic entertainment, 385
    opportunities in, 382–385
    private-sector, 403–404
    professionals in, 63–64
    women and, 401
Leonard, Fred, 43
"level playing field," 143, 229
Lewis, Dio, 24, 25
liability, physical education and, 259, 296
life expectancy, 222
lifespan involvement, 1. *See also* lifespan physical activity
    popularity of, 4
lifespan physical activity
    ageless and genderless, 5
    early years, 5–8
    emerging characteristics, 17–19
    facilities, 14–17
    forever, 14
    framework for professionals, 20
    limitations, 19–20
    older adults, 13–14
    responsibility of all to make it available to all, 20
    sport/games festivals, 17
    watershed period, 5
    young adulthood, 10–13
    youth-the transition years, 8–10
lifespan physical education, 264
lifestyle changes, 224
lifestyle education, 83–84
    wellness as center of, 406–407
lifestyle management, 4, 406–407
lifetime sport movement, in post-WWII era, 57–58
lifetime sports, 55–56, 59
light-emitting-diode (LED), 321
Ling, Per Henrik, 30–31, 68
Ling system, 32
lipid, 171

literature. See sport literature
Little Gym, 6
Little League baseball, 49, 53, 112, 113, 114
load. See progressive overload
Locke, Lawrence, 356
logic, 368
Logsdon, Bette, 247
Louisana School for Math, Science, and the Arts, 272
Love, Davis, III, 354
low back pain, 168, 171, 223
low-impact activities for older adults, 14
Low-Impact Aerobics (Fonda/video), 209
low-income groups. *See also* socioeconomic status
    limitations in sport, fitness, and physical education
        for, 19–20, 59, 83, 399
    obesity in, 18
Loy, John, 335, 342
LPGA. *See* Ladies Professional Golfers Association
LRE. *See* least restrictive environment
Lung Association, 389

Madison Junior High School, 272, 273
magnet schools, 249
mainstream, 256
main-theme curricula, 289
major depressive disorder (MDD), 231
Major League Baseball (MLB), 53, 148
Major League Soccer (MLS), 157
Malamud, Bernard, 370
malpractice suits, 296
Manley, Audrey, 167
Man O'War, 41
Manross, Mark, 276
Man, Sport and Existence (Slusher), 369
marathons, 59
Marx, Karl, 29
Maryland Avenue School, 271–272
masculinity-femininity ideals, 70–71
massage therapists, 390
Master of Public Health (M.P.H.), 390
master's athletics, 13–14
master's degree in fitness, 218–219
masters sport
    Web sites about, 163
    competition, 13–14, 128–129
mathematical modeling, 323
Mays, Willie, 54
McCloy, C. H., 50
McCloy, Charles, 39, 43
    classification index, 39, 42

McCullagh, James C., 135
McCurdy, James, blood pressure and heart rate standards, 39
McGwire, Mark, 148
McKenzie, R. Tait, 40
McNab, Tom, 370
McNeill, Alexander, 406
Mead, George Herbert, 337
mechanical kinesiology, 318. *See also* biomechanics; kinesiology
mechanics, 318
Mechanics of Athletics, The (Dyson), 319
Medford, Oregon, Boys Study, 330
media. *See* films; popular media; sport humanities; sport literature; television
medical gymnastics, 31
Medicine and Science in Sports, 61
Medicine and Science in Sports and Exercise, 309
medicine, sport. *See* sport medicine
Meggyesy, Dave, 79, 339
mental health, 174
mental imaging, 351
Merchant, Larry, 339
Merriwell, Frank, 71, 107
MET. *See* metabolic equivalent
metabolic equivalent (MET), 188–190
metaphysics, 368
Metheny, Eleanor, 60, 61, 78, 80, 92, 247, 369
Metzner, Henrich, 33
Miami (Ohio) University fitness and recreation center, 11
Michener, James, 339
Michigan Intercollegiate Athletic Association, 122
Michigan State, 40
Middle Ages, sport and, 90
middle-school programs
    "new PE," 272
    P.E.4LIFE, 273
mimicry or pretense in games, 338
minorities. *See also* African Americans; black people; gender; minority issues; race; women
    limitations in sport, fitness, and physical education for, 59
    low incidence of, in coaching and administration, 132
    obesity in, 18
    as participants in collegiate and professional sport, 131
minority issues, 157–158
    post-World War I era, 41

misinformation, 226
moderate-to-vigorous physical activity (MVPA)
   difficulty of monitoring and qualifying, 195
   formula for, 224
   measuring, 187–188
   range of activity, 176
Modern Educational Dance (Laban), 77
modified games, 140–141
modified sports, 144
moguls, 97
Monday Night Football, 54
Moody, Helen Wills, 41
moral development, tied to sport and fitness, 76
moral philosophy, 106
Morgan, William, 35
Morrill Land Grant Act (1862), 29
motion analysis, 321
motivation, 225
motor behavior Web sites, 376
motor behavior specialists
   preparation to become, 332
   what they do, 332
motor control, 326
   areas of study within, 331
   current issues and problems in, 332–334
   current status, 330–332
   defined, 328–329
   development of, 329–330
   early efforts, 6
   as a field of study, 328–329
   professional interest in, 327
   questions investigated in, 327–328
motor development, 326
   areas of study within, 331
   current issues and problems in, 332–334
   current status, 330–332
   defined, 328–329
   development of, 329–330
   as a field of study, 328–329
   professional interest in, 327
   questions investigated in, 327–328
motor learning, 61, 326
   areas of study within, 331
   current issues and problems in, 332–334
   current status, 330–332
   defined, 328–329
   development of, 329–330
   as a field of study, 328–329
   professional interest in, 327
   questions investigated in, 327–328

motor-performance fitness, 169, 172
   components of, 170
movement curriculum, 77–79
movement education, 60, 246–248, 271–272
   vs. traditional model, 288
movement exploration, 248
movement vocabulary, 6
Moving and Growing, 78
Moving Children, 233
Mt. Holyoke Female Seminary, 25
multiactivity curriculum, in secondary physical education, 289
multiactivity-program approach, 244–245
multicultural education, dance as, 393
multipurpose athletic clubs, 14–15
muscles, 178
   adaptation to training stresses, 179
   agonist-antagonist pairs, 183
   endurance and strength, 181–184
muscular Christianity, 25, 68–70, 76
muscular endurance, 170
"Muscular Fitness and Health" (Kraus and Hirschland), 55
MVPA. *See* moderate-to-vigorous physical activity
My Pedagogic Creed (Dewey), 73

Nader, Ralph, 56
NAGWS. *See* National Association for Girls and Women in Sport
NAIA. *See* National Association of Intercollegiate Athletes
Naismith, James, 35
Namath, Joe, 54
Nash, Jay B., 40, 42, 76, 369, 43
NASPE. *See* National Association for Sport and Physical Education
NASPSPA. *See* North American Society for the Psychology of Sport and Physical Activity
NASSM. *See* North American Society for Sport Management
NATA. *See* National Athletic Trainers' Association
National Alliance for Youth Sports, 116, 139
   nine programs of (listed), 117
National Archery Association, 25
National Association for Girls and Women in Sport (NAGWS), 63, 156
National Association for Sport and Physical Education (NASPE), 41, 62, 63, 113, 142, 294
   academic-discipline movement, 62
   as allied association, 63

NASPE (*continued*)
  assessment of student progress, 294–295
  coaching guidelines, 142
  coaching standards, 121
  competency standards for sport-management curricula, 130–131
  content standards for physical education programs, 242, 294
  formation of, 41
  national coaching summit, 121
  national goals and standards, 245–246
  national standards, 280–282
  "Parent's Checklist for Quality Youth Sport Programs," 113
  physically educated person, 242, 243
  sport pedagogy and, 360
  Youth Sports Coalition, 113
National Association of Amateur Athletics, 25
National Association of Intercollegiate Athletes (NAIA), 122–123
National Athletic Administrators Association, 120
National Athletic Trainers' Association (NATA), 131, 147, 213–215
  Board of Certification (NATABOC), 214
  Education Task Force, 214
National Basketball Association (NBA), 53, 112, 125
  Chamberlin's 100-point game, 100
  diversity in staff, 157
National Board for Professional Teaching Standards, 280
National Bowling Congress, 24
National Center for Health Statistics, 388
National Children and Youth Fitness Study I, 195
National Children and Youth Fitness Study II, 185, 186, 195, 196, 286
National Clearinghouse for Youth Sports Information, 117
National Coalition for Promoting Physical Activity, 207
National Collegiate Athletic Association (NCAA), 4
  Athletic Congress of, 100
  basketball finals, 4, 54, 90, 367
  coaching and, 151–152
  divisions, 122–123, 151
  drug-testing issue, 152
  economic disparities and, 152
  founding of, 40
  recruiting violations, sanctions against, 151–152
  student-athlete study, 153–154
National Commissions for Health Education Credentialing, 390

National Conference on State Parks, 383
National Congress of State Games, 17
National Consortium for Physical Education and Recreation for Individuals with Disabilities (NCPERID), 282
National Council for Accreditation of Coaching Education (NCACE), 121
National Council of the YMCA, 43
National Council on Educational Standards and Testing, 280
National Council on Youth Sports, 112–113
national curriculum, 295
National Dance Association (NDA), 63, 393
National Education Association (NEA), 38, 40, 308
National Federation of Coaches Associations, 120
National Federation of Interscholastic Coaches Education Program (NFICEP), 120
National Federation of State High School Associations, 116, 119–120, 150
National Football League (NFL), 53
National Forest Service, 384
national governing bodies, 124
National Hockey League (NHL), 125
  diversity in, 157
National Institutes of Health, 176, 270–271
nationalism, 68
National Junior College Athletic Association (NJCAA), 123
National League, 125
National Park Service, 40, 49, 384
National Recreation and Park Association (NRPA), 383
National Recreation Association, 40, 383
National School Demonstration, 212
National School Population Fitness Survey, 195
National Society for Sport History (NSSH), 371
National Standards for Athletic Coaches, 121
National Strength and Conditioning Association, 215
  certification, 213
  instructor certification, 212
National Strength and Conditioning Association (NSCA), 214
National Study of Professional Education in Health and Physical Education, 50
National Therapeutic Recreation Society, 384
National Youth Administration (NYA), 47, 49
National Youth Sport Coaches Association (NYSCA), 116, 117
National Youth Sports Officials Association (NYSOA), 117
Nation at Risk, A, 56

naturalism, 74
Natural, The (Malamud), 370, 374
Nautilus, 184
Nazi Olympics, 53
NCAA. *See* National Collegiate Athletic Association
NCACE. *See* National Council for Accreditation of Coaching Education, 121
NCPERID. *See* National Consortium for Physical Education and Recreation for Individuals with Disabilities
NDA. *See* National Dance Association
NEA. *See* National Education Association
Needham High School, 270
negligence, 296
Negro professional leagues, 41
new physical education, 37, 47, 243–244
    Clark Hetherington, 38–39
    early twentieth century, 76–77
    European antecedents, 74–75
    Luther Halsey Gulick, 38–39
    philosophical challenge to, 60
    progressive-education theory, 73
    reemergence of play, 75–76
    Rosiland Cassidy, 38–39
    school sport and, 73–77
    Thomas Wood and, 38
New Physical Education, The (Wood and Cassidy), 38
new populations, as theme for the future, 400–401
New York Athletic Club, 72
New York City Marathon, 57
New York Turnverein, 33
New York University, 40, 41, 42, 74
New Zealand high schools, 159, 405–406
NFICEP. *See* National Federation of Interscholastic Coaches Education Program
NHL. *See* National Hockey League
Nicklaus, Jack, 53
Nietzsche, Friedrich Wilhelm, 76
Nissen, Hartwig, 31
NJCAA. *See* National Junior College Athletic Association
noncompetitive games, 95
nonparticipant sport involvement, 129
    athletic training, 131
    sport and technology, 132–133
    sport management and administration, 130–131
    vocations, 129–133
nonprofessional athlete, 112
nonprofit organizations, 384, 385

"no pain, no gain," 140, 181
Nordquist, Doug, 137
normative philosophy, 369
norm-referenced scores, 185, 196
North American Society for Sport History, 62
North American Society for Sport Management (NASSM), competency standards for sport-management curricula, 130–131
North American Society for the Psychology of Sport and Physical Activity (NASPSPA), 61, 330, 347
North Dallas Forty (Gent), 370
Northeastern University, 143
Novak, Michael, 91, 102–103, 110, 369
NRPA. *See* National Recreation and Park Association
NSCA. *See* National Strength and Conditioning Association, 214
nutrition. *See* diet
NYSCA. *See* National Youth Sport Coaches Association

Oberlin College, 40, 43
Obertueffer, Delbert, 369
obesity, 59, 168, 174, 199, 223, 299
    in adults, 18
    in children, 18, 171
    in minorities, 18
    populations of special concern, 179
    prevalence of, 228
officiating
    sport, 129
    women in, 156
Ohio High School Athletic Association (OHSAA), 118
Ohio State, 40
Ohio State University recreation program, 10–11
OHSAA. See Ohio High School Athletic Association
older adults
    activity patterns among, 200–201
    depression and, 231
    fitness among, 230–231
    fitness levels among, 200–201
    fitness tests for, 188
    learning to be active, 14
    Master's athletics, 13–14
    physical activities forever, 14
    resistance training for, 186
    statewide sport festivals, 128
Olde Sawmill Elementary School, 267–268
Olympic Games
    2000, 126
    in ancient Greece, 23

Olympic Games (*continued*)
  Chariots of Fire depiction of, 367
  coach education programs, 124
  development programs, 158
  as festival, 97
  first, in ancient Greece, 154
  high jump, 316
  inequity and, 154–155
  Los Angeles (1984), 137–138
  Mexico City (1968), 61, 100, 316, 347
  modern, beginning of (1896), 71–72
  revival of, 33, 35, 53
  Rome, 100, 347
  success of recent, 90
  women in, 154–155
Olympic Scientific Congresses, 360
Olympic Tennis Club, 15
"olympism," 35
online scouting network (OSN), 132
On the Principles for a Policy of Sport for All, 159
open competition, 58
organizational consolidation, 49–50
organizations
  fitness Web sites, 236
  Web sites, 300
organized recreational sport, 125–129
organized sport. *See also* sport organizations
  emergence of, 34–37
  premature entry into, 139
orthotic, 320
osteoarthritis, 174
osteoporosis, 171, 174
otherwise qualified phrase, 128
Outcomes Project, 245–246
Outerbridge, Mary, 24
out-of-school sport, 9–10
Out of Their League (Meggyesy), 79, 339
Outward Bound, 72–73, 81
overall mortality, 174
overuse injuries, 139–140

PACE. *See* Program for Athletic Coaches Education
Paddock, Charlie, 41
Palmer, Arnold, 54
Paralympic Games, 126
parental pressures, 149–150
parent form of a game, 140
Parents Association for Youth Sports, 117
"Parent's Checklist for Quality Youth Sport Programs,"
  113

Parks and Recreation, 383
Parks, Rosa, 56
participation
  coed, in secondary schools, 290–292
  costs of, 143
  healthy behaviors and, 234
  informal (young adults), 13
  kinds of, 112
  new forms of, 79–80
  numbers of girls and boys involved, 117
  shift to, from spectating, 48–49
  softball, 12
  of youth, 113
pass-to-play rules, 147–148
PATH Foundation, 235–236
pay-to-play plans, 150–151, 399
PCPFS. *See* President's Council on Physical Fitness and
  Sport
PCPFS Research Digest, 212
P.E.4LIFE, 248, 272, 273
pedagogical kinesiology, 321
pedagogy
  defined, 357–358
  sport. *See* sport pedagogy
Pennsylvania State University, 319
people with disabilities, sport for, 126–128
  organizations for, 127
  Web sites about, 162
PEPI. *See* Physical Education Public Information
  project
Perceptual and Motor Skills, 329
perceptual-motor learning, 328
performance enhancement
  drugs, intercollegiate sport and, 152
  role, of sport psychologists, 350
  sport psychology and, 350
  supplements, school sport and, 148–149
Perrin, Ethel, 43
personal and social responsibility model, 80
personal performance sports, 97
Pestalozzi, Johann Heinrich, 74
philosophical influences, 66–84, 67
  amateurism, 71–72
  Beecher system, 25
  British ideals, 71–72
  chronology of, 69
  early twentieth century, 76–77
  experiential and adventure education, 81
  fair play, 71–72
  fitness renaissance, 81–84, 82–84

German system, 25
gymnastic philosophies, 68
humanistic philosophies, 79–80
humanistic sport, 79–80
human movement philosophy, 60, 77–79, 77–79
masculinity-femininity ideals, 70–71
muscular Christianity, 25, 68–70
physical education, 79–80
play education, 80
Puritan prohibitions, 25
reemergence of play, 75–76
shift allowing physical education in schools, 25
sport education, 80–81, 80–81
wellness movement, 81–84, 82–84
Philosophic Society for the Study of Sport (PSSS), 62, 371
philosophy
    defined, 67
    moral, 106
    sport, 367
Philosophy of Sport and Physical Education Academy, 371
philosophy (pedagogy), 368–371
photography. *See* sport photography
physical activity
    defined, 169
    forever, 14
    guidelines, for toddlers and preschoolers, 203
    health benefits, 174
    infrastructure for the United States, 235–237
    moderate-intensity, 177
    programs for children and youths, 201–208
    public-policy concern, 83
    research issues in, 234–235
    sedentary, 177
Physical Activity and Health, 168, 306
Physical Activity for Children: A Statement of Guidelines, 201, 203–204
"Physical Activity Guidelines for Children" (NASPE), 176
physical-activity infrastructure, 235–237
physical activity (PA), CDC recommendations for, 201–208
physical-activity programs, preschool, 6
Physical Activity Pyramid, 176, 177
Physical Best (AAHPERD), 206, 233
"Physical Best-FITNESSGRAM®" program, 206
physical culture, 26
Physical Dimensions curriculum for high schools (Kansas), 273–274, 275

physical education. *See also* elementary-school programs; new physical education
    1885–1900, 29–34
    academic-discipline movement, 60–64
    academic-integration model, 248–249
    access and equity, 43
    adapted, 256, 257, 282, 300
    adventure-education approach, 253–255
    assessment, 294–295
    basic concepts, 242–262
    as basic subject, 294
    Beecher system, 31–32
    beginning of, 38
    beginning of science of, 42–43
    Boston Conference, 33–34
    Bucher's definitions, 244
    central meaning, 260–261
    coeducational, 290–292
    communication, effect on, 28–29
    competition, good and bad, 298–299
    content standards, 242, 294
    credibility with the public, 295
    daily, House Congressional Resolution 97, 265
    Dio Lewis system, 32
    "discipline of," 59
    distributing, more equitably, 398–399
    eclectic curriculum, 255
    education, effect on, 29
    education through the physical, 41–42, 242–245
    elementary, 7–8
    fitness issues in, 231–234
    gender equity, 296–297, 401
    general problems in, 293–299
    German system, 30
    goals of, 54
    Great Depression era (1930–1940), 48–50
    health-related, 248
    heritage of, 23–24
    Hetherington's four objectives for, 42
    historical influences on, 244
    Hitchcock system, 32–33
    immigration, effect on, 28
    importance of in schools, 4
    industrialization, effect on, 28
    innovative steps toward, 233
    intellectual climate, effect on, 29
    liability, 259, 296
    mid-1950s and on, 56–60
    minimum standards, 257
    movement education, 246–248

physical education (*continued*)
  NASPE's national goals and standards, 245–246
  national curriculum, 295–296
  new physical education, 37–39
  new populations, 400–401
  new settings for, 14–17
  objectives, 42
  outcomes, 295
  philosophical forces in, since 1950, 77–84
  philosophies, 25–26
  post-World War I era, 40–43
  post-World War II era, 52–56, 54–55, 308–309
  professional response to criticisms, 233–234
  Rousseau's argument about, 74
  Sargent system, 33
  school. *See* school sport
  in schools since the 1950s, 59–60
  science of, beginning, 42–43, 42–43
  scientific activity and, 59
  scientific understanding of, 19, 26, 32–33
  shaping of, 39–40
  skill equity, 297–298
  social-development model, 249–251
  sport-education model, 251–253
  in the sport/fitness culture, 299–300
  state requirements for, 257–259
  for students with disabilities, 256–257
  subject matter of, 255
  Swedish system, 29, 30–31
  technology in, 274, 276–278
  Title IX, 259–260. *See also* Title IX
  toward an expanded, 404–405
  transition period, 40
  transportation, effect on, 28–29
  umbrella concept, 26, 39–40, 47, 61
  urbanization, effect on, 28
  in urban schools, 292–293
  WWII era, 50–52
Physical Education Central, 276
Physical Education Curriculum, The (La Porte), 50, 245
physical education facility. *See* sport facility
Physical Education for Progress (PEP) bill, 212
Physical Education: Perspectives, Inquiry, Applications
  (Gensemer), 305
physical education programs
  comprehensive health-related elementary-school
    model, 265–266
  comprehensive high school, 272
  districtwide wellness initiative, 273

  early-elementary movement, 271–272
  elementary adventure program, 269–270
  high school emphasizing community linkages, 272–273
  high school fitness emphasis, 270
  high-school lifetime physical-activity program, 267
  high school personal-growth curriculum, 268–269
  "new PE" at middle school, 272
  P.E.4LIFE, 273
  preschool programs, 266–267
  research-based national elementary program, 270–271
  state wellness curriculum for high schools, 273–274
  successful, 274
  upper-elementary sport-education, 267–268
Physical Education Public Information (PEPI) project,
  245
physical-education teachers
  certification differences among states, 279–280
  certification for teaching adapted physical education,
    282
  day in the life, 278–279
  national standards for, 280–282
  preparing to become, 279–282
  what they do, 278
physical-fitness instruction, 212–213
  adult fitness bachelor's degree, 218
  certification for, 215–219. *See also* certification
  fitness master's degree, 218–219
  physical therapy, 217–218
  strength and conditioning specialist certification,
    215–217
  YMCA fitness instructor certification, 217
physically educated person, 242, 243
physical rehabilitation, 332
physical therapy, 317
  certification, 217–218
physical training, 26
Physician and Sports Medicine, The, 309
physiology. *See also* exercise physiology
  defined, 307
PL 94–142, 126, 256
"Plan for Life," 17
play, 26
  characteristics of, 93
  child's, and adult play, 94–95, 338
  concept of, 75, 337
  continuum of sport and, 93–94
  defined, 93

Friedrich Froebel and, 75
games, sport, and, relations among (figure), 338
general, 42
sport as a form of, 93–94
play education, 80
playful competition, 251
Playground and Recreation Association, 40
Playground Association of America, 39
playground movement, 39
playgrounds, design of, 6
play, in sport education, 251
play of. See play
Playorena, 267
Police Athletic League, 383
popular media, 225–226
Positive Coaching Alliance, 139
Posse, Baron Nils, 31, 33
Posse Normal School of Gymnastics, 31
post-1950 era
    aerobics era, 58–59
    educational movement of, 77–84
    fitness renaissance, 58–59
    reformist movement in education and, 61
    school physical education and, 59–60
    sport in perspective, 57
    trends, 57–58
post-Civil War era, development of organized sport in, 24–25
post-World War I era, 40–43, 47
post-WWII era
    exercise physiology, 308–309
    expansion and growth, 52–56
    fitness crisis, 55–56
    intercollegiate sport, 121–122
    in physical education, 54–55
poverty. See low-income groups; socioeconomic status
power, 170
praxis, 340
preschoolers, physical activity guidelines for, 203
preschool programs, 6, 266–267
"Presidential Fitness Week," 55
Presidential Sports Award, 211
President's Challenge Physical Activity and Fitness Awards program, 211
President's Council on Physical Fitness and Sport (PCPFS), 211
President's Council on Youth Fitness, 55, 211
primary rules, of games, 96
private-membership groups, 384

private-sector, 384
    Depression-era intervention of, 49
    equitable distribution and, 399
    fitness is fashionable, 59
    health-enhancement programs in, 390
    shift of opportunities for fitness to, 18–19
    sport clubs, 15
privatization of leisure, recreation, sport, and fitness, 399
profession
    birth of, 23–24
    context for emergence of, 26
    disciplines and, collaboration between, 402–403
    emergence of, 22–25
    fitness Web sites, 236
    timeline for emergence of, 27–28
professional athletes, 112
Professional Golfers Association "First Swing" golf program, 273
professional philosophy, 67
professionals
    disagreement among, on elementary physical education, 288
    expanded focus for with new populations, 400–401
    interest in motor skills, 327
    new, 19
    possibilities for, framework for, 20
    preparing classroom teachers to teach elementary PE, 286
professional sport, 124–125
professional sport entertainment, 130
profiles, 321
program director (ACSM), 216
Program for Athletic Coaches Education (PACE), 120
progressive-education theory, 73
progressive overload, 180
Promoting Better Health for Young People through Physical Activity and Sport, 212
promotion, sport. See sport promotion
PSSS. See Philosophic Society for the Study of Sport
psychobiological approaches (in sport psychology), 349
Psychological Advisory Committee of the United States Olympic Committee, 352
psychology. See also sport psychology
    cognitive, 345
    faculty, 30
    major figures in, 38–39
    "self," 79
    sociology and, of sport and exercise, 342–343
    third-force or humanistic, 79

Psychology of Athletics (Griffith), 347
Psychology of Coaching (Griffith), 347
Psychomotor Learning (Kerr), 325
psychophysiological approaches (in sport psychology), 349
"psych-soc," 342–343
public health challenge, as theme for the future, 397–398
Public Law 94–142, 126
Public Laws, 126, 256–259
public recreation and park agencies, 384
public sector, equitable distribution and, 398–399
Public Works Administration, 49
Puritan philosophies, 25, 26, 36, 68–70, 76, 90

qualitative biomechanical analysis, 321
quality of life, 174
quantitative biomechanical analysis, 321
Quest, 78, 333

Rabbit Run (Updike), 370
race. *See also* minorities
    equity issues, 227–229
    limitations in sport, fitness, and physical education for, 19–20, 83
rappelling, in elementary adventure program, 269–270
reaction time, 170
records
    importance of, 100–101
    in sport education, 251–252
recovery time, 180
recreation. *See also* Organized recreational sport
    age and, 386
    America's "giant opportunity," 385
    areas of service and employment, 384–385
    armed-forces, 384
    campus, 384
    college recreational intramural programs, 123
    commercial, 384
    community, for young adults, 11–12
    defined, 383
    Depression-era popularity of, 48–49
    employee services and, 384
    inner-city problems, 386
    post-World War II era, 383
    professional organizations, 383–384
    professional preparation, 383
    reduction and elimination of constraints, 385–386
    restorative goal of, 385

    for service personnel, 54–55
    therapeutic, 384
    university programs, 10–11
    Web sites about, 394
recreational participant, 112
recreational sport, organized, 125–129
recreation and leisure-services industry, 382
recreation industry, delivery of programs, 382–385
recreation movement, beginning, 40
recruiting violations, intercollegiate sport and, 151–152
referee, role of, 99
registered clinical exercise physiologist (ACSM), 216
Rehabilitation Act (1973), 126, 128, 256
rehabilitative services, 213–215
Reisman, David, 337
relaxation training, 351
religion
    decline of opposition to sport and exercise, 28
    sport as natural, 91–92
repetition maximums (RMs), 182
Report on Physical Activity and Health, 212
Research Consortium, 63
research issues, in fitness and physical activity, 234–235
Research Quarterly, 47, 329
Research Quarterly of Exercise and Sport, 308
research specialization, 52
resistance exercises, 31, 201
resistance training, 171, 183–184
responsibility-in-the-gym model, 250
rest and recovery activities, 51
Review of Sport and Leisure, 339
Revolt of the Black Athlete, The (Edwards), 339
Richardson, Dot, 211
risk sports, 83
rivalry, 98
road racing, 57
Robinson, Jackie, 157
role conflict, 291–292
role strain, 291
Roman Empire
    ancient, 23
    athletics in, 90
Roosevelt, Franklin D., 47
Roosevelt, Theodore, 76
Rose Bowl, 54, 151
Rotella, Robert, 354
Round Hill School, 25, 30
Rousseau, Jean-Jacques, 29, 74
Royal Central Institute of Gymnastics (Stockholm), 31

Rudolph, Wilma, 54, 100
Rugby School, 70, 107
rules
   codification of, 99
   nature of games and, 107–108
   pass-to-play, 147–148
   primary, 96
   secondary, 96
   violations of, 107–108
runner's philosopher (George Sheehan), 67
Ruth, Babe, 41

"sado-asceticism," 140
Sage, George, 338
Sanatory Gymnasium (Cambridge), 33
sanctions, 151
San Diego State University, 270–271
Sargent, Dudley, 24, 25–26, 33, 39, 42, 308
   Universal Test for Strength, Speed, and Endurance,
     39
Sargent Jump Test, 43
Sargent Normal School of Physical Training, 43
Sargent School for Women, 43
Sargent School of Physical Education, 33
Sargent system, 33
Sargent tests, 42–43
Schiller, Friedrich von, 75–76
Schollander, Don, 79, 339
school. See also elementary-school programs; high
    school programs; school sport; secondary school
    programs
   health education in, 388–389
   magnet or alternative, 249
   physical education since the 1950s, 59–60
   urban, 292–293, 386
School and Society (Dewey), 73
school-based experience, 280
school coaches
   interschool sport and, 120–121
   professional associations for, 120–121
   as teacher-coach, 149
School Health Policies and Program Study, 258
School physical-education programs, 1930–1940, 48
school programs, during WWII, 51
school spirit, 145
school sport, 144–151
   booster clubs, 149–150
   coach as teacher-coach, 149
   eligibility and pass-to-play rules, 147–148

   exclusion and the varsity model, 145–146
   ideas for reforming, 148
   inclusive model, 159
   injuries, 146–147
   new physical education and, 73–77
   parental pressures, 149–150
   parents and coaches out of control, 150
   pay-to-play plans, 150–151
   performance-enhancing supplements, 148–149
   specialization, 148
science
   early approach in physical education, 26
   health-fitness/activity patterns and adult hypokinetic
     disease, 196
   Hitchcock system and, 32–33
   of physical education, beginnings of, 42–43
   renewed emphasis on, 79
   understanding sport, fitness, and physical education
     through, 19
Science of Swimming, The (Councilman), 319
Scientific Consensus Conference on Physical Activity,
    Health, and Well-Being (1995), 192
scientific understanding of sport, fitness, and physical
    education, 19
scientist, sport. See sport scientist
Scott, Jack, 79
Season on the Brink, A. (Feingold), 368
seasons, in sport education, 251
secondary rules, of games, 96
secondary-school programs
   "busy, happy, and good," 288
   coed participation, 290–292
   difficult teaching situations, 289–290
   intramural programs, 293
   issues in, 288–293
   multiactivity curriculum, 289
   physical education in urban high schools, 292–293
   rethinking, 292
   role conflict in, 291–292
secondary schools. See high school programs; secondary
    school programs
Second International Sport Psychology Congress, 61
second-order philosophy, 368–369
sedentary activities, 177
sedentary lifestyle, chronic illnesses related to, 223
self-contained classroom, 286
"self" psychologies, 79
self-regulation (in sport psychology), 349
senior citizens. See older adults

"separate but equal," 56
settings
    home gymnasiums, 16
    multipurpose athletic clubs, 14–15
    specialized sport/fitness centers, 15–16
    sport clubs, 15
    sport-games festivals, 17
    sport-medicine centers, 16
    worksite, 16–17
sexual behavior, 388
Shape of the Nation Survey (2002), 258
Shector, Leonard, 79
Sheed, Wilfred, 92, 135
Sheehan, George, 66, 67
Sheehan, Thomas, 366
Shoeless Joe (Kinsella), 102, 370
Shoemaker, Willie, 54
Silent Spring, The (Carson), 56
Simon, Robert, 333
SIRC. *See* Sport Information Research Centre
skill equity, 297–298
skinfold test, 186, 195
Slusher, Howard, 369
"Smart Start," 6
Smith College, 32, 35
smokers, 223, 224
smoking, 388–389, 391
soccer, 6–7, 23
social development, checklist for, 269
social-development model, 249–251, 292
social gradient in health and fitness, 176, 178
social institution, sport as, 98–99. *See also* institutional-
    ization of sport
socialization, time line for, 51
social psychology (in sport psychology), 349
Social Security Act of 1935, 47
socioecological view, 178
socioeconomic status. *See also* low-income groups
    equity issues, 227–229
    and lack of involvement in the wellness movement,
        391
    unequal access based on, 143
sociology, 336. *See also* sport sociology
"Soft American, The" (Kennedy), 55, 211
softball
    co-rec leagues, 125
    invention of, 35
    as most popular participation sport, 12
    popularity of, 48

software programs
    FITNESSGRAM®, 207
    kinematic measurements and, 320–321
    for kinesiology and biomechanics, 320–321
    physical education, 276
SPARK. *See* Sports, Play, and Active Recreation for Kids
specialization, 280
    for elementary school teachers, 286–287
    primary liability of, 141
    school sport and, 148
    in sport sociology, 339
specialized sport/fitness centers, 15–16
Special Olympics, 126–128
specificity, 179
spectatoritis, 102
spectator sport. *See also* sport spectating
    girls and, 71
    Indianapolis 500, 40
    professional teams, 4
    shift from, to participation, 48–49
    television's influence on, 102
    WWI era, 50–51
speculative philosophy, 369
speed, 170
spinal disorders, 171
sport. *See also* issues and problems in sport
    access and equity, 43
    on the college campus (1852–1900), 35–36
    communication, effect on, 28–29
    competition in, 97–98
    continuum of play and, 93–94
    decline of opposition to, 28
    defined, 338
    democratization of, 49
    developmentally inappropriate, 140
    distributing, more equitably, 398–399
    education, effect on, 29
    education through the physical, 41–42
    in elementary schools, 8
    emergence of organized, 34–37
    equity issues. See equity issues
    expansion of, 53–54
    fitness involvement, 12–13
    games, play and, relations among (figure), 338
    gender equity in, 401
    Great Depression era (1930–1940), 48–50
    heritage of, 23–24
    high-school interschool program, 8–9
    humanistic, 79–80

immigration, effect on, 28
impact on family life, 143
importance of, 91
industrialization, effect on, 28
informal participation, 13
institutionalization of, 96–97
intellectual climate, effect on, 29
intercollegiate, beginning of, 36–37
interscholastic, 116–121
intramural, 39–40
learned skills, 357
lifetime, 55–56
masters, 128–129
mid-1950s and on, 56–60
natural religion, 91–92
new populations, 400–401
new settings for, 14–17
nonparticipant involvement, 129–133
opportunities for children, 6–7
out-of-school, 9–10
personal performance, 97
in perspective, 160
philosophical forces in, since 1950, 77–84
as physically active game, 338
post-1950 era, 57–58
post-Civil War era, 24–25
post-World War I era, 42–43
post-World War II era, 52–56
professional, 124–125
recreational. See recreational sport
risk, 83
school. See school sport
scientific understanding of, 19
standardized (institutionalized), 34
statistics about, 111
technology and, 132–133
television's influence on growth of, 54. See also
    television
transition time between local games and organized
    sport, 24
transportation, effect on, 28–29
types of beauty in, 104–106
university recreation programs, 10–11
urbanization, effect on, 28
veterans, 128–129
World War II era, 50–52
sport academies, 115
sport administration, 129
sport aesthetics, 103–106. See also beauty in sport

sport and activity industry, six segments of, 130
Sport: A Philosophic Inquiry (Weiss), 369
sport biomechanics, 129
Sport Brain, 210
sport broadcasting, 129
sport camps, 57–58, 129
sport clubs, 15
sport-club system, 158
sport commentators, 375
sport counseling, 129. See also sport psychologists
sport culture
    beginning of, 40
    inclusive rather than exclusionary, 405–406
Sport, Culture, and Society (Loy and Kenyon), 338
SPORTDiscus, 133
sport education, 60, 80–81
    defining characteristics, 251–252
    philosophy of, 82
    as physical-education model, 251–253
    upper-elementary-school program, 267–268
sport-education model, 251–253, 292
sport entertainment, professional and amateur, 130
sport-equipment
    design, 129
    industries, 54, 58
sport ethics, 106–108
sport-facility
    design, 129
    management, 129
sport fan, 103
sport festivals, Web sites about, 163
sport films, 102, 370, 374
sport fitness, 129
sport/fitness centers, specialized, 15–16
sport/fitness culture, 299–300
Sport for All movement, 158, 159–160, 208
"sport for peace" model, 292
SportFun, 208
sport/games festivals, 17
sport history, 61, 368, 370–371, 373
sport humanities, 366–378
    areas of study within, 373
    current issues and problems in, 375, 377
    current status, 371–375
    defined, 368–370
    development of, 367, 370–371
    as fields of study, 368–370
    films, 370
    historical investigations, 368, 370–371

sport humanities (*continued*)
  literature, 369–371
  philosophy, 368–369, 370–371
  questions investigated in, 368
  Web sites about, 377
sport-humanities specialists
  preparation to become, 374–375
  what they do, 374
Sport Information Research Centre (SIRC), 133
sport job opportunities, 130
sport journalism, 129
sport leadership, 129
sport literature, 54, 79, 102, 309, 339, 370, 371, 373
Sport Literature Association (SLA), 371
sport management, 384
sport management and administration, 130–131
sport medicine, 129, 213
  professional organizations, 214
sport-medicine centers, 16
sport organizations
  genesis of, 99–100
  masters or veterans sports, 128–129
  for people with disabilities, 126–128
sport participation, kinds of, 112. *See also* participation
sport pedagogists
  preparation to become, 362
  what they do, 362
sport pedagogy, 62, 356
  areas of study within, 361
  current issues and problems in, 363–364
  current status, 360–363
  defined, 357–359
  development of, 359–360
  field of curriculum, 358–359
  field of instruction, 358–359
  as a field of study, 357–359
  questions investigated in, 357
  Web sites about, 377
sport performer, 99
sport philosophy, 61, 373. *See also* exercise physiology
sport photography, 129
sport physiology, 78, 129
sport problems and issues
  child and youth sport, 138–144
  cooperation and competition, 137–138
  equity issues, 154–158
  general or social problems?, 136–137
  intercollegiate sport, 151–154
  school sport, 144–151
  sport systems, 158–160

sport programs, collegiate, 121–123
sport promotion, 129
sport psychologists
  certification of, 345–347
  consulting, 346, 350
  counseling role, 350–351
  focus on mental aspects, 346
  preparation to become, 351–353
  what they do, 349–350
sport psychology, 61, 78, 129, 344
  academic, 348–349
  current issues and problems in, 353–354
  current status, 348–353
  defined, 345–347
  development of, 347–348
  as a field of study, 345–347
  interventions, 350, 351
  topic areas and questions in, 349
  Web sites, 376
sport publicity, 129
sports, 26
sports biomechanics, 59
Sport Science, 315
sport-science programs, 79
sport sciences, 320
sport scientist, 129
sport services, 130
Sports Illustrated
  featuring sport problems and issues, 339
  President Kennedy's article in, 55, 211
  weekly coverage in, 367
Sports in America (Michener), 339
sportsmanship, 106. *See also* fair play
sport sociologists
  preparation to become, 341
  what they do, 341
sport sociology, 78, 335
  areas of study within, 340
  current issues and problems in, 341–343
  current status, 339–341
  development of, 338–339
  as a field of study, 336–338
  as subdiscipline area, 61
  as value free field, 342
  Web sites about, 376
Sport Sociology Academy, 339
sports officiating, 129
sport specialist, 141
sport spectating, 102–103. *See also* spectator
  sports

Sports, Play, and Active Recreation for Kids (SPARK), 248, 270–271, 286
sport studies, 129, 371–372
sport-studies programs, 79
sport systems
  alternative goals for, 158–159
  Sport for All, 159–160
  sport in perspective, 160
sport training, 57
spot reducing, 309
Springfield College, 25, 43
Sputnik, 56, 59
Stagg, Amos Alonzo, 37
stairway to lifetime fitness, 225
standardization, 49–50
Stanford University, 38
Start Smart, 117
State Champion Award, 212
State Games, 17
state requirements for physical education, 257–259, 279–280
statewide sport festivals, Web sites about, 163
static flexibility, 172, 184
steroids, anabolic, 152
Story, Thomas, 40
strength, 170, 172
Strength and Conditioning, 216
strength and conditioning specialist certification, 215–217
strength training, 177, 181–184
  for children, 206
stress management, 385
student-athletes, intercollegiate, treatment of, 153–154
student behavior (sport pedagogy), 361
students with disabilities, physical education for, 256–257. *See also* adapted physical education; modified sports
subdiscipline areas, 61
suburbs, 52
summative assessments, 295
summer games, 17
Sun City, Arizona, 384
Super Bowl, 4, 54, 367
  as festival, 97
supplemental contract (for coaches), 149
Swan, Lynn, 211
Swedish system, 29, 30–31, 33, 68

tactical awareness, 60
Take Time for Paradise (Giamatti), 369

target games, 96
target heart-rate zone, 175
teacher behavior (sport pedagogy), 361
teacher-coach, 149
teacher education (sport pedagogy), 357, 358
teacher effectiveness (sport pedagogy), 361
teacher issues (sport pedagogy), 361
teachers
  difficult teaching situations, 289–290
  elementary specialist, 286–287
  gender equity and, 297
  physical-education. See physical-education teachers
Teachers College (Columbia University), 38, 39, 40, 41, 42, 74
teaching and curriculum, Web sites about, 300
Teaching Games for Understanding, 60
teaching situations, difficult, 289–290
technology. *See also* software programs; Web sites; World Wide Web
  developments in sports and, 210
  effect on sport biomechanics, 320–322
  in home fitness centers, 210
  influence of, on sport and fitness, 19
  in physical education, 274, 276–278
  sport and, 132–133
Technology and Physical Education program, 274
telecommunications, 276
television
  catering to adults, 198–199
  creation of informed spectators, 103
  major influence on growth of sport, 54
  revolutionized sport spectating, 102
  sport channels, 19
  sport coverage on, 367
Tenneco, Inc., 16, 209
Tennessee Valley Authority, 49
territory or invasion games, 96
therapeutic recreation, 384
Therapeutic Recreation Journal, 383
third-force psychology, 79
Third World Masters Games, 231
Thorndike, Edward, 38–39, 50
Thorpe, Jim, 40
threshold of training, 180
Tilden, Bill, 41
time, as issue for elementary physical education professionals, 285–286
Time magazine, 193
Tin Cup, 102
Tinning, Richard, 173

Title IX, 37, 121, 126, 401; *See also* gender equity; women
  assumption of, 290
  coaching and administration positions, 132
  coaching opportunities and, 132
  coed participation, 60, 290
  cultural change and, 401
  effects of, 260
  equity for girls and women, 154
  focus of, 155
  framework of, 57
  gender equity and, 297
  girls and women, 154–157
  impetus for growth of intercollegiate sports for women, 122
  increase of sport opportunities, 131
  influences of, 259
  intercollegiate sport, 122
  interscholastic sport, 117
  legal and moral implications, 260
  minority athletes and, 132
  moral imperative, 401
  passage of, 57
  people with disabilities and, 126
  physical education and, 259–260
  plan to remediate problems under, 156
  school coaches, 121
  secondary-school programs, 296–297
  three point test for compliance, 156
  Web sites about, 163
  work yet to be done, 155–156
tobacco use, 388
toddlers, physical activity guidelines for, 203
Tom Brown's Schooldays (Arnold), 70, 107
Tones of Theory, 62
tourism, 385
"Toward a Sociology of Sport," 335
training. *See also* athletic training; fitness training
  athletic, 131
  threshold of, 180
transportation, effect of, on sport, fitness, and physical education, 28–29
travel, 385
treadmill test, 186
triathlons, 59
Trilling, Blanche, 37, 43
Turners, the, 68
Turnplatz, 30
Turnverein, 23, 25, 30

tutorials, 276
Type II diabetes, 171

Ulrich, Celeste, 247, 406
ultimate Frisbee, 96
UNESCO. *See* United Nations Educational, Scientific and Cultural Organization
unified sports, 127–128
unit approach to curriculum design, 50, 245
United Nations Educational, Scientific and Cultural Organization (UNESCO), 159–160
United States
  physical-activity infrastructure, 235–237
  sport heritage in, 23–29
United States Masters Swimming organization, 128
United States Olympic Committee, 126
United States Public Health Service. See *Healthy People 2000; Healthy People 2010*
unity of man, 74
Universal Gym, 184
Universal Test for Strength, Speed, and Endurance, 39
University of California at Los Angeles (UCLA), 38
University of Chicago, 73
University of Illinois, 40, 347
University of Iowa, 43
University of Michigan, 43
University of Nebraska, 47
University of Oregon, 41
University of Virginia, 282
University of Wisconsin, 37, 41, 392
university recreation programs, 10–11
Unsafe at Any Speed (Nader), 56
Updike, John, 370
urban high schools, physical education in, 292–293
urbanization, effect of, on sport, fitness, and physical education, 28
USA Volleyball Coaching Accreditation Program (CAP), 124
U.S. Congress, House Concurrent Resolution 97 (1987), 4, 264–265
U.S. Department of Health and Human Services, 389
U.S. Department of Health, Education, and Welfare, 211
use-it-or-lose-it syndrome, 201
user fees, 150, 399
U. S. National Commission on Excellence in Education, 56
U.S. News and World Report, 193
U.S. Olympic Committee, 126
  Elite Athlete Project, 319

Psychological Advisory Committee of, 352
on sport for people with disabilities, 126
U.S. Olympic movement, Amateur Sports Act, 126, 256
U.S. Public Health Service. See also Healthy People 2000; *Healthy People 2010*
U.S. Supreme Court, 56
U.S. Surgeon General, 168, 212, 306, 391, 397

value free research and scholarship in sport sociology, 342
VanderZwaag, Harold, 366
varsity model of competition, 113, 145–146, 197, 405
Vealey, Robin S., 344
Veblen, Thorstein, 337
vertigo and games, 338
veterans sport, 128–129
video, *Low-Impact Aerobics* (Fonda), 209
Vietnam conflict, 56–57
Virginia Tech, 276
vocational opportunities, 129–133
volleyball, invention of, 35
voluntary organizations, 384

Wagner Act of 1935, 47
Walker, LeRoy, 121
walking, 226
War Fitness Conference (1943), 50
Warren, John, 24
WAVA. *See* World Association of Veteran Athletes
Weber, Max, 337
Web sites
adapted physical education, 300
American Academy of Sports Medicine, 61
American Fitness Alliance (AFA), 206
American Physical Therapy Association, 217
biomechanics, 376
Bluegrass State Games, 17
Center for the Study of Sport in Society, 143, 157
child and youth sport, 162
dance, 394
exercise physiology, 376
exercise psychology, 376
fitness for adults, 236
fitness for children and youth, 236
fitness-related professions and organizations, 236
general organizations and associations, 300
health, 394
intercollegiate sport, 162
interscholastic sport, 162

kineisology, 376
masters sport, 163
motor behavior, 376
National Athletic Trainers' Association, 147, 213
National Congress of State Games, 17
other sites, 163
people with disabilities, sport for, 162
Physical Education Central , 276, 277
President's Council on Physical Fitness and Sport, 212
recreation, 394
resources for positive spectating and parenting in sport, 139
sport humanities, 377
Sport Information Research Centre (SIRC), 133
sport pedagogy, 377
sport psychology, 376
sport sociology, 376
Sports, Play, and Active Recreation for Kids (SPARK), 270
state games and sport festivals, 163
teaching and curriculum, 300
United States Masters Swimming organization, 128
viewing and analyzing movement of athletes, 320
women in sport, 163
workplace, benefits to, 208
worksite fitness and wellness programs, 208
weight consciousness, 227
weight reduction, spot reducing and, 309
weight training. *See also* strength training physiological changes and benefits from, 183
Weismuller, Johnny, 41
Weiss, Paul, 92, 369, 371
Wellesley College, 31
wellness, 170, 387
as the center of lifestyle education, 406–407
defined, 169
as theme for the future, 406
wellness initiative in schools, 273
wellness movement, 4, 82–84, 236
concept of, 387
districtwide initiative, 205, 236, 273
lifestyle education and, 406–407
worksite programs, 16–17, 208–209
wellness programs, 208
federal efforts to promote, 210–212
informal home-based activities, 209–210
Western Athletic Conference, 122
Western Conference (Big Ten), 37

Western Female Institute, 25, 31
Wheeling, West Virginia, 226
Wilberg, Robert, 333
Wilkinson, Bud, 55
Williams, Jesse Fiering, 42, 43, 76, 241, 369
winning, outside pressure for, 142
Winter Games for the Disabled, 126
Winter State Games, 17
Wisconsin Growth Study, 330
Wolffe, Joseph B., 61
women. *See also* gender equity; Title IX
    barrier to participation in contact sports, 156
    early twentieth century activity and, 77
    equity issues, 227–229
    equity issues in sport, 154–158
    as founding members of Association for the Advance-
        ment of Physical Education, 24
    founding of calisthenics for, 31–32
    four "virtues" of, 31, 154
    in high school coaching, 121
    increased economic power of, 401
    intercollegiate sport for, 37
    involvement in sport expansion, 35
    masculinity-femininity ideals, 70–71
    new sense of possibilities, 52
    as pioneers, 43
    in sport, Web sites about, 163
    Title IX, 57, 154–158
    in World War II armed services, 50
Women's Christian Temperance Union, 24
women's movement, 57
    sport as an arena for, 83
Women's Professional Volleyball League, 124
Women's Sport & Fitness, 209
Wood, Thomas, 22, 38–39, 41–42, 43, 73, 74, 76
worksite fitness
    costs of inadequate, 208
    health programs and, 389–390
worksite health programs, 16–17, 208–209, 389–390
Works Progress Administration (WPA), 47, 49
World Association of Veteran Athletes (WAVA), 128
World Cup, as festival, 97
World Leisure and Recreation Association, 384
World Masters Athletics Association, 128
World Masters Games, 13, 128
World Series, 4, 40, 54
World Veterans Track and Field Championships, 13
World War I, 48
World War II era, motor learning and, 329

World War II, post. See post World War II era
World Wheelchair Games, 126
World Wide Web. *See also* Web sites
    on line scouting network (OSN), 132
    source of information for sports, 19, 102, 132
    as source of sport, fitness, and physical education
        information, 19
    success of, in physical education, 276–278
Worthington Hills Elementary School, 269–270
Wright, Harry, 34

X games, 83, 97
XI Paralympic Games, 126

Yale University, 91, 92, 369, 371
YMCA. *See* Young Men's Christian Association
young adults
    community recreation, 11–12
    fitness involvement, 12–13
    informal participation, 13
    university recreation programs, 10–11
Young Men's Christian Association (YMCA), 28, 40,
    43
    ASEP Basic Education course and, 116
    begun in England, 25
    certification programs, 213, 217, 229, 390
    Charles H. McCloy, 43
    early movement, 24
    early twentieth century, 76
    first American, 25
    fitness facilities, 14–15, 212
    fitness instructor certification, 217
    focus of, 72
    during the Great Depression, 49
    invention of basketball and volley ball, 35
    recreation and, 40, 382, 383
    sponsorship of sports, 114
    use of sport to reach youths, 28
    volunteer coaches from ASEP, 142
Young Women's Christian Association (YWCA), 40
    facilities, 212
    during the Great Depression, 49
    recreation, 40, 382, 383
    sponsorship of sports, 114
You Stay Alive recognition system, 207
Youth Risk Behavior Surveillance, 258
youth sport, 57. *See also* child and youth sport; high
        school programs; secondary school programs
    beginning of, 53